Intellectual Property Rights and United States International Trade Laws

Wayne W. Herrington

George W. Thompson

OCEANA PUBLICATIONS, INC.
Dobbs Ferry, New York

You may order this or any other Oceana publications by visiting Oceana's website at http://www.oceanalaw.com

Library of Congress Control Number: 2002103203

ISBN 978-0-379-21438-3

TABLE OF CONTENTS

CUSTOMS SERVICE ENFORCEMENT AGAINST GOODS THAT INFRINGE OR COUNTERFEIT A TRADEMARK, TRADE NAME, OR COPYRIGHT

ENFORCEMENT OF RIGHTS UNDER TRADE AGREEMENTS

APPENDICES

INDEX

Preface

This book addresses the intersection of two areas of law: international trade and intellectual property. It covers investigations by the United States International Trade Commission under Section 337 of the Tariff Act of 1930, United States Customs Service protection against imports that infringe intellectual property rights, and proceedings before the United States Trade Representative concerning violations by foreign nations of international agreements or standards respecting intellectual property. For each of these subjects, we review the administrative agencies charged with enforcing the laws, their procedures, and, where applicable, judicial review of their decisions. Our goal was to prepare a text that the neophyte and occasional practitioner could use as a primer on these topics, and that the specialist could turn to as a research reference.

We are grateful to Ms. Betty Rivers and Ms. Sylvia Nur for their assistance in preparing the text.

About the Authors

Wayne W. Herrington is counsel to Finnegan, Henderson, Farabow, Garrett, and Dunner in Washington, D.C. He was previously Senior Counsellor and Special Advisor on Intellectual Property and Technology with the Office of the General Counsel at the United States International Trade Commission, where his responsibilities included representing the Commission before the United States Court of Appeals for the Federal Circuit and the United States Court of International Trade. He served as law clerk to the Honorable Giles S. Rich, Associate Judge of the United States Court of Customs and Patent Appeals (now the United States Court of Appeals for the Federal Circuit). He received his J.D. from Columbia University and an LL.M. in Patent Law and Trade Regulation from George Washington University. He has written and lectured extensively on issues relating to intellectual property and international trade.

George W. Thompson is a partner in the Washington, D.C. office of the law firm Neville Peterson LLP, before which he was an attorney in the Office of General Counsel of the U.S. International Trade Commission. He is co-author of the books *Exporting: Regulations, Documentation, Procedures* and *International Ocean and Air Transportation*, is the Supervisory Editor and primary author of *Transnational Contracts* (Oceana Publications), and is a contributing author for Oceana's treatise *Customs Law and Administration*. He also is an Adjunct Professor at the graduate School of Public Policy of George Mason University, where he teaches the courses International Contract Negotiation and ABCs of Importing and Exporting. Mr. Thompson is a graduate of the State University of New York and Cornell Law School.

INTELLECTUAL PROPERTY ACTIONS AT THE INTERNATIONAL TRADE COMMISSION (Section 337 of the Tariff Act of 1930)

I. INTRODUCTION

Section 337 of the Tariff Act of 1930 (19 U.S.C. § 1337) ("Section 337"), which has actually been in existence in one form or another since 1922, is administered by the United States International Trade Commission, an independent agency of the United States. Under Section 337, owners of United States intellectual property rights who believe those rights are being infringed by imports (particularly patent owners and their exclusive licensees) can petition the Commission (via complaint) to institute adjudicative proceedings called investigations to obtain orders excluding infringing articles from entry into the United States and/or cease and desist orders prohibiting the violators from continuing their infringing activities. An understanding of Section 337 begins with an understanding of the agency which administers it—the United States International Trade Commission.

II. THE UNITED STATES INTERNATIONAL TRADE COMMISSION

The United States International Trade Commission ("the Commission") is an independent agency of the United States.[1] It was originally established in 1916 as the Tariff Commission.[2] The original mission of the Commission was to relieve the Congress of the burden it had borne up to that time of conducting the detailed fact-finding investigations which were a necessary prelude to the enactment of tariff legislation. Subsequently, the Commission acquired additional functions, all related to customs and international trade matters. It was renamed the United States International Trade Commission in the Trade Act of 1974.[3]

A. The Commissioners

The Commission is composed of six Commissioners,[4] who are nominated by the President and must receive the advice and consent of the Senate before taking office. 19 U.S.C. § 1330(a). No more than three Commissioners may be of the same political party. 19 U.S.C. § 1330(a). Thus, the Commission is usually composed of three Republicans and three Democrats. In making appointments, members of different political parties must be appointed alternately "as nearly as may be practicable." 19 U.S.C. § 1330(a). Commissioners are ordinarily appointed for nine-year terms, unless they are completing the remaining term of another Commissioner who has resigned or otherwise left office. 19 U.S.C.

---

1 *I.e.*, it is not part of any cabinet department in the Executive Branch.

2 Act of September 8, 1916, c. 463, Title VII, § 700 *et seq.*, 39 Stat. 795 (current version at 19 U.S.C. § 1330 *et seq.*).

3 Act of January 3, 1975, P.L. 93-618, Title I, § 171(a), 88 Stat. 2009 (codified at 19 U.S.C. § 2231). The history of the Commission is recounted in John M. Dobson, *Two Centuries of Tariffs, The Background and Emergence of the United States International Trade Commission* (Washington, Government Printing Office 1976).

4 Biographies of the five Commissioners currently in office are reproduced at Appendix A.

§ 1330(b). They may not be reappointed, unless their initial term was for five years or less. 19 U.S.C. § 1330(a).

From among the Commissioners, a chairman and vice-chairman are designated by the President for two-year terms. 19 U.S.C. § 1330(c). There are statutory restrictions on which Commissioners may be so designated. 19 U.S.C. § 1330(c). One important restriction is that the Commissioners so designated may not be from the same political party. 19 U.S.C. § 1330(c)(3)(B).

As a general rule, a majority of a quorum of the Commissioners is required to approve any proposition before the Commission. *Frischer & Co. v. Bakelite Corporation,* 39 F.2d 247, 255 (CCPA 1930). A quorum is defined by statute as a majority of the Commissioners in office. 19 U.S.C. § 1330(c)(6). There are some exceptions to the majority-of-the-quorum requirement. These exceptions have been created by statute or by Commission rule. Among these exceptions is the statutory provision that where the Commission is authorized to make an investigation on its own motion or on complaint or application, an evenly divided vote of the Commissioners voting is sufficient to institute such investigation. 19 U.S.C. § 1330(d)(5). The Commission's investigations under Section 337 of the Tariff Act of 1930 are among the investigations included under this provision.

B. Powers of the Commission

The Commission has very broad general powers to conduct proceedings and gather information to perform its functions. These powers are set out at 19 U.S.C. §§ 1331, 1333. Among them is the authority to issue subpoenas to any person in the United States and to request the assistance of the courts in enforcing those subpoenas. 19 U.S.C. § 1333(a)-(c); *U.S. International Trade Commission v. E.&J. Gallo Winery,* 637 F. Supp. 1262 (D.D.C. 1985). These general powers are the tools which the Commission uses to conduct the specific proceedings for which Congress has made it responsible.

C. Proceedings Conducted by the Commission

The most important proceedings[5] conducted by the Commission are: (1) investigations of unfair practices in the import trade (usually patent infringement)

---

5 Most Commission proceedings are referred to as investigations, a designation stemming from the Commission's original role as a fact-finding agency which made reports and recommendations to the Congress and the President, a role it still plays under some of its statutory authorities. Commission investigations are usually titled after the imported commodity which is the subject of the investigation. In some types of investigations (*e.g.*, investigations under the antidumping and countervailing duty laws), the name of the exporting country is also part of the title. All investigations are also given an investigation number which reflects the statutory authority under which they are conducted. An example of how a Section 337 investigation is titled and numbered is *Certain Neodymium-Iron-Boron Magnets, Magnet Alloys, and Articles Containing Same*, Inv. No. 337-TA-372. The "337" in the investigation number indicates that the investigation is being conducted under Section 337. The "TA-372" indicates that the

under Section 337 of the Tariff Act of 1930 (19 U.S.C. § 1337); (2) investigations conducted to determine whether a relevant U.S. industry is materially injured or threatened with material injury by imports that are sold at less than fair value ("dumped") or by imports which benefit from certain subsidies provided through foreign government programs (19 U.S.C. §§ 1671, 1673 *et. seq.*); (3) general fact-finding investigations under Section 332 of the Tariff Act of 1930 (19 U.S.C. § 1332), and (4) investigations conducted under Section 201 of the Trade Act of 1974 (19 U.S.C. § 2251) to determine whether an article is being imported in such increased quantities that it is a substantial cause of serious injury, or the threat thereof, to the U.S. industry producing the like or directly competitive article ("global safeguard actions"). The foregoing is not a complete list of the Commission's activities. A more complete summary of the various proceedings and activities of the Commission can be found in the current version of the *United States Government Manual* or the most recent *Year in Review* (formerly, *Annual Report*) of the Commission. The Commission's website, www.usitc.gov, contains this and other information as well.

D. The Commission Staff

In performing its functions, the Commission is assisted by a staff of some 400, including lawyers, economists, and commodity specialists. These are organized as set out in the chart on the following page.

A glance at the Commission's organizational chart reveals several staff entities which play important roles in the administration of Section 337.

The General Counsel is the Commission's chief legal advisor. The Office of the General Counsel is composed of the General Counsel, the Deputy General Counsel, three Assistant General Counsels (including an Assistant General Counsel for Section 337) and a staff of attorney-advisors. The General Counsel advises the Commission on the disposition of all cases and matters before it, seeks court enforcement of any subpoenas issued by the Commission or under its authority, and defends the Commission's decisions before its reviewing courts.[6]

The Office of the Administrative Law Judges is composed of the Commission's administrative law judges (ALJs), their law clerks, and support staff. The primary and virtually exclusive role of the Commission's administrative law judges is to preside over the evidentiary hearings (including pre-hearing matters) in Section 337 investigations instituted by the Commission and to issue initial

investigation is the three hundred and seventy-second Section 337 investigation conducted after the enactment of the Trade Act of 1974, which, as discussed *infra*, substantially revised Section 337.

6 The Commission is one of the few Federal agencies which may be represented in the courts by its own attorneys, as opposed to attorneys from the Department of Justice, though it may request representation by the Department of Justice. 19 U.S.C. § 1333(g). The grant of litigation authority to the Commission was an important feature of the Trade Act of 1974.

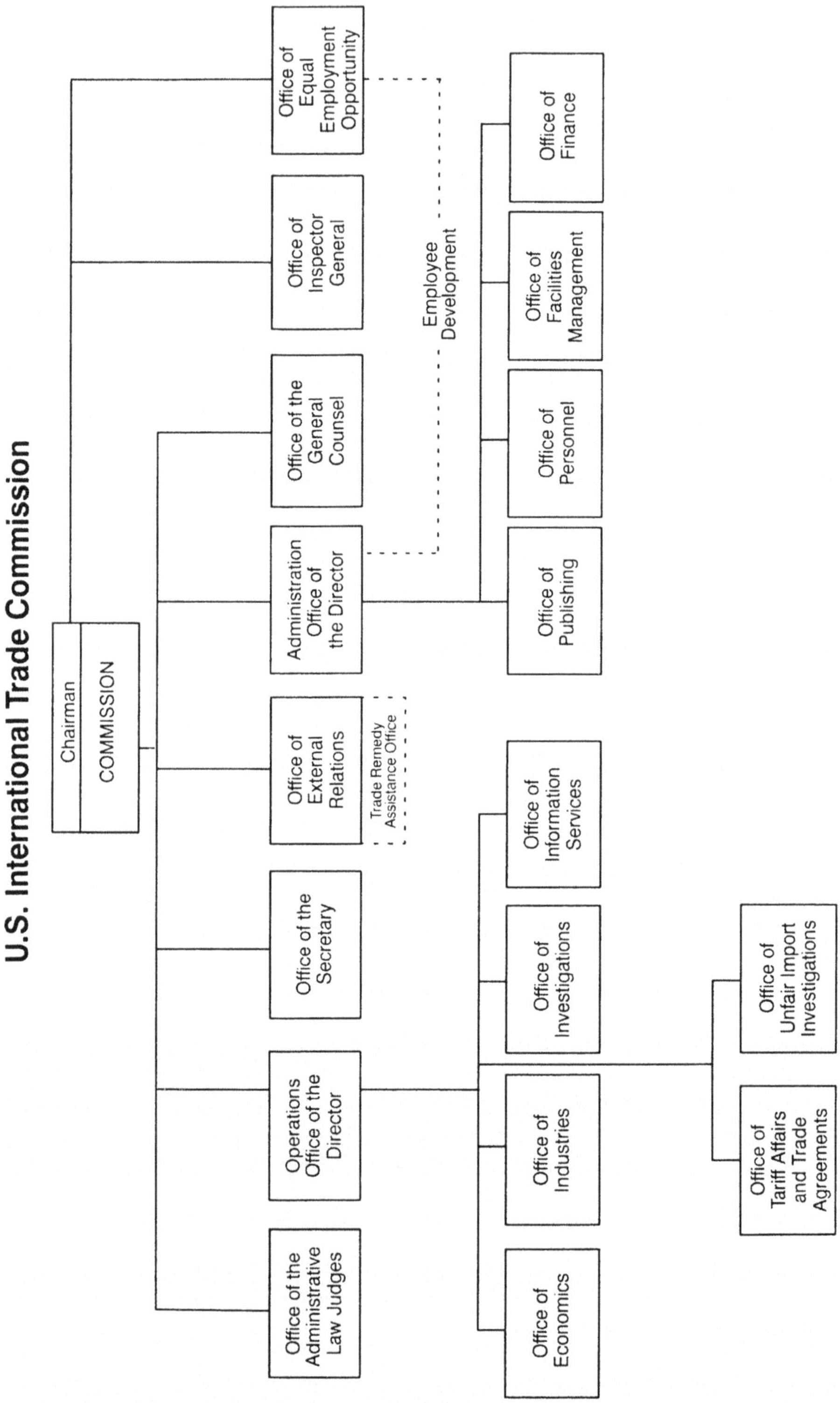
U.S. International Trade Commission
Chairman
COMMISSION
Office of Equal Employment Opportunity
Office of Inspector General
Office of the General Counsel
Administration Office of the Director
Office of External Relations
Trade Remedy Assistance Office
Office of the Secretary
Operations Office of the Director
Office of the Administrative Law Judges
Employee Development
Office of Finance
Office of Facilities Management
Office of Personnel
Office of Publishing
Office of Information Services
Office of Investigations
Office of Industries
Office of Economics
Office of Unfair Import Investigations
Office of Tariff Affairs and Trade Agreements

determinations in those investigations as to whether a violation of Section 337 exists. At the present time, the Commission has four administrative law judges.

The Office of Unfair Import Investigations (OUII) is composed of a Director, two Supervisory Commission investigative attorneys, and a staff of Commission investigative attorneys. The primary role of OUII is to provide the Commission investigative attorney, who acts as a third party in Section 337 investigations to assure that the record is complete and that all issues are fully aired. OUII attorneys also advise prospective complainants on the requirements of the Commission's rules regarding Section 337 and will, if requested (and staff time permitting), review draft complaints for compliance with those rules.

The Office of the Secretary is the official point of contact with the Commission. The Dockets Section of the Office of the Secretary receives all filings with the Commission and officially issues and serves notices and orders of the Commission.

E. Commission Rules

The Commission conducts each of its proceedings in accordance with statutory authority. Pursuant to that authority and its general rulemaking authority under 19 U.S.C. § 1335, the Commission has also issued general and specific rules which govern those proceedings. The Commission's rules of general applicability are found at 19 C.F.R. Part 201. These rules govern all Commission investigations, including those under Section 337, in the absence of a more specific rule. The Commission has also issued rules specific to each type of investigation it conducts. The Commission's specific rules for Section 337 cases are found at 19 C.F.R. Part 210. The Commission's rules may be cited by citing to 19 C.F.R. and the particular section being referred to. Frequently, however, the Commission and practitioners simply refer to a particular rule as "Commission Rule," followed by a reference to the particular section being referred to. Thus, 19 C.F.R. § 210.4 may simply be referred to as Commission Rule 210.4. As discussed *infra*, in addition to the applicable rules of the Commission itself, each Section 337 investigation will be subject to ground rules issued by the Commission administrative law judge designated to preside over it.

III. THE STATUTE: SECTION 337 OF THE TARIFF ACT OF 1930

Section 337 was originally enacted as Section 316 of the Tariff Act of 1922, which was reenacted as Section 337 of Tariff Act of 1930, and has since been substantially amended. Probably the most important amendment was the wholesale revision of Section 337 in the Trade Act of 1974, which among other things, required for the first time that Section 337 investigations be conducted under the adjudicative provisions of Administrative Procedure Act. The modern version of Section 337 dates from this revision. There have been subsequent important amendments to Section 337 in the Trade Agreements Act of 1979 ("TAA

1979"), the Omnibus Trade and Competitiveness Act of 1988 ("OTCA"), and the Uruguay Round Agreements Act ("URAA") in 1994, as well as lesser amendments. The Uruguay Round Agreements Act amendments are notable because they were precipitated by a ruling of a dispute panel convened under the General Agreement on Tariffs and Trade (GATT), which had found many features of Section 337 (as it then existed) as violating the national treatment provisions of GATT.

A copy of the current version of Section 337 is reproduced at Appendix A.

A. Substantive Provisions: Unfair Practices in the Import Trade

Section 337(a), the principal substantive provision of Section 337, prohibits certain unfair practices in the import trade as set out in subparagraphs (A)-(E) of Section 337(a)(1). These unfair practices will be discussed *infra*. However, it is first necessary to discuss the context of these practices, *i.e.*, the import trade, because it is that context which the Commission and its reviewing court have treated as determining whether the Commission has subject matter jurisdiction in any given case.

1. Subject Matter Jurisdiction

Subparagraph (A) of Section 337(a)(1) limits the unfair practices it covers to those occurring "in the importation of articles . . . into the United States, or in the sale of such articles by the owner, importer, or consignee. . . ." Subparagraphs (B)-(E) of Section 337(a)(1) prohibit "[t]he importation into the United States, the sale for importation, or the sale within the United States after importation by the owner, importer, or consignee, of articles" that violate the intellectual property rights specified in those subparagraphs.[7] Both the Commission and its reviewing courts have treated "importation," "sale for importation," and "sale after importation" as jurisdictional. *See Enercon GmbH v. International Trade Commission*, 151 F.3d 1376, 1380-1383 (Fed. Cir. 1998), *affirming Certain Variable Speed Wind Turbines and Components Thereof*, Inv. No. 337-TA-376 (USITC Pub. 3003 (Nov. 1996)). Therefore, it is necessary to understand what is meant by each of these terms. In doing so, it must be kept in mind that while Section 337 addresses unfair practices and intellectual property rights, it is part of Title 19 of the United States Code, *i.e.*, the customs laws.

a. Importation; Reimportation

Under the customs laws, including Section 337, "importation" is defined broadly by case law as the act of bringing articles within the jurisdictional limits of the United States with intent to unlade them. *See, e.g., Porto Rico Brokerage Co.*,

7 Subparagraph (E), added in 1999, refers to "the owner, importer, or *consigner*." (Emphasis supplied.) The reference to "consigner" is apparently an inadvertent error, as subparagraphs (B)-(D) refer to "consignee."

Inc. v. United States, 76 F.2d 605 (CCPA 1935), *aff'd on rehearing*, 80 F.2d 521 (CCPA 1936). This definition covers the more familiar circumstance where the goods have been "unladed" and passed through Customs. The definition of importation is broad enough to include reimportation and the Commission has taken the position that reimportation is importation under Section 337. *Certain Sputtered Carbon-Coated Computer Disks and Products Containing Same, Including Disk Drives*, Inv. No. 337-TA-350 (Commission Opinion of October 27, 1993) (USITC Pub. 2701 (Nov. 1993)).

b. Sale for Importation

The term "sale for importation" presumes that importation has not yet occurred. The Commission's reviewing court (the United States Court of Appeals for the Federal Circuit) has held that Congress intended to give the term "sale" its ordinary meaning and that that meaning includes those situations in which a contract has been made between two parties who agree to transfer title and possession of specific property for a price. *Enercon*, 151 F.3d at 1381-82. In *Enercon*, the Federal Circuit found that U.C.C. § 2-106(1), which the Commission had used to define "sale," was in accord with the ordinary meaning of that term and that the Commission reasonably construed "sale for importation" as including the formation of a contract for goods in accordance with U.C.C. 2-204(1). *Enercon*, 151 F.3d at 1381-83. The court found no requirement that a "sale for importation" required delivery of the goods, or even delivery of control of the goods, to the purchaser or his agent. It also noted that U.C.C. 2-204(1) provides that "a contract for [the] sale of goods may be made in any manner sufficient to show agreement, including conduct by both parties which recognizes the existence of such a contract . . . even through the moment of its making is undetermined." *Enercon*, 151 F.3d at 1383.

Whether a contract has been formed is a factual conclusion. *Id.* at 1383. At the Commission level, the party arguing that a contract exists must establish that conclusion by a preponderance of the evidence. *Id.* On appeal, the Commission's factual conclusion of whether a contract has been formed will be affirmed if supported by substantial evidence. *Id.* In *Enercon*, the court found that there was substantial evidence, including the writings and the conduct of the parties, that the parties had entered into a contract for the sale of articles for importation into the United States. *Id.*

c. Sale after Importation

The definition of "sale after importation" follows logically from the foregoing definitions of "sale" and "importation."

d. Articles

This term obviously covers tangible products, the type that pass through the ports of entry of the United States every day. The ordinary meaning of the term would seem to preclude asserting Section 337 against electronic transmissions. However, some recent Commission decisions seem to indicate that the Commission may feel that it can assert jurisdiction over electronic transmissions, at least for the purpose of issuing cease and desist orders. *See, Certain Hardware Logic Emulation Systems and Components Thereof,* Inv. No. 337-TA-383 (USITC Pub. 3089 (March 1998)). The question has not yet been addressed by the Commission's reviewing court.

e. Definition of "United States"

Section 337(m) defines "United States" as "the customs territory of the United States as defined in general note 2 of the Harmonized Tariff Schedule of the United States," which in turn defines United States as consisting of the States, the District of Columbia, and Puerto Rico.

f. Owner, Importer, or Consignee

The owner of an article has legal title to it, though not necessarily possession. The importer of an article need not be its owner. A consignee of an article has possession of the article, but does not have legal title to it.

2. Unfair Practices Covered by Section 337

The unfair practices in the import trade which are prohibited by Section 337 are listed in Sections 337(a)(1)(A)-(E), but may be grouped for convenience into non-intellectual-property cases (Section 337(a)(1)(A)) and intellectual property cases (Section 337(a)(1)(B)-(E)).[8] Historically, the overwhelming majority of Section 337 cases have been brought for intellectual property infringement, especially patent infringement.

a. Non-Intellectual-Property Cases (Section 337(a)(1)(A))

Section 337(a)(1)(A) prohibits:

> Unfair methods of competition and unfair acts in the importation of articles (other than articles provided for in subparagraphs (B), (C), (D), and (E)) into the United States, or in the sale of such articles by the owner, importer, or consignee, the threat or effect of which is—
>
> (i) to destroy or substantially injure an industry in the United States;
>
> (ii) to prevent the establishment of such an industry; or
>
> (iii) to restrain or monopolize trade and commerce in the United States.

Very few cases are brought under this provision, which covers a wide variety of unfair practices, such as misappropriation of trade secrets, violations of the antitrust laws, passing off, and false advertising.

---

8 More precisely, the distinction is between cases involving infringement of an intellectual property right created by Federal law (Section 337(a)(1)(B)-(E)) and all other unfair practices. Some of these unfair practices include infringement of intellectual property rights, but not ones created by Federal law, *e.g.*, trade secrets and non-Federally registered trademarks.

b. Intellectual Property Cases (Section 337(a)(1)(B)-(E))

Section 337(a)(1)(B)-(E) covers cases involving infringement of a patent, copyright, Federally-registered trademark, mask work, or vessel hull design. These are discussed separately below.

i. Patent and Copyright Infringement

Section 337(a)(1)(B) prohibits:

> The importation into the United States, the sale for importation, or the sale within the United States after importation by the owner, importer, or consignee, of articles that—
>
> (i) infringe a valid and enforceable United States patent or a valid and enforceable United States copyright registered under title 17; or
>
> (ii) are made, produced, processed, or mined under, or by means of, a process covered by the claims of a valid and enforceable United States patent.

Section 337(a)(1)(B)(i) refers to patent and copyright infringement as defined under applicable Federal law.[9] Section 337(a)(1)(B)(ii) is a provision unique to Section 337. It was originally enacted in 1940 as Section 337a to overrule the decision of the United States Court of Customs and Patent Appeals in *In re Amtorg Trading Corporation*, 75 F.2d 826 (CCPA), *cert. denied*, 296 U.S. 576 (1935). It was reenacted in its present form in the OTCA in 1988.[10] The OTCA also enacted 35 U.S.C. § 271(g), covering process patent infringement under the patent laws, a provision which, like other acts of infringement defined by 35 U.S.C. § 271, is embraced by Section 337(a)(1)(B)(i). This means that there are two provisions in Section 337 covering process patent infringement. However, 35 U.S.C. § 271(g) is subject to certain express limitations and provisions that Section 337(a)(1)(B)(ii) is not. Presumably, the two provisions are not co-extensive. It is clear, however, that while Section 337(a)(1)(B)(ii) prohibits imports made using patented processes, it does not prohibit imports made by a process using patented articles. *Amgen, Inc. v. United States International Trade Commission*, 902 F.2d 1532 (Fed. Cir. 1990).

Cases for patent infringement form the overwhelming majority of Section 337 cases. Very few cases are brought for copyright infringement, perhaps because other provisions of law are more advantageous.

ii. Trademark Infringement

Section 337(a)(1)(C) prohibits:

> The importation into the United States, the sale for importation, or the sale within the United States after importation by the owner, importer, or consignee, of articles that infringe a valid and enforceable United States trademark registered under the Trademark Act of 1946.

---

9 There are, of course, some types of infringement which would not occur in importation, sale for importation, or sale after importation and therefore would not, as a practical matter, arise in Section 337 cases.

10 The history of Section 337(a)(1)(B)(ii) is recounted in *Amgen, Inc. v. United States International Trade Commission*, 902 F.2d 1532, 1538-40 (Fed. Cir. 1990)

By its terms this provision applies to trademarks registered under the Trademark Act of 1946 (the Lanham Act). It does not apply to unregistered marks or marks registered under state law (or any Federal law other than the Trademark Act of 1946). Only a few cases are brought under this provision, again perhaps because other provisions of law are more advantageous. One case to note, however, is *Certain Agricultural Tractors Under 50 Power Take-Off Horsepower*, Inv. No. 337-TA-380 (USITC Pub. 3026 (March 1997)), finding trademark infringement in a case involving so-called "gray-market goods." The Federal Circuit subsequently affirmed the Commission's decision. *Gamut Trading Co. v. International Trade Commission*, 200 F.3d 775 (Fed. Cir. 1999).

iii. Mask Work Infringement

Section 337(a)(1)(D) prohibits:

> The importation into the United States, the sale for importation, or the sale within the United States after importation by the owner, importer, or consignee, of a semiconductor chip product in a manner that constitutes infringement of a mask work registered under chapter 9 of title 17.

Only one case has been brought under this provision.

iv. Vessel Hull Design Infringement

Section 337(a)(1)(E) prohibits:

> The importation into the United States, the sale for importation, or the sale within the United States after importation by the owner, importer, or consigner [*sic*], of an article that constitutes infringement of the exclusive rights in a design protected under chapter 13 of title 17.

This provision was added in 1999. The "design" referred to is a design for a vessel hull, protection for which is provided for by the Digital Millennium Copyright Act. No cases have been brought under this provision.

v. Basis for Commission Decisions on Validity and Infringement of Intellectual Property Rights; Defenses Available

The Commission decides the substantive questions of validity and infringement of patents, copyrights, Federally-registered trademarks, mask works, and vessel hull designs by following the decisions of the Federal courts in these areas. In patent cases, the Commission follows the decisions of the United States Court of Appeals for the Federal Circuit. Section 337(c) provides that "[a]ll legal and equitable defenses may be presented in all cases." However, there are some defenses which will not apply in Section 337 cases, *i.e.*, those unique to claims for damages, such as failure to mark patented articles with notice of the patent.

3. Industry Requirement

a. Intellectual-Property-Based Cases (Section 337(a)(2)-(3))

In order to establish a violation of Section 337 in intellectual-property-based cases, a complainant must establish the existence of an "industry in the United

States" in addition to establishing the existence of an unfair act (such as patent infringement). For intellectual-property-based cases, the requirement is expressed in Section 337(a)(2), which provides that a Section 337 violation may be found—

> . . . only if an industry in the United States, relating to the articles protected by the patent, copyright, trademark, mask work, or design concerned, exists or is in the process of being established.

The criteria for determining whether a domestic industry defined by Section 337(a)(2) exists are set out in Section 337(a)(3) as follows:

> For purposes of paragraph (2), an industry in the United States shall be considered to exist if there is in the United States, with respect to the articles protected by the patent, copyright, trademark, mask work, or design concerned—
>
> (A) significant investment in plant and equipment;
>
> (B) significant employment of labor or capital; or
>
> (C) substantial investment in its exploitation, including engineering, research and development, or licensing.

Only one of these criteria need be met. Section 337(a)(3)(A) and Section 337(a)(3)(B) refer to activities with respect to an article covered by the involved intellectual property right. They are the most frequent bases for alleging the existence of a domestic industry. Section 337(a)(3)(C) contemplates that the complainant is relying on activities involving the intellectual property right itself.

In practice, the Commission has characterized the domestic industry requirement as having a "technical" prong and an "economic" prong. *See, Certain Variable Speed Wind Turbines and Components Thereof,* Inv. No. 337-TA-376 (Comm'n Opn. pp. 14-18) (USITC Pub. 3003 (Nov. 1996)).

To satisfy the technical prong where the complainant is relying on Section 337(a)(3)(A) or Section 337(a)(3)(B), the complainant must show that its own product or that of its licensees is covered by the intellectual property right it is asserting. *Id.* In patent cases, this means that the complainant must show that that product is covered by at least one claim of the asserted patent. *Id.* It is not necessary, however, for that claim to be the same claim asserted to be infringed. *Certain Microsphere Adhesives, Process for Making Same, and Products Containing Same, Including Self-Stick Repositionable Notes,* Inv. No. 337-TA-366 (Comm'n Opn. pp. 7-16) (USITC Pub. 2949 (Jan. 1996)). To satisfy the technical prong under Section 337(a)(3)(C), the complainant need not have a product at all, since the focus of that provision is on the intellectual property right itself.

To satisfy the economic prong of the domestic industry requirement, the complainant must demonstrate the existence of at least one of the relevant "significant" or "substantial" activities of Section 337(a)(3) with respect to the protected product or intellectual property right. *Certain Variable Speed Wind Turbine and Components Thereof,* Inv. No. 337-TA-376 (Comm'n Opn. pp. 14-18) (USITC Pub. 3003 (Nov. 1996)) This is a factual determination which is made on a case-by-case basis. There is no requirement that the industry be of any particular size. *Id.* In practice, little domestic activity is actually required and thus it is possible for even imported products to satisfy the requirement, if there is sufficient domestic post-importation activity with respect to them. *See, e.g., Certain Salinomycin Biomass and Preparations Containing Same*, Inv. No. 337-TA-370 (USITC Pub. 2978 (July 1996) (Unreviewed ID)). These activities cannot be cataloged in their entirety, but could, for example, include packaging, servicing, and repair. However, the legislative history indicates that mere sales activity is insufficient. Of course, if the complainant is relying on exploitation of the intellectual property right under Section 337(a)(3)(C), it need not have a product at all, since the statute specifically provides for the sufficiency of significant investment in the exploitation of that right, including engineering, research and development, or licensing.

b. Non-Intellectual-Property-Based Cases (Section 337(a)(1)(A))

There is also an "industry" requirement for at least some non-intellectual-property cases, *i.e.*, those brought under Section 337(a)(1)(A)(i)-(ii), though there is no express statutory definition of "industry" for Section 337(a)(1)(A)(i)-(ii) as there is for Section 337(a)(1)(B)-(E). However, as written, Section 337(a)(1)(A) substantially corresponds to the substantive provision of Section 337 as it existed prior to the 1988 amendments in the OTCA, and thus it would be expected that the Commission would follow the precedent established for defining a domestic industry under that prior provision, which, in any event, is similar to that set forth in Section 337(a)(3)(A)-(B). Section 337(a)(1)(A)(iii) does not have an "industry" requirement, but does refer to "trade and commerce." Here the Commission would be expected to follow its precedent of looking to the antitrust and unfair competition laws for guidance.

c. Time for Determining Existence of Industry

The Federal Circuit has held that the time for determining the existence of a domestic industry is as of the time the complaint is filed. *Bally-Midway Mfg. Co. v United States International Trade Commission*, 714 F.2d 1117, 1121-22 (Fed. Cir. 1983). The Commission may therefore not make a determination that there is no violation of Section 337 simply because the domestic industry ceases to exist during the pendency of the investigation because of the activities of the accused infringers. *Id.* The Commission takes the position, however, that after the conclusion of the investigation and the issuance of a remedial order, it can suspend or revoke its remedial order if the domestic industry requirement is no longer met. To that end, in one case where the complainant had become bankrupt and was in the process of ceasing operations, the Commission conditioned its relief on reports from the complainant as to the status of its operations. *Certain Variable Speed Wind Turbines and Components Thereof*, Inv. No. 337-TA-376 (USITC Pub. 3003 (Nov. 1996)).

4. Injury Requirement

There is no injury requirement for cases brought under Section 337(a)(1)(B)-(E), *i.e.,* for intellectual-property-based cases. There remains an injury requirement for cases under Section 337 (a)(1)(A), however. Thus, in non-intellectual-property-based cases, the unfair imports must have the threat or effect to (1) "destroy or substantially injure an industry in the United States," (2) "prevent the establishment of such an industry," or (3) "restrain or monopolize trade and commerce in the United States." 19 U.S.C. § 1337(a)(1)(A)(i)-(iii).

5. Statutory Exceptions to Coverage of Practices by Section 337 (Section 337(b)(3))

There are certain practices which Congress has decided should not be pursued (or at least not primarily pursued) under Section 337. These are set out in Section 337(b)(3) and consist of practices which fall within the antidumping or countervailing duty laws and certain acts which Congress has determined cannot form the basis of an action for copyright infringement.

a. Dumping and Unlawful Subsidies

Imports involving less-than-fair value sales (dumping) or benefiting from the provision of unlawful subsidies are subject to their own, separate statutory regimes, which are jointly administered by the Commission and the Department of Commerce. These regimes, specifically set out in 19 U.S.C. §§ 1671,1673 *et seq.*, are commonly referred to as the countervailing duty and antidumping laws and it is those laws, not Section 337, that constitute the primary avenue for seeking relief from the unfair practices they cover.

i. Complaint or Investigation Based Solely on Acts within Antidumping or Countervailing Duty Laws

Under Section 337(b)(3), the Commission is not permitted to institute a Section 337 investigation if it has reason to believe that the matter before it is based solely on alleged acts and effects which are within the purview of the countervailing duty or antidumping laws. If it has already instituted such an investigation, it must terminate it.

ii. Complaint or Investigation Based Partly on Acts Within Antidumping or Countervailing Duty Laws

If the matter before the Commission is only based in part on allegations covered by the antidumping and/or countervailing duty laws and also in part on alleged acts and effects which could form an independent basis for a Section 337 investigation, the Commission may institute or continue a Section 337 investigation into the entire matter.

iii. Notification to Department of Commerce; Investigation by Commerce

The Commission may notify the United States Department of Commerce if it has reason to believe a matter before it is covered in whole or in part by the countervailing duty or antidumping laws. The Department of Commerce may then commence an investigation under those laws.

As noted above, if the matter before the Commission is covered wholly by the countervailing duty or antidumping laws, the Commission may not institute a Section 337 investigation and, if it has, it must terminate that investigation. However, if the matter before the Commission is only covered in part by the countervailing duty or antidumping laws, the Commission may institute a Section 337 investigation or continue such an investigation. In the latter case, if the Department of Commerce commences a countervailing duty or antidumping proceeding, the Commission may suspend its Section 337 investigation during the time the matter is before the Department of Commerce for final decision. Any final decision by the Department of Commerce in its investigation will be "conclusive upon the Commission with respect to the issue of less-than-fair-value sales or subsidization and the matters necessary for such decision."

b. Complaint or Investigation Based on Certain Types of Alleged Copyright Infringement

Copyright infringement generally comes within Section 337(a)(1)(B)(i). However, if the Commission has reason to believe that the matter before it relates to alleged copyright infringement with respect to which action is prohibited by 17 U.S.C. § 1008, the Commission may not institute a Section 337 investigation with respect to that alleged unfair act. 19 U.S.C. § 1337(b)(3). If it has already done so, it must terminate that investigation. *Id.*

B. Remedial Orders

If the Commission concludes that a violation of Section 337 exists, it may issue an exclusion order, a cease and desist order, or both. The Commission has a great deal of latitude in selecting the appropriate remedial order and the terms of any such order. *Hyundai Electronics Industries Co., Ltd. v. United States International Trade Commission*, 899 F.2d 1204, 1208-09 (Fed. Cir. 1990); *Viscofan, S.A. v. United States International Trade Commission*, 787 F.2d 544, 548 (Fed. Cir. 1986).

1. Exclusion Orders (Section 337(d)-(e))

Exclusion orders are orders excluding the involved articles from entry into the United States and are enforced by the United States Customs Service at the ports of entry. They are usually framed in terms of the exclusion of articles covered by the intellectual property right found to have been infringed. There are two types of exclusion orders: limited and general. A limited exclusion order is limited to articles from a named firm which was a respondent in the Commission's investigation, *e.g.*, "articles made by X coming within claim 1 of United States Patent No.______." A general exclusion order is not limited as to source and will apply to non-parties as well. However, to obtain a general exclusion order, the criteria of Section 337(d)(2) must be satisfied. Specifically, the complainant must show that "a general exclusion from entry of articles is necessary to prevent circumvention of an exclusion order limited to products of named persons" or that "there is a pattern of violation of this section and it is difficult to identify the source of infringing products." Section 337(d)(2) was added by the URAA, but reflects preexisting Commission case law. For an example of a case where a general exclusion order was issued, *see Certain Neodymium-Boron-Magnets, Magnet Alloys, and Articles Containing Same*, Inv. No. 337-TA-372 (USITC Pub. 2964 (May 1996)). An exclusion order is ordinarily directed to entries for consumption unless it has been shown that it should be directed to other types of entries as well. *See, e.g., Certain Variable Speed Wind Turbines and Components Thereof*, Inv. No. 337-TA-376 (USITC Pub. 3003 (Nov. 1996)).

2. Cease and Desist Orders (Section 337(f))

A cease and desist order is an order to a named person who was a respondent in the Commission's investigation to cease and desist certain activities to prevent further violation of Section 337. A cease and desist order will normally be issued if the complainant establishes the existence of "commercially significant" inventory of the infringing articles held by the respondent in the United States. *Certain Neodymium-Iron-Boron Magnets, Magnet Alloys, and Articles Containing Same*, Inv. No. 337-TA-372 (Comm'n Opn. pp. 13-14) (USITC Pub 2964 (May 1996)). Consent orders are a kind of cease and desist order, *i.e.*, they are consent orders to cease and desist. As discussed *infra*, under Section 337(f), the Commission itself enforces its cease desist orders and if it finds such an order to have been violated it may replace it with an exclusion order. It may also assess a civil penalty of not more than the greater of $100,000 a day or twice the domestic value of articles entered or sold for each day such articles are imported or sold in violation of a cease and desist order.

3. Remedial Orders for Downstream Products

Complainants sometimes seek remedial orders not only against the products specifically covered by the intellectual property right involved in the investigation, but also articles which incorporate those products, *i.e.*, downstream products. When this occurs, the Commission must balance the right of the intellectual property owner to a complete remedy against the potential disruption to legitimate international trade such an order might cause. The Commission performs this balancing by considering certain factors set out in *Certain Erasable Programmable Read-Only Memories, Components Thereof, Products Containing Such Memories, and Processes for Making Such Memories ("EPROMs")*, Inv. No. 337-TA-276 (Comm'n Opn. at 125) (USITC Pub. 2196 (May 1989)), *aff'd, Hyundai Electronics Industries Co., Ltd. v. United States International Trade Commission*, 899 F.2d 1204 (Fed. Cir. 1990). These factors include, but are not limited to (1) the value of the infringing articles compared to the value of the downstream products in which they are incorporated, (2) the identity of the manufacturer of the downstream products (*i.e.*, are the downstream products manufactured by the party found to have committed the unfair act, or by third parties), (3) the incremental value to the complainant of the exclusion of the downstream products, (4) the incremental detriment to the respondents of such exclusion, (5) the burdens imposed on third parties resulting from the exclusion of downstream products, (6) the availability of alternative downstream products which do not contain the infringing articles, (7) the likelihood that imported downstream products actually contain the infringing articles and are thereby subject to exclusion, (8) the opportunity for evasion of an exclusion order which does not include downstream products, and (9) the enforceability by the Customs Service of an order including downstream products. *Id.*

It is the complainant's burden to justify an order against downstream products and the Commission, in the recent past, has been reluctant to award such relief except in limited ways. Thus, in *EPROMs*, the Commission refused to order exclusion of such downstream products as computers which incorporated the covered memory chips, but did find justification for exclusion of motherboards containing those chips. The Commission is more willing to order downstream product relief where to fail to do so would result in the effective denial of any relief.

The grant of downstream product relief may provoke a negative reaction from the Office of the United States Trade Representative during the Presidential review period, possibly resulting in disapproval of any Commission order including such relief.

4. Seizure and Forfeiture Orders (Section 337(i))

Section 337(i) authorizes the Commission to order seizure and forfeiture of an article that is subject to an exclusion order when (1) the owner, importer, or consignee has previously attempted to import the article; (2) it was previously denied entry because of the exclusion order; and (3) the Secretary of the Treasury (*i.e.*, Customs) provided notice of the exclusion order and that a further attempt to enter the article would result in seizure and forfeiture. The intent of Section 337(i) is to deter importers from knowingly attempting to circumvent an exclusion order by "port shopping" or by other repeated attempts to enter goods or like goods subject to an exclusion order. A seizure and forfeiture order is not issued at the end of the Commission's investigation, but rather during the course of Customs' enforcement of an exclusion order.

C. Public Interest Factors Precluding Relief (Section 337(d)-(f))

While a finding of a violation of Section 337 will ordinarily result in the issuance of a remedial order, this is not a certainty because Section 337(d)-(f) provides that the Commission may nevertheless refuse to issue remedial orders if after examining their effect "upon the public health and welfare, competitive conditions in the United States economy, the production of like or directly competitive articles in the United States, and United States consumers," it finds that such orders should not be issued. The Commission has only rarely invoked consideration of these public interest factors to deny relief where it has found a violation of Section 337.[11]

D. Important Procedural Aspects of Section 337

1. Applicability of the Administrative Procedure Act

Section 337(c) provides that Commission determinations under Section 337 are to be made "on the record after notice and opportunity for a hearing in conformity with the provisions of subchapter II of chapter 5 of title 5 [of the United States Code]," placing Section 337 proceedings under the adjudicative provisions of the Administrative Procedure Act. Section 337 proceedings are the only Commission proceedings subject to these provisions. The Commission takes the position that these provisions certainly apply from the time it institutes a Section 337 investigation until it issues its final determination on whether a violation of Section 337 exists (or the investigation is earlier terminated). However, the Commission believes that these provisions do not apply to its institution proceedings (during which it determines whether to institute a Section 337 investigation) or to certain proceedings related to its Section 337 investigations. Further, even within the context of its Section 337 investigations, the Commission takes the position that these provisions do not apply to the issues of remedy, the public interest, and bonding, as discussed *infra*.

2. Time Limits

Section 337(b)(1) requires that the Commission complete its Section 337 investigations "at the earliest practicable time" after publication of the notice of investigation in the *Federal Register*. To this end, Section 337(b)(1) requires the Commission to "establish a target date for its final determination" within 45 days after institution of the investigation. The "target date" is an administrative deadline and may be extended. As a matter of policy, the Commission has determined to establish target dates similar to the 12 and 18-month statutory deadlines for completion that were in effect prior to the amendment of Section 337 by the URAA. Most target dates have been set at 11 to 15 months from publication of the notice of investigation in the *Federal Register*. Some of these have been extended.

The Commission has delegated its authority to initially set target dates to its administrative law judges, who are free to issue orders setting target dates up to 15 months. Commission Rule 210.51. Orders setting a target date at 15 months or less are final and not subject to interlocutory review by the Commission. To set

11 The Commission did, however, deny relief on this basis in *Certain Crankpin Grinders*, Inv. No. 337-TA-60 (USITC Pub. 1022 (1979)) and in *Certain Inclined-Field Acceleration Tubes and Components Thereof*, Inv. No. 337-TA-67 (USITC Pub. 1119 (1980)).

a longer target date, or to extend an existing target date past 15 months, the administrative law judge must issue his or her order as an initial determination, providing an opportunity for possible Commission review.

In setting a target date, the administrative law judge may (but is not required to) request the parties to submit "target date statements" and replies thereto, arguing for a particular target date. Typically, complainants seek shorter dates than respondents, though the parties sometimes will agree on a target date. Generally, the benchmark for target dates is 12 months. A longer target date may be set if the case presents such features as, for example, assertion of several intellectual property rights, the existence of numerous parties, or complex technology.

It should be noted that the statutory requirement for setting a target date applies only to original investigations. It does not apply to investigations remanded to the Commission by its reviewing court, nor does it apply to so-called related proceedings (discussed *infra*). Nevertheless, the Commission may (and often does) set administrative deadlines governing remanded investigations and related proceedings to assure that these are completed on a timely basis.

IV. OVERVIEW OF SECTION 337 PROCEEDINGS

The primary proceeding which the Commission conducts under Section 337 is its investigation as to whether there is a violation of Section 337. In addition, the Commission conducts certain proceedings which bear on certain matters related to Commission Section 337 investigations, but which can be or must be conducted separately. The Commission refers to these latter proceedings as related proceedings. The Commission's rules define what constitutes an investigation and a related proceeding.[12]

---

12 Commission Rule 210.3 defines an investigation as "a formal Commission inquiry instituted to determine whether there is a violation of section 337 of the Tariff Act of 1930. An investigation is instituted upon publication of a notice in the *Federal Register*. The investigation entails postinstitution adjudication of the complaint. An investigation can also involve the processing of one or more of the following: a motion to amend the complaint and notice of investigation; a motion for temporary relief; a motion to designate "more complicated" the temporary relief stage of the investigation; an interlocutory appeal of an administrative law judge's decision on a particular matter; a motion for sanctions for abuse of process, abuse of discovery, or failure to make or cooperate in discovery, which if granted, would have an impact on the adjudication of the merits of the complaint; a petition for reconsideration of a final Commission determination; a motion for termination of the investigation in whole or part; and procedures undertaken in response to a judgment or judicial order issued in an appeal of a Commission determination or remedial order issued under section 337 of the Tariff Act of 1930."

Commission Rule 210.3 defines related proceedings as "preinstitution proceedings, sanction proceedings (for the possible issuance of sanctions that would not have a bearing on the adjudication of the merits of a complaint or a motion under this part [19 C.F.R. Part 210]), bond forfeiture proceedings, proceedings to enforce, modify, or revoke a remedial or consent order, or advisory opinion proceedings."

Typical related proceedings include those to determine whether to institute a Section 337 investigation, enforcement of cease and desist orders or consent orders, and certain sanction proceedings.

Nearly all Section 337 investigations are instituted on the basis of complaints filed by private parties, though the Commission does have authority to institute investigations on its own motion. The proceeding by which the Commission decides whether to institute a Section 337 investigation is referred to by several names. In practice, it is usually referred to as an institution proceeding, though the Commission's rules also refer to it as pre-institution proceeding or an initiation proceeding.

Once instituted, the investigation may generally be divided into two phases: proceedings before the administrative law judge (ALJ) and proceedings before the Commission itself. There are at least three parties to an investigation: the complainant(s), the respondent(s), and the Commission investigative attorney.

Unless the investigation is terminated sooner, the proceedings before the ALJ result in: (1) an initial determination on whether a violation of Section 337 exists and (2) a recommended determination on what type of remedial order should be issued and the amount of the bond that must be posted to permit temporary entry during the Presidential review period.

The ALJ's initial determination and recommended determination are subject to review by the Commission itself. If the Commission decides to review the initial determination, it will conduct review proceedings on the question of violation of Section 337 based on the existing evidentiary record. Further, whether it conducts review proceedings or not, if the possibility of the issuance of a remedial order exists, the Commission will seek submissions on remedy, public interest and bonding by parties and non-parties.

To remedy any violation it has found, the Commission may issue an exclusion order prohibiting the importation of infringing articles and/or a cease and desist order directed against persons having been found to be in violation of Section 337.

If the Commission finds a violation of Section 337 and issues a remedial order, it will forward its determination and order to the President, who may disapprove them for policy reasons. Commission determinations under Section 337 are subject to review by the United States Court of Appeals for the Federal Circuit, whose decisions are in turn reviewable by the United States Supreme Court by writ of certiorari.

The following flowchart (taken from the Commission's *Year in Review* for fiscal year 2000) illustrates the timetable for a Section 337 investigation:

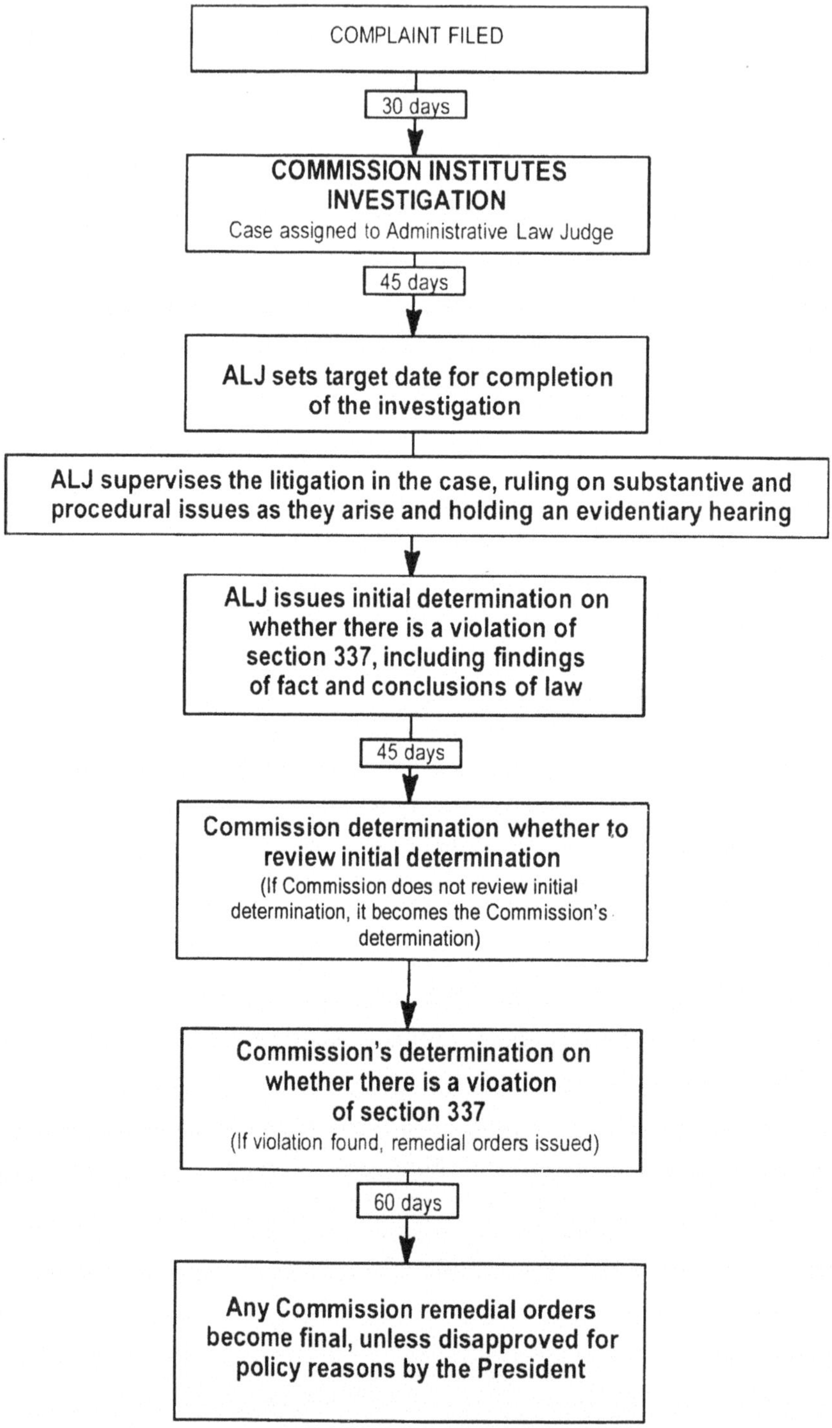

V. GENERAL RULES FOR WRITTEN SUBMISSIONS AND COMPUTATION OF TIME

The Commission has prescribed rules covering the form of written submissions, filing and service, and computation of time, which apply to Section 337 investigations and related proceedings. It should be noted that there are special rules governing the filing and service of complaints and motions for temporary relief, as discussed *infra*.

A. Written Submissions (Commission Rules 201.8, 201.16, 210.4)

1. Form

All written submissions must be on letter size paper (8½ inches by 11 inches). However, copies of documents prepared for a court or another agency (such as court pleadings or patent file wrappers) may be of a larger size.

All submissions must be clear and legible.

The name of the person signing the original must be typewritten or otherwise reproduced on each copy.

If the document contains confidential information, it must be labeled to indicate that it contains confidential information. As a matter of good practice, this label should be bolded or otherwise call attention to itself. Preferably, the label should appear at the top (or bottom) of every page of the document, so that if the pages become separated, it can readily be determined that they came from a confidential document and treated accordingly.

2. Where Filed; Mode of Filing

Written submissions are filed at the Office of the Secretary of the Commission. They are deemed filed on the day they are actually received. Thus, while it is possible to file by mail or overnight courier, such submissions will be deemed to be filed as of the date of actual receipt. As a matter of practice, the Office of the Secretary currently does not accept filings via facsimile or electronic transmission. A cover sheet (available from the Office of the Secretary or the Commission's website) should accompany any filing. The cover sheet calls for certain information which is used to index the document on the Commission's Electronic Document Imaging System (EDIS).

3. Service

Unless an applicable rule, the Commission, or the presiding administrative law judge specifically provides otherwise, every written submission filed by a party or proposed party must be served on all other parties in the manner specified in Commission Rule 201.16(b).

a. Mode of Service

Commission Rule 201.16(b) provides for mail service or actual delivery to a party or counsel for a party (if the party is represented by counsel). If service is by mail, it must be by first class mail, postage prepaid. If the addressee is outside the United States, mail service must be by first class air mail, postage prepaid. Service by mail is complete on mailing, but three calendar days are added for any response to a document served by mail, unless the addressee is located in a foreign country, in which case 10 calendar days are added.

b. Proof of Service

Each document served must be filed with a certificate of service showing the date and manner of service. Such a certificate constitutes proof of service. Commission Rule 201.16(c). The Office of the Secretary will not accept a document required to be served which is not accompanied by a certificate of service and will so notify the submitter.

4. Number of Copies for Filing with Original

A prescribed number of copies must be filed with the original of any written submission. There is a special rule with regard to the number of copies of the complaint which must be filed with the Commission. With regard to other written submissions, the number of copies which must be filed depends on whether the submission is addressed to (*i.e.*, is to be acted on by) the Commission itself or to the administrative law judge. In the former case, a signed original (or a copy designated as an original) and fourteen copies are required. Commission Rules 201.8(d), 210.4(f)(2). In the latter case, an original and six copies are required.[13] Commission Rule 210.4(f)(2). As a general rule, when the investigation is before the Commission, all submissions will be addressed to the Commission. When the investigation is before the ALJ, most submissions will be addressed to the ALJ but some may be addressed to the Commission.[14] The original and at least one copy must be printed on one side only and left unbound. Commission Rule 201.8(d) provides that the "unbound" original and copy may be "stapled or held together by a clip." However, as a matter of practice the Office of the Secretary will not accept "unbound" originals or copies that are stapled, so these must always be held together by a clip, such as a binder clip. Of course, the remaining copies may be stapled. Further, as a matter of practice, the Office of the Secretary will not accept "unbound" originals and copies that include tabbed pages (as for exhibits). Rather, untabbed pages with the exhibit numbers printed on their face must be substituted for the tabbed pages. The remaining copies may include tabbed pages.

There are additional rules governing the number of copies of those documents which contain confidential information and for which public versions must be

---

13 The Commission has recently issued a notice relaxing its copy requirements. 66 F.R. 58523-24 (Nov. 21, 2001).

14 For example, a motion for partial summary determination would be addressed to the ALJ and would be filed as an original and six copies. The ALJ grants such motions by initial determination which are subject to Commission review on petition while the remainder of the case continues to proceed before the ALJ. A petition for review is addressed to the Commission, not the ALJ, and thus would be filed as an original and fourteen copies.

filed. Under Commission Rule 201.8(d), four additional copies of such documents must be filed in which the confidential business information has been deleted and these copies must be marked "non-confidential" or "public version." As a matter of practice, two of the four copies of each of these so-called non-confidential or public versions should be treated as the "unbound" original and copy of the non-confidential version. Of course, as noted above, the confidential version must be labeled to indicate that it contains confidential information.

5. Requirement and Time for Filing Public Versions

Commission Rule 201.8, which is a rule of general applicability, requires non-confidential or public versions of all submissions which contain confidential information. However, Commission Rule 210.4(f)(3)(i), which is specific to Section 337 cases (and therefore governs over Commission Rule 201.8) requires public versions only for specified submissions, to be filed at specified times.

Thus, a public version is required for a complaint, a supplement to a complaint, a motion for temporary relief, and documentation supporting a motion for temporary relief. Public versions of these submissions must be filed concurrently with the confidential versions.

A public version is also required for a response to a complaint and all supplements and exhibits thereto, all submissions relating to a motion to amend the complaint or notice of investigation, and all submissions addressed to the Commission. Public versions of these documents need not be filed concurrently with the confidential versions, but must be filed within ten calendar days of filing the confidential versions.

By order, the Commission or the administrative law judge may require the filing of public versions of other confidential submissions at specified times.

If a submitter's ability to prepare a non-confidential version of a submission is dependent upon receipt of the non-confidential version of an initial determination, or a Commission order or opinion, or a ruling by the administrative law judge or the Commission as to whether some or all of the information at issue is entitled to confidential treatment, the non-confidential copies of the submission must be filed within 10 calendar days after service of the Commission or administrative law judge document in question.

The time periods set out above for filing public versions apply unless the Commission, the administrative law judge, or another rule specifically provides otherwise.

B. Computation of Time (Commission Rules 201.14, 201.16(d))

1. General Rule

Unless the Commission, the administrative law judge, or an applicable rule prescribes otherwise, the computation of time in Section 337 proceedings is governed by Commission Rules 201.14 and 201.16(d). Under Commission Rule

201.14, any period of time prescribed or allowed begins on the next business day following the day on which the act or event initiating such period of time. This means that if, for example, a motion is served on a Friday, the period for filing and serving a response does not begin on Saturday (as would be the case in a Federal district court action) but on the following Monday.[15]

If the last day of the period so computed it is a Saturday, Sunday, or Federal legal holiday, the period runs until the end of the next business day. A Federal legal holiday refers to any full calendar day designated as a legal holiday by the President or the Congress of the United States. Commission Rule 201.14.

2. Special Rule for Periods of Less Than Seven Days

When the period of time prescribed or allowed is less than 7 days, intermediate Saturdays, Sundays, and Federal legal holidays are excluded from the computation.

3. Additional Time After Service by Mail

As noted above, Commission Rule 201.16(d) prescribes additional time to take action with respect to a document (*e.g.*, a motion) where that document was served by mail.

VI. CONFIDENTIAL INFORMATION (Section 337(n); Commission Rule 201.6)

A. Generally

Section 337(n) governs the disclosure of confidential information submitted to the Commission or exchanged among the parties in Section 337 proceedings. Section 337(n) leaves it to the Commission to define what constitutes confidential information and the Commission has done so in Commission Rule 201.6(a)(1). As defined by the Commission, confidential business information is information which concerns or relates to the

> trade secrets, processes, operations, style of works, or apparatus, or to the production, sales, shipments, purchases, transfers, identification of customers, inventories, or amount or source of any income, profits, losses or expenditures of any person, firm, partnership, corporation, or other organization or other information of commercial value, the disclosure of which is likely to have the effect of either impairing the Commission's ability to obtain such information as is necessary to perform its statutory functions, or causing substantial harm to the competitive position of the person, firm, partnership, corporation, or other organization from which the information was obtained, unless the Commission is required by law to disclose such information.

Section 337(n)(1) prohibits the disclosure of confidential information except pursuant to a protective order issued under the authority of the Commission,

15 As a result of this provision, many practitioners serve motions no later than Thursday.

unless the permission of the submitter has been obtained for such disclosure. Notwithstanding this provision, Section 337(n)(2) provides for disclosure of confidential information to certain enumerated persons, specifically:

(a) An officer or employee of the Commission who is directly concerned with

- carrying out the investigation or related proceeding in connection with which the information is submitted.
- the administration of a bond pursuant to Section 337(e), (f) or (j).
- the administration or enforcement of an exclusion order issued pursuant to Section 337(d), (e), or (g), a cease and desist order issued pursuant to Section 337(f), or a consent order issued pursuant to Section 337(c).
- proceedings for the modification or rescission of a temporary or permanent order issued under Section 337(d)-(g), (i), or a consent order.
- maintaining the administrative record of the investigation or related proceeding.

(b) An officer or employee of the United States Government who is directly involved in Presidential review under Section 337(j).

(c) An officer or employee of the United States Customs Service who is directly involved in administering an exclusion order under Section 337(d), (e), or (g) resulting from the investigation or related proceeding in connection with which the information is submitted.

B. Obtaining Confidential Treatment

1. Prior to Institution of the Investigation

During the time the Commission is considering whether to institute a Section 337 investigation (*i.e.*, during institution proceedings), there is no protective order in effect. However, confidential treatment for submissions may be sought by filing a request addressed to the Secretary. Ordinarily, only the complainant will be seeking confidential treatment during the institution phase. Commission Rule 201.6 sets out the procedure for requesting confidential treatment, but as a matter of practice, the complainant simply files a request (usually in the form of a letter to the Secretary) along with the complaint, briefly explaining the justification for the request for confidential treatment and certifying in writing under oath that substantially identical information is not available to the public. The Secretary notifies the requester by letter as to the action taken on the request. As a matter of practice, these requests are almost always granted.

2. After Institution

After institution of the investigation, the confidential treatment of submissions or information is governed by a protective order, issued by the administrative law judge within a few days of institution.

VII. INITIATION OF A SECTION 337 INVESTIGATION

The Commission has authority to institute Section 337 investigations "on complaint under oath or upon its initiative." 19 U.S.C. § 1337(b)(1). Historically,

Section 337 cases have been initiated by complaint filed by a private party, usually the intellectual property owner or another person who has standing to bring an action under the intellectual property right. The Commission has only rarely instituted investigations on its own initiative and even in those cases, close examination shows that the investigation was actually based on a complaint or derived from a pre-existing investigation that was based on a complaint.

The filing of a complaint does not itself commence an investigation. Rather, the Commission must vote on whether to institute an investigation. By rule, the Commission has given itself 30 days (which may be extended) to consider the complaint.[16] As with other types of investigations based on complaint or petition, the Commission will institute a Section 337 investigation if one half of the Commissioners voting agree that an investigation should be instituted. 19 U.S.C. § 1330(d)(5). If the Commission votes to institute an investigation, it will issue a notice of investigation, which it will then publish in the *Federal Register,* usually within a week after it issues the notice. Publication of the notice of investigation in the *Federal Register* marks the official beginning of the investigation. Many (but not all) subsequent dates in the investigation are determined by reference to the date of publication of the notice of investigation in the *Federal Register.*

A. The Complaint

The required contents of the complaint are set out in Commission Rule 210.12. That same rule also provides that, in certain cases, additional materials must be provided with the complaint. The complaint will be considered properly filed if it conforms with the Commission's rules or if it substantially complies with those rules and "good and sufficient reason" is given for the failure to fully comply with those rules.[17]

Unlike complaints in Federal district court actions for patent infringement, Section 337 complaints must contain considerable factual pleadings. There are two reasons for this. First, since the Commission is taking the affirmative act of voting on institution, it must assure itself that there is adequate basis to proceed. Second, as a matter of policy, the Commission wishes to provide a respondent with as much information as possible at the beginning of an investigation to avoid potential unfairness, since Section 337 investigations are subject to time limits. This second aspect was particularly important prior to the amendment of

16 This 30-day "institution," "initiation" or "pre-institution" proceeding is a "related proceeding" under the Commission's rules.

17 Under Commission Rule 201. 8, each document filed with the Commission for the purpose of initiating any investigation, including a Section 337 investigation, will be considered properly filed if it conforms with the pertinent rules therefor. In Section 337 cases, the document filed for the purpose of initiating the investigation is the complaint. Substantial compliance with the pertinent rules may be accepted by the Commission provided "good and sufficient reason" is stated for the inability to comply fully with the rules. Commission Rule 201.8.

Section 337 by the URAA, when Section 337 provided short statutory deadlines for the completion of investigations (one year, extendable to 18 months in "more complicated" cases), thus affording only limited discovery to respondents. That importance largely remains because the Commission has chosen to set its administrative deadlines ("target dates") very close to the previous statutory deadlines.

Ordinarily, if the complaint contains the information required by Commission Rule 210.12, is accompanied by any required additional materials, and makes out an alleged violation of Section 337, institution is assured. There have, however, been instances where the Commission has refused to institute an investigation because the complaint contained inadequate information or where it was clear from the information presented that an investigation should not be instituted. The Commission has also delayed institution or conducted a preliminary investigation where it felt that certain factual or legal issues needed to be pursued prior to institution.

B. Contents of the Complaint (Commission Rule 210.12)

1. Oath and Signatures (Commission Rule 210.12(a)(1))

Commission Rule 210.12(a)(1) provides that the complaint must be "under oath and signed by the complainant or his duly authorized officer, attorney, or agent. . . ." As a matter of practice, the complaint is usually signed by the attorney for the complainant and has attached thereto a verification consisting of an oath or declaration that the person subscribing has personal knowledge and/or knowledge on information and belief of the facts stated therein and that they are true (or believed to be true, where knowledge is on information and belief). If an unsworn declaration is made in lieu of an oath, the declaration is made under penalty of perjury. *See*, 28 U.S.C. § 1746. Since most complainants are corporations, most verifications are signed by an officer of the corporation. Sometimes verifications are made by in-house counsel (who may or may not be an officer of the corporation). Occasionally, the oath or declaration is signed by outside counsel or another agent designated by the complainant. The person who signs the verification will be a target for a deposition. Outside counsel should therefore ordinarily not sign the oath or declaration.

The rule requires that the name, address, and telephone number of the complainant must appear on the first page of the complaint. The rule also requires that the name, address, and telephone number of the officer, attorney or agent signing the oath or declaration appear on the first page of the complaint.

2. Statement of Facts (Commission Rule 210.12(a)(2))

Commission Rule 210.12(a)(2) requires that the complaint include a "statement of the facts constituting the alleged unfair methods of competition and unfair acts." This is usually satisfied by a recitation of those ultimate facts which, if established, make out the unfair practice alleged. Thus, for example, where the unfair practice alleged is to be patent infringement under 35 U.S.C. § 271(a) by the importation, sale for importation, or sale after importation of an accused article, the recitation of ultimate facts would be that:

- the accused article is being imported into the United States, sold for importation into the United States, or sold after importation into the United States;
- the complainant is the owner or exclusive licensee of the asserted patent;
- the accused article is covered by at least one claim of the patent; and
- the sale or importation of the accused article is without authority of the patentee.

3. Specific Instances of Unlawful Importation or Sales (Commission Rule 210.12(a)(3))

Commission Rule 210.12(a)(3) requires that the complaint describe "specific instances of alleged unlawful importations or sales." The specific instances referred to are specific importations or sales of the accused articles. Complainants usually do not have any direct knowledge of a specific importation since Customs entry papers are not publicly available.[18] However, importation is easily inferred from the presence of the imported article in the United States coupled with evidence that the accused article is of foreign origin. Presence in the United States is usually made known by the article being placed on sale in the United States. The complainant usually recites one or more instances of such offers for sale, referring to the specific entity and location making the offer and the specific item being offered and the date. The complainant will sometimes make purchases of such articles directly or indirectly. Evidence of foreign origin is frequently available as a consequence of customs marking requirements, which may result in the name of the country of origin appearing on the article itself or on its package or container. Photographs of the article and/or its packaging, including portions showing manufacturer and/or country of origin, as well as copies of receipts, and indeed the articles and their packaging, may be submitted as exhibits.

4. Tariff Numbers (Commission Rule 210.12(a)(3))

Commission Rule 210.12(a)(3) requires that the complaint provide the tariff numbers for the accused articles. For importations prior to January 18, 1989, the relevant tariff numbers are the applicable item numbers in the Tariff Schedules of the United States (TSUS). For importations on or after January 1, 1989, the relevant tariff numbers are the applicable item numbers in the Harmonized Tariff Schedule of the United States (HTSUS or HTS).

It is now unlikely that importations prior to January 1, 1989, will be the subject of a Section 337 complaint and therefore the question of providing TSUS

---

18 Complainants may, however, be able to take advantage of a patent import survey conducted by the Customs Service under 19 C.F.R. § 12.39a to determine such importation.

numbers is not likely to arise. As to HTS numbers, the complainant will ordinarily not know what HTS numbers the importations in question came in under, since customs entry documents are not publicly available. However, given knowledge of the article, the complainant may offer its opinion or belief of where the articles should be classified under the HTS, *i.e.*, HTS numbers. This is sufficient to meet the rule.

5. Proposed Respondents (Commission Rule 210.12(a)(4))

Commission Rule 210.12(a)(4) requires that the complaint state the name and address of each person alleged to be violating Section 337. These persons are referred to as proposed respondents and are usually listed on the front page of the complaint. The rule also requires that the complaint state the nature of the business of each proposed respondent, if known. There is ordinarily no difficulty in meeting these requirements.

6. Other Court or Agency Litigation (Commission Rule 210.12(a)(5))

Commission Rule 210.12(a)(5) requires that the complaint include "a statement as to whether the alleged unfair methods of competition and unfair acts, or the subject matter thereof, are or have been the subject of any court or agency litigation and, if so, include a brief summary of such litigation." This requirement is usually met by identifying the other litigation by title and court number, with a brief statement of the nature and status of the proceedings.

7. Domestic Industry/Trade and Commerce (Commission Rule 210.12(a)(6))

a. Intellectual-Property-Based Cases

Commission Rule 210.12(a)(6)(i) addresses complaint requirements for alleging the existence of a domestic industry for cases brought under Section 337(a)(1)(B)-(E), *i.e.*, cases where the alleged unlawful unfair practice is the infringement of certain intellectual property rights, *i.e.*, patents, copyrights, mask works, Federally-registered trademarks, and vessel hull designs. As noted above, these cases are by far the most numerous brought under Section 337, with patent cases being the overwhelming majority. For such cases, Commission Rule 210.12(a)(6)(i) requires that the complaint provide "a description of the relevant domestic industry as defined in section 337(a)(3) that allegedly exists or is in the process of being established, including the relevant operations of any licensees." The rule provides that relevant information includes but is not limited to: (A) significant investment in plant and equipment; (B) significant employment of labor or capital; and (C) substantial investment in the exploration of the subject patent, copyright, trademark, or mask work, including engineering, research and development, or licensing. These, of course, are the domestic industry criteria set out in Section 337(a)(3).

b. Non-Intellectual-Property-Based Cases

Commission Rule 210.12(a)(6)(ii) addresses the information required for an allegation of domestic industry in cases not involving alleged violations of the intellectual property rights set out in Section 337(a)(1)(B)-(E), *i.e.*, cases brought under Section 337(a)(1)(A)(i)-(ii). The requirement is stated simply as "a description of the domestic industry affected, including the relevant operations of any licensees."

c. Antitrust-Based Cases

Commission Rule 210.12(a)(6)(iii) addresses the situation where the alleged unfair practices "have the threat or effect of restraining or monopolizing trade and commerce in the United States . . .," *i.e.*, cases brought under Section 337 (a)(1)(A)(iii) (usually antitrust violations). In such cases, the complaint must include "a description of the trade and commerce affected."

8. Complainant's Business (Commission Rule 210.12(a)(7))

Commission Rule 210.12(a)(7) requires that the complaint include "a description of the complainant's business and its interests in the relevant domestic industry or the relevant trade and commerce." For intellectual-property-based cases, the rule additionally requires "a showing that at least one complainant is the owner or exclusive licensee of the subject intellectual property." In intellectual property cases (and especially patent cases), the complainant (and/or its licensees) is frequently co-extensive with the domestic industry.

9. Specific Theory for Non-Intellectual-Property Based Cases (Commission Rule 210.12(a)(8))

Commission Rule 210.12(a)(8) sets out additional requirements where the unfair practice is not based on an intellectual property right under Commission Rule 210.12(a)(6)(i), *i.e.*, cases not based on Section 337(a)(B)-(E). In essence, this rule addresses the injury requirement for cases brought under Section 337(a)(1)(A). In such cases, the complaint must state "a specific theory and provide corroborating data to support the allegation(s) in the complaint concerning the existence of a threat or effect to destroy or substantially injure a domestic industry, to prevent the establishment of a domestic industry, or to restrain or monopolize trade and commerce in the United States." In all such instances, the rule provides that the complaint should ordinarily include the following:

a) volume and trend of production of the involved domestic article;

b) volume and trend of sales of the involved domestic article;

c) volume and trend of inventories of domestic article;

d) description of facilities employed in the production of the involved domestic article;

e) description of the number and type of workers employed in the production of the involved domestic article;

f) profit-and-loss information covering overall operations;

g) profit-and-loss information covering operations concerning the involved domestic article;

h) pricing information with respect to the involved domestic article;

i) when available, volume and sales of imports; and

j) other pertinent data (not defined in the rule).

While not stated in the rule, the complaint should indicate what type of injury is being suffered and describe the nexus between that injury and the alleged unfair practice.

10. Additional Requirements for Patent-Based Cases (Commission Rule 210.12(a)(9))

There are additional requirements set out in Commission Rule 210.12(a)(9) where the complaint is based on patent infringement, as nearly all are. These additional requirements are:

a) Identification of each asserted patent and a certified copy of each such patent. Only the original complaint need include the certified copy of the patent. The other copies of the complaint need only include copies of the certified copy of the asserted patent.

b) Identification of the ownership of each asserted patent and a copy of each assignment relating thereto. Again, only the original complaint need include the certified copy of each assignment. The other copies of the complaint need only include copies of the certified copies of the assignments.

c) The identification of each licensee under each of the involved patents.

d) When known, a list of

- each foreign patent corresponding to each involved U.S. patent;
- each corresponding foreign patent application (not already issued as a patent); and
- each corresponding foreign patent application that has been denied.

The list must provide an indication of the prosecution status of each corresponding foreign patent application.

e) A nontechnical description of the invention of each involved U.S. patent.

f) A reference to the specific claims in each U.S. patent that allegedly cover the article imported or sold by each person named as violating Section 337 or that allegedly cover the process under which such article was produced.

g) A showing that each person named as violating Section 337 is importing or selling the article covered by, or produced under the involved process covered by, the asserted specific claims of each asserted U.S. patent. The rule requires that this showing be made by "appropriate allegations." It also requires that "when practicable" the showing be made by a claim chart that applies an exemplary claim of each asserted patent to a representative involved domestic article or process and to a representative involved article of each person named as violating Section 337 or to the process under which such article was produced. As noted above, it is not necessary that the complainant rely on the same claims for domestic industry that it asserts are infringed.

h) Drawings, photographs, or other visual representations of both the involved domestic article or process and the involved article of each person named as violating Section 337 or the process used in producing the imported article. When a claim chart is furnished under Commission Rule 210.12(a)(9)(vii), the parts of such drawings, photographs, or other visual representations should be labeled so that they can be read in conjunction with the claim chart.

11. Request for Relief (Commission Rule 210.12(a)(10))

Commission Rule 210.12(a)(10) requires that the complaint include a request for relief. Typically, such a request includes a request that the Commission institute an investigation, determine that a violation of Section 337 exists, and issue an exclusion order and/or cease and desist orders. If temporary relief is requested under Section 337(e) and/or (f), a motion for temporary relief must either accompany the complaint or be filed prior to institution of the investigation.

12. Submission of Articles as Exhibits (Commission Rule 210.12(b))

Commission Rule 210.12(b) requires that "if practicable," the complainant must, at the time the complaint is filed, submit samples of both the domestic article and all imported articles that are the subject of the complaint.

13. Additional Materials (Commission Rule 210.12(b)-(g))

Commission Rule 210.12(c)-(g) provides for the submission of additional materials for certain intellectual-property-based cases. These additional materials are distinct from the additional requirements for patent-based cases in Commission Rule 210.12(a)(9). The rules governing these additional materials are self-contained as to copies. No further copies are required beyond those specified in Commission Rule 210.12(c)-(g).

a. Additional Material to Accompany Patent-Based Complaint (Commission Rule 210.12(c))

Commission Rule 210.12(c) requires that the following additional materials be submitted in patent-based cases:

a) three copies of each license agreement arising out of each asserted patent. If a standard license agreement is used, three copies of that standard agreement may be provided along with a list of the licensees operating under that agreement.

b) one certified copy of the prosecution history for each asserted patent, plus three additional copies of that certified copy. This requirement sometimes poses difficulties for complainants because the Patent and Trademark Office may not be able to provide a certified copy on a timely basis or, indeed, may have misplaced the prosecution history and thus not be able to provide even an uncertified copy. As a matter of practice, the Commission will, for the purposes of institution, accept an uncertified copy of the prosecution history or a copy reconstructed from the complainant's files. However, the Commission expects that a certified copy will eventually be provided during the course of the investigation.

c) four copies of each patent and applicable papers of each technical reference mentioned in the prosecution history of each asserted patent.

b. Additional Materials to Accompany Complaint Based on Federally-Registered Trademark (Commission Rule 210.12(d))

Commission Rule 210.12(d) provides for the following additional materials for cases based on a Federally-registered trademark:

a) one certified copy of the Federal registration and three additional copies;

b) three copies of each license agreement (if any) concerning use of the trademark. If a standard license agreement is used, three copies of that agreement and a list of licensees operating under it will suffice.

c. Additional Materials to Accompany Complaint Based on Non-Federally Registered Trademark (Commission Rule 210.12(c))

Commission Rule 210.12(e) provides for the following additional materials for cases based on a non-Federally-registered trademark:

a) a detailed and specific description of the alleged trademark;

b) information concerning prior attempts to register the alleged trademark; and

c) information on the status of current attempts to register the alleged trademark.

d. Additional Material to Accompany Complaint Based on Copyright (Commission Rule 210.12(f))

Commission Rule 210.12(f) provides for the submission of following additional materials to be submitted in copyright-based cases:

a) one certified copy of the Federal registration and three additional copies;

b) three copies of each license agreement (if any) concerning use of the copyright. If a standard license agreement is used, three copies of that agreement and a list of the licensees operating under it will suffice.

e. Additional Materials to Accompany Complaint Based on Registered Mask Work (Commission Rule 210.12(g))

Commission Rule 210.12(g) provides for the submission of the following additional materials in cases based on a registered mask work:

a) one certified copy of the Federal registration and three additional copies;

b) three copies of each license agreement (if any) concerning use of the mask work. If a standard license agreement is used, three copies of that agreement and a list of licensees operating under it will suffice.

C. Review of Draft Complaint by OUII

Prospective complainants may request the Commission's Office of Unfair Import Investigations to advise them with regard to the requirements for complaints and to review any draft complaint. Seeking such advice and review will greatly assist in ensuring that the complaint will meet the requirements of the Commission's rules and will facilitate institution of an investigation based on that complaint.

D. Filing and Service of the Complaint (Commission Rule 210.8)

A complaint must be filed as an original with 14 copies of the confidential version of the complaint and 14 copies of the public version of the complaint. Further, the complainant must file an additional copy of each of the confidential version and the public version of the complaint for each proposed respondent named in the complaint and an additional public version of the complaint for each foreign government of any proposed respondent. The complainant is not required to serve the complaint on the proposed respondents. Such service is effected by the Commission itself if and when it institutes an investigation based on that complaint, as discussed *infra.* However, if the complaint is accompanied by a motion for temporary relief, the complainant must serve public versions of the complaint and the motion for temporary relief on filing, as discussed *infra.*

E. Duty to Supplement Complaint (Commission Rule 210.12(h))

Commission Rule 210.12(h) provides that a complainant must supplement the complaint prior to institution of an investigation if he obtains information upon the basis of which he knows or reasonably should know that a material legal or factual assertion in the complaint is false or misleading. Many so-called supplements are filed, not to make corrections to the complaint, but to add information on allegations. These are more properly considered amendments to the complaint.

F. Amendment of Complaint (Commission Rule 210.14)

1. Pre-Institution

The complaint may be amended at any time prior to institution of the investigation. However, the later an amendment is filed and the more substantive it is, the more likely it is that the Commission will extend its usual 30-day deadline for acting on the complaint.

2. Post-Institution

After institution, the complaint (and notice of investigation) may be amended only by grant of an appropriate motion to amend. Such a motion is addressed to the administrative law judge designated to preside over the investigation. It will be granted only for good cause shown and upon such conditions as are necessary to avoid prejudice to the public interest and the rights of the parties to the investigation. If the grant of such a motion would require amendment of the notice of investigation, such grant must be by initial determination, making it subject to immediate Commission review. All other dispositions of such motions are by order.

G. Commission Action on Receipt of Complaint (Commission Rules 210.9-.11)

On receipt of a complaint, the Commission has 30 days to determine whether to institute an investigation based on that complaint, though it may extend that period.

Copies of the complaint are distributed to the Commissioners, the Office of the General Counsel, and the Office of Unfair Import Investigations. Subsequently, OUII will forward a recommendation as to what action the Commission should take with respect to the complaint. In almost every case, OUII recommends institution of an investigation. This is to be expected because in most cases OUII will have reviewed the complaint prior to its formal filing. As noted above, a Section 337 investigation will be instituted if half the Commissioners participating vote to institute; a majority vote is not required.

In considering whether to institute an investigation on the basis of a complaint, the Commission normally considers only the complaint, any supplements and amendments thereto, and the recommendation of OUII. There is no provision for the Commission to receive or consider submissions from the proposed respondents or anyone else other than the complainant. Indeed, the proposed respondents will ordinarily not have been served with a copy of the complaint on filing (except in cases where temporary relief has been requested). Nevertheless, proposed respondents are frequently aware of the complaint and sometimes file submissions in an attempt to persuade the Commission not to institute an investigation. The Commission, in its discretion, may consider such submissions, but they are hardly ever successful even in delaying the Commission vote, much less avoiding institution, since they usually simply recite defenses which the Commission feels should be considered in the first instance by the ALJ after the investigation is instituted. However, there may be some circumstances where such a submission could be successful.[19]

1. Commission Action on Institution

If, as is almost always the case, the Commission votes to institute an investigation based on the complaint, it will issue a notice of investigation and serve that notice and the public version of the complaint (including any amendments and supplements) on the respondents named in the notice of investigation and on the embassies of their countries. The Commission will also serve the notice of investigation on the U.S. Department of Health and Human Services, the U.S. Department of Justice, the Federal Trade Commission, the Customs Service, and "such other agencies and departments as the Commission considers appropriate." As a matter of practice, such service is usually by certified mail by the Office of the Secretary. If the Secretary's efforts to serve the complaint and notice of investigation by certified mail are not successful, the complainant may seek leave from the presiding administrative law judge to attempt to effect personal service. If such personal service is successful, the complainant must notify the administrative law judge and file proof of such service with the Office of the Secretary.

The notice of investigation, not the complaint, governs the scope of the investigation, though in most cases their scope is coextensive. The notice recites the scope of the complaint (as amended and supplemented) and the scope of the investigation. It identifies the complainant, the respondents, the Commission investigative attorney assigned to the case, and also (under current practice) the administrative law judge assigned to the case. Issuance of the notice transfers the investigation to the administrative law judge. The notice of investigation is published in the *Federal Register* within about a week of its issuance. Under the Commission's rules, publication in the *Federal Register* marks the official commencement of the investigation.[20]

2. Commission Action on Non-Institution

In the rare instance where the Commission decides not to institute an investigation, it will dismiss the complaint and provide the complainant and all proposed

19 For example, the existence of a prior judgment of invalidity of the asserted patent, even if currently subject to appeal, should foreclose institution. The existence of such a judgment is subject to administrative notice and has a preclusive effect even if the judgment is on appeal.

20 This statement is subject to two caveats. First, the assigned administrative law judge may issue his or her ground rules and protective order prior to publication of the notice in the *Federal Register*. Second, the time for filing and serving the answer to the complaint and notice of investigation runs from their service by the Commission, which usually precedes publication of the notice in the *Federal Register* by a few days.

respondents with written notice of the dismissal and the reasons therefor. This notice is not published in the *Federal Register*. The reasons for dismissal are usually given only briefly.

H. Withdrawal of the Complaint (Commission Rule 210.10)

1. Withdrawal of the Complaint Prior to Commission Vote on Institution

Under the Commission's rules, a complainant has the right to withdraw the complaint prior to the Commission's vote on institution by simply filing a notice of withdrawal with the Commission. Commission Rule 210.10(a)(5)(i). The rule does not specify whether a partial withdrawal (*i.e.*, withdrawal as to one of several parties or claims) is permitted, but in practice the Commission has permitted such partial withdrawals. If the complaint is being withdrawn pursuant to a settlement agreement, a copy of the agreement must be filed with the Commission along with the notice of withdrawal. Commission Rule 210.10(a)(5)(i). If, as is often the case, the settlement agreement contains confidential business information as defined by Commission Rule 201.6(a), at least one copy of the agreement with such information deleted must be filed as well. *Id.*[21]

2. Withdrawal of the Complaint After Commission Vote to Institute

A complainant who wishes to withdraw the complaint after formal institution of the investigation (*i.e.*, publication of the notice of investigation in the *Federal Register*) must file a motion with the administrative law judge or, if the investigation is before the Commission, with the Commission as discussed *infra*.[22]

VIII. INITIAL STEPS BY RESPONDENT; OBTAINING CONFIDENTIAL VERSION OF COMPLAINT; RESPONSE TO COMPLAINT AND NOTICE OF INVESTIGATION; COUNTERCLAIMS

A. Initial Steps; Obtaining Confidential Version of Complaint

Once the Commission votes to institute an investigation, it issues a notice of investigation and serves each respondent and the embassy of the respondent's country with the public version of the complaint and with the notice of investigation. Shortly thereafter, the designated ALJ will issue the ground rules for the

---

21 The Commission rule anomalously states that the public version must accompany "the motion," but the rule provides only for withdrawal by notice, not by motion. The reference to "the motion" should be read as referring to the notice of withdrawal.

22 The rules leave a gap in the procedure to be followed for withdrawing the complaint after the Commission vote to institute but before publication of the notice of investigation in the *Federal Register*.

investigation and a protective order governing the submission and handling of confidential information. One of the first steps for respondents is to obtain the confidential version of the complaint and the confidential exhibits. This is done by having outside counsel notice an appearance and subscribe to the protective order. Ordinarily, only outside counsel may have access to confidential information under the protective order. After subscribing to the protective order, outside counsel may send a letter to the Secretary of the Commission requesting the confidential version of the complaint and exhibits. The Office of the Secretary usually makes these available within a day or two of receipt of the request. At the same time, respondent and its counsel will have to turn to preparing a response to the complaint and notice of investigation.

B. The Response (Commission Rule 210.13)

1. Time for Filing Response

In cases not involving requests for temporary relief (*i.e.*, most cases) each respondent named in the notice of investigation has twenty days from the date of service of the complaint and notice of investigation to file and serve its response to the complaint and notice of investigation. As noted above, the Commission ordinarily serves the complaint and notice of investigation as soon as it issues its notice of investigation and usually does so by mail. Under the Commission's rules, when a person is served by mail, additional time is added to the time for response. For respondents located in the United States, three days are added; for respondents located abroad, ten days are added. Commission Rule 201.16(d). Thus, domestic respondents ordinarily have 23 days to respond to the complaint and foreign respondents have 30 days.[23]

2. Requirements for Response

The response must conform to Commission Rules 201.8, 210.4, and 210.5, discussed above. It must be made under oath (or, pursuant to 1 U.S.C. § 1, declaration) and must be "signed by respondent or his duly authorized officer, attorney, or agent." The name, address, and telephone number of the respondent and any such officer, attorney, or agent must be given on the first page of the response.

Commission Rule 210.13(b) provides that each respondent must respond to each allegation in (1) the complaint and (2) the notice of investigation and must "set

---

23 The difference in response times for domestic and foreign respondents who have been served by mail can create a problem where the two respondents are related (*e.g.*, parent-subsidiary) and desire to file simultaneous or combined responses. This can be obviated by filing a motion addressed to the presiding administrative law judge noting the relationship between the respondents and requesting that the domestic respondent be given an additional seven days to file its response so that the responses for the domestic and foreign respondents are due on the same day. Such motions are rarely objected to and are usually granted.

forth a concise statement of the facts constituting each ground of defense."[24] For each fact alleged in the complaint and notice, there must be a specific admission, denial, or explanation. If the respondent is without knowledge of an alleged fact, it may make a statement to that effect.

If a respondent fails to so respond to the allegations in the complaint and notice, those allegations may be deemed to have been admitted.

3. Additional Information Required to be Provided in Response

In addition to responding to the allegations in the complaint and notice, each response must include, when available, "statistical data on the quantity and value of imports of the involved article." Respondents who are importers must also provide the HTS numbers for importations of the accused imports occurring on or after January 1, 1989 and the TSUS numbers for importations prior to January 1, 1989.

Each respondent must also include in its response:

a. a statement concerning the respondent's capacity to produce the subject article, and

b. a statement concerning the relative significance of the United States market to the respondent's operations.

Respondents who are not manufacturers of the accused imports must state the name and address of their suppliers.

4. Affirmative Defenses

Respondents must plead affirmative defenses with as much specificity as possible.

5. Additional Requirements for Response in Patent Case

Under Commission Rule 210.13(b), when the alleged unfair practices are based on the claims of a U.S. patent, the respondent is "encouraged" to make the following showings:

(a) If it is asserted in defense that the article imported or sold by respondents is not covered by, or produced under a process covered by, the claims of each involved U.S. patent, "a showing of noncoverage for each involved claim in each U.S. letters patent in question shall be made." This showing may be made "by appropriate allegations and, when practicable, by a chart that applies the involved claims of each U.S. letters patent in question to a

---

24 In those (unusual) situations where the notice of investigation covers fewer allegations than those in the complaint, the respondent should only be required to respond to those allegations in the complaint which have been continued in the notice of investigation.

representative involved imported article of the respondent or to the process under which such article was produced."

(b) Drawings, photographs, or other visual representations of the involved imported article of respondent or the process utilized in producing such article. When a claim chart is furnished under Commission Rule 210.14(b)(1), the parts of those drawings, photographs, or other visual representations "should" be labeled so that they can be read in conjunction with the claim chart.

(c) If the claims of any asserted U.S. patent are asserted to be invalid or unenforceable,

- the basis for such assertion;
- when prior art is relied on, a showing of how the prior art renders each claim invalid or unenforceable and a copy of such prior art.

Commission Rule 210.13(b)(3) provides that for good cause, the ALJ may "waive any of the substantive requirements imposed under this paragraph or may impose additional requirements." It is unclear whether this provision is limited to Commission Rule 210.13(b)(3) or could extend to Commission Rule 210.13(b)(1) and 210.13(b)(2).

Commission Rule 210.13(c) provides that at the time a response is filed, "if practicable, the respondent shall submit the accused article imported or sold by the respondent, unless the article has already been submitted by the complainant."

C. Counterclaims (Section 337(c); Commission Rule 210.14)

1. Mode and Time for Filing

Section 337(c) provides that a respondent "may raise any counterclaim in a manner provided by the Commission." The Commission has implemented this provision in Commission Rule 210.14(e) which provides that counterclaims must be filed in a separate document. That rule also provides that counterclaims may be filed at any time after institution of the investigation, but not later than ten business days before the commencement of the evidentiary hearing on violation before the presiding administrative law judge.

2. Mandatory Removal of Counterclaims to District Court for Adjudication

While a respondent must file its counterclaims with the Commission, the Commission will not adjudicate them. Rather, Section 337(c) (and Commission Rule 210.14(e)) provide that immediately after filing a counterclaim, the respondent must file a notice of removal with a United States district court in which venue for any of the counterclaims raised by the party would exist under 28 U.S.C. § 1391.

The district courts have jurisdiction over such removed counterclaims in accordance with 28 U.S.C. § 1368, which grants the district court original jurisdiction of any civil action based on a counterclaim raised under Section 337(c) "to the extent that it arises out of the transaction or occurrence that is the subject matter of the opposing party's claim" in the Commission's investigation. Thus, 28 U.S.C. § 1368 only grants the district court jurisdiction over compulsory counterclaims raised and removed pursuant to Section 337(c). Respondents must separately establish district court jurisdiction for permissive counterclaims which have been raised and removed pursuant to Section 337(c).

Under Section 337(c) and 28 U.S.C. § 1446(f), any counterclaim raised and removed pursuant to Section 337(c) will relate back to the date of the original complaint on which the Commission's Section 337 investigation is based. Pursuant to 28 U.S.C. § 1446(f), the district court will resolve such removed counterclaim "in the same manner as an original complaint under the Federal Rules of Civil Procedure," except that the district court will not require payment of the filing fee for original complaints.

Section 337(c) provides that action on a counterclaim raised and removed pursuant to Section 337(c) "shall not delay or affect the proceeding under this section, including the legal and equitable defenses that may be raised under this subsection [Section 337(c)]." Presumably, this passage is intended to put parties and tribunals on notice that while counterclaims which call for declarations of invalidity, unenforceability and non-infringement of the asserted intellectual property right may be raised and removed to a district court for adjudication, the Commission will retain jurisdiction over and will adjudicate the corresponding defenses of invalidity, unenforceability, and non-infringement. Thus, the Commission may proceed to consideration of those defenses which may be raised in its investigation without awaiting district court adjudication of the corresponding counterclaims.

IX. SECTION 337 INVESTIGATIONS: ADMINISTRATIVE LAW JUDGE PHASE

Once the Commission institutes a Section 337 investigation, it assigns it to one of its administrative law judges to conduct an evidentiary hearing and issue an initial determination on whether a violation of Section 337 exists, as well as a recommended determination on remedy and bonding.

A. The Administrative Law Judge System

In proceedings conducted under the adjudicative provisions of the Administrative Procedure Act, an agency may itself conduct the evidentiary hearing. 5 U.S.C. § 556(b)(1). Alternatively, one of its members may do so. 5 U.S.C. § 556(b)(2). Most agencies, including the Commission, use a third option: having the evidentiary hearing conducted by an administrative law judge. 5 U.S.C.

§ 556(b)(3). Under the ALJ system, ALJs issue initial decisions that are subject to review by the agency. 5 U.S.C. § 557.

An ALJ is an employee of the agency for administrative purposes, but the agency does not have a free hand in his or her selection or discipline. ALJs must be selected from a roster of eligibles provided by the Office of Personnel Management (OPM). Persons become eligible to be listed on the roster by possessing certain qualifications determined by OPM and by passing written and oral examinations administered by OPM. Alternatively, agencies may offer appointment to ALJs already serving with other agencies or to persons who have previously served as ALJs and who are eligible for reinstatement as such.

B. Administrative Law Judges at the Commission

The Commission currently employs four ALJs, who, with their staff, are organized as the Commission's Office of Administrative Law Judges. At the present time, the organization of this office does not include a chief administrative law judge position, though it has so provided in the past. Each judge has a law clerk and a secretary.

The Commission's Office of Administrative Law Judges exists primarily to provide ALJs for its Section 337 investigations. The assigned ALJ will eventually set a target date for completion of the investigation, establish a procedural schedule, oversee discovery by the parties, conduct an evidentiary hearing, receive briefing and argument, and ultimately issue an initial determination as to whether a violation of Section 337 exists, as well as a recommended determination on remedy and bonding. Under its current practice, the Commission assigns an ALJ to a Section 337 investigation on institution of that investigation. Those assignments are made on a rotating basis, as nearly as practicable, as required by 5 U.S.C. § 3105. This means that it is often possible to determine which ALJ will be assigned to an investigation before an investigation is instituted.[25]

C. Action by the ALJ After Assignment: Issuance of Protective Order and Ground Rules

Within a few days after an investigation is assigned to an ALJ, he or she typically issues two orders: (1) a protective order governing the submission and treatment of confidential information and (2) that particular ALJ's ground rules

25 Indeed, some counsel, armed with knowledge of this selection procedure, attempt to time the filing of a complaint to "pre-select" a particular ALJ. The method is not foolproof, however, especially if several complaints are filed on or near the same day, since they may not be taken up and assigned to an ALJ in the precise order in which they were filed. Further, if a complaint is related to a current (and thus previously assigned) investigation, the ensuing investigation based on that complaint may be assigned to the same ALJ, no matter what the rotation system might otherwise dictate. And, of course, eventually, the initial determination of the ALJ is subject to limited *de novo* review by the Commission.

which will govern the case. The issuance of the ground rules may be accompanied by a notice of a preliminary conference, a call for discovery statements, and/or a call for target date statements, all discussed *infra*. Alternatively, these may be called for independently.

The automatic issuance of the protective order differs from Federal district court practice, where such orders are not automatically entered. Rather, the parties to a district court action ordinarily negotiate the terms of a proposed protective order and then move the court to issue the negotiated order. Protective orders issued by the Commission's ALJs typically limit the disclosure of confidential information to outside counsel and independent experts and require both to "subscribe to" the protective order before they can receive confidential information. Subscribing to the protective order is usually done via a letter to the Secretary of the Commission, which is filed with the Commission and served on the other parties. The protective order usually provides that independent experts may not subscribe to the protective order and receive confidential information unless their curriculum vitae and other information have been provided to the other parties and those other parties have not objected to the expert receiving confidential information.

The ground rules, whether attached to a preliminary conference order or issued independently, are extensive and address every phase of the proceedings before the administrative law judge.

Despite their seemingly standard language, the protective order and the ground rules must be reviewed carefully in every case, since their provisions vary from ALJ to ALJ and there is sometimes a variation from language used in previous cases by the same ALJ. This is more the case for the ground rules than the protective order. Both the protective order and the ground rules may be amended *sua sponte* by the ALJ or on motion. However, both the protective order and the ground rules, and any amendments thereto, must be consistent with the Commission's rules.

D. Discovery Statements

As noted above, the administrative law judges may call for the submission of discovery statements very early in the case, usually about the same time they issue the protective order and ground rules. In these statements, if they are ordered, the parties are required to address such matters as what the issues are, whether the issues can be narrowed or be the subject of dispositive motions, the possibility of settlement, the extent and type of discovery anticipated, the type of information they intend to offer to support their case and what they will be seeking from others, and a proposed procedural schedule. The order requiring discovery statements may contemplate that the parties confer and attempt to agree on the matters discussed in their discovery statements, especially the proposed procedural schedule. It may also contemplate that the parties will submit their own statements or that a joint discovery statement be filed, with dissenting parties being able to file their own, alternative, statements.

Since the discovery statement, if ordered, is usually required very early in the investigation, the parties may have little to say about the matters required to be discussed therein, except for the procedural schedule. Thus, as a matter of practice, the most important function of the discovery statement is as a vehicle to set the procedural schedule. To this end, parties frequently confer on the procedural schedule whether expressly required to do so or not.

E. Discovery

With a few exceptions, discovery by the parties may commence as soon as the notice of investigation is published in the *Federal Register* and may therefore have begun even before the date set for the submission of discovery statements and prior to any preliminary conference. Discovery is supervised by the ALJ. The type of discovery available is similar to that available in the Federal district courts and is discussed in detail *infra*.

F. Pre-Hearing Conferences

Commission Rule 210.35(a) provides that at an ALJ may order counsel or other representatives of the parties to meet with him or her for one or more conferences to consider simplification and clarification of the issues, the scope of the hearing, the necessity or desirability of amendments to the pleadings, stipulations and admissions of either fact or the content and authenticity of documents, expedition in the discovery and presentation of evidence, and "other matters as may aid in the orderly and expeditious disposition of the investigation."

An ALJ may conduct two major pre-hearing conferences, one at the beginning of the investigation (denoted a "preliminary conference") and one just prior to the evidentiary hearing (denoted a "pre-hearing" or pre-trial" conference.) These conferences are transcribed by a reporter. Intermediate live and telephonic conferences may be scheduled as well. Alternatively, an ALJ may schedule only a pre-trial conference and, as appropriate, intermediate conferences.

G. Answer

The answer to the complaint and notice of investigation will be due shortly after the Commission assigns the investigation to an ALJ, perhaps even before the date set for any preliminary conference. The content of the answer is discussed *supra*.

H. Target Date; Target Date Statements (Section 337(b)(1); Commission Rule 210.51)

The target date is the date by which the Commission must complete the investigation and must be set within 45 days after publication of the notice of investigation in the *Federal Register*. It is ordinarily set by the ALJ, who may do so *sua sponte* or after requesting target date proposals ("target date statements") from the parties. If the ALJ sets a target date which is 15 months or less from the date of the publication of the notice of investigation in the *Federal Register*, he or she will set the date by final order, *i.e.*, the target date will not be subject of Commission review. If the ALJ sets the target date beyond 15 months or extends an earlier target date beyond 15 months, he or she must do so by initial determination, which is subject to Commission review.

The setting of administrative deadlines for completion of the investigation was introduced by the amendments to Section 337 in the URAA. Prior to those amendments, the statute required that Section 337 investigations be completed within one year of the publication of the notice of investigation in the *Federal Register*, with the possibility of a six-month extension in "more complicated" cases. As a matter of policy, the Commission has decided that its administrative deadlines, or target dates, should be set at or near the earlier statutory deadlines. In most cases the target dates have been set between 11 and 15 months, though some of these have been extended.

I. The Procedural Schedule; Order of Proceedings

Early in the investigation, after the receipt of any discovery statements and the conclusion of any preliminary conference, the ALJ will issue an order establishing a procedural schedule for various pre-trial matters, the trial itself, and perhaps post-trial submissions. The schedule may be amended by order of the ALJ as a result of a motion filed by a party or *sua sponte*. The items in the procedural schedule vary somewhat among the ALJs and according to the nature of the case. The list below is a combined list of the more important items in approximate chronological order.

1. Settlement Conference and Report

An ALJ may require the private parties to confer on the possibility of settlement at certain stages of the proceedings and to report on the results of their discussions.

2. Identification of Expert Witnesses

On the assigned date in the procedural schedule, each party may be required to identify those experts it expects to testify at the hearing. The required identification usually calls for a statement of how the experts are to be qualified as experts, their expertise, and a copy of their curriculum vitae. These expert witnesses may ultimately submit expert reports and be subject to deposition on those reports.

3. Tentative List of Witnesses

On the assigned date in the procedural schedule, each party may be required to provide a tentative list of witnesses that it expects to call to testify at the hearing, with an identification of each witness's relationship to the party. Both fact and expert witnesses may be required to be listed.

4. Expert Reports

The procedural schedule will usually set times for submission of initial and rebuttal expert reports. The Commission's rules do not expressly address expert reports. In general, these should be prepared in the same way and with the same level of detail as expert reports in an action in a United States district court. However, as with other items in the procedural schedule, the ground rules issued in the case should be consulted for any comments, suggestions, or requirements. As a general rule, the ALJs may be expected to follow district court practice as to the content of expert reports and the manner in which such reports may be supplemented and expert testimony received.

5. Notice of Art

The notice of art is usually relevant only in patent cases. The purpose of the notice is to indicate the art on which a party will rely for any purpose. These purposes include, but are not limited to, claim construction, invalidity, infringement, and inequitable conduct.

6. Submission of Statements Regarding Witness Statements

An ALJ may provide the parties with an opportunity to submit some or all of their direct testimony in the form of a document known as a witness statement. If an ALJ intends to provide this opportunity, he or she may assign a date in the procedural schedule for each party to submit a statement proposing the use of witness statements in lieu of live direct testimony.

7. Discovery Cutoff and Completion

The ALJ will set a date in the procedural schedule for discovery cut-off and completion. Depending on the particular ALJ and scheduling order, the term "cut-off" may refer to the last day on which discovery requests can be served, so that the date for discovery cut-off may be somewhat earlier than the date for completion of discovery. In other scheduling orders, the term may be used to indicate the completion of discovery. If there is any ambiguity as to the meaning of the term in any particular schedule, that ambiguity should be resolved promptly. Of course, some discovery may continue beyond the discovery completion date as the result of an order to compel.

8. Deadline for Motions to Compel Discovery

Motions to compel discovery may be filed throughout the pre-trial period up to the deadline set by the ALJ in the procedural schedule. The deadline for motions to compel discovery is set later than the dates for cut-off and completion of discovery. Orders compelling discovery may result in the ordered discovery being taken or obtained after the general deadline for cut-off and completion of discovery.

9. Joint Narrative Statement of the Issues

One of the Commission's ALJs (Judge Terrill) requires the parties to submit a Joint Narrative Statement of the Issues, defined in his ground rules as a concise, neutral statement of each issue, each party's position on that issue, and the names of its supporting witnesses on those positions.

10. Direct Exhibits; Physical and Demonstrative Exhibits

The procedural schedule will set a date for the filing and exchange of direct exhibits and exhibit lists. The details of filing and exchange will be set out in the ALJ's ground rules. Most direct exhibits are documentary exhibits and are filed and served. Direct physical and demonstrative exhibits are not usually filed and served. However, they must be made available for inspection by the other parties and, of course, must ultimately be brought to the hearing. Some exhibits may be confidential and the manner of maintaining confidentiality during trial and after admission into the record will be set forth in the ground rules. Some judges may require a declaration justifying confidentiality which must be submitted at a time designated in the procedural schedule.

Of course, filing and serving the exhibits does not mean they are admitted. Indeed, at this point they should be regarded as proposed exhibits. They are subject to objection which may result in their not being admitted. Questions of admissibility are dealt with via motions *in limine*, at the pre-hearing (*i.e.*, pre-trial) conference, and during the hearing (and sometimes even afterward).

The time for filing and serving direct exhibits is subject to some variation and may not be the same for each party. The complainant is always first, but the schedule may require the respondent and Commission investigative attorney to file and serve their exhibits at the same time as the complainant or at subsequent times. The schedule may permit the Commission investigative attorney to file and serve direct exhibits after the private parties. Generally, the private parties provide the overwhelming majority of exhibits. The Commission investigative attorney normally relies on the exhibits of the private parties and offers a few additional exhibits of his or her own.

11. Objections to Direct Exhibits

The scheduling order usually sets a date for filing and serving objections to direct exhibits. Objections must at least briefly state the grounds therefor.

Commission Rule 210.37(b) sets out the requirements for admissibility:

> Relevant, material, and reliable evidence shall be admitted. Irrelevant, immaterial, unreliable, or unduly repetitious evidence shall be excluded. Immaterial or irrelevant parts of an admissible document shall be segregated and excluded as far as practicable.

Hearsay is not itself an objection to proffered evidence; however, it may form the basis of an objection for unreliability.

12. Rebuttal Exhibits

The scheduling order will set a time for filing and serving rebuttal exhibits. The above comments on direct exhibits apply to rebuttal exhibits. The rebuttal exhibit list must usually state what direct exhibit it is rebutting.

13. Objections to Rebuttal Exhibits

The scheduling order will set a time for filing and serving objections to rebuttal exhibits. The above comments on objections to direct exhibits apply to objections to rebuttal exhibits. An additional objection that can be made to a rebuttal exhibit is that it is not a proper rebuttal exhibit, *i.e.*, it does not purport to rebut a direct exhibit.

14. Pre-Hearing Statements and Briefs

The scheduling order will set a date for filing and serving pre-hearing statements or briefs. The order may provide for complainant and respondent to file their pre-hearing statements at the same time, with the Commission investigative attorney filing a few days later. The pre-hearing statement is an important document outlining the party's case. Its format and contents are specified by the ALJ's ground rules. There is no reply.

15. Tutorial

Some scheduling orders provide for a tutorial for the ALJ on the technology which is the subject of the investigation. The tutorial is usually presented a few days prior to trial.

16. Pre-Hearing Conference

The scheduling order will set a pre-hearing conference to occur just prior to the commencement of the evidentiary hearing, usually on the first day of the hearing itself. The purpose of this conference is to address any administrative and procedural details relating to the trial and to rule on objections to exhibits. The admissibility of some exhibits may, however, be deferred until the evidentiary hearing. The pre-hearing conference is transcribed by a reporter. Thus, all rulings on exhibits will be of record, as required by Commission Rule 210.37(e).

17. Evidentiary Hearing

Commission Rule 210.36 requires that the opportunity for an evidentiary hearing be provided in all Section 337 investigations in accordance with the requirements of the Administrative Procedure Act. Such hearings are usually scheduled to begin two to four months prior to the due date for the ALJ to issue the initial determination on whether there is a violation of Section 337. Hearings are usually set for periods of one or two weeks. Commission Rule 210.37(b), implementing the Administrative Procedure Act, sets out the requirements for the admissibility of evidence:

> Relevant, material, and reliable evidence shall be admitted. Irrelevant, immaterial, unreliable, or unduly repetitious evidence shall be excluded. Immaterial or irrelevant parts of an admissible document shall be segregated and excluded as far as practicable.

The ALJ's ground rules will specify the order of trial and the manner of examination of witnesses. In some cases, some or all of the witnesses may give their direct testimony by witness statement, a document consisting of written questions by counsel and the witness's written responses. If a witness statement is used, it is signed by the witness at the hearing and cross-examination begins immediately. The unsigned witness statement must usually be provided as a direct exhibit at the time for filing and serving direct exhibits.

Opening arguments may be permitted.

The Commission's policy is to conduct the hearing in public as much as possible, but the very large amount of confidential information in Section 337 cases makes this very difficult to do and hearings are frequently closed to the public for long periods of time.

18. Post-Hearing Briefs, Proposed Findings of Fact, Proposed Conclusions of Law

Post-hearing briefs, proposed findings of fact, and proposed conclusions of law are provided for by Commission Rule 210.40 and the dates for their submission are set out in the procedural schedule. These are usually the most extensive and among the most important documents filed in the case. The format and content of these documents are specified in the ALJ's ground rules.

19. Post-Hearing Reply Briefs, Rebuttal Findings of Fact and Conclusions of Law

Like the documents to which they respond, post-hearing reply briefs and rebuttal findings of fact and conclusions of law are usually the most extensive and among the most important documents filed in the case. Likewise, the format and content of these documents are specified in the ALJ's ground rules.

20. Closing Argument

Closing argument, which is usually scheduled, is one of the most important events in the investigation since the ALJ will have an opportunity to ask counsel questions (and counsel will have the opportunity to respond). Closing argument may be scheduled for a date well after the hearing and take the better part of one or two days.

J. Initial Determination on Violation of Section 337 (Commission Rule 210.42(a)(1))

In this document, the ALJ rules on whether there is a violation of Section 337. This document is usually extensive and divided into three parts: an opinion, findings of fact and conclusions of law. It is usually referred to (somewhat confusingly) as the "final initial determination" to distinguish it from the initial determinations (*i.e.*, rulings on certain motions) the ALJ may issue up to the issuance of the final initial determination. The ALJ files the initial determination with the Commission and it is served on the parties. At the same time, the ALJ certifies the evidentiary record to the Commission.

Under Commission Rule 210.42(a)(1)(i), the final initial determination must be filed and served three months before the target date, if the target is set at 15 months or less. If the target date is set at more than 15 months, the initial determination is due four months before the target date.

K. Recommended Determination on Remedy and Bonding (Commission Rule 210.42(a)(1)(ii))

In this document, the ALJ makes a recommendation to the Commission as what remedy should be issued and the amount of bond the respondents must post to permit temporary importation during the Presidential review period. While Commission Rule 210.42(a)(1)(ii) provides that this document must be issued within 14 days after the initial determination, in practice it is frequently issued with and, indeed, as part of the initial determination. There is a distinction between the two documents, however. An initial determination will become the determination of the Commission by operation of law if it is not reviewed by the Commission, as discussed *infra*. This is not true for a recommended determination, which must be specifically adopted by the Commission in order to become a Commission determination.

X. DISCOVERY (Commission Rules 210.27-.34)

The Commission's rules provide for discovery by all the methods familiar to practitioners in the Federal courts. These include depositions (Commission Rule 210.28), interrogatories (Commission Rule 210.29), requests for production of documents and things and entry upon land (Commission Rule 210.30), requests for admission (Commission Rule 210.31), and subpoenas (Commission Rule 210.32). The times for responding to discovery requests are set by the administrative law judge in his or her ground rules. The times set for responses to requests for written discovery are usually considerably shorter than in Federal district court proceedings, the usual response time being 10 days from service of the request. The Commission's rules provide for the issuance of protective orders and, as noted above, a protective order governing the production and treatment of confidential information is issued *sua sponte* by the administrative law judge at the beginning of every investigation. The ground rules of the administrative law judge address discovery and also provide for the treatment of information claimed to be the subject of privilege or work product immunity. The Commission's rules provide for sanctions for abuse of discovery and for failure to make or cooperate in discovery.

There are some differences in the language of the Commission's rules on discovery and the corresponding Federal Rules of Civil Procedure. Nevertheless, since the Commission's rules were derived from the Federal Rules, the case law developed by Federal district courts on the Federal Rules is applied by analogy to the Commission's rules where the language is similar.

A. Scope of Discovery (Commission Rule 210.27(b))

Generally, discovery will be permitted if the information sought appears reasonably calculated to lead to the discovery of admissible evidence, even if the information sought would be inadmissible at the evidentiary hearing.

Specifically, unless otherwise ordered by the administrative law judge, a party may obtain discovery regarding any matter, not privileged, which is relevant to the following:

a. the claim or defense of the party seeking discovery or the claim or defense of any other party, including the existence, description, nature, custody, condition, and location of any books, documents, or other tangible things;

b. the identity and location of persons having knowledge of any discoverable matter;

c. the appropriate remedy for a violation of Section 337;

d. the appropriate bond for the respondents under Section 337(j)(3) during Presidential review of the potential remedial order which may be issued by the Commission.

B. Form of Discovery Requests, Responses, and Objections (Commission Rule 210.27(d)(1))

The first page of every request for discovery or response or objection thereto must have a caption setting forth:

a. the name of the Commission;

b. the title of the investigation or related proceeding;

c. the docket number or investigation number, if any, assigned to the investigation or related proceeding.

C. Signing of Discovery Requests, Responses, and Objections (Commission Rule 210.27(d)(2))

1. If Party Represented by an Attorney

If a party is represented by an attorney, every request for discovery or response or objection thereto made by that party must be signed by at least one attorney of record in the attorney's individual name. The address of the attorney so signing must be stated.

2. If Party Not Represented by an Attorney

If a party is not represented by an attorney, the party must sign the request, response, or objection. The address of the party must be stated.

3. Significance of Signing; Certification

The signature of an attorney or party constitutes a certification that to the best of the signer's knowledge, information, and belief formed after a reasonable inquiry, the request, objection or response is:

a. consistent with Commission Rule 210.5(a) (relating to confidential information, if applicable) and other relevant provisions of 19 C.F.R. Chapter II, and warranted by existing law or a good faith argument for the extension, modification, or reversal of existing law;

b. not interposed for any improper purpose, such as to harass or to cause unnecessary delay or needless increase in the cost of litigation; and

c. not unreasonable or unduly burdensome or expensive, given the needs of the case, the discovery already had in the case, and the importance of the issues at stake in the litigation.

It should be noted that this certification based on the signature of an attorney or party is distinct from the verification required for responses to interrogatories and requests for admission.

4. Failure to Sign; Consequences

Commission Rule 210.27(d) provides that if a request, response, or objection is not signed, "it shall be stricken" unless it is signed promptly after the omission is called to the attention of the party making the request, response, or objection. This is a somewhat puzzling provision since discovery requests, responses, and objections are not filed with the Commission. The rule also provides that a party "shall not be obligated to take any action" with respect to the request, response, or objection until it is signed. For discovery requests, this provision means that there is no obligation to respond and object until the request is signed. The provision might seem to have no meaning for unsigned responses or objections. However, unsigned responses or objections could be regarded as defective as such, possibly giving rise to the usual consequences for failure to make discovery or timely file a response and objections.

5. Improper Certification

If an attorney or party has, without substantial justification, certified a request, response, or objection in violation of the requirements of Commission Rule 210.27(d), the ALJ or the Commission, on motion or *sua sponte*, may impose an appropriate sanction on the attorney or the party or both.

D. Supplementation of Responses to Discovery Requests (Commission Rule 210.27(c))

Commission Rule 210.27(c) governs the supplementation of responses to discovery requests. A party has a duty to supplement or correct a previous response to include information thereafter acquired if ordered to do so by the Commission or the administrative law judge. A party is under a duty seasonably to amend a prior response to an interrogatory, request for production, or request for admission if the party learns that the response is in some material respect incomplete or incorrect and if the additional or corrective information has not otherwise been made known to the other parties during the discovery process or in writing.

In addition to the foregoing, a duty to supplement responses may also be imposed by agreement of the parties, or at any time prior to a hearing through new requests for supplementation of prior responses.

E. Discovery Requests, Responses and Objections Not Filed; Service

Discovery requests, responses, and objections are not filed with the Commission or required to be served on the ALJ. They are always served on the parties to the investigation. In some cases, individual administrative law judges have ordered that they be served on him or her. Such service does not constitute a filing and the requests, responses, and objections do not thereby become part of the Commission record. (They can become part of the record if attached to a motion or accepted as exhibits at the evidentiary hearing.)

F. Discovery by the Commission Investigative Attorney

The Commission investigative attorney is a party to the investigation and is entitled to take discovery. As a matter of practice, the Commission investigative attorney usually serves brief written discovery and only rarely notices depositions, relying on the discovery efforts of the private parties, including participating in depositions noticed by the private parties.

G. Discovery from the Commission, Commission Employees, and the Commission Investigative Attorney

Discovery is hardly ever attempted from the Commission, Commission employees, or the Commission investigative attorney in the course of a Section 337 investigation. It is highly unlikely that these would have information within the scope of discovery and there are restrictions on whether and to what extent discovery can be taken from them at all.

H. Interrogatories (Commission Rule 210.29)

Any party may serve written interrogatories on any other party.

1. When Interrogatories May Be Served

A party may serve interrogatories on any other party after the date of publication of the notice of investigation in the *Federal Register*.

2. Limit on Number of Interrogatories

The Commission's rules do not place any limit on the number of interrogatories a party may serve. However, the ground rules of the administrative law judge may limit the number of interrogatories.

3. Time for Service of Response and Objections to Interrogatories

Commission Rule 210.29(b)(2) expressly provides that the administrative law judge will set the time for responses and objections to interrogatories. This matter is dealt with in the ground rules issued by the administrative law judge in each case. The response times set are short, usually ten days from service of the interrogatories (compared to thirty days in Federal district court actions). The ground rules will also set out the manner in which the time for responses may be extended, *i.e.*, whether by informal means (agreement of the parties) or formal means (motion).

4. Contents of Response

The response must repeat the interrogatory being answered immediately preceding the answer. Commission Rule 210.29(b)(2) provides that each interrogatory must be answered separately and fully in writing unless it is objected to.

If the interrogatories are answered in whole or in part, the response must be signed under oath (or declaration) by the person answering. Objections must be signed by the attorney making them. These requirements are usually met by having the attorney sign the response, with the understanding (sometimes expressly indicated) that he or she is signing for objections only. A verification, consisting of an oath or declaration signed by the person making the answers, is attached to the response.

5. Contention Interrogatories

Commission Rule 210.29(b)(3) permits contention interrogatories, *i.e.*, interrogatories which call for an answer which involves an opinion or contention that relates to fact or the application of law to fact. However, the administrative law judge may order that such an interrogatory need not be answered until after designated discovery has been completed or until or a pre-hearing conference or a later time. Such an order may be issued as a result of a motion for a protective order filed by the party to whom the interrogatories are directed. It may also be issued as part of a ruling on a motion to compel filed by the party serving the interrogatories.

6. Option to Produce Records

A party to whom an interrogatory is directed may, instead of providing a direct narrative response, refer the requesting party to records from which the answer may be discovered or ascertained. This option may be exercised if the burden of discovery and ascertaining the answer is substantially the same for the party serving the interrogatory as for the party served. A party who chooses this option must specify the documents from which the answer may be ascertained. The specification must be sufficient in detail so that the requesting party can locate the documents as readily as the party served. If the documents have not already been produced, the answering party must provide the requesting party reasonable opportunity to inspect the documents and make copies, compilations, abstracts or summaries.

I. Request for Production of Documents and Things and Entry Upon Land (Commission Rule 210.30)

Any party may serve on any other party (1) a request for the production of documents or things or (2) a request to permit entry upon designated land or other property in the possession or control of the party upon whom the request is served for the purpose of inspecting and measuring, surveying, photographing, testing or sampling the property or any designated object or operation thereon.

1. When Requests May Be Served

Any party may serve a request under Commission Rule 210.30 on any other party after the date of publication of the notice of investigation in the *Federal Register.*

2. Contents of the Request

The request must set forth the items to be inspected, whether by individual item or by category, and describe each item and category with reasonable particularity. The request must specify a reasonable time, place, and manner of making the inspection and performing the related acts.

3. Time for Response

Commission Rule 210.30(b)(2) expressly provides that the administrative law judge will set the time for responding to a request under Commission Rule 210.30 and this matter is dealt with in the ground rules issued by the administrative law judge in each case. The response times that are set are short, usually ten days from service of the request (compared to thirty days in Federal district court actions). The ground rules of some ALJs permit at least some opportunity to agree on an extension of this time. However, other ALJs may require that extensions of time be sought by formal means, *i.e.*, by motion.

4. Contents of Response

The response must state, with respect to each item or category, that inspection and related activities will be permitted as requested, unless the request is objected to, in which case the reasons for the objection must be stated. If objection is made to only part of any item or category, that part must be specified and, of course, the objection set out.

A party who produces documents for inspection must produce them as they are kept in the usual course of business or organize and label them to correspond to the categories in the request.

5. Persons Not Parties

Commission Rule 210.30(c) provides that Commission Rule 210.30 "does not preclude issuance of an order against a person not a party to permit entry upon land," an apparent reference to the Commission's subpoena power.

J. Requests for Admission (Commission Rule 210.31)

Any party may serve written requests for admission on any other party. Such requests may seek the admission of "the truth of any matters relevant to the investigation . . . that relate to statements or opinions of fact or of the application of law to fact." Such requests may also include requests to admit the genuineness of any documents described in the request. In that case, the party serving the request must serve copies of any documents referred to therein with the requests. Service of the documents is not required if they have already been furnished to or are otherwise known to be in possession of the party served and the request makes a statement to that effect.

1. When Requests for Admission May Be Served

The respondent and the Commission investigative attorney may serve requests for admission on the complainant after the date the notice of investigation is published in the *Federal Register*. The Commission's rules do not specify when the complainant may serve requests for admission. Commission Rule 210.31(a) expressly leaves this to the administrative law judge and it is usually set forth in the ALJ's ground rules for the case.

2. Contents of Requests for Admission

Each matter as to which an admission is requested must be set forth separately. If the request relates to a document, a copy of that document must accompany the request. A copy of the document is not required if it has been otherwise furnished or is known to be in the possession of the other party and the request contains a statement to that effect.

3. Time for Answers and Objections

Commission Rule 210.31(b) expressly provides that the administrative law judge will set the time for filing answers and objections to requests for admission. The ALJ usually sets the time period for such answers and objections in his or her ground rules for the case. The periods set are short, usually ten days from service of the request. Some ALJs permit the parties to agree to at least limited extensions of time for serving answers and objections. Other ALJs require a motion to obtain an extension.

4. Contents of Answers and Objections

A party answering a request for admission must repeat the request for admission immediately preceding his answer. Presumably this requirement also applies to requests which are objected to. The answer must be sworn or verified.

If an answer is made to a request, the party answering the request must (1) admit the matter, (2) specifically deny the matter, or (3) set forth in detail the reasons why it cannot truthfully admit or deny the matter.

If a denial is made, it must "fairly meet" the substance of the admission. If, in good faith, a party must qualify an answer or deny only a part of the matter as to which an admission is requested, the party must specify what part of the matter is true and qualify or deny the remainder.

If an answering party gives lack of information or knowledge as a reason for failure to admit or deny, it must state that it has made reasonable inquiry and that the information known to or readily obtainable by it is insufficient to enable it to admit or deny.

If a party objects to a request, it must state the reasons for its objection. A party who considers that a matter as to which an admission has been requested presents a genuine issue for a hearing may not object to the request on that ground alone; rather, the party must deny the matter or give reasons why it cannot admit or deny it.

5. Effect of Failure to Answer or Object

If a party fails to timely answer or object to requests for admission, the matters for which admission is sought may be deemed to be admitted.

6. Motion to Contest Sufficiency of Answers or Objections

This motion is specific to requests for admission and is analogous to a motion to compel, which is specifically provided for in the Commission's rules on interrogatories and document requests, but not in its rule on requests for admission.

If the party serving requests for admission believes that the answers are insufficient or that the objections are not justified, it may move to determine the sufficiency of answers or objections. If the administrative law judge determines that an answer is insufficient, *i.e.*, does not comply with requirements of the rule, he or she may order either that the matter be admitted or that an amended answer be served. As to objections, the answering party will have the burden of showing that its objection is justified. If it fails to do so, the administrative law judge must order that an answer be served.

In lieu of the foregoing orders, the ALJ may defer final disposition of the motion to a pre-hearing conference or at a designated time prior to the evidentiary hearing.

7. Effect of Admissions

Commission Rule 210.31(d) provides that a matter which has been admitted "may be conclusively established" unless the administrative law judge permits withdrawal or amendment of the admission.

8. Withdrawal or Amendment of Admission

Under Commission Rule 210.31(d), the administrative law judge may, on motion, permit withdrawal or amendment of an admission when the presentation of the issues in the investigation will be served and the party who obtained the admission fails to show that such withdrawal or amendment will prejudice that party in maintaining its position on the issues in the investigation.

9. Effect of Admissions on Other Proceedings

Commission Rule 210.31(d) provides that any admission made by a party thereunder is "for the purpose of the pending investigation only and is not an admission for any other purpose, nor may it be used against him in any other proceeding."

K. Depositions (Commission Rule 210.28)

Commission Rule 210.28 provides that any party may take the deposition "of any person, including a party" by deposition upon oral examination or written questions. By its terms, the quoted phase includes persons who are not parties. However, the failure of a non-party to comply with a notice of deposition is quite different from failure of a non-party to comply, since discovery sanctions are available against a party, but not a non-party.[26]

---

26 Of course, a non-party may be made subject to compulsion to comply via a subpoena ad testificandum, but the sanctions for non-compliance with a subpoena are different from failure of a party to comply with a notice of deposition. Further, enforcement of a Commission subpoena requires court intervention.

1. When Depositions May Be Taken; Time for Notice

Commission Rule 210.28(a) provides that a party may take a deposition following publication of the notice of investigation in the *Federal Register.* It also provides that the administrative law judge will determine "the permissible dates or deadlines for taking such depositions."

Commission Rule 210.28(c) provides that depositions be on notice and that the administrative law judge will determine the "appropriate period" for providing such notice. The administrative law judges usually set this "appropriate period" in the ground rules they issue for each case. For example, the ground rules may provide for ten days notice if the deponent is located in the United States and fifteen days notice if the deponent is located outside of the United States. The notice must be served on the other parties to the investigation.

2. Contents of Notice of Deposition

The notice of deposition must state:

- the time and place for taking the deposition;
- the name and address of each person to be examined;[27]
- if a subpoena duces tecum is to be served on the person to be examined, the designation of the material to be produced as set forth in the subpoena must be attached to or included in the notice.

If the deposition is to be conducted by telephone, the notice should so state. Similarly, if parties have stipulated or the ALJ has ordered that the deposition be recorded by other than stenographic means, the notice should so state.

3. Telephonic Depositions

Commission Rule 210.28(c) specifically provides for the possibility of telephonic depositions. If the deposition is to be by telephone, the notice should include a statement to that effect. No stipulation or order is necessary to conduct a deposition by telephone. However, if a telephonic deposition is objected to by any party, that party may move to have the deposition taken "live," *i.e.,* with the deponent present.

4. Recording of Deposition by Other Than Stenographic Means; Video Depositions

The Commission's rules contemplate that the deposition will be recorded by stenographic means. If a party or parties wish to have the deposition recorded by

27 If the name of any person to be examined is not known, the notice of deposition must provide "a general description sufficient to identify him or the particular class or group to which he belongs." Commission Rule 210.28(c).

other than stenographic means, this can be done by stipulation or by obtaining an order from the administrative law judge. (The ALJ may have already included this possibility in his or her ground rules.) Thus, if it is desired that the deposition be recorded by video instead of stenographic means, a stipulation or order would be required. However, if the deposition is being recorded by stenographic means and it is simply desired that it also be recorded by video, a stipulation or order may not be required, though in the absence of either, the only official "recording" may be the one by stenographic means.

5. Persons Before Whom Depositions May Be Taken

Depositions may be taken before a person having power to administer oaths under the laws of the United States or of the place where the examination is held. The court reporter who records the deposition in the United States usually has the power to administer such oaths and thus serves two roles at the deposition.

6. Taking of Deposition

The procedure for taking a deposition is to swear in the witness and then have the party issuing the notice begin the direct examination of the witness. Any adverse party may cross-examine the witness. While the Commission's rules do not expressly provide for redirect examination, this frequently takes place. In multi-party cases, the parties must agree as to the sequence of examination. The Commission investigative attorney, if he or she chooses to attend, usually examines the witness last, subject to possible follow-up examination by the other parties based on the testimony elicited.

Objections to questions or documents must be in "short form," stating the grounds of objections relied upon, a provision which may be read as prohibiting speaking objections. At least one administrative law judge has expressly prohibited speaking objections in his ground rules. The Commission's rules provide that "[e]vidence objected to shall be taken subject to the objections, except that privileged communications and subject matter need not be disclosed." Of course, the "evidence" referred to is not (at least not yet) evidence in the sense of having been admitted into the evidentiary record.

After the record of the deposition is reduced to writing, the deposition must be signed by the witness, unless the parties waive signing or the witness is ill, cannot be located, or refuses to sign. The deposition transcript must also be certified by the person before whom the deposition was taken.

When the deposition is recorded by stenographic means, the stenographer must certify on the transcript that the witness was sworn in the stenographer's presence and that the transcript is a true record of the testimony of the witness. As noted, when a court reporter is used in the United States, the stenographer and the person administering the oath are the same person.

When a deposition is recorded by other than stenographic means and is thereafter transcribed, the person transcribing it must certify that the person heard the witness sworn on the recording and that the transcript is a correct transcription of the recording.

As noted above, there may be instances where the witness does not sign the transcript. This can occur when the parties stipulate to waiver of signature or when the witness is ill, cannot be found, or refuses to sign. When the witness does not sign, the person administering the oath must state that fact on the record and set out the reason therefor.

The court reporter or other person preparing the transcript must forward one copy to each party who was present or represented at the deposition.[28]

7. Special Procedure for Depositions of Non-Party Officers or Employees of the Commission or Other Government Agencies

If a party wishes to obtain the deposition (1) of an officer or employee of the Commission other than the Commission investigative attorney, or (2) of an officer or employee of another Government agency, or wishes to obtain documents or other physical exhibits in the custody, control, and possession of such officer or employee, a special procedure must be followed. Specifically, that party must first file a written motion with the administrative law judge for leave to apply for a subpoena under Commission Rule 210.32(c). In that motion, the party must show how the information expected to be obtained is (1) within the scope of discovery permitted by Commission Rule 210.27(b) or Commission Rule 210.61 and (2) that the information cannot be obtained by alternative means without undue hardship.

8. Admissibility of Depositions

The Commission's rules prescribe the circumstances under which depositions may be considered for admission into evidence. Even if these circumstances are met, objection may be made at the hearing to receiving in evidence any deposition or part thereof for any reason that would require exclusion of the evidence if the witness were then present and testifying.

---

28 This would, by definition, include the Commission investigative attorney. In any event, under Commission Rule 210.28(f), whenever a party takes a deposition, it must promptly serve a copy of the deposition transcript on the Commission investigative attorney. Such service does not constitute a determination that the transcript is admissible in evidence or that it may be used in the investigation.

A deposition may be used as evidence against any party who was present or represented at the taking of the deposition or who had reasonable notice thereof as follows:

- Any deposition may be used by any party for the purpose of contradicting or impeaching the testimony of a deponent who has been called as a witness at the evidentiary hearing;
- The deposition of a party may be used by an adverse party for any purpose;
- The deposition of a witness, whether or not a party, may be used by any party for any purpose if the administrative law judge finds:
  - that the witness is dead;
  - that the witness is out of the United States, unless it appears that the absence of the witness was procured by the party offering the testimony;
  - that the witness is unable to attend or testify because of age, illness, infirmity, or imprisonment;
  - that the party offering the deposition has been unable to procure the attendance of the witness by subpoena;[29] or
  - upon application and notice, that such exceptional circumstances exist as to make it desirable in the interest of justice and with due regard to the importance of presenting the oral testimony of witnesses at a hearing, to allow the deposition to be used.

9. Use of Only Part of Deposition

If only part of a deposition is offered in evidence by a party, an adverse party may require the offering party to introduce any other part that ought in fairness to be considered with the part introduced, and any party may introduce any other parts.

10. Effect of Errors and Irregularities in Depositions

a. In Notice of Deposition

All errors and irregularities in the notice of deposition are waived unless written objection is served promptly on the party issuing the notice of deposition.

---

29 In this connection it should be noted that the Commission has nationwide subpoena power, *i.e.*, its subpoenas are not subject to the geographic limitations of Federal district court subpoenas.

b. As to Disqualification of Person Before Whom Deposition Is To Be Taken

If the person before whom the deposition is to be taken is thought to be unqualified (*i.e.*, there is noncompliance with Commission Rule 210.28(b)), an objection based on such disqualification must be made (1) before the taking of the deposition begins or (2) as soon thereafter as the disqualification becomes known or could be discovered with reasonable diligence.

c. As to Taking of the Deposition

i. Certain Objections Not Waived for Failure to Make During or Prior to Deposition

Certain objections are not waived by failure to make them before or during the deposition, unless the ground for objection is one that might have been obviated or removed if presented at that time. These objections are:

- objections to the competency of the witness, and
- objections to the competency, relevancy, or materiality of the witness' testimony.

ii. Certain Objections Waived for Failure to Make at Deposition

Certain objections are waived unless "seasonable" objection is made at the taking of the deposition. These objections are to:

- Errors or irregularities occurring at the oral examination in
  - the manner of taking the deposition
  - the form of the questions or answers
  - the oath or affirmation, or
  - the conduct of the parties.
- Errors of any kind which might be obviated, removed, or cured if promptly presented.

d. Deposition upon Written Interrogatories; Waiver of Objections to Form of Questions

Where the deposition is upon written interrogatories, objections to the form of questions are waived unless the objections are reduced to writing and served upon the party propounding the questions. Commission Rule 210.28(i)(3)(iii) expressly leaves the deadline for serving such objections to be set by the administrative law judge.

e. As to Completion and Return of Deposition

Unless a motion to suppress the deposition or part thereof is made with reasonable promptness after the defect is, or with due diligence might have been ascertained, objections are waived as to errors and irregularities in the manner in which the testimony is transcribed or the deposition is prepared, signed, certified, sealed, endorsed, transmitted, filed, or otherwise dealt with by the person before whom it was taken.

L. Protective Orders (Commission Rule 210.34)

Commission Rule 210.34 governs the issuance of protective orders by the administrative law judge. By far the most important of these orders and the only protective order which is issued (as a matter of course) in every investigation is the protective order governing the submission and treatment of confidential business information.

1. Obtaining Protective Orders

Commission Rule 210.34 extends to a wide variety of protective orders and provides that, on motion by a party or by the person against whom discovery is sought or on his or her own initiative and for good cause shown, the ALJ "may make any order that may appear necessary and appropriate for the protection of the public interest or that justice requires to protect a party or person from annoyance, embarrassment, oppression, or undue burden or expense. . . ." The rule provides a non-inclusive list of such orders, *i.e.*,

- that the discovery not be had;
- that the discovery may be had only on specified terms and conditions, including a designation of the time or place;
- that discovery may be had only by a method of discovery other than that selected by the party seeking discovery;
- that certain matters not be inquired into, or that the scope of discovery be limited to certain matters;
- that discovery be conducted with no one present except persons designated by the administrative law judge;
- that a deposition, after being sealed, be opened only by order of the Commission or the administrative law judge;
- that a trade secret or other confidential research, development, or commercial information not be disclosed or be disclosed only in a designated way;
- that the parties simultaneously file specified documents or information enclosed in sealed envelopes to be opened as directed by the Commission or the administrative law judge.

2. Denial of Motion for Protective Order

A denial of a motion for a protective order, whether in whole or in part, may include an order requiring that discovery be made "on such terms and conditions as are just."

3. Issuance or Amendment of Protective Order by Commission

Commission Rule 210.34(a) provides that the Commission, as well as the ALJ, may issue protective orders and that the Commission may continue or amend a protective order issued by the administrative law judge.[30]

M. Subpoena Practice (Commission Rule 210.32)

Under its organic act, the Commission is authorized to issue subpoenas in aid of any of its investigations, including those under Section 337. 19 U.S.C. § 1333(a); *U.S. International Trade Commission v. E. & J. Gallo Winery*, 637 F. Supp. 1262 (D.D.C. 1985). There are significant differences between subpoena practice at the Commission and that before United States district courts. First, Commission subpoenas must be applied for and therefore are not routinely issued in blank. Second, Commission subpoenas may be served anywhere within the United States, *i.e.*, they are not subject to the geographical limitations of Federal district court subpoenas. Third, Commission subpoenas are enforced by and at the discretion of the Commission itself through summary proceedings for an enforcement order in a United States district court, not by contempt proceedings before the Commission.

1. Subpoenas Available

Commission Rule 210.32 governs subpoenas issued in Section 337 proceedings. It provides for both subpoenas ad testificandum and subpoenas duces tecum for discovery and evidentiary purposes.

2. Form of Subpoenas

The Commission's rules do not provide for any particular form for subpoenas. However, the ground rules of the administrative law judge may prescribe a suggested or mandatory form. All subpoenas must identify the proceeding and the subpoenaed party. In the case of a subpoena duces tecum, the date, time, and place where documents are to be produced must be set out. Further, the categories of documents and things must be identified. In the case of a subpoena ad testificandum, the subpoena must state the date, time, and place where testimony is to be taken. In the case of a subpoena ad testificandum to a legal person (*i.e.*, a "30(b)(6)" subpoena), the categories for which testimony is sought must be identified. Subpoenas usually contain instructions and definitions of the terms used therein. These usually include instructions for dealing with documents or things which are subject to a claim of privilege by providing for the submission of a privilege log. Subpoenas also include instructions for dealing with documents, things or testimony which are claimed to constitute confidential business

---

30 Ordinarily, protective orders issued by the ALJ are automatically continued before the full Commission.

information by indicating that the protective order is applicable and attaching a copy of the protective order.

3. Applications for Subpoenas

Commission Rule 210.32 provides that applications for subpoenas in Section 337 cases are made to the administrative law judge. These applications may (and usually are) made *ex parte*, accompanied by the proposed subpoenas. The ground rules of the administrative law judge may require that the original application and proposed subpoenas be accompanied by one or more copies thereof. Subpoena applications are usually brief, describing the testimony or documents being sought, why they are sought, and why a subpoena is necessary to obtain them. In the case of a subpoena duces tecum, Commission Rule 210.32(a)(2) requires that the application "specify the material to be produced as precisely as possible, showing the general relevancy of the material and the reasonableness of the scope of the subpoena."

4. Issuance of the Subpoena

Assuming the application and proposed subpoenas are in order, the administrative law judge will ordinarily sign the subpoena, usually within a day or two, and usually without any alterations. There have been occasions where an administrative law judge has issued a subpoena with further limitations on its scope, when he or she felt that its full scope was not supported by the application. There have also been occasions when an administrative law judge has altered the return date for the subpoena. The chambers of the ALJ notifies the applicant when the subpoena has been signed. Subpoenas are usually served by the requesting party immediately on receipt from the administrative law judge.

5. Certain Subpoenas Prohibited or Restricted

By Commission rule, certain subpoenas are prohibited or restricted. Thus, the administrative law judge may not entertain a subpoena for production of documents grounded upon the Freedom of Information Act, *i.e.*, a person may not use the Commission's subpoena rule to circumvent the procedure under FOIA.

Commission Rule 210.32(c)(1) subjects an application for a subpoena requiring the production of non-party Commission materials or the production of records or personnel of other Government agencies to special requirements and procedures. Such applications must "specify as precisely as possible the material to be produced, the nature of the information to be disclosed, or the expected testimony of the official or employee, and shall contain a statement showing the general relevancy of the material, information, or testimony and the reasonableness of the scope of the application, together with a showing that such material, information, or testimony or their substantial equivalent could not be obtained without undue hardship or by alternative means."

Under Commission Rule 210.32(c)(2), the administrative law judge may issue such a subpoena "when warranted," but the rule specifically contemplates limiting their scope and provides that to the extent they are granted, the ALJ "shall provide such terms and conditions for the production of the material, the disclosure of the information, or the appearance of the official or employee as may appear necessary and appropriate for the protection of the public interest."

6. Witness Fees

Under Commission Rule 210.32(f), any person compelled to appear in person to depose or testify in response to a subpoena must be paid the same fees and mileage as witnesses in proceedings in the Federal courts. The only exception is for salaried Federal employees summoned to depose or testify as to matters related to their public employment. Such employees are paid in accordance with the applicable Federal regulations, irrespective of the party at whose instance they are summoned.

The fees and mileage are paid by the party at whose instance the deponent or witness appears. The fees are due no later than the date for compliance with the subpoena. However, failure to timely tender such fees will not invalidate the subpoena.

7. Motion to Quash

The subpoenaed person may move to quash the subpoena. The time for filing and serving the motion to quash is indicated in the subpoena.

8. Enforcement of Subpoenas

The Commission has no contempt power and its subpoenas must be enforced through the Federal courts. To obtain court enforcement, the party who requested the subpoena may petition the administrative law judge to certify a request for judicial enforcement to the Commission. Alternatively, the administrative law judge may act *sua sponte*. The request must be accompanied by copies of the relevant papers and a written report from the ALJ concerning the purpose, relevance, and reasonableness of the subpoena. The Commission may then (but need not) proceed with judicial enforcement of the request. If it does decide to so proceed, it is not required to enforce the entire request. The Commission will issue a notice as to whether it has granted the request. Enforcement of the subpoena is by the Commission itself, by bringing an action for enforcement in a United States district court, usually the United States District Court for the District of Columbia, as in the *Gallo* case noted above. In such a district court enforcement proceeding, the Commission is represented by attorneys from its Office of the General Counsel or, if requested, from the Department of Justice. The result is usually an enforcement order by the district court, the violation of which may be grounds for exercise of the contempt power of the court.

XI. MOTIONS PRACTICE

Motions are simply requests to a tribunal to take or order certain action. Commission Rule 210.15 generally governs motions practice in Section 337 proceedings. However, certain types of motions have their own specific rules. These include motions for default (Commission Rules 210.16-.17), summary determination (Commission Rule 210.18), intervention (Commission Rule 210.19), declassification of confidential information (Commission Rule 210.20), termination of the investigation (Commission Rule 210.21), suspension of the investigation (Commission Rule 210.23), sanctions (Commission Rule 210.25), and temporary relief (Commission Rules 210.22, 210.52-.69).

Where a motion is governed by a specific provision, that provision must be followed in addition to the general provision. Where a specific provision conflicts with the general provision, the specific provision governs.

Depending upon the nature of the motion and the stage of the proceedings, a motion may be addressed to the Commission or the ALJ. When an investigation or related proceeding is before the Commission, the Commission's rules provide that the motion is addressed to the Chairman of the Commission. In practice, however, such motions are addressed to the Commission. When an investigation or related proceeding is before the administrative law judge, the motion is directed to him or her.[31]

In addition to the Commission's rules governing motions, practitioners must also consult the ground rules of the administrative law judge, which may impose additional requirements, both generally and for specific types of motions.[32] The ground rules may not, however, waive a requirement of the Commission's rules (unless the rule grants the ALJ authority to do so) nor can the ground rules impose requirements inconsistent with the Commission's rules. Further, the ground rules are limited to those motions addressed to the ALJ.[33]

A. Content

All written motions must state the particular order, ruling, or action desired and the grounds therefor. Commission Rule 210.15(b). Frequently, the ground rules of the ALJ may impose specific format requirements, such as a requirement that the motion and the memorandum in support be filed as separate documents or that a proposed order accompany the motion.

---

31 Following the usual practice, a motion is "addressed" to the Commission by simply having the header on the first page if the motion refer to "United States International Trade Commission." To "address" a motion to the administrative law judge, an additional line is added to refer to the ALJ presiding over the case (*e.g.*, "Before Administrative Law Judge (Name)"). Indeed, this practice is not only followed for motions, but for all submissions.

32 For example, an ALJ's ground rules may require the parties to meet and confer before filing any motion relating to a discovery dispute.

33 Most motions are, however, addressed to the ALJ.

B. Filing and Service

Motions must be filed with the Office of the Secretary and served on all other parties to the case. In the case of a motion to amend the complaint and notice of investigation to name an additional respondent after institution, the motion must be served on the proposed additional respondent.

C. Responses

Under Commission Rule 210.15, a response is due within 10 days after service of the motion or within such longer or shorter time as may be designated by the administrative law judge or the Commission. The ALJs usually set shorter times in their ground rules. Further, a party filing a motion may request that an even shorter response time be set for that specific motion, though such requests are not lightly granted. The ALJ may also shorten the response time for a specific motion *sua sponte*. The parties will, of course, be notified if a shorter response time is set.

All non-moving parties are entitled to file a response to a motion. In the case of a motion to amend the complaint or notice of investigation to name an additional respondent after institution, the proposed respondent may also respond. Indeed, the Commission's rules provide that the proposed respondent "shall respond or he may be deemed to have consented to the granting of the relief asked for in the motion."

The Commission and the ALJ may waive the requirements of Commission Rule 210.15 with respect to motions for extensions of time and may rule on such motions *ex parte*.

D. Replies

The moving party has no right of reply except as may be permitted by the Commission or the administrative law judge. The usual procedure is to file a motion for leave to file a reply with the proposed reply attached. Such a motion for leave should be filed promptly, since any delay may result in the motion being ruled on before the motion for leave is filed.

E. Rulings on Motions

The Commission rules on motions addressed originally to it by issuing an order. The administrative law judge rules on motions addressed to him or her by issuing an initial determination or order, depending on the nature of the motion. By Commission rule, certain motions addressed to the ALJ are granted or denied by initial determination.[34] Other motions are granted by initial

34 These motions certainly include a motion for temporary relief (Commission Rules 210.42(b), 210.66) and may include a motion for the forfeiture or return of complainant's temporary relief bond. Commission Rules 210.42(b), 210.70. However, Commission Rule 210.42(c) states that only the grant of the latter motion is by initial determination and that its denial is by order.

determination, but denied by order.[35] Rulings on motions which do not fall into one of these two categories are made by order only, whether the motion is granted or denied.

F. Review of Rulings on Motions

Where the initial ruling on the motion is by the Commission itself, any further review by the Commission is by a request for reconsideration.

Where the initial ruling on the motion is by the ALJ, a motion for reconsideration by the administrative law judge may be filed, though such a motion is not specifically provided for in the Commission's rules. If Commission review of the ALJ's ruling is sought, the procedure for obtaining review depends on whether the ruling was made by initial determination or by order. Motions for temporary relief and rulings thereon are subject to their own regime discussed *infra.*

1. Where Ruling Is by Initial Determination

An initial determination which constitutes a ruling on a motion is distinguished from the ALJ's final initial determination on whether a violation of Section 337 exists. However, like that final initial determination, it will become the Commission's determination after a prescribed period of time, usually 30 or 45 days, depending on the type of motion, unless the Commission determines to review it. Commission Rule 210.42(h). Thus, when a motion is ruled upon by initial determination, a party seeking review must do so within the time limits set by the Commission's rules and cannot wait until the final initial determination is issued. The procedure for such review is governed by Commission Rules 210.43-.45 and is analogous (but not identical) to review of a final initial determination discussed *infra.*

2. Where Ruling is Made by Order: Interlocutory Appeals

Rulings made by order are not reviewable by the Commission until the administrative law judge issues his or her final determination (on whether a violation of Section 337 exists) unless an interlocutory appeal is authorized or permitted.

---

35 These motions include a motion to amend the complaint or notice of investigation pursuant to Commission Rule 210.14(b); a motion for finding of default pursuant to Commission Rule 210.16; a motion for summary determination pursuant to Commission Rule 210.18; a motion for intervention pursuant to Commission Rule 210.19; a motion for termination pursuant to Commission Rule 210.21; a motion to suspend an investigation pursuant to Commission Rule 210.23; a motion for forfeiture or return of respondents' bonds pursuant to Commission Rule 210.50(d); a motion to set a target date exceeding 15 months pursuant to Commission Rule 210.51(a); and a motion for forfeiture or return of a complainant's temporary relief bond pursuant to Commission Rule 210.70. *See* Commission Rule 210.42(c). These motions also include a motion to declassify information made pursuant to Commission Rule 210.20(b). *See* Commission Rules 210.20(b), 210.42(a)(2).

There are two types of interlocutory appeals: those which may be made without leave of the administrative law judge and those which require such leave. In both cases, the Commission retains discretion to entertain the appeal.

There are two types of interlocutory rulings which do not require leave of the administrative law judge before appeal may be sought. These are: (1) a ruling which requires the disclosure of Commission records or requires the appearance of Government officials pursuant to commission Rule 210.32(c)(2) and (2) a ruling which denies an application for intervention under Commission Rule 210.19.

Appeals from the foregoing two types of rulings may be sought by filing an application for review with the Commission within five days after service of the administrative law judge's ruling. There is a 15 page limit on such applications. An answer to the application for review may be filed within five days after service of the application.

The application for review should specify the person or party taking the appeal, designate the ruling or part thereof from which appeal is being taken, and specify the reasons and present arguments as to why Commission review is sought.

The Commission may entertain any such appeal in its discretion. If the Commission decides to entertain the appeal, it will issue an order placing the matter on its docket for review. Any such review order will set out the scope of the review and the issues to be considered. It will also provide for the filing of any briefs if the Commission wishes briefing in addition to the application for review and any responses thereto. In the case of an appeal of a ruling by the administrative law judge under Commission Rule 210.32(c)(2), the Commission may stay the return date of the order.

For interlocutory orders not covered by Commission Rule 210.24(a), appeals may only be taken with leave of the administrative law judge. Leave is granted if the administrative law judge determines, in writing, with supporting justification, that the interlocutory ruling involves a controlling question of law or policy as to which there is substantial ground for difference of opinion and either an immediate appeal from the ruling may materially advance the ultimate completion of the investigation or subsequent review will be an inadequate remedy. Commission Rule 210.24(b)(1).

A special rule is followed where review is sought of a ruling by the administrative law judge under Commission Rule 210.5(c)(1) as to whether information designation by the supplier is entitled to confidential treatment under Commission Rule 210.5(b). For such a ruling, the administrative law judge grants leave simply by providing written justification. Commission Rule 210.24(b)(2).

If leave to appeal is granted, the party seeking review may file a written application for review (limited to 15 pages) with the Commission within five days after service of the administrative law judge's determination to grant leave. An answer may be filed five days after service of the application. The grant of such an appeal is discretionary with the Commission. Unless otherwise ordered, if the Commission permits an appeal, its review will be confined to the application for review and any answer thereto.

The filing of an application for review will not stay the investigation before the administrative law judge, unless the administrative law judge or the Commission orders a stay.

XII. DEFAULT (Section 337(g); Commission Rules 210.16–.17)

The Commission's rules recognize two forms of default: statutory default, based on Section 337(g), and non-statutory default.

A. Statutory Default

Section 337(g) defines certain circumstances under which a respondent will be found in default and specifies the consequences of such default.

Section 337(g)(1) applies to cases where the complainant is not seeking a general exclusion order. It provides that if:

- a respondent fails to respond or otherwise fails to appear to answer the complaint and notice of investigation, after service thereof; and
- that respondent fails to show good cause why he should not be found in default; and
- the complainant seeks relief limited solely to that person,

then, the Commission shall

- presume the facts alleged in the complaint to be true; and
- upon request, issue an exclusion order or a cease and desist order (or both) limited to the defaulting respondent;

unless

- after consideration of certain public interest factors, it finds that such relief should not be issued.

Section 337(g)(2) addresses the question of default when the complainant seeks a general exclusion order. It is in addition to the authority of the Commission to issue a general exclusion order when a respondent appears to contest a Section 337 proceeding. Under Section 337(g)(2), the Commission may also issue a general exclusion order where no respondent appears to contest the investigation if

- a violation of Section 337 is established by substantial, reliable, and probative evidence, and
- the requirements of Section 337(d)(2) (relating to general exclusion orders) are met.

The provisions of Section 337(g)(2) thus require the complainant to put on its evidence in a (truncated) oral hearing or with documents.

Commission Rule 210.16 is intended to implement Section 337(g). It provides that a party shall be found in default if it fails to respond to the complaint and notice of investigation in the manner prescribed by Commission Rule 210.13, or (in cases involving a motion for temporary relief) Commission Rule 210.59(c), or "otherwise fails to answer the complaint and notice," and fails to show cause why it should not be found in default.[36]

If a respondent has failed to respond or appear as called for by Section 337(g) and Commission Rule 210.16(a)(1), the administrative law judge, on motion or *sua sponte*, may issue an order directing that respondent show cause why it should not be found in default. If the respondent fails to make the necessary showing, the administrative law judge will issue an initial determination finding that respondent in default, which will be the subject of possible Commission review. If the Commission decides not to review that initial determination, or affirms it, the Commission will have made a determination of default with respect to that respondent. If the administrative law judge denies a motion for default under Commission Rule 210.16(a)(1), he or she will do so by order.

There are some immediate consequences to a party found in default pursuant to Commission Rule 210.16. Specifically, a party found in default will be deemed to have waived its rights:

- to appear,
- to be served with documents, and
- to contest the allegations at issue in the investigation.

Commission Rule 210.16(b)(3).

While these consequences follow immediately from a Commission determination of default, such a determination does not automatically result in the immediate issuance of relief, *i.e.*, a remedial order. In order to obtain immediate relief against a defaulting respondent, the complainant must specifically request such relief. The complainant does so by filing a declaration with the Commission that it is seeking immediate entry of relief against the respondent in default. The facts alleged in the complaint will be presumed to be true with respect to the defaulting respondent.

On receipt of the declaration, the Commission "may" issue an exclusion order, a cease and desist order, or both, affecting the defaulting respondent, but only after it considers the effect of such orders on certain public interest factors and

36 As Commission Rule 210.16(a)(2) makes clear, a party may also be found in default as a sanction for abuse of process or for failure to make or cooperate in discovery.

concludes that such relief should still be issued. As a matter of practice, if all the respondents are found in default at the same time, the Commission will usually issue relief immediately, if it is not contrary to the public interest. If, however, only some of the respondents have been found in default, the Commission will defer issuing relief until there has been action on all respondents, *i.e.*, until the conclusion of the investigation. This is because if other parties remain contesting the case, the possibility remains that the issuance of relief may be precluded, *e.g.*, in a patent-based case, the patent might ultimately be declared invalid, making relief even against defaulting respondents inappropriate.

In any motion requesting the entry of default or the termination of the investigation with respect to the last remaining respondent, the complainant must declare whether it is seeking a general exclusion order. The Commission may issue a general exclusion order if the requirements of Section 337(g)(2) are met and if the Commission concludes that such an order is not precluded by consideration of certain public interest factors.

B. Failure to Act Other Than Statutory Forms of Default (Commission Rule 210.17)

Commission Rule 210.17 provides that certain failures to act other than the defaults covered by Commission Rule 210.16 may provide a basis for the presiding administrative law judge or the Commission to draw adverse inferences and to issue findings of fact, conclusions of law, determinations (including a determination on violation of Section 337), and orders that are adverse to the party who fails to act. As specified in the rule, such failures include, but are not limited to:

1. Failure to respond to a motion that materially alters the scope of the investigation or a related proceeding;

2. Failure to respond to a motion for temporary relief pursuant to Commission Rule 210.59;

3. Failure to respond to a motion for summary determination under Commission Rule 210.18;

4. Failure to appear at a hearing before the administrative law judge after filing a written response to the complaint or motion for temporary relief, or failure to appear at a hearing before the Commission;

5. Failure to file a brief or other written submission requested by the administrative law judge or the Commission during an investigation or a related proceeding;

6. Failure to respond to a petition for review of an initial determination, a petition for reconsideration of an initial determination, or an application for interlocutory review of an administrative law judge's order;

7. Failure to file a brief or other written submission requested by the administrative law judge or the Commission;

8. Failure to participate in temporary relief bond forfeiture proceedings under Commission Rule 210.70.

The presiding administrative law judge or the Commission may take action under Commission Rule 210.17 *sua sponte* or on motion by a party.

XIII. AVOIDANCE OF TRIAL: SUMMARY DETERMINATION (Commission Rule 210.18)

Summary determination is the Commission's analog to summary judgment in Federal district court actions and is covered by Commission Rule 210.18.

Any party may move for summary determination in his favor on all or some of the issues in the investigation. Thus, the rule specifically provides for partial summary determination.

A. Time for Filing Motion

The complainant may move for summary determination at any time after 20 days following the date of service of the complaint and notice of investigation. Any other party (including, of course, a respondent) may move for summary determination at any time after the date of publication of the notice of investigation in the *Federal Register*. However, in each case, the motion must be filed at least thirty days before the evidentiary hearing on permanent relief. If the investigation involves a motion for temporary relief, the administrative law judge will set the deadline for filing motions for summary determination in connection with such request for temporary relief. Any affidavits in support of the motion for summary determination must accompany the motion.

Responses to motions for summary determination are due 10 days after service and there is no right of reply. A nonmoving party may file opposing affidavits within 10 days after service of the motion, *i.e.*, at the same time the response to the motion is filed and served. When a motion for summary determination is made and supported in accordance with Commission Rule 210.18, a party opposing the motion may not rest upon mere allegations or denials of the opposition party's pleading, but must, in its response, set forth specific facts by affidavits, answers to interrogatories, or as otherwise provided, showing that there is a genuine issue of fact for the evidentiary hearing. If the opposing party does not so respond, summary determination, if appropriate, will be rendered against it.

The rules governing the timing of motion for summary determinations ensure that such filings are made while the investigation is pending before the administrative law judge. The ALJ may, in his or her discretion or at the request of any party, set the matter for oral argument and "call for the submission of briefs or memoranda."

B. Affidavits

Affidavits submitted in connection with motions for summary determination must be made on personal knowledge of the affiant. They must set forth such facts as would be admissible in evidence and must affirmatively show that the affiant is competent to testify to the matters stated therein. If the affidavit refers to papers or parts of papers, sworn or certified copies of those papers must be attached to the affidavit or filed and served with the affidavit.

The administrative law judge may permit affidavits to be supplemented or opposed by depositions, answers to interrogatories, or further affidavits. (This increases the probability that the administrative law judge will permit replies and surreplies.)

In accordance with 1 U.S.C. § 1, the term "affidavits" under the Commission's rules encompasses affirmations (declarations).

C. Ruling; Basis

Summary determination will be granted if the "pleadings and any depositions, answers to interrogatories, and admissions on file, together with the affidavits, if any, show that there is no genuine issue as to any material fact and that the moving party is entitled to a summary determination as a matter of law."

D. Order of Summary Determination

The granting of a motion for summary determination constitutes an initial determination and is subject to possible Commission review by the procedure set forth in Commission Rules 210.43-46. The denial of summary determination is by order and is subject to Commission review, if at all, by the interlocutory review procedures of Commission Rule 210.24.

E. Refusal of Summary Determination; Continuations

If it appears from the affidavits of a party opposing summary determination that that party cannot, for reasons stated, present by affidavit facts essential to justify the party's opposition, the administrative law judge may refuse to grant summary determination. Alternatively, the administrative law judge may order a continuance to permit affidavits to be obtained or depositions to be taken or discovery to be had or "may make such other order as is appropriate."

F. Order Establishing Facts

If the administrative law judge does not grant summary determination on the whole case or for all the relief requested and an evidentiary hearing is necessary, he or she, by examining the pleadings and interrogating counsel, if necessary, must "if practicable" ascertain what material facts are actually and in good faith controverted. The administrative law judge will then make an order specifying the facts that appear without substantial controversy and directing such further proceedings as are warranted. The facts so specified will be deemed established for the purposes of the investigation.

XIV. INTERVENTION (Commission Rule 210.19)

A. Intervention Generally

Any person wishing to intervene in an investigation or related proceeding must file and serve a written motion seeking such status.[37] The certificate of service must show that the motion has been served on each party to the investigation or related proceeding according to Commission Rule 201.16(b). Any party may file a response to the motion in accordance with Commission Rule 210.15(c). Any response must be accompanied by a certificate showing that the response was served on the proposed intervenor and all other parties. The Commission, or the administrative law judge by initial determination, may grant the motion "to the extent and upon such terms as may be proper under the circumstances." The denial of a motion for intervention is by (interlocutory) order, but is specially reviewable as of right under Commission Rule 210.24(a)(2).

Non-parties seek intervention for a wide variety of reasons, including disqualification of counsel. The proposed intervenor and the parties should know that unless the order granting intervention limits the intervenor's status, the intervenor has all the rights of a party, *i.e.*, where the Commission's rules specify that a "party" has a particular right or obligation, that rule applies to an intervenor as well. This follows from Commission Rule 210.3, which defines "party" as including an intervenor.

B. Intervention as a Respondent

In certain circumstances, a non-party may seek to intervene as a respondent, usually in order to provide a basis for a motion for a mandatory stay of a parallel district court action under 28 U.S.C. § 1659. The Commission has recently provided criteria for the grant of such a motion in *Certain Network Interface Cards and Access Points for use in Direct Sequence Spread Spectrum Wireless Local Area Networks and Products Containing Same*, Inv. No. 337-TA-455 (Comm'n Opn. of July 17, 2001). Essentially, the Commission requires that the articles of the proposed intervenor-respondent could be found in violation of Section 337 and therefore be excluded from entry into the United States if the remedy sought by the complainant as granted, *i.e.*, the Commission requires that the proposed intervenor show that it could have been named as a respondent.

37 A motion for intervention is also referred to as an "application" for intervention.

XV. DECLASSIFICATION OF CONFIDENTIAL INFORMATION (Commission Rule 210.20)

Under Commission Rule 210.20, any party may move to declassify documents or portions thereof that have been designated confidential by the submitter but that do not satisfy the confidentiality criteria set forth in Commission Rule 201.6(a). Such motions may be brought during the investigation or after conclusion of the investigation. If the investigation is before a presiding administrative law judge, the motion is directed to him or her. Under that same rule, if the investigation is not before a presiding administrative law judge, then it is addressed to and ruled upon by the chief administrative law judge or such ALJ as he or she may designate.[38] *See also* Commission Rule 210.5.

Prior to the issuance of the public version of the initial determination on whether there is a violation of Section 337 or an initial determination that would otherwise terminate the investigation if adopted by the Commission, the grant or denial of a motion to declassify is by order and subject to the special interlocutory order review procedure set out in Commission Rule 210.24(b)(2). After the issuance of such public version, the grant of a motion to declassify must be by initial determination and is subject to Commission review proceedings for initial determinations. The denial of such a motion remains by order and is reviewable, if at all, by the interlocutory review procedure of Commission Rule 210.24(b).

XVI. SUSPENSION OF INVESTIGATION (Section 337(b)(3); Commission Rule 210.23)

Any party may move to suspend the investigation because of the pendency of proceedings before the Department of Commerce pursuant to Section 337(b)(3). The administrative law judge or the Commission may also raise the issue *sua sponte*. The grant of such a motion by an administrative law judge is by initial determination; its denial is by order.

XVII. TERMINATION OF INVESTIGATION WITHOUT ADJUDICATION ON THE MERITS (Commission Rule 210.21)

A. By Withdrawal of the Complaint and Otherwise

Commission Rule 210.21(a)(1) provides that any party may move at any time prior to the issuance of the initial determination on violation of Section 337 for an order to terminate an investigation in whole or in part as to any or all respondents on the basis of withdrawal of the complaint or certain allegations

38 As noted above, the current organization of the Commission's Office of Administrative Law Judges is such that there is no chief administrative law judge. Presumably, the Commission itself will now make the designation indicated.

contained therein. Commission Rule 210.21(a)(1) also provides for the termination of investigations for "good cause" other than the grounds listed in Commission Rule 210.21(a)(2). The ALJ may grant the motion in an initial determination "upon such terms and conditions as he deems proper." Motions under Commission Rule 210.21(a)(1) are filed and granted, though it should be noted that there is no express basis in Section 337 for them as there is in Section 337(c) for terminations based on consent orders and agreements between the private parties, as discussed below.

B. By Consent Order or Agreement Between Private Parties

Section 337(c) provides that the Commission may terminate an investigation by issuing a consent order or on the basis of an agreement between the private parties to the investigation, including an agreement to present the matter for arbitration. This provision is implemented by Commission Rules 210.21(a)(2), (b)-(c).

1. Consent Orders

a. Nature

A consent order is an agreed-to cease and desist order. The Commission has express authority to terminate investigations based on consent orders under Section 337(c).

b. Procedure

i. Prior to Institution of Investigation

The Commission's rules do not provide for the issuance of consent orders generally prior to the institution of an investigation. They do provide that, prior to institution of a Section 337 investigation, a person who is the subject of a preliminary investigation under Section 603 of the Trade Act of 1974 (19 U.S.C. § 2482) may submit a proposal for disposition of the matter under investigation in the form of a consent order stipulation that incorporates a proposed consent order executed by or on behalf of such person and that complies with the requirements of Commission Rule 210.21(c)(3), discussed *infra*. Commission Rule 210.21(c)(1)(i).

ii. Subsequent to Institution of the Investigation

After institution of the investigation, a respondent may file a motion to terminate the investigation as to it on the basis of a consent order. The motion must be accompanied by a stipulation that incorporates a proposed consent order. The stipulation must comply with the requirements of Commission Rule 210.21(c)(3)(i). If the stipulation contains confidential business information, a redacted version of the stipulation must also accompany the motion. The following paragraphs provide details with respect to a motion to terminate an investigation on the basis of a consent order.

c. Who May File

The motion may be filed by one or more respondents, specifically those who have undertaken the stipulation. The stipulating respondent may (but is not required to) file the motion jointly with other parties to the investigation.

d. Time for Filing Motion

After institution, a motion to terminate an investigation based on a consent order may be filed as of right at any time prior to commencement of the evidentiary hearing before the ALJ. Commission Rule 210.21(c)(ii). After the commencement of the evidentiary hearing, the movant must make a showing of good cause for such a motion to be considered. *Id.*

e. Effect of Filing Motion

The filing of a motion to terminate based on a consent order does not stay proceedings before the ALJ unless the ALJ so orders. Commission Rule 210.21(c)(1)(ii). Ordinarily, if a stay is sought, the movant asks for it in the motion to terminate.

f. Action on Motion by ALJ

The ALJ grants a motion to terminate on the basis of a consent order by issuing an initial determination. Commission Rule 210.21(c)(1)(ii). If the initial determination contains confidential business information, the ALJ must also simultaneously issue a redacted version of the initial determination. *Id.* The ALJ denies the motion by issuing an order (not an initial determination) to that effect.

g. Commission Disposition of Consent Order

The ALJ's initial determination granting a motion to terminate an investigation based on a consent order is subject to Commission review pursuant to the petition for review procedure provided for by Commission Rules 210.43-.45. However, since such motions are frequently made jointly or at least not objected to, petitions for review of initial determinations granting those motions are not usually filed by the parties and the Commission does not ordinarily review them on its own motion.

On receipt of an initial determination granting a motion to terminate on the basis of a consent order, the Commission will provide notice of the initial determination and the proposed consent order stipulation to the U.S. Department of Health and Human Services, the U.S. Department of Justice, the Federal Trade Commission, the U.S. Customs Service, and "such other departments and agencies as the Commission deems appropriate." Commission Rule 210.21(c)(2)(i).

Regardless of whether the Commission reviews the initial determination under its petition for review rules, it will consider the effect of the settlement by consent order upon the public health and welfare, competitive conditions in the United States economy, the production of like or directly competitive articles in the United States, and United States consumers. Commission Rule 210.21(c)(2)(ii).

If the Commission affirms (or, equivalently, does not review) the ALJ's initial determination and that affirmance results in termination of the investigation in its entirety, it will issue a notice to that effect in the *Federal Register. Id.* If the Commission affirms the ALJ's initial determination, but such affirmance does not result in termination of the investigation in its entirety (usually because of the existence of non-settling respondents), the Commission will issue an order indicating its affirmance. An order of termination by consent order need not constitute a determination that there has been a violation of Section 337.

If the Commission reverses the ALJ's initial determination, the parties will not be bound by the consent order proposal in later actions before the Commission. Commission Rule 210.21(c)(2)(ii).

h. Withdrawal from Consent Order Stipulation

In the absence of good cause shown, a party may not withdraw from a consent order stipulation once it has been submitted. Commission Rule 210.21(c)(1)(ii).

i. Contents of Consent Order Stipulation Generally

Every consent order stipulation must contain:

- The proposed consent order (frequently attached as an exhibit).
- An admission of all jurisdictional facts.
- An express waiver of all rights to seek judicial review or otherwise challenge or contest the validity of the consent order.
- A statement that the signatories to the consent order stipulation will cooperate with and will not seek to impede by litigation, or other means, the Commission's efforts to gather information which may be required under 19 C.F.R. Part 210, Subpart I as part of the administration or enforcement of the consent order.
- A statement that the enforcement, modification, and revocation of the consent order will be carried out pursuant to 19 C.F.R. Part 210, Subpart I, incorporating by reference the Commission's Rules of Practice and Procedure.

j. Additional Contents of Consent Order Stipulation in Intellectual-Property-Based Investigations

Commission Rule 210.21(c)(3)(i)(B) specifies additional contents for the consent order stipulation in intellectual-property-based cases. These additional contents are:

- A statement that the consent order will not apply "with respect to any claim of any intellectual property right that has expired or been found or adjudicated invalid or unenforceable by the Commission or a court or agency of competent jurisdiction, provided that such finding or judgment has become final and nonreviewable."

– A statement that each signatory to the stipulation who was a respondent in the investigation will not seek to challenge the validity of the intellectual property right "in any administrative or judicial proceeding to enforce the consent order." It should be noted that this provision does not foreclose a respondent from challenging validity in an action for infringement brought by the intellectual property right owner in a district court since such an infringement action is independent of any proceeding to enforce the consent order.[39]

k. Optional Stipulation of No Admission of Unfair Practice

Commission Rule 210.21(c)(3)(C) provides that the consent order stipulation may contain a statement that the signing thereof is "for settlement purposes only and does not constitute an admission by any respondent that an unfair act has been committed."

l. Effect of Consent Order

The Commission treats consent orders as cease and desist orders and enforces them in the same way. The Federal Circuit affirmed this treatment of consent orders in *San Huan New Materials High Tech, Inc. v. International Trade Commission*, 161 F.3d 1347 (Fed. Cir. 1998)

2. Termination by Agreement Between the Parties: Settlement

As noted above, Section 337(c) provides for termination of an investigation in whole or in part on the basis of "an agreement between the private parties to the investigation, including an agreement to present the matter for arbitration." The most common type of such an agreement is a settlement agreement which may constitute or include a licensing agreement. Most motions to terminate on the basis of a settlement agreement are joint motions by the private parties who are signatories to the settlement agreement.

a. Required Contents of Motion

A motion for termination by settlement must include:

1. Copies of the licensing or other settlement agreement.

2. Copies of any supplemental agreements.

3. A statement that there are no other agreements, written or oral, express or implied, between the parties concerning the subject matter of the investigation.

If any of the settlement, licensing or supplemental agreements contain confidential business information, redacted copies of such agreements must accompany the motion.

---

39 Query whether a declaratory judgment action to challenge validity may properly be brought by the respondent in a Federal district court where the only "reasonable apprehension" of litigation is of a proceeding to enforce the consent order, as opposed to an infringement proceeding in a Federal district court.

b. Procedure/Ruling by the ALJ; Commission Action

The ALJ grants a motion for termination by settlement agreement by issuing an initial determination, which is subject to Commission review on petition by a party to the investigation or *sua sponte*, though such review is unusual. Along with the initial determination, the ALJ certifies the motion and the involved agreements to the Commission. If the initial determination or the agreements contain confidential business information, the ALJ must simultaneously file redacted versions with the Commission. On receipt, the Commission provides the public version of the initial determination and agreements to the U.S. Department of Health and Human Services, the U.S. Department of Justice, the Federal Trade Commission, the U.S. Customs Service, "and such other departments and agencies as the Commission deems appropriate."

If the Commission does not review or affirms the ALJ's initial determination and that action results in termination of the entire investigation, the Commission will publish a notice of such termination in the *Federal Register.* If the Commission does not review or affirms the ALJ's initial determination but such action does not result in termination of the entire investigation, the Commission will issue an order of affirmance (or of non-review, if that is the case) of the ALJ's initial determination.

If the Commission reverses an initial determination by the ALJ terminating the investigation on the basis of a settlement agreement, it will issue an order to that effect. The Commission's rules do not specifically provide for the consequences of a reversal. The parties should provide for such a contingency in their settlement agreement. If the settlement is based on a licensing agreement and the license agreement remains in force after reversal of the ALJ's initial determination, it is difficult to see how any Commission remedial order could affect the licensed respondent, since such orders are prospective only.

3. Termination Based on Arbitration Agreement

Section 337(c) specifically provides for terminations based upon an agreement by the private parties to refer the matter to arbitration. This provision was added to Section 337(c)by the Uruguay Round Agreements Act.

a. Procedure

Requests to terminate an investigation in whole or in part based on an arbitration agreement are made by motion to the ALJ or the Commission, depending upon which of them the investigation is before. Commission Rule 210.21(d).

The motion must include the arbitration agreement as an attachment. If that agreement contains confidential business information, a redacted version of the agreement must also be filed. If the motion is filed while the investigation is pending before the ALJ, he or she will grant the motion by issuing an initial determination to that effect. If the initial determination or the agreement contains confidential business information, the ALJ must file redacted versions along with the confidential versions of the documents.

If the Commission affirms (or, equivalently, does not review) the ALJ's initial determination (or itself grants the motion) and such disposition results in termination of the investigation in its entirety, the Commission will issue a notice to that effect in the *Federal Register*. If such affirmance or grant does not result in termination of the investigation in its entirety (because, *e.g.*, of non-settling parties), the Commission will issue an order of affirmance (or non-review) or grant, as the case may be. The Commission's rules do not specifically state what the consequences of reversal or denial are.

b. Effect

A Commission order of termination on the basis of arbitration is effective immediately. Such an order does not constitute a determination as to whether a violation of Section 337 exists. Commission Rule 210.21(d).

XVIII. SANCTIONS AND SANCTION PROCEEDINGS (Commission Rule 210.25 and related rules)

Section 337(h) permits the Commission to issue rules prescribing sanctions for abuse of process and abuse of discovery "to the extent authorized by Rule 11 and Rule 37 of the Federal Rules of Civil Procedure." The Commission's principal rules prescribing sanctions are Commission Rule 210.4(d)(1) (abuse of process), Commission Rule 210.27(d)(3) (abuse of discovery), Commission Rule 210.33(b)-(c) (failure to make or cooperate in discovery) and Commission Rule 210.34(c) (violation of a protective order).

Sanctions may be sought by motion. Commission Rule 210.25(a)(1). However, when the investigation is before the ALJ, he or she may raise the sanction issue *sua sponte*. Commission Rule 210.25(a)(2). Likewise, when the investigation is before the Commission, it may raise the issue *sua sponte*. When the sanction sought would not have a bearing on the adjudication of the merits of a complaint or another pending motion, it may be dealt with in an independent "related proceeding."

A. Time for Filing Sanctions Motions

1. Abuse of Process

A motion alleging abuse of process should be filed "promptly" after the requirements of Commission Rule 210.4(d)(1)(i) have been satisfied. Commission Rule 210.25(a)(1). The requirements of Commission Rule 210.4(d)(1)(i) reflect a "safe harbor" rule, *i.e.*, as a precondition of filing a motion for sanctions for abuse of process, the moving party must serve its motion for sanctions on the non-moving parties and give the accused party or person seven days to withdraw or correct the challenged document. If the accused party does not withdraw or correct the document within that period, the accusing party may then file the motions for sanctions. The Commission has made it clear that any warning short of one fulfilling the procedural requirements of the safe harbor rule will not support the subsequent filing of a motion for sanctions. *See Certain Hardware Logic Emulation Systems and Components Thereof*, Inv. No. 337-TA-383 (Commission Opinion on Appeal of Order No. 96) (reproduced in USITC Pub. 3154 (January 1999)). The safe harbor rule does not apply if the ALJ raises the issue of sanctions on his or her own motion under Commission Rule 210.25(a)(2). In that circumstance, the ALJ may issue an order to the attorney, law firm, party, or proposed party to show cause why it has not violated Commission Rule 210.4(c).

2. Abuse of Discovery; Failure to Make or Cooperate in Discovery; Violation of Protective Order

A motion alleging abuse of discovery, failure to make or cooperate in discovery, or violation of a protective order should be filed "promptly after the allegedly sanctionable conduct is discovered." Commission Rule 210.25(a)(1).

B. To Whom Motion for Sanctions is Addressed

Depending upon the circumstances, a motion for sanctions is addressed to the administrative law judge or the Commission.

1. When Motion is Addressed to ALJ

A motion for sanctions is addressed to the ALJ "if the allegedly sanctionable conduct occurred and is discovered while the administrative law judge is presiding in an investigation or in a related proceeding." Commission Rule 210.25(b).

2. When Motion is Addressed to the Commission

A motion for sanctions is addressed to the Commission if (1) the allegedly sanctionable conduct occurred while the Commission is presiding or (2) after the investigation or related proceeding is terminated. Commission Rule 210.25(c).

3. Gaps in the Rules

Commission Rule 210.25 does not state to whom a motion for sanctions is addressed if the alleged sanctionable conduct occurred while the ALJ was presiding but is not discovered until later, when the Commission is presiding. In such a circumstance, Commission Rule 210.15 would appear to permit the motion to be addressed to the Chairman of the Commission (*i.e.*, the Commission itself) providing the possibility for the entire Commission to consider it, though the Commission could remand the matter to the ALJ.

4. Mode of Decision on Motions for Sanctions Where Motion is Addressed to ALJ

Where a motion for sanctions is addressed to the ALJ in a pending investigation and the ALJ rules on the motion prior to or concurrently with the initial determination on violation of Section 337, the ALJ will rule on the motion by separate order. Where a motion for sanctions is addressed to the ALJ in a related proceeding, the ALJ's ruling must be by order.

5. Mode of Decision on Motions for Sanctions Where Motion is Addressed to Commission

If the allegedly sanctionable conduct occurred while the investigation or related proceeding is before the Commission or if the motion for sanctions is filed after the investigation or related proceeding is terminated, the motion if filed with the Commission.

The Commission may act on the motion itself issuing an order granting or denying the motion. It may also (and is likely to) assign the motion to an ALJ for a recommended determination. If the Commission assigns the motion to an ALJ, it will issue an order to that effect, setting forth the procedures and deadlines to be followed in arriving at the recommended determination. Commission Rule 210.25(c). That same order will also set out the deadline and procedures for seeking Commission review of the recommended determination. Commission Rule 210.25(e).

C. Deferred Ruling by the ALJ

If a motion for sanctions is filed with the ALJ during an investigation, the ALJ may defer adjudication of the motion for a period of up to 90 days after issuance of the final determination concerning violation of Section 337 or termination of the investigation. Such a deferred ruling must be made in the form of a recommended determination. Commission Rule 210.25(f).

D. Commission Review of ALJ Sanction Rulings

1. Ruling Issued Before ID on Violation

If the ALJ's order concerning sanctions is issued prior to the initial determination concerning violation of Section 337 or termination of the investigation, Commission review may be obtained through the interlocutory appeal procedure of Commission Rule 210.24(b)(1). Such an appeal requires leave of the ALJ which, if granted, must be followed by an application for Commission review which the Commission may grant in its discretion. If the application is granted, appeal will be permitted. Such an appeal may be decided on the application papers or on the basis of further briefing as required or permitted by the Commission.

2. Commission Review of ALJ Ruling on Sanctions Made with ID

If the ALJ's order concerning sanctions is issued concurrently with the initial determination, the order may be appealed via a petition the contents of which conform to the requirements of Commission Rule 210.43(b), *i.e.*, the requirements for a petition for review of an initial determination. The Commission will issue a notice specifying the period for filing and responding to the petition. The Commission will rule on the order after disposition of the initial determination on violation or termination of the investigation.

3. Commission Review of Deferred Ruling on Sanctions by ALJ

If the ALJ has issued a deferred ruling on sanctions under Commission Rule 210.25(f) by issuing a recommended determination, any party may file written comments with the Commission 14 days after service of the recommended determination. Replies to the comments may be filed within 7 days after service thereof. The Commission will rule on the recommended determination after reviewing the arguments of the parties as set out in their comments and replies and after "taking any other steps the Commission deems appropriate." Commission Rule 210.25(f).

4. Commission Review of ALJ Ruling Under Commission Rule 210.25(c)

If the ALJ has issued a recommended determination on sanctions after being assigned to do so by the Commission pursuant to Commission Rule 210.25(c), the deadlines and procedures for Commission review will be specified in the Commission's order of assignment. Commission Rule 210.25(e).

E. Sanctions—Substantive Law

As noted above, there are four circumstances where the Commission may order sanctions: abuse of process (Commission Rule 210.4(d)(1)); abuse of discovery (Commission Rule 210.27(d)(3)); failure to make or cooperate in discovery (Commission Rule 210.33(b)-(c)); and violation of a protective order (Commission Rule 210.34(c)).

1. Abuse of Process (Commission Rule 210.4(d)(1)); Safe Harbor Provisions

Commission Rule 210.4(c) provides:

> (c) Representations. By presenting to the presiding administrative law judge or the Commission (whether by signing, filing, submitting, or later advocating) a pleading, written motion, or other paper, an attorney or unrepresented party or proposed party is certifying that to the best of the person's knowledge, information, and belief, formed after an inquiry reasonable under the circumstances—
>
> (1) It is not being presented for any improper purpose, such as to harass or to cause unnecessary delay or needless increase in the cost of the investigation or related proceeding;
>
> (2) The claims, defenses, and other legal contentions therein are warranted by existing law or by a non-frivolous argument for the extension, modification, or reversal of existing law or the establishment of new law;

(3) The allegations and other factual contentions have evidentiary support or, if specifically so identified, are likely to have evidentiary support after a reasonable opportunity for further investigation or discovery; and

(4) The denials of factual contentions are warranted on the evidence or, if specifically so identified, are reasonably based on a lack of information or belief.

If a party believes that another party has violated Rule 210.4(c), Commission Rule 210.4(d) provides that that party may file a motion seeking the imposition of "an appropriate sanction upon the attorneys, law firms, or parties" believed to have violated Rule 210.4(c). Such a motion, however, is subject to the "safe harbor" rule of Rule 210.4(d), discussed above.

2. Sanctions for Abuse of Process

A sanction for abuse of process must be limited to what is sufficient to deter the repetition of such conduct or comparable conduct by others similarly situated. It may consist of, or include, directives of a nonmonetary nature, an order to pay a penalty, or, if imposed on motion and warranted for effective deterrence, an order directing payment to the movant of some or all of the reasonable attorney's fees and other expenses incurred as a direct result of violation. Absent exceptional circumstances, a law firm will be held jointly responsible for violations committed by its partners, associates, and employees. The movant, if prevailing on the motion, may be awarded reasonable expenses and attorney's fees for bringing the motion, "if warranted." However, the same rule applies to the accused party, should it prevail.

There are certain restrictions on sanctions for abuse of process. First, monetary sanctions may not be imposed against the United States, the Commission, or the Commission investigative attorney. Second, monetary sanctions may not be awarded against a represented party or proposed party for a violation of Commission Rule 210.4(c)(2) (dealing with legal claims, defenses and contentions). Third, monetary sanctions may not be imposed on the Commission's or the ALJ's initiative unless the Commission or the ALJ have issued an order to show cause prior to termination of the investigation or related proceeding as to the relevant party and the termination is the result of a motion to withdraw the complaint or other document that was the basis of the investigation or related proceeding, a settlement agreement, a consent order agreement, or an arbitration agreement. Fourth, monetary sanctions imposed to compensate the Commission for expenses incurred by the Commission investigative attorney or the Commission's Office of Unfair Import Investigations must include reimbursement for some or all the costs reasonably incurred as a direct result of the violation, but will not include attorney's fees.

3. Abuse of Discovery (Commission Rule 210.27(d)(3))

The ALJ or the Commission on motion or *sua sponte* under Commission Rule 210.25 may impose sanctions for abuse of discovery, which is defined as certifying a discovery request, response or objection in violation of Commission

Rule 210.27(d)(2) without "substantial justification." The signature of a party or the attorney for a party on such a request, response, or objection constitutes a certification that to the best of signer's knowledge, information, and belief formed after a reasonable injury, the request, response, or objection is:

- Consistent with Commission Rule 210.5(a) (if applicable)[40] and other relevant provisions of 19 C.F.R. Chapter II,[41] and warranted by existing law or a good faith agreement for the extension, modification, or reversal of existing law;
- Not interposed for any improper purpose, such as to harass or to cause unnecessary delay or needless increase in the cost of litigation; and
- Not unreasonable or unduly burdensome or expensive, given the needs of the case, the discovery already had in the case, and the importance of the issues at stake in the litigation.

4. Sanctions for Abuse of Discovery

Commission Rule 210.27(d)(3) provides that an "appropriate sanction" may be imposed for abuse of discovery. The Commission's rules do not specifically define what an "appropriate sanction" may be but do state that it "may include an order to pay the other parties the amount of reasonable expenses incurred because of the violation, including a reasonable attorney's fee, to the extent authorized by Rule 26(g) of the Federal Rules of Civil Procedure." Commission Rule 210.27(d)(4).

5. Exceptions to Monetary Sanctions for Abuse of Discovery

Commission Rule 210.27(d)(4) provides that monetary sanctions for abuse of discovery will not be imposed against the United States, the Commission, or a Commission investigative attorney. Commission Rule 210.25(d)(5) provides that monetary sanctions for discovery abuse will not extend to reimbursement of the Commission for attorney's fees (*i.e.*, the salary of the Commission investigative attorney). However, that same rule provides that monetary sanctions may be imposed to reimburse the Commission for expenses incurred by a Commission investigative attorney or the Commission's Office of Unfair Import Investigations.

6. Failure to Make or Cooperate in Discovery (Commission Rule 210.33(b)-(c))

The sanctions available for failure to make or cooperate in discovery include both non-monetary and monetary sanctions.

---

40 Commission Rule 210.5(a) governs the definition and submission of confidential business information.

41 19 C.F.R. Chapter II are the Commission's rules in their entirety.

7. Non-Monetary Sanctions for Failure to Make or Cooperate in Discovery

Non-monetary sanctions may be imposed if a party or an officer or agent of a party fails to comply with an order compelling discovery. Such orders include, but are not limited to:

- an order for the taking of a deposition;
- an order for the production of documents;
- an order to answer interrogatories;
- an order issued pursuant to a request for admission; or
- an order to comply with a subpoena

The non-monetary sanctions which the ALJ may impose include, but are not limited to:

- an inference that the admission, testimony, documents, or other evidence would have been adverse to the party;
- a ruling that for the purposes of the investigation the matter or matters concerning the order or subpoena issued be taken as established adversely to the party;
- a ruling that the party may not introduce into evidence or otherwise rely upon testimony by the party, officer, or agent, or documents, or other material in support of his position in the investigation;
- a ruling that the party may not be heard to object to the introduction and use of secondary evidence to show what the withheld admission, testimony, documents, or other evidence would have shown;
- a ruling that a motion or other submission by the party concerning the order or subpoena issued be stricken or a ruling by initial determination that a determination in the investigation be rendered against the party, or both; or
- an order for any other non-monetary sanction available under Rule 37(b) of the Federal Rules of Civil Procedure.

8. Forms of Ruling Granting Non-Monetary Sanctions for Failure to Make or Cooperate in Discovery

Generally, a ruling granting non-monetary sanctions may be in the form of a written or oral order. Presumably, an oral order will be indicated in a transcript so that it is part of the record. As noted above, a ruling granting the sanction of rendering a determination in an investigation is made by initial determination and thus, presumably, written. Rulings granting sanctions may also be made by inclusion "in the initial determination of the administrative law judge," presumably a reference to the final initial determination on violation of Section 337 or an initial determination terminating the investigation.

9. Insufficiency of Non-Monetary Sanctions for Failure to Make or Cooperate in Discovery

The purpose of non-monetary sanctions is to "compensate for the lack of withheld testimony, documents, or other evidence" and the selection of the specific non-monetary sanction is made to accomplish this purpose. However, there may be cases where non-monetary relief will not be sufficient to accomplish this purpose. In such cases, the ALJ must certify to the Commission a request that court enforcement of the subpoena or other discovery order be sought.

10. Monetary Sanctions for Failure to Make or Cooperate in Discovery

Monetary sanctions may be imposed "[i]f a party or an officer, director, or managing agent of the party or person designated to testify on behalf of a party fails to obey an order to provide or permit discovery."

In such circumstances, the ALJ or the Commission may "make such orders in regard to the failure as are just." Specifically, the ALJ or the Commission, in lieu of or in addition to imposing the non-monetary sanctions discussed above and to the extent provided in Rule 37(b)(2) of the Federal Rule of Civil Procedure, upon motion or *sua sponte* under Commission Rule 210.25, may require the party failing to obey the order or the attorney advising that party or both to pay reasonable expenses, including attorney's fees, caused by the failure, unless the ALJ or the Commission finds that "the failure was substantially justified or that other circumstances make an award of expenses unjust."

11. Exceptions to Monetary Sanctions for Failure to Make or Cooperate in Discovery

Commission Rule 210.33(c)(1) provides that monetary sanctions for failure to make or cooperate in discovery will not be imposed against the United States, the Commission, or a Commission investigative attorney.[42] Commission Rule 210.33(c)(2) provides that monetary sanctions for failure to make or cooperate in discovery will not extend to reimbursement of the Commission for attorney's fees (*i.e.*, the salary of the Commission investigative attorney). However, that same rule provides that monetary sanctions may be imposed to reimburse the Commission for expenses incurred by a Commission investigative attorney or the Commission's Office of Unfair Import Investigations.

12. Violation of Protective Order (Commission Rule 210.34(c))

While not entirely clear from Commission Rule 210.34(c), the protective order being referred to therein the violation of which may result in sanctions, is the

---

42 It is unclear what, if any, discovery could be sought from the United States, the Commission, or a Commission investigative attorney in any Section 337 investigation or related proceeding.

protective order issued by the ALJ at the beginning of the investigation to protect confidential business information.[43]

13. Sanctions for Violation of Protective Order

Any individual who has agreed to be bound by the terms of a protective order issued pursuant to Commission Rule 210.34(a) (this usually means a protective order governing confidential business information) and who is found to have violated the terms of the protective order, may be subject to one or more of the following sanctions:

(1) An official reprimand by the Commission;

(2) Disqualification from or limitation of further participation in a pending investigation;

(3) Temporary or permanent disqualification from practicing in any capacity before the Commission pursuant to Commission Rule 201.15(a);

(4) Referral of the facts underlying the violation to the appropriate licensing authority in the jurisdiction in which the individual is licensed to practice.

14. Action Required by Party Making Unauthorized Disclosure of Information (Commission Rule 210.34(b))

Commission Rule 210.34(b) provides that if confidential business information submitted in accordance with the terms of a protective order is disclosed to any person other than in a manner authorized by the protective order, the party responsible for the unauthorized disclosure must immediately bring all pertinent facts relating to such disclosure to the attention of (1) the submitter of the information, and (2) the administrative law judge or the Commission. Further, the rule requires that "without prejudice to other rights and remedies of the submitter of the information," the party making the unauthorized disclosure must "make every effort to prevent further disclosure of such information by the party or the recipient of such information."

15. Sanctions Not Specified in Commission Rule 210.25(d)

Commission Rule 210.34(d) provides for certain responsibilities and sanctions not referred to in Commission Rule 210.25. These relate to reporting requests for confidential information.

---

43 This conclusion is inferred from Commission Rule 210.34(a), which provides for protective orders of all types. Commission Rule 210.34(c), covering violations of protective orders, refers only to violations of a protective order by "[a]ny individual who has agreed to be bound by the terms of a protective order issued pursuant to paragraph (a) of this section. . . ." A protective order governing confidential information is the only order usually required to be subscribed to.

a. Reporting Requests for Confidential Information

Under Commission Rule 210.34(d)(1), each person subject to a protective order issued pursuant to Commission Rule 210.34(a) (an apparent reference to a protective order governing confidential information) must report in writing to the Commission immediately upon learning that confidential business information disclosed to him or her pursuant to the protective order is the subject of a subpoena, court or administrative order (other than an order of a court reviewing a Commission decision), discovery request, agreement, or other written request seeking disclosure by him or any other person, of that confidential business information to persons who are not, or may not be, permitted access to that information pursuant to either a Commission protective order or Commission Rule 210.5(b).

The purpose of this requirement is to put the Commission on notice so that it may commence or intervene in proceedings to protect the confidential business information. Of course, the party or person subject to the request or order should not only comply with the rule requiring notice, it should object to such disclosure in the proceeding in which the request or order is made.

b. Sanctions for Failure to Report

If a person subject to the reporting requirement of Commission Rule 210.34(d)(1) willfully fails to timely report a request for confidential business information, the Commission, after providing notice and an opportunity to comment, may "impose a sanction" (not specified in the rule) "or it may take other action." Commission Rule 210.34(d)(2).

XIX. COMMISSION REVIEW OF FINAL INITIAL DETERMINATIONS

An initial determination on whether there is a violation of Section 337 is sometimes referred to as a final initial determination. As with other initial determinations, the Commission may review a final initial determination through grant of a petition for review filed by one or more parties or on its own motion. However, the Commission is not required to grant a petition for review simply because a party has filed one. Further, if the Commission does decide to review the ALJ's initial determination, it may limit its review to selected issues.

A. Review by Grant of Petition for Review

1. Petition for Review; Contents

A party seeking Commission review of a final initial determination must file and serve a petition seeking such review within ten days of service of the initial determination. Oppositions to such petitions must be filed within five business days of the service of the petition. There are certain circumstances under which a party may not be permitted to file a petition for review. Thus, a party may not petition for review on any issue as to which it has been found in default. Further, a party or proposed respondent who failed to file a response to a motion addressed in an initial determination may be deemed to have consented to the relief requested in that motion and may not petition for review of the issues raised therein. This latter restriction would, by its terms, apply to a final initial determination made on the basis of a motion for summary determination as well as any motions decided as part of the final initial determination.[44]

The contents of a petition for review are prescribed by Commission Rule 210.43(b). Such petition must:

1. Identify the party seeking review.

2. Specify the issues upon which review of the initial determination is sought.

3. For each issue for which review is sought, specify one or more of the following grounds:

    (a) That a finding or conclusion of material fact is clearly erroneous;

    (b) That a legal conclusion is erroneous, without governing precedent, rule or law, or constitutes an abuse of discretion; or

    (c) That the determination is one affecting Commission policy.

4. Set forth a concise statement of the facts material to the consideration of the specified issues.

5. Present a concise argument providing the reasons that review by the Commission is necessary or appropriate to resolve an important issue of fact, law or policy.

2. Failure to File Petition for Review; Failure to Raise Issues in Petition

A party's failure to file a petition for review of an initial determination will constitute abandonment of all issues decided adversely to that party in the initial determination. Commission Rule 210.43(b)(3). If a party does file a petition for review, but fails to seek review of an issue decided adversely to it, the Commission will deem such issue as having been abandoned by that party. However, the fact that a party has not filed a petition for review or has failed to seek review of one or more issues will not preclude the Commission from ordering review on its own motion of any or all issues decided in the initial determination.

3. "Contingent" Petitions for Review

Sometimes a party will file what it denominates a "contingent" petition for review, ostensibly seeking review only if the Commission grants a petition for review expected to be filed by another (usually adverse) party. The Commission

---

44 Both restrictions would, of course, apply to (interlocutory) initial determinations ruling on motions prior to issuance of the final initial determination on violation.

makes no distinction between "contingent" petitions for review and other petitions for review and treats "contingent" petitions for review as ordinary petitions for review. Commission Rule 210.43(b)(3).

4. Grant or Denial of Review

The Commission must ordinarily decide whether to grant or deny a petition for review of a final initial determination on violation within 45 days after service of that initial determination, though it may extend this time by order. Commission Rule 210.43(d)(1). The Commission's decision to grant or deny a petition is based solely on the petition and the oppositions thereto, without oral argument or further written submissions unless ordered by the Commission. Commission Rule 210.43(d)(2).

Commission review of a final (or interlocutory) initial determination is discretionary and, if granted, may be granted in whole or in part. Commission Rule 210.43(d)(1). The Commission will ordinarily grant a petition for review and order review proceedings if it appears that a finding of fact is clearly erroneous, that a conclusion of law is "erroneous, without governing precedent, rule or law, or constitutes an abuse of discretion," or if the petition "raises a policy matter connected with the initial determination, which the Commission thinks it necessary or appropriate to address." Commission Rule 210.43(d)(2). As noted above, the Commission's rules require a petition for review to address these criteria. However, while these criteria are applicable to the grant or denial of a petition, they are not applicable to the review proceeding itself, as explained below.

The petition will be granted if one of the participating Commissioners votes for review. Commission Rule 210.43(d)(3).

The effect of granting review is just that: it triggers a review proceeding (discussed below) which will ultimately result in a final determination by the Commission. To the extent the petition is denied with respect to any part of the initial determination, that part of the initial determination becomes the Commission's determination.

The recommended determination on remedy and bonding is not subject to the petition for review procedure, but does not automatically become the determination of the Commission if review is not ordered. In order for the recommended determination to become the Commission determination, it must be affirmatively adopted by the Commission. Parties nevertheless often address these issues in their petitions for review and their review briefs.

B. Commission Review on its Own Motion

The Commission may review an initial determination (or an issue therein) on its own motion. The criteria for Commission review on its own motion are the same as for whether to grant a petition for review and such review will be ordered if one Commissioner votes for review. Any such review is conducted on the same basis as review based on the grant of a petition. The question of Commission review on its own motion does not arise often since the parties frequently file petitions for review.

C. Decision Whether to Review; The Review Proceeding

The Commission will issue a notice as to whether or nor it has determined to conduct a review proceeding, a notice which the Commission usually publishes in the *Federal Register.* If the Commission has determined to conduct a review proceeding, the notice will specify the issues to be reviewed and set a briefing schedule. Commission Rule 210.43(d)(3). In addition to publishing the notice in the *Federal Register* and serving it on the parties, the Commission may also serve the notice on the U.S. Department of Health and Human Services, the U.S. Department of Justice, the Federal Trade Commission, the Customs Service, and such other agencies as it deems appropriate.

As a matter of practice, the Commission usually requires written submissions from the parties on the issues under review about two weeks from the date of the issuance of the notice of review. Reply submissions are usually due a week later. The notice will also establish a schedule for written submissions from the parties, Federal agencies, and interested members of the public on the issues of remedy, the public interest, and bonding by the respondents. Commission Rule 210.46(a). In their written submissions, the parties may present their arguments concerning the recommended determination on the issues of remedy and bonding by respondents. The written submission of a party usually addresses the issues on review and on remedy, public interest, and bonding in a single document.

While the Commission can limit the page length of the written submissions, it usually does not.

A party may, as part of its written submission, request a Commission hearing for the purpose of oral argument. The Commission may grant such a request if one participating Commissioner votes to do so. However, it is very rare for a request for oral argument to be granted.

D. Nature of Commission Review

The Commission will review only the issues set out in its notice of review. Commission Rule 210.45. It is important to note that Commission review of final (and interlocutory) initial determinations is not in the nature of an appellate review, notwithstanding the appellate-like criteria for granting a petition for review or ordering review *sua sponte*. Rather, Commission review of an initial determination is a limited *de novo* review. It is limited in the sense that it is limited to the evidentiary record certified to the Commission by the administrative law judge. Thus, the Commission will not consider new evidence not previously offered (though it can rule on evidentiary objections and offers of proof and can remand the case to the ALJ to reopen the evidentiary record). Commission review is *de novo*, because the Commission "examines for itself the record on the issues under review." *Certain Acid-Washed Denim Garments*, Inv. No. 337-TA-324 (USITC Pub. 2576 (Nov. 1992)). The Commission may affirm, reverse, modify, set aside or remand for further proceedings, in whole or in part, the initial determination of the administrative law judge. Commission Rule 210.45(c). The Commission may also make any findings or conclusions that in its judgment are proper based on the record in the proceeding. *Id.* If the Commission's determination on review terminates the investigation in its entirety, the Commission will publish notice to that effect in the *Federal Register. Id.*

E. Commission Action on Issues of Public Interest, Remedy, and Bonding

As noted above, if the Commission contemplates the issuance of a remedial order, it will seek and consider written submissions from the parties, Federal agencies and members of the public on the questions of (1) what remedy would be appropriate to address the violation of Section 337 which has been or may be found, (2) whether the issuance of a remedy is precluded by the consideration of the public interest factors enumerated in Section 337(d)-(f), and (3) the amount of the bond to be posted by the respondents to permit entry during the Presidential review period. It is possible that the Commission will issue such a notice seeking such submissions even it does not order review of the initial determination, *i.e.*, if it decides not to review a final initial determination finding a violation of Section 337.

In addition to the written submissions of the parties and other persons and agencies on the issues of public interest, remedy, and bonding, the Commission will also have before it the ALJ's recommended determination on remedy and bonding and the record certified to it by the ALJ which will include the evidence of record before the ALJ on those two issues. In contrast to the issues on review, however, the Commission takes the position that it can accept additional information on public interest, remedy, and bonding from the parties and non-parties as part of their written submissions.

F. Commission Final Determination

The Commission will issue its final determination after the conclusion of any review proceeding. If it has not conducted a review proceeding, and the unreviewed initial determination is affirmative, the Commission will issue its final determination after receiving and considering the written submissions on public interest, remedy and bonding. If it has decided not to review a negative initial determination, its decision not to review constitutes its final determination in the investigation. In any event, the Commission must issue its final determination by the target date set for the completion of the investigation.

If the Commission's final determination is affirmative, it will issue notice thereof, as well as any remedial orders and publish notice thereof in the *Federal Register*. If the Commission has reviewed the initial determination, it will issue an opinion on its resolution of those issues or may simply indicate it is adopting the initial determination. The Commission usually issues an opinion on the questions of remedy, public interest, and bonding.

If the Commission's final determination is negative, *i.e.*, it concludes that there is no violation of Section 337, it will issue a notice and an order terminating the investigation. If it has reviewed the initial determination, it may issue an opinion on its resolution of the issues on review.

In arriving at its final determination, the Commission may limit the grounds for its decision to one or more dispositive issues and not take a position on the other issues before it, a procedure approved by its reviewing court in *Beloit Corp. v. Valmet Oy*, 742 F.2d 1421 (Fed. Cir. 1984).

The Commission serves the final determination on the parties and publishes notice thereof in the *Federal Register*. If the final determination is affirmative, the Commission will also transmit its determination and order, as well as the record, to the President for review and to the Secretary of the Treasury for enforcement of any exclusion order by the Customs Service.

G. Petitions for Reconsideration

A party may file a petition for reconsideration within 14 days after service of the Commission's determination or any action ordered to be taken thereunder, setting forth the relief desired and the grounds in support thereof. Commission Rule 210.47. A petition for reconsideration must be confined to "new questions raised by the determination or action ordered to be taken thereunder and upon which the petitioner had no opportunity to submit arguments." *Id.* A party wishing to oppose such a petition must file an answer within five days after service of the petition on the opposing party. *Id.*

The filing of a petition for reconsideration will not stay the effective date of the Commission's determination or any action the Commission has ordered to be taken thereunder or toll the running of any statutory time period affecting the Commission determination or the action it has ordered to be taken thereunder, "unless specifically so ordered by the Commission."[45] On reconsideration, the Commission may affirm, set aside, or modify its determination, including any action ordered by it to be taken thereunder. Commission Rule 210.48. When appropriate, the Commission may order the administrative law judge to take additional evidence. *Id.* It should be noted that the Commission currently takes the view that once a notice of appeal of the final determination has been filed, it

45 Of course. the Commission cannot issue any order affecting the Presidential review period or the time for appeal.

loses jurisdiction and it will then not act on a pending petition for reconsideration, even if the petition was filed prior to the notice of appeal.

XX. PRESIDENTIAL REVIEW OF COMMISSION DETERMINATION AND ORDER

Under Section 337(j), if the Commission determines that there is a violation of Section 337, it must transmit to the President a copy of its determination, the action it has taken with respect thereto (*i.e.*, the remedial order it has issued), and the record on which its determination is based.

The President has 60 days from the day on which he receives a copy of the Commission's determination to disapprove the Commission's determination "for policy reasons" and notify the Commission of such disapproval. In practice, the Presidential review is conducted by the Office of the United States Trade Representative (USTR) which is part of the Executive Office of the President, with the primary responsibility borne by USTR's Office of General Counsel. In conducting this review, USTR obtains the views of other agencies through the Trade Policy Staff Committee. USTR also receives representations from the countries of the affected exporters and responsible USTR officials may also meet with the parties or their representatives. The Presidential review proceeding is not subject to the Administrative Procedure Act. Ultimately, the Trade Representative will make the final policy decision on behalf of the President. During the period of Presidential review, the Commission's determination (and remedial orders) are effective upon publication of the Commission's determination in the *Federal Register* except that articles subject to an exclusion order or a cease and desist order may be entered under bond prescribed by the Secretary of the Treasury in an amount determined by the Commission to be sufficient to protect the complainant from any inquiry.

If the President disapproves the Commission's determination, that determination and any remedial order "shall have no force or effect" as from the date of notice of such disapproval.

Such disapprovals are very rare. Since 1975, the President has only disapproved a Commission determination five times, the most recent being in *Certain Dynamic Random Access Memories, Components Thereof and Products Containing Same ("DRAMs")*, Inv. No. 337-TA-242, which occurred in 1987. 52 F.R. 46011 (Dec. 3, 1987) In some of these cases (such as *DRAMs*), the Commission was able to correct the aspect that precipitated Presidential disapproval. There is no provision in Section 337 for judicial review of Presidential disapproval. Indeed, such review may not be available at all. *See, Duracell, Inc. v. United States International Trade Commission*, 778 F.2d 1578 (Fed. Cir. 1985).

The Commission's determination becomes final if (1) the President does not disapprove such determination within the 60-day Presidential review period, or (2) the President notifies the Commission before the close of that review period that he approves the Commission's determination. In the case of (1) the date the Commission's determination becomes final is the close of the 60-day period. In the case of (2), the Commission's determination becomes final on the day the President notifies the Commission of his approval. As a matter of practice, unless the President has determined to disapprove the Commission's determination (and order), he simply lets the 60-day period expire without issuing any written notification. Thus, it is usually necessary to make telephone inquiries to the Office of the General Counsel at USTR or the Commission to determine the outcome of Presidential review.

The effect of Presidential non-disapproval is to make the Commission's determination final for purposes of appeal, to preclude any further importation under bond, and, under the usual bond terms, to require redelivery of affected articles previously imported under bond. If such redelivery cannot be made, there may be proceedings to determine whether the bond posted by a respondent to permit importation during the Presidential review period should be forfeited to the complainant in whole or in part.

XXI. TEMPORARY RELIEF (Section 337(e); Commission Rules 210.52-.69)

A. Generally

Section 337(e) authorizes the Commission to issue temporary or preliminary relief effective for the duration of a Section 337 investigation if it determines that there is "reason to believe" that there is a violation of Section 337. Such temporary relief may take the form of a temporary exclusion order, a temporary cease and desist order, or both. Temporary relief is analogous to preliminary injunctive relief in United States district courts. Indeed, the statute provides that the Commission may grant preliminary relief "to the same extent as preliminary injunctions and temporary restraining orders may be granted under the Federal Rules of Civil procedure." 19 U.S.C. § 1337(e)(3). The issuance of temporary relief is therefore governed by considering and balancing the same four factors governing the issuance of preliminary injunctions. *Rosemount, Inc. v. U.S. International Trade Commission*, 910 F.2d 819 (Fed. Cir. 1990). These factors are "(1) the movant's likelihood of success on the merits; (2) whether or not the movant will suffer irreparable injury during the pendency of the litigation if the preliminary injunction is not granted; (3) whether or not that injury outweighs the harm to other parties if the preliminary injunction is issued; and (4) whether the grant or denial of the preliminary injunction is in the public interest." *Rosemount,* 910 F.2d at 821, *citing, inter alia, Illinois Tool Works, Inc. v. Grip-Pak, Inc.*, 906 F.2d 679, 681 (Fed. Cir. 1990). Under Section 337(j), the grant of temporary relief by the Commission is subject to Presidential review and possible disapproval, as is the case for its decisions on permanent relief. Section 337(c) provides that the Commission's decisions on temporary relief are subject to appeal to the United States Court of Appeals for the Federal Circuit.

Review by that court is under an abuse of discretion standard, the same standard used for reviewing district court decisions on preliminary injunctions. *Id.*

Temporary relief is sought by motion, which must be filed with the complaint or at least prior to institution of the investigation. The Commission must determine whether to "provisionally accept" (*i.e.*, entertain) the motion and does so at the same time it decides whether to institute an investigation based on the complaint. If the Commission decides to institute an investigation, it may or may not accept the motion for temporary relief. Of course, if the Commission decides not to institute an investigation, it will not accept the motion for temporary relief.

If the Commission decides to institute an investigation and accepts the motion for temporary relief, it must determine whether to grant the motion within 90 days of the publication of the notice of investigation in the *Federal Register* (150 days if the case is designated as "more complicated"). The procedural means by which the Commission makes this decision is through a temporary relief proceeding, the details of which are discussed below. Essentially, the temporary relief proceeding takes place concurrently with the investigation itself and thus is a kind of proceeding within a proceeding.

If the Commission decides that temporary relief is appropriate, it will ordinarily condition the issuance of such relief on the posting of a bond by the complainant. This bond is analogous to a preliminary injunction bond and may be forfeited to the respondent if, at the end of the investigation, the Commission concludes that the respondent has not violated Section 337.

Temporary relief may take the form of a temporary exclusion order. However, even if the Commission issues a temporary exclusion order, it will not be a complete bar to entry of the subject articles, since Section 337(e)(1) provides that such articles may be entered under bond. The form of the bond is prescribed by the Secretary of the Treasury (*i.e.*, the Customs Service). The amount of the bond is set by the Commission as part of the temporary relief proceeding. Under Section 337(e)(1), the Commission must set the bond at an amount "sufficient to protect the complainant from any injury." If the respondent fails to post the bond, its articles covered by the exclusion order will be refused entry. If the respondent posts the bond, its articles may be entered. However, if the Commission concludes its investigation with a determination that the respondent has violated Section 337 and the President does not disapprove the Commission's determination and order, the respondent may be required to export or destroy the articles under Customs Service supervision. If the respondent fails to do so, it may forfeit some or all of the bond amount to the complainant. The Commission may issue temporary cease and desist orders in addition to or in lieu of a temporary exclusion order. Such cease and desist orders may be enforced by replacement with a temporary exclusion order or enforced independently.

There are only a few cases where a complainant has sought temporary relief, and fewer where such relief was granted.

B. Procedure

1. Motion for Temporary Relief

As noted above, a motion for temporary relief must be filed with the complaint or at least prior to institution of the investigation.

a. Contents of Motion for Temporary Relief

The motion for temporary relief must contain:

1. A detailed statement of specific facts bearing on the four factors the Federal Circuit has stated that a United States district court must consider in granting a preliminary injunction.

2. A detailed statement of facts bearing on:

   a. Whether the complainant should be required to post a bond as a prerequisite to the issuance of temporary relief; and

   b. The appropriate amount of the bond, should the Commission determine that a bond will be required.

b. Documents to Accompany Motion

In addition to the motion itself, the complainant filing a motion for temporary relief must also submit the following documents and information:

1. A memorandum of points and authorities in support of the motion for temporary relief;

2. Affidavits (or declarations) executed by persons with knowledge of the facts asserted in the motion for temporary relief; and

3. All documents, information, and other evidence in the complainant's possession that it intends to submit in support of the motion for temporary relief.

If the motion and accompanying documents contain confidential business information, the complainant must request confidential treatment for such information and submit public versions of the motion and accompanying documents.

c. Service of Motion

Where a complaint is accompanied by a motion for temporary relief, the complainant must simultaneously serve a copy of the public versions of the complaint and motion for temporary relief on each proposed respondent and the embassy of each country from which the accused imports come. Service must be made on the day the complaint and motion are filed with the Commission. The Commission's rules are quite strict about how service is to be accomplished and proven. Thus, Commission Rule 210.54 provides that service must be by "messenger, courier, express mail, or equivalent means." A certificate of service must accompany the complaint and motion when they are filed (that same day). Further, actual proof of service (or "proof of a serious but unsuccessful effort to make such service") must be filed within 10 days of filing the complaint and motion. If a certificate of service or actual proof of service is not timely filed, the Commission may extend its usual 35-day deadline for determining whether to institute an investigation and whether to provisionally accept the motion for temporary relief.

d. Content of Service Copies

While respectful of the complainant's need to redact confidential information from the service copies of the complaint and motion, the Commission's rules also reflect a concern for providing adequate notice to the proposed respondents.

If the complainant has designated attachments to the complaint as being confidential in their entirety, it must provide a nonconfidential summary of what each such attachment contains. If the complainant redacts confidential information in the complaint or motion for temporary relief, the remainder of the complaint and motion must contain enough factual information about each element of the violation alleged in the complaint and motion to enable each proposed respondent to comprehend the allegations against it.

If the Commission determines that the complainant has made excessive designations of confidentiality, it may require the complainant to file and serve new public versions of the complaint and motion. If the Commission does so, the 35-day time period for the Commission to determine whether to institute an investigation and whether to provisionally accept the motion will begin anew.

e. Notice Accompanying Service Copies

Commission Rule 210.56(a) requires the complainant to serve on the proposed respondents and involved embassies a notice advising them as to the nature of the proceedings and the procedure to be followed with respect to the complaint and motion. The text of the notice is specified in the rule. Among other things, the notice must specify the date the complaint and motion are filed. If these are filed after the date specified, the complainant must serve a supplementary notice giving the correct date of filing. Commission Rule 210.56(b).

f. Motion Filed After Complaint

Ordinarily, the complainant must file and serve the motion for temporary relief on the same day as the complaint. It is possible to file and serve the motion after that date (but prior to institution), if the complainant makes a showing that "extraordinary circumstances" exist that warrant temporary relief and that the moving party was not aware, and with due diligence could not have been aware, of those circumstances at the time the complaint was filed. Such a delayed filing and service of the motion will restart the period for the Commission to determine whether to institute an investigation based on the complaint and whether to provisionally accept the motion for temporary relief.

g. Amendment of Motion for Temporary Relief

A motion for temporary relief may be amended at any time prior to institution of the investigation. Such an amendment must be filed and served as for the original motion. If the amendment (1) expands the scope of the investigation, (2) changes the complainant's assertions on the issue of whether a bond is to be required as a prerequisite to the issuance of temporary relief or (3) changes the appropriate amount of the complainant's bond, the 35-day period for the Commission to determine whether to institute an investigation and to provisionally accept the motion starts anew.

2. Provisional Acceptance of Motion

The Commission will determine whether to provisionally accept the motion for temporary relief at the same time it determines whether to institute an investigation based on the complaint. Under Commission Rule 210.58, the Commission has 35 days from filing of the complaint and motion to make that determination, unless it extends the time therefor or exceptional circumstances exist.

The Commission reviews the motion for sufficiency in the same manner as it reviews the complaint, *i.e.*, it determines whether the motion complies with the Commission's rules. If the Commission determines that the motion is in compliance with the rules and if it also determines to institute an investigation, it will "provisionally accept" the motion. Under the rule, provisional acceptance simply means that the motion has been accepted for the purpose of "referral to the chief administrative law judge, who will assign the motion to a presiding administrative law judge" (the administrative law judge presiding over the investigation). Since the Commission's Office of Administrative Law Judges is no longer organized to have a chief administrative law judge, the Commission, in its notice of investigation, directly refers the motion to the administrative law judge designated in that notice as presiding in the investigation.

As noted above, if the Commission determines not to institute an investigation based on the complaint, the question of temporary relief is moot, and the Commission will not accept the motion. The converse is not true, however. If the Commission determines not to provisionally accept a motion for temporary relief, it may nevertheless determine to institute an investigation.

3. Service of Motion and Complaint

Official service of the motion for temporary relief is made by the Commission itself at the same time it serves the complaint. However, as noted above, the complainant must nevertheless have served the public versions of the complaint and motion on the proposed respondents and the embassies of their countries when it files the complaint and motion.

4. Responses to the Motion and Complaint

a. Generally; Time for Responses

Commission Rule 210.59 provides that "any party" may file a response to a motion for temporary relief.

In an "ordinary" investigation, the time for filing the response to the motion (and to the complaint and notice of investigation) is 10 days after service of the motion by the Commission. In a "more complicated" case, the time for response is 20 days after service by the Commission, unless otherwise ordered by the administrative law judge.

b. Contents of the Response to Motion

The response to the motion for temporary relief must comply with Commission Rules 201.8, 210. 4 and 210.5 and must contain the following:

1. A statement that sets forth with particularity any objection to the motion for temporary relief;

2. A statement of specific facts the U.S. Court of Appeals for the Federal Circuit would consider in determining whether to affirm lower court decisions granting or denying preliminary injunctions;

3. A memorandum of points and authorities in support of the respondent's response to the motion;

4. Affidavits (or declarations), where possible, executed by persons with knowledge of the facts specified in the response.

Each response must address:

1. To the extent possible, the complainant's assertions as to whether it should be required to post a bond as a condition of obtaining temporary relief;

2. The appropriate amount of any bond to be posted by the complainant.

c. Filing and Service of Response to Complaint and Notice of Investigation

In an investigation where the Commission has accepted a motion for temporary relief, the deadline for filing and service of the response to the complaint and notice of investigation is the same as that for the response to the motion. Thus, the responses to the complaint and notice of investigation and to the motion for temporary relief are filed and served at the same time.

5. Designating an Investigation "More Complicated"

As noted above, Section 337(e)(2) provides that the Commission must make its final determination on temporary relief within 90 days of the publication of the notice of investigation in the *Federal Register* unless it declares the investigation "more complicated," in which case its final determination on temporary relief will be due 150 days after publication of the notice of investigation in the *Federal Register*. The Commission may designate an investigation as "more complicated" when it issues its notice of investigation. If it does not do so, the administrative law judge may do so on motion or *sua sponte*. Such a designation by the administrative law judge will, by rule, constitute a final determination of the Commission and notice thereof will be published in the *Federal Register*. The notice must state the reasons for designating the investigation as "more complicated," *e.g.*, "complexity of the issues raised in the motion for temporary relief or the responses thereto, or for other good cause shown." Commission Rule 210.60.

6. Discovery and Compulsory Process

As with discovery in cases not involving motions for temporary relief, the administrative law judge sets all discovery deadlines and generally does so in his or her ground rules. In cases involving temporary relief motions, the manner and timing of service of discovery requests are usually subject to special requirements to ensure timeliness and the ALJ may set shorter response times to discovery requests as they relate to temporary relief. The scope of discovery in cases involving temporary relief encompasses the additional issues associated with requests for temporary relief and therefore is somewhat broader than in cases not involving a motion for temporary relief. Thus, discovery also includes:

(a) any matter relevant to the motion for temporary relief and the responses thereto, including the issues of bonding by the complainant; and

(b) the issues the Commission considers pursuant to Section 337(e)(1), (f)(1), and (j)(3), *viz*:

(1) the appropriate form of relief (notwithstanding the form of relief requested in the motion for temporary relief);

(2) whether consideration of the public interest preclude that form of relief; and

(3) the amount of the bond to be posted by the respondents to secure importations or sales of the subject imported merchandise while the temporary relief order is in effect.

7. Evidentiary Hearing

Commission Rule 210.62 requires that a hearing "in accordance with the Administrative Procedure Act" be provided in connection with every motion for temporary relief. As a matter of practice, the administrative law judge ordinarily provides for an oral evidentiary hearing which may last about a week. At that hearing, the parties may offer evidence on the issues relating to temporary relief. At any such hearing, the administrative law judge may (but is not required to) receive evidence on the issues of remedy, the public interest and bonding by the respondents under Section 337(e)(1), (f)(1), and (j)(3).

8. Proposed Findings and Conclusions of Law

Commission Rule 210.63 expressly leaves to the administrative law judge the question of whether and to what extent the parties will be permitted to file proposed findings of fact, proposed conclusions of law, and supporting briefs on temporary relief.

9. Interlocutory Appeals

Commission Rule 210.64 precludes interlocutory appeals to the Commission on any matter connected with a motion for temporary relief decided by an administrative law judge prior to the issuance of the initial determination on the motion for temporary relief.

10. Certification of the Record

The administrative law judge must certify the evidentiary record on which his or her initial determination granting or denying temporary relief is based and must do so at the time he or she issues that initial determination.

11. Initial Determination on Temporary Relief; Commission Action Thereon

a. Time for Issuance of Initial Determination

i. Ordinary Investigation

The administrative law judge must issue his or her initial determination on temporary relief (and certify the record on which it is based) within 70 days after the publication of the notice of investigation in the *Federal Register.*

ii. "More Complicated" Investigation

The administrative law judge must issue his or her initial determination on temporary relief within 120 days after publication of the notice of investigation in the *Federal Register.*

b. Scope of the Initial Determination

The initial determination must address:

a. the substantive requirements for the grant of temporary relief, *i.e.*, the factors the Federal Circuit has stated a United States district court must consider in granting a preliminary injunction;

b. whether the complainant should be required to post a bond as a prerequisite to the issuance of temporary relief;

c. the amount of the complainant's bond, if one is to be required.

The initial determination may address the issues of remedy, the public interest, and bonding by respondents.

c. Effect of Initial Determination

The initial determination will become the Commission's determination 20 calendar days after issuance (30 calendar days after issuance in a "more complicated" case) unless the Commission modifies, reverses, or sets aside the initial determination in whole or in part during that period. If the initial determination is issued prior to the expiry of the 70-day (or 120-day) period, the additional time is added to the time for the Commission to act. Thus, in an ordinary, case, if the initial determination is issued on the 65th day after publication of the notice of investigation in the *Federal Register* (*i.e.*, 5 days early), it will not become the Commission's determination until 25 calendar days after issuance. In computing the foregoing deadlines, intermediate Saturdays, Sundays and Federal holidays are included. If the last day of the period in a Saturday, Sunday, or Federal holiday, the effective date of the initial determination will be extended to the next business day.

d. Written Comments on the Initial Determination

There is no petition for review procedure for initial determinations on temporary relief. Rather, each party is entitled to file written comments concerning "any clear error of material fact, error of law, or policy matter" warranting modification, reversal, or setting aside of the initial determination. These are limited to 35 pages (45 pages in a "more complicated" case) and must be filed within 7 calendar days (10 calendar days in a "more complicated" case) after issuance of the initial determination. In computing the deadlines for filing written comments, intermediate Saturdays, Sundays, and Federal holidays are included. If the initial determination is issued on a Friday, however, the filing deadline will be measured from the first business day after issuance. If the last day of the filing period is a Saturday, Sunday, or Federal holiday, the filing deadline is extended to the next business day. The parties must serve their comments on each other by messenger, courier, express mail, or "equivalent means."

e. Comments by Government Agencies

The Commission will serve notice of the initial determination on temporary relief on certain Federal agencies, specifically the U.S. Department of Health and Human Services, the U.S. Department of Justice, the Federal Trade Commission, the U.S. Customs Service, and (rarely) such other agencies as it considers appropriate. These agencies have 10 calendar days from the date of service of the notice to file comments on the initial determination. Except for the Customs Service, comments by Federal agencies are rare.

f. Responses to Written Comments of Parties

Each party may file a response to the written comments of the other parties.

Such reply comments are limited to 20 pages (30 pages in a "more complicated" case) and must be filed within 10 calendar days of issuance of the initial determination (14 calendar days in a "more complicated" case). In no case will the period for reply comments be less than two calendar days.

g. Commission Action on Initial Determination

The Commission will not modify, reverse, or set aside an initial determination on temporary relief unless it finds that:

1. A finding of material fact is clearly erroneous;
2. There is an error of law; or
3. There is a policy matter warranting such action by the Commission

If the Commission determines to modify, reverse, or set aside the initial determination, it will issue a notice and, if appropriate, an opinion. If the Commission does not modify, reverse, or set aside the initial determination within the time provided, it will automatically become the determination of the Commission.

The Commission will issue notice of its determination by the statutory deadline or "as soon as possible thereafter" and will serve its notice on the parties. If the Commission's determination is affirmative, *i.e.*, if its disposition of the initial determination is a determination that there is reason to believe a violation of Section 337 exists and that a temporary relief order will be issued, it will also publish notice of its determination in the *Federal Register.* If the Commission determines that the complainant must post a bond as a prerequisite to the issuance of temporary relief, the Commission will set forth in the original notice or in a supplemental notice the conditions for any such bond (in addition to those set out in the initial determination) and the deadline for filing the bond with the Commission.

h. Remedy, the Public Interest and Bonding by Respondents

Commission Rule 210.67 prescribes the procedure for arriving at the Commission's determination of the appropriate form of temporary relief, whether the public interest factors enumerated in Section 337(e)(l), (f)(1) preclude such relief, and the amount of the bond under which respondents' merchandise will be permitted to enter the United States during the period temporary relief is in effect.

While the motion for temporary relief is before the administrative law judge, he or she may permit discovery, receive evidence, and make findings on these issues (at least on public interest), but is not required to address the issues of remedy, the public interest, and bonding by the respondents pursuant to Section 337(e)(1), Section 337(f)(1), and Section 337(j)(3). If the administrative law judge does make findings pertaining to the public interest, those findings may be superseded by findings of the Commission.

On the 65th day after institution of the investigation (the 110th day in a "more complicated" case), all parties are to file written submissions with the Commission addressing those issues. These written submissions are to refer to information and evidence already in the record, but additional information and evidence germane to these issues may also be provided. Interested persons may also file written submissions on these issues.

On or before the 90-day (or 150-day) deadline, the Commission will issue its determination or what relief is appropriate, whether such relief is precluded by the above-mentioned public interest factors, and the amount of respondent's bond to permit importation during the period temporary relief is in effect. To the extent the Commission's findings on public interest are inconsistent with those of the administrative law judge, the Commission's findings will govern.

12. Complainant's Temporary Relief Bond

a. Generally

The Commission will ordinarily require the complainant to post a bond as a condition for the issuance of temporary relief.

The bond may consist of one or more of the following:

(1) The surety bond of a surety or guarantee corporation that is licensed to do business with the United States in accordance with 31 U.S.C. §§ 9304-9306 and 31 C.F.R. Parts 223 and 224;

(2) The surety bond of an individual, a trust, an estate, or a partnership, or a corporation, whose solvency and financial responsibility will be investigated and verified by the Commission; or

(3) A certified check, a bank draft, a post office money order, cash, a United States bond, a Treasury note, or other Government obligation within the meaning of 31 U.S.C. § 9301 and 31 C.F.R. Part 225, which is owned by the complainant and tendered in lieu of a surety bond, pursuant to 31 U.S.C. § 9303(c) and 31 C.F.R. Part 225.

b. Restrictions and Requirements for Bonds

The complainant's temporary relief bond is subject to the same restrictions and requirements applicable to individual and corporate sureties on Customs bonds, as set forth in 19 C.F.R. Part 113.

i. Individual Sureties; Affidavit

If the surety is an individual, that individual must file an affidavit which specifies that individual's assets, liabilities, and net worth and provides that the individual will notify the Commission of any transfer or change in the assets set out therein.

A form of the affidavit is set out at Appendix A to Commission Rule 210.68.

ii. Information to Appear on or Accompany Bond

The bond must contain a provision which authorizes the Government to "collect or sell the bond" if the Commission orders forfeiture of the bond under Commission Rule 210.70. If the bond is in the form of a certified check, bank draft, post office money order, cash, United States bond, Treasury note, or other obligation, these must be accompanied by an instrument which authorizes the Government to "collect or sell" the offered instrument. In either case, certain information must appear on the face of the bond or the instrument of authorization, namely:

(1) The investigation caption and docket number;

(2) The names, addresses, and seals (if appropriate) of the principal, the surety, the obligee, as well as the "attorney in fact" and the registered process agent (if applicable) (*see* Customs Service regulations in 19 C.F.R. Part 113 and Treasury Department regulations in 31 C.F.R. Parts 223-225).

(3) The terms and conditions of the bond obligation, including the reason the bond is being posted, the amount of the bond, the effective date and duration of the bond (as prescribed by the Commission order, notice, determination, or opinion requiring the complainant to post a bond); and

(4) A section at the bottom of the bond or other instrument for the date and authorized signature of the Secretary of the Commission to reflect the Commission's approval of the bond.

iii. Additional Requirements for Sureties Posting Financial Instrument in Lieu of Bond

If a complainant wishes to post a financial instrument (*i.e.*, certified check, bank draft, post office money order, cash, United States bond, or other Government obligation) in lieu of a surety bond, the complainant must so notify the Commission immediately upon receipt of the Commission document requiring the posting of a bond. The complainant must also contact the Secretary of the Commission to make arrangements for Commission receipt, handling, management, and deposit of the involved financial instrument, in accordance within 31 U.S.C. § 9303, 31 C.F.R. Parts 202, 208, and 225 and other governing Treasury regulations and circulars. It is possible that the applicable Treasury regulations and/or circulars may require that the financial instrument being tendered in lieu of a bond be collateralized.

c. Commission Approval of Complainant's Bond

All bonds posted by complainants must be approved by the Commission before the temporary relief provided for will be issued. The Commission has, by rule, delegated the responsibility for such bond approval to the Secretary.

i. Investigation by the Secretary

Prior to action on the bond, the Secretary or the Commission's Office of Investigations may investigate the veracity of all factual information set forth in the bond and the accompanying documentation (*e.g.*, power of attorney), as well as any additional verification required by 31 C.F.R. Parts 223-225.

ii. Grounds for Rejection of Bond

The Secretary may reject a bond on one or more of the following grounds:

(1) Failure to comply with the instructions in the Commission's determination, order, or notice directing the complainant to post a bond;

(2) Failure of the surety or the bond to provide information or supporting documentation required by the Commission, the Secretary, Commission Rule 210.68, 31 C.F.R. Parts 223-224, or because of a limitation prescribed in a governing statute, regulation, or circular;

(3) Failure of an individual surety to execute and file with the bond, an affidavit of the type shown in Appendix A of Commission Rule 210.68, which sets forth information about the surety's assets, liabilities, net worth, real estate and other property of which the initial surety is the sole owner, other bonds on which the individual surety is a surety (and which must be updated at 4-month intervals while the bond is in effect, measured from the date on which the bond is approved by the Secretary on behalf of the Commission or by the Commission);

(4) Any question about the solvency or financial responsibility of the surety, or any question of fraud, misrepresentation, or perjury which comes to light as a result of the verification inquiry during the bond approval process; and

(5) Any other reason deemed appropriate by the Secretary.

iii. Appeal of Disapproval of Bond to the Commission

A complainant may appeal the decision of the Secretary rejecting a bond to the Commission. The appeal is limited to matters of law only and is commenced by filing a petition with the Commission in the form of a letter to the Chairman within 10 days after service of the rejection letter.

d. Monitoring of Complainant's Bond

Even though the Commission approves the bond and issues temporary relief, it retains jurisdiction over both. If any question concerning the continued solvency of the individual or the legality or enforceability of the bond or undertaking develops, the Commission may take the following actions, *sua sponte* or on motion:

(1) Revoke the Commission approval of the bond and require complainant to post a new bond; or

(2) Revoke or vacate the temporary remedial order for public interest reasons or changed conditions of law or fact (criteria that are the basis for modification or rescission of final Commission action pursuant to Commission Rules 210.76(a)(1) and 210.76(b)); or

(3) Notify the Treasury Department if the problem involves a corporate surety licensed to do business with the United States under 31 U.S.C. §§ 9303-9306 and 31 C.F.R. Parts 223-224; or

(4) Refer the matter to be the U.S. Department of Justice if there is a suggestion of fraud, perjury, or related conduct.

XXII. FORFEITURE OR RETURN OF RESPONDENT'S BOND (Commission Rule 210.50(d))

As previously noted, respondents may be required to post a bond to permit importation (1) during the investigation, if temporary relief is granted, or (2) during the Presidential review period, if temporary or permanent relief is issued. If a respondent is required to post a bond, the question of whether the bond should be returned or forfeited in whole or in part will arise at the close of investigation and at the end of the Presidential review period.

If the Commission finds no violation of Section 337 at the conclusion of an investigation in which it has issued temporary relief, any temporary importation bond posted will be returned. If the Commission finds a violation of Section 337 (or reason to believe a violation exists) and issues a remedial order, but the President disapproves the Commission's determination and order, any bond posted to permit importation during the Presidential review period will be returned. A respondent may file a motion for return of its bond. The Commission's rules do not specify when such a motion must be filed, but a prudent respondent will act expeditiously.

If the Commission finds a violation of Section 337 and the President does not disapprove the Commission's determination and order, a complainant may file a motion for forfeiture of respondent's bond within 30 days after the expiration of the Presidential review period.

Any nonmoving party may file a response to a motion within 15 days after filing of the motion unless otherwise ordered by the administrative law judge.

A motion for forfeiture or return of a respondent's bond in whole or in part will be adjudicated by the administrative law judge in an initial determination with a 45-day effective date, which is subject to Commission review under Commission Rules 210.42-.45. Commission Rule 210.50(d). In determining whether to grant the motion, the administrative law judge and the Commission will be guided by practice under Rule 65 of the Federal Rules of Civil Procedure (taking into account that the roles of the parties are reversed in this instance).

If the Commission determines that a respondent's bond should be forfeited to a complainant, and if the bond is being held by the Secretary of the Treasury, the Commission Secretary will promptly notify the Secretary of the Commission's determination.

XXIII. FORFEITURE OR RETURN OF COMPLAINANT'S TEMPORARY RELIEF BOND (Commission Rule 210.70)

The question of forfeiture or return of a complainant's temporary relief bond arises at the end of the Commission's investigation. If the Commission finds that the respondents who were subject to temporary relief did violate Section 337, the complainant may move for the return of the bond it has posted. The

Commission's rules do not set a deadline for filing such a motion, but the complainant will wish to act expeditiously. If the Commission finds that one or more respondents who were subject to temporary relief did not violate Section 337, "to the extent alleged in the motion for temporary relief and provided for in the temporary relief order," those respondents may move to commence proceedings to determine whether complainant's bond should be forfeited to them in whole or in part. An eligible respondent must file such motion within 30 days after filing of the Commission determination on violation.

A non-moving party may file a response to a motion for return or for forfeiture of complainant's bond under Commission Rule 210.70(a) within 15 days after such motion is filed, unless otherwise ordered by the administrative law judge.

A motion for return or forfeiture of complainant's temporary relief bond is adjudicated by the administrative law judge, who must issue an initial determination thereon. The initial determination is subject to the review procedures of Commission Rules 210.42-45. Unless reviewed within 45 days, it will become the Commission's final determination. In determining whether to grant a motion under Commission Rule 210.70(a), "the administrative law judge and the Commission will be guided by practice under Rule 65 of the Federal Rules of Civil Procedure." Commission Rule 210.70(c).

XXIV. MODIFICATION OR RESCISSION OF COMMISSION ORDERS (Section 337(k); Commission Rule 210.76)

A. Generally

Section 337(k)(1) provides that, except as provided in Section 337(f) and Section 337(j),[46] any remedial order issued by Commission "shall continue in effect until the Commission finds . . . that the conditions which led to such exclusion from entry or order no longer exist."

Commission Rule 210.76 contains two provisions for modification or rescission of Commission remedial orders. The first of these, Commission Rule 210.76(a)(1), is the older of the two. The second, Commission Rule 210.76(a)(2), is based on Section 337(k)(2).

1. Commission Rule 210.76(a)(1)

Under Commission Rule 210.76(a)(1), whenever "any person" believes that "changed conditions of fact or law, or the public interest" require that an exclusion order, cease and desist order, or consent order be modified or set aside, in

46 Section 337(f), which provides for the issuance of cease and desist orders, also provides that the Commission may modify or revoke a cease and desist order and replace a revoked cease and desist order with an exclusion order. Section 337(j) provides that Commission orders will be effective during the Presidential review period except that articles may be entered under bond.

whole or in part, that person may file a petition with the Commission requesting such relief.

2. Commission Rule 210.76(a)(2)

Commission Rule 210.76(a)(2) rests on Section 337(k)(2) and is framed so as to consider the circumstances of Section 337(k)(2) as being a special case under Commission Rule 210.76(a)(1), though it may be argued that Section 337(k)(2) is the exclusive method intended by Congress for the modification or rescission of remedial orders.

Commission Rule 210.76(a)(2), consistent with Section 337(k)(2), covers the circumstance where the petitioner previously has been found in violation of Section 337 (*i.e.*, is a former respondent) and seeks (1) a Commission determination that it is no longer in violation of Section 337 or (2) modification of rescission of a remedial order. In any proceeding initiated as a result of the petition under Commission Rule 210.76(a)(2), the burden of proof is on the petitioner and relief may be granted by the Commission only on the basis of new evidence or evidence that could not have been presented in the prior proceeding or "on grounds that would permit relief from a judgment or order under the Federal Rules of Civil Procedure."

B. Procedure for Initiating Modification/Rescission Proceedings

1. By Petition

A petition filed under Commission Rule 210.76(a)(1) or Commission Rule 210.76(a)(2) must state the changes desired and the changed circumstances warranting the requested action. It must also include materials and argument in support the requested action, and must be served on all parties to the investigation in which the remedial order sought to be modified or rescinded was issued. Any person may file an opposition to the petition within 10 days of service of the petition.

2. On the Commission's Own Motion

The Commission may also consider modification or rescission of a remedial order on its own initiative.

C. Commission Action

After considering the petition and any oppositions thereto, the Commission may take immediate action to grant or deny modification or rescission. It may also institute a proceeding and hold a public hearing at which "interested persons" may appear and be heard, after which it may act on petition. The Commission may also delegate any hearing (or, indeed, the entire proceedings) to an administrative law judge who may take evidence and certify a recommended determination (along with the record) to the Commission. The Commission will consider the recommended determination and record and may require further briefing and argument. Eventually, the Commission will issue a final determination granting or denying modification or rescission. The Commission's final determination may be appealed to the United States Court of Appeals for the Federal Circuit. *Allied Corp. v. United States International Trade Commission,* 850 F.2d 1573 (Fed. Cir.1988); *Crucible, Inc. v. United States International Trade Commission,* 127 F.3d 1057 (Fed. Cir. 1997).

XXV. ADVISORY OPINIONS (Commission Rule 210.79)

A. Generally

On the request of "any person," the Commission may issue an advisory opinion as to whether that person's proposed cause of action or conduct would violate a Commission exclusion order, cease and desist order, or consent order.

B. Proceedings for Obtaining Advisory Opinions

The Commission's rules do not provide for a specific or exclusive procedure for rendering advisory opinions. Indeed, Commission Rule 210.79(a) makes it clear that advisory opinions are discretionary and that they will be issued "upon such investigation as it [the Commission] deems necessary." Therefore, the procedure is set out in the Commission's order granting the request. As a matter of practice, the Commission (after it has decided to grant the request) will refer the proceeding to an administrative law judge for an "initial advisory opinion," analogous to an initial determination. This initial advisory opinion is made subject to Commission review procedures similar to those for initial determinations and will eventually result in a Commission final advisory opinion. Commission Rule 210.79(a) provides that "[a]dvisory opinion proceedings are not subject to sections 557, 555, 556, 557, and 702 of title 5 of the United States Code." However, in practice, many advisory proceedings are conducted in a manner very similar to original investigations of whether a violation of Section 337 exists.

C. Advisory Opinions Discretionary

The Commission is not required to institute an advisory opinion proceeding simply because one has been requested. The Commission will consider "whether the issuance of such an advisory opinion would facilitate the enforcement of section 337 of the Tariff Act of 1930, would be in the public interest, and would benefit consumers and competitive conditions in the United States, and whether the person has a compelling business need for the advice and has framed his request as fully and accurately as possible."

D. Revocation of Advisory Opinions

The Commission may at any time reconsider any advisory opinion and revoke its advice, where the public interest requires. In that event, the Commission will notify the requester of the advisory opinion of its intent as well as an opportunity to present its views to the Commission. The Commission will not proceed against a person for violation of an exclusion order, cease and desist order, or consent order with respect to any action that was taken in good faith reliance on a Commission advisory opinion, if all relevant facts were accurately presented to the Commission and if that action was promptly discontinued upon notification of revocation of the Commission's advisory opinion.

E. No Judicial Review of Commission Advisory Opinions

Commission advisory opinions are not appealable. *Allied Corp. v. United States International Trade Commission*, 850 F.2d 1573 (Fed. Cir. 1988).

XXVI. JUDICIAL REVIEW OF COMMISSION DETERMINATIONS

A. Generally

The Commission's decisions under Section 337 are reviewable by appeal or (rarely) by mandamus. The Commission's reviewing court is the United States Court of Appeals for the Federal Circuit.

B. The United States Court of Appeals for the Federal Circuit

The United States Court of Appeals for the Federal Circuit was created by the Federal Courts Improvement Act of 1982 by effectively merging the then-existing United States Court of Customs and Patent Appeals (CCPA) and the appellate division of the then-existing United States Court of Claims. The new court was given all the jurisdiction of these two courts and certain additional jurisdiction as well. Since the CCPA had been the reviewing court for the Commission's decisions under Section 337, the Federal Circuit succeeded to that jurisdiction, which is set out at 28 U.S.C. § 1295(a)(6) and 19 U.S.C. § 1337(c). In its first decision, *South Corp. v. United States*, 690 F.2d 1368 (Fed. Cir. 1982), the Federal Circuit adopted the prior precedent of the CCPA and the Court of Claims.

The Federal Circuit is a court under Article III of the Constitution and consists of a chief judge and eleven associate judges. The court sits year-round in Washington, D.C., hearing cases at the beginning of every month. On occasion, the court will hold its monthly hearings elsewhere. At its inception, the court sat in panels of three or five judges, but has since followed the practice of sitting in panels of three judges. The court may hear or rehear an appeal in banc, but this is unusual. Panels are obliged to follow the decisions of previous panels (or, if applicable, prior precedent of the CCPA or the Court of Claims). Prior panel decisions or other applicable precedent can only be overturned by an in banc decision of the court. Decisions of Federal Circuit are reviewable by United States Supreme Court by writ of certiorari.

C. Commission Decisions Reviewable; Final Determinations

Section 1295(a)(6) of Title 28, United States Code provides that the Federal Circuit has jurisdiction over "final determinations" of the Commission under Section 337 of the Tariff Act (19 U.S.C. § 1337).

Section 337(c) contains more detailed provisions about what Commission decisions are appealable. These may be cataloged as follows:

(a) Determinations under Section 337(d) as to whether a violation of Section 337 exists.

(b) Determinations under Section 337(e) as to whether there is reason to believe a violation of Section 337 exists.

(c) Determinations under Section 337(f) as to whether to issue a permanent or temporary cease and desist order in addition to or in lieu of, respectively, a permanent exclusion order under Section 337(d) or a temporary exclusion order under Section 337(e), as well as determinations enforcing cease and desist orders (and consent orders).

(d) Determinations under Section 337(g) that a respondent is in default.

(e) Determinations as to whether the Commission should grant any relief after consideration of the so-called "public interest factors," *i.e.*, public health and welfare, competitive conditions in the United States economy, the production of like or directly competitive articles in the United States, and United States consumers, consideration of which is required by Sections 337(d)-(g).

(f) Determinations as to "the amount and nature of bond." Such determinations would include:

- the amount and nature of the bond which may be required of a complainant as a condition of granting temporary relief under Section 337(e);
- the amount and nature of the temporary importation bond which may be required of an importer during the period of investigation if temporary relief is granted under Section 337(e) or (f);
- the amount and nature of the temporary importation bond which may be required of an importer during the Presidential review period upon the grant of temporary relief or permanent relief.

(g) Determinations as to "the appropriate remedy." This appears to be related to the choice of remedial order and the terms of such orders.

(h) Determinations with respect to the forfeiture of bonds under Section 337(d), (e), or (j), *i.e.*, forfeiture of

(1) temporary importation bonds posted during the Presidential review period in cases where the Commission issues either permanent or temporary relief, and

(2) temporary importation bonds posted to permit importation during the investigation when the Commission has issued temporary relief.

i. Determinations with respect to the imposition of sanctions under Section 337(h) for abuse of discovery or abuse of process.

D. Who May Appeal

Section 337(c) provides that "[a]ny person adversely affected" by a Commission final determination (at least one under Section 337(d), (e), (f), or (g)) may appeal that determination. The Federal Circuit has taken this language literally. *LSI Computer Systems, Inc. v. United States International Trade Commission*, 832 F.2d 588 (Fed. Cir. 1987). Thus, a person may appeal even if not a party to the Commission proceeding. *Id.* And this is true even if the person was aware of the investigation and could have become a party, but chose not to do so. *Id.*

E. Parties to the Appeal

The appellant is the person adversely affected by the Commission's final determination and order, whether it was a party to the Commission's investigation or not. *See, LSI, supra.* In most appeals, however, the appellant was a party (a losing party) in the Commission's investigation. The appellee is always the Commission, which is usually represented in the appeal by an attorney from its Office of General Counsel. The winning party in the Commission investigation is not automatically a party to the appeal, but must seek to become a party by moving to intervene on the side of the Commission. Motions to intervene are rarely objected to and are usually granted.

F. Time for Appeal

An appeal must be taken within 60 days "after the [Commission's] determination becomes final." Careful attention must be paid to this language, because affirmative and negative Commission determinations on violation of Section 337 (or reason to believe a violation exists) become final at different times. A negative final determination, *i.e.*, a determination that there is no violation of Section 337 (or that there is no reason to believe a violation of Section 337 exists) is final as soon as the Commission makes that determination. However, an affirmative final determination, *i.e.*, a final determination that there is a violation of Section 337 (or that there is reason to believe a violation of Section 337 exists) is not final for purposes of appeal unless the President has affirmatively indicated approval during the Presidential review period or that period expires without any action being taken by the President.[47]

---

47 There is currently a controversy about whether Commission affirmative final determinations on violation or reason to believe a violation exists can be immediately appealed as interlocutory orders under 28 U.S.C. § 1292(c)), *i.e.*, without awaiting the outcome of President review. The Federal Circuit has actually entertained such appeals, noting definitively in one case that it had jurisdiction. However, the Court's order in that case was unpublished. *See Jazz Photo Corp. v. International Trade Commission* (Appeal No. 99-1431) (Unpublished Order of July 6, 1999).

G. Divisibility of Final Determinations; Effect on Time for Appeal

In patent cases, the Federal Circuit considers Commission final determinations to be rendered on a patent-by-patent basis. *See Allied Corp. v. United States International Trade Commission*, 782 F.2d 982 (Fed. Cir. 1986). In multi-patent cases, this means that the Commission's "final determination" is really a bundle of final determinations, one final determination for each patent. This rule raises no questions where the Commission's final determinations are made at the same time and are all affirmative or all negative. In that circumstance, all the final determinations will be subject to the same appeal period. If, however, the Commission's determinations on some patents are affirmative, but negative for other patents, there will be two separate appeal periods and two separate appeals by different parties. (These appeals may, however, be consolidated once the second appeal has been taken.) Further, it is possible that separate final determinations may be made at different times whether they are all the same (all affirmative or negative) or not. For example, the Commission may (1) affirm (or not review) a summary determination of invalidity of one patent or (2) on consideration of a final initial determination, decide not to review the ALJ's determination of invalidity or non-infringement of one patent, leaving its decision on other patents for future determination during a review proceeding. In both examples, the Commission will have made a final negative determination as to the first patent, a determination for which the appeal period begins running as soon as the determination is made, notwithstanding that the Commission has not yet made its decision on the other patents in the case.

In connection with the foregoing discussion, there are two further considerations. First, what if the case involved only one patent with multiple claims and the Commission went affirmative on some claims but negative on others? It would seem that multiple claims in a patent should be treated in the same manner as multiple patents, with the same possibility of different appeal periods. The second consideration is whether the reasoning in *Allied* can be extended beyond patent cases. There seems to be no reason why it should not.

H. Issues Before the Court Limited to Those Commission Has Decided

The issues before the court in any appeal are limited to those the Commission has actually decided. *Beloit Corp. v. Valmet Oy*, 742 F.2d 1421 (Fed. Cir. 1984). Thus, where the Commission adopted an ALJ's final initial determination on the issue of non-infringement, but specifically declined to take a position on the other issues determined in that final initial determination, the only issue decided by the Commission, and thus the only issue before the court on appeal, was the issue of non-infringement. *Id.*

I. Alternative Grounds for Affirmance

A party who has won before the Commission on the ultimate final determination of no violation of Section 337 has no standing to appeal issues it has lost on. *Surface Technology, Inc. v. United States International Trade Commission*, 780 F.2d 29 (Fed. Cir. 1985) This would encompass, for example, a party who has successfully argued noninfringement, but whose argument of invalidity has been rejected by the Commission. However, assuming it has successfully intervened in the appeal, the winning party in the Commission's investigation may argue issues decided against it by the Commission if those issues would provide an alternative ground for affirmance of the Commission's final determination. *See, Surface Technology, supra.* Thus, in the foregoing example, the party winning the case at the Commission on noninfringement may not only argue in support of the Commission's determination of noninfringement, it may also argue that the Commission was incorrect to have rejected that party's argument that the asserted patent is invalid, since that argument, if adopted, would also support the Commission's conclusion of no violation of Section 337. Of course, consistent with *Beloit*, the Commission would have actually had to have made a decision on the issue of invalidity. Alternative grounds for affirmance are raised and argued in the winning party's brief, which is usually filed and served at the same time as the Commission's brief, since the winning party will have intervened on the side of the Commission. The Commission, of course, is limited to defending its final determination on the grounds on which it was made.

J. Standard of Appellate Review

The Federal Circuit reviews legal determinations of the Commission *de novo*. *Corning Glass Works v. United States International Trade Commission*, 799 F.2d 1559 (Fed. Cir. 1986). While the court will grant some deference to the Commission's construction of laws which the Commission is charged with the primary administration of, such deference does not include the Commission's construction of the patent laws. *Id.* In contrast, the court reviews the Commission's factual findings under the deferential "substantial evidence" standard and will not overturn those findings unless they are not supported by substantial evidence, which is defined as "such relevant evidence as a reasonable mind might accept as adequate to support a conclusion." *Corning*, 799 F.2d at 1566, *quoting*, *Consolo v. Federal Maritime Commission*, 383 U.S. 607, 619-20 (1966). Substantial evidence is distinct from the notion of the weight of the evidence and the factual findings of an administrative agency, such as the Commission, may be upheld even if two inconsistent conclusions could be reached from the evidence adduced. *Consolo*, 383 U.S. at 619-20.

Even more deferential is the standard of review for the Commission's assessment of the public interest factors, the amount and nature of any bond, and the selection and terms of any remedial order, all of which are reviewed under an abuse of discretion standard. *Hyundai Electronics Industries, Ltd. v. United States International Trade Commission*, 899 F.2d 1204, 1208-1209 (Fed. Cir. 1990). Likewise, the Commission's evidentiary decisions, including those concerning privilege, are reviewed under the abuse of discretion standard. *Winbond Electronics Corporation v. International Trade Commission*, 262 F.3d 1363, 1370 (Fed. Cir. 2001). Abuse of discretion is also the standard for review of the Commission's final determinations granting or denying temporary relief. *Rosemount, Inc. v. United States International Trade* Commission, 910 F.2d 819, 821 (Fed. Cir. 1990). While abuse of discretion is regarded as a highly deferential standard, there are cases where the court has found it to exist. *See, e.g., Biocraft Laboratories, Inc. v. United States International Trade Commission,* 947 F.2d 483 (Fed. Cir. 1991).

K. Applicable Rules

It should be carefully noted that only some of the Federal Rules of Appellate Procedure ("Appellate Rules") and the rules of the Federal Circuit ("Federal Circuit Rules") are applicable to appeals from administrative agencies, such as the Commission.

Appellate Rules 15-20 are specific to review or enforcement of orders of an administrative agency. Appellate Rule 20 makes all the rules of the Federal Rules of Appellate Procedure applicable to such review, except Rules 3-14 (which govern appeals from district courts and the Tax Court) and Rules 22-23 (relating to *habeas corpus* and 28 U.S.C. § 2255 proceedings). The rules of practice published by the Federal Circuit include both the Federal Rules of Appellate Procedure and the court's own rules. *United States Court of Appeals for the Federal Circuit Rules of Practice* (Washington, D.C. May 1, 2001). In the version of the Federal Rules of Appellate Procedure rules in that publication, the portions which the Federal Circuit feels are inapplicable to its proceedings are crossed out. The court has thus crossed out those portions of the Federal Rules of Appellate Procedure which relate to "enforcement" of an agency order, and has entirely crossed out Appellate Rule 15.1 (relating to NLRB appeals), Appellate Rule 17(a) (relating to the filing of the agency record), and Appellate Rule 19 (relating to settlement of a judgment enforcing an agency order in part).

Federal Circuit Rules 15-20 are the court's own rules specific to appeals from agency decisions. Federal Circuit Rule 20 makes all Federal Circuit rules applicable to appeals from agencies, except Federal Circuit Rules 3-12 (relating to appeals from district courts, the Court of International Trade, the United States Court of Federal Claims, and the United States Court of Appeals for Veterans Claims). The court's rules include useful practice notes, though it should be remembered that these do not have the binding effect of rules.

L. Procedure for Appeal

The following is a brief outline of the course of an appeal at the Federal Circuit. It does not purport to cover all requirements of the court's rules, which must be consulted to ensure that all requirements are met.

1. Notice of Appeal/Petition for Review

This is the first paper filed in the appeal and it is filed with the Federal Circuit, not the Commission. Fed. R. App. P. 15(a); Fed. Cir. R. 15(a)(2). The proper term for this paper is a notice of appeal, not a petition for review, since Section 337(c) refers to an appeal to the court. The notice of appeal is a simple document. It must state the name of the party seeking review, the name of the agency, and specify the order or part thereof for which review is sought. It must be accompanied by the appropriate appeal fee. Fed. R. App. P. 15(e). The court's rules provide a sample form for review of decisions of administrative agencies (Fed. Cir. R. Form 2). The original notice and three copies must be filed with the court. Fed. Cir. R. 15(a)(4). Further, a copy must be served on each party to the Commission investigation. The appellant must provide the court with a list of those so served, and provide a copy of the notice for the clerk to serve on the Commission. Fed. Cir. R. 15(c). The appellant need not serve a copy of the notice on the Commission; such service is the duty of the clerk. However, many appellants do serve the Commission with the notice of appeal as a matter of courtesy.

2. Docketing the Appeal/Notice of Docketing

Once the clerk's office at the Federal Circuit receives the notice of appeal, it dockets the appeal and serves all parties with a notice of docketing. Fed. Cir. R. 15(b)(2)-(3). The date of docketing is usually the day the notice of appeal is filed or the next day.

3. Filing Papers with the Court

Documents may be filed with the clerk's office during business hours or in the court's lockbox, which is open until midnight. Documents filed in the lockbox are removed the following morning and treated as having been filed the previous day, *i.e.*, the day they were placed in the lockbox.

4. Intervention

The winning party in the Commission investigation must seek intervention in order to participate in the appeal. This is done by filing a motion under Fed. R. App. P. 15(d). Such motions are rarely objected to and are usually granted. Intervention is usually sought by the winning party in the Commission investigation. However, unlike the Commission, the intervenor is not limited to the actual basis for the Commission's determination, but may also argue grounds rejected by the Commission if those grounds would justify the Commission's determination. *Surface Technology, Inc. v. United States International Trade Commission*, 780 F.2d 29 (Fed. Cir. 1985) Thus, for example, an intervenor who had successfully argued noninfringement, but whose argument of invalidity had been rejected by the Commission, could argue invalidity as an alternative ground for affirmance of the Commission's determination.

5. Motions Practice; Motion to Dismiss

Motions practice at the Federal Circuit is governed by Appellate Rule 27 and Federal Circuit Rule 27. Motions to dismiss for lack of jurisdiction or to remand should be made as early in the appeal process as possible. *See,* Fed. Cir. R. 27(f).

6. Commission Record/Certified List

The court does not ordinarily require that the Commission's record in the investigation on appeal be filed, though it may do so in certain cases. What the court does require is that the Commission file and serve the parties with the so-called certified list within 40 days after the clerk serves the notice of appeal on the Commission. Fed. R. App. P. 17; Fed. Cir. R. 17. This is a list of every document and exhibit filed with the Commission during the investigation. It includes the pleadings, motions, responses, orders, exhibits, and rulings in the case, including the final determination which is the subject of the appeal. Historically, the Commission has taken the full 40 days to file and serve the certified list.

7. Main Brief of Appellant

The appellant's main brief is due 60 days after service of the certified list or of the date of docketing, whichever is later. Fed. Cir. R. 31. Since the Commission usually files the certified list well after docketing, the appellant's brief is usually due 60 days after service of the certified list.[48] The rules specify the contents of briefs. Fed. R. App. P. 28; Fed. Cir. R. 28.

If an appellant fails to file an initial brief, the clerk may dismiss the appeal. Fed. Cir. R. 31(d).

8. Brief of Appellee (Commission)

The brief of the appellee, *i.e.*, the Commission, is due 40 days after service of the appellant's brief. Fed. Cir. R. 31(a)(2) Typically, the brief of an intervenor who has intervened on the side of the Commission (as is the usual case) will be due at the same time as the Commission's brief.

9. Reply Brief

The reply brief of the appellant is typically due 14 days after service of the appellee's brief, but must, in any event, usually be filed at least three days before oral argument, if scheduled. Fed. R. App. P. 31(a). If the reply brief is served

---

48 When a motion is filed that, if granted, would terminate the appeal (*e.g.*, a motion to dismiss for lack of jurisdiction) the time for filing briefs may be extended until disposition of the motion. See, Fed. Cir. R. 31(c).

within four business days of oral argument, it must be served in such a manner as to reach all parties prior to such argument. Fed. Cir. R. 31(a)(5).

10. Appendix to the Briefs

The appellant is responsible for preparing and filing the appendix to the briefs. Fed. R. App. P. 30(a). The appendix must include certain documents specified by the rules as well as those portions of the record designated by the parties. Fed. R. App. P. 30; Fed. Cir. R. 30. The court encourages the parties to agree on the contents of the appendix and its rules provide a rather cumbersome procedure for designating the contents of the appendix in the absence of such an agreement. Fed. Cir. R. 30(b). In practice, many parties are able to agree on the contents of the appendix. One method used is to simply assign a range of numbers to the parties, who use those numbers to identify the portions of the record that they cite in their brief, providing the appellant with numbered copies of those documents from which the appellant prepares the appendix. The appellant must file and serve the appendix within seven days after the filing and service of the last reply brief. Fed. Cir. R. 30(a)(4). If the appellant fails to file the appendix, the clerk may dismiss the appeal. Fed. Cir. R. 30(a)(8).

11. Oral Argument

Oral argument is governed by Appellate Rule 34 and Federal Circuit Rule 34. Oral argument is normally held in appeals from Commission determinations, though it is possible to submit a case on the briefs. Counsel only have a limited time for argument and should expect questions from the court.

12. Opinion; Judgment

The court's decision on appeal is known as a judgment. If the judgment is one of affirmance, the court may issue its judgment without opinion if certain conditions are met. Fed. Cir. R. 36. If the court issues an opinion, that opinion may be published or unpublished. If published, the opinion is citeable as precedent in subsequent cases. If unpublished, it may only be cited in subsequent cases under the conditions set forth in the court's rules. Fed. Cir. R. 47.6.

13. Petition for Rehearing; Rehearing En Banc

A party may file a petition for rehearing by the panel which originally heard and decided the appeal. Fed. R. App. R. 40; Fed. Cir. R. 40. Such petitions are often combined with a petition for rehearing in banc, as permitted by Federal Circuit Rule 35(d). Petitions for rehearing are rarely successful.

14. Mandate

The court will normally issue its mandate seven days after the expiry of the time for filing a petition for rehearing or, if a petition for panel rehearing, petition for rehearing en banc, or motion to stay the mandate has been filed, within seven days after entry of a denial thereof, whichever is later. Fed. R. App. R. 41(b).

15. Stays Pending Appeal

The Federal Rules of Appellate Procedure and the Federal Circuit's rules provide for the possibility of obtaining a stay pending appeal. Fed. R. App. P. 18; Fed. Cir. R. 18. Ordinarily, the appellant must have sought a stay from the Commission as precondition to seeking a stay pending appeal from the court; if the appellant has not sought a stay from the Commission, it must explain why it was not practicable to have done so. Fed. R. App. 18(a): Fed. Cir. R. 18(d).

16. Accelerated Appeals

Neither the Federal Rules of Appellate Procedure nor the rules of the Federal Circuit expressly provide for accelerated or expedited appeals. However, the Federal Circuit may order that appeals be expedited in whole or in part, sometimes doing so *sua sponte*. For example, in *Dupont Merck Pharmaceutical Co. v. Bristol-Myers Squibb Co.*, 62 F.3d 1397 (Fed. Cir. 1995), a patent appeal from a district court, the court issued an order on July 14, 1995, expediting briefing and oral argument. Argument was actually held two weeks later, on July 31, 1995. The court issued its decision on August 8, 1995. In an appeal from the International Trade Commission in a Section 337 case, the court *sua sponte* ordered an expedited appeal on December 21, 2000, treating the briefs on the then-pending stay motions as briefs on the merits, permitting supplemental briefing on January 5 and January 9, 2001, and ordering oral argument for January 16, 2001. *Winbond Electronics Corp. v. International Trade Commission*, Appeal Nos. 01-1031, -1032, -1034 (Unpublished Order of December 21, 2000). The court issued its decision on January 30, 2001.

Parties should not count on such expedition as in these cases, but they may, of course, ask for it.

Requests for expedition are made by motion to the Court, explaining why expedition is necessary.

17. Mandamus

The Federal Circuit does have jurisdiction to review court and agency decisions by mandamus. Petitions for mandamus are governed by Appellate Rule 21 and Federal Circuit Rule 21. However, review by mandamus is not as of right and is subject to requirements that a requesting party will ordinarily find difficult to meet. Specifically, the petitioner would have to show a clear right to the relief sought, a clear duty on the part of the respondent to do the act in question, and the lack of any other adequate remedy. *See Maier v. Orr*, 754 F.2d 973, 983, *reh'g denied*, 758 F.2d 1578 (Fed. Cir. 1985).

XXVII. ENFORCEMENT OF REMEDIAL ORDERS

The Commission's exclusion orders are enforced by the United States Customs Service at the ports of entry. The Commission's cease and desist orders (and consent orders) are enforced by the Commission itself.

A. Enforcement of Exclusion Orders by Customs; Judicial Review

The Customs Service is responsible for enforcing the Commission's exclusion orders. 19 U.S.C. § 1337(d). Once the Commission issues an exclusion order, it forwards it to the Customs Service for enforcement. When it does so, it also forwards its determination supporting the order and a letter giving contact information for the intellectual property owner and listing the then-current licensees.

The Customs Service also has access to the entire Commission record underlying its determination and order. In general, exclusion orders are administered by the Intellectual Property Rights Branch of Customs' Office of Regulations and Rulings, but are processed by Customs' Office of Field Operations. On receipt of the exclusion order and supporting information letter, the Customs Service issues a directive ("exclusion order notice") to the various ports of entry providing directions as to how to enforce the order. At the end of the Presidential review period, the Customs Service may issue a further notice to the ports of entry. In the usual case (*i.e.*, where the President has not disapproved the Commission's determination and order), the agency so advises the ports. Temporary importation under bond will then no longer be permitted, and the ports will order redelivery and exportation or destruction of articles permitted entry under bond during the Presidential review period. Failure by the importer to comply with orders for redelivery may result in forfeiture of some or all of the amount of the bond to the complainant. Whether and to what extent forfeiture of the bond will be ordered is determined by the Commission in an administrative bond forfeiture proceeding, the result of which is appealable to the Federal Circuit.

Customs Service officials at the ports of entry are initially responsible for determining whether articles offered for entry come within the exclusion order and therefore subject to exclusion from entry. If necessary, they will make this decision with the assistance of Customs laboratories and may seek advice and assistance from Customs Headquarters, specifically, the Intellectual Property Rights Branch of the Office of Regulations and Rulings. The Customs Service provides written notification of exclusion from entry to the importer.

Exclusions from entry pursuant to Commission orders, like other exclusions from entry, are subject to administrative review within the Customs Service through the administrative protest procedure. 19 U.S.C. § 1514(a)(4); *Canadian Tarpoly Co. v. United States International Trade Commission*, 640 F.2d 1322, 1325 n.2 (CCPA 1981). A Customs protest is commenced by filing Customs Form 19, along with such additional information and argument the importer feels may convince Customs to reverse its decision to exclude. By statute, if Customs fails to decide that protest within 30 days, the protest will be deemed to have been denied on the 30th day. 19 U.S.C. § 1499(c)(5)(B).

Denials of protests may be reviewed by civil action in the United States Court of International Trade. 28 U.S.C. § 1581(a); *Canadian Tarpoly Co. v. United States International Trade Commission*, 640 F.2d 1322, 1325 n.2 (CCPA 1981). An adverse decision from the Court of International Trade may be appealed to the Federal Circuit. 28 U.S.C. § 1295(a)(5). Unlike an appeal from a final determination of the Commission, a notice of appeal from the Court of International Trade is filed with that court, not the Federal Circuit. 28 U.S.C. § 2645(c). Such appeals must be filed "within the time and in the manner prescribed for appeals to United States courts of appeals from the United States district courts." *Id.* Since the United States is a party to civil actions contesting the denial of protests, the time for filing the appeal is sixty days from entry of judgment. *See,* 28 U.S.C. § 2107(b). Once the notice of appeal is filed, it is processed by the clerk's office at the Court of International Trade and then forwarded to the Federal Circuit, where the clerk's office at that court completes the processing and assigns a docket number to the appeal.

B. Preimportation Rulings by Customs; Judicial Review

It is possible to obtain a formal ruling from the Customs Service, prior to importation, as to whether Customs will enforce an exclusion order against a particular article. This request is made under Part 177 of the Customs Regulations. The request should be addressed to the Intellectual Property Rights (IPR) Branch, Office of Regulations and Rulings, though this is not expressly set out in Part 177. The request must provide Customs with enough information and documentation, including samples, if necessary, to permit Customs to determine whether the articles come within the order. The formal request may be preceded by and/or followed by discussions with the IPR Branch. While confidential treatment may be requested for any submissions made, the ruling itself is ordinarily public.

Judicial review of Customs' preimportation rulings is by way of civil action in the Court of International Trade. However, the jurisdictional basis for such a civil action is different from that for review of a denial of a protest. Review of preimportation rulings is provided by 28 U.S.C. § 1581(h) and, perhaps in some cases, by 28 U.S.C. § 1581(i).

Jurisdiction under 28 U.S.C. § 1581(h) is more difficult to obtain than under 28 U.S.C. § 1581(a), which govern denials of protests. This is because it must be shown that irreparable harm will occur if there is no judicial review of Customs' preimportation ruling. Showing such irreparable harm is akin to the showing that must be made by a party seeking a preliminary injunction. The appeal of an adverse decision of the Court of International Trade in a civil action contesting a preimportation ruling is to the Federal Circuit and the procedure is the same as in the case of an appeal from an adverse decision in a civil action contesting the denial of a protest.

C. Preliminary Injunctions in the Court of International Trade

During the pendency of a civil action in the Court of International Trade, a party may request the issuance of a preliminary injunction against Customs' enforcement of an exclusion order pending resolution of the merits by the Court of International Trade. This makes the most sense in civil actions seeking review of preimportation rulings under 28 U.S.C. § 1581(h), since irreparable harm must be shown to obtain jurisdiction in any event. In the case of a civil action seeking review of the denial of a protest, it may make more sense to seek expedited proceedings, at least in the alternative, obviating the need to show irreparable harm.

Preliminary injunctions in the Court of International Trade are subject to the same criteria as in United States district courts and proceedings are similar. Further, while the court may dispose of a motion for preliminary injunction on the basis of evidence that would not be admissible at trial (*e.g.*, declarations), it is not required to do so and may order an evidentiary hearing, with live direct testimony and cross-examination.

D. Enforcement of Cease and Desist Orders by the Commission

As provided in Section 337(f)(2), the Commission itself enforces its cease and desist orders and consent orders (which are a kind of cease and desist order, *i.e.*, a consent order to cease and desist).[49] To enforce these orders, the Commission may conduct either an informal or a formal enforcement proceeding to determine whether a violation of the order has occurred and what action to take (replacement of cease and desist order or consent order with an exclusion order and/or assessment of a civil penalty).

Informal enforcement proceedings may be conducted by the Commission through the Office of Unfair Import Investigations with respect to any act or omission by anyone in possible violation of a Commission remedial order. Commission Rule 210.75 (a). Informal proceedings may consist of correspondence or conferences with the persons concerned. *Id.*

Formal enforcement proceedings, ostensibly covered by Commission Rule 210.75(b), are in practice conducted in a manner similar to an original investigation and, like an original investigation, may be instituted on the Commission's own motion or as a result of a complaint. If a formal enforcement proceeding is instituted, the complaint will be served on the alleged violator and a notice of institution will be published in the *Federal Register.* Commission Rule 210.75(b). The respondent has 15 days after service to respond to the complaint. *Id.* Commission Rule 210.75(b) does not require any specific type of formal enforcement

49 The Commission's enforcement rule, Commission Rule 210.75, refers anomalously to proceedings to enforce exclusion orders, as well as cease and desist orders and consent orders. Indeed, there are several portions of that rule which the Commission does not apply in practice. This section is limited to the actual practice of the Commission.

proceeding, and though referring to the possibility of a hearing, states that such a hearing will not be subject to the adjudicative provisions of the Administrative Procedure Act, which apply to original investigations. However, Commission Rule 210.75(b)(3) does provide for the possibility of referring the matter to an administrative law judge for the issuance of an initial determination which would be subject to Commission review and would become the final determination of the Commission if not reviewed within 90 days after service. The Commission has usually opted for this procedure, which is very similar to the procedure followed in original investigations, including opportunity for discovery.

If the enforcement proceeding results in a finding that the Commission's remedial order has been violated, it may modify that order, replace a cease and desist order or a consent order with an exclusion order, and/or assess a civil penalty. As provided in Section 337(f)(2), the penalty assessed may be "not more than the greater of $100,000 or twice the domestic value of the articles entered or sold" for each day the order is violated. That the Commission itself may assess civil penalties for violation of a cease and desist order or a consent order was confirmed by the United States Court of Appeals for the Federal Circuit in *San Huan New Materials High Tech, Inc. v. International Trade Commission*, 161 F.3d 1347 (Fed. Cir. 1998). Commission decisions in enforcement proceedings, at least where they result in the assessment of a civil penalty, are appealable to the United States Court of Appeals, as in *San Huan*. Under Section 337(f)(2) the Commission may seek the assistance of the United States district courts to collect the penalty assessed. Under that same provision, the Federal district courts "may issue mandatory injunctions incorporating the relief sought by the Commission as they deem appropriate in the enforcement of such final orders of the Commission [cease and desist orders and consent orders]."

XXVIII. MANDATORY STAY OF PARALLEL DISTRICT COURT PROCEEDINGS (28 U.S.C. § 1659)

A respondent may find that in addition to facing a Section 337 proceeding, it is also facing a parallel proceeding in a United States district court. For example, a complainant may not only bring a patent infringement proceeding at the Commission, it may also bring a patent infringement action in a United States district court, forcing a respondent to "fight on two fronts." The possibility of such parallel proceedings was a major reason that a GATT Panel found Section 337 to violate the national treatment provisions of the GATT, since domestic articles would not be subject to parallel Commission and district court proceedings. In subsequently amending Section 337 in the URAA, the Congress decided not to eliminate parallel proceedings, but to give precedence to the Commission proceeding by providing for a mandatory stay of the district court action for the duration of the Commission investigation and also providing for the possible use of the Commission record in the district court action after the conclusion of the Commission proceeding.

A. Mandatory Stay Generally

The mandatory stay provision is found at 28 U.S.C. § 1659. It applies to civil actions "involving parties that are also parties to a proceeding before the United States International Trade Commission under Section 337 of the Tariff Act of 1930." The archetypal such civil action would be a patent infringement action. However, the language is broad enough to encompass a declaratory judgment action, including an action based on counterclaims which have been raised and removed pursuant to Section 337(c).

B. Who May Request Mandatory Stay

Only a party to the civil action who is also a respondent in the proceeding before the Commission may request the mandatory stay.

C. Time for Requesting Mandatory Stay

The eligible party in the district court action must request the mandatory stay within:

(1) 30 days after the party is named as a respondent in the proceeding before the Commission, or

(2) 30 days after the district court action "is filed,"

whichever is later.

D. Matters Subject to Mandatory Stay

The mandatory stay covers district court proceedings "with respect to any claim that involves the same issues involved in the proceeding before the Commission."

In patent cases, this provision has generally been interpreted to apply only to the extent that the same patents are alleged to be infringed. As a result, complainants have sometimes alleged infringement of different or at least some additional patents in the district court proceeding, even if the same accused articles are involved, so that they may continue to force the respondent to fight on two fronts. Whether Congress intended or could be deemed to have intended such a result is unclear and the matter has yet to be definitively resolved. District courts may use their discretionary authority to stay proceedings with respect to all patents before them.

E. Duration of Mandatory Stay

The mandatory stay provided by 28 U.S.C. § 1659(a) is in effect "until the determination of the Commission becomes final." Thus, it is clear that it will remain in effect at least until the Commission issues its final determination. For affirmative cases, the stay will probably be in effect until the end of the Presidential review period. It is unclear whether the stay would automatically continue if an appeal were taken from the Commission's final determination.

F. Use of Commission Record in District Court After Stay

After dissolution of the mandatory stay, 28 U.S.C. § 1659(b) provides for transmission of the Commission record to the district court and that it "shall be admissible" in the district court action "to the extent permitted under the Federal Rules of Evidence and the Federal Rules of Civil Procedure."

It is unclear how and to what extent the Commission record will be admitted, if it is admitted at all, since the Commission is not bound by the Federal Rules of Civil Procedure or the Federal Rules of Evidence. Indeed, the Commission is permitted to and does receive hearsay evidence, providing it meets the standard for evidence under the Administrative Procedure Act.

G. Stay or Injunction of Commission Proceedings

While it is possible to obtain a stay of parallel district court proceedings, most courts have been reluctant to stay or enjoin Commission proceedings in favor of district court proceedings. However, where a pre-existing agreement, *e.g.*, a licensing agreement, precludes a private party from commencing Commission proceedings in favor of court proceedings or arbitration, such agreements may be enforced, at least to the extent of prohibiting the private party in violation of the agreement from proceeding against the other party to the agreement in a Commission investigation instituted on its complaint. *See Texas Instruments, Inc. v. Tessera, Inc.*, 231 F.3d 1325 (Fed. Cir. 2000).

XXIX. EFFECT OF COMMISSION DETERMINATIONS ON DISTRICT COURT PROCEEDINGS

A. No Issue Preclusion Effect Given to Commission Determinations

A determination of the Commission on patent issues, even if affirmed by the Federal Circuit is not given preclusive effect. *Texas Instruments, Inc.* v. *Cypress Semiconductor Corp.*, 90 F.3d 1558, 1568-1570 (Fed. Cir. 1996). While decisions of administrative agencies such as the Commission when acting in a judicial capacity (as the Commission does in Section 337 cases) may be given preclusive effect, they will not be given preclusive effect when Congress, either expressly or implicitly, has indicated they should not. *Id.* In the case of Section 337, the Federal Circuit found that when Congress passed the Trade Reform Act of 1974, allowing respondents in Section 337 proceedings to plead, and the Commission to consider, all legal and equitable defenses, including patent invalidity and unenforceability, the legislative history indicated that Congress did not intend Commission Section 337 determinations on patent issues to have preclusive effect:

> In patent-based cases, the Commission considers, for its own purposes under Section 337, the status of imports with respect to the claims of U.S. patents. The Commission's findings neither purport to be, nor can they be, regarded as binding interpretation of the U.S. patent laws in particular factual contexts. Therefore, it seems clear that any disposition of a Commission action by a Federal Court should not have res judicata or collateral estoppel effect in cases before such courts.

S. Rep. No. 1298, 93rd Cong., 2d Sess. 196 (1974), reprinted in 1974 U.S.C.C.A.N. 7186, 7329.

The court noted that it had consistently held that Congress did not intend decisions of the Commission on patent issues to have preclusive effect. *Id.*[50] The court also stated that neither the subsequent amendments to Section 337 nor the creation of the Federal Circuit evidenced a contrary Congressional intent. *Id.*[51] The absence of preclusive effect for Commission determinations does not mean that district courts are free to ignore decisions of the Federal Circuit reviewing Commission determinations, since published decisions of the Federal Circuit create precedent which the district courts and even subsequent panels of the Federal Circuit are bound to follow. However, as to the same claim raised in the Commission proceeding, accused infringers can raise whatever defenses they believe are justified, regardless of whether they had previously raised them at the Commission and lost. *Id.* The district court can, however, give the Commission's determination persuasive value. *Id.* On appeal, the Federal Circuit is free to "thoroughly review" the district court's decision. *Id.* The court further stated: "[a]s a court we are bound to follow our own precedents, and, to the extent we have previously ruled on a matter, a subsequent panel will have powerful incentives not to deviate from that prior holding, short of thoroughly justified grounds." *Id.*

B. No Claim Preclusion Effect Given to Commission Determinations

The Federal Circuit has held that, at least in patent cases, a determination of the Commission does not result in claim preclusion in a subsequent proceeding for patent infringement in a district court. *Bio-Technology General Corp., v. Genentech, Inc.*, 80 F.3d 1553, 1563-1564 (Fed. Cir. 1996). The basis for the

---

50 The court cited *Tandon Corp.* v. *United States International Trade Commission*, 831 F.2d 1017, 1019 (Fed. Cir. 1987), *Texas Instruments, Inc.* v. *United States International Trade Commission*, 851 F.2d 342, 344 (Fed. Cir. 1988), and *Corning Glass Works* v. *United States International Trade Commission*, 799 F.2d 1559, 1570 n. 12 (Fed. Cir. 1986).

51 In a footnote the court stated that allowing prior Commission decisions on patent infringement questions to have preclusive effect "would potentially deprive the parties of their Seventh Amendment right to a jury trial on the issue of infringement." *Texas Instruments*, 90 F.3d at 1569 n. 10. However, the court also noted authority that application of collateral estoppel to a legal action based on an equitable determination does not violate the Seventh Amendment right to a jury trial. *Id.*

court's holding was that claim preclusion would not be applied "if the initial forum did not have the power to award the full measure of relief sought in the later litigation." *Id.*, citing *Davidson v. Capuano*, 792 F.2d 275, 278 (2d Cir. 1986). As the court pointed out, the Commission, the initial forum in *BTG*, cannot award damages.

The court also pointed to the legislative history of the Trade Reform Act of 1974 as supporting its view that "ITC decisions with respect to patent issues should have no claim preclusive effect in later district court litigation." The court noted that in a previous case the Commission had taken the position that its decisions have no res judicata effect in district court litigation. *Id.*, citing *Corning Glass Works v. United States International Trade Commission*, 799 F.2d 1559, 1570, n.12. The court concluded that "in view of jurisdictional limitations on the relief available in the ITC, we hold that the ITC's prior decision cannot have claim preclusive effect in the district court." *Id.*, citing *Texas Instruments, Inc. v. United States International Trade Commission*, 851 F.2d 342, 344 (Fed. Cir. 1988).

C. Non-Patent Cases

The legislative history and the Federal Circuit cases discussed above are specific to patent cases. There have been cases where non-patent determinations of the Commission have been awarded preclusive effect. For example, in *Baltimore Luggage Company v. Samsonite Corporation*, 727 F. Supp. 202 (D. Md. 1989), the district court granted Samsonite's motion for summary judgment that Baltimore Luggage's assertions of antitrust violations and unfair competition were barred by res judicata because in a prior Commission investigation, Baltimore Luggage raised these issues as affirmative defenses and lost. The Commission, appearing as amicus curiae, opposed Samsonite's motion. The court found the relevant legislative history limited to patent cases, noting that the district courts have exclusive jurisdiction over those cases, but not trademark cases. The court relied on the decision in *Union Mfg. Co., Inc.*, v. *Han Baek Trading Co.*, 763 F.2d 42 (2d Cir. 1985). The court also rejected the argument that the Commission's determination on these defenses had been vacated by the Federal Circuit and thus deprived of preclusive effect. Rather, the court stated that Baltimore Luggage had failed to raise the Commission's determination on these defenses when it intervened in Samsonite's appeal and therefore the Commission's determination as to them was never before the Federal Circuit to be vacated.

D. Preclusive Effect of District Court Judgments

A judgment of a district court will have a preclusive effect on a subsequent Commission proceeding, barring any claim before the Commission which would be barred in a second infringement action in a district court. *See The Young Engineers, Inc. v. U.S. International Trade Commission*, 721 F.2d 1305, 1313-1317

(Fed. Cir. 1983). Such claim preclusion does not bar every charge of infringement based on the asserted patent, only conduct of the same nature as that involved in the prior litigation. *Id.*

XXX. A NOTE ON SECTION 337 AND THE GATT

Section 337 has been attacked three times as being inconsistent with provisions of the General Agreement on Tariff and Trade (GATT).

In the *Automotive Spring Assemblies* case BISD 305/107, the panel designated by the Contracting Parties first examined the consistency of the specific exclusion order issued by the Commission in one of its investigations, concluded that it fell within Article XX(d) of the GATT, and then gave a mixed and less than definitive decision on the compliance of Section 337 itself with the GATT.

In the second case, referred to as the *Aramid Fibers* case, BISD 365/345, the European Community successfully attacked Section 337 as it existed in 1986 as violative of Article III(4) of the GATT and only justified by Article XX(d) of the GATT in certain instances. The panel assigned to the case issued its final report in 1988 and it was adopted by the GATT Council in 1989. The United States eventually amended Section 337 in 1994, as part of the Uruguay Round Agreements Act, ostensibly to comply with the GATT Panel Report.

In January 2000, the European Union requested consultations under the provisions of the Dispute Settlement Agreement of the World Trade Organization, stating that the URAA amendments to Section 337 had not eliminated Section 337's inconsistency with Article III(4) of the GATT and stating further that Section 337 was in violation of the Agreement on Trade-Related Aspects of Intellectual Property Rights (TRIPS). The requested consultations have been held, but the European Union has never requested that a panel be constituted to address its allegations.

CUSTOMS SERVICE ENFORCEMENT AGAINST GOODS THAT INFRINGE OR COUNTERFEIT A TRADEMARK, TRADE NAME, OR COPYRIGHT

XXXI. STATUTORY AUTHORITY FOR ENFORCEMENT AGAINST IMPORTED GOODS THAT INFRINGE OR COUNTERFEIT A TRADEMARK, TRADE NAME, OR COPYRIGHT

A. Trademark and Trade Name Provisions

Titles 15 and 19 of the United States Code include provisions that prohibit the importation into the U.S. of merchandise and/or containers that infringe a United States-registered trademark or a domestic or foreign trade name or provide a counterfeit of a registered trademark. The statutes provide for Customs Service enforcement, which can take the form of exclusion of infringing merchandise or seizure and possible forfeiture of infringing and counterfeit goods, as well as the assessment of civil penalties against parties involved in the importation or attempted importation of the proscribed goods.

Section 42 of the Lanham Act, codified at 15 U.S.C. § 1124, requires imported merchandise that copies or simulates a trademark registered in the United States or the name of a domestic foreign manufacture, manufacturer or trader to be denied entry into the U.S. Imports bearing the name of a foreign manufacture, manufacturer or trader may similarly be excluded, as long as the foreign country involved "by treaty, convention, or law affords similar privileges to citizens of the United States." The statute also prohibits entry to imported merchandise that "bear[s] a mark or name calculated to induce the public to believe that the article is manufactured in the United States, or that it is manufactured in any foreign country or locality other than the country or locality in which it is in fact manufactured."

To facilitate these prohibitions, the statute authorizes domestic and foreign parties to record their names, trademarks, and places where their goods are manufactured with the Treasury Department, the cabinet department that oversees the Customs Service. The Treasury Department is directed to disseminate this information to Customs Service officers, who enforce the exclusion requirement. In practice, the Treasury Department has delegated its statutory responsibility to the Customs Service.

A trademark owner or other party whose intellectual property is protected under the statute may seek to compel the Customs Service to enforce the statute through a Federal district court action. *Lever Bros. Co. v. United States*, 877 F.2d 101 (D.C. Cir. 1989); *see Montres Rolex, S.A. v. Snyder,* 718 F.2d 524, 527-28 (2d Cir. 1983), *cert. denied*, 465 U.S. 1100 (1984). The statute also gives rise to a private right of action allowing the intellectual property owner to proceed directly against the alleged infringing party. *E.g., Societe des Produits Nestle, S.A. v. Casa Helvetia Inc.*, 982 F.2d 633 (1st Cir. 1992).

Sections 43(b) and 43(a)(1) of the Lanham Act, 15 U.S.C. §§ 1125(b) and 1125(a)(1), require the exclusion from entry of any goods or container therefor that is marked or labeled to contain:

> any word, term, name, symbol, or device, or any combination thereof, or any false designation of origin, false or misleading description of fact, or false or misleading representation of fact, which—
>
> (A) is likely to cause confusion, or to cause mistake, or to deceive as to the affiliation, connection, or association of such person with another person, or as to the origin,

> sponsorship, or approval of his or her goods, services, or commercial activities by another person. . . .

Section 43(a)(1) also permits a district court action by a person alleging damage from another party's use of such false or misleading labels or containers.

In addition to the seizure authority set forth in the preceding provisions, the Customs Service may seize and forfeit goods that violate Sections 1124 and 1125 pursuant to 19 U.S.C. § 1595a(c)(2)(C). 19 U.S.C. § 1595a(b) also authorizes imposition of a penalty against the importer and other parties involved in the transaction:

> Every person who directs, assists financially or otherwise, or is in any way concerned in any unlawful activity mentioned in the preceding subsection shall be liable to a penalty equal to the value of the article or articles introduced or attempted to be introduced.

19 U.S.C. § 1526(a) prohibits the importation of "merchandise of foreign manufacture"or a "label, sign, print, package, wrapper, or receptacle" for such merchandise that bears a registered trademark that is owned by a United States citizen or a corporation or association organized under the laws of the U.S. Such goods are subject to seizure and forfeiture under 19 U.S.C. § 1526(b), as long as the trademark has been recorded with the Treasury Department. The statutory prohibition excludes merchandise for which the trademark owner has given written consent for importation, 19 U.S.C. § 1526(a), and small quantities of merchandise accompanying travelers for their personal use, 19 U.S.C. § 1526(d).

Section 1526(a) does not require that the imported merchandise be infringing; to the contrary, it covers genuine trademarked merchandise produced abroad, and to that extent is broader in coverage than 15 U.S.C. §§ 1124 and 1125. On the other hand, the statute's reach extends only to registered trademarks; unlike 15 U.S.C. § 1124, it does not cover trade names. Section 1526(a) also does not apply when the domestic and foreign trademark owners are the same parties or are related to each other or to a common owner, or when one owner controls the other or both are subject to control by another party. *K Mart Corp. v. Cartier, Inc.*, 486 U.S. 281 (1988).

19 U.S.C. § 1526(e) prohibits the importation of merchandise bearing a counterfeit trademark, and directs that such merchandise must be seized and forfeited. Thereafter, the goods must either be destroyed or, with the trademark owner's permission, have the counterfeit mark removed, following which they may be donated to a charitable organization, used by the federal government, or sold at public auction. Certification marks are covered by this provision, as well as trademarks. *United States v. 4500 Audek Model No. 5601 AM/FM Clock Radios*, 220 F.3d 539 (7th Cir. 2000). In addition to forfeiture of the goods, the statute provides that persons involved in the importation or attempted importation of counterfeit goods are subject to a civil fine. 19 U.S.C. § 1526(f).

The statute also establishes a private right of action for damages and injunctive relief. 19 U.S.C. § 1526(c).

Although the statutes permit, and in the case of counterfeits require, that proscribed goods be seized, the Customs Service is also authorized to remit a seizure. The agency has been granted general remission authority in 19 U.S.C. § 1618, and 19 U.S.C. § 1595a(c)(5)(A) specifies that this authority is applicable to seizures made under 19 U.S.C. § 1595a(c)(2)(C). 19 U.S.C. § 1595a(c)(5)(A) also authorizes the Customs Service to permit the exportation of merchandise that was seized under 19 U.S.C. § 1595a(c)(2)(C).

B. Copyright Provisions

17 U.S.C. § 602(a) prohibits the importation of copies or phonorecords obtained outside the U.S. unless authorized by the owner of a copyright on those works. The prohibition does not apply imports for use by the Federal government or a state or local government, unless the work is for use in schools or is an audiovisual work imported for purposes other than archival use. It also excludes works imported for the private use of the importer (limited to one copy or phonorecord at any one time) or as part of an arriving traveler's personal baggage. In addition, it excludes one copy of an audiovisual work and up to five copies or phonorecords of any other work imported by or for an organization operated for scholarly, educational, or religious purposes and not for private gain. *Id.*

17 U.S.C. § 602(a) directs the Treasury Department to adopt regulations to enforce Section 602. The statute provides that such regulations

> may require, as a condition for the exclusion of articles under Section 602—
>
> (1) that the person seeking exclusion obtain a court order enjoining importation of the articles; or
>
> (2) that the person seeking exclusion furnish proof, of a specified nature and in accordance with prescribed procedures, that the copyright in which such person claims an interest is valid and that the importation would violate the prohibition in Section 602; the person seeking exclusion may also be required to post a surety bond for any injury that may result if the detention or exclusion of the articles proves to be unjustified.

17 U.S.C. § 602(b). The statute permits seizure and forfeiture of articles imported in violation of these prohibitions, and appears to require destruction of forfeited articles. 17 U.S.C. § 602(c).

Seizure and forfeiture of copies or phonorecords "manufactured, reproduced, distributed, sold, or otherwise used, intended for use, or possessed with intent to use in violation of" 17 U.S.C. § 506(a) (which provides criminal sanctions for willful copyright infringement) is authorized under 17 U.S.C. § 509. This section also permits seizure and forfeiture of "all plates, molds, matrices, masters, tapes, film negatives, or other articles by means of which such copies or phonorecords may be reproduced, and all electronic, mechanical, or other devices for manufacturing, reproducing, or assembling such copies or phonorecords." 17 U.S.C. § 509(a). Section 509 specifies that seizures effected under it are governed by the procedures established under general provisions of the customs laws relating to seizures and forfeitures and their remission. 17 U.S.C. § 509(b).

XXXII. THE CUSTOMS SERVICE REGULATIONS

The Customs Service is a service of the Treasury Department. 31 U.S.C. § 308. It has the primary enforcement role in excluding prohibited imports from entry into the United States. The Customs Service's regulations implement the statutory provisions concerning exclusion of articles with infringing or counterfeit trademarks, trade names, or copyrights. Specifically, they provide procedures for trademark and trade name registration, treatment of potentially infringing or counterfeit goods, and importers' options in the event their merchandise is prevented from entering the U.S.

A. Recordation of Trademarks

A trademark owner seeking protection against infringing imports may apply to record its trademark with the Customs Service. Recordation is a condition precedent for Customs Service enforcement against articles bearing copying or simulating trademarks, as well as against gray market imports. 19 C.F.R. §§ 133.22(a), 133.23(a); *see Weil Ceramics & Glass, Inc. v. Dash*, 618 F. Supp. 700 (D.N.J. 1985), *rev'd on other grounds*, 878 F.2d 659 (3d Cir. 1989) (registration required for gray market protection) and *Customs Headquarters Rulings 451754* (Nov. 13, 1991) (recordation a prerequisite for seizure of goods bearing confusingly similar marks) and *731605* (Nov. 15, 1988) (recordation's expiration removes restrictions on infringing imports).

On the other hand, recordation is not required for the agency to proceed against merchandise bearing a counterfeit trademark. 19 C.F.R. § 133.21(a), (b); *Customs Headquarters Ruling 451754* (Nov. 13, 1991). Nevertheless, even those trademark owners that are concerned solely with counterfeit imports should consider recording their marks with the Customs Service, as doing so will place the trademark in a national database that makes it more readily accessible to Customs inspectors.

Recordation is limited to marks that have current registrations with the Patent and Trademark Office. 19 C.F.R.§ 133.1(a).[52] A foreign trademark that has not been registered in the U.S. is ineligible for Customs Service protection. *Customs Headquarters Ruling 460963* (March 11, 1996).

Applications to record trademarks must be in writing, and provide the following information:

- The name, complete business address, and citizenship of the trademark owner or owners (if a partnership, the citizenship of each partner; if an association or

52 Section 133.1(a) provides:

> (a) Eligible trademarks. Trademarks registered by the U.S. Patent and Trademark Office under the Trademark Act of March 3, 1881, the Trademark Act of February 20, 1905, or the Trademark Act of 1946 (15 U.S.C. § 1051 *et seq.*) except those registered on the supplemental register under the 1946 Act (15 U.S.C. § 1096), may be recorded with the U.S. Customs Service if the registration is current.

corporation the State, country, or other political jurisdiction within which it was organized, incorporated, or created);

- The places of manufacture of goods bearing the recorded trademark;
- The name and principal business address of each foreign person or business entity authorized or licensed to use the trademark and a statement as to the use authorized; and
- The identity of any parent or subsidiary company or other foreign company under common ownership or control which uses the trademark abroad. For this purpose:

  (1) Common ownership means individual or aggregate ownership of more than 50 percent of the business entity; and

  (2) Common control means effective control in policy and operations and is not necessarily synonymous with common ownership.

19 C.F.R. § 133.2(a)-(d). The reason for the inquiry regarding the trademark owner's "common ownership and control" with a foreign company using the trademark is to limit protection to trademarks with different foreign and domestic owners. The Customs Service's longstanding interpretation of 19 U.S.C. § 1526(a) is that its prohibitions are inapplicable when the domestic and foreign trademarks are owned and/or controlled by the same or related companies. *See* 19 C.F.R. § 133.23(a) and *K Mart Corp. v. Cartier, Inc.*, 486 U.S. 281, 285 (1988) (discussing predecessor to Section 133.23(a)). Except in "*Lever Brothers*" circumstances discussed below, the Customs Service will not provide protection when the domestic and foreign trademarks have common ownership or control. 19 C.F.R. § 133.23.

1. Additional Requirement for "Lever Rule" Recordations

The regulation includes an additional requirement for U.S. trademark owners that have common ownership and control with the foreign trademark owner and wish to apply for protection against imported goods that have material physical differences from merchandise bearing the same trademark in the United States.

> Lever-rule protection. For owners of U.S. trademarks who desire protection against gray market articles on the basis of physical and material differences (see Lever Bros. Co. v. United States, 981 F.2d 1330 (D.C. Cir. 1993)), a description of any physical and material difference between the specific articles authorized for importation or sale in the United States and those not so authorized. In each instance, owners who assert that physical and material differences exist must state the basis for such a claim with particularity, and must support such assertions by competent evidence and provide summaries of physical and material differences for publication. Customs determination of physical and material differences may include, but is not limited to, considerations of:
>
> (1) The specific composition of both the authorized and gray market product(s) (including chemical composition);
>
> (2) Formulation, product construction, structure, or composite product components, of both the authorized and gray market product;

> (3) Performance and/or operational characteristics of both the authorized and gray market product;
>
> (4) Differences resulting from legal or regulatory requirements, certification, etc.;
>
> (5) Other distinguishing and explicitly defined factors that would likely result in consumer deception or confusion as proscribed under applicable law.

19 C.F.R. § 133.2(e). This regulation was adopted in response to the appellate decisions in *Lever Bros. Co. v. United States*, 877 F.2d 101 (D.C. Cir. 1989) and 981 F.2d 1330 (D.C. Cir. 1993). The court concluded that common ownership of domestic and foreign trademarks did not bar exclusion of certain unauthorized imports pursuant to 15 U.S.C. § 1124: "Section 42 of the Lanham Act precludes the application of Customs' affiliate exception with respect to physically, materially different goods." 981 F.2d at 1338.

An applicant seeking protection under this provision would be well-advised to provide painstaking documentation of the differences between the imported and domestic trademarked products. The factors set forth in the regulation are broad enough to encompass a vast array of product differences, and the fifth factor, 19 C.F.R. § 133.2(e)(5), is a catch-all that permits applicants to identify additional differences that they consider to be important.

The *Federal Register* notices proposing and adopting the rules makes it clear that an application for "*Lever Brothers*" protection must be well-documented, and should address at least some of the characteristics set forth in the regulation

> In each case, any proffered characteristic must be supported by competent evidence. Customs recognizes that it cannot anticipate all of the considerations that may lead to a finding of "physical and material difference," but Lever suggests certain categories of information which are appropriate. The last criterion above leaves open the possibility that unspecified information may be considered at Customs' discretion.
>
> Owners claiming gray market protection under the proposed provision should be aware that Customs will require the grounds for claiming physical and material differences to be stated with particularity. Any such request lacking in specificity will be rejected.

Gray Market Imports and Other Trademarked Goods; Proposed Rule, 63 Fed. Reg. 14662, 14664 (March 26, 1998). The specified factors are "a starting point for determining if protection is warranted." *Gray Market Imports and Other Trademarked Goods; Final Rule*, 64 Fed. Reg. 9058, 9060 (Feb. 24, 1999). The Customs Service "will consider other characteristics that can be described with particularity and that would likely result in consumer deception or confusion under the law. The bases explicitly enumerated for granting Lever-rule protection are not all inclusive." *Id.*

To the extent possible, the application should identify the asserted differences on a detailed product-specific basis, *e.g.*, by reference to catalog or stock number. A well-documented application will help to avoid a Customs Service finding that the application was too general to support a finding of differences between specific products, and will also serve to bolster the applicant's case in court in the event the agency either denies the application or allows it to languish without a decision. Also, if "*Lever Brothers*" protection is granted, a detailed product-specific identification of the goods covered will assist Customs inspectors in identifying infringing goods.

2. Additional Documents

The trademark or trade name recordation application "shall be accompanied by" the following additional documents:

- A status copy of the certificate of registration certified by the U.S. Patent and Trademark Office showing title to be presently in the name of the applicant; and
- Five copies of the certificate, or of a U.S. Patent and Trademark Office facsimile. The copies may be reproduced privately and shall be on paper approximately 8 x 10-1/2 inches in size. If the certificate consists of two or more pages, the copies may be reproduced on both sides of the paper.

19 C.F.R. § 133.3(a). The application must also be accompanied by a check or money order, payable to "United States Customs Service," in the amount of $190.00 for each trademark to be recorded, and $190.00 for each additional class of goods for which the mark will be recorded. 19 C.F.R. § 133.3(a). The application must be sent to the Intellectual Property Rights Branch, U.S. Customs Service, 1300 Pennsylvania Avenue, NW., Washington, DC 20229. Business proprietary information submitted with the application to record will be exempt from public disclosure, but "the trademark owner must submit a summary of the physical and material differences, which need not disclose proprietary information." 64 Fed. Reg. at 9061.

The Customs Service will publish in the *Federal Register* notice of any requests it receives for trademark recordation, "giving interested parties an opportunity to comment on the request for protection, before making a final determination in the matter." 19 C.F.R. § 133.2(f); 64 Fed. Reg. at 9059. Once protection has been granted, attempted imports of unauthorized physically and materially different goods will be detained, so that "the burden is on the importer to show either that the goods are identical and Lever-rule protection should not apply, or that an exception is applicable." *Id.* at 9061. The agency will also notify the applicant upon approval or denial of the recordation request, 19 C.F.R. § 133.1(b), and will publish *Federal Register* notice when it approves a trademark's recordation. The Customs Service is under no time limit to evaluate the application and render a decision approving or denying it.

3. Length of Recordation and Renewal

The regulation provides that the recordation remains in force for the duration of the twenty year PTO registration period or renewal period. Note that the trademark law provides that a trademark remains in force for a ten year period, subject to renewal or cancellation, 15 U.S.C. § 1058(a). Nevertheless, this unexplained inconsistency in the regulations should have no practical effect, as long as the trademark owner renews its recordation with the Customs Service within the prescribed period following PTO renewal, as discussed below. The Customs Service will cancel a recordation upon final cancellation or revocation of the trademark before the PTO. 19 C.F.R. § 133.4(b),(c).

The recordation may be renewed by an application submitted no later than three months after the current PTO registration expires. The renewal application must include a status copy of the certificate of registration, certified by the PTO, that shows renewal of the trademark and title to be in the name of the applicant, along with a "statement describing any change of ownership or in the name of owner, in compliance with Secs. 133.5 and 133.6 of this part, and any change of addresses of owners or places of manufacture." 19 C.F.R. § 133.7(a)(1),(2). The renewal application must be accompanied by an $80.00 check or money order, payable to the United States Customs Service, for each class (if coverage for more than one is sought). 19 C.F.R. § 133.7(a)(3).

During the three-month post-expiration period, a trademark owner faced with "unavoidable delay[]" in filing its application may request an extension of the submission deadline. Although the regulation is unclear on this point, it appears to permit an extended period for submitting the application altogether, as well as for submitting any individual piece(s) of the renewal application that are unavailable when an otherwise timely application is submitted. The request for an extension should "set forth the circumstances due to which application is delayed." If the Customs Service is persuaded, it may grant the applicant a "reasonable extended period" within which to complete the renewal application process. 19 C.F.R. § 133.7(b).

A trademark owner that fails to submit the renewal application or request for extension within the designated three-month period is no longer eligible for the renewal process and must apply for recordation all over again. 19 C.F.R. § 133.7(c). Considering that essentially the same information must be submitted in both an initial and renewal application, this may not at first blush appear to be more than a minor inconvenience costing $110.00 more per trademark or class. However, implicit in the regulation is that the original recordation will lapse, and the Customs Service will not afford trademark protection during the period between the recordation's expiry and the new application's approval. 19 C.F.R. § 133.7(a) provides that "[t]o continue uninterrupted Customs protection for trademarks, the trademark owner shall submit a written application to renew" in a timely manner, indicating that protection will be interrupted if timely application to renew is not made. *See also Customs Headquarters Ruling 731605* (Nov. 15, 1988).

The Customs Service must be informed in the event there is a change in a recorded trademark's ownership for the mark to continue receiving protection; the new owner's failure to do so may compromise its ability to receive the benefits of recordation. The new owner is required to apply for continuation of the recordation by submitting an application containing all of the information required by Section 133.2 and setting forth any time limit on the rights of ownership that were transferred. In addition, the new owner must submit "a status copy of the certificate of registration certified by the U.S. Patent and Trademark Office showing title to be presently in the name of the new owner," and pay an $80.00 fee to United States Customs Service to cover all previously-recorded trademarks encompassed by the new owner's application. 19 C.F.R. § 133.5.

Similarly, the Customs Service must be informed if there is a change in the trademark owner's name, even in the absence of a change of the mark's ownership. The notice must include "a status copy of the certificate of registration certified by the U.S. Patent and Trademark Office showing title to be presently in the name as changed," along with an $80.00 check or money order payable to the United States Customs Service.

B. Recordation of Trade Names

The Customs regulations also provide the standards and procedures for recordation of a trade name; such recordation is a prerequisite to Customs Service enforcement against potentially infringing imports. The recording process is quite similar to that in place for trademarks.

First, the regulations specify substantive restrictions on names that may be recorded. "The name or trade style" must have been "used for at least 6 months to identify a manufacturer or trader" before it is acceptable for recordation. The Customs Service will not record as trade names "[w]ords or designs used as trademarks," regardless of whether they are registered with the PTO. Also, the Customs Service will record the complete business name, "unless convincing proof establishes that only a part of the complete name is customarily used." 19 C.F.R. § 133.11. As noted below, the application must include a statement demonstrating compliance with the first two requirements.

The application must be in writing and addressed to: Intellectual Property Rights Branch, U.S. Customs Service, 1300 Pennsylvania Avenue, NW., Washington, DC 20229. It must include the following information:

- The name, complete business address, and citizenship of the trade name owner or owners (if a partnership, the citizenship of each partner; if an association or corporation, the State, country, or other political jurisdiction within which it was organized, incorporated or created).
- The name or trade style to be recorded.
- The name and principal business address of each foreign person or business entity authorized or licensed to use the trade name, and a statement as to the authorized use.
- The identity of any parent or subsidiary company, or other foreign company under common ownership or control which uses the trade name abroad, as defined in 19 C.F.R. § 133.2(d).

- A description of the merchandise with which the trade name is associated.
- An accompanying statement of the owner, partners, or principal corporate officer, as well as statements by at least two other persons not associated with or related to the applicant but having actual knowledge of the facts, stating that to the person's best knowledge and belief:

  (1) The applicant has used the trade name in connection with the class or kind of merchandise described in the application for at least six (6) months;

  (2) The trade name is not identical or confusingly similar to any other trade name or registered trademark used in connection with such class or kind of merchandise; and

  (3) The applicant has the sole and exclusive right to the use of such trade name in connection with the merchandise of that class or kind.

19 C.F.R. §§ 133.12, 133.13(a). The application fee is $190.00 per trade name; a check or money order for this amount, payable to "United States Customs Service," must accompany the application. 19 C.F.R. § 133.13(b).

Following receipt of the application, the Customs Service will publish *Federal Register* notice of the trade name's tentative recordation, and the procedures and time period for interested parties to file their opposition. 19 C.F.R. § 133.14(a). After "consideration of any claims, rebuttals, and other relevant evidence, notice of final approval or disapproval of the application shall be published in the *Federal Register* and the Customs Bulletin." 19 C.F.R. § 133.14(b).

The Customs Service will provide protection against infringing imports for the duration of the trade name's use. The recordation shall be cancelled at the recording party's request or the agency's obtaining evidence of the name's disuse. A recording party's failure to respond to a Customs Service inquiry concerning continued use of the name is evidence of disuse, and may suffice to warrant cancellation. 19 C.F.R. § 133.15.

C. Recordation of Copyrights

The regulations permit a copyright owner to record with the Customs Service a claim to copyright that has been registered under the Copyright Act of July 30, 1947, as amended, or the Copyright Act of 1976, as amended. 19 C.F.R. § 133.31(a),(b). The eligible copyright "owner" for recordation purposes includes "any person who has acquired copyright ownership through an exclusive license, assignment, or otherwise, and claims actual or potential injury because of actual or contemplated importations of copies (or phonorecords) of eligible works." 19 C.F.R. § 133.31(b). In addition, "'[c]opyright owner,' with respect to any one of the exclusive rights comprised in a copyright, refers to the owner of that particular right." *Id.*

The application must be in writing and provide the following information:

- The name and complete address of the copyright owner or owners.
- If the applicant is a person claiming actual or potential injury by reason of actual or contemplated importations of copies or phonorecords of the eligible work, a statement setting forth the circumstances of such actual or potential injury.
- The country of manufacture of genuine copies or phonorecords of the protected work.
- The name and principal address of any foreign person or business entity authorized or licensed to use the protected work, and a statement as to the exclusive rights authorized
- The foreign title of the work, if different from the U.S. title.
- In the case of an application to record a copyright in a sound recording, a statement setting forth the name(s) of the performing artist(s), and any other identifying names appearing on the surface of reproduction of the sound recording, or its label or container.

19 C.F.R. § 133.32.

1. Additional Documents

The following documents must be submitted with the application.

- An "additional certificate" of copyright registration issued by the U.S. Copyright Office. If the name of the applicant differs from the name of the copyright owner identified in the certificate, the application shall be accompanied by a certified copy of any assignment, exclusive license, or other document recorded in the U.S. Copyright Office showing that the applicant has acquired copyright ownership in the copyright.
- Five (5) photographic or other likenesses reproduced on paper approximately 8" x 10-1/2" in size of any copyrighted work. An application shall be excepted from this requirement if it covers a work such as a book, magazine, periodical, or similar copyrighted matter readily identifiable by title and author or if it covers a sound recording. Five likenesses of a component part of a copyrighted work, together with the name or title, if any, by which the part depicted is identifiable, may accompany an application covering an entire copyrighted work.

19 C.F.R. § 133.33(a). A check for $190.00 for each copyright to be recorded, payable to the United States Customs Service, must accompany the application. 19 C.F.R. § 133.33(b). The package should be sent to: Intellectual Property Rights Branch, U.S. Customs Service, 1300 Pennsylvania Avenue, Washington, DC 20229. 19 C.F.R. § 133.32.

2. Length of Recordation and Renewal

The copyright recordation is effective, and protection against infringing imports commences, as of the date of approval. The Customs Service will notify the applicant of its disposition of the application, and, if it approves the application, will issue instructions to its own officials concerning the scope of protection afforded under the recordation. 19 C.F.R. §§ 133.31, 133.34(a). As a general rule, the recordation remains in effect for a period of twenty (20) years from the date of recordation. However, it shall cease sooner upon the expiration of the recordant's copyright ownership, the recordant's filing a request for cancellation with the Customs Service, or the final cancellation or revocation of the underlying copyright registration by the U.S. Copyright Office. 19 C.F.R. § 133.34(b),(c).

The recordant may renew the recordation beyond the twenty-year limit upon filing an application for renewal with the Customs Service. The regulations do not specify the contents of that application. A document identifying the previously-recorded copyright and the owner's name and address should suffice, although the renewal applicant should also note any changes in the information it was required to submit under 19 C.F.R. § 133.32 in the original application to record.

The renewal application must be accompanied by the following materials:

- Proof that the recordant's copyright ownership is valid. The proof required shall vary with the date that the work was first copyrighted as follows:
  - Works in which copyright subsists on or after January 1, 1978. An affidavit signed by the recordant attesting to the continued validity of the copyright, stating the date the copyright was registered with the U.S. Copyright Office, whether the author of the work is still alive and, if not, the date of his death, and any additional information that the Customs Service may require of the recordant.
  - Works under statutory copyright on December 31, 1977. If the copyright is still in its first term when recordation expires, a certificate of registration issued by the U.S. Copyright Office or, if the copyright has been renewed, a certificate of renewal registration issued by the U.S. Copyright Office.
- A statement describing any change of ownership or name of owner, in compliance with 19 C.F.R. §§ 133.35 and 133.36, and any change of address of the owner.

The renewal application must be accompanied by a check or money order made payable to "U.S. Customs Service," and shall be addressed to the Intellectual Property Rights Branch, U.S. Customs Service, 1300 Pennsylvania Avenue, Washington, DC 20229. 19 C.F.R. § 133.37(c).

The term of renewal is effective for twenty years or until the recordant's ownership interest in the copyright expires, whichever occurs sooner. The recordation may be renewed for unlimited successive terms, as long as the recordant's ownership interest remains unexpired. 19 C.F.R. § 133.37(a).

The application to renew must be submitted at least three months before expiration of the current recordation. 19 C.F.R. § 133.37(b). Failure to meet the deadline precludes renewal, meaning that the recordant must reapply to record the copyright all over again. 19 C.F.R. § 133.37(d). Implicit in this requirement is that copyright protection will lapse during any gap period between expiration of the original recordation and approval of the reapplication. There is no grace period akin to that provided for trademark recordation renewals under 19 C.F.R. § 133.7(b).

Following transfer of ownership of a recorded copyright, the new owner must apply to the Customs Service to continue the recordation. The new owner's application must include the information required under 19 C.F.R. § 133.32, *i.e.*, the new owner's name and address, a statement of any claimed actual or potential injury due to imports, the country in which genuine copies of the copyrighted work are manufactured, the name and address of any authorized or licensed users abroad and a statement of the exclusive rights authorized, the foreign title of the work, and, for a sound recording, the name of the performing artist and any other identifying names on the work or its label or container. It must also set forth any time limit on the rights of ownership transferred. 19 C.F.R. § 135.32(a)(1), (2).

The new owner must also submit with the application "[a] certified copy of any assignment, exclusive license, or other document recorded in the U.S. Copyright Office showing the applicant has acquired an ownership interest in the copyright," as well as a check or money order for $80.00, payable to the United States Customs Service. This fee covers all previously-recorded copyrights covered by the application. 19 C.F.R. § 133.35(b)(1), (2). The application should be sent to the Intellectual Property Rights Branch, U.S. Customs Service, 1300 Pennsylvania Avenue, Washington, DC 20229.

The Customs Service must be notified in the event the copyright owner's name changes. The notification should describe the change, and must be accompanied by "[a] certified copy of any document recorded in the U.S. Copyright Office showing the change in the name of the owner" as well as payment of the $80.00 fee, made in the manner described above. The fee will cover all recorded copyrights covered by the notification. 19 C.F.R. § 133.36(a), (b).

The Customs Service will notify applicants concerning the disposition of any applications to record, renew, or continue a copyright, or notifications of the owner's name change. 19 C.F.R. § 133.31(c).

XXXIII. REGULATORY ENFORCEMENT PROCEDURES

Following proper recordation of a trademark, trade name, or copyright, the Customs Service will act to prevent potentially infringing articles from entering the United States. As with the other laws enforced by the Customs Service, the enforcement scheme for intellectual property rights anticipates that the agency may inspect, detain, and either seize or return goods presented for importation. It also provides the importer and intellectual property owner with the opportunity to present their views to the agency, and authorizes judicial review of any finding of infringement and the consequent remedy applied by the agency.

The details of enforcement procedures vary in several important respects for trademarks/trade names and copyrights. However, both are rooted in the Customs entry process, a thumbnail sketch of which follows.

A. The Entry Process in General

After merchandise arrives in the United States from another country, it is held in Customs custody pending release to the importer or importer's agent. The release from Customs custody is effected by "entry" of the merchandise. The term entry refers both to the physical movement of goods and the administrative process authorizing that movement. The vast majority of entries are made "for consumption," meaning that the goods are released into the "Customs territory" of the United States for the importer to use, sell, or otherwise dispose of as it sees fit. Goods may also be entered for transportation and exportation, meaning that they are merely transiting the U.S. *en route* to a third country, or may be entered for placement in a foreign-trade zone or subzone or in a customs bonded warehouse; these latter three types of entry place restrictions on the importer's disposition of the goods within the United States.

Generally, an entry for consumption must be effected within five (5) days after the conveyance carrying merchandise arrives at a U.S. port. 19 C.F.R. §§ 141.5, 142.2(a). The importer or its agent is required to file a customs entry form describing the merchandise and providing information concerning its tariff classification. dutiable value, and country of origin. The Customs Service also requires the presentation of a commercial invoice that provides "a detailed description of the merchandise," or a pro forma invoice as a substitute, along with a packing list. 19 C.F.R. §§ 142.3, 141.86, 142.6(a). The regulations provide to importers the option of filing the entry summary before the goods arrive in the U.S. port; however, under this option the same documentation must be provided as when the entry papers are filed after arrival. 19 C.F.R. § 141.63(a).

The Customs Service has plenary authority to inspect merchandise upon its arrival in the United States, and may demand that an importer provide samples of merchandise for inspection. 19 U.S.C. § 1499(a); *see generally* 19 C.F.R. Part 151, Subpart A. Entry may not be effected unless and until the merchandise is presented for inspection upon the Customs Service's request. 19 U.S.C. § 1499(a). Following presentation of the merchandise for inspection, the agency has five days within which to make a determination of admissibility into the United States; a failure to release merchandise within that period is considered a decision to detain it. 19 U.S.C. § 1499(c)(1); 19 C.F.R. § 151.16(b). Merchandise that the agency determines is inadmissible into the United States is subject to detention, and will not be released to the importer for entry. As a general rule, if no decision concerning admissibility is made within thirty (30) days from the date of its presentation to the Customs Service for examination, the merchandise is considered to be excluded from entry. 19 U.S.C. § 1499(c)(5)(A).

The Customs Service is authorized to inspect merchandise even after entry, by requiring the importer to provide samples or examination packages. 19 C.F.R. § 151.11. If the importer fails to comply, or does so and the merchandise is thereupon found to have been ineligible for admission into the United States, the Customs Service may issue a demand for redelivery, meaning that the goods must be returned to Customs custody. *Id.*; 19 C.F.R. §§ 141.113(c), (d). The agency may also issue a demand for redelivery without having first requested a sample, if it believes that the goods should not have been released in the first place.

An importer will have obvious difficulties complying with such a post-entry demand to redeliver the merchandise to Customs custody, especially if the goods have been sold, commingled in inventory, used in manufacturing, or otherwise disposed of, or have been sold and are awaiting shipment. Failure to redeliver the merchandise may result in the assessment of liquidated damages against the importer. *Id.*; 19 C.F.R. Part 172.

Following entry of the merchandise, the Customs Service has one year in which to make a final determination regarding the admissibility, classification, and appraised value of the merchandise covered by the entry; this process is known as "liquidation" of the entry. 19 U.S.C. § 1504(a). As a general rule, if the agency fails to act within the one year period, the entry is "deemed liquidated" at the classification, rate of duty, and duty amount asserted in the entry by the importer. However, when additional information is necessary to determine the applicable duties, upon notice to the importer the liquidation period may be extended annually by the Customs Service, for up to three one-year periods. In addition, the entry's liquidation may be suspended by operation of law, for example when a court has enjoined liquidation as part of its judicial review of an antidumping determination.

After liquidation, the entry is considered "final" unless (1) within 90 days the importer files a protest challenging the factual and/or legal bases for the Customs Service's action, or (b) within one year the importer files a request for reliquidation, pursuant to 19 U.S.C. § 1520, asserting that a clerical error, mistake of fact, or other inadvertence not amounting to an error in the construction of law caused an error in the liquidation. If the latter relief is sought and denied by the Custom Service, the importer may file a protest against such denial.

Thus, an importer who wishes to challenge a Customs Service liquidation decision must file a protest within the prescribed period. If it fails to do so, the agency is barred from taking corrective action, however meritorious the importer's claim otherwise may be. Each protest must be in writing, identify the importer and the import entry concerned, and set forth a reasonably clear statement regarding the decision challenged and the importer's protest claim and the reasons therefor. 19 U.S.C. § 1514. Protests are normally decided by Customs officials at the Customs district where the protest is filed but, in appropriate cases, the importer may request that the protest be forwarded to Customs Service Headquarters for further review.

A protest may also be filed against a Customs Service decision to exclude merchandise from entry. As discussed below, such a protest provides an avenue for seeking administrative relief, and also is a necessary step for a judicial challenge to the exclusion in the U.S. Court of International Trade. 28 U.S.C. § 1581(a).

B. The Administrative Ruling Process

An importer has a clear interest in knowing whether its merchandise will be permitted to enter the United States, as well as such matters as the applicable tariff classification and dutiable value, both at the time of entry and at the time of liquidation. To provide definitive guidance on such questions, the Customs Service has established a pre-importation ruling process.

19 U.S.C. § 1625 authorizes the Customs Service to establish a program for issuing binding rulings to importers, and establishes procedural safeguards for the issuance and revocation of rulings. Because intellectual property matters within the Customs Service's authority may be the subject of rulings, both importers and intellectual property owners should be aware of the procedures and consequences for issuance of rulings.

Section 1625(a) directs that rulings must be made publicly available within ninety days of their issuance. Section 1625(b) requires the Customs Service to establish an internal appeal process for importers who are dissatisfied with their rulings, and requires expedited consideration in cases of business necessity. Section 1625(c) establishes an important procedural protection for importers that have received rulings that the Customs Service subsequently decides to modify or revoke. If a ruling to be modified or revoked has been in effect for at least 60 days, or the Customs Service plans to modify the treatment previously accorded to substantially identical transactions, notice of this intent must be published in the *Customs Bulletin*. The statute provides for a minimum 30-day comment period following publication, requires subsequent publication of the final decision, and directs that any resulting change in treatment is not effective until 60 days after such publication.

Such reliance on a ruling is limited to the party that sought and received it.

> A ruling letter is subject to modification or revocation without notice to any person, except the person to whom the letter was addressed. Accordingly, no other person should rely on the ruling letter or assume that the principles of that ruling will be applied in connection with any transaction other than the one described in the letter.

19 C.F.R. § 177.9(c).

The ruling process protects importers in several ways. It allows them to know beforehand whether their goods will be admitted to the U.S. and what their duty liability will be, by providing, *e.g.*, the classification and valuation that the

Customs Service intends to apply to a particular product or transaction. While such rulings bind both the Customs Service and the importer, they are subject to appeal and, following the entry's liquidation, protest if the importer disagrees with the agency's position. In addition, they cannot be modified or revoked without public notice, opportunity to comment, and a delayed effective date. In short, the ruling process allows importers to determine the agency's position before importation, and rely on it in conducting their business thereafter.

The Customs Service will issue advance rulings on intellectual property issues, such as whether a particular product or package infringes a trademark or copyright that has been registered with the agency. Because infringing items are subject to exclusion from entry and possible seizure, seeking the agency's prior guidance on the admissibility of such merchandise may be the only way to avoid loss of the goods or, at best, delayed entry.

An importer or other party who obtains an adverse ruling should be aware that the ruling may be given some judicial deference in a subsequent court challenge. In *United States v. Mead Corp.*, 121 S. Ct. 2164 (2001), the Supreme Court held that Customs classification rulings were not entitled to judicial deference under the standard set forth in *Chevron U.S.A. Inc. v. Natural Resources Defense Council, Inc.*, 467 U.S. 837 (1984). However, the Court did conclude that reviewing courts may consider such rulings under the less deferential standard in *Skidmore v. Swift & Co.*, 323 U.S. 134 (1944). As interpreted by *Mead*, the circumstances and extent of *Skidmore* deference may vary, depending on the issue, the quality of the ruling, the conclusion's consistency with other rulings, and other factors that may make it "persuasive" to the court.

Relying on *Mead*, the United States Court of Appeals for the Federal Circuit has deferred to Customs' revocation of a previous tariff classification ruling in *Heartland By-Products, Inc. v. United States*, Appeal Nos. 00-1287, 00-1289 (Aug. 31, 2001). The court found the challenged ruling persuasive in light of the fact that it was issued pursuant to a notice and comment process, addressed the points raised by the commenters and hence was given "thorough consideration," and was "supported by a logical and well-reasoned explanation." In addition, Customs' "'specialized experience' in classifying goods . . . lends further persuasiveness to" the ruling. While the revocation ruling was inconsistent with a previous ruling, this was diminished as a factor because the previous inconsistent ruling was the one being revoked, was not issued under a notice and comment procedure, and did not address the specific issue covered in the second ruling. Based on this reasoning, the court concluded that the challenged ruling had the "power to persuade," and upheld it.

The Court of International Trade has considered the degree of deference warranted under *Mead* and *Skidmore* in several classification cases. *Carrini, Inc. v. United States*, Slip Op. 01-91 (Aug. 2, 2001) (Customs' position unpersuasive due to its inconsistency with precedent); *Genesco Inc. v. United States*, Slip Op. 00-57 (May 23, 2000) (Treasury Decision underlying protest denial accorded

"*Skidmore* respect" based on notice and comment procedure, need to define terms, and reasonableness of Customs' interpretation). Note that *Genesco* was a pre-*Mead* application of the *Skidmore* rule.

An importer or other party that is weighing the pros and cons of applying for a ruling should give careful consideration to the consequences of an adverse result on a subsequent lawsuit to challenge the Customs Service's position. Because the quality of Customs rulings varies, and the thoroughness of a ruling's discussion often reflects the amount and quality of information presented by the requester, it is nearly impossible to predict the degree of deference that will be afforded by a reviewing court. Of course, the *Skidmore* standard for deference is inherently unpredictable: it essentially holds that an administrative pronouncement is persuasive if a court finds it to be persuasive, and unpersuasive if a court finds it so.

Although *Mead* dealt specifically with a classification ruling, its scope would appear likely to encompass rulings in other areas covered by the Customs Service's jurisdiction, including intellectual property protection. One point that the courts will have to address is whether the Customs Service has the necessary "specialized experience" in evaluating intellectual property infringement to lend persuasiveness to its rulings under the *Mead* and *Skidmore* decisions.

If the importer foregoes seeking a ruling, and instead seeks to import merchandise without having gotten one, it faces the possibility of an unpleasant surprise, such as a finding of non-admissibility, detention or seizure of its goods, or other unanticipated restrictions. Even if the importer takes that risk, and thereafter protests against the adverse Customs Service action, it may not avoid judicial deference to the agency's position. That is because Customs Headquarters may issue a ruling in response to a protest, particularly when the importer has asked for "further review" under 19 C.F.R. § 174.23. Although reviewing courts have not yet addressed whether such a ruling issued in response to a protest is entitled to *Skidmore* deference the same as a ruling issued in response to an importer's request, the rationale for the latter appears equally applicable to the former.

The Customs Service has established a regulatory structure for the ruling process in 19 C.F.R. Part 177. The regulations permit an importer to request, in writing, "a definitive interpretation of applicable law, or other appropriate information." Ruling requests should cover future transactions:

> Generally, a ruling may be requested under the provisions of this part only with respect to prospective transactions—that is, transactions which are not already pending before a Customs Service office by reason of arrival, entry, or otherwise.

19 C.F.R. § 177.1(a). If a transaction is currently pending, *i.e.*, the entry has not been liquidated, a Customs Service office may seek "internal advice" from Customs Service headquarters that results in a published decision. Although a completed transaction, such as a liquidated entry, cannot be the subject of a ruling request, the Customs Service will issue protest decisions in response to an importer's protest. 19 C.F.R. §§ 177.1(a)(2)(i), (ii).

The Customs Service will not issue a ruling in response to an oral request, and any oral advice provided by a Customs Service official is not binding on the agency. 19 C.F.R. § 177.1(b).

A ruling may be requested by "any person who, as an importer or exporter of merchandise, or otherwise, has a direct and demonstrable interest in the question or questions presented in the ruling request, or by the authorized agent of such person." 19 C.F.R. § 177.1(c).

Although the vast majority of rulings are sought by or on behalf of importers of merchandise, the Customs Service will entertain ruling requests from recordants of intellectual property rights who seek the agency's position on whether a potential import will be considered infringing. There is little doubt that the recordant or owner of intellectual property has a "direct and demonstrable interest" in such questions as whether a specific product or design is infringing or counterfeit, and whether it will be permitted to enter the United States. The statutes authorizing intellectual property owners to record with the Customs Service reflects a Congressional recognition of their interest in obtaining agency enforcement against infringing imports.

A ruling request must be in writing, 19 C.F.R. § 177.2(a), and meet the following requirements:

> (b) Content—(1) Generally. Each request for a ruling must contain a complete statement of all relevant facts relating to the transaction. Such facts include the names, addresses, and other identifying information of all interested parties (if known); the name of the port or place at which any article involved in the transaction will arrive or be entered, or which will otherwise have jurisdiction with respect to the act or activity described in the transaction; and a description of the transaction itself, appropriate in detail to the type of ruling requested.
>
> Description of transaction—(i) Generally. The Customs transaction to which the ruling request relates must be described in sufficient detail to permit the proper application of relevant Customs and related laws.
>
> * * *
>
> (5) Prior or current transactions. Each request for a ruling must state whether, to the knowledge of the person submitting the request, the same transaction, or one identical to it, has ever been considered, or is currently being considered by any Customs Service office or whether, to the knowledge of the person submitting the request, the issues involved have ever been considered, or are currently being considered, by the United States Court of International Trade, the United States Court of Appeals for the Federal Circuit, or any court of appeal therefrom. Where the transaction described in the ruling request is but one of a series of similar and related transactions, that fact must also be stated.
>
> (6) Statement of position. If the request for a ruling asks that a particular determination or conclusion be reached in the ruling letter, a statement must be included in the request setting forth the basis for that determination or conclusion, together with a citation of all relevant supporting authority.
>
> (7) Privileged or confidential information. Information which is claimed to constitute trade secrets or privileged or confidential commercial or financial information regarding the business transactions of private parties the disclosure of which would cause substantial harm to the competitive position of the person making the request (or of another interested

> party), must be identified clearly and the reasons such information should not be disclosed, including, where applicable, the reasons the disclosure of the information would prejudice the competitive position of the person making the request (or of another interested party) must be set forth.
>
> (c) Signing; instructions as to reply. The request for a ruling must be signed by a person authorized to make the request, as described in Sec. 177.1(c). A ruling requested by a principal or authorized agent may direct that the ruling letter be addressed to the other.

19 C.F.R. § 177.2(b), (c).

Ruling requests concerning intellectual property matters should be addressed to:

> Commissioner of Customs
> United States Customs Service
> 1300 Pennsylvania Avenue, N.W.
> Washington, D.C. 20229
> Attention: Office of Regulations and Rulings
> Intellectual Property Rights Branch

XXXIV. PROCEDURES AND TIMETABLE

A. Enforcement Provisions for Goods Suspected of Copying or Simulating a Recorded Trademark or Trade Name

Merchandise suspected of bearing a copying or simulating trademark or trade name may not be imported into the United States, and instead must remain in the custody of the Customs Service pending resolution of their infringing status. 19 C.F.R. §§ 133.22(b), 133.25. The importer of the detained goods is provided the opportunity to seek their release, while the trademark or trade name owner is kept apprised of the seizure and is permitted to submit to Customs its comments concerning the questions of infringement and appropriate remedy.

1. Detention of Merchandise

The regulations establish procedures for the Customs Service to follow when items that it believes are infringing are presented for entry: such articles "shall be denied entry and subject to detention. . . ." 19 C.F.R. § 133.22(b). Echoing the applicable statutes, 19 U.S.C. § 1526(a) (foreign merchandise) and 15 U.S.C. § 1124 (foreign and domestic merchandise), the regulation's denial and detention requirement applies to "articles of foreign or domestic manufacture," thus making it immaterial whether the article presented for importation was produced in the United States or abroad.

Merchandise suspected of infringing a recorded trademark or trade name must be detained for thirty (30) days from the date of its presentation to the Customs Service for examination. 19 C.F.R. §§ 133.22(b), (c), 133.25(a). The agency must notify the importer of the detention within five (5) days, *id.*, although, as a practical matter, the importer generally learns of the detention when its goods are not released from Customs Service custody. The notice of detention must be in writing, 19 C.F.R. § 133.25(d), and should follow the form set forth in Exhibit A.

Exhibit A
Letter to be sent to importer where goods have been detained for bearing confusingly similar marks or constituting restricted gray market goods.

Dear Sir/Madam:

In accordance with 19 CFR §§ 133.23 and 133.25 (Title 19, Code of Federal Regulations, sections 133.22 and 133.25), implementing section 526 of the Tariff Act of 1930, as amended Title 19, United States Code, section 526 (19 U.S.C. § 1595a(c)(2)(C)), and section 42 of the Lanham Trademark Act (15 U.S.C. § 1124), articles bearing unauthorized uses of an American trademark, or confusingly similar copies or simulations of U.S. trademarks recorded with Customs are prohibited importation or denied entry into the United States.

You are hereby notified that under 19 CFR §§ 133.23 and 133.25, your importation of ____, entry number_________________________, is being detained by U.S. Customs for the following violation of U.S. trademark law:

( ) A confusingly similar copy or simulation, in violation of 15 U.S.C. § 1124, subject to forfeiture under 19 U.S.C. § 1595a(c)(2)(C).

( ) An unauthorized "gray market" importation, in violation of 19 U.S.C. § 1526(a), subject to forfeiture under 19 U.S.C. § 1526(b).

U.S. Customs Recordation Number:

Description of Trademark:

U.S. Patent & Trademark Office Registration Number:

The imported articles shall be detained for a period of 30 days from the date presented to Customs. You may obtain release of the detained articles within the 30-day detention period if you can establish that an exemption under 19 CFR § 133.22(c) is applicable. If release of the merchandise is not affected within this 30-day period, the goods shall be seized and subjected to forfeiture under 19 U.S.C. § 1595a(c)(2)(C) for a violation of 15 U.S.C. § 1124, as implemented by 19 CFR § 133.22.

Sincerely,

Area/Port Director of Customs

Similar restrictions apply to infringing articles accompanying an importer and certain imports made by mail. 19 C.F.R. § 133.24. The most frequent example of the former situation arises when a traveler returning from abroad had acquired trademarked goods during his sojourn and attempts to bring them into the U.S. on his person or in his baggage. Under the regulation, such items are subject to detention—a fact that undoubtedly surprises many travelers who legally purchased goods abroad—with notice thereof provided orally by the Customs inspector at the time the goods are discovered. 19 C.F.R. § 133.24(b)(1).

The provisions for infringing goods imported by mail apply to noncommercial shipments (which are usually purchases by or gifts to individuals) or commercial shipments valued at no more than $250.00. 19 C.F.R. § 133.24(a). Notice of such detentions should be given on Customs Form 8. 19 C.F.R. § 133.24(b)(2). Not all mail imports are covered by this procedure; those valued at more than $250.00 are subject to the provisions of 19 C.F.R. § 133.22.

Articles covered by Section 133.24 are subject to a thirty-day detention period, starting on the date that notice of detention is provided. 19 C.F.R. § 133.24(a). Detained articles may be released if any of the circumstances provided in 19 C.F.R. § 133.22(c) (discussed below) are met. 19 C.F.R. § 133.24(c)(1). In addition, the importer may request the Customs Service to export or destroy the seized merchandise rather than seek its release. 19 C.F.R. §§ 133.24(c)(2), (3). Alternatively, the importer may remove or obliterate the trademarks, either in the presence of a Customs officer and to that officer's satisfaction or elsewhere, in which case the articles must be returned for examination by a Customs officer to assure that the trademark or trade name has been satisfactorily removed. The goods will be released from detention following satisfactory removal or obliteration of the mark or name. *Id.*

Even if infringing goods have been released from Customs custody, for example, because Customs officials failed to realize that the infringed trademark had been recorded, the agency may issue a notice of redelivery to the importer requiring its return in accordance with 19 C.F.R. § 133.26:

> If it is determined that merchandise which has been released from Customs custody is subject to the restrictions of Sec. 133.22 or Sec. 133.23 of this subpart, the port director shall promptly make demand for the redelivery of the merchandise under the terms of the bond on Customs Form 301, containing the bond conditions set forth in Sec. 113.62 of this chapter, in accordance with Sec. 141.113 of this chapter. If the merchandise is not redelivered to Customs custody, a claim for liquidated damages shall be made in accordance with Sec. 141.113(h) of this chapter.

In turn, 19 C.F.R. § 141.113(c) provides:

> If at any time after entry the port director finds that any merchandise contained in an importation is not entitled to admission into the commerce of the United States for any reason not enumerated in paragraph (a) or (b) of this section, he shall promptly demand the return to Customs custody of any such merchandise which has been released.

Although the demand for return to Customs custody must be made "promptly" after discovery of the goods' inadmissability, as a practical matter the Customs Service has a thirty-day period in which to issue the demand. A demand for redelivery is timely only if issued within thirty days from (1) the date the goods were released from Customs custody at the time of entry (except for textiles, which have a 180-day period), or (2) the commencement of an additional "conditional release" period resulting from a post-entry request for samples or an examination package. 19 C.F.R. §§ 113.62(d) and 141.113(c); *Customs Headquarters Ruling 224872* (July 5, 1994). An untimely demand for redelivery cannot be enforced. *Customs Headquarters Rulings 227686* (Aug. 12, 1999) and *114693* (Dec. 10, 1999).

The Customs Service may require the importer to provide samples or examination packages of merchandise that has been released from Customs custody. 19 C.F.R. § 151.11. The reason for such a request would be to permit an evaluation of whether the released goods infringed a recorded trademark, or were otherwise improperly admitted to the United States; the Customs Service can demand redelivery of the merchandise following examination of the samples. The importer's failure to comply with a demand for samples can result in a notice of redelivery for the entire merchandise covered by the entry. *Id.*; 19 C.F.R. § 141.113(d).

The agency's enforcement authority is not limited to entries of merchandise for consumption. The statute and regulations do not distinguish between consumption and other types of entries, and several courts have concluded that the statutory reach extends beyond consumption entries.

United States v. Watches, 692 F. Supp. 1317 (S.D. Fla. 1988), arose from a Customs Service seizure of counterfeit watches and parts that were part of an "in-bond" entry through the United States. The seized goods had been exported from Hong Kong for delivery to Paraguay, and were simply transiting the U.S. *en route* to their ultimate destination. The seller-claimants sought return of the seized merchandise on the ground that an in-bond entry is not an importation over which the Customs Service has been granted seizure authority.

The court rejected this argument, finding that the term "import" was broad enough to encompass in-bond entries, so the fact that the merchandise "was not intended to be introduced into the stream of commerce of the United States . . . the use of the word 'entry' in 15 U.S.C. Sec. 1124 should not be limited to the definition in 19 C.F.R. Sec. 141.0a, but rather given its much broader meaning encompassing every type of entry used throughout the customs regulations." Consequently, the merchandise was subject to seizure.

Because the court's conclusion hinged on the scope of the word "import" under the Lanham and Tariff Acts, its analysis is applicable to infringing and gray market goods as well as counterfeits.

Similarly, *A.T. Cross Co. v. Sunil Trading Corp.*, 467 F. Supp. 47 (S.D.N.Y. 1979), held that counterfeit foreign-origin goods held in a foreign-trade zone for subsequent shipment to another country were within the Lanham Act's purview. Again, although the decision arose from a dispute between two private parties in the context of a challenge to the court's jurisdiction, its reasoning would equally apply to Customs Service enforcement action against counterfeits in a foreign-trade zone. The court noted that "Customs officials are given a substantial amount of authority not only in admitting and exporting goods from the zone, but also in dealing with the goods while therein." The Customs Service's general authority over zone activity, coupled with its statutory instruction to enforce provisions of the Lanham Act, would permit it to seize counterfeits held in a zone.

In *Ocean Garden, Inc. v. Marktrade Co., Inc.*, 953 F.2d 500 (9th Cir. 1991), the court concluded that infringing foreign merchandise placed in a foreign-trade zone in the United States for exportation to a third country was subject to Lanham Act restrictions. Although the issue before the court was whether a

Federal district court had jurisdiction over a trademark infringement lawsuit against a Mexican enterprise, its reasoning would also serve to confirm that the Customs Service has trademark enforcement authority over goods placed in a foreign-trade zone, regardless of whether they were counterfeit or "merely" infringing.

The court also defined infringing articles as "prohibited merchandise" that cannot properly be allowed in a foreign-trade zone under 19 C.F.R. §§ 146.31 and 146.1(b)(13), and implied that the Customs Service would have authority to detain and forfeit items that were admitted to a zone in violation of this proscription.

The Customs Service takes the view that certain infringing goods may be placed in a foreign-trade zone or bonded warehouse, where they may be stored for exportation or brought into compliance with legal requirements, including the trademark laws. *Customs Headquarters Ruling 466891* (June 18, 1999) permitted gray market cigarettes whose packaging would otherwise be in violation of 15 U.S.C. § 1125(a) to be entered into a foreign-trade zone for repackaging and subsequent entry for consumption. The ruling noted that infringing goods under Section 1125(a) were restricted, not prohibited, merchandise, and thus could be placed in a zone.

> Cigarettes that do not bear the required markings are considered restricted, not prohibited, merchandise. They are considered restricted because cigarettes not permitted entry for labeling violations may be entered if a defect in labeling is cured. The [Foreign Trade Zones] Act allows merchandise to be reconditioned, relabeled, repacked, etc., within a [zone]. If merchandise is not in compliance with the law, it can be brought into a[] [zone] to either be brought into compliance, or exported.

Customs Headquarters Ruling 466891 also held that similar operations could take place in a Customs bonded warehouse. *Accord, Customs Headquarters Ruling 455953* (Aug. 5, 1993).

Although the ruling dealt specifically with goods in violation of 15 U.S.C. § 1125(a), its conclusion stemmed from the broad sweep of the Foreign Trade Zones Act, 19 U.S.C. § 81a(c). Because trademark-infringing articles are generally considered restricted merchandise, they are eligible for placement in a foreign-trade zone. Such goods may be stored or exported in their original condition, and may be repackaged or otherwise processed so they are no longer infringing; at that point, they could be entered for consumption. By the same token, the Foreign Trade Zones Act prohibits placement of merchandise "prohibited by law" in a zone. This proscribes goods bearing a counterfeit trademark, which the Customs Service considers to be prohibited merchandise, from placement in a zone even for exportation.

United States v. Watches and *A.T. Cross* leave no doubt that the Customs Service's authority to exclude or seize counterfeit merchandise is not limited to attempted entries for consumption. *Ocean Garden* takes a more restrictive view of the types of merchandise that may be placed in a foreign-trade zone than the agency has in its own rulings. Whether a court that has been asked to enjoin the zone entry of trademark-infringing goods would defer to the Customs Service's statutory interpretation has yet to be determined.

2. Grounds for Release of Detained Merchandise

During the thirty-day detention period provided under 19 C.F.R. § 133.22(c), the importer may seek to establish that the merchandise should be released from detention and allowed to enter the United States. *Id.* The Customs Service may grant extensions of this period "for good cause shown" by the importer. 19 C.F.R. § 133.25(a).

The regulation permits the goods' release upon the importer's demonstrating any of the following circumstances:

> (1) The objectionable mark is removed or obliterated as a condition to entry in such a manner as to be illegible and incapable of being reconstituted, for example by: (i) Grinding off imprinted trademarks wherever they appear; (ii) Removing and disposing of plates bearing a trademark or trade name;
>
> (2) The merchandise is imported by the recordant of the trademark or trade name or his designate;
>
> (3) The recordant gives written consent to an importation of articles otherwise subject to the restrictions set forth in paragraph (b) of this section or Sec. 133.23(c) of this subpart, and such consent is furnished to appropriate Customs officials;
>
> (4) The articles of foreign manufacture bear a recorded trademark and the one-item personal exemption is claimed and allowed under Sec. 148.55 of this chapter.

19 C.F.R. § 133.22(c).

To qualify under the first ground for release, the mark must be permanently removed by such means as "grinding, filing or scraping. . . . Covering over marks with tape, epoxy, resin, solder, glue or other materials is unsatisfactory." *Customs Headquarters Ruling 707797* (June 10, 1977). The Customs Service will not perform the removal or obliteration process on the importer's behalf. *Id.*

The second ground would arise when the Customs Service has—perhaps mistakenly—withheld entry even though the importer is the recordant of the merchandise, or when the importer has designated another entity to import the articles.

Third, the importer can obtain the trademark recordant's written consent to importation of the goods. The Customs Service does not appear to require that such consent be presented in a specific form, *see Customs Headquarters Ruling 731890* (Jan. 13, 1989).

Finally, the importer may make use of the personal exemption authorized under 19 U.S.C. § 1526(d)(1) and (2) and 19 C.F.R. § 148.55. The exemption applies to articles accompanying a person arriving in the United States from abroad that are for the person's personal use. The regulation places a strict limit on exempt quantities: only "one article of the type bearing the protected trademark" may be imported by an individual at any one time. 19 C.F.R. § 148.55(c) Also, an individual may use the exemption only once "for the same type of article in any 30-day period immediately prior to his arrival in the United States." 19 C.F.R. § 148.55(b)(1). Moreover, the importer may not sell an exempt article for a period of one year from the date of importation; doing so subjects the article to forfeiture. 19 C.F.R. § 148.55(b)(2). Finally, the exemption applies only to articles of foreign manufacture, 19 C.F.R. § 148.55(a), so that a domestically-produced item purchased abroad would be outside its scope.

The personal exemption of Section 148.55 is suited for use only by an individual traveler who has had articles accompanying him detained under 19 C.F.R. § 133.24.

Strangely absent from the listed bases for releasing detained merchandise is any reference to proof of noninfringement as a basis for releasing detained goods. In practice, the Customs Service will entertain arguments from the importer that the detained goods are not infringing, and should be released on that ground.

If the importer demonstrates to the Customs Service's satisfaction either noninfringement or the applicability of one of the 19 C.F.R. § 133.22(c) circumstances during the detention period, the goods shall be released for entry. 19 C.F.R. § 133.22(e). Such release may take place before the thirty-day detention period has expired. *Id.* Note that exportation of the merchandise is not an option during the detention stage, except for goods that either accompanied the importer or were brought in by a mail importation, as set forth in 19 C.F.R. § 133.24(c)(2) and (3).

On the other hand, if the importer fails to obtain release, the goods are subject to seizure and subsequent forfeiture. 19 C.F.R. § 133.22(f).

3. The Trademark or Trade Name Owner's Role in the Administrative Proceedings

The regulations also direct that the intellectual property owner be informed that merchandise has been denied entry. Such notice is optional before a notice of detention has been issued (*i.e.*, following the importer's presentation of the goods for entry and a tentative Customs Service decision to detain), and mandatory thereafter. 19 C.F.R. § 133.25(b).

Specifically, prior to issuance of the notice of detention, the Customs Service "may disclose" to the trademark or trade name owner "any of the following information"; after the notice of detention, the agency "shall disclose" this information to the owner "if available":

(1) The date of importation;

(2) The port of entry;

(3) A description of the merchandise;

(4) The quantity involved; and

(5) The country of origin of the merchandise.

The post-detention notice to the intellectual property owner must be given "within 30 days, excluding weekends and holidays, of the date of detention." 19 C.F.R. § 133.25(b). The form of notice is provided as Exhibit B.

Exhibit B
Letter to be sent to trademark holder in cases where gray market goods or goods bearing confusingly similar marks have been detained.

Dear Sir/Madam:

In accordance with 19 CFR § 133.25, Customs Regulations (Title 19, Code of Federal Regulations), implementing section 526 of the Tariff Act of 1930, as amended, Title 19, United States Code, Section 526 (19 U.S.C. § 1526), trademark holders are entitled to receive certain information from Customs relative to the detention of goods bearing violative trademarks.

Customs has detained goods which bear the following trademark which constitute unauthorized uses of an American trademark, or confusingly similar copies or simulations of U.S. trademarks recorded with Customs, and is notifying you, the trademark holder, of the action:

Description of Trademark:

U.S. Customs Recordation Number:

U.S. Patent & Trademark Office Registration Number:

In accordance with 19 CFR § 133.25 you are hereby notified of the following detention information:

Date of Importation:

Port of Entry:

Description of Merchandise:

Quantity:

Country of Origin:

In accordance with 19 CFR § 133.25, you may obtain a sample of the detained goods upon request, provided you meet certain conditions.

Sincerely,

Area/Port Director of Customs

In addition to this information, the Customs Service may provide a sample of the merchandise to the trademark or trade name owner "for examination or testing to assist in determining whether the article imported bears an infringing trademark or trade name. " 19 C.F.R. § 133.25(c). A sample may be provided at any time between the goods' presentation for entry and a Customs Service decision to seize the merchandise. *Id.* Before the sample is released, the Customs Service shall "remove or obliterate any information indicating the name and/or address of the manufacturer, exporter, and/or importer, including all bar codes or other identifying marks." *Customs Directive No. 2310-008A* (April 7, 2000) ¶ 5.2.3.

The trademark or trade name owner interested in obtaining a sample must provide to the Customs Service a surety bond "conditioned to hold the United States, its officers and employees, and the importer or owner of the imported article harmless from any loss or damage resulting from the furnishing of" the sample. *Id.* The form and amount of the bond are determined by the port director of the Customs port in which the merchandise was detained. *Id.* As a general rule, the bond amount will be 110 percent of the CIF (cost, insurance and freight) value of the sample, plus any applicable duties and fees; the minimum bond amount is $100.00. When a sample is valued below $100.00, the owner may provide a cash deposit in lieu of a bond. *Customs Directive No. 2310-008A* ¶ 5.2.2.

The sample must be returned upon the agency's demand, or after the examination or testing is completed. If the trademark or trade name owner cannot do so because the sample was damaged, destroyed, or lost, it must provide the following certification to the Customs Service: "The sample described as [insert description] and provided pursuant to 19 CFR 133.25(c) was (damaged/destroyed/lost) during examination or testing for trademark infringement." 19 C.F.R. § 133.25(c). Failure to return the sample will result in forfeiture of the bond or cash deposit to the Customs Service. *Customs Directive No. 2310-008A* ¶ 5.2.2.

The regulations do not specifically delineate a role for the trademark or trade name owner in evaluating whether detained articles are infringing. However, the notification and sample provisions would seem to implicitly anticipate that the owner will be permitted to make its views known to the Customs Service; for example, it would make no sense to provide a sample for testing if the results could not be reported to the agency. On the other hand—and in contrast with the procedures for imports suspected of copyright infringement—there is no formal authorization for the intellectual property owner to present its views to the Customs Service. Similarly, there is no procedure for the intellectual property owner to administratively or judicially appeal a Customs Service decision to allow entry of the goods.

B. Enforcement Provisions for Suspected Gray Market Goods

Customs Service enforcement procedures for gray market goods are similar to those for copying or simulating articles. "Restricted gray market goods," as defined in 19 C.F.R. § 133.23(a), are subject to denial of entry and detention.[53] 19 C.F.R. § 133.23(c). The importer must be notified in writing of the detention within five days, 19 C.F.R. § 133.25(a), (d); the notice should convey the same information as that for infringing goods, as set forth in Exhibit A. Goods subject to restriction may be detained for a thirty-day period "from the date on which the goods are presented for Customs examination." 19 C.F.R. §§ 133.23(d), 133.25(a). The Customs Service has discretion to extend the thirty-day period. *Id.*

Unlike Section 133.22(a), which applies to articles of either domestic or foreign origin, the regulation's gray market restrictions are limited to goods of foreign manufacture. 19 C.F.R. § 133.23(a).

---

53 The type of goods subject to gray market restrictions are discussed below, in chapter XLIII.

An article that would otherwise be subject to detention as "physically and materially different" will be permitted entry if it meets the following labeling requirement:

> the merchandise or its packaging bears a conspicuous and legible label designed to remain on the product until the first point of sale to a retail consumer in the United States stating that: "This product is not a product authorized by the United States trademark owner for importation and is physically and materially different from the authorized product." The label must be in close proximity to the trademark as it appears in its most prominent location on the article itself or the retail package or container. Other information designed to dispel consumer confusion may also be added.

19 C.F.R. § 133.23(b).

1. Grounds for Release of Detained Merchandise

During the detention period, the importer may seek to demonstrate that one of the four exceptions provided in 19 C.F.R. § 133.22(c) applies to the goods: (1) the trademark or trade name is removed or obliterated so as to be illegible and incapable of being reconstituted, (2) the merchandise is imported by the recordant of the trademark or trade name or his designate. (3) the recordant consents to the importation in writing, or (4) the articles are of foreign manufacture and the importer claims the personal exemption provided in 19 C.F.R. § 148.55.

In addition, the importer may attempt to demonstrate that one of the following circumstances applies to the goods:

> (1) The trademark or trade name was applied under the authority of a foreign trademark or trade name owner who is the same as the U.S. owner, a parent or subsidiary of the U.S. owner, or a party otherwise subject to common ownership or control with the U.S. owner (in an instance covered by Secs. 133.2(d) and 133.12(d) of this part); and/or
>
> (2) For goods bearing a genuine mark applied under the authority of the U.S. owner, a parent or subsidiary of the U.S. owner, or a party otherwise subject to common ownership or control with the U.S. owner, that the merchandise as imported is not physically and materially different, as described in Sec. 133.2(e), from articles authorized by the U.S. owner for importation or sale in the United States; or
>
> (3) Where goods are detained for violation of Sec. 133.23(a)(3), as physically and materially different from the articles authorized by the U.S. trademark owner for importation or sale in the U.S., a label in compliance with Sec. 133.23(b) is applied to the goods.

19 C.F.R. § 133.23(d). The first two of these defenses relate to whether the goods are "restricted" in the first place, *i.e.*, the regulation explicitly permits the importer to raise a substantive defense to the detention. The third permits release of the goods upon application of the label provided for in 19 C.F.R. § 133.23(b); it applies only to goods detained as "physically and materially different."

As with copying or simulating goods, the regulation provides for seizure of restricted gray market goods unless their release was granted within the thirty-day period (or any extension thereof granted by the Customs Service). 19 C.F.R. § 133.23(f).

2. The Trademark or Trade Name Owner's Role in the Administrative Proceedings

The trademark or trade name owner has the same notification rights regarding detained gray market goods that it does for copying or simulating articles. The owner may be given notice prior to the notice of detention's issuance. Within thirty days of the date of detention, it is entitled to notice of the date of importation and port of entry, the quantity and description of the merchandise, and the country of origin. 19 C.F.R. § 133.25(b); Exhibit B. The trademark or trade name owner may obtain a sample of the detained goods, subject to the bonding requirements of 19 C.F.R. § 133.25(c).

Once again, the regulation does not provide for the intellectual property owner's participation before the Customs Service concerning the disposition of the detained items. The owner's views may be particularly important to place before the Customs Service if the importer raises the Section 133.23(d)(1) or (2) defenses that the detained merchandise is not restricted under the regulations. The trademark or trade name owner would seem particularly well suited to comment on the relationship between the foreign and domestic owners, and on the nature and materiality of any physical differences between the imported goods and trademarked merchandise sold in the U.S.

C. Enforcement Provisions for Goods Suspected of Bearing a Counterfeit Trademark

Goods "of domestic or foreign manufacture" suspected of bearing a counterfeit trademark are not detained, but instead are subject to seizure and subsequent forfeiture. 19 C.F.R. § 133.21(b). This regulation does not provide a procedure under which the importer may challenge the Customs Service's designation of the goods as counterfeit. Such an opportunity may be particularly important in light of the sometimes fine line between counterfeit and "merely" copying or simulating goods.

The importer of counterfeit goods will be informed in writing that they have been seized. The letter should follow the format in Exhibit C.

Exhibit C
Letter to be sent to importer informing him that goods have been seized for bearing counterfeit marks.

Dear Sir/Madam:

In accordance with 19 CFR § 133.21, Customs Regulations (Title 19, Code of Federal Regulations), implementing section 526 of the Tariff Act of 1930, as amended, Title 19, United States Code, Section 526 (19 U.S.C. § 1526(e)), articles bearing counterfeit trademarks are subject to seizure and forfeiture.

You are hereby notified that under 19 CFR § 133.21, your importation of ___________ ____, entry number_______________________, has been seized by U.S. Customs as bearing counterfeits of the following registered U.S. trademark:

Description of Trademark:

U.S. Customs Recordation Number:

U.S. Patent & Trademark Office Registration Number:

You may exercise you right to petition this seizure pursuant to Part 171, Title 19, Code of Federal Regulations.

Sincerely,

Area/Port Director of Customs

The Customs Service considers that it has authority to seize counterfeit goods regardless of whether the genuine trademark has been recorded with the agency. 19 C.F.R. § 133.21(a) defines "a 'counterfeit trademark' [as] a spurious trademark that is identical to, or substantially indistinguishable from, a registered trademark." 19 C.F.R. § 133.22(a), by contrast, limits the definition of "copying or simulating" trademark or trade name to one that "resemble[s] a recorded mark or name." Consequently, importers of counterfeit goods cannot avoid having their shipments stopped by using only trademarks that are recorded with the Customs Service. However, the sanctions may vary depending on whether the counterfeited trademark was recorded.

1. Grounds for Release of Seized Merchandise

The regulation provides a Draconian remedy for seized counterfeit goods: unless the trademark owner consents to the "importation of the articles, exportation, entry after obliteration of the trademark, or other appropriate disposition" within thirty days of being notified of the seizure, the goods are subject to forfeiture. 19 C.F.R. § 133.21(b), (e).[54] The regulation does not provide for an extension of the thirty-day period. There is no option of removing or obliterating the counterfeit trademark, nor is the personal exemption of 19 C.F.R. § 148.55 applicable.

In the absence of the trademark owner's consent to importation or other remedy, 19 C.F.R. § 133.21(e) directs that the seized goods must be disposed of as provided in 19 C.F.R. § 133.52(c), which in most cases means they will be destroyed.

2. The Trademark Owner's Role in the Administrative Proceedings

The trademark owner is entitled to notice of the seizure within thirty days, along with the following information when available: date of importation, port of entry, description of the merchandise, quantity involved, name and address of the manufacturer, country of origin of the merchandise, name and address of the exporter, and name and address of the importer. Note that the owner will be informed of the identities and locations of the counterfeits' manufacturer, exporter,

54 Section 133.21(b) speaks only of the trademark owner authorizing "importation," while Section 133.21(e) permits the trademark owner to authorize "exportation, entry after obliteration of the trademark, or other appropriate disposition" in addition to importation.

and importer, which should prove useful in the event it pursues private remedies; such information is not disclosed for infringing or gray market goods. The letter format is provided as Exhibit D.

Exhibit D
Letter to be sent to trademark holder in cases where goods bearing counterfeit marks have been seized.

Dear Sir/Madam:

In accordance with 19 CFR § 133.21, Customs Regulations (Title 19, Code of Federal Regulations), implementing section 526 of the Tariff Act of 1930, as amended, Title 19, United States Code, Section 526 (19 U.S.C. § 1526(e)), articles bearing counterfeit trademarks are subject to seizure and forfeiture.

Customs has seized goods which bear marks which constitute counterfeit copies of the following trademark and is notifying you, the trademark holder, of the action:

Description of Trademark:

U.S. Customs Recordation Number:

U.S. Patent & Trademark Office Registration Number:

In accordance with 19 CFR § 133.21, you are hereby notified of the following seizure information:

Date of Importation:

Port of Entry:

Description of Merchandise:

Quantity:

Name/address of Manufacturer:

Name/address of Exporter:

Name/address of Importer:

Country of Origin:

In accordance with 19 CFR § 133.21, you may obtain a sample of the seized goods upon request, provided you meet certain conditions.

Sincerely,

Area/Port Director of Customs

The trademark owner may receive a sample of the goods following seizure, under the same bonding and bond forfeiture provisions applicable to samples of infringing merchandise. 19 C.F.R. § 133.21(d); *Customs Directive No. 2310-008A* (April 7, 2000) ¶ 5.1.2.

D. Enforcement Provisions for Goods Suspected of Copyright Infringement

The copyright enforcement regulations differ from those applicable to trademark infringement and counterfeit by distinguishing between articles presented for importation that the Customs Service has determined to be infringing, and those which it merely suspects are infringing. The former situation receives treatment similar to that accorded infringing or counterfeit trademarks. In the latter situation, however, the regulations set forth detailed administrative procedures for the agency, importer and copyright owner to follow before a finding of infringement is made. In particular, they provide an explicit role for the copyright owner in the infringement determination.

1. Infringing Copies

The Customs Service is directed to seize copies or phonorecords presented for importation that it determines to be infringing or "piratical." Specifically, each Customs port director shall seize both "any imported article which he determines is an infringing copy or phonorecord of a copyrighted work protected by Customs" and "an imported article if the importer does not deny a representation that the article is an infringing copy or phonorecord as provided in Sec. 133.43(a)." 19 C.F.R. § 133.42(c). Phonorecords are defined in 17 U.S.C. § 101 as:

> material objects in which sounds, other than those accompanying a motion picture or other audiovisual work, are fixed by any method now known or later developed, and from which the sounds can be perceived, reproduced, or otherwise communicated, either directly or with the aid of a machine or device. The term 'phonorecords' includes the material object in which the sounds are first fixed.

Customs Headquarters Ruling 467741 (Oct. 15, 1999) (holding that a doll in which a musical recording has been placed is a "phonorecord").

When the agency determines that a good is "clearly piratical," it institutes a seizure under this section. *Customs Directive No. 2310-005A* (April 7, 2000) ¶¶ 6.3.2 and 6.4.1. A "clearly piratical" item is one in where there is "overwhelming and substantial similarity between the copyrighted elements of the protected work and the imported item so as to clearly indicate that one work was based upon the other." *Id.* ¶ 6.3.2. A Customs Service official may make such a determination based on "[c]lear-cut copies, controlling decisions issued by" the Customs Service's Intellectual Property Rights Branch, "or (in specifically authorized instances only) decisions or orders issued by a court of law. . . ." *Id.* ¶ 6.4.1. Seizure is effected by issuance of a notice of seizure to the importer, which should follow the format of Exhibit E.

Exhibit E
Notice of Seizure to Importer, Clearly Piratical Copyrights Recorded with Customs.

Dear Sir or Madam:

In accordance with Customs Regulations 19 CFR § 133.42, Customs Regulations (Title 19, Code of Federal Regulations), implementing section 603 of the Copyright Act of 1976 (17 U.S.C. § 603), articles constituting clearly piratical copies of registered copyrights are subject to seizure and forfeiture.

You are hereby notified that under section 133.42 of the Customs Regulations, your importation of ______________________________, entry number ____________ has been seized by U.S. Customs as constituting clearly piratical copies of the following registered and recorded copyright:

Title:

U.S. Copyright Office Registration Number:

U.S. Customs Recordation Number:

If you admit that these items are, in fact, piratical, you may abandon such items to Customs and assent to their forfeiture; or you may petition for relief from forfeiture of the articles pursuant to 19 CFR §§ 171 and 172.

Sincerely,

Area/Port Director

Within thirty days (excluding weekends and holidays) after issuance of the seizure notice, the Customs Service must provide the following information to the copyright owner: the date of importation, port of entry, description of the merchandise and quantity involved, name and address of the manufacturer, exporter and importer, and country of origin of the merchandise. 19 C.F.R. § 133.42(d). The owner may also obtain from the Customs Service a sample of the seized merchandise, which it may use "for examination, testing, or any other use in pursuit of a related private civil remedy for copyright infringement." As a condition for receiving a sample, the owner must post a surety bond. If it fails to return the sample to the Customs Service, the owner must provide a certification concerning the sample's disposition, and the bond will be forfeitcd. 19 C.F.R. § 133.42(e).

Although the regulation is silent on the importer's options to disprove the finding of infringement, as a practical matter the Customs Service will entertain arguments on this point. If the agency does not release the seized goods as non-infringing, they are subject to forfeiture. Unlike the trademark or trade name infringement provisions, there is no personal exemption for merchandise that has been detained for copyright infringement.

Goods that the Customs Service has released from custody and permitted to enter the United States, but later concludes are infringing, may be subject to a demand for redelivery. The importer's failure to return them shall give rise to a claim for liquidated damages being assessed against it by the Customs Service. 19 C.F.R. § 133.46.

2. Suspected Infringing Copies

When the Customs Service "has any reason to believe that an imported article may be an infringing copy or phonorecord of a recorded copyrighted work," it must withhold delivery. The importer is entitled to notice, and must further be advised "that if the facts so warrant he may file a statement denying that the article is in fact an infringing copy and alleging that the detention of the article will result in a material depreciation of its value, or a loss or damage to him." Unless the agency receives "within 30 days of a denial by the importer that the article constitutes an infringing copy or phonorecord, it shall be considered to be such a copy and shall be subject to seizure and forfeiture." 19 C.F.R. § 133.43(a). The form of the notification letter is provided as Exhibit F. The Customs Service will demand redelivery of suspected infringing merchandise that has already been released from Customs custody and assert a liquidated damages claim for failure to comply, in accordance with19 C.F.R. § 133.46.

Exhibit F
Notice of Detention to the Importer, Possibly Piratical Recorded Copyright

Dear Sir or Madam:

In accordance with Customs Regulations 19 CFR § 133.43 and 17 USC § 603, the importation (including "in-transit" shipments) of piratical copies of a recorded copyrighted work is prohibited. You are hereby advised that there is reason to believe that your importation of ________________________ may constitute a piratical copy of the following registered and recorded copyrighted work:

Title:

U.S. Copyright Office Registration Number:

U.S. Customs Recordation Number:

In the absence of receipt within 30 days of a denial by you that the article constitutes a piratical copy, it shall be considered to be such a copy and shall be subject to seizure and forfeiture. If this merchandise is already in your possession, you may satisfy the requirement of this notice by giving Customs "constructive" custody until such time as the issue of piratical copying is resolved. This may be accomplished by a letter granting us constructive custody and affirming that the subject merchandise will be held intact by you pending further instructions from this office and the posting of a single entry bond for three times the value of the merchandise. The merchandise may not be sold, used, assigned, leased or disposed of without U.S. Customs permission.

If you believe the facts warrant, you may file a statement denying that the article is in fact a piratical copy and stating that the detention or redelivery of the article will result in a material depreciation of its value or a loss or damage to you.

Upon receipt of your denial, a sample of the merchandise in question will be sent to the copyright holder. If he claims that there is a violation of his copyright, both you and he will have up to 30 days to submit additional evidence and legal briefs in support of your respective positions, before we forward the matter to the Commissioner of Customs for decision.

In addition, you have several further options. If you agree that these items are, in fact, piratical, or if you wish to waive your right to contest piracy, you may abandon such items to Customs at the time of redelivery and assent to their forfeiture, or you may petition for relief from forfeiture of the articles.

Sincerely,

Area/Port Director

If the importer files the Section 133.43(a) denial, the copyright owner shall be informed by the Customs Service within thirty days that delivery of suspected infringing goods was withheld, and should be given the following information: the date of importation, port of entry, and description of the merchandise and quantity involved and its country of origin. 19 C.F.R. § 133.43(b).

In addition, the owner will be provided with a notice that the imported article will be released to the importer unless, within thirty days from the date of the notice, he files with the Customs Service:

(i) A written demand for the exclusion from entry of the detained imported article; and

(ii) A bond, in the form and amount specified by the port director, conditioned to hold the importer or owner of the imported article harmless from any loss or damage resulting from Customs detention in the event the Commissioner or his designee determines that the article is not an infringing copy prohibited importation under section 602 of the Copyright Act of 1976 (17 U.S.C. § 602) (See part 113 of this chapter).

Id. See Exhibit G.

Exhibit G
Letter to Copyright Holder, Possibly Piratical Recorded with Customs.

Dear Sir or Madam:

The Customs Service has detained a shipment of ________________________ which may constitute a violation of the following copyrighted work:

Title:

U.S. Copyright Office Registration Number:

U.S. Customs Recordation Number:

Pursuant to Customs Regulations 19 CFR § 133.43, a sample is hereby submitted for your review. The importer denies that the articles are piratical copies, and alleges that their continued detention will result in a material loss or damage to him. Please be advised that these imported articles will be released to the importer unless, within 30 days from the date of this letter, you file:

1. A written demand for the exclusion of these items; and

2. A bond on Customs Form 301 (copy enclosed) in the amount of _________ conditioned to hold U.S. Customs, and the importer or owner, harmless from the loss or damage resulting from Customs detention in the event that these items are determined not to be piratical.

If you file the demand and bond, you and the importer will be notified of a time period for filing further evidence, briefs or material. You, the copyright holder, have the burden of proving infringement.

At the conclusion of the regulatory and statutory time periods, the entire file will be forwarded to the Commissioner of Customs for review and decision.

Sincerely,

Area/Port Director

The bond amount is the value of the merchandise in question. In lieu of a bond, the copyright owner may be permitted to tender a check in the bond amount. *See Luxury Int'l, Inc. v. United States*, 69 F. Supp. 2d 1364 (Ct. Int'l Trade 1999) ("*Luxury Int'l I*"), noting the Customs Service's acceptance of a check as security pursuant to 19 C.F.R. § 113.40. The bond may not be withdrawn by the copyright owner until the Customs Service reaches a decision regarding infringement. 19 C.F.R. § 133.43(d)(4).

Although the thirty-day period for filing a demand and posting a bond appears to be mandatory, the copyright owner will not be penalized for missing the deadline if a Customs Service error was the cause. *See Luxury Int'l, Inc. v. United States*, 90 F. Supp. 2d 1294 (Ct. Int'l Trade 2000) ("*Luxury Int'l II*"), holding that the copyright owner acted timely despite the Customs Service's erroneous failure to accept within thirty days a check proffered as the required security. The copyright owner may also receive a sample of the merchandise prior to seizure, subject to the same bonding and return requirements provided for seized infringing articles. 19 C.F.R. § 133.43(c).

Thus, following receipt of notice from the agency, it is the copyright owner who determines whether the Customs Service pursues the suspected infringement. If the owner files a written demand for exclusion of the detained goods and posts the bond, the Customs Service in the port where the merchandise was detained will establish a period of up to thirty days for the importer and owner to "submit any evidence, legal briefs or other pertinent material to substantiate the claim or denial of infringement." 19 C.F.R. § 133.43(d)(1); *see* Exhibit H. Before submitting such materials the parties are required to exchange with each other their previous submissions to the Customs Service, "including the importer's denial of infringement and the copyright owner's demand for exclusion." 19 C.F.R. § 133.43(d)(1)(i). The subsequent Section 133.43(d)(1) submissions must include "a written statement confirming that a copy has already been provided to the opposing party." *Id.* This apparently refers to both the previous submissions and the "evidence, legal briefs or other pertinent material."

Exhibit H
Notice to Copyright Owner and Importer (Exclusion Demand)

Dear Sir or Madam:

Relative to the exclusion of the suspected piratical copies of: ________________________, entry number ______________________ for suspected violation of the following protected works:

Title of Copyright:

U.S. Copyright Office Registration Number:

U.S. Customs Recordation Number.

Issue is joined as to the claim. Pursuant to 19 CFR § 133.43(c)(1)(I) [*sic*], within thirty (30) days from the date of this letter, both parties, or their duly-authorized agents, may submit to Customs any additional information or documentation substantiating its claim. The copyright holder has the burden of proof in this matter. Within this 30-day period, both parties should submit to each other and to Customs:

1. Copies of any and all arguments, legal briefs, evidence, or other pertinent material submitted, whether part of the initial claim or subsequent discovery.

2. A written statement, signed by the party or duly-authorized agent, confirming that copies of the above were in fact provided to the importer within the 30-day time period.

Please be advised that no additional material to substantiate the claim or denial of infringement will be accepted by this office after this 30-day period expires.

Sincerely,

Area/Port Director

The regulation provides the parties with up to thirty days to file rebuttal briefs, which must also have a written statement of service on the opposing party, at which point the argument period is cut off. *Id.* The Customs Service must notify the parties of their opportunity to file briefs and information, the schedule therefor, and the service requirement. The copyright owner, as the party claiming the imported merchandise is an infringing copy, bears the burden of proof. 19 C.F.R. § 133.43(d)(1)(i). The form of notification is provided as Exhibit I.

Exhibit I
Notice to Copyright Owner and Importer, Rebuttal Period

Dear Sir or Madam:

Relative to the exclusion of the suspected piratical copies of________________, entry number ________________ for suspected violation of the following protected works:

Title of Copyright:

U.S. Copyright Office Registration Number:

U.S. Customs Recordation Number:

Pursuant to 19 CFR § 133.43(c)(1)(I) [*sic*], the parties have submitted to Customs, and exchanged copies of any and all arguments, legal briefs, evidence, or other pertinent material, whether part of the initial claim or subsequently discovered, and a written statement, signed by the parties or duly authorized agent confirming that copies of the above were in fact provided to the importer within the initial 30-day time period.

The parties will be afforded an additional 30-day "rebuttal period" (beginning as of the date of this letter) in which to exchange and submit to Customs:

1. Copies of any and all arguments, legal briefs, evidence, or other pertinent material submitted in rebuttal to arguments submitted, and

2. A written statement, signed by the importer or duly-authorized agent, confirming that copies of the above were in fact provided to the other party within the 30-day rebuttal period.

Please be advised that no additional material to substantiate the claim or denial of infringement will be accepted by this office once this 30-day rebuttal period expires.

Sincerely,

Area/Port Director

Following submission of rebuttal briefs, the Customs port will forward the entire case file and samples of the merchandise to Customs headquarters for resolution. 19 C.F.R. § 133.43(d)(1)(ii). The parties will be notified of the resulting decision.

A determination that the detained article is an infringing copy of a recorded copyright will result in seizure of the merchandise and institution of forfeiture proceedings, and return of the copyright owner's bond. 19 C.F.R. § 133.44(a). However, seizure may be forestalled if the importer has commenced a protest action in the United States Court of International Trade.[55] If Customs headquarters determines that the article is not infringing, the detention is lifted and the

55 The Court of International Trade's protest jurisdiction over the Customs Service's trademark, trade name, and copyright enforcement is discussed in chapter XXXVIII.

importer is free to import the goods. The Customs Service will also forward the copyright owner's bond to the importer, meaning that the importer will collect the full amount of the bond. 19 C.F.R. § 133.43(b).

There are circumstances in which the case will not be forwarded to Customs headquarters, but instead will be resolved in the local Customs port. If the copyright owner "fails to present sufficient evidence or proof to substantiate a claim of infringement, the port director shall release the detained shipment to the importer and all further importations of the same article, by whomever imported, without further notice to the copyright owner." 19 C.F.R. § 133.43(d)(2). Although this appears to allow the Customs port to make a determination on the merits without forwarding the case to Customs headquarters, the regulations are unclear on when local resolution under this provision is appropriate.

Also, the copyright owner's failure to meet specified procedural requirements will permit local resolution. The goods shall be released, and future shipments permitted to enter unmolested, "[i]f the copyright owner disclaims that the specified imported article is an infringing copy of his recorded copyrighted work." *Id.* The goods will also be released if the copyright owner fails to file a written demand for exclusion and post a bond under 19 C.F.R. § 133.43(b)(1)(i) and (ii). 19 C.F.R. § 133.43(d)(3). Unlike a Section 133.43(d)(2) release, the regulation does not direct unfettered entry for future shipments of identical articles.

The person that recorded the copyright with the Customs Service need not be the same one that files the Section 133.43(b)(i) demand for exclusion and participates in the subsequent administrative proceedings. In *Luxury Int'l II*, the Court of International Trade held that the copyright registrant/owner could pursue the exclusion remedy even though another party that had licensed ownership rights from the registrant had recorded the copyright with the Customs Service.

> . . . because Elorg owns the rights at issue and Tetris is the exclusive licensee, both entities fall within the meaning of 'copyright owner' as defined by *19 C.F.R. § 133.31*. Because the regulations do not require that the copyright owner who recorded the copyright be the same copyright owner to protect the copyright, and because Elorg and Tetris are copyright owners, Elorg and Tetris were entitled to take the steps provided in Customs regulations to keep Luxury's merchandise from entering the United States stream of commerce.

90 F. Supp. 2d at 1298.

The copyright owner has the option of bypassing the 19 C.F.R. § 133.43 administrative proceedings altogether by seeking a court injunction, regardless of whether it recorded the copyright with the Customs Service. To do so, the owner must "submit a certified copy of the court order to the Commissioner of Customs, Attention: Office of the Chief Counsel, Washington, DC 20229." 19 C.F.R. 133.43(e). If the owner seeks enforcement for an unrecorded copyright, it must pay $190 "and, if the work is a three-dimensional or other work not readily identifiable by title and author, [submit] 5 photographic or other likenesses reproduced on paper approximately 8" x 10\1/2" in size." *Id.*

XXXV. FORFEITURE PROCEEDINGS

Unless infringing goods that have been detained for trademark infringement or as restricted gray market merchandise are released within the period prescribed under the regulations, they are subject to seizure and subsequent forfeiture by the Customs Service. 15 U.S.C. § 1124; 19 U.S.C. § 1595a(c)(2)(C); 19 C.F.R. §§ 133.22(f), 133.23(f). Seized goods bearing counterfeit trademarks are similarly subject to forfeiture, 19 U.S.C. §§ 1526(f) and 1595a(c)(2)(C) and 19 C.F.R. §§ 133.21(b), 133.42(c), as are goods seized for copyright infringement. 17 U.S.C. § 603; 19 U.S.C. § 1595a(c)(2)(C); 19 C.F.R. §§ 133.42(c), 133.44(a). The procedures are identical regardless of the intellectual property right violated by the imported merchandise, with several provisions specific to goods bearing a counterfeit trademark.

There are two types of forfeiture proceedings, administrative and judicial. The former applies when the goods seized have a forfeiture value of $500,000 or less, while the latter applies to goods valued above the threshold. The Customs Service is required to determine the domestic value of the seized goods, 19 U.S.C. § 1606 and 19 C.F.R. § 162.43(a); this value determines the type of forfeiture proceedings that are applicable. The party claiming ownership of the seized merchandise—the claimant—may also request judicial forfeiture regardless of the value involved, thereby bypassing administrative forfeiture proceedings.

A. Administrative Forfeiture

Seized merchandise with a value of $500,000 or less is subject to administrative forfeiture, as is seized merchandise which is prohibited from importation, such as counterfeit goods. 19 U.S.C. § 1607(a). Forfeiture proceedings are initiated by the Customs Service's issuance of a notice of seizure and intent to forfeit and sell or otherwise dispose of the merchandise to "each party who appears to have an interest in the seized article." The notice should include the following items:

(1) The provisions of law alleged to have been violated;

(2) A description of the specific acts or omissions forming the basis of the alleged violations;

(3) If the alleged violations involve the entry or attempted entry of merchandise,

(i) A description of the merchandise and the circumstances of its entry or attempted entry, and

(ii) The identity of each entry, if specific entries are involved.

19 C.F.R. § 162.31(b)(1)-(3). Notice must "be published for at least three successive weeks in a newspaper circulated at the Customs port and in the judicial district where the property was seized" with all known parties-in-interest given notice of such publication. 19 U.S.C. § 1607(a); 19 C.F.R. § 162.45(b)(1).

After the administrative forfeiture proceedings are underway, a claimant to the merchandise may file a petition for administrative relief. 19 U.S.C. § 1618; 19 C.F.R. §§ 133.51(b) and 171 Subpart B. A claimant choosing to petition for relief must agree "to defer judicial or administrative forfeiture proceedings until completion of the administrative process"; otherwise, "summary forfeiture proceedings will be begun." 19 C.F.R. § 162.31(a).

In response to the petition, the government may grant relief upon the condition that the claimant exports or destroys the seized merchandise regardless of the intellectual property right that was infringed. 19 C.F.R. § 133.51(b)(1). For trademark or trade name cases, release of the goods may be conditioned upon removal of infringing trademarks or trade names from the merchandise, after which the goods may be released for importation. 19 C.F.R. § 133.51(b)(2). Foreign-manufactured books or periodicals that violate 17 U.S.C. § 601 (the "manufacturing clause") may be released for importation, as long as the copyright owner has filed a statement of abandonment in the Copyright Office, and the notice of copyright is completely obliterated. In light of the manufacturing clause's current narrow applicability, this latter ground for relief is unlikely to be used with much frequency.

The Customs Service is likely to permit exportation of the seized goods when the claimant did not know that they were infringing. *See Customs Headquarters Rulings 732376* (May 31, 1990) ("the district director may allow the return of the imported articles to the country of export whenever he is satisfied that the importer had no reasonable grounds for believing that his act (of importing the infringing articles) constitute a violation of law"), *733189* (March 28, 1990) and *732056* (Feb. 1, 1989) (same). However, if the importer had previously attempted to import infringing merchandise, it not only casts doubt on its lack of knowledge, but also raises the possibility of attempted entry of the merchandise at another port. In that case, permission to export the merchandise is unlikely to be given, and the Customs Service is likely to order its destruction. *Customs Headquarters Ruling 732005* (Sept. 15, 1989). Any duties collected on merchandise that was entered before the intellectual property violations were discovered shall be refunded to the importer. 19 C.F.R. § 133.53.

A claimant that is dissatisfied with the Customs Service's response to its petition may file a supplemental petition for relief. 19 C.F.R. § 171.33.

The administrative proceedings may result in condemnation of the merchandise or its return to the claimant, with or without assessment of a penalty. Merchandise with infringing trademarks or trade names that the Customs Service decides against returning will either be retained for the agency's use or sold, after the infringed trademark or name is removed. 19 C.F.R. § 133.52(a). Articles with counterfeit trademarks, or that violate the copyright laws, shall be destroyed. 19 C.F.R. § 133.52(c), (b).

B. Judicial Forfeiture

Seizures that are ineligible for administrative forfeiture are referred to the United States attorney for the judicial district where the seizure was made for commencement of judicial proceedings. 19 U.S.C. § 1610. A claimant that is otherwise eligible for administrative forfeiture may seek immediate court review by filing a claim with the Customs Service within twenty (20) days of the date on which notice of seizure was first published. The claimant must also provide a penal bond to cover the government's costs and expenses if the judicial proceedings result in condemnation of the seized merchandise. The required bond amount is the lower of ten (10) percent of the value of the merchandise or $5,000, with a minimum bond amount of $250. After receiving the claim and bond, the Customs Service will forward the matter to the appropriate United States attorney for commencement of condemnation proceedings. 19 U.S.C. § 1608; 19 C.F.R. § 162.47.

XXXVI. ASSESSMENT OF FINES FOR COUNTERFEIT TRADEMARKED MERCHANDISE

The 1996 Anticounterfeiting Consumer Protection Act requires that persons involved in the importation of counterfeit trademarked goods are subject to assessment of a civil fine under 19 U.S.C. § 1526(f) in addition to seizure and forfeiture. The statute directs that:

> (1) Any person who directs, assists financially or otherwise, or aids and abets the importation of merchandise for sale or public distribution that is seized under subsection (e) of this section shall be subject to a civil fine.
>
> (2) For the first such seizure, the fine shall be not more than the value that the merchandise would have had if it were genuine, according to the manufacturer's suggested retail price, determined under regulations promulgated by the Secretary.
>
> (3) For the second seizure and thereafter, the fine shall be not more than twice the value that the merchandise would have had if it were genuine, as determined under regulations promulgated by the Secretary.
>
> (4) The imposition of a fine under this subsection shall be within the discretion of the Customs Service, and shall be in addition to any other civil or criminal penalty or other remedy authorized by law.

Liability is not limited to the importer; other persons who "direct[], assist[] financially or otherwise, or aid[] or abet[]" are also covered. The Customs Service considers that the statute "subjects all parties who can exercise control over the import transaction to its application." *Guidelines for the Assessment and Mitigation of Civil Fines Under 19 U.S.C. § 1526(f)*, T.D. 99-76, 33 *Cust. Bull. & Dec.* No. 43 at 19 (Oct 27, 1999) (*Guidelines*).

The statutory fine amounts are quite harsh: for the first seizure of counterfeit goods from a specific person, the maximum fine is the retail value of genuine trademarked goods, and for subsequent seizures the maximum is twice the genuine goods' retail value. Although these statutory limits are subject to reduction in administrative mitigation proceedings, parties involved in importing counterfeit goods face substantial monetary liability.

Procedures for assessment of fines are set forth in 19 C.F.R. § 162.31, and are identical to those governing forfeitures. In short, they require that all "interested parties" be provided with notice of the proceeding, along with information concerning the alleged violation and amount of penalty and notification of the right to petition for relief. Individuals suspected of involvement in the violation "may be named individually or jointly and severally in penalty notices." *Guidelines*, 33 *Cust. Bull. & Dec.* No. 43 at 24.

The *Guidelines* provide factors for Customs officers to consider in determining the amount of fines assessed under Section 1526(f). The agency's policy is to initially assess a fine at the full statutory amount. For purposes of the assessment, the "value that the merchandise would have had if it were genuine" will be based on the manufacturer's suggested retail price (MSRP). *Id.* Such a formulation could result in assessment of higher fines than are warranted under the statute, as the MSRP may not be the price at which merchandise is actually sold at retail. If an identical genuine good is not available, the fine can be based on the MSRP for a similar class or kind of genuine good. *Id.* at 22.

The amount assessed in the initial Section 162.31 notice will not necessarily be the amount finally determined to be appropriate. Under the *Guidelines*, the Customs Service is authorized to reduce the amount of the fine, based on the specific circumstances of the case and the application of "mitigating" and "aggravating" factors. The *Guidelines* provide the following suggested dispositions of fine proceedings.

1. First offense (under 19 U.S.C. § 1526(f)), with mitigating, and no aggravating, factor(s):

   10–30% of the applicable MSRP of the genuine good (the assessed fine amount).

2. First offense (under 19 U.S.C. § 1526(f)), with aggravating factor(s):

   30–50% of the MSRP of the genuine good.

3. First offense (under 19 U.S.C. § 1526(f)), with evidence of knowledge as to the counterfeit nature of the goods, with no aggravating factors:

   50–80% of the MSRP of the genuine good.

4. Second offense (under 19 U.S.C. § 1526(f)), with mitigating, and no aggravating, factor(s):

   10–30% of twice the MSRP of the genuine good.

5. Second offense (under 19 U.S.C. § 1526(f)), with aggravating factor(s), or third or subsequent offense (under 19 U.S.C. § 1526(f)):

   50–80% of twice the MSRP of the genuine good.

6. Second offense (under 19 U.S.C. § 1526(f)), with evidence of knowledge as to the counterfeit nature of the goods:

   No mitigation.

The specified mitigating factors are:

1. Lack of knowledge of the counterfeit nature of the trademark.
2. Prior good record of importations under 19 U.S.C. § 1526.
3. Inexperience in importing.
4. Cooperation with Customs officers in ascertaining the facts establishing the violation.

5. Inability to pay the fine (demonstrated by documentary evidence including, but not limited to, income tax returns for the prior three years).

The *Guidelines* identify the following aggravating factors.

1. More than two prior importations of merchandise seized and forfeited under 19 U.S.C. § 1526(e).
2. Criminal violation relating to the subject transaction.
3. Submission of falsified documentation (*i.e.*, false description, false country of origin, etc.), or other deceptive practices in connection with the subject importation.

Id. at 24-25. Repeat offenders are subject to a higher statutory fine as well as diminished (or no) mitigation of the statutory amount.

Because Section 1526(f) applies only to merchandise imported "for sale or public distribution," it does not reach goods imported for personal use, *e.g.*, by a returning traveler. As the *Guidelines* note, such goods would remain subject to seizure and forfeiture.

Following completion of the mitigation proceedings, fines that have been assessed but not been paid will be referred to the Justice Department for collection. *Id.* at 23.

XXXVII. LIQUIDATED DAMAGES PROCEEDINGS

An importer's failure to return merchandise to Customs custody following a timely demand can result in an assessment of liquidated damages. The basis for a liquidated damages claim is that the importer failed to meet the conditions of the surety bond on which it is listed as the principal.[56] One of the required bond conditions is that the importer return merchandise to Customs custody following a demand for redelivery. 19 C.F.R. § 113.62(d). The Customs Service may seek liquidated damages for the importer's failure to do so. If liquidated damages are assessed and the importer does not pay them, the agency may proceed against the surety on the bond.

Procedures for assessment of liquidated damages are set forth in 19 C.F.R. Part 172. Following a failure to redeliver (or other ground for assessing liquidated damages), the Customs Service will issue the bond principal—usually, the importer—a notice of liquidated damages and demand for payment. The amount of damages claimed may be up to three times the value of the goods declared at entry. 19 C.F.R. § 142.113(h). The bond surety will also be advised that the demand has been made. 19 C.F.R. § 172.1(a).

The importer has the right to petition the Customs Service for relief from the liquidated damages claim. A petitioner may argue that the goods covered by the redelivery notice were not infringing or counterfeit and, if successful, should

56 A surety bond is generally required as a condition for importing merchandise into the United States. *See* 19 C.F.R.§ 113.12.

have the claim cancelled without any monetary liability. The petitioner may also assert that there were mitigating circumstances for its failure to return the goods, and request cancellation of the claim based on the petitioner's payment of a lower monetary amount.

The Customs Service has issued guidelines for determining the circumstances in which cancellation of a bond is appropriate in T.D. 94-38 (April 14, 1994). Failure to redeliver merchandise that violates either a copyright or a trademark is treated under the following guidelines:

1. If the importer fails to redeliver violative merchandise, but after assessment of liquidated damages receives a retroactive licensing of the merchandise from the copyright holder or the trademark holder, the liquidated damages claim is cancelled upon payment of an amount between one and five percent of the value of the merchandise, but not less than $100.

2. If the copyright holder or trademark holder does not authorize entry of the merchandise, a claim arising from a first-time violation is cancelled upon payment of an amount between twenty percent and fifty percent of the value of the merchandise, depending on whether there are aggravating or mitigating circumstances.

3. In subsequent violations, when there is no authorization from the copyright holder or trademark holder, the claim is cancelled upon payment of at least fifty percent of the value of the merchandise. To receive any further relief in these circumstances, the importer must show that there are extraordinary mitigating circumstances.

4. As a general rule, when the merchandise bears a counterfeit trademark, the Customs Service will not cancel the liquidated damages claim upon payment of a lesser amount. Some relief may be granted if the merchandise is genuine.

Although the copyright and trademark guidelines do not identify mitigating or aggravating circumstances applicable to resolution of liquidated damages claims, the Treasury Decision that sets them forth elsewhere specifies such factors for certain country of origin marking violations. These factors may provide guidance concerning the analysis that the Customs Service will undertake in evaluating claims arising from copyright or trademark violations.

The Treasury Decision provides the following examples of aggravating factors:

1. The offender is uncooperative, *e.g.*, fails to provide information to the Customs Service when requested.

2. There have been a large number of violations of this type by the offender in relation to the total number of transactions in which it engages.

3. The offender is experienced in importing.

4. The offender has shown willful disregard or carelessness toward its legal responsibilities.

Examples of mitigating circumstances are:

1. The Customs Service has committed an error that contributed to the importer's violation, *e.g.*, the offender can demonstrate that it acted in accordance with instructions issued by agency personnel.

2. The offender shows cooperation with Customs Service personnel in resolving the case.

3. The offender takes immediate remedial action.

4. The offender has a lack of importing experience.

> 5. There have been a small number of violations of this type by the offender in relation to the total number of transactions in which it engages.

The importer's failure to provide a sample of merchandise when requested by the Customs Service can also give rise to a liquidated damages claim. T.D. 94-38 directs that the failure to provide a sample to determine whether there is a copyright or trademark violation shall be resolved as if the substantive violation had occurred. Thus, a liquidated damages claim stemming from a failure to provide a sample of a product that is suspected of infringing a copyright shall be treated as a "failure to redeliver copyright-violative merchandise where no retroactive license is given." On the other hand, if a sample is provided outside the time period provided in the Customs Service notice, a lower amount of damages may be assessed. Specifically, if the sample is provided following issuance of the liquidated damages claim and the importer can establish that (1) the sample was from the shipment in question and (2) the merchandise was not infringing or counterfeit, the liquidated damages claim "may be cancelled upon payment of an amount between one and five percent of the value of the merchandise in the shipment, but not less than $100."

XXXVIII. ADMINISTRATIVE PROTESTS

Certain actions of the Customs Service are subject to an administrative appeal through the protest procedure. A protest not only affords an opportunity for further administrative consideration, but in most cases is a mandatory predicate for judicial review of Customs Service decisions in the Court of International Trade.

19 U.S.C. § 1514(a) specifies the agency decisions that may be the subject of a protest. Section 1514(a)(4) defines those decisions concerning enforcement of intellectual property rights may be protested.

> Except as provided in subsection (b) of this section, section 1501 of this title (relating to voluntary reliquidations), section 1516 of this title (relating to petitions by domestic interested parties), and section 1520 of this title (relating to refunds and errors), decisions of the Customs Service, including the legality of all orders and findings entering into the same, as to
>
> * * *
>
> > - the exclusion of merchandise from entry or delivery or a demand for redelivery to customs custody under any provision of the customs laws, except a determination appealable under section 1337 of this title;
>
> shall be final and conclusive upon all persons (including the United States and any officer thereof) unless a protest is filed in accordance with this section. . . .

The regulations setting forth the actions to be taken in the event that imports of counterfeit or infringing goods are attempted speak only of seizure, or detention followed by seizure, and make no reference to "exclusion of merchandise from entry" as called for under the protest statute. *See* 19 C.F.R. §§ 133.21(b) (counterfeit trademarks), 133.42(c) (infringing copyrights), 133.22(b), (f) (trademark-infringing goods), 133.23(d), (f) (restricted gray market merchandise), and 133.43(a) and 133.44(a) (suspected copyright infringement).

Under 19 U.S.C. § 1499(c)(5), a detention of merchandise for more than thirty (30) days after its initial presentation for examination may be deemed a protestable exclusion from entry. Section 1499(c)(5)(A) provides that:

> The failure by the Customs Service to make a final determination with respect to the admissibility of detained merchandise within 30 days after the merchandise has been presented for customs examination, or such longer period if specifically authorized by law, shall be treated as a decision of the Customs Service to exclude the merchandise for purposes of section 1514(a)(4) of this title.

Thus, the Customs Service's failure to either release the goods from detention or make a formal determination of inadmissibility within the specified time period is itself a protestable event. An importer who wishes to file a protest must do so within ninety (90) days of this deemed decision. 19 U.S.C. § 1514(a).[57] A protest that is neither granted nor denied within thirty (30) days of filing is deemed to have been denied on that date. 19 U.S.C. § 1499(c)(5)(B) and 19 C.F.R. § 174.21(b); *Customs Headquarters Ruling 962006* (Dec. 21, 1999). In turn, the date of denial begins the 180-day statute of limitations for filing a lawsuit in the Court of International Trade. 19 U.S.C. § 1499(c)(5)(C); 28 U.S.C. § 1581(a).

The statutory detention period is identical to that imposed under 19 C.F.R. § 133.25(a) for trademark-infringing and restricted gray market items. At the end of the thirty-day period, the Customs Service must decide whether to release the goods—in which case there is no protestable decision—or seize them. If it decides on the latter course, the timing of events becomes crucial in determining whether a protestable event occurs. If the Customs Service issues a seizure notice on the thirtieth day, there is no exclusion of merchandise under Section 1499(c)(5)(A) but, instead, a seizure. *CDCOM (U.S.A.) Int'l, Inc. v. United States*, 963 F. Supp. 1214 (Ct. Int'l Trade 1997); *Tempco Marketing v. United States*, 957 F. Supp. 1276 (Ct. Int'l Trade 1997). On the other hand, if the seizure notice is issued after the thirtieth day, the merchandise is deemed to have been excluded even though it is subsequently seized. *See Milin Industries, Inc. v. United States*, 691 F. Supp. 1454, 1455, 1457-58 (Ct. Int'l Trade 1988) (exclusion of merchandise for failure to present textile visas was protestable following seizure) and *Genii Trading Co. v. United States*, 17 CIT 195 (1997) (noting *Milin Industries* but nevertheless declining to exercise jurisdiction).

The importer's ability to file a protest and thereafter appeal to the Court of International Trade depends on whether detained goods were first excluded, or instead were seized without exclusion. A seizure cannot be protested. *CDCOM (U.S.A.) Int'l*, 963 F. Supp. at 1217, citing *Int'l Maven, Inc. v. McCauley*, 678 F. Supp. 300, 302 (Ct. Int'l Trade 1988); *Customs Headquarters Ruling*

---

57 A failure to protest and pursue remedies in the Court of International Trade will not prevent the import from prosecuting a district court action seeking a declaratory judgment of non-infringement and cancellation of registered, recorded trademarks. *Stuhlbarg Int'l Sales Co., Inc. v. John D. Brush & Co., Inc.*, 240 F.3d 832 (9th Cir. 2001).

223077 (Sept. 16, 1991). Consequently, the protest remedy is unavailable for merchandise that is initially seized without prior detention for trademark counterfeiting, or for which the detention period does not exceed the thirty days prescribed under 19 U.S.C. § 1499(c)(5)(A).

The same rule regarding timing appears applicable to the Customs Service's copyright enforcement activities. The immediate seizure of a product under 19 C.F.R. § 133.42(a) would not be protestable. By contrast, a thirty-plus day detention period would be protestable, notwithstanding a subsequent seizure of the merchandise. *See Luxury Int'l I*, 69 F. Supp. 2d at 1368:

> Luxury filed a protest to contest Customs' decision to continue to exclude its goods, and Customs denied the protest. Under the plain meaning of 28 U.S.C. § 1581(a), 19 U.S.C. § 1514 and § 1515, the Court has the power to hear Luxury's complaint regarding Customs' denial of its protest against the continued exclusion of its goods.[58]

The relationship between the Section 133.43(b)-(d) procedure for administratively determining whether goods are infringing—a process that will take longer than thirty days—and the thirty-day rule of 19 U.S.C. § 1499(c)(5)(A), is unclear.[59] Under the latter statute, a failure to determine admissibility within that period is not protestable only if a "longer period [is] specifically authorized by law." 17 U.S.C. § 1603(b), which authorizes the administrative procedure for resolving suspected copyright infringement, does not "specifically authorize[]" a longer period. To insure that it acts in a timely manner, an importer that plans to protest the failure to release its merchandise for suspected copyright violations would be well-advised to file a protest within ninety days of the "deemed decision" to exclude its merchandise, even though administrative proceedings to assess the infringement issue may then be pending.[60]

The Customs Service will entertain protests against exclusion of goods for alleged trademark violations. In *Customs Headquarters Ruling 729488* (May 20, 1990), for example, the agency determined that certain goods covered by a protest were not trademark-infringing, and ordered their release to the importer. *See also Customs Headquarters Ruling 732508* (July 5, 1989).

19 U.S.C. § 1514(a)(4) also authorizes an importer to protest a demand for redelivery. An importer that cannot redeliver goods may seek a substantive determination on whether they are infringing through this procedure. *E.g.*,

---

58 The protest in *Luxury Int'l* was lodged against the Customs Service's decision to continue detaining the importer's merchandise in the face of the copyright owner's purportedly deficient tender of cash in lieu of a bond.

59 19 C.F.R. § 133.43(a) directs that suspected infringing goods shall have delivery withheld for thirty days. Such goods are detained only thereafter, if the importer denies infringement and the copyright owner files a demand for exclusion.

60 The *Luxury Int'l* court remanded the substantive violation issue to the Customs Service, and effectively stayed proceedings on the protest appeal until after receiving a remand determination.

Customs Headquarters Ruling 733249 (May 2, 1990). If the protest is successful, the importer can avoid a liquidated damages claim for failure to redeliver. *See Customs Headquarters Ruling 724253* (Oct. 24, 1984). The statute does not distinguish between notices to redeliver for infringement and for counterfeiting, so that the question of whether merchandise has a counterfeit trademark can be raised in a protest against a demand for redelivery.

XXXIX. COURT OF INTERNATIONAL TRADE JURISDICTION FOR DENIED ADMINISTRATIVE PROTESTS

A. Basic Procedures

The Court of International Trade has exclusive jurisdiction over an action commenced to challenge the Customs Service's denial of a protest. 28 U.S.C. § 1581(a). The applicable statute of limitations is 180 days from the "date of mailing of notice of denial of a protest." 28 U.S.C. § 2636(a)(1). Under 19 U.S.C. § 1499(c)(5)(B), a protest against exclusion of merchandise is deemed to have been denied thirty days after its filing in the absence of a grant or denial within that period. This deemed denial rule applies to protests lodged against both deemed exclusions under 19 U.S.C. § 1499(c)(5)(B) and affirmative decisions to exclude merchandise. *See also* 19 U.S.C. § 1515(b) (protest deemed denied thirty days after mailing by certified or registered mail if importer has requested accelerated disposition). An action filed before the protest is denied or deemed denied is premature, and the Court of International Trade will lack jurisdiction over it. *Seaside Food, Inc. v. United States*, 21 CIT 189 (1997).

A protest action is commenced by the filing of a summons. 28 U.S.C. § 2632(b); Court of International Trade Rule 3(a)(1). A complaint need not be filed until eighteen (18) months after the summons, Court of International Trade Rule 83(a), but the plaintiff in an action seeking release of detained merchandise would probably wish to move a bit faster than that. The complaint may be filed with the summons. Following commencement of the action, the Customs Service is required to transmit to the court the entry documents and other materials related to the challenged administrative determination. 28 U.S.C. § 2635(a); Court of International Trade Rule 70. The court will base its determination on the record made before it, 28 U.S.C. § 2640(a)(1), *i.e.*, it is not limited to the administrative record. See also 28 U.S.C. § 2641(A) (permitting parties to introduce evidence).

Intervention in protest actions is prohibited. 28 U.S.C. § 2631(j)(1)(A). Nevertheless, the domestic copyright owner was permitted to intervene in *Luxury Int'l*, pursuant to Court of International Trade Rule 24(a). The court found that the copyright owner met the criteria for intervention, in that it had a stake in the proceeding due to its posting of a security under 19 C.F.R. § 133.43(b)(6)(ii) and faced potential harm to its reputation in the event infringing goods were released into U.S. commerce. The parties do not appear to have addressed 28 U.S.C. § 2631(j)(1)(A)'s applicability to the action.

B. Jurisdictional Issues

Because, as discussed above, a seizure is not protestable, the denial of a protest against a seizure would be outside the Court of International Trade's jurisdiction. *Tempco Marketing*, 957 F. Supp. at 127. A number of cases have involved protests where merchandise was initially detained and thereafter seized, necessitating analyses of whether the protest addressed an exclusion or seizure and hence could give rise to the action. To resolve this question, the court has adopted the following four-part test.

1. Whether the protest itself states that it challenges exclusion or seizure of the goods.
2. Whether the plaintiff received a notice of seizure.
3. Whether the government has control of the merchandise.
4. Whether, following the seizure, the importer was given a choice between immediate forfeiture and petitioning for relief.

Genii Trading Co., 21 CIT at 196, citing *Int'l Maven*; *CDCOM (U.S.A.) Int'l*, 963 F. Supp. at 1217 n.8; *Tempco Marketing*, 957 F. Supp. at 1278.

Although this test was certainly appropriate in *Int'l Maven*, which addressed whether the Customs Service had in fact seized the goods and not first excluded them, it is misplaced in evaluating whether the court has jurisdiction over a deemed exclusion that is followed by a seizure. Specifically, the test overlooks the fact that a deemed exclusion is, by statute, an explicitly-protestable event, regardless of whether a seizure follows. The fact that the importer received a notice of seizure or was given the choice between immediate forfeiture and petitioning for relief has no bearing on whether a protestable deemed exclusion occurred under 19 U.S.C. § 1499(c)(5)(A)—the statute itself establishes that it has. Similarly, the government will have had control of merchandise during the detention and exclusion period; government control is not an exclusive hallmark of a seizure, but generally precedes it. Consequently, while the four-part test may provide guidance in determining whether a government action constitutes a seizure, it offers little practical guidance in determining whether a protestable deemed exclusion of merchandise has occurred.

The court has not held that a subsequent seizure supersedes and renders incontestable a previous deemed exclusion, which might be one basis for denying jurisdiction. To the contrary, in *Milin Industries*, 691 F. Supp. at 1457, the court found that it had jurisdiction over an exclusion of goods despite a subsequent seizure, and even though the protest against exclusion was not filed until after the seizure occurred. *Milin Industries* involved an exclusion for lack of textile visas, and an underlying dispute as the goods' tariff classification, rather than trademark infringement. Nevertheless, its analysis is equally applicable in trademark and copyright cases.[61]

The court in *Genii Trading Co.* and *Tempco Marketing* also declined to exercise jurisdiction on the ground that the cases involved questions of trademark law, over which Federal district courts had exclusive jurisdiction pursuant to 28 U.S.C. § 1331. This position highlights a split in the court's approach to cases involving substantive intellectual property questions. In a number of cases, the court has concluded that its jurisdictional reach does not include intellectual property issues, even though they arise in the context of Customs Service action. In other cases, the court has shown no difficulty in resolving issues of trademark and copyright law.

The first decisions declining to exercise jurisdiction were issued in 1982 and 1983. In *Lois Jeans & Jackets, U.S.A., Inc. v. United States*, 566 F. Supp. 1523 (Ct. Int'l Trade 1983), the court found procedural irregularities in the Customs Service's change of position concerning whether the importer's merchandise was counterfeit and rendered a judgment in the plaintiff's favor. The court noted that "the infringement issue is not within the exclusive jurisdiction of the Court of International Trade nor within the Court's special expertise in matters relating to international trade," 566 F. Supp. at 1528, and that parallel infringement proceedings were simultaneously underway in Federal district court. Because the interests of "judicial expertise, economy and efficiency" were best served in the district court, the Court of International Trade did not address the trademark issues. *See also Lois Jeans & Jackets, U.S.A., Inc. v. United States*, 5 CIT 216 (1983) (court noted pending district court action on substantive trademark questions and stayed further proceedings in its action pending the outcome of that case).

In a nearly contemporaneous decision, *Bally/Midway Mfg. Co. v. Regan*, 565 F. Supp. 1045 (Ct. Int'l Trade 1983), the court found that it lacked jurisdiction over a domestic copyright owner's action against the Customs Service's failure to exclude from entry allegedly infringing merchandise. Jurisdiction would not lie under 28 U.S.C. § 1581(i) because the case did not involve an embargo or other quantitative restriction, nor under 28 U.S.C. § 1581(h) because it did not involve pre-importation review. The action was transferred to Federal district court,

61 In the *Luxury Int'l* litigation, "the Court issued an order prohibiting Customs from instituting seizure proceedings pending resolution of the case or until the Court granted permission to commence seizure proceedings." 90 F. Supp. 2d at 1296. The decision did not explain whether this was a precautionary step to guard against possible loss of jurisdiction in the event seizure proceedings were instituted by the Customs Service. To the extent the Court of International Trade anticipated that a seizure made after commencement of an action would deprive it of jurisdiction, it could issue an "All Writs Act" injunction to preserve its jurisdiction. *See Zenith Radio Corp. v. United States*, 710 F.2d 806 (Fed. Cir. 1983).

apparently due to that court's exercise of exclusive jurisdiction over copyright matters under 28 U.S.C. § 1338.[62]

Although *Lois Jeans & Jackets* and *Bally/Midway* flirted with the idea that the Court of International Trade lacked jurisdiction over substantive intellectual property matters and that exclusive jurisdiction lay in Federal district courts, they did not explicitly adopt this position. In *Int'l Maven*, an action challenging a seizure of allegedly counterfeit goods, the court made this leap in the context of rejecting jurisdiction under 28 U.S.C. § 1581(i).[63]

> The underlying dispute in this action would require a determination on the substantive law governing trademark and counterfeit goods. Under 28 U.S.C. §§ 1331 and 1338, the district courts have original jurisdiction over actions based on federal statutes relating to trademarks.

678 F. Supp. at 303 (citations omitted). Accordingly, the court found that it lacked Section 1581(i) jurisdiction, as the complaint did not deal with Customs Service "administration and enforcement" of a matter otherwise within the court's jurisdiction.

Although the quoted *Int'l Maven* discussion concerned jurisdiction under 28 U.S.C. § 1581(i), and did not address whether substantive trademark issues were cognizable under 28 U.S.C. § 1581(a) following denial of a valid protest, the decisions in *Genii Trading Co.* and *Tempco Marketing* arguably have extended it that far. Because both cases found that the importer had not protested an exclusion under the four *Int'l Maven/Milin Industries* factors, they did not squarely address the issue of whether the court should refuse an otherwise-valid protest case solely because it raised substantive trademark issues. At a minimum, however, those cases have held that the presence of substantive trademark issues provides an additional reason for not accepting Section 1581(a) jurisdiction.[64]

The Ninth Circuit in *Stuhlbarg Int'l* cited *Tempco Marketing* and *Milin Industries* for the proposition that the Court of International Trade lacks jurisdiction over substantive trademark matters. The court rejected the domestic trademark owner's argument that the importer should have been required to exhaust protest remedies. The underlying dispute—the trademark's validity—was

---

62 A slightly earlier case, *Kidco, Inc. v. United States*, 4 CIT 103 (1982), similarly rejected jurisdiction over a copyright owner's action challenging the Customs Service's enforcement procedures, on the ground that no embargo or other quantitative restriction was in place. Although the court noted the existence of parallel proceedings in Federal district court, it did not assert that it lacked jurisdiction over copyright matters that might arise under 28 U.S.C. § 1581(a).

63 The first fatal defect in plaintiff's case was that it had protested a seizure, which was not a decision covered under 19 U.S.C. §§ 1514(a) and 1515 and 28 U.S.C. § 1581(a).

64 Although *Genii Trading Co.* and *Tempco Marketing* concerned trademark matters, their reasoning would be equally applicable to copyrights.

outside the Court of International Trade's jurisdiction, and the inherent delays in the protest procedure rendered it inadequate.[65]

Another line of cases takes the view that the court's protest jurisdiction is broad enough to permit adjudication of substantive copyright and trademark disputes arising between an importer and the Customs Service. In *Schaper Manufacturing Co. v. Regan*, 566 F. Supp. 894 (Ct. Int'l Trade 1983)—decided shortly after *Bally/Midway*—the court assumed jurisdiction over a domestic copyright owner's lawsuit concerning alleged deficiencies in the Customs Service's enforcement procedure. It noted that the complaint related to administration and enforcement of the Customs regulations, thereby distinguishing it from *Bally/Midway*. In evaluating the "gravamen of the complaint," the court acknowledged its reference to the copyright laws in Title 17, United States Code. It found that the action did not involve a question of copyright infringement but rather Customs Service enforcement, and thus was outside the district court's exclusive grant of jurisdiction over copyright matters. Rather, the allegation went to the agency's "administration and enforcement" of the laws and regulations restricting importation of infringing copyrights, and was thus cognizable under 28 U.S.C. § 1581(i).[66]

In discussing the scope of its jurisdiction, the *Schaper* court noted the government's concession "that the right of protest and subsequent judicial review by this court under 19 U.S.C. § 1514 is available to the importer challenging the determination of customs to exclude merchandise because of its piratical character. *See Norwood Imports v. United States*, 48 Cust. Ct. 1 (1961)."[67] This statement implies that the court could hear all aspects of a protest against exclusion, including the substantive copyright issues. The court further indicated that a district court's exclusive jurisdiction over copyright matters would not arise until a claim for infringement between private parties was filed there.

In *M.W. Kasch Co. v. United States*, 640 F. Supp. 1335 (Ct. Int'l Trade 1986), the court declined to dismiss an action contesting the denial of a protest against

65 The Customs Service itself considers that it "has no authority to question the validity of the [trademark] registration." *Customs Headquarters Ruling 460360* (June 30, 1995).

66 *Schaper's* continued vitality is questionable in light of its identification of copyright enforcement as "a concomitant part of the function of raising 'revenue from imports'." Based on this conclusion, the court located its jurisdictional grant in 28 U.S.C. § 1581(i)(4), which provides jurisdiction over the Customs Service's "administration and enforcement with respect to" "any law of the United States arising from—revenue from imports or tonnage." The Supreme Court's jurisdictional discussion in *K Mart Corp. v. Cartier, Inc.*, 485 U.S. 176 (1988), would preclude the use of 28 U.S.C. § 1581(i)(3) and (4), relating to administration and enforcement of "embargoes or other quantitative restrictions," as an alternative ground for jurisdiction under Section 1581(i).

67 The court did not have to determine the scope of its protest jurisdiction under 28 U.S.C. § 1581(a), as *Schaper* did not involve a protest. Rather, the court looked to its authority to review a protest as a guide to its authority to hear a domestic copyright owner's complaint against administration of the customs laws.

detention of merchandise for copyright infringement. The court (and apparently the parties) did not address whether a detention was protestable.[68] From the discussion in *M.W. Kasch*, it appears that the protest was filed against a detention, and that no decision to exclude the merchandise had been rendered by the Customs Service.

However, the court did reject the government's argument that the district court's exclusive jurisdiction over copyright matters under 28 U.S.C. § 1338 precluded the Court of International Trade from resolving whether the plaintiff's merchandise was infringing. Relying in part on *Schaper*,[69] the court found that:

> However narrow the definition of "exclusion of merchandise . . . under any provision of the customs laws " within the meaning of 19 U.S.C. § 1514(a)(4), such definition still encompasses the acts of Customs complained of herein.

640 F. Supp. at 1340. The court also noted that a district court hearing a previously-filed companion case had opined that the matter fell within the Court of International Trade's exclusive jurisdiction. *Id.* at 1335, 1340.

In *Luxury Int'l II*, the court relied on its protest jurisdiction to review the Customs Service's substantive decision that the imports infringed a recorded copyright. Although the discussion was brief—"Customs acted properly pursuant to its authority to make determinations concerning copyright infringement," 90 F. Supp. at 1299—it is noteworthy for having addressed the issue at all.

Finally, in *Ross Cosmetics*, 17 CIT 814 (1993) ("*Ross Cosmetics I*"), *following remand*, 18 CIT 979 (1994) ("*Ross Cosmetics II*"), the court addressed trademark counterfeiting and infringement issues that arose from a pre-importation ruling issued by the Customs Service. The court's jurisdictional competence to consider these issues was neither questioned by the government nor commented on by the court. The *Ross Cosmetics* decisions certainly demonstrated the Court of International Trade's ability to address complex trademark matters.

---

68 This 1986 decision preceded the legislative enactment, codified at 19 U.S.C. § 1499(c)(5)(A), directing that the Customs Service's failure to render a decision concerning the admissibility of merchandise within thirty days was itself a protestable decision; that legislation was adopted in 1993, in the *North American Free Trade Agreement Implementation Act*, § 613, 107 Stat. 2171.

69 Both *Schaper* and *M.W. Kasch* cited *Norwood Imports v. United States*, 48 Cust. Ct. 1 (1961), decided by the Court of International Trade's predecessor tribunal, the Customs Court. As explained in *M.W. Kasch*, in *Norwood*:

> . . . the plaintiff invoked the court's jurisdiction as a result of a protest pursuant to [19 U.S.C. § 1514] to claim that Customs had erroneously excluded artificial geraniums from entry into the country on the ground that they were piratical copies. It is unclear from the report of the decision whether jurisdiction was contested by the government, but, in any event, the court reached the merits in deciding the case.

XL. COURT OF INTERNATIONAL TRADE JURISDICTION FOR PRE-IMPORTATION RULINGS

From an importer's perspective, the primary problem with protest jurisdiction is that it requires an importation, or an attempted importation, before the court is empowered to hear the dispute. This means that the importer will either have its goods detained and thereafter seized or seized at the outset, and face the probability of forfeiture and possible penalties in addition to the cost of losing the goods as a condition of proceeding to court. Unless the importer wishes to orchestrate a nominal value "test" shipment to underlie its protest claim, the prospect of protesting and only then proceeding into court is undesirable and potentially expensive.

The Court of International Trade has been provided with exclusive jurisdiction over pre-importation challenges to a ruling issued by the Customs Service, permitting the importer to bypass the import and protest requirement. Pursuant to 28 U.S.C. § 1581(h),

> The Court of International Trade shall have exclusive jurisdiction of any civil action commenced to review, prior to the importation of the goods involved, a ruling issued by the Secretary of the Treasury, or a refusal to issue or change such a ruling, relating to classification, valuation, rate of duty, marking, restricted merchandise, entry requirements, drawbacks, vessel repairs, or similar matters, but only if the party commencing the civil action demonstrates to the court that he would be irreparably harmed unless given an opportunity to obtain judicial review prior to such importation.

Section 1581(h) jurisdiction appears to be readily applicable to an importer's challenge to a ruling that its goods are infringing or counterfeit, and thus will be denied entry to the United States if importation is attempted. Indeed, jurisdiction was founded on 28 U.S.C. § 1581(h) in *Ross Cosmetics*, *see* 17 CIT at 814, in which the importer challenged a Customs Service ruling that the packaging proposed for its merchandise constituted counterfeit use of several trademarks. *Ross Cosmetics* is noteworthy both because it reviewed a trademark-related ruling under Section 1581(h) jurisdiction, and because it showed the Court of International Trade's willingness to critically evaluate the Customs Service's factual and legal findings regarding trademark matters.

The Court of International Trade has identified four requirements for jurisdiction under Section 1581(h):

> (1) review must be sought prior to importation; (2) review sought must be for a ruling; (3) the ruling must relate to certain subject matter; and (4) the importer must show that irreparable harm will result unless judicial review prior to importation is obtained.

American Frozen Food Institute, Inc. v. United States, 855 F. Supp. 388, 393 (Ct. Int'l Trade 1994), citing *Nat'l Juice Products Ass'n v. United States*, 628 F. Supp. 978, 982 (Ct. Int'l Trade 1986). *American Frozen Food* also noted that "the burden of establishing that jurisdiction exists" rests on the plaintiff. 855 F. Supp. at 393.

The *American Frozen Food* factors appear to be readily applicable to review of intellectual property rulings. First, it is unlikely that an importer will attempt entry of an article that a ruling has determined to be infringing or counterfeit, as such merchandise is subject to detention and/or seizure. Because the timing of an importation is inherently within the importer's control, minimal planning will insure that no imports of the merchandise in question are attempted prior to commencement of a lawsuit under Section 1581(h). Of course, if the importer wishes to attempt making an importation before filing its case, it can thereafter proceed to court under Section 1581(a) protest jurisdiction.

Second, as long as the importer followed the proper procedures for seeking a ruling under the Customs Service's 19 U.S.C. § 1625 ruling program and actually received one from the Customs Service, it would meet the requirement that "review sought must be for a ruling."

Third, the ruling would relate to subject matter within the purview of Section 1581(h), *i.e.*, a ruling issued under the Customs Service's 19 U.S.C. § 1625 ruling program. Such a ruling would concern "a ruling issued by the Secretary of the Treasury" that relates to "restricted merchandise" (and, arguably, "entry requirements"), and would fall within the specified subject matter.

The biggest potential stumbling block to the court taking jurisdiction is the fourth requirement, that the importer demonstrate that it would be irreparably harmed if pre-importation review is not allowed. The government has challenged jurisdiction in a number of other Section 1581(h) cases, however. Although none of these involved an intellectual property issue, they do provide guidance as to the showing required by the court for the proper invocation of Section 1581(h) jurisdiction.

In *American Frozen Food*, 855 F. Supp. at 393-94, the plaintiff demonstrated that it would incur substantial irrecoverable costs to redesign packaging and faced potential additional future compliance costs due to a procedurally-defective rulemaking procedure. The court agreed that the costs and indefinite period before issuance of a final rule qualified as irreparable harm. The court in *CPC Int'l, Inc. v. United States*, 896 F. Supp. 1240, 1234 (Ct. Int'l Trade 1995), found that a ruling "that would cause the importer to incur costs expenditures, business disruption or other financial losses, for which the importer has no legal redress to recover in court" is "irreparable harm within the purview of § 1581(h)." The plaintiff in *Holford USA Ltd., Inc. v. United States*, 912 F. Supp. 555 (Ct. Int'l Trade 1995), sought review of a ruling that effectively would have excluded its merchandise from the United States or forced it to incur substantial costs; the court agreed that these sufficed to show irreparable harm.

These decisions provide guidance as to the type and extent of potential harm that an importer could point to in seeking review of an intellectual property ruling.[70] The potential forfeiture of seized merchandise under an adverse ruling provides

70 The issue of irreparable harm was not addressed in the *Ross Cosmetics* decision, apparently because the government did not contest the basis for jurisdiction.

an additional indicator of irreparable harm—without pre-importation review, the importer would face the loss of its merchandise. In the case of items that a ruling determines to have a counterfeit trademark, the importer would face the further harm of monetary penalties under 19 U.S.C. § 1526(f) and criminal proceedings under 18 U.S.C. § 2320. Importers of copyrights deemed infringing may also face criminal sanctions under 17 U.S.C. § 506 and 18 U.S.C. §§ 2318, 2319, and/or 2319A.

A domestic intellectual property owner that sought a ruling as to whether certain goods would be considered infringing or counterfeit by the Customs Service could also seek review under this jurisdictional provision. The ruling program permits such domestic parties to seek rulings, so the second and third *American Frozen Food* factors could be met: review would be sought for a ruling, and would relate to a matter subject to Section 1581(h)'s coverage.

Regarding the first *American Frozen Food* factor, specific merchandise that was the subject of the ruling request could be imported before the court case was commenced, or even before the ruling was issued; the timing of importation is inherently outside the domestic intellectual property owner's control. On the other hand, the plaintiff could argue that the ruling would have prospective application, as it would affect imports made after the court has ruled. The Court of International Trade recently found that Section 1581(h) actions may consider issues that are applicable to actual entries of merchandise, as long as those entries were only contemplated at the time the action was commenced. *Heartland By-Products, Inc. v. United States*, Slip Op. 02-22 (Feb. 26, 2002). By limiting the relief sought to entries that were made after the action's commencement, the domestic intellectual property owner would likely conform to Section 1581(h)'s requirement.

A plaintiff seeking 28 U.S.C. § 1581(h) review of a ruling's conclusion that goods are not infringing or counterfeit would also have a conceptual basis for proving irreparable harm. The argument would be that pursuing judicial review after the goods have been imported will not remedy the harm caused by the allegedly infringing or counterfeit imports.[71] The Court of International Trade

71 Because the Court of International Trade's protest jurisdiction is limited to importers, a domestic intellectual property owner could not obtain jurisdiction under 28 U.S.C. § 1581(a). Jurisdiction under 28 U.S.C. § 1581(i) is doubtful. The restrictions on infringing or counterfeit imports do not provide "revenue," nor do they impose "tariffs, duties, fees, or other taxes on the importation of merchandise for reasons other than the than the raising of revenue." Accordingly, subsections 1581(i)(1) and (2) are inapplicable. Subsection 1581(i)(3) is unavailable in light of the Supreme Court's finding in *K Mart Corp. v. Cartier, Inc.*, 485 U.S. at 184-86, that the 19 U.S.C. Part 133 regulations do not establish "embargoes or other quantitative restrictions on the importation of merchandise." Subsection 1581(i)(4) relates to "administration and enforcement" of other areas over which the court has been provided jurisdiction. However, a domestic intellectual property owner's lawsuit would not involve administration and enforcement of a protestable matter under 28 U.S.C. § 1581(a), *K Mart Corp.*, 485 U.S. at 190-91, nor of a matter covered under Section 1581(i)(1)-(3). Consequently, Section

has recognized that a party's lost profits, lost good will, and tarnished good name could qualify as irreparable harm for Section 1581(h) purposes. *Thyssen Steel Co. v. United States*, 712 F. Supp. 202, 205 (Ct. Int'l Trade 1989). Even if money damages for the former harm could be awarded in a Federal district court action, the latter two may not be susceptible to a monetary remedy. "Trademark infringement by its very nature results in irreparable injury since the attendant loss of goodwill, reputation and business cannot adequately be quantified and the trademark owner cannot adequately be compensated." *Pepsico, Inc. v. Torres*, 27 U.S.P.Q.2d 1948 (C.D. Cal. 1993) (citations omitted).

XLI. DISTRICT COURT JURISDICTION FOR FORFEITURES

An importer or other claimant to goods seized by the Customs Service decisions can await the outcome of administrative mitigation proceedings, including resolution of its petition(s) for relief. As the Court of International Trade has noted, "[i]n the majority of cases, this petition for remission or mitigation settles the dispute, eliminating the need for judicial intervention [citations omitted]. If this process does not resolve the issue, then by the government bringing a judicial condemnation proceeding, the claimant is permitted to assert his claim or interest in the property." [Citation omitted.] *Int'l Maven, Inc.*, 678 F. Supp. at 302.

Federal district courts have exclusive jurisdiction over such seizures pursuant to 28 U.S.C. § 1356:

> The district courts shall have original jurisdiction, exclusive of the courts of the States, of any seizure under any law of the United States on land or upon waters not within admiralty and maritime jurisdiction, except matters within the jurisdiction of the Court of International Trade under section 1582 of this title.

In such actions, the government is required to "show the existence of facts sufficient to establish probable cause" that the alleged violation occurred, including the elements of the underlying intellectual property violation. *United States v. One Lot of Approximately Twenty Thousand Pairs of Counterfeit Blue Jeans*, 601 F. Supp. 476, 479 (W.D.N.C. 1985). Once the government has done so, the burden of proof shifts to the claimant. *Id.*, citing 19 U.S.C. § 1615.

The court will review the underlying merits of the alleged intellectual property violation, *see United States v. 10,510 Packaged Computer Towers*, 152 F. Supp. 2d 1189 (N.D. Cal. 2001). Judicial review of the Customs Service's disposition of forfeited articles appears to be limited to considering whether the agency followed statutory and regulatory requirements. *United States v. One Lot of Approximately Twenty Thousand Pairs of Counterfeit Blue Jeans*, 601 F. Supp. at 482.

1581(i)(4) is an unlikely source of jurisdiction. It appears that, outside of Section 1581(h), the domestic plaintiff's only judicial recourse against Customs Service enforcement decisions would be to file an action in Federal district court under 28 U.S.C. §§ 1331 and/or 1338. *See Societe des Produits Nestle, S.A. v. Casa Helvetia, Inc.*, 982 F.2d 633 (1st Cir. 1992).

XLII. FACTORS IN EVALUATING THE JUDICIAL FORUM TO CHOOSE

The Court of International Trade may provide a more hospitable venue for importers seeking to undo the Customs Service's exclusion of their products, or demand for redelivery of products to Customs custody. The standard of review applicable to protest cases arising from 19 U.S.C. § 1499(c)(5)(A) is that the government must establish the alleged violation by a preponderance of the evidence:

> Notwithstanding section 2639 of title 28, once an action respecting a detention is commenced, unless the Customs Service establishes by a preponderance of the evidence that an admissibility decision has not been reached for good cause, the court shall grant the appropriate relief which may include, but is not limited to, an order to cancel the detention and release the merchandise.

19 U.S.C. § 1499(c)(5)(C). This standard places a greater burden on the government to prove the underlying violation than the "probable cause" standard applicable to district court actions under 28 U.S.C. § 1356. However, it applies only when the Customs Service has failed to reach a determination concerning eligibility for entry. If a determination that the merchandise is inadmissible is made, the burden of proving the decision incorrect is placed on the plaintiff. 28 U.S.C. § 2639(a)(1); *see North American Free Trade Agreement Implementation Act*, H.R. Rep. 103-361 Part I, 103d Cong., 1st Sess. (1993) at 109-10.

The Court of International Trade may also provide faster review of the matter. An importer could file its case within sixty days from the date of initial detention (thirty to await the protestable "deemed exclusion," plus thirty to await the "deemed denial" of the protest). Additionally, an action contesting the exclusion of merchandise should be given under Court of International Trade Rule 3(g)(4).

Pre-importation review of a ruling pursuant to 28 U.S.C. § 1581(h) avoids the expense and delay of actually importing merchandise that the Customs Service has ruled is inadmissible. This procedure thus relieves the potential importer of concern that its goods will be forfeited.

XLIII. THE SUBSTANTIVE LAW APPLIED BY THE CUSTOMS SERVICE

A. "Copying or Simulating" Trademarks

The Customs regulations define "[a] 'copying or simulating' trademark or trade name" as "one which may so resemble a recorded mark or name as to be likely to cause the public to associate the copying or simulating mark or name with the recorded mark or name." 19 C.F.R. § 133.22(a). Although the regulations do not provide any further guidance concerning the way in which the Customs Service will interpret the "copying or simulating" standard, the agency and its reviewing court have made it clear that they apply the general principles of trademark law.

1. The *Ross Cosmetics* Decisions

In *Ross Cosmetics*, *supra*, the Court of International Trade had to determine whether an importer's proposed packaging was likely to cause confusion by comparing the articles it enclosed with named trademarked articles. Although the case dealt specifically with the requirements for comparative advertising claims, it also provided a useful general discussion of the standards for determining trademark infringement for Customs Service enforcement purposes.

> The basic test for statutory trademark infringement is 'likelihood of confusion', which has been construed by courts to mean a probability of confusion rather than a possibility of confusion. *See* 2 McCarthy on Trademarks and Unfair Competition §23.01[3][a]. In order to determine whether a likelihood of confusion exists, courts apply and balance multiple factors. *Id.* §23.03[1]. The commonly used factors include: the degree of resemblance between the existing marks, the similarity of the marketing methods and channels of distribution; where the goods are not directly competitive, the likelihood that the senior user will expand into the field of the junior user; the degree of distinctiveness of the mark; the characteristics of the prospective purchasers and the degree of care they exercise; the intent of the alleged infringer; and evidence of actual confusion. *Id.*

18 CIT at 986-987.

The *Ross Cosmetics* litigation involved an importer's challenge to *Customs Headquarters Ruling 451142* (June 27, 1991), which held that the importer's proposed package labeling would constitute counterfeit use of certain registered trademarks. The imported articles were various perfumes that supposedly smelled like certain "famous brand" trademarked perfumes. The proposed packaging would bear the statements "COMPARE TO [famous brand name] YOU WILL SWITCH TO [importer's brand name]" and "OUR PRODUCT IS IN NO MANNER ASSOCIATED WITH OR LICENSED BY THE MAKERS OF [famous brand name]." The three trademarks in question that had been recorded with the Customs Service, and the importer's corresponding brand, were "Youth Dew/Morning Dream," "Giorgio/Gorgeous," and "Opium/Oblivion."[72]

In *Ross Cosmetics I*, the court implicitly accepted the view that "the mere use of the names registered as trademarks in and of itself is not considered a violation of trademark protection," thus following the mainstream judicial view that a competitor's use of another's trademarked name is not *per se* infringing. The court faulted the Customs Service's assertion that the imported articles posed a likelihood of confusion based solely on a comparison of the import packaging with facsimile copies of the recorded trademarks' PTO registrations. Rather, the proper analysis required that the importer's "proposed packages should be compared with the actual packages bearing the registered trademarks or reasonable reproductions representing the design and color of the trademarks."

---

72 The court also provided useful analyses of the Customs Service's authority concerning counterfeit goods, the differences between counterfeit and infringing goods, and the circumstances in which comparative advertising may qualify as counterfeit use of a trademark; these are discussed in Section 3 below.

The court also noted the agency's position that the words "no" or "not" are ineffective disclaimers, and stated that the disclaimer's effectiveness had to be evaluated "in the context of the entire package" based on comparisons of the importer's packaging to that of the recorded trademarks, taking into account the color and design of each. The Customs Service had failed to conduct this comparison, and instead relied solely on disclaimer language which it assumed to be ineffective.

The court further rejected the Customs Service's argument that the importer had the burden of "disproving the likelihood of confusion," particularly because the agency had proceeded based on an inadequate record and failed to seek additional information on its own or from the importer. Because of all these inadequacies, the case was remanded for the agency to conduct the appropriate packaging comparisons.

In its remand determination, the Customs Service concluded that three of the importer's proposed packages were non-infringing, but that the other three constituted counterfeit or infringing use of registered trademarks and should not be permitted to enter the U.S. *Ross Cosmetics II* addressed the importer's objections to the remand's adverse findings as to two of the products; the controversy as to the third was rendered moot by a settlement stipulation between the importer and trademark owner in separate litigation. The court disagreed that the packaging was counterfeit, and went on to find that one of the considerations was whether the packaging infringed the trademarks.

The court agreed that the importer's "Gorgeous" product infringed the "Giorgio" trademark. "Giorgio" had inherent distinctiveness and thus was "a strong mark entitled to a broad scope of protection." The two names were used on identical products, as defined by trademark product class. There was "a high degree of similarity between the two packages" as indicated by their use of alternating stripes of identical color and width, crests of nearly-identical colors, product name placement in nearly identical positions, and the similar "consonants, vowels, and sounds" in both product names. These close similarities suggested that the importer deliberately designed its packaging to be similar to that of the recorded mark. While the imports' lower quality meant they would likely be sold in different channels of distribution than "Giorgio," there was evidence of overlap in commercial channels. Finally, the likelihood that the imports would be bought on "impulse" made it unlikely that a purchaser would closely examine the differences in packaging.

Having agreed that there was a likelihood of confusion, the court then evaluated the adequacy of the import packaging disclaimer. The name "Giorgio" was located in a prominent position at the top of the package, while the disclaimer was located at the bottom and was written in relatively small type size. The disclaimer thus "could be easily overlooked by consumers and therefore is insufficient to dispel the likelihood of confusion."

The court reached a similar conclusion regarding the importer's "Love Birds" packaging. The factors weighing in favor of an infringement finding were that the registered trademark was distinctive and thus inherently strong, the two names in question were used on identical products, and the imports would be purchased on impulse. In addition, there were several packaging similarities, including a yellow background and a front panel oval with birds in flight depicted in it. The import packaging displayed the registered trademark "L'Air du Temps" more prominently than the import's own name, and had the disclaimer at the bottom in small typeface. On the other hand, the two products did not appear to be sold in the same retail outlets. On balance, the court found that the evidence in favor of both infringement and inadequacy of the disclaimer supported the Customs Service's finding of a likelihood of confusion from the import packaging.[73]

Ross Cosmetics was decided under a deferential standard of review that precluded the court from conducting its own fact finding. As the court noted in *Ross Cosmetics II*, review *de novo* could lead to a different outcome. 18 CIT at 989. Because of the case's procedural posture, the court's analysis was limited to determining whether "there is a rational connection between the facts found and the determination made by" the Customs Service. *Id.*

Nevertheless, the *Ross Cosmetics* decisions provide the only guidance from the Court of International Trade to the Customs Service concerning the standards that the latter should apply in evaluating whether imported articles are either infringing or counterfeit, and whether a disclaimer suffices to negate a finding of likelihood of confusion. In this regard, they stand as crucial precedent for the court, the agency, and importers and trademark owners alike.

2. Administrative Rulings

Interestingly, the Customs Service has not acknowledged the *Ross Cosmetics* precedent in its published rulings concerning trademark infringement. Rather, to the extent that they cite a precedential basis for their analysis, Customs Service rulings tend to rely on *Polaroid Corp. v. Polarad Electronics Corp.*, 287 F.2d 492 (2d Cir.), *cert. denied*, 368 U.S. 820 (1961). In the agency's view, *Polaroid* presents the following factors to be used in determining whether there is a likelihood of confusion: (1) the degree of similarity between the marks; (2) similarity of the products; (3) actual confusion; (4) sophistication of the buyers; (5) the defendant's good faith in adopting the mark; (6) the strength of the registered mark; and (7) channels of trade. *Customs Headquarters Rulings 462025* (June

73 Because the "L'Air du Temps" trademark was not recorded with the Customs Service, *see* 17 CIT at 814, the court should have concluded its analysis upon finding that the import packaging was not counterfeit. Recordation under 19 C.F.R. § 133.1 is a condition precedent to Customs Service enforcement against a "copying or simulating" article. Consequently, the Customs Service lacked authority to take action against the infringing imports, and the court should not have taken up the question of whether the imports infringed.

20, 1996), *460360* (June 30, 1995), *459411* (May 26, 1995), *459012* (May 2, 1995), and *459018* (Jan. 5, 1995).

In evaluating the degree of similarity, the Customs Service will consider whether the imported and recorded marks:

> are similar in appearance and sound. *See Communications Satellite Corporation v. Comcet, Inc.*, 429 F.2d 1245 (4th Cir. 1970); *American Cyanamid Co. v. United States Rubber Co*, 356 F.2d 1008, 53 C.C.P.A. 994, 148 U.S.P.Q. 729 (1966); *David Sherman Corp. v. Heublein, Inc.*, 340 F.2d 377 (8th Cir. 1965) and *G. D. Searle & Co. v. Chas Pfizer & Co.*, 265 F.2d 385 (7th Cir. 1959)."

Customs Headquarters Ruling 459012 (May 2, 1995). Based on this standard, the agency found "that the words 'LYCRI' and 'LYCRO' are 'confusingly similar' to the recorded marks" with the word "LYCRA."

Also applying the first factor in *Polaroid*, the Customs Service found little similarity between imported embroidered patches having a star, a dog or wolf, and the word "Cowboys," and the trademarked National Football League team design consisting "of a football helmet with a star in the middle on each side. The only similarity between the embroidered patch and the recorded design is that they both contain a star." Because the patch did not provide an immediate suggestion of association with football generally or the Dallas Cowboys particularly, and the word "Cowboys" was not part of the recorded trademark, the Customs Service found a minimal degree of similarity. *Customs Headquarters Ruling 458516* (Jan. 5, 1995).

Customs Headquarters Ruling 460360 (June 30, 1995) applied the degree of similarity factor to a configuration trademark. It adopted the standard set forth in *Chemlawn Servs. Corp. v. GNC Pumps, Inc.*, 690 F. Supp. 1560 (1988), stating that it would consider "whether the suspect mark incorporates the distinctive features which are unique to the registered configuration trademark so as to cause confusion between consumers."

The ruling also held that the imported product's inclusion of the manufacturer's own brand name "is a significant factor in reducing likelihood of confusion among consumers as to the source of the product. *Ziebart Intern. Corp. v. After Market Associates*, 802 F.2d 220 (7th Cir. 1986), cited in *G. Heileman Brewing Co. v. Anheuser-Busch, Inc.*, 873 F.2d 985 (7th Cir. 1989)." *Compare Customs Headquarters Ruling 719127* (1983) ("courts around the country have acknowledged that an infringer does not avoid infringement by putting his own name or mark on the goods together with the infringing mark. . . . An infringement on a registered trademark is an infringement without consideration of the placement of the name of a manufacturer or other designs.")

Beyond merely noting whether the imported and trademarked goods are similar, the rulings have not separately addressed the second *Polaroid* factor, the degree of similarity between the products.

Consideration of the third, fourth and fifth *Polaroid* factors—actual confusion, sophistication of the buyers, and the alleged infringer's good faith in adopting the mark—is virtually always absent from Customs rulings, apparently because the parties requesting them failed to include information on these points. *E.g.*, *Customs Headquarters Ruling 462025* ("[i]nsufficient evidence was presented for us to evaluate the strength of the recorded mark and [requester's] good faith in adopting the mark. Also, no evidence was presented for us to evaluate actual confusion among consumers.") In light of the judicial deference that may be accorded to a ruling under *Mead*, an importer would be foolish to submit a ruling request with such deficiencies.

The fourth factor, sophistication of an article's purchasers, was given paramount importance in *Customs Headquarters Ruling 709649* (May 1, 1979), which considered whether an imported pectolytic enzyme product called "Pectinex" was confusingly similar to the recorded trademark "Pectinol." Both the imported and trademarked products were sold to fruit processors. The ruling found that the imported product posed little likelihood of confusion, as both products were sold to sophisticated professional buyers who were unlikely to be confused by similar trademarks, "due to the fact that the law recognizes and attributes superior knowledge and awareness to that class of purchaser." In addition, the recorded trademark's use of the descriptive word "pectin" was given little significance; instead, the ruling looked to the non-descriptive suffixes "ex" and "ol", and stated that they "neither look nor sound alike."

Concerning strength of the recorded trademark, the Customs Service has adopted the view that a "fanciful and a famous mark which has gained recognition throughout the world through advertising and sales campaigns" will be considered "strong." *Customs Headquarters Ruling 27818* (March 12, 1986).

Finally, regarding channels of trade, the Customs Service looks to "whether there is a relationship in use, promotion, distribution, or roles, between the parties' goods. *Forum Corp. Of North America v. Forum, Ltd.*, 903 F.2d 434 (7th Cir. 1990)." *Customs Headquarters Ruling 460360* (mass merchant retailers selling to hobbyists and do-it-yourself users, and jobbers catering to professionals, provide different channels of trade and intended consumers).

3. Comparative Advertising

In addition to the ruling at issue in *Ross Cosmetics*, the Customs Service has issued several other opinions concerning comparative advertising. In *Customs Headquarters Ruling 451291* (July 5, 1991), the imported packages contained perfumes, and stated on their front panels "Our version of (a famous brand)." An immediately-following asterisk denoted the disclaimer "Trademark of (the holder of the trademark) not connected with Mystic Impressions" on the package's front panel and was repeated, in French, on its top flap. Based on the close proximity of the trademark and the disclaimer, and the fact that both were of the same size and type face, the Customs Service found that the package was not likely to cause consumer confusion.

The packaging at issue in *Customs Headquarters Ruling 468896* (March 5, 2000) contained accessories to be used with cellular telephones manufactured by other companies; the latter had recorded their trademarks with the Customs Service. The front panel included the importer's own trademark and, in significantly smaller typeface, the statement "Fits [name of cellular telephone brand]." The rear panel set forth the importer's trademark and also contained, in boldface, the statement "[name of cellular telephone brand] is the registered trademark of an independently owned and operated company. This product has not been licensed or endorsed by the manufacturer of [name of cellular telephone brand] products. All other company names and product names are trademarks or registered trademarks of their respective companies."

This disclaimer sufficed to avoid the likelihood of consumer confusion, based on the presence of the importer's trademark on the front and back panels and relatively limited use of the recorded trademarks, along with the use of the descriptive word "Fits" and the explicit disclaimer.

In *Customs Headquarters Ruling 731514* (Dec. 9, 1988), the agency concluded that the following language appearing on a product's box was not likely to cause consumer confusion, even though the recorded mark appeared at least once on every top and side panel of the box:

FOR NINTENDO (R)

FOR USE WITH NINTENDO ENTERTAINMENT SYSTEM

NINTENDO (R) COMPATIBLE JOYSTICK

FOR NINTENDO (R) ENTERTAINMENT SYSTEM

COMPATIBLE WITH NINTENDO (R) ENTERTAINMENT SYSTEM

"Nintendo and Kraft are registered trademarks of Nintendo of America, Inc. and Kraft Systems Inc. respectively."

The ruling found that the recorded trademark was not used in a predominant fashion on the box, and was often in close proximity to the name of the importer, and was used along with other references to the product's functional attributes. Noting that "[a] competitor can . . . use another's registered trademark to describe aspects of its own goods but not to create confusion as to the origin of the product," *Selchow & Righter Co. v. Decipher, Inc.*, 598 F. Supp. 1489 (1984), the ruling concluded that "[t]he words and phrases on the package in question make it clear that" the box merely denoted the enclosed product's compatibility with the trademarked product. *Accord*, *Customs Headquarters Ruling 731762* (Sept. 27, 1988).

B. Gray Market Imports

Gray market goods have been defined as "foreign manufactured goods, for which a valid United States trademark has been registered, that are legally purchased abroad and imported into the United States without the consent of the American trademark holder." *Weil Ceramics & Glass, Inc. v. Dash*, 878 F.2d

659, 662 n.1 (3d Cir. 1989), *cert. denied*, 493 U.S. 853. There are two types of gray market situations within the Customs Service's purview. The first occurs when trademarked imported merchandise is identical to trademarked domestic merchandise; in that case, the corporate relationship between the domestic and foreign trademark owners will determine whether the goods may be entered. The second occurs when the imported and domestic merchandise purportedly has material, physical differences. The relationship between the foreign and domestic trademark owners is irrelevant in this scenario. Instead, the nature and extent of the product differences will determine whether the goods are subject to exclusion or specific labeling requirements to avoid consumer confusion.

Customs Service treatment of gray market goods has been shaped by court decisions to a greater extent than has enforcement in other intellectual property areas. The primary reason is that the Customs Service regulations have been challenged in several lawsuits by trademark owners dissatisfied with the scope of protection afforded against gray market imports. These cases clarified the extent of the agency's authority and caused adoption of conforming amendments to the regulations to the extent the regulations did not comport with statutory requirements. To a lesser extent, judicial decisions have a bearing on Customs Service enforcement because the statutes underlying the agency's gray market restrictions also provide a private right of action, so that lawsuits between private parties have colored our understanding of the statutes. While the outcomes of these private actions may not be binding on the Customs Service, at a minimum they provide both trademark recordants and importers with guidance concerning the types of facts and arguments to present to the agency.

1. Relationship Between Foreign and Domestic Trademark Owners ("*K Mart Corp.*"-Type Cases)

In *K Mart Corp. v. Cartier, Inc.*, 486 U.S. 281, 287 (1988), the Supreme Court defined the most common gray market situations thusly:

> The gray market arises in any of three general contexts. The prototypical gray-market victim (case 1) is a domestic firm that purchases from an independent foreign firm the rights to register and use the latter's trademark as a United States trademark and to sell its foreign-manufactured products here. Especially where the foreign firm has already registered the trademark in the United States or where the product has already earned a reputation for quality, the right to use that trademark can be very valuable. If the foreign manufacturer could import the trademarked goods and distribute them here, despite having sold the trademark to a domestic firm, the domestic firm would be forced into sharp intrabrand competition involving the very trademark it purchased. Similar intrabrand competition could arise if the foreign manufacturer markets its wares outside the United States, as is often the case, and a third party who purchases them abroad could legally import them. In either event, the parallel importation, if permitted to proceed, would create a gray market that could jeopardize the trademark holder's investment.
>
> The second context (case 2) is a situation in which a domestic firm registers the United States trademark for goods that are manufactured abroad by an affiliated manufacturer. In its most common variation (case 2a), a foreign firm wishes to control distribution of its wares in this country by incorporating a subsidiary here. The subsidiary then registers

> under its own name (or the manufacturer assigns to the subsidiary's name) a United States trademark that is identical to its parent's foreign trademark. The parallel importation by a third party who buys the goods abroad (or conceivably even by the affiliated foreign manufacturer itself) creates a gray market. Two other variations on this theme occur when an American-based firm establishes abroad a manufacturing subsidiary corporation (case 2b) or its own unincorporated manufacturing division (case 2c) to produce its United States trademarked goods, and then imports them for domestic distribution. If the trademark holder or its foreign subsidiary sells the trademarked goods abroad, the parallel importation of the goods competes on the gray market with the holder's domestic sales.
>
> In the third context (case 3), the domestic holder of a United States trademark authorizes an independent foreign manufacturer to use it. Usually the holder sells to the foreign manufacturer an exclusive right to use the trademark in a particular foreign location, but conditions the right on the foreign manufacturer's promise not to import its trademarked goods into the United States. Once again, if the foreign manufacturer or a third party imports into the United States, the foreign-manufactured goods will compete on the gray market with the holder's domestic goods.

With this understanding of the gray market permutations in mind, the Court upheld the then-existing Customs Service regulations concerning related-party ownership. "We hold that the Customs Service regulation is consistent with 526 insofar as it exempts from the importation ban goods that are manufactured abroad by the 'same person' who holds the United States trademark, 19 CFR 133.21(c)(1) (1987), or by a person who is 'subject to common . . . control' with the United States trademark holder, 133.21(c)(2)." *Id.* at 293. On the other hand, the Court struck down as inconsistent with the statute the regulation that proscribed enforcement when use abroad of the trademark or trade name owner had been authorized by the U.S. owner that was not related to the foreign manufacturer.[74]

Following *K Mart Corp.*, the Customs Service revised its regulations to restate the common ownership or control exceptions. The current regulation defines "restricted gray market articles" as:

> foreign-made articles bearing a genuine trademark or trade name identical with or substantially indistinguishable from one owned and recorded by a citizen of the United States or a corporation or association created or organized within the United States and imported without the authorization of the U.S. owner.

19 C.F.R. § 133.23(a). The regulation limits such restricted goods to those on which the trademark or trade name was either "[a]pplied by a licensee (including a manufacturer) independent of the U.S. owner," or:

> [a]pplied under the authority of a foreign trademark or trade name owner other than the U.S. owner, a parent or subsidiary of the U.S. owner, or a party otherwise subject to common ownership or control with the U.S. owner (see Secs. 133.2(d) and 133.12(d) of this

74 Justices Brennan and Scalia each authored concurring and dissenting opinions in *K Mart Corp.* that provided extensive discussion of the background to 19 U.S.C. § 1526 and the statute's varying interpretations by the Customs Service, in particular regarding the question of related party coverage.

> part), from whom the U.S. owner acquired the domestic title, or to whom the U.S. owner sold the foreign title(s);

19 C.F.R. § 133.23(a)(i), (ii). The first provision would cover "independent" foreign parties to which the U.S. trademark owner had licensed the right to use the trademark or trade name. Although the regulation does not define "independent," a fair inference is that it is a licensee that is not under "common ownership or control" with the U.S. owner. Whether a relationship between the foreign and domestic parties that falls short of "common ownership or control" nevertheless renders the foreign licensee non-independent is not clear.

The second provision exempts from gray market protection trademarks that are applied abroad under the authority of the U.S. trademark owner or its parent or subsidiary (whether domestic or foreign), or an entity under "common ownership or control with the U.S. [trademark or trade name] owner." The provision thus effects the *K Mart Corp.* decision that domestic and foreign trademarks held by related parties are ineligible for gray market protection.

Common ownership or control is defined in 19 C.F.R. § 133.2(d)(1) and (2).

> (1) Common ownership means individual or aggregate ownership of more than 50 percent of the business entity; and
>
> (2) Common control means effective control in policy and operations and is not necessarily synonymous with common ownership.

The definition of common ownership provides a straightforward more than fifty percent equity stake standard. Common control is rather more loosely defined. It goes beyond common ownership and requires "effective control in policy and operations." For example, a minority shareholder that nevertheless provides corporate direction could be found to exercise control.

The Customs Service has published few rulings concerning the types of corporate relationships that will foreclose gray market protection. However, several court cases arising from disputes between private parties as well as agency enforcement actions, or lack thereof, provide guidance on this question.

The cases concerning common ownership uniformly reach the unsurprising conclusion that a corporate beyond the regulation's threshold will prevent exclusion of gray market goods. In *Weil Ceramics*, *supra*, the appellate court dismissed an action brought by a trademark owner against an unauthorized importer of trademarked goods. The plaintiff had initially registered the trademark when it was unrelated to the foreign trademark owner, but subsequently was acquired by a foreign corporation that shared a common corporate parent with the foreign manufacturer of the trademarked goods. The U.S. company argued that because it had been independently incorporated prior to its acquisition and owned the trademark in the United States distinguished its situation from the holding in *K Mart Corp.*

The appellate court disagreed that these distinctions made a difference. *K Mart Corp.* focused not on whether the U.S. trademark owner had been established by the foreign owner simply to control distribution, but instead on whether there was a corporate relationship. The fact that the U.S. company was a subsidiary of the foreign company related to the foreign trademark owner placed it under *K Mart Corp.* regardless of when and by whom it was first established and whether it owned the trademark. The *Weil Ceramics* court extended this related parties analysis to encompass actions brought under 15 U.S.C. §§ 1124 and 1114, and thus went beyond the *K Mart Corp.* decision's reliance on 19 U.S.C. § 1526. *See also Yamaha Corp. of America v. United States*, 961 F.2d 245, 250 (D.C. Cir. 1992) (upholding dismissal of action because 19 U.S.C. § 1526 "itself excludes from its general protected class those U.S. trademark holders that are wholly owned American subsidiaries of the foreign trademark owners").

By contrast, the court upheld an injunction against unauthorized imports in *Premier Dental Products v. Darby Dental Supply Co.*, 974 F.2d 850 (3d Cir. 1986), *cert. denied*, 479 U.S. 950. Although the domestic trademark owner had an exclusive distributorship agreement with the foreign trademark owner, it was independent of the foreign company and had developed its own good will in the trademarked product. The unauthorized imports jeopardized this good will by diminishing consumer confidence that goods with the trademark originated with a single source, and thus sufficed to demonstrate sufficient irreparable harm to warrant an injunction. On this point, the court explicitly disagreed with the outcome in *Bell & Howell: Mamiya Co. v. Masel Supply Co.*, 719 F.2d 42 (2d Cir. 1983), which denied gray market protection because of the U.S. trademark owner's failure to demonstrate consumer confusion due to gray market imports.

Several pre-*K Mart Corp.* appellate decisions cited in *Weil Ceramics* also concluded that gray market imports should not be excluded when the foreign and domestic trademark owners are related. *NEC Electronics v. CAL Circuit Abco, Inc.*, 810 F.2d 1506 (9th Cir. 1987), *cert. denied*, 484 U.S. 851, rejected an attempt to enjoin unauthorized imports under 15 U.S.C. §§ 1114 and 1125 because the U.S. trademark owner was the foreign trademark owner's wholly-owned subsidiary and was subject to the latter's primary control. The court noted that its conclusion comported with the Customs Service's interpretation of 19 U.S.C. § 1526. Similarly, in *Parfums Stern, Inc. v. United States Customs Service*, 575 F. Supp. 416 (S.D. Fla. 1983), the court refused to enjoin the Customs Service from releasing gray market goods from its custody where the foreign and domestic trademark owners "appear[] to be a single international enterprise operating through an amoeba-like structure" that involved related individuals and corporations.[75]

The outer bounds of the scope of common control were explored in *United States v. Eighty-Three Rolex Watches*, 992 F.2d 508 (5th Cir. 1993). The appeal involved the Customs Service's seizure and forfeiture of ROLEX watches that

75 The court did not describe the exact corporate relationship between the domestic and foreign trademark owners with more specificity.

an unauthorized party had attempted to import, in a situation with trademark ownership as follows. The foreign trademark was owned by the Swiss manufacturer of ROLEX watches, Manufacture des Montres Rolex S.A. Bienne (Bienne). Bienne had made the Swiss corporation Montres Rolex S.A. (Geneva) the worldwide distributor of ROLEX watches and had authorized it to register combination trademarks that included the name "ROLEX," although Bienne remained the sole owner of the ROLEX trademark. The U.S. trademark owner, Rolex Watch U.S.A. Inc. (Rolex), was "wholly owned through two intervening subsidiaries" by a different Swiss corporation, which also had an 86 percent ownership stake in Geneva. One shareholder/officer/director in Bienne also held a small amount of Geneva's stock, and Geneva and Bienne jointly owned a building where each leased space; this was the extent of the companies' relationship.

The court rejected the importer/claimant's assertion that the foreign and domestic trademark owners were subject to common control. The fact "that both Bienne and Geneva perform essential functions in manufacturing and selling Rolex products" did not indicate common control. In the court's view, the type of control envisioned by the regulation was "the sort of control that a parent corporation would exercise over a subsidiary or that a common owner might exercise over both organizations." 992 F.2d at 515, citing *United States v. Eighty-Nine (89) Bottles of Eau de Joy*, 797 F.2d 767 (9th Cir. 1986), which in turn cited *Coalition to Preserve the Integrity of American Trademarks v. United States*, 598 F. Supp. 844, 850 (D.C.D.C. 1984). Neither a longstanding business relationship nor cooperation in production and marketing equated to common control.

In the Customs Service's view, a corporate ownership (or control) relationship between a U.S. trademark owner and a trademark owner in any foreign country precludes gray market protection. It does not matter that protection is being sought only against imports from a specific foreign country where the trademark owner or licensee is independent of the U.S. trademark owner.

> Customs' interpretation of section 133.23(a)(2) is that where the U.S. trademark owner owns the subject trademark in *any* foreign country, or where a parent or subsidiary of the trademark owner, or party otherwise subject to common ownership or control owns the subject trademark in *any* foreign country, the subject trademark is not eligible for gray market protection.

Customs Headquarters Ruling 469076 (Nov. 19, 2001) (emphasis in original); *Customs Headquarters Ruling 469561* (July 25, 2000).[76] This interpretation is questionable in light of 19 C.F.R. § 133.23(a)(2)'s reference to restricted gray market goods as those where the trademark was "[a]pplied under the authority of a foreign trademark owner . . . other than the U.S. owner [or] a parent or subsidiary of the U.S. owner. . . ." The regulation focuses on the U.S. trademark

76 One of the authors of this text is a member of the law firm representing the party that sought gray market protection in *Customs Headquarters Ruling 469076*.

owner's relationship to the owner of the trademark placed on specific goods for which gray market protection is sought. The fact that a U.S. trademark owner may be related to a trademark owner in Country A but not in Country B is irrelevant to the question of whether goods from Country B should be restricted.

2. Physically and Materially Different Goods ("*Lever Brothers*"-Type Cases)

In *Lever Bros. Co. v. United States*, 877 F.2d 101 (D.C. Cir. 1989) and 981 F.2d 1330 (D.C. Cir. 1993), the court rejected the Customs Service's reliance on the related party doctrine when the imported trademarked merchandise had material and physical differences from domestic goods bearing the same trademark. The court had tentatively interpreted 15 U.S.C. § 1124 to "'bar[] foreign goods bearing a trademark identical to the valid U.S. trademark but physically different,' without regard to affiliation between the producing firms or the genuine character of the trademark abroad," 877 F.2d at 111, remanded the matter to the district court to permit the parties to more extensively brief the issue, and thereafter confirmed its initial conclusion following a thorough review of Section 1124's legislative, judicial, and regulatory history. 981 F.2d at 1333-37, 1338-39. In the court's view, Section 1124 prohibits the importation of trademarked goods that are not "genuine." Because "[t]rademarks applied to physically different foreign goods are not genuine from the viewpoint of the American consumer," 981 F.2d at 1339, they were subject to exclusion under 15 U.S.C. § 1124.

The domestic and imported goods were described as follows.

> [Lever Brothers], an American company, and its British affiliate, Lever Brothers Limited ('Lever UK'), both manufacture deodorant soap under the 'Shield' trademark and hand dishwashing liquid under the 'Sunlight' trademark. The trademarks are registered in each country. The products have evidently been formulated differently to suit local tastes and circumstances. The U.S. version lathers more, the soaps smell different, the colorants used in American 'Shield' have been certified by the FDA whereas the colorants in British 'Shield' have not, and the U.S. version contains a bacteriostat that enhances the deodorant properties of the soap. The British version of 'Sunlight' dishwashing soap produces less suds, and the American version is formulated to work best in the 'soft water' available in most American cities, whereas the British version is designed for 'hard water' common in Britain.
>
> The packaging of the U.S. and U.K. products is also somewhat different. The British 'Shield' logo is written in script form and is packaged in foil wrapping and contains a wave motif, whereas the American 'Shield' logo is written in block form, does not come in foil wrapping and contains a grid pattern. There is small print on the packages indicating where they were manufactured. The British 'Sunlight' comes in a cylindrical bottle labeled 'Sunlight Washing Up Liquid.' The American 'Sunlight' comes in a yellow, hourglass-shaped bottle labeled 'Sunlight Dishwashing Liquid.'

981 F.2d at 1331. The *Lever Brothers* discussion thus provides guidance as to some of the types of differences that may qualify as material: product composition, performance, and packaging.

Following *Lever Brothers*, the Customs Service amended its regulations to permit a U.S. trademark or trade name owner to receive gray market protection against imports with material physical differences. *Gray Market Imports and Other Trademarked Goods; Final Rule*, 64 Fed. Reg. 9058, 9060 (Feb. 24, 1999). The new regulations provide the type of information required when a trademark or trade name is recorded to receive gray market protection. 19 C.F.R. § 133.2(e); *see* chapter XXXII, *infra*.

As with "related party" gray market disputes, most court cases concerning exclusion of merchandise for alleged material physical differences have involved private parties. While this may diminish their direct relevance to Customs Service enforcement, they certainly indicate judicial views of the type of product differences that warrant gray market relief and arguably should guide Customs Service analysis as well.

Societe des Produits Nestle, S.A. v. Casa Helvetia Inc., 982 F.2d 633 (1st Cir. 1992), involved the defendant's unauthorized sale in the United States of chocolate that bore plaintiff's U.S.-registered trademarks and had been produced under license in Venezuela. Plaintiff manufactured its own trademarked goods in Italy and shipped them to the U.S. The Venezuelan and Italian merchandise differed "in presentation, variety, composition, and price," 982 F.2d at 635, which raised the question of whether they were "material." Although the court was unwilling to establish a formulaic rule for resolving this question, it left no doubt about its view that the standard was not a difficult one.

> There is no mechanical way to determine the point at which a difference becomes 'material.' Separating wheat from chaff must be done on a case-by-case basis. Bearing in mind the policies and provisions of the Lanham Act as they apply to gray goods, we can confidently say that the threshold of materiality is always quite low in such cases.

982 F.2d at 641. Following a brief discussion of several precedents construing 15 U.S.C. § 1124, including *Lever Brothers*, the court defined the type of differences that would qualify.

> We conclude that the existence of any difference between the registrant's product and the allegedly infringing gray good that consumers would likely consider to be relevant when purchasing a product creates a presumption of consumer confusion sufficient to support a Lanham Act claim. Any higher threshold would endanger a manufacturer's investment in product goodwill and unduly subject consumers to potential confusion by severing the tie between a manufacturers's protected mark and its associated bundle of traits.
>
> The alleged infringer, of course, may attempt to rebut this presumption, see *Coach Leatherware*, 933 F.2d [162] at 170 [(2d Cir. 1991)]; *cf. Resource Developers, Inc. v. Statue of Liberty-Ellis Island Found.*, 926 F.2d 134, 140 (2d Cir. 1991) (shifting the burden "to the defendant to demonstrate the absence of consumer confusion" in an action for damages), but in order to do so he must be able to prove by preponderant evidence that the differences are not of the kind that consumers, on average, would likely consider in purchasing the product.

Id. The court determined that there were differences in quality control, composition, configuration (*i.e.*, product shape), packaging, and price. It found that each of these was material, as each could cause customer confusion between the gray market and authorized products. Because of these differences and the fact that their sale in the U.S. was not authorized by the trademark owner, they were not "genuine" within the meaning of 15 U.S.C. § 1124. Additionally, they were likely to confuse consumers into believing that the gray market goods were sponsored by the domestic trademark owner, and thus ran afoul of 15 U.S.C. § 1125(a)(1).

The Court of Appeals for the Federal Circuit approvingly cited *Societe des Produits Nestle* in *Gamut Trading Co. v. U.S. Int'l Trade Comm'n*, 200 F.3d 775 (Fed. Cir. 1999), an appeal from the Commission's finding of a section 337 violation due to the importation of materially-different used tractors. The differences between the imported and domestic trademarked goods included performance characteristics and varying replacement parts and service requirements. In addition, the imported models lacked English-language warning labels, instructions, and operating and service manuals. The court agreed that these were material, notwithstanding that some of them may have been "readily apparent to consumers," as the administrative record indicated that consumers associated the gray market product with the U.S. trademark owner. 200 F.3d at 781.

The *Gamut Trading* opinion also is noteworthy for its concurrence with *Societe des Produits Nestle* that there is a

> low threshold of materiality, requiring no more than showing that consumers would be likely to consider the differences between the foreign and domestic products to be significant when purchasing the product, for such differences would suffice to erode the goodwill of the domestic source.

Id. at 779. Because the Federal Circuit is the court of appeals for challenges to Customs Service decisions under 28 U.S.C. § 1581(a), it will be interesting to watch whether it takes this position in reviewing agency and lower court decisions concerning *Lever Brothers*-type cases.

An injunction against importation and sale in the U.S. of unauthorized gray market soft drinks that had been bottled for sale in Mexico was issued in *Pepsico, Inc. v. Torres*, 1993 U.S. Dist. LEXIS 17588, 27 U.S.P.Q.2d 1948 (C.D. Cal. 1993). The decision was premised on 19 U.S.C. § 1526 (citing *PepsiCo, Inc. v. Giraud*, 7 U.S.P.Q.2d 1371 (D.P.R. 1988)), and did not mention 15 U.S.C. § 1124. The differences that the court found between the Mexican and U.S. products included different labels and potential deterioration in the former caused by shipping delays.

The court dismissed an action seeking relief against gray market imports in *Summit Technology, Inc. v. High-Line Medical Instruments Co., Inc.*, 922 F. Supp. 299 (C.D. Cal. 1996). The allegedly infringing goods were of United States manufacture and had been exported by the U.S. trademark owner, which claimed that they were materially different from domestically-sold trademarked articles due to the absence of U.S. Food and Drug Administration approval, lower qualify controls, and other reasons that were not specified in the decision. The imported articles also had been used abroad. The court concluded that there was no likelihood of consumer confusion as to the source of the products, because they had been produced in the U.S. Moreover, the court held, gray market protection was available only against goods of foreign origin.

C. Counterfeit Imports

1. Distinguishing Counterfeit from "Merely Infringing" Goods

The Customs Service regulation adopts the Lanham Act's (15 U.S.C. § 1127) definition of "counterfeit": "A 'counterfeit' is a spurious mark which is identical with, or substantially indistinguishable from, a registered mark." 19 C.F.R. § 133.21(a). In practice, distinguishing between counterfeit and merely infringing goods has bedeviled the agency, just as it has reviewing courts. Goods that display a fake trademark that is identical to the real one pose a relatively easy enforcement target; once the goods have been identified, and the Customs inspector determines that their source was not the trademark owner, there is little more analysis required.

Evaluating whether imported goods bear an unauthorized "substantially indistinguishable" trademark, or instead is confusingly similar, appears to be more art than science. The distinction is a crucial one, however, because the procedures and sanctions available to the Customs Service will vary depending on which category covers the imported merchandise.

The *Ross Cosmetics II* decision provided general guidance on distinguishing counterfeit and infringing articles.

> Usually, 'counterfeit merchandise is made so as to imitate a well-known product in all details of construction and appearance so as to deceive customers into thinking that they are getting genuine merchandise.' 3 J. Thomas McCarthy, McCarthy on Trademarks and Unfair Competition § 25.01[5][a] (3d ed. 1992).
>
> The second category consists of 'merely infringing' goods which are not counterfeits but bear marks likely to cause public confusion. This category includes merchandise which bears a mark that 'copies or simulates' a registered mark so as to be likely to cause the public to associate the copying or simulating mark with the registered mark. *See* 15 U.S.C. § 1124; 19 C.F.R. § 133.21; *see also Montres Rolex, S.A. v. Snyder,* 718 F.2d 524, 527-28 (2d Cir. 1983), *cert. denied*, 465 U.S. 1100 (1984) (distinguishing copying or simulating mark that is counterfeit mark from copying or simulating mark that is a merely infringing mark). Also included in this category is merchandise which uses any word, name, symbol, or any combination thereof, in such a manner that is likely to cause public confusion as to the origin, sponsorship, or approval of the merchandise by another person. *See* 15 U.S.C. § 1125(a)(2).

18 CIT at 984-85.

Applying this standard, the court rejected Customs' remand determination that the imported merchandise was counterfeit. The imports were not counterfeits because they "do not imitate the well known products . . . in all details of construction and appearance." *Id.* The court further rejected Customs' position that the imports' packaging reference to registered trademarks was a *per se* counterfeit use. The mere "use of another person's trademark is not prohibited by law unless it creates a reasonable likelihood of confusion as to the source, identity, or sponsorship of the product." *Id.* (citations omitted). At a minimum, *Ross Cosmetics II* would take most comparative advertising cases out of the counterfeit realm altogether, unless the imported article was identical in all or nearly all respects to the trademarked one. The use of comparative advertising statements on otherwise-identical imported goods arguably would suffice to place them in the infringing rather than counterfeit category.

2. Administrative Rulings

Imported jeans bearing marks identical to two recorded ("Pierre Cardin" and "Jordache") and one unrecorded ("Sergio Valente") trademarks were deemed counterfeit in *Customs Headquarters Ruling 726641* (Jan. 2, 1985). The ruling noted that the first step in a counterfeiting analysis is to determine whether the marks are "spurious," *i.e.*, are "marks that are applied to goods without authorization of the trademark owner." Citing *Montres Rolex, supra*, the ruling said that the second step is:

> to compare the accused mark with the protected mark as it appears on the trademark owner's merchandise . . . from the perspective of an average purchaser rather than an expert. If, upon examination of the marks as they appear on the imported merchandise, an average purchaser would find them to be 'the spitting image' of, or 'substantially indistinguishable' from the trademark owners' merchandise, then a 'counterfeit' trademark violation is established.

Imports that had marks identical to the recorded trademarks were clearly counterfeit.

Comparing the remaining imports with the registered but unrecorded trademark was slightly more difficult, as the Customs Service did not have a copy of the registered mark to use for comparison and thus could not consider the import label "Sergio Valente," standing alone, to be a counterfeit. Instead, the ruling looked to other common design elements of the unrecorded trademark and the imports to reach a finding of counterfeiting. The ruling did not provide the source of the agency's knowledge of those design elements of the trademark that underlay its comparison.

The imported goods also had a design identical to that of a recorded trademark in *Customs Headquarters Ruling 452057* (Oct. 17, 1991). As described in the ruling:

> [t]he shirt forwarded for our review is a solid colored, pull-over shirt. The label sewn to the inside of the collar indicates that the shirt was made in Indonesia. The only design on the shirt is the stitched man on horseback holding a raised polo mallet. The registered and recorded trademark is the design of a polo player on horseback holding a raised mallet. After comparing the design on the imported shirt to the registered and recorded trademark, we conclude that absent a document authorizing the manufacturer to use this trademark it is a counterfeit use of the trademark.

A similar situation arose in *Customs Headquarters Ruling 459018* (Jan. 5, 1995). The recorded trademark included the words "Jonathan Martin" and a unicorn design, while the imported goods used the trademarked name and a slight variant of the design (a unicorn head rather than the entire figure). The Customs Service found that "this minor difference does not negate our finding that this label is 'counterfeit' since it clearly copies the key features of the trademarked design." *See also Customs Headquarters Ruling 729377* (June 20, 1986).

In *Customs Headquarters Ruling 459411* (May 26, 1995), the recorded trademark was the word "Gecko," which was registered for use on clothing, including hats. The imported caps had the term "Gecko Hawaii" printed on them. The Customs Service found that the imports were counterfeit because "the recorded mark has been copied in its entirety and appears on caps, articles which are closely akin to hats, the class of goods for which the mark is registered."

Counterfeit use of a recorded trademark was detected in *Customs Headquarters Ruling 451915* (Oct. 10, 1991). The recorded mark consisted of a design, which was copied exactly on the imported goods. The imports had additional statements concerning conformity with government and private standards, and asserted that these precluded a finding of counterfeiting.

The Customs Service disagreed:

> [i]t has long been established that the addition of words to a trademark does not preclude the finding of infringement. See Menendez v. Holt, 128 U.S. 514 (1888) (appellant's name accompanied the trademarked words and the Court stated that such use is an aggravation and not a justification); A.T. Cross Company v. Jonathan Bradley Pens, Inc., 470 F.2d 689 (2d Cir. 1972) (addition of words does not save the day).

Similarly, the fact that the goods had the importer's own name on them, rather than that of the trademark owner, would not prevent them from being considered counterfeit. It was unnecessary for the Customs Service to find that the purchasing public would associate the goods with the trademark owner. "In reaching a determination that the imported ladders infringe the registered and recorded trademark, it is not necessary for us to engage in an actual finding of confusion. The Keds Corporation v. Renee International Trading Corp., 888 F.2d 215, 218 (1st Cir. 1989)."

The agency considered the standards for evaluating imports with "sound-alike" names in *Customs Headquarters Ruling 459012* (May 5, 1995). The recorded trademark was "Lycra," and the imported articles variously bore the names "LAICRA," "LICRA," "LIKRA" and "LYKRA." The ruling found that the sound-alike imports were counterfeit using the "phonetic test" set forth in *G. D. Searle & Co. v. Chas Pfizer & Co.*, 265 F.2d 385 (7th Cir. 1959), based on their "degree of similarity in sound" to the recorded trademark.

> . . . the terms 'LAICRA', 'LICRA', 'LIKRA' and 'LYKRA' are almost identical in visual appearance to the recorded marks and contain only slight variations in spelling. For example, the letter Y in 'LYCRA' is replaced by the letters AI in 'LAICRA' and I in the terms 'LICRA' and 'LIKRA'. The letter C in 'LYCRA' is replaced by the letter K in 'LYKRA'. Also, like the 'LYCRA' marks, the words 'LAICRA', 'LICRA', 'LIKRA' and 'LYKRA' all begin with the letter L and end with the letter A. . . . we find that they sound exactly alike. Each of these terms contains two syllables which like the 'LYCRA' marks have the same stress pattern with primary accent on the first syllable (LAI, LI and LY) and secondary accent on the second syllable (CRA and KRA).

The ruling also considered the fact that the sound-alike terms appeared on garments, as did the recorded trademark to indicate a "close nexus" between the imported and trademarked items. *Compare Customs Headquarters Ruling 450725* (March 20, 1991) (use of term "Ray-B" on sunglasses was not counterfeit of trademark "Ray-Ban," also used on sunglasses, but was "confusingly similar.")

Customs Headquarters Ruling 450180 (Aug. 24, 1990) involved the recorded trademark "BRITISH KNIGHTS," used on shoes, and imported shoes marked variously "BRITISH KNIGHTS," "BRITISH NIGHTS" and "BRITISH HIGHTS." Those marked with the first name were clear counterfeits. The second name was "substantially indistinguishable" from the recorded trademark.

> When comparing the registered and recorded mark with the suspected mark, the comparison must be of the overall impression created by the mark. Aveda Corporation v. Evita Marketing, Inc., 706 F. Supp. 1419, 1429 (D. Minn. 1989 (quotation omitted). The lack of the letter 'K' removes only one letter from the overall appearance of the mark, but leaves 13 letters identical to the registered and recorded mark. Additionally, it is significant that even without the letter 'K' the sound of the two marks remains identical. Sounds of marks are an element in the determination of similarity of marks.

However, the third name was not considered counterfeit:

> Compared phonetically the two marks have the same number of syllables and the same stress pattern. The overall appearance remains similar to the recorded mark, but is not as similar as the two marks discussed above. However, since this mark still appears on the same type of product, footwear, and has a very similar sound as the protected mark we conclude that the mark is a confusingly similar mark. [Citations omitted.]

An article's ostensible use of "comparative" advertising was found to be counterfeit *Customs Headquarters Ruling 454063* (April 13, 1993). The recorded trademark was the letters "GM." The imported merchandise was key caps (apparently for automotive use) marked "FOR GM," where the word "FOR" was approximately one quarter of the size of the letters "GM," and the latter was underlined while the former was not.

The Customs Service rejected the importer's argument that its use of the word "FOR" qualified as a permissible use of the trademark. Rather than being used for advertising purposes, the presence of the recorded trademark falsely indicated an association between the goods and the trademark owner. Additionally, the emphasis on the letters "GM," rather than the word "FOR," showed that the trademark and not the purported disclaimer predominated. "It is an accepted axiom that greater force and effect is given to the dominant feature of a mark. Giant Food Inc. v. Nation's Foodservice, Inc., 710 F.2d 1565, 1570 (Fed. Cir. 1983); Blumenfeld Development Corporation v. Carnival Cruise Lines, Inc., 669 F. Supp. 1297, 1320 (E.D. Pa. 1987)."

D. Copyright Infringement

Customs Service rulings on copyright infringement look to judicial decisions for guidance; the agency does not have its own unique jurisprudence on the issue.

The agency considers that it has authority to make both factual determinations and findings of law, in accordance with judicial precedent, and this view has judicial blessing. *The Miss America Organization v. Mattel, Inc.*, 945 F.2d 536, 544 (2d Cir. 1991): "Congress has granted Customs some independence and autonomy in making determinations of infringement regarding items imported into the United States. . . ." The court noted that the agency "has developed expertise in determining whether articles are or may be infringing," *id.* at 539. *See Customs Headquarters Ruling 453234* (Aug. 18, 1992) (citing *Miss America*).

To prove copyright infringement, the complaining party must first demonstrate that it owns a valid copyright in the allegedly infringing article. Copyright ownership may be demonstrated by a U.S. Copyright Office certificate of registration. *Customs Headquarters Rulings 469770* (July 7, 2000) and *469468* (May 22, 2000). Because the Customs regulations require proof of ownership as a condition for recording a copyright, this first element of copyright infringement would in most cases be established *prima facie* by the Customs Service's recordation of the copyright. *See* 19 C.F.R. § 133.33(a)(1).

However, the Customs Service will entertain arguments from an importer that the registered and recorded copyright is, in fact, not deserving of protection because of its similarity to works in the public domain. *Customs Headquarters Ruling 453234* (Aug. 18, 1992), *on reconsideration*, *Customs Headquarters Ruling 456375* (Aug. 23, 1993). Although the Customs Service is loath to find the copyright invalid in such circumstances, it will either refrain from taking enforcement action against allegedly infringing imports or afford extremely narrow protection to the copyright:

> Customs is keenly aware that the issuance of a registration certificate by the U.S. Copyright Office constitutes prima facie presumption of validity. Durham Industries. Inc. v. Tomy Corporation, 630 F.2d 905 (2d Cir. 1980); Masquerade Novelty, Inc. v. Unique Industries. Inc., 912 F.2d 663 (3rd Cir. 1990). However the scope of protection afforded a work covered by a copyright is a separate inquiry. See Feist, 499 U.S. at , 111 S. Ct. at 1289; Atari Games Corporation v. Ralph Oman, 979 F.2d 242, 244 n.4 (D.C. Cir. 1992).

Customs Headquarters Ruling 456375. Thus, the agency will review the validity of a copyright, but in the context of determining whether there is infringement. *Id.*; *Customs Headquarters Ruling 453234*.

Second, the owner must establish that the article illegally copied the copyrighted work. *Id.* Copying can be demonstrated by direct evidence of copying, *Customs Headquarters Ruling 450973* (Nov. 14, 1991), including "an admission by the importer or testimony by a witness to the copying," *Customs Headquarters Ruling 456337* (March 9, 1994). The copyright owner may prove copying by indirect or circumstantial evidence such as proof of access to the copyrighted work or similarities between the two works that are unlikely to have occurred without copying. Latman, *supra* at 191. Courts have held that a copyright owner may indirectly prove access to a protected work by showing that the defendant had a reasonable opportunity to view or copy the protected work, for example, in cases where the work has been widely disseminated.

In the absence of such direct evidence, copying may be established by showing that "(1) the alleged infringer had access to the copyrighted work, and (2) the protected elements of the two works are substantially similar." *Customs Headquarters Ruling 469770*, citing *Atari, Inc. v. North American Philips Consumer Electronics Corp.*, 672 F.2d 607, 614 (7th Cir. 1982). Access to the copyrighted work "is presumed where an item is generally available on the open market." *Id.*, citing *Amstein v. Porter*, 154 F.2d 464, 468 (2d Cir. 1946). Advertising of the copyrighted work through, for example, in brochures or on a World Wide Web homepage, also allows an inference of its widespread dissemination, *Customs Headquarters Ruling 469468*, as does the copyrighted work's use in a widely-circulated theatrical movie. *Customs Headquarters Ruling 456337*. Access may also be inferred from a substantial similarity between the copyrighted and allegedly infringing work. *Customs Headquarters Ruling 732843* (June 12, 1990). Similarly, copying may be inferred when "similarities between the two works that are unlikely to have occurred without copying." *Customs Headquarters Ruling 456337*.

On the other hand, mere copying of the protected work will not in itself support a finding of infringement. "A finding of 'substantial similarity' means that the infringing article copies a substantial and material amount of the protected work . . . simply establishing that a protected work has been copied is insufficient to prove infringement." *Customs Headquarters Rulings 458962* (Sept. 26, 1994) and *459411* (May 26, 1995).

The standard for determining "substantial similarity" has been stated in numerous administrative rulings. *Customs Headquarters Ruling 467741* (Oct. 15, 1999), for example, stated that:

> As a general matter, substantial similarity is determined by reference to the 'ordinary observer' test, *i.e.*, 'whether an average lay observer would recognize the alleged copy as having been appropriated from the copyrighted work.' Ideal Toy Corp. v. Fab-Lu Ltd., 360 F.2d 1021, 1022 (2d Cir. 1966). See also, Atari v. North American Philips, 672 F.2d at 614 (The test is 'whether the accused work is so similar to the plaintiff's work that an ordinary reasonable person would conclude that the defendant unlawfully appropriated the plaintiff's protectable expression by taking material of substance and value.'). See, *e.g.*, Peter Pan Fabrics, Inc. v. Martin Weiner Corp., 274 F.2d 487, 489 (2d Cir. 1960) (holding that 'the ordinary observer, unless he set out to detect the disparities, would be disposed to overlook them, and regard their aesthetic appeal as the same.').

Accord, *Customs Headquarters Rulings 469468* and *468099* (July 30, 1999). "Another way of stating the test is whether an ordinary observer who is not attempting to discover disparities between the two articles would be disposed to overlook them and regard their aesthetic appeal as the same." *Customs Headquarters Ruling 460135* (March 5, 1996). Copying will be found when the "similarity between the works is so striking as to preclude the possibility that the works were arrived at independently," *Customs Headquarters Ruling 732843* (June 12, 1990). Minor differences will be disregarded. *Id.*; *Customs Headquarters Rulings* 468099 (July 30, 1999) and *469468* (May 22, 2000).

Several rulings have also noted that courts may apply the "'total concept and feel test' by which an article is found to be infringing if the 'mood evoked by the total combination of its elements is substantially similar to the copyrighted work.' Roth Greeting Cards v. United Card Co., 429 F.2d 1106 (9th Cir. 1970)." *Customs Headquarters Ruling 456337* (March 9, 1994) and *468099*. Although this standard is usually cited as an aside, it has provided the rule of decision in several rulings. The Customs Service rulings have not addressed the practical differences, if any, that it sees between the "ordinary observer" and "total concept and feel" tests.

At least one ruling has followed the two part test set forth in *Sid & Marty Kroft Television Productions, Inc. v. McDonald's Corp.*, 562 F.2d 1157, 1162 (9th Cir. 1977). *Customs Headquarters Ruling 469770* interpreted this standard as follows:

> The first step, referred to as the 'extrinsic test', requires a determination of substantial similarity between the ideas which includes an analysis of the specific criteria that can be listed and analyzed, such as the type of artwork at issue, the materials used, the subject matter, and the setting for the subject. Since it is an extrinsic test, analytic dissection and expert testimony are appropriate. The second step, labeled the 'intrinsic test', involves a determination of substantial similarity between the expressions of the ideas which depends not on expert testimony or analytic dissection, but instead on the response of the ordinary reasonable person, that is, the determination focuses largely on whether the suspect work captures the 'total concept and feel' of the copyrighted work. See Spectravest Inc. v. Mervyn's Inc., 673 F. Supp. 1486 (N.D. Cal. 1987); Baxter v. MCA Inc., 812 F.2d 421, 424 (9th Cir. 1987).

It is not yet clear whether the *Sid & Marty Kroft* approach will supplant one or both of the other standards hitherto applied by the Customs Service.

1. Rulings Under the "Ordinary Observer" Standard

Customs Headquarters Ruling 456337 addressed whether imported shoes contained images that infringed copyrights recorded by the Walt Disney Company. The distinctive features of the first copyrighted figure, "Ariel" the mermaid, included "long red hair," "a purple shell-shaped bra top," "a sea shell-shaped design on both sides at the waist," and "a flower in her hands." The imported article had identical features, and differed only by having a flower in her hair, a different-colored bottom outfit, and held a flower in one hand instead of two. These differences were "clearly insignificant" compared with the fundamental similarities. Substantial similarity could also be found because the imported article would be "recognizable by an ordinary observer as having been taken from the copyrighted work," citing *Roth Greeting Cards v. United Card Co.*, 429 F.2d 1106. 1110 (9th Cir. 1970) and *Bradbury v. Columbia Broadcasting System Inc.*, 287 F.2d 478 (9th Cir. 1961).

The second and third copyrighted figures, "Flounder" the fish and "Sebastian" the crab, were copied exactly on the imported articles. The fish character on the imported goods had a central location and visibility to the causal observer and thus was substantially similar even though it was "surrounded by other aquatic characters." Similarly, the imports' use of only the top portion of the copyrighted crab included unique features of the copyrighted design.

Customs Headquarters Ruling 460135 found that copyrighted lion characters had "unique expression through the shaping of the animals' head, the shape and position of the ears, nose and eyes, facial expression, and presentation of body features such as a mane or tail." The imported items had nearly identically copied these features to such an extent "that an average observer would recognize the copy as having been appropriated from the [copyrighted] character."

Both the copyrighted and allegedly infringing work in *Customs Headquarters Ruling 467741* (Oct. 15, 1999) were dolls that contained voice recordings of an identical public domain prayer. However, the differences in their sound—a girl's voice in one as opposed to a synthetic or mechanical sounding voice in the other—were more significant these similarities. Likewise, the dolls in which the recordings were contained were dissimilar in such features as height and clothing. substantial similarity.

By contrast, *Customs Headquarters Ruling 459411* found that the copyrighted and imported goods were substantially similar in that both depicted a lizard wearing sunglasses and contained several identical words. Even though there were "slight variations in the feet, tail and mouth of the lizard on the imported article . . . the expression of the caricature of a lizard is the same" and the imports infringed.

2. Rulings Under the "Total Concept and Feel" Standard

As explained in *Customs Headquarters Ruling 469770* (July 7, 2000), application of this approach "involves a determination of substantial similarity between the expressions of the ideas which depends not on expert testimony or analytic dissection, but instead on the response of the ordinary reasonable person." In "total concept and feel" rulings, the Customs Service seems to rely on a visual impression of the articles' appearance, with a listing of the similarities or differences provided as backup confirmation of the validity of that impression. *See, e.g.*, *Customs Headquarters Ruling 469468* (May 22, 2000): "Dissection of similarities is inappropriate because it distracts the reasonable observer from a comparison of the total concept and feel of the works" (quoting *Aliotti v. R. Dakin & Co.*, 831 F.2d. 898, 901 (9th Cir. 1987)).

Customs Headquarters Ruling 469468 concerned imported plates with a design that was "virtually identical to the copyrighted design."

> As they appear on the sample plates, both designs are comprised of a series of vertical lines bordered by circles running along the inner and outer rim of the plate, and tapering slightly from the outer to the inner circle. The two designs differ only in minor respects, *e.g.*, the copyrighted design consists of a repeating series of four tapered, vertical lines whereas the challenged design is comprised of five tapered, vertical lines. Based on our examination of the two works, we find that the design on the [imported] plate has the total concept and

> feel of [recordant's] copyrighted . . . design and that the ordinary observer would be disposed to overlook any minor differences and would regard the designs as having the same aesthetic appeal.

No infringement was found in *Customs Headquarters Ruling 468099* (July 30, 1999). The "total concept and feel" of the imported and copyrighted teddy bears was dissimilar in light of technical differences in construction, the fact that one was seated and the other standing, and the imported articles' association with sports compared with the copyrighted items' appeal to sentimentality.

In practice, regardless of the nominal approach followed, Customs Service rulings tend to look to the same factors in evaluating the substantial similarity issue.

XLIV. TRADEMARK-RELATED MARKING REQUIREMENTS

The Customs Service also enforces the country of origin marking statute, which provides that:

> every article of foreign origin (or its container, as provided in subsection (b) hereof) imported into the United States shall be marked in a conspicuous place as legibly, indelibly, and permanently as the nature of the article (or container) will permit in such manner as to indicate to an ultimate purchaser in the United States the English name of the country of origin of the article.

19 U.S.C. § 1304(a). The referenced subsection (b) requires that an article's container be marked, if the article itself is excepted from marking.

The Customs regulations implementing this statute have a specific marking requirement for imported goods bearing a trademark that references the U.S. or a location therein.

> **§ 134.47 Souvenirs and articles marked with trademarks or trade names.**
>
> When as part of a trademark or trade name or as part of a souvenir marking, the name of a location in the United States or 'United States' or 'America' appear, the article shall be legibly, conspicuously, and permanently marked to indicate the name of the country of origin of the article preceded by 'Made in,' 'Product of,' or other similar words, in close proximity or in some other conspicuous location.

The country of origin marking must "be legible, indelible, and permanent." 19 C.F.R. § 134.41(a). To meet the "permanence" requirement, the marking "should be at least sufficient to insure that in any reasonably foreseeable circumstance, the marking shall remain on the article (or its container) until it reaches the ultimate purchaser unless it is deliberately removed," and "must survive normal distribution and store handling." *Id.* To be "conspicuous," "[t]he ultimate purchaser in the United States must be able to find the marking easily and read it without strain." 19 C.F.R. § 134.41(b).

This marking requirement applies not only to articles imported directly into the United States, but also to those articles produced in the U.S. incorporating foreign-origin materials or parts that do not undergo a "substantial transformation" into a new and different article of commerce, as well as imported articles that are repacked in the United States prior to distribution. 19 C.F.R. § 134.26. Articles that do not meet the marking requirements are subject to exclusion from entry (19 U.S.C. § 134.3), demand for redelivery if entry has occurred (*Id.*) and assessment of liquidated damages if such redelivery is not made (19 C.F.R. § 134.54), and assessment of special marking duties (19 U.S.C. § 1304(f) and 19 C.F.R.§ 134.54).

There are a number of Customs Service rulings that provide practical guidance concerning compliance with this marking requirement. The agency is willing to accept a filed application with the PTO as proof of a trademark's existence and scope for purposes of Section 134.47. *Customs Headquarters Rulings 561260* (June 18, 1999), *560806* (March 19, 1998), and *560791* (April 29, 1998). The importer's ability to prove that the reference to the United States is part of a trademark is crucial, for if it is not part of a trademark, the more restrictive marking requirements of 19 C.F.R. § 134.46 apply.[77] As discussed in *Customs Headquarters Ruling 560791*,

> [t]he critical difference between the two provisions is that 19 CFR 134.46, when applicable, requires that the name of the actual country of origin shall appear 'in close proximity' to the non-origin reference and in lettering of at least comparable size. By contrast, 19 CFR 134.47, which applies regardless of whether the U.S. locality in the trade name may mislead or deceive the ultimate purchase, requires that the actual country of origin appear in close proximity or 'in some other conspicuous location'.

See Customs Headquarters Ruling 562070 (June 20, 2001) (because the name "American Original" was not proven to be a registered trademark, 19 C.F.R. § 134.46 was applicable and required statement of country of origin in close proximity to the name).

Customs Service rulings have established that variations of "United States" and "America" fall within Section 134.47's mandate, for example, "Automotive Aftermarket of the Americas" (*Customs Headquarters Ruling 561325* (Oct. 25, 1999)), "America's Finest Outfitter" (*Customs Headquarters Ruling 561260*), and "American Rod & Gun"(*Customs Headquarters Ruling 560806*).

Rulings also have addressed the "conspicuousness" requirement. *Customs Headquarters Ruling 561325* held that a box having the trademark on four panels of a

---

77 **§ 134.46 Marking when name of country or locality other than country of origin appears.**

In any case in which the words 'United States,' or 'American,' the letters 'U.S.A.,' any variation of such words or letters, or the name of any city or location in the United States, or the name of any foreign country or locality other than the country or locality in which the article was manufactured or produced appear on an imported article or its container, and those words, letters or names may mislead or deceive the ultimate purchaser as to the actual country of origin of the article, there shall appear legibly and permanently in close proximity to such words, letters or name, and in at least a comparable size, the name of the country of origin preceded by 'Made in,' 'Product of,' or other words of similar meaning.

box must have the country of origin marking on at least two box panels. *Accord, Customs Headquarters Ruling 733046* (May 4, 1990). *Customs Headquarters Ruling 561260* approved a paper tag attached to outdoor products, on the front of which were printed the trademark and the importer's name and U.S. address. The ruling found that "[a]lthough the font used to print the country of origin marking is smaller than the surrounding type, the marking is separated from the other product information in such a way that it is easily located." Similar marking was deemed acceptable in *Customs Headquarters Ruling 560806. Compare New York Customs Ruling E80581* (May 12, 1999) (additional country of origin marking required on hang tag that had trademark referencing "St. Louis, U.S.A"). In *New York Customs Ruling D86756* (Feb. 3, 1999), the agency considered the name "Ozark Trail" on the front of a package to trigger the special marking requirements, but allowed the country of origin to be printed on the back of the package in part because the reference to the U.S. location was "indirect."

XLV. PATENT SURVEYS

The Customs Service will conduct a survey of imports to identify merchandise that appears to infringe a U.S.-registered patent when requested by the patent's owner. When the agency identifies such items in the course of a survey, it will provide the requesting patent owner with the names and addresses of the importers of the apparently infringing merchandise. A patent survey may provide a useful tool to identify respondent parties for purposes of drafting a Section 337 or district court complaint.

The procedures for requesting a survey are set forth in 19 C.F.R. § 12.39a and expanded in Customs Directive No. 2310-009 (Dec. 9, 1999). Under the regulation, the survey application must set forth the following information:

- The patent owner's name and address.
- A description of the merchandise believed to infringe the patent (if available).
- The country of manufacture of the merchandise believed to infringe the patent (if available).

Directive 2310-009 requires that the following additional information be included.

For non-chemical articles:

- The appropriate Harmonized Tariff Schedule (HTS) number according to the applicant;
- If the product is being exported or imported by the applicant, the HTS number(s) being used;
- All trademarks and trade names being used for the product;

- A sample, if possible;
- Name(s) of any final product(s) incorporating the patented article(s);
- How the patents are used;
- Port(s) at which such goods may likely be entered, if known; and
- Name and telephone number of a technical specialist who may be contacted for further inquiries.

For chemical articles, in addition to the preceding information, the application must provide:

- Chemical Abstracts Service Registry (CAS) number(s), if assigned;
- All names being used for the chemical (*i.e.*, proprietary and chemical), especially trade names;
- A chemical analysis, if possible;
- Whether the chemical product is an active ingredient; and
- If the chemical is an active ingredient, the types of final product(s) in which it will it be found and the names of such final product(s).

The application also must be accompanied by a certified copy of the patent registration issued by the PTO, three additional copies of the registration, and a check for the applicable fee.

The applicant can request that the import survey cover periods of two, four or six months. The fee charged will vary depending on the time period requested. As provided in 19 C.F.R. § 24.12(a)(3), the fees are $1,000 for the two-month survey, $1,500 for four months, and $2,000 for six months. The check should be payable to order of "United States Customs Service."

An application for a patent survey should be sent to:

U.S. Customs Service
Office of Regulations & Rulings
Intellectual Property Rights Branch,
Room 3.4A
1300 Pennsylvania Ave., NW.
Washington, D.C. 20229

If the patent survey application is accepted, the Customs Service will attempt to identify potentially infringing imports at each port of entry and report the results to the applicant on a monthly basis. Directive 2310-009 provides the following sample letter for reporting the results.

Dear Sir/Madam:

This Patent Import Survey Report is issued in response to your request that U.S. Customs perform a Patent Import Survey, as provided for by Title 19, Code of Federal Regulations, Section 12.39a (19 CFR § 12.39a).

We have attempted to identify importations of goods, which appear to infringe your patent as described in the Patent Survey Application No. _____________.

This port (has/has not) identified importations of goods which appear to infringe the patent which is the subject of the Patent Survey Application listed above. We are providing the name and address of such importer(s) below:

Name of importer:

Address of importer:

Sincerely,

Area/Port Director

cc: U.S. International Trade Commission

Office of the General Counsel
500 E Street, SW.
Washington, D.C. 20436

ENFORCEMENT OF RIGHTS UNDER TRADE AGREEMENTS

XLVI. U.S. GOVERNMENT SANCTIONS AGAINST FOREIGN INTELLECTUAL PROPERTY VIOLATIONS

A. Overview of Section 301

United States law permits the Executive Branch to investigate and sanction foreign practices that either infringe or fail to protest American intellectual property rights or violate agreements to which a foreign government is a party. The primary responsibility for such investigations is vested in the Office of the United States Trade Representative (USTR). The agency's role is summarized on its internet website: "Like the National Security Council or Council of Economic Advisors, USTR is part of the Executive Office of the President. Through an interagency structure, the USTR coordinates trade policy, resolves disagreements, and frames issues for Presidential decision." Of direct relevance to U.S. intellectual property rights owners, USTR has the primary responsibility for conducting negotiations and dispute resolution proceedings in the World Trade Organization (WTO), overseeing bilateral trade negotiations with other countries, and establishing policies to govern tariff preferences under the Generalized System of Preferences (GSP) and other programs.

The primary legal mechanism available to USTR for addressing intellectual property disputes with foreign governments is Section 301 of Trade Act of 1974, codified at 19 U.S.C. § 2411 *et seq.* Its provisions allow USTR to identify, investigate, and seek to resolve three broad types of foreign violations. First, USTR can pursue a foreign government's failure to adhere to international agreements concerning intellectual property matters, such as the Agreement on Trade-Related Aspects of Intellectual Property Rights (TRIPS Agreement) adopted under the auspices of the WTO. Second, USTR can investigate a foreign government's activities (or lack thereof) that adversely affect U.S. intellectual property owners, even if the complained-of act is not the subject of an international agreement. Third, USTR can raise activities by foreign private parties, such as unauthorized copying of movies, that it wants the foreign government to prevent. In practice, the three types of disputes can overlap: for example, foreign private parties' unauthorized copying may constitute an infringement of American-owned intellectual property rights, while the foreign government's failure to take action against them may provide a failure to meet obligations under the TRIPS Agreement.

B. Substantive Reach of Section 301

The statute requires USTR to take specified remedial action when it determines that (1) U.S. rights under any trade agreement are being denied, (2) a foreign country is violating, or otherwise denying to the United States, the benefits of a trade agreement, or (3) a foreign country has taken "unjustifiable" action that burdens or restricts U.S. commerce. 19 U.S.C. § 2411(a)(1). The agency also has discretionary authority to take action when it finds that an "act, policy, or practice of a foreign country is unreasonable or discriminatory and burdens or restricts United States commerce, and action by the United States is appropriate." 19 U.S.C. § 2411(b).

Certain foreign practices that may affect American-owned intellectual property rights are specifically mentioned as actionable under Section 301. A foreign practice may be "unreasonable" if it is "unfair and inequitable," even though it does not violate a trade agreement. Included among the specifically-defined "unreasonable" practices are those that deny "fair and equitable" "provision of adequate and effective protection of intellectual property rights notwithstanding the fact that the foreign country may be in compliance with the specific obligations of the [TRIPS] Agreement. . . ." 19 U.S.C. § 2411(d)(3)(B)(i)(II). Such unreasonable practices might occur when the foreign country fails to provide:

> adequate and effective means under the laws of the foreign country for persons who are not citizens or nationals of such country to secure, exercise, and enforce rights and enjoy commercial benefits relating to patents, trademarks, copyrights and related rights, mask works, trade secrets, and plant breeder's rights.

19 U.S.C. § 2411(d)(3)(F)(i).

Similarly defined as unreasonable is the foreign country's failure to provide "nondiscriminatory market access opportunities for United States persons that rely upon intellectual property protection. . . ." 19 U.S.C. § 2411(d)(3)(B)(i)(III). This is defined to "include[] restrictions on market access related to the use, exploitation, or enjoyment of commercial benefits derived from exercising intellectual property rights in protected works or fixations or products embodying protected works." 19 U.S.C. § 2411(d)(3)(F)(ii).

In addition, "unjustifiable" practices "include, but are not limited to, any act, policy, or practice" contrary to the "international legal rights of the United States" and "which denies national or most-favored-nation treatment or the right of establishment or protection of intellectual property rights." 19 U.S.C. § 2411(d)(4)(A), (B).[78]

Not specifically mentioned, but actionable under 19 U.S.C. § 2411(b), is a violation of the TRIPs agreement or the intellectual property provisions of another trade agreement.

---

78 In brief, "national treatment" means that imported goods and foreign persons must be treated as favorably as domestic goods, services, or persons. A country's providing a longer term of patent protection to its own nationals than it does to foreign persons would exemplify a denial of national treatment. "Most favored nation treatment" requires that a country not discriminate between goods, services or persons from different countries, *i.e.*, it cannot treat one trading partner more favorably than another. An example of a breach of most favored nation treatment is Country A's granting a longer term of patent protection to citizens of Country B than it does to citizens of Country C.

C. Exceptions to Mandatory Action

There are several exceptions to Section 2411(a)'s mandate. USTR is not required to act against a foreign practice when the WTO Dispute Settlement body, or the dispute settlement mechanism under another trade agreement, has determined that the complained-of foreign practice is not violating the agreement or otherwise denying U.S. rights thereunder. Mandatory action may also be forestalled when USTR determines that the foreign country involved is "taking satisfactory measures to grant the rights of the United States under a trade agreement," or has agreed to eliminate the practice in question or implement another "imminent solution" acceptable to USTR. If removing the foreign practice is impossible, the foreign country and USTR may reach agreement under which the former provides compensatory trade benefits (such as reduced tariffs on specified products) to the United States. Finally, USTR need not act when doing so would have disproportionately adverse economic effects in the U.S. or "cause serious harm to the national security of the United States." 19 U.S.C. § 2411(a)(2).

D. Remedial Actions Available to USTR

The statute provides a broad array of remedial actions for USTR to pursue. First, it may "suspend, withdraw, or prevent" trade agreement concessions by the U.S. that the foreign country would otherwise enjoy. 19 U.S.C. § 2411(c)(1)(A). Second, USTR may order the imposition of "duties or other import restrictions on the goods of" that country, or "fees or restrictions on the services of" that country that are provided in the United States. 19 U.S.C. § 2411(c)(1)(B). This means, for example, that USTR could order an increase in the rate of customs duties applicable to imports from the offending country, or impose numerical quotas on the quantity of goods from that country permitted to enter the U.S. Third, if the offending country is a beneficiary under the GSP, the Caribbean Basin Economic Recovery Act (CBERA), or the Andean Trade Preference Act (ATPA), USTR may revoke or otherwise limit duty-free status for some or all of its merchandise. 19 U.S.C. § 2411(c)(1)(C). Finally, USTR may negotiate a binding agreement under which the other country agrees to eliminate the disputed practice, or provide satisfactory compensation (such as reduced tariffs on American products) to the U.S. 19 U.S.C. § 2411(c)(1)(D). Any such compensation should benefit the U.S. "trade sector" disadvantaged by the foreign practice, unless doing so is "not feasible" or benefits to a different U.S. economic sector would be "more satisfactory." 19 U.S.C. § 2411(c)(4).

Although the amount of trade affected by the remedial action ordered by USTR should be commensurate with that affected by the foreign practice, 19 U.S.C. § 2411(a)(3), USTR's actions need not be limited to the "goods or economic sector" of the foreign country involved in the practice under consideration. 19 U.S.C. § 2411(c)(3). Thus, a Section 301 investigation concerning automobiles could result in additional duties on the foreign country's textile products.

E. Procedures and Timetables Under Section 301

The statute permits an "interested person" to file a petition with USTR seeking action under Section 301. 19 U.S.C. § 2412(a)(1). An "interested person" is broadly defined; it "includes, but is not limited to, domestic firms and workers, representatives of consumer interests, United States product exporters, and any industrial user of any goods or services that may be affected by actions taken under subsection (a) or (b) of" Section 301. 19 U.S.C. § 2411(d)(9). The regulation confirms the broad standing granted under Section 301:

> An interested person is deemed to be any party who has a significant interest affected by the act, policy, or practice complained of, for example: A producer, a commercial importer, or an exporter of an affected product or service; a United States person seeking to invest directly abroad, with implications for trade in goods or services; a person who relies on protection of intellectual property rights; a trade association, a certified union or recognized union or group of workers which is representative of an industry engaged in the manufacture, production or wholesale distribution in the United States of a product or service so affected; or any other private party representing a significant economic interest affected directly by the act, policy or practice complained of in the petition.

15 C.F.R. § 2006.0. Thus, as a practical matter, any party that can demonstrate that the alleged foreign practice has or may adversely affect it should qualify as an interested person.

The regulations provide detailed requirements for the petition's contents. It must state that it requests action under Section 301, identify the petitioner(s) and the "person, firm or association, if any, which petitioner represents," and describe the petitioner's economic interest affected by the foreign government practice at issue. 15 C.F.R. § 2006.1(a)(1). Next, it must describe the foreign practice it wishes to see addressed, *i.e.*, the trade agreement rights being denied "or the other act, policy or practice which is the subject of the petition," and the Section 301 provision that covers the foreign practice. 15 C.F.R. § 2006.1(a)(2). Copies of applicable foreign laws, regulations, or other measures should be attached when available to the petitioner, or at least cited fully when unavailable. 15 C.F.R. § 2006.1(a)(3). The petition should identify the foreign country and allegedly violated trade agreement and the intellectual property right (or product, service or investment matter) covered by the petition, and demonstrate how the foreign practice denies U.S. rights under or otherwise violates a trade agreement, or is "unjustifiable, unreasonable, or discriminatory and burdens or restricts United States commerce." 15 C.F.R. § 2006.1(a)(4)-(6).

Additionally, the petition must provide information concerning the degree to which the foreign practice burdens or restricts U.S. commerce, *i.e.*, the monetary consequence and the method for calculating it, and the volume of trade involved. 15 C.F.R. § 2006.1(a)(7). It must note whether the petitioner also is or has filed for relief under another statute. 15 C.F.R. § 2006.1(a)(8).

A petition asserting that the foreign country "denies adequate and effective protection of intellectual property rights" should identify, if possible, the extent to which the U.S. provides "reciprocal opportunities" for "foreign nationals and firms." 15 C.F.R. § 2006.1(b)(2). It should also provide the following information:

> (A) Identification of the intellectual property right for which protection has been sought,
>
> (B) Indication of how persons who are not citizens or nationals of such foreign country are denied the opportunity to secure, exercise, and enforce rights relating to patents, process patents, registered trademarks, copyrights, or mask works, and
>
> (C) The relevant laws of the foreign country and an analysis of how the foreign country's law or policies conform to provisions of international law or international agreements to which both the United States and the foreign country are parties.

15 C.F.R. § 2006.1(b)(2)(ii).

Petitions that fail to meet the requirements as to form and content may be rejected, although USTR has discretion to take further action even under a deficiently-drawn petition. 15 C.F.R. § 2006.2. Also, USTR may initiate an investigation even without a petition's filing; this would include self-initiation. 19 U.S.C. § 2412(b).

For petitions that are accepted for docketing, the agency must determine within 45 days from the date of filing whether to initiate an investigation. Notice of the initiation decision will be published in the *Federal Register.* 19 U.S.C. § 2412(a)(2), (3); 15 C.F.R. § 2006.3. Following initiation, USTR may seek additional information from the relevant foreign government and begin consultations in an attempt to reach a mutually-agreeable resolution. 19 U.S.C. § 2413; 15 C.F.R. § 2006.4, 2006.5. If such consultations fail, USTR is directed to initiate formal dispute settlement proceedings by the earlier of (1) the close of the consultation period provided in the international agreement underlying the dispute, or (2) 150 days after consultations began. 15 C.F.R. § 2006.6.

USTR will solicit public comments following initiation of an investigation, through a public hearing (if requested) and submission of written briefs, in accordance with a schedule published in the *Federal Register.* 15 C.F.R. § 2006.7-2006.9. The schedule for reaching a final determination hinges on whether the dispute stems from a trade agreement. If no trade agreement is involved, the decision is due within twelve (12) months from the date of initiation. If a trade agreement is involved, the decision is due by the earlier of (1) thirty (30) days after dispute resolution proceedings under the agreement are completed, or (2) 18 (eighteen) months after the initiation date. 19 U.S.C. § 2414(a)(2). The statute does not provide sanctions for missing these deadlines, however, and merely requires that Congress be notified in the event "a dispute is not resolved before the close of the minimum dispute settlement period provided for in a trade agreement." 19 U.S.C. § 2414(a)(4).

F. Special 301

19 C.F.R. § 2242(a)(1) (called "Special 301") directs USTR to annually identify foreign countries that:

> (A) deny adequate and effective protection of intellectual property rights, or
>
> (B) deny fair and equitable market access to United States persons that rely upon intellectual property protection. . . .

Denial of adequate and effective protection of intellectual property rights occurs when

> the foreign country denies adequate and effective means under the laws of the foreign country for persons who are not citizens or nationals of such foreign country to secure, exercise, and enforce rights relating to patents, process patents, registered trademarks, copyrights and mask works.

19 C.F.R. § 2242(d)(2). Denial of fair and equitable market access arises if:

> the foreign country effectively denies access to a market for a product protected by a copyright or related right, patent, trademark, mask work, trade secret, or plant breeder's right, through the use of laws, procedures, practices, or regulations which—
>
> (A) violate provisions of international law or international agreements to which both the United States and the foreign country are parties, or
>
> (B) constitute discriminatory nontariff trade barriers.

19 C.F.R. § 2242(d)(3).

USTR is further authorized to specify "priority foreign countries" from among those identified under Section 2242(a)(1), based on the following criteria:

> (1) In identifying priority foreign countries under subsection (a)(2) of this section, the Trade Representative shall only identify those foreign countries—
>
> (A) that have the most onerous or egregious acts, policies, or practices that—
>
> (i) deny adequate and effective intellectual property rights, or
>
> (ii) deny fair and equitable market access to United States persons that rely upon intellectual property protection,
>
> (B) whose acts, policies, or practices described in subparagraph (A) have the greatest adverse impact (actual or potential) on the relevant United States products, and
>
> (C) that are not—
>
> (i) entering into good faith negotiations, or
>
> (ii) making significant progress in bilateral or multilateral negotiations,
>
> to provide adequate and effective protection of intellectual property rights.

19 U.S.C. § 2242(a)(2), (b). USTR is to make its determination of priority foreign countries in consultation "with the Register of Copyrights, Commissioner of Patents and Trademarks, other appropriate officers of the Federal Government." 19 U.S.C. § 2242(b)(2)(A). In addition, USTR should rely on "available sources" and information submitted to it, including under a Section 2412 petition. 19 U.S.C. § 2242(b)(2)(B). The agency will specifically solicit public

submissions on the issue. *See, e.g.*, *Identification of Countries Under Section 182 of the Trade Act of 1974: Request for Public Comment*, 66 Fed. Reg. 66492 (Dec. 26, 2001).

Having determined the countries that meet these criteria, within thirty (30) days USTR must initiate a section 301 investigation of the priority foreign countries, unless doing so "would be detrimental to United States economic interests." In the event it does not initiate an investigation with respect to one or more priority foreign countries, USTR must provide Congress with a written report setting forth the reasons for not initiating. 19 U.S.C. § 2412(b)(2). If an investigation is commenced, it can result in the imposition of trade sanctions against the named country. *E.g.*, *Determination of Action To Increase Duties on Certain Products of Ukraine Pursuant to Section 301(b): Intellectual Property Laws and Practices of the Government of Ukraine*, 67 Fed. Reg. 120 (Jan. 2, 2002) (imposing duty rates of 100 percent *ad valorem* on specific articles imported from Ukraine).

In addition to the required annual report and designation of foreign countries, under 19 U.S.C. § 2242(c)(1)(B), USTR is authorized to make "out of cycle" identifications of countries meeting the criteria of 19 U.S.C. § 2242(d)(2) and (3).

G. Generalized System of Preferences

The GSP is a statutory program under which the United States grants a tariff preference to certain merchandise originating in "beneficiary developing countries." 19 U.S.C. § 2461 *et seq.* Eligible countries must be designated as beneficiaries by the President to receive the tariff preference for their products.

The statute provides several factors to be taken into account in designating a country as a GSP beneficiary or considering its removal if it has already been designated. Under 19 U.S.C. § 2462(c)(5), one of those factors is "the extent to which such country is providing adequate and effective protection of intellectual property rights."

USTR conducts annual reviews of beneficiary countries' continued eligibility for GSP status. As part of these reviews, USTR will entertain claims that a foreign country has denied intellectual property protection and hence warrants removal from the ranks of GSP beneficiaries. If USTR determines that a beneficiary country is doing so, the offender may lose some or all of its benefits under the GSP program. Such action may also be taken in conjunction with a Section 301 proceeding. *E.g.*, *Determination of Action To Suspend GSP Benefits Under Section 301(b); Further Proposed Action and Publication of Preliminary Product List; and Request for Public Comment: Intellectual Property Laws and Practices of the Government of Ukraine*, 66 Fed. Reg. 42246 (Aug. 10, 2001).

XLVII. PROCEEDINGS BEFORE THE WORLD TRADE ORGANIZATION

Pursuant to Section 301, USTR may be required to refer another country's apparent violations of trade agreements for dispute resolution proceedings. Perceived violations of WTO agreements would be referred to the WTO for resolution.

The WTO is a multilateral organization, to which more than 140 countries are members, that oversees the negotiation and enforcement of agreements governing international trade.

The *Agreement Establishing the World Trade Organization* (LT/UR/A/2 (April 15, 1994)) includes, as Annex 2, the *Understanding on Rules and Procedures Governing the Settlement of Disputes* (LT/UR/A-2/DS/U/1). This *Understanding* provides the procedural rules applicable when one WTO member believes that another member has violated the terms of a WTO agreement. Thus, if USTR concludes in a Section 301 proceeding that another WTO member country was not in compliance with the WTO *Agreement on Trade-Related Aspects of Intellectual Property Rights*, or had taken action (or inaction) in violation of another WTO agreement, under the *Understanding* its prescribed course is to seek dispute resolution proceedings. Such proceedings before the WTO are handled by the organization's Dispute Settlement Body (DSB), which consists of all representatives of all member countries.

WTO dispute resolution proceedings are commenced by a request for consultations.[79] At the consultation stage, the governments involved discuss the alleged violation and, in theory, seek a negotiated settlement. The consultation stage can last up to sixty days.

Assuming consultations are unsuccessful in resolving the matter, the complaining country may request appointment of a panel at a DSB meeting. A panel typically will consist of three members, who may be representatives from other WTO member countries or outside experts. The prospective respondent country may prevent, or "block" a panel from being formed at the first DSB meeting following the complainant's request. The *Understanding* does not permit subsequent blocking of a panel's formation by the prospective respondent. Although the entire DSB can vote by consensus to block a panel's formation, in practice this is unlikely to occur given that the complainant can single-handedly thwart a consensus finding. The process of permitting a panel to be formed can take up to several months, depending on whether formation was blocked in the first DSB meeting where the panel was requested.

After the DSB authorizes formation of a panel and the members have been appointed, the parties submit written documents that are akin to briefs in U.S. courts. These documents are submitted simultaneously, *i.e.*, the complainant

79 The following discussion draws from the text of the *Understanding* and the WTO's on-line publication, *Settling Disputes: The WTO's 'most individual contribution'*.

does not file first with a subsequent reply from the respondent. The panel will then hold an initial hearing for the parties to present their positions and the panelists to ask questions; this process is broadly analogous to oral argument in a U.S. appellate court. The parties thereafter submit written rebuttal statements, after which the panel will hold a second hearing. Third countries that have an interest in the matter under dispute may also participate in the written and oral advocacy stages of the proceeding.

After the second hearing, the panel will prepare an initial draft report summarizing the dispute's factual background and the parties' arguments and circulate it to the parties for correction and comment. It will subsequently prepare an interim report setting forth any amendments to the initial draft along with its tentative findings and conclusions for the parties' review and comments, following which it will prepare a final version of the report. The final report will specify whether the panel found that the complained-of activity violated a WTO agreement.

The panel report will be circulated to WTO members, and will be adopted by the DSB unless there is a consensus of members against doing so.

One or more countries dissatisfied with the panel report may appeal it to the DSB's Appellate Body. The Appellate Body consists of seven experts who have been appointed for four-year terms; each appeal is heard by three of its members. The Appellate Body's decision will be set forth in an appellate report, which can be rejected by a consensus vote of DSB members but otherwise will be adopted by the DSB.

If a panel or Appellate Body finding is that the respondent country has violated a WTO agreement, that country will be expected to follow the panel or appellate report and should state its intention to do so within thirty days of the report's adoption by the DSB. If immediate compliance is not possible, a reasonable period of time for compliance is likely to be granted by the DSB.

Failure to undertake changes that remove the violation require consultations between the complainant and respondent to determine appropriate "compensation," which may take the form of concessions designed to increase the complainant's access to the respondent's market. If the parties cannot agree on compensation levels, the complainant may seek DSB authorization to impose retaliatory measures against the respondent. Unless a consensus of the DSB is opposed, authorization for such measures will generally be granted. Retaliatory measures would typically take the form of the complainant country imposing increased tariffs against products from the respondent. The amount of trade subject to retaliation should approximate the amount of trade affected by the respondent's underlying violation.

The WTO's dispute resolution system should forestall unilateral action by a member country that believes another member has violated an agreement. Indeed, unilateral action against a country that has incontrovertibly violated one of its WTO commitments would itself be a violation of the *Understanding*.

APPENDICES

APPENDIX A
SECTION 1337 STATUTE AND REGULATIONS

UNITED STATES CODE
TITLE 19—CUSTOMS DUTIES
CHAPTER 4—TARIFF ACT OF 1930
SUBTITLE II—SPECIAL PROVISIONS
PART II—UNITED STATES INTERNATIONAL TRADE COMMISSION

Sec. 1337 Unfair practices in import trade

(a) Unlawful activities; covered industries; definitions

(1) Subject to paragraph (2), the following are unlawful, and when found by the Commission to exist shall be dealt with, in addition to any other provision of law, as provided in this section:

(A) Unfair methods of competition and unfair acts in the importation of articles (other than articles provided for in subparagraphs (B), (C), (D), and (E)) into the United States, or in the sale of such articles by the owner, importer, or consignee, the threat or effect of which is—

(i) to destroy or substantially injure an industry in the United States;

(ii) to prevent the establishment of such an industry; or

(iii) to restrain or monopolize trade and commerce in the United States.

(B) The importation into the United States, the sale for importation, or the sale within the United States after importation by the owner, importer, or consignee, of articles that—

(i) infringe a valid and enforceable United States patent or a valid and enforceable United States copyright registered under Title 17; or

(ii) are made, produced, processed, or mined under, or by means of, a process covered by the claims of a valid and enforceable United States patent.

(C) The importation into the United States, the sale for importation, or the sale within the United States after importation by the owner, importer, or consignee, of articles that infringe a valid and enforceable United States trademark registered under the Trademark Act of 1946.

(D) The importation into the United States, the sale for importation, or the sale within the United States after importation by the owner, importer, or consignee, of a semiconductor chip product in a manner that constitutes infringement of a mask work registered under chapter 9 of Title 17.

(E) The importation into the United States, the sale for importation, or the sale within the United States after importation by the owner, importer, or consigner, of an article that constitutes infringement of the exclusive rights in a design protected under chapter 13 of title 17.

(2) Subparagraphs (B), (C), and (D) of paragraph (1) apply only if an industry in the United States, relating to the articles protected by the patent, copyright, trademark, mask work, or design concerned, exists or is in the process of being established.

(3) For purposes of paragraph (2), an industry in the United States shall be considered to exist if there is in the United States, with respect to the articles protected by the patent, copyright, trademark, mask work, or design concerned—

(A) significant investment in plant and equipment;

(B) significant employment of labor or capital; or

(C) substantial investment in its exploitation, including engineering, research and development, or licensing.

(4) For the purposes of this section, the phrase "owner, importer, or consignee" includes any agent of the owner, importer, or consignee.

(b) Investigation of violations by Commission

(1) The Commission shall investigate any alleged violation of this section on complaint under oath or upon its initiative. Upon commencing any such investigation, the Commission shall publish notice thereof in the *Federal Register.* The Commission shall conclude any such investigation and make its determination under this section at the earliest practicable time after the date of publication of notice of such investigation. To promote expeditious adjudication, the Commission shall, within 45 days after an investigation is initiated, establish a target date for its final determination.

(2) During the course of each investigation under this section, the Commission shall consult with, and seek advice and information from, the Department of Health and Human Services, the Department of Justice, the Federal Trade Commission, and such other departments and agencies as it considers appropriate.

(3) Whenever, in the course of an investigation under this section, the Commission has reason to believe, based on information before it, that a matter, in whole or in part, may come within the purview of part II of subtitle IV of this chapter, it shall promptly notify the Secretary of Commerce so that such action may be taken as is otherwise authorized by such part II. If the Commission has reason to believe that the matter before it (A) is based solely on alleged acts and effects which are within the purview of section 1671 or 1673 of this title, or (B) relates to an alleged copyright infringement with respect to which action is prohibited by section 1008 of Title 17, the Commission shall terminate, or not institute, any investigation into the matter. If the Commission has reason to believe the matter before it is based in part on alleged acts and effects which are within the purview of section 1671 or 1673 of this title, and in part on alleged acts and effects which may, independently from or in conjunction with those within the purview of such section, establish a basis for relief under this section, then it may institute or continue an investigation into the matter. If the Commission notifies the Secretary or the administering authority (as defined in section 1677(1) of this title) with respect to a matter under

this paragraph, the Commission may suspend its investigation during the time the matter is before the Secretary or administering authority for final decision. Any final decision by the administering authority under section 1671 or 1673 of this title with respect to the matter within such section 1671 or 1673 of this title of which the Commission has notified the Secretary or administering authority shall be conclusive upon the Commission with respect to the issue of less-than-fair- value sales or subsidization and the matters necessary for such decision.

(c) Determinations; review

The Commission shall determine, with respect to each investigation conducted by it under this section, whether or not there is a violation of this section, except that the Commission may, by issuing a consent order or on the basis of an agreement between the private parties to the investigation, including an agreement to present the matter for arbitration, terminate any such investigation, in whole or in part, without making such a determination. Each determination under subsection (d) or (e) of this section shall be made on the record after notice and opportunity for a hearing in conformity with the provisions of subchapter II of chapter 5 of Title 5. All legal and equitable defenses may be presented in all cases. A respondent may raise any counterclaim in a manner prescribed by the Commission. Immediately after a counterclaim is received by the Commission, the respondent raising such counterclaim shall file a notice of removal with a United States district court in which venue for any of the counterclaims raised by the party would exist under section 1391 of Title 28. Any counterclaim raised pursuant to this section shall relate back to the date of the original complaint in the proceeding before the Commission. Action on such counterclaim shall not delay or affect the proceeding under this section, including the legal and equitable defenses that may be raised under this subsection. Any person adversely affected by a final determination of the Commission under subsection (d), (e), (f), or (g) of this section may appeal such determination, within 60 days after the determination becomes final, to the United States Court of Appeals for the Federal Circuit for review in accordance with chapter 7 of Title 5. Notwithstanding the foregoing provisions of this subsection Commission determinations under subsections (d), (e), (f), and (g) of this section with respect to its findings on the public health and welfare, competitive conditions in the United States economy, the production of like or directly competitive articles in the United States, and United States consumers, the amount and nature of bond, or the appropriate remedy shall be reviewable in accordance with section 706 of Title 5. Determinations by the Commission under subsections (e), (f), and (j) of this section with respect to forfeiture of bonds and under subsection (h) of this section with respect to the imposition of sanctions for abuse of discovery or abuse of process shall also be reviewable in accordance with section 706 of Title 5.

(d) Exclusion of articles from entry

(1) If the Commission determines, as a result of an investigation under this section, that there is a violation of this section, it shall direct that the articles concerned, imported by any person violating the provision of this section, be excluded from entry into the United States, unless, after considering the effect of such exclusion upon the public health and welfare, competitive conditions in the United States economy, the production of like or directly competitive articles in the United States, and United States consumers, it finds that such articles should not be excluded from entry. The Commission shall notify the Secretary of the Treasury of its action under this subsection directing such exclusion from entry, and upon receipt of such notice, the Secretary shall, through the proper officers, refuse such entry.

(2) The authority of the Commission to order an exclusion from entry of articles shall be limited to persons determined by the Commission to be violating this section unless the Commission determines that—

(A) a general exclusion from entry of articles is necessary to prevent circumvention of an exclusion order limited to products of named persons; or

(B) there is a pattern of violation of this section and it is difficult to identify the source of infringing products.

(e) Exclusion of articles from entry during investigation except under bond; procedures applicable; preliminary relief

(1) If, during the course of an investigation under this section, the Commission determines that there is reason to believe that there is a violation of this section, it may direct that the articles concerned, imported by any person with respect to whom there is reason to believe that such person is violating this section, be excluded from entry into the United States, unless, after considering the effect of such exclusion upon the public health and welfare, competitive conditions in the United States economy, the production of like or directly competitive articles in the United States, and United States consumers, it finds that such articles should not be excluded from entry. The Commission shall notify the Secretary of the Treasury of its action under this subsection directing such exclusion from entry, and upon receipt of such notice, the Secretary shall, through the proper officers, refuse such entry, except that such articles shall be entitled to entry under bond prescribed by the Secretary in an amount determined by the Commission to be sufficient to protect the complainant from any injury. If the Commission later determines that the respondent has violated the provisions of this section, the bond may be forfeited to the complainant.

(2) A complainant may petition the Commission for the issuance of an order under this subsection. The Commission shall make a determination with regard to such petition by no later than the 90th day after the date on which the Commission's notice of investigation is published in the *Federal Register*. The Commission may extend the 90-day period for an additional 60 days in a case it designates as a more complicated case. The Commission shall publish in the *Federal Register* its reasons why it designated the case as being more complicated. The Commission may require the complainant to post a bond as a prerequisite to the issuance of an order under this subsection. If the Commission later determines that the respondent has not violated the provisions of this section, the bond may be forfeited to the respondent.

(3) The Commission may grant preliminary relief under this subsection or subsection (f) of this section to the same extent as preliminary injunctions and temporary restraining orders may be granted under the Federal Rules of Civil Procedure.

(4) The Commission shall prescribe the terms and conditions under which bonds may be forfeited under paragraphs (1) and (2).

(f) Cease and desist orders; civil penalty for violation of orders

(1) In addition to, or in lieu of, taking action under subsection (d) or (e) of this section, the Commission may issue and cause to be served on any person violating this section, or believed to be violating this section, as the case may be, an order directing such person to cease and desist from engaging in the unfair methods or acts involved, unless after considering the effect of such order upon the public health and welfare, competitive

conditions in the United States economy, the production of like or directly competitive articles in the United States, and United States consumers, it finds that such order should not be issued. The Commission may at any time, upon such notice and in such manner as it deems proper, modify or revoke any such order, and, in the case of a revocation, may take action under subsection (d) or (e) of this section, as the case may be. If a temporary cease and desist order is issued in addition to, or in lieu of, an exclusion order under subsection (e) of this section, the Commission may require the complainant to post a bond, in an amount determined by the Commission to be sufficient to protect the respondent from any injury, as a prerequisite to the issuance of an order under this subsection. If the Commission later determines that the respondent has not violated the provisions of this section, the bond may be forfeited to the respondent. The Commission shall prescribe the terms and conditions under which the bonds may be forfeited under this paragraph.

(2) Any person who violates an order issued by the Commission under paragraph (1) after it has become final shall forfeit and pay to the United States a civil penalty for each day on which an importation of articles, or their sale, occurs in violation of the order of not more than the greater of $100,000 or twice the domestic value of the articles entered or sold on such day in violation of the order. Such penalty shall accrue to the United States and may be recovered for the United States in a civil action brought by the Commission in the Federal District Court for the District of Columbia or for the district in which the violation occurs. In such actions, the United States district courts may issue mandatory injunctions incorporating the relief sought by the Commission as they deem appropriate in the enforcement of such final orders of the Commission.

(g) Exclusion from entry or cease and desist order; conditions and procedures applicable

(1) If—

(A) a complaint is filed against a person under this section;

(B) the complaint and a notice of investigation are served on the person;

(C) the person fails to respond to the complaint and notice or otherwise fails to appear to answer the complaint and notice;

(D) the person fails to show good cause why the person should not be found in default; and

(E) the complainant seeks relief limited solely to that person;

the Commission shall presume the facts alleged in the complaint to be true and shall, upon request, issue an exclusion from entry or a cease and desist order, or both, limited to that person unless, after considering the effect of such exclusion or order upon the public health and welfare, competitive conditions in the United States economy, the production of like or directly competitive articles in the United States, and United States consumers, the Commission finds that such exclusion or order should not be issued.

(2) In addition to the authority of the Commission to issue a general exclusion from entry of articles when a respondent appears to contest an investigation concerning a violation of the provisions of this section, a general exclusion from entry of articles, regardless of the source or importer of the articles, may be issued if—

(A) no person appears to contest an investigation concerning a violation of the provisions of this section,

(B) such a violation is established by substantial, reliable, and probative evidence, and

(C) the requirements of subsection (d)(2) of this section are met.

(h) Sanctions for abuse of discovery and abuse of process

The Commission may by rule prescribe sanctions for abuse of discovery and abuse of process to the extent authorized by Rule 11 and Rule 37 of the Federal Rules of Civil Procedure.

(i) Forfeiture

(1) In addition to taking action under subsection (d) of this section, the Commission may issue an order providing that any article imported in violation of the provisions of this section be seized and forfeited to the United States if—

(A) the owner, importer, or consignee of the article previously attempted to import the article into the United States;

(B) the article was previously denied entry into the United States by reason of an order issued under subsection (d) of this section; and

(C) upon such previous denial of entry, the Secretary of the Treasury provided the owner, importer, or consignee of the article written notice of—

(i) such order, and

(ii) the seizure and forfeiture that would result from any further attempt to import the article into the United States.

(2) The Commission shall notify the Secretary of the Treasury of any order issued under this subsection and, upon receipt of such notice, the Secretary of the Treasury shall enforce such order in accordance with the provisions of this section.

(3) Upon the attempted entry of articles subject to an order issued under this subsection, the Secretary of the Treasury shall immediately notify all ports of entry of the attempted importation and shall identify the persons notified under paragraph (1)(C).

(4) The Secretary of the Treasury shall provide—

(A) the written notice described in paragraph (1)(C) to the owner, importer, or consignee of any article that is denied entry into the United States by reason of an order issued under subsection (d) of this section; and

(B) a copy of such written notice to the Commission.

(j) Referral to President

(1) If the Commission determines that there is a violation of this section, or that, for purposes of subsection (e) of this section, there is reason to believe that there is such a violation, it shall—

(A) publish such determination in the *Federal Register*, and

(B) transmit to the President a copy of such determination and the action taken under subsection (d), (e), (f), (g), or (i) of this section, with respect thereto, together with the record upon which such determination is based.

(2) If, before the close of the 60-day period beginning on the day after the day on which he receives a copy of such determination, the President, for policy reasons, disapproves

such determination and notifies the Commission of his disapproval, then, effective on the date of such notice, such determination and the action taken under subsection (d), (e), (f), (g), or (i) of this section with respect thereto shall have no force or effect.

(3) Subject to the provisions of paragraph (2), such determination shall, except for purposes of subsection (c) of this section, be effective upon publication thereof in the *Federal Register*, and the action taken under subsection (d), (e), (f), (g), or (i) of this section with respect thereto shall be effective as provided in such subsections, except that articles directed to be excluded from entry under subsection (d) of this section or subject to a cease and desist order under subsection (f) of this section shall, until such determination becomes final, be entitled to entry under bond prescribed by the Secretary in an amount determined by the Commission to be sufficient to protect the complainant from any injury. If the determination becomes final, the bond may be forfeited to the complainant. The Commission shall prescribe the terms and conditions under which bonds may be forfeited under this paragraph.

(4) If the President does not disapprove such determination within such 60-day period, or if he notifies the Commission before the close of such period that he approves such determination, then, for purposes of paragraph (3) and subsection (c) of this section such determination shall become final on the day after the close of such period or the day on which the President notifies the Commission of his approval, as the case may be.

(k) Period of effectiveness; termination of violation or modification or rescission of exclusion or order

(1) Except as provided in subsections (f) and (j) of this section, any exclusion from entry or order under this section shall continue in effect until the Commission finds, and in the case of exclusion from entry notifies the Secretary of the Treasury, that the conditions which led to such exclusion from entry or order no longer exist.

(2) If any person who has previously been found by the Commission to be in violation of this section petitions the Commission for a determination that the petitioner is no longer in violation of this section or for a modification or rescission of an exclusion from entry or order under subsection (d), (e), (f), (g), or (i) of this section—

(A) the burden of proof in any proceeding before the Commission regarding such petition shall be on the petitioner; and

(B) relief may be granted by the Commission with respect to such petition—

(i) on the basis of new evidence or evidence that could not have been presented at the prior proceeding, or

(ii) on grounds which would permit relief from a judgment or order under the Federal Rules of Civil Procedure.

(l) Importation by or for United States

Any exclusion from entry or order under subsection (d), (e), (f), (g), or (i) of this section, in cases based on a proceeding involving a patent, copyright, mask work, or design under subsection (a)(1) of this section, shall not apply to any articles imported by and for the use of the United States, or imported for, and to be used for, the United States with the authorization or consent of the Government. Whenever any article would have been excluded from entry or would not have been entered pursuant to the provisions of such subsections but for the operation of this subsection, an owner of the patent, copyright, mask work, or design adversely affected shall be entitled to reasonable and entire compensation in an action before the United States Court of Federal Claims pursuant to the procedures of section 1498 of title 28.

(m) "United States" defined

For purposes of this section and sections 1338 and 1340[1] of this title, the term "United States" means the customs territory of the United States as defined in general note 2 of the Harmonized Tariff Schedule of the United States.

(n) Disclosure of confidential information

(1) Information submitted to the Commission or exchanged among the parties in connection with proceedings under this section which is properly designated as confidential pursuant to Commission rules may not be disclosed (except under a protective order issued under regulations of the Commission which authorizes limited disclosure of such information) to any person (other than a person described in paragraph (2)) without the consent of the person submitting it.

(2) Notwithstanding the prohibition contained in paragraph (1), information referred to in that paragraph may be disclosed to—

(A) an officer or employee of the Commission who is directly concerned with—

(i) carrying out the investigation or related proceeding in connection with which the information is submitted,

(ii) the administration of a bond posted pursuant to subsection (e), (f), or (j) of this section,

(iii) the administration or enforcement of an exclusion order issued pursuant to subsection (d), (e), or (g) of this section, a cease and desist order issued pursuant to subsection (f) of this section, or a consent order issued pursuant to subsection (c) of this section,

(iv) proceedings for the modification or rescission of a temporary or permanent order issued under subsection (d), (e), (f), (g), or (i) of this section, or a consent order issued under this section, or

(v) maintaining the administrative record of the investigation or related proceeding,

(B) an officer or employee of the United States Government who is directly involved in the review under subsection (j) of this section, or

(C) an officer or employee of the United States Customs Service who is directly involved in administering an exclusion from entry under subsection (d), (e), or (g) of this section resulting from the investigation or related proceeding in connection with which the information is submitted.

1 Sec. 1340 of this title was omitted from the Code.

CODE OF FEDERAL REGULATIONS
TITLE 19—CUSTOMS DUTIES
CHAPTER II—UNITED STATES INTERNATIONAL TRADE COMMISSION
SUBCHAPTER A—GENERAL
PART 201—RULES OF GENERAL APPLICATION

Subpart E—Opening Commission Meetings to Public Observation Pursuant to 5 U.S.C. 552b

Sec. 201.33 Purpose and scope.

Sec. 201.34 Definitions.

Sec. 201.35 Notices to the public.

Sec. 201.36 Closing a portion or portions of a meeting or a series of meetings.

Sec. 201.37 Changing the time, place, subject matter, or determination to open or close a meeting following a public notice.

Sec. 201.38 Requests by interested persons that the Commission close a portion of a Commission meeting.

Sec. 201.39 General Counsel's certification of Commission action in closing a meeting or a series of meetings.

Sec. 201.40 Records-retention requirements.

Sec. 201.41 Public inspection and copying of records; applicable fees.

Subpart F—National Security Information

Sec. 201.42 Purpose and scope.

Sec. 201.43 Program.

Sec. 201.44 Procedures.

Subpart G—Enforcement of Nondiscrimination on the Basis of Handicap in Programs or Activities Conducted by the U.S. International Trade Commission

Sec. 201.101 Purpose.

Sec. 201.102 Application.

Sec. 201.103 Definitions.

Secs. 201.104-201.109 [Reserved]

Sec. 201.110 Self-evaluation.

Sec. 201.111 Notice.

Secs. 201.112-201.129 [Reserved]

Sec. 201.130 General prohibitions against discrimination.

Secs. 201.131-201.139 [Reserved]

Sec. 201.140 Employment.

Secs. 201.141-201.148 [Reserved]

Sec. 201.149 Program accessibility: Discrimination prohibited.

Sec. 201.150 Program accessibility: Existing facilities.

Sec. 201.151 Program accessibility: New construction and alterations.

Secs. 201.152-201.159 [Reserved]

Sec. 201.160 Communications.

Secs. 201.161-201.169 [Reserved]

Sec. 201.170 Compliance procedures.

Sec. 201.171-201.999 [Reserved]

Subpart H—Debt Collection

Sec. 201.201 Definitions.

Sec. 201.202 Purpose and scope of salary and administrative offset rules.

Sec. 201.203 Delegation of authority.

Sec. 201.204 Salary offset.

Sec. 201.205 Salary adjustments.

Sec. 201.206 Administrative offset.

Sec. 201.207 Administrative offset against amounts payable from Civil Service Retirement and Disability Fund

Sec. 201.208 Tax refund offset.

Sec. 201.0 Seal

(a) Pursuant to section 331(g) of the Tariff Act of 1930, as amended (19 U.S.C. 1331(g)), the United States International Trade Commission has adopted an official seal, the depiction of which follows:[OMITTED]

(b) Custody and certification obligations. The Secretary shall have custody of the seal of the United States International Trade Commission and he, or the Acting Secretary, may execute under seal any certification required to authenticate any books, records, papers, or other documents as true copies of official records of the United States International Trade Commission.

Sec. 201.1 Applicability of part

This part relates generally to functions and activities of the Commission under various statutes and other legal authority. Rules having special application appear separately in parts 202 through 207, inclusive, of this chapter. In case of inconsistency between a rule of general application and a rule of special application, the latter is controlling.

Subpart A—Miscellaneous

Sec. 201.2 Definitions

As used in this chapter—

(a) Commission means the United States International Trade Commission;

(b) Inspector General means the Inspector General of the Commission;

(c) Tariff Act means the Tariff Act of 1930, 19 U.S.C. 1202-1677j;

(d) Trade Expansion Act means the Trade Expansion Act of 1962, 19 U.S.C. 1801-1991;

(e) Trade Act means the Trade Act of 1974, 19 U.S.C. 2101-2487;

(f) Trade Agreements Act means the Trade Agreements Act of 1979, Public Law 96-39, 93 Stat. 144;

(g) Rule means a section of the Commission Rules of Practice and Procedure (19 CFR chapter II);

(h) Secretary means the Secretary of the Commission.

(i) Except for adjudicative investigations under subchapter C of this chapter, party means any person who has filed a complaint or petition on the basis of which an investigation has been instituted, or any person whose entry of appearance has been accepted pursuant to Sec. 201.11 (a) or (c). Mere participation in an investigation without an accepted entry of appearance does not confer party status.

(j) Person means an individual, partnership, corporation, association, or public or private organization.

Sec. 201.3 Commission offices, mailing address, and hours

(a) Offices.

The Commission's offices are located in the United States International Trade Commission Building on 500 E Street SW., Washington, DC.

(b) Mailing address.

All communications to the Commission should be addressed to the "Secretary, U.S. International Trade Commission, 500 E Street SW., Washington, DC 20436."

(c) Hours.

The hours of the Commission are from 8:45 a.m. to 5:15 p.m., eastern standard or daylight savings time, whichever is in effect in Washington, DC.

Sec. 201.3a Missing children information

(a) Pursuant to 39 U.S.C. 3220, penalty mail sent by the Commission may be used to assist in the location and recovery of missing children. This section establishes procedures for such use and is applicable on a Commission-wide basis. The Program and Planning Branch, Office of Management Services, 202-724-1234, shall be the point of contact for matters related to the implementation of this section.

(b) Missing children information shall be inserted in or affixed to such mailings of Commission monthly calendars, notices, press releases, and other documents as the Commission may direct. Such missing children information shall be obtained exclusively from the National Center for Missing and Exploited Children.

(c) The procedure established in subsection (b) above will result in missing children information being inserted in an estimated 25 percent of the Commission's penalty mail and will cost an estimated $1,500 for the first year of implementation. The Director of Administration shall make such changes in the procedure as he deems appropriate to maximize the use of missing children information in the Commission's mail.

Sec. 201.4 Performance of functions

(a) Conduct of business.

A majority of the members of the Commission constitutes a quorum. The Commission may meet and exercise its powers at any place, and may, by one or more of its members, or by such agents as it may designate, prosecute any inquiry necessary to its duties in any part of the United States or in any foreign country.

(b) Alteration or waiver of rules.

Rules in this chapter may be amended, waived, suspended, or revoked by the Commission only. A rule may be waived or suspended only when in the judgment of the Commission there is good and sufficient reason therefor, provided the rule is not a matter of procedure required by law.

(c) Authority to make decisions.

Authority to interpret the Commission's rules and the laws applying to the Commission, and to make findings, determinations, or other decisions not relating to matters of internal management, is retained in the Commission itself and is not delegated.

(d) Presentation of matter that may come within the purview of other laws.

Whenever any party or person, including the Commission staff, has reason to believe that (1) a matter under investigation pursuant to section 337 of the Tariff Act of 1930, or (2) a matter under an investigation pursuant to section 201 of the Trade Act of 1974 (19

U.S.C. 2251), which is causing increased imports may come within the purview of another remedial provision of law not the basis of such investigation, including but not limited to the antidumping provisions (19 U.S.C. 1673) or the countervailing duty provisions (19 U.S.C. 1303, 1671 et seq.) of the Tariff Act of 1930, then the party or person may file a suggestion of notification with the Commission that the appropriate agency be notified of such matter or circumstances, together with such information as the party or person has available. The Commission Secretary shall promptly thereafter publish notice of the filing of such suggestion and information, and make them available for inspection and copying to the extent permitted by law. Any person may comment on the suggestion within 10 days after the publication of said notice. Thereafter, the Commission shall determine whether notification is appropriate under the law and, if so, shall notify the appropriate agency of such matters or circumstances. The Commission may at any time make such notification in the absence of a suggestion under this rule when the Commission has reason to believe, on the basis of information before it, that notification is appropriate under law.

Sec. 201.5 Attendance fees and mileage

(a) Deponents and witnesses.

Any person compelled to appear in person to depose or testify in response to a subpoena shall be paid the same fees and mileage as are paid witnesses in the courts of the United States: Provided, that salaried employees of the United States summoned to depose or testify as to matters related to their public employment, irrespective of at whose instance they are summoned, shall be paid in accordance with applicable Government regulations.

(b) Responsibility.

The fees and mileage referred to in this section shall be paid by the party at whose instance deponents or witnesses appear: Provided, that when it is the Commission, one or more Commissioners, or one of its employees at whose instance deponents or witnesses appear, such fees and mileage shall be paid by the Commission.

Sec. 201.6 Confidential business information

(a) Definitions.

(1) Confidential business information is information which concerns or relates to the trade secrets, processes, operations, style of works, or apparatus, or to the production, sales, shipments, purchases, transfers, identification of customers, inventories, or amount or source of any income, profits, losses, or expenditures of any person, firm, partnership, corporation, or other organization, or other information of commercial value, the disclosure of which is likely to have the effect of either impairing the Commission's ability to obtain such information as is necessary to perform its statutory functions, or causing substantial harm to the competitive position of the person, firm, partnership, corporation, or other organization from which the information was obtained, unless the Commission is required by law to disclose such information. The term "confidential business information" includes "proprietary information" within the meaning of section 777(b) of the Tariff Act of 1930 (19 U.S.C. 1677f(b)). Nonnumerical characterizations of numerical confidential business information (e.g., discussion of trends) will be treated as confidential business information only at the request of the submitter for good cause shown.

(2) Nondisclosable confidential business information is privileged information, classified information, or specific information (e.g., trade secrets) of a type for which there is a clear and compelling need to withhold from disclosure. Special rules for the handling of such information are set out in Sec. 207.7 of this chapter.

(b) Procedure for submitting business information in confidence.

(1) A request for confidential treatment of business information shall be addressed to the Secretary, United States International Trade Commission, 500 E Street SW., Washington, DC 20436, and shall indicate clearly on the envelope that it is a request for confidential treatment.

(2) In the absence of good cause shown, any request relating to material to be submitted during the course of a hearing shall be submitted at least three (3) working days prior to the commencement of such hearing.

(3) With each submission of, or offer to submit, business information which a submitter desires to be treated as confidential business information, under paragraph (a) of this section, the submitter shall provide the following, which may be disclosed to the public:

(i) A written description of the nature of the subject information;

(ii) A justification for the request for its confidential treatment;

(iii) A certification in writing under oath that substantially identical information is not available to the public;

(iv) A copy of the document

(A) Clearly marked on its cover as to the pages on which confidential information can be found;

(B) With information for which confidential treatment is requested clearly identified by means of brackets; and

(C) With information for which nondisclosable confidential treatment is requested clearly identified by means of triple brackets (except when submission of such document is withheld in accord with paragraph (b)(4) of this section); and

(v) A nonconfidential copy of the documents as required by Sec. 201.8(d).

(4) The submission of the documents itemized in paragraph (b)(3) of this section will provide the basis for rulings on the confidentiality of submissions, including rulings on the confidentiality of submissions offered to the Commission which have not yet been placed under the possession, control, or custody of the Commission. The submitter has the option of providing the business information for which confidential treatment is sought at the time the documents itemized in paragraph (b)(3) of this section are provided or of withholding them until a ruling on their confidentiality has been issued.

(c) Identification of business information submitted in confidence.

Business information which a submitter desires to be treated as confidential shall be clearly labeled "confidential business information" when submitted, and shall be segregated from other material being submitted.

(d) Approval or denial of requests for confidential treatment.

Approval or denial of requests shall be made only by the Secretary or Acting Secretary. A denial shall be in writing, shall specify the reason therefor, and shall advise the submitter of the right to appeal to the Commission.

(e) Appeals from denial of confidential treatment.

(1) For good cause shown, the Commission may grant an appeal from a denial by the Secretary of a request for confidential treatment of a submission. Any appeal filed shall be addressed to the Chairman, United States International Trade Commission, 500 E Street SW., Washington, DC 20436, and shall clearly indicate that it is a confidential submission appeal. An appeal may be made within twenty (20) days of a denial or whenever the approval or denial has not been forthcoming within ten (10) days (excepting Saturdays, Sundays, and Federal legal holidays) of the receipt of a confidential treatment request, unless an extension notice in writing with the reasons therefor has been provided the person requesting confidential treatment.

(2) An appeal will be decided within twenty (20) days of its receipt (excepting Saturdays, Sundays, and Federal legal holidays) unless an extension notice in writing with the reasons therefor, has been provided the person making the appeal.

(3) The justification submitted to the Commission in connection with an appeal shall be limited to that presented to the Secretary with the original or amended request. When the Secretary or Acting Secretary has denied a request on the ground that the submitter failed to provide adequate justification, any such additional justification shall be submitted to the Secretary for his consideration as part of an amended request. For purposes of paragraph (e)(1) of this section, the twenty (20) day period for filing an appeal shall be tolled on the filing of an amended request and a new twenty (20) day period shall begin once the Secretary or Acting Secretary has denied the amended request, or the approval or denial has not been forthcoming within ten (10) days of the filing of the amended request. A denial of a request by the Secretary on the ground of inadequate justification shall not obligate a requester to furnish additional justification and shall not preclude a requester from filing an appeal with the Commission based on the justification earlier submitted to the Secretary.

(f) Appeals from approval of confidential treatment.

(1) For good cause shown, the Commission may grant an appeal from an approval by the Secretary of a request for confidential treatment of a submission. Any appeal filed shall be addressed to the Chairman, United States International Trade Commission, 500 E Street, S.W., Washington, DC 20436, shall show that a copy thereof has been served upon the submitter, and shall clearly indicate that it is a confidential submission appeal. An appeal may be made within twenty (20) days of the approval by the Secretary of a request for confidential treatment or whenever the approval or denial has not been forthcoming within ten (10) days (excepting Saturdays, Sundays, and Federal legal holidays) of the receipt of a confidential treatment request, unless an extension notice in writing with the reasons therefor has been provided the person requesting confidential treatment.

(2) An appeal will be decided within twenty (20) days of its receipt (excepting Saturdays, Sundays, and Federal legal holidays) unless an extension notice, in writing with the reasons therefor, has been provided the person making the appeal.

(g) Granting confidential status to business information.

Any business information submitted in confidence and determined to be entitled to confidential treatment shall be maintained in confidence by the Commission and not disclosed except as required by law. In the event that any business information submitted to the Commission is not entitled to confidential treatment, the submitter will be permitted to withdraw the tender unless it is the subject of a request under the Freedom of Information Act or of judicial discovery proceedings.

(h) Scope of provisions.

The provisions of Secs. 201.6(b) and 201.6 (d) through (g) shall not apply to adjudicative investigations under Subchapter C, Part 210, of the Commission's rules of practice and procedure.

Subpart B—Initiation and Conduct of Investigations

Sec. 201.7 Investigative authority and initiation of investigations

(a) Investigative authority.

In order to expedite the performance of its functions, the Commission may engage in investigative activities preliminary to and in aid of any authorized investigation, consolidate proceedings before it, and determine the scope and manner of its proceedings;

(b) Initiation of investigations.

Investigations may be initiated by the Commission on the Commission's own motion, upon request of the President or the United States Trade Representative, upon resolution of the Committee on Ways and Means of the House of Representatives or the Committee of Finance of the Senate, upon resolution of either branch of Congress, or upon application, petition, complaint, or request of private parties, as required or provided for in the pertinent statute, Presidential proclamation, Executive Order, or in this chapter.

Sec. 201.8 Filing of documents

(a) Where to file; date of filing.

Documents shall be filed at the office of the Secretary of the Commission in Washington, DC. Such documents, if properly filed, will be deemed to be filed on the date on which they are actually received in the Commission.

(b) Conformity with rules.

Each document filed with the Commission for the purpose of initiating any investigation shall be considered properly filed if it conforms with the pertinent rules prescribed in this chapter. Substantial compliance with the pertinent rules may be accepted by the Commission provided good and sufficient reason is stated in the document for inability to comply fully with the pertinent rules.

(c) Specifications for documents.

Each document filed under this chapter shall be clear and legible.

(d) Number of copies.

A signed original (or a copy designated as an original) and fourteen (14) copies of each document shall be filed. All submissions shall be on letter-sized paper (8\1/2\ inches by

11 inches), except copies of documents prepared for another agency or a court (e.g. patent file wrappers or pleadings papers). The original and at least one copy of all submissions shall be printed on one side only and shall be unbound (although they may be stapled or held together by means of a clip). In the event that confidential treatment of the document is requested under Sec. 201.6, at least four (4) additional copies shall be filed, in which the confidential business information shall have been deleted and which shall have been conspicuously marked "nonconfidential" or "public inspection." The name of the person signing the original shall be typewritten or otherwise reproduced on each copy.

(e) Identification of party filing document.

Each document filed with the Commission for the purpose of initiating any investigation shall show on the first page thereof the name, address, and telephone number of the party or parties by whom or on whose behalf the document is filed and shall be signed by the party filing the document or by a duly authorized officer, attorney, or agent of such party. (Also, any attorney or agent filing the document shall give his address and telephone number.) The signature of the person signing such a document constitutes a certification that he had read the document, that to the best of his knowledge and belief the statements contained therein are true, and that the person signing the document was duly authorized to sign it.

Sec. 201.9 Methods employed in obtaining information

In obtaining information necessary to carry out its functions and duties, the Commission may employ any means authorized by law. In general, the Commission obtains pertinent information from its own files, from other agencies of the Government, through questionnaires and correspondence, through field work by members of the Commission's staff, and from testimony and other information presented at the hearings.

Sec. 201.10 Public notices

As appropriate, notice of the receipt of documents properly filed, of the institution of investigations, of public hearings, and of other formal actions of the Commission will be given by publication in the Federal Register. In addition to such publication, a copy of each notice will be posted at the Office of the Secretary to the Commission in Washington, DC, and, as appropriate, copies will be sent to press associations, trade and similar organizations of producers and importers, and others known to have an interest in the subject matter.

Sec. 201.11 Appearance in an investigation as a party

(a) Who may appear as a party.

Any person may apply to appear in an investigation as a party, either in person or by representative, by filing an entry of appearance with the Secretary. Each entry of appearance shall state briefly the nature of the person's reason for participating in the investigation and state the person's intent to file briefs with the Commission regarding the subject matter of the investigation. The Secretary shall promptly determine whether the person submitting the entry of appearance has a proper reason for participating in the investigation. In any investigation conducted under part 207 of this chapter, industrial users, and if the merchandise under investigation is sold at the retail level, representative consumer organizations, will be deemed to have a proper reason for participating in the investigation. If it is found that a person does not have a proper reason for participating in the investigation, that person shall be so notified by the Secretary and shall not be entitled to appear in the investigation as a party. A person found to have a proper reason for participating in the investigation shall be permitted to appear in the investigation as a party, and acceptance of such person's entry of appearance shall be signified by the Secretary's inclusion of such person on the service list established pursuant to paragraph (d) of this section.

(b) Time for filing.

(1) Except in the case of investigations conducted under part 207 of this chapter, each entry of appearance shall be filed with the Secretary not later than twenty-one (21) days after publication of the Commission's notice of investigation in the Federal Register.

(2) In the case of investigations conducted under subpart B of part 207 of this chapter, each entry of appearance shall be filed with the Secretary not later than seven (7) days after publication of the Commission's notice of investigation in the Federal Register. A party that files a notice of appearance during such time need not file an additional notice of appearance during the portion of the investigation conducted under subpart C of part 207 of this chapter.

(3) Notwithstanding paragraph (b)(2) of this section, a party may file an entry of appearance during the final phase of an investigation conducted under part 207 of this chapter no later than twenty-one (21) days prior to the hearing date listed in the Federal Register notice published pursuant to Sec. 207.24(b) of this chapter.

(4) In the case of reviews conducted under subpart F of part 207 of this chapter, each entry of appearance shall be filed with the Secretary not later than twenty-one (21) days after publication in the Federal Register of the notice of institution described in Sec. 207.60(d) of this chapter.

(5) Notwithstanding paragraph (b)(4) of this section, a party may file an entry of appearance in a review conducted under subpart F of part 207 of this chapter within the period specified in the notice issued under Sec. 207.62(c) of this chapter. This period shall be at least 45 days.

(c) Late filing.

Any entry of appearance filed with the Secretary after the filing date established in paragraph (b) of this section shall be referred to the Chairman, or other person designated to conduct the investigation, who shall promptly determine whether to accept such entry for good cause shown by the person desiring to file the notice. The Secretary shall promptly notify the submitter of a decision to deny the entry, or if the entry is accepted, include such person on the service list established pursuant to paragraph (d) of this section.

(d) Service list.

Upon the expiration of the time for filing notices of appearance established in paragraph (b) of this section, the Secretary shall prepare a service list. The service list shall contain the names and addresses of all persons, or their representatives, who are parties to the investigation pursuant to Sec. 201.2(h) and paragraph (a) of this section. Upon the acceptance of a late entry of appearance pursuant to paragraph (c) of this section, the Secretary shall amend the service list to include the name and address of the person whose notice has been accepted and shall promptly forward such notice to all parties to the investigation.

Sec. 201.12 Requests

Any party to a nonadjudicative investigation may request the Commission to take particular action with respect to that investigation. Such requests shall be by letter addressed to the Secretary, shall be placed by him in the record, and shall be served on all other parties. The Commission shall take such action or make such response as it deems appropriate.

Sec. 201.13 Conduct of nonadjudicative hearings

(a) In general.

Public hearings are held by the Commission when required by law or, if not required by law, when in the judgment of the Commission there is good and sufficient reason therefor. Public hearings will be held at the time and place specified in notices issued under Sec. 201.10. Public hearings are ordinarily held in the Hearing Room of the International Trade Commission Building, in Washington, DC, but may be held elsewhere at the Commission's discretion.

(b) Presiding officials.

(1) Who presides. Public hearings or conferences in nonadjudicative investigations will be conducted by the Commission or by one or more Commissioners. When the Commission deems it necessary, such hearings will be conducted by one or more designated employees. In all cases the transcript of the testimony at a hearing will be presented for the consideration of the Commission.

(2) Powers and duties. The Commission, one or more of the Commissioners, or one or more designated employees shall have all the powers to conduct fair and impartial hearings, to take necessary action to avoid delay in the disposition of proceedings, including the prescription of time allocated to testimony, argument, and questioning, to regulate the course of hearings and the conduct of the parties and their counsel therein, and to maintain order.

(c) Participation in a hearing.

(1) Who may participate. A party may participate in the hearing, either in person or by representative. A nonparty who has testimony or arguments that may aid the Commission's deliberations may also participate, under such conditions as may be established by the presiding officials at the hearing.

(2) Notices of participation. Notices of participation in a hearing shall be filed with the Secretary at least three (3) days in advance of the date set for the hearing or two (2) days in advance of the date set in the notice of investigation for a prehearing conference, whichever shall first occur, except that the presiding officials may waive this requirement for good cause. Witnesses on behalf of persons filing notices of participation need not file separate notices.

(d) Witness list.

Each person who files a notice of participation pursuant to paragraph (c) of this section shall simultaneously file with the Secretary a list of the witnesses he intends to call at the hearing.

(e) Order of the testimony.

Unless otherwise ordered by the presiding officials, witnesses will give testimony in the order designated by the Secretary to the Commission. Each witness, after being duly sworn, will be permitted to proceed with his or her testimony without interruption except by presiding officials.

(f) Supplementary material.

Up to five double-spaced pages of supplementary material, other than remarks read into the record, will be accepted for the record. Supplementary material exceeding five pages may be accepted upon a showing of such cause as may be deemed sufficient by the presiding officials. As used herein, the term supplementary material refers to (1) additional graphic material such as charts and diagrams used to illuminate an argument or clarify a position and (2) information not available to a party at the time its prehearing brief was filed.

(g) Questioning of witnesses.

After completing testimony, a witness may be questioned by any member of the Commission or by its staff. Any participant may, with the permission of the presiding officials, direct questions to the witness, but only for the purpose of assisting the Commission in obtaining relevant and material facts with respect to the subject matter of the investigation.

(h) Oral argument.

When, in the opinion of the presiding officials, time permits and the nature of the proceedings and the complexity or importance of the questions of fact or law involved warrant, the presiding officials may allow oral argument after conclusion of the testimony in a hearing. The presiding officials will determine in each instance the time to be allowed for argument and the allocation thereof.

(i) Briefs.

(1) Parties. Briefs of the information produced at the hearing and arguments thereon may be presented to the Commission by parties to the investigation. Unless otherwise ordered, fourteen (14) clear copies shall be filed with the Secretary to the Commission. Time to be allowed for submission of briefs will be set after conclusion of testimony and oral argument, if any.

(2) Nonparties. Any person who is not a party to an investigation may submit a short statement for the record regarding the subject matter of an investigation.

(j) Verification of testimony.

Oral or written information submitted at hearings will, upon order of the Commission, be subject to verification from books, papers, and records of the persons submitting the information and from any other available sources.

(k) Hearing transcripts.

A verbatim transcript of all hearings will be taken. The Commission does not distribute transcripts of the records of such hearings. Any person may inspect the transcript of a hearing at the Commission's office in Washington, DC, or purchase it from the official reporter.

(l) To facilitate the conduct of hearings, parties intending to use easels, audio visual, and similar equipment in the course of hearing presentations should advise the Secretary of their intent to use such equipment at least three (3) working days before the hearing.

(m) Closed sessions.

(1) Upon a request filed by a party to the investigation no later than seven (7) days prior to the date of the hearing (or three (3) days prior to the date of a conference conducted under Sec. 207.15 of this chapter) that

(i) Identifies the subjects to be discussed;

(ii) Specifies the amount of time requested; and

(iii) Justifies the need for a closed session with respect to each subject to be discussed, the Commission (or the Director, as defined in Sec. 207.2(c) of this chapter, for a conference under Sec. 207.15 of this chapter) may close a portion of a hearing (or conference under Sec. 207.15 of this chapter) held in any investigation in order to allow such party to address confidential business information, as defined in Sec. 201.6, during the course of its presentation.

(2) In addition, during each hearing held in an investigation conducted under section 202 of the Trade Act, as amended, or in an investigation under title VII of the Tariff Act as provided in Sec. 207.24 of this chapter, following the public presentation of the petitioner(s) and that of each panel of respondents, the Commission will, if it deems it appropriate, close the hearing in order to allow Commissioners to question parties and/or their representatives concerning matters involving confidential business information.

Sec. 201.14 Computation of time, additional hearings, postponements, continuances, and extensions of time

(a) Computation of time.

Computation of any period of time prescribed or allowed by the rules in this chapter, by order of the Commission, or by order of the presiding officer under part 210 of this chapter shall begin with the first business day following the day on which the act or event initiating such period of time shall have occurred. The last day of the period so computed is to be included, unless it is a Saturday, Sunday, or Federal legal holiday, in which event the period runs until the end of the next business day. When the period of time prescribed or allowed is less than 7 days, intermediate Saturdays, Sundays, and Federal legal holidays shall be excluded from the computation. As used in this rule, a Federal legal holiday refers to any full calendar day designated as a legal holiday by the President or the Congress of the United States.

(b) Additional hearings, postponements, continuances, and extensions of time.

(1) Prior to its final determination in any investigation, the Commission may in its discretion for good cause shown grant additional hearings, postponements, or continuances of hearings.

(2) The Chairman of the Commission or such other person as is designated to conduct the investigation shall determine whether to grant for good cause shown extensions of time for performing any act required by or pursuant to the rules contained in this chapter.

(3) A request that the Commission take any of the actions described in this section shall be filed with the Secretary and served on all parties to the investigation.

Sec. 201.15 Attorneys or agents

(a) In general.

No register of attorneys or agents who may practice before the Commission is maintained. No application for admission to practice is required. Any person desiring to appear as attorney or agent before the Commission may be required to show to the satisfaction of the Commission his acceptability in that capacity. Any attorney or agent practicing before the Commission, or desiring so to practice, may for good cause shown be suspended or barred from practicing before the Commission, or have imposed on him such lesser sanctions as the Commission deems appropriate, but only after he has been accorded an opportunity to present his views in the matter.

(b) Former officers or employees.

No former officer or employee of the Commission who personally and substantially participated in a matter which was pending in any manner or form in the Commission during his employment shall be eligible to appear before the Commission as attorney or agent in connection with such matter. No former officer or employee of the Commission shall be eligible to appear as attorney or agent before the Commission in connection with any matter which was pending in any manner or form in the Commission during his employment, unless he first obtains written consent from the Commission.

Sec. 201.16 Service of process and other documents

(a) By the Commission.

Except when service by another method shall be specifically ordered by the Commission, the service of a process or other document of the Commission shall be served by anyone duly authorized by the Commission and be effected—

(1) By mailing or delivering a copy of the document to the person to be served, to a member of the partnership to be served, to the president, secretary, other executive officer, or member of the board of directors of the corporation, association, or other organization to be served, or, if an attorney represents any of the above before the Commission, by mailing or delivering a copy to such attorney; or

(2) By leaving a copy thereof at the principal office of such person, partnership, corporation, association, or other organization, or, if an attorney represents any of the above before the Commission, by leaving a copy at the office of such attorney.

(b) By a party other than the Commission.

Except when service by another method shall be specifically ordered by the Commission, the service of a document of a party shall be effected:

(1) By mailing or delivering copies of the document to the Secretary to the Commission (the number of copies being as provided for in Sec. 201.8(d) of this part) and a nonconfidential version thereof to each other party, or, if the party is represented by

an attorney before the Commission, by mailing or delivering a nonconfidential version thereof to such attorney; or

(2) By leaving copies thereof at the office of the Secretary of the Commission (the number of copies being as provided for in Sec. 201.8(d) of this part) and at the principal office of each other party, or, if a party is represented by an attorney before the Commission, by leaving copies at the office of such attorney.

(3) When service is by mail, it is complete upon mailing of the document.

(4) When service is by mail, it shall be by first class mail, postage prepaid. In the event the addressee is outside the United States, service shall be by first class airmail, postage prepaid.

(c) Proof of service; certificate.

(1) Each document filed with the Secretary to the Commission by a party in the course of an investigation (as provided in Sec. 201.8 of this part) shall be served on each other party to the investigation.

(2) Each document served by a party shall include a certificate of service, setting forth the manner and date of such service. The certificate of service shall be deemed proof of service of the document. In the event a document is not accompanied by a certificate of service, the Secretary shall not accept such document for filing and shall promptly notify the submitter.

(d) Additional time after service by mail.

Whenever a party or Federal agency or department has the right or is required to perform some act or take some action within a prescribed period after the service of a document upon it and the document is served upon it by mail, three (3) calendar days shall be added to the prescribed period, except that when mailing is to a person located in a foreign country, ten (10) calendar days shall be added to the prescribed period.(19 U.S.C. 1335 and the Administrative Procedure Act, 5 U.S.C. 551, et seq.)

Subpart C—Availability of Information to the Public Pursuant to 5 U.S.C. 552

Sec. 201.17 Procedures for requesting access to records

(a) Requests for records.

(1) A request for any information or record shall be addressed to the Secretary, United States International Trade Commission, 500 E Street SW., Washington, DC 20436 and shall indicate clearly both on the envelope and in the letter that it is a "Freedom of Information Act Request."

(2) Any request shall reasonably describe the requested record to facilitate location of the record. If the request pertains to a record that is part of the Commission's file in an investigation, the request should identify the investigation by number and name. A clear description of the requested record(s) should reduce the time required by the Commission to locate and disclose releasable responsive record(s) and minimize any applicable search and copying charges.

(3) Except as provided in paragraph (b) of this section, requests will be processed in the order in which they are filed.

(4) Requests for transcripts of hearings should be addressed to the official hearing reporter, the name and address of which can be obtained from the Secretary. A copy of such request shall at the same time be forwarded to the Secretary.

(5) Copies of public Commission reports and other publications can be requested by calling or writing the Publications Office in the Office of the Secretary. Generally, such publications can be obtained more quickly from this office. Certain Commission publications are sold by the Superintendent of Documents, U.S. Government Printing Office, and are available from that agency at the price set by that agency.

(6) A day-to-day, composite record will be kept by the Secretary of each request with the disposition thereof.

(b) Expedited processing.

(1) Requests for records under paragraph (a)(1) of this section will be taken out of order and given expedited treatment whenever it is determined that they involve:

(i) Circumstances in which the lack of expedited treatment could reasonably be expected to pose an imminent threat to the life or physical safety of an individual;

(ii) An urgency to inform the public about an actual or alleged federal government activity, if made by a person primarily engaged in disseminating information;

(iii) The loss of substantial due process rights; or

(iv) A matter of widespread and exceptional media interest in which there exist possible questions about the government's integrity which affect public confidence.

(2) A request for expedited processing may be made at the time of the initial request for records or at any later time.

(3) A requester who seeks expedited processing must submit a statement, certified to be true and correct to the best of that person's knowledge and belief, explaining in detail the basis for requesting expedited processing. For example, a requester within paragraph (b)(1)(ii) of this section, if not a full-time member of the news media, must establish that he or she is a person whose main professional activity or occupation is information dissemination, though it need not be his or her sole occupation. A requester within paragraph (b)(1)(ii) of this section also must establish a particular urgency to inform the public about the government activity involved in the request, beyond the public's right to know about government activity generally. The formality of certification may be waived as a matter of administrative discretion.

(4) Within ten calendar days of receipt of a request for expedited processing, the Secretary will decide whether to grant it and will notify the requester of the decision. If a request for expedited treatment is granted, the request will be given priority and will be processed as soon as practicable. If a request for expedited processing is denied, any appeal of that decision will be acted on expeditiously.

(c) Public reading room.

The Commission maintains a public reading room in the Office of the Secretary for access to the records that the FOIA requires to be made regularly available for public inspection and copying. Reading room records created by the Commission on or after November 1, 1996, are available electronically. This includes a current subject-matter index of reading room records, which will indicate which records are available electronically.

Sec. 201.18 Denial of requests, appeals from denial

(a) Written requests for inspection or copying of records shall be denied only by the Secretary or Acting Secretary, or, for records maintained by the Office of Inspector General, the Inspector General. Denials of written requests shall be in writing, shall specify the reason therefor, and shall advise the person requesting of the right to appeal to the Commission. Oral requests may be dealt with orally, but if the requester is dissatisfied he shall be asked to put the request in writing.

(b) An appeal from a denial of a request must be received within sixty days of the date of the letter of denial and shall be made to the Commission and addressed to the Chairman, United States International Trade Commission, 500 E Street SW., Washington, DC 20436. Any such appeal shall be in writing, and shall clearly indicate both on the envelope and in the letter that it is a "Freedom of Information Act Appeal."

(c) Except when expedited treatment is requested and granted, appeals will be decided in the order in which they are filed, but in any case within twenty days (excepting Saturdays, Sundays, and legal holidays) unless an extension, noticed in writing with the reasons therefor, has been provided to the person making the request. Notice of the decision on appeal and the reasons therefor will be made promptly after a decision. Requests for expedited treatment should conform with the requirements in Sec. 201.17(c) of this part.

(d) The extensions of time mentioned in paragraphs (a) and (b) of this section shall be made only for one or more of the following reasons:

(1) The need to search for and collect the requested records from field facilities or other establishments that are separate from the office processing the request;

(2) The need to search for, collect, and appropriately examine a voluminous amount of separate and distinct records which are requested in a single communication; or

(3) The need for consultation, which shall be conducted with all practicable speed, with another agency having a substantial interest in the determination of the request or among two or more components of the agency having a substantial subject-matter interest therein.

(e) The extensions of time mentioned in paragraphs (a) and (b) of this section shall not exceed ten working days in the aggregate.

Sec. 201.19 Notification regarding requests for confidential business information

(a) In general.

Business information provided to the Commission by a business submitter which the Commission has designated as "confidential business information" will not be disclosed pursuant to a Freedom of Information Act (FOIA) request except in accordance with this section.

(b) Definitions.

The following definitions are to be used in reference to this section:

Confidential business information means commercial or financial information that has been designated as confidential business information by the Commission under Sec. 201.6 of this part.

Submitter means any person or entity who provides confidential business information, directly or indirectly, to the Commission. The term includes, but is not limited to, corporations, producers, importers, and state and foreign governments.

(c) Notice to submitters.

Except as provided for in paragraph (e) of this section, the Commission will, to the extent permitted by law, provide a submitter with prompt written notice of a FOIA request or administrative appeal encompassing its confidential business information whenever required under paragraph (d) of this section, in order to afford the submitter an opportunity to object to disclosure pursuant to paragraph (f) of this section. Such written notice will describe the nature of the confidential business information requested. The requester will also be notified that notice and opportunity to object to are being provided to a submitter.

(d) When notice is required.

Notice will be given to a submitter in writing at submitter's last known address whenever:

(1) The information the subject of the FOIA request or appeal has been designated by the Commission as confidential business information; and

(2) The Commission has reason to believe that the information may not be protected from disclosure under FOIA Exemptions 3 or 4.

(e) Exceptions to notice requirement.

The notice requirements of paragraph (c) of this section will not apply if:

(1) The Commission determines that the information should not be disclosed;

(2) The information lawfully has been published or has been officially made available to the public; or

(3) Disclosure of the information is required by law (other than 5 U.S.C. 552).

(f) Opportunity to object to disclosure.

In general, the Commission has 10 working days in which to respond to a FOIA request. Through the notice described in paragraph (c) of this section, the Commission will afford a submitter an opportunity, within the period afforded to the Commission to make its decision in response to the FOIA request, to provide the Commission with a detailed written statement of any objection to disclosure. Such statement shall be filed at least one working day before the Commission is required to respond to the FOIA request, and it shall specify all grounds for withholding any of the information under any exemption of FOIA. In the case of FOIA Exemptions 3 or 4, it shall demonstrate why the information should continue to be considered confidential business information within the meaning of Sec. 201.6 of this part and should not be disclosed. The submitter's claim of continued confidentiality should be supported by a certification by an officer or authorized representative of the submitter. Information provided by a submitter pursuant to this paragraph may itself be subject to disclosure under FOIA.

(g) Notice of intent to disclose.

The Commission will consider carefully a submitter's objections and specific grounds for nondisclosure prior to determining whether to disclose the information. Whenever the Commission decides to disclose such information over the objection of a submitter, the Commission will forward to the submitter a written notice which will include:

(1) A statement of the reasons for which the submitter's disclosure objections were not sustained;

(2) A description of the information to be disclosed; and

(3) A specified disclosure date. Such notice of intent to disclose will be forwarded to the submitter a reasonable number of days prior to the specified disclosure date and the requester will be notified likewise.

(h) Notice of FOIA lawsuit.

Whenever a requester brings suit seeking to compel disclosure of information that the Commission has designated as confidential business information, the Commission will promptly notify the submitter at its last known address. For the purpose of this paragraph, the Secretary may assume such address to be that given on the submission.

Sec. 201.20 Fees

(a) In general.

Fees pursuant to 5 U.S.C. 552 shall be assessed according to the schedule contained in paragraph (b) of this section for services rendered by agency personnel in responding to and processing requests for records under this subpart. All fees so assessed shall be charged to the requester, except where the charging of fees is limited under paragraph (c) of this section or where a waiver or reduction of fees is granted under paragraph (d) of this section. The Secretary will collect all applicable fees. Requesters shall pay fees by check or money order made payable to the Treasury of the United States.

(b) Charges.

In responding to requests under this subpart, the following fees shall be assessed, unless a waiver or reduction of fees has been granted pursuant to paragraph (d) of this section:

(1) Search.

(i) No search fee shall be assessed with respect to requests by educational institutions, noncommercial scientific institutions, and representatives of the news media as defined in paragraphs (j) (6), (7), and (8) of this section, respectively. Search fees shall be assessed with respect to all other requests, subject to the limitations of paragraph (c) of this section. The secretary may assess fees for time spent searching even if agency personnel fail to locate any respective record or where records located are subsequently determined to be entirely exempt from disclosure.

(ii) For each quarter hour spent by agency personnel in salary grades GS-2 through GS-10 in searching for and retrieving a requested record, the fee shall be $4.00. When the time of agency personnel in salary grades GS-11 and above is required, the fee shall be $6.50 for each quarter hour of search and retrieval time spent by such personnel.

(iii) For computer searches of records, which may be undertaken through the use of existing programming, requester shall be charged the actual direct costs of conducting the search, although certain requesters (as defined in paragraph (c)(2) of this section) shall be entitled to the cost equivalent of two hours of manual search time without charge. These direct costs shall include the cost of operating a central processing unit for that portion of operating time that is directly attributable to searching for records responsive to a request, as well as the costs of operator/programmer salary apportionable to the search (at no more than $6.50 per quarter hour of time so spent).

(2) Duplication. Duplication fees shall be assessed with respect to all requesters, subject to the limitations of paragraph (c) of this section. For a paper photocopy of a record (no more than one copy of which need be supplied), the fee shall be $0.10 per page. For copies produced by computer, such as tapes or printouts, the Secretary shall charge the actual direct costs, including operator time, of producing the copy. For other methods of duplication, the Secretary shall charge the actual direct costs of duplicating a record.

(3) Review.

(i) Review fees shall be assessed with respect to only those requesters who seek records for a commercial use, as defined in paragraph (j)(5) of this section. For each quarter hour spent by agency personnel in reviewing a requested record for possible disclosure, the fee shall be $6.50.

(ii) Review fees shall be assessed only for the initial record review, *i.e.*, all of the review undertaken when a component analyzes the applicability of a particular exemption to a particular record or record portion at the initial request level. No charge shall be assessed for review at the administrative appeal level of an exemption already applied. However, records or record portions withheld pursuant to an exemption that is subsequently determined not to apply may be reviewed again to determine the applicability of other exemptions not previously considered. The costs of such a subsequent review are properly assessable, particularly where that review is made necessary by a change of circumstances.

(c) Limitations on charging fees.

(1) No search or review fee shall be charged for a quarter-hour period unless more than half of that period is required for search or review.

(2) Except for requesters seeking records for a commercial use (as defined in paragraph (j)(5) of this section), the Secretary shall provide without charge—

(i) The first 100 pages of duplication (or its cost equivalent), and

(ii) The first two hours of search (or its cost equivalent).

(3) Whenever a total fee calculated under paragraph (b) of this section is $25.00 or less, no fee shall be charged.

(4) The provisions of paragraphs (c)(2) and (3) of this section work together. For requesters other than those seeking records for a commercial use, no fee shall be charged unless the cost of search is in excess of two hours plus the cost of duplication in excess of 100 pages exceeds $25.00.

(d) Waiver or reduction of fees.

(1) Records responsive to a request under 5 U.S.C. 552 shall be furnished without charge or at a charge reduced below that established under paragraph (b) of this section where the Secretary determines, based upon information provided by a requester in support of a fee waiver request or otherwise made known to the Secretary that disclosure of the

requested information is in the public interest, because it is likely to contribute significantly to public understanding of the operations or activities of the Government and is not primarily in the commercial interest of the requester. Requests for a waiver or reduction of fees shall be considered on a case-by-case basis.

(2) In order to determine whether the first fee waiver requirement is met—*i.e.*, that disclosure of the requested information is in the public interest because it is likely to contribute significantly to public understanding of the operations or activities of the government—the Secretary shall consider the following four factors in sequence:

(i) The subject of the request: Whether the subject of the requested records concerns "the operations or activities of the government." The subject matter of the requested records, in the context of the request, must specifically concern identifiable operations or activities of the federal government—with a connection that is direct and clear, not remote or attenuated. Furthermore, the records must be sought for their informative value with respect to those government operations or activities; a request for access to records for their intrinsic informational content alone will not satisfy this threshold consideration.

(ii) The informative value of the information to be disclosed: Whether the disclosure is "likely to contribute" to an understanding of government operations or activities. The disclosable portions of the requested records must be meaningfully informative on specific government operations or activities in order to hold potential for contributing to increased public understanding of those operations and activities. The disclosure of information that already is in the public domain, in either a duplicative or a substantially identical form, would not be likely to contribute to such understanding, as nothing new would be added to the public record.

(iii) The contribution of an understanding of the subject by the public likely to result from disclosure: Whether disclosure of the requested information will contribute to "public understanding." The disclosure must contribute to the understanding of the public at large, as opposed to the individual understanding of the requester or a narrow segment of interested persons. A requester's identity and qualifications—e.g., expertise in the subject area and ability and intention to effectively convey information to the general public—shall be considered. It will be presumed that a representative of the news media (as defined in paragraph (j)(8) of this section) who has access to the means of public dissemination readily will be able to satisfy this consideration. Requests from libraries or other record repositories (or requesters who intend merely to disseminate information to such institutions) shall be analyzed, like those of other requesters, to identify a particular person who represents that he actually will use the requested information in scholarly or other analytic work and then disseminate it to the general public.

(iv) The significance of the contribution to public understanding: Whether the disclosure is likely to contribute "significantly" to public understanding of government operations or activities. The public's understanding of the subject matter in question, as compared to the level of public understanding existing prior to the disclosure, must be likely to be enhanced by the disclosure to a significant extent. The Secretary shall not make separate judgments as to whether information, even though it in fact would contribute significantly to public understanding of the operations or activities of the government, is "important" enough to be made public.

(3) In order to determine whether the second fee waiver requirement is met—*i.e.*, that disclosure of the requested information is not primarily in the commercial interest of the requester—the Secretary shall consider the following two factors in sequence:

(i) The existence and magnitude of a commercial interest: Whether the requester has a commercial interest that would be furthered by the requested disclosure. The Secretary shall consider all commercial interests of the requester (with reference to the definition of commercial use in paragraph (j)(5) of this section), or any person on whose behalf the requester may be acting, but shall consider only those interests which would be furthered by the requested disclosure. In assessing the magnitude of identified commercial interests, consideration shall be given to the role that such FOIA-disclosed information plays with respect to those commercial interests, as well as to the extent to which FOIA disclosures serve those interests overall. Requesters shall be given a reasonable opportunity in the administrative process to provide information bearing upon this consideration.

(ii) The primary interest in disclosure: Whether the magnitude of the identified commercial interest of the requester is sufficiently large, in comparison with the public interest in disclosure, that disclosure is "primarily in the commercial interest of the requester." A fee waiver or reduction is warranted only where, once the "public interest" standard set out in paragraph (d)(2) of this section is satisfied, that public interest can fairly be regarded as greater in magnitude than that of the requester's commercial interest in disclosure. The Secretary shall ordinarily presume that, where a news media requester has satisfied the "public interest" standard, that will be the interest primarily served by disclosure to that requester. Disclosure to data brokers or others who compile and market government information for direct economic return shall not be presumed to primarily serve the "public interest."

(4) Where only a portion of the requested records satisfies both of the requirements for a waiver or reduction of fees under this paragraph, a waiver or reduction shall be granted only as to that portion.

(5) Requests for the waiver or reduction of fees shall address each of the factors listed in paragraphs (d) (2) and (3) of this section, as they apply to each record request.

(e) Notice of anticipated fees in excess of $25.00.

Where the Secretary determines or estimates that the fees to be assessed under this section may amount to more than $25.00, he shall notify the requester as soon as practicable of the actual or estimated amount of the fees, unless the requester has indicated in advance his willingness to pay fees as high as those anticipated. (If only a portion of the fee can be estimated readily, the Secretary shall advise the requester that the estimated fee may be only a portion of the total fee.) In cases where a requester has been notified that actual or estimated fees may amount to more than $25.00, the request will be deemed not to have been received until the requester has agreed to pay the anticipated total fee. A notice of the requester pursuant to this paragraph shall offer him the opportunity to confer with agency personnel in order to reformulate his request to meet his needs at a lower cost.

(f) Aggregating requests.

Where the Secretary reasonably believes that a requester or a group of requesters acting in concert is attempting to divide a request into a series of requests for the purpose of evading the assessment of fees, the Secretary may aggregate any such requests and charge accordingly. The Secretary may presume that multiple requests of such type made within a 30-day period have been made in order to evade fees. Where requests are separated by a longer period, the Secretary shall aggregate them only where there exists a reasonable basis for determining that said aggregation is warranted, e.g., where the requests involve clearly related matters. Multiple requests involving unrelated matters shall not be aggregated.

(g) Advance payments.

(1) Where the Secretary estimates that a total fee to be assessed under this section is likely to exceed $250.00, the Secretary may require the requester to make an advance payment of an amount up to the entire estimated fee before beginning to process the request, except where the Secretary receives a satisfactory assurance of full payment from a requester with a history of prompt payment.

(2) Where a requester has previously failed to pay a records access fee within 30 days of the date of billing, the Secretary may require the requester to pay the full amount owed, plus any applicable interest (as provided for in paragraph (h) of this section), and to make an advance payment of the full amount of any estimated fee before he begins to process a new request or continues to process a pending request from that requester.

(3) For requests other than those described in paragraphs (g) (1) and (2) of this section, the Secretary shall not require the requester to make an advance payment, *i.e.*, a payment made before work is commenced or continued on a request. Payment owed on work already completed is not an advance payment.

(4) Where the Secretary acts under paragraph (g) (1) or (2) of this section, the administrative time limits described in subsection (a)(6) of the FOIA for the processing of an initial request or an appeal, plus permissible extensions of these time limits, shall be deemed not to begin to run until the Secretary has received payment of the assessed fee.

(h) Charging interest.

The Secretary may assess interest charges on an unpaid bill starting on the 31st day following the day on which the bill was sent to the requester. Once a fee payment has been received by the Secretary, even if not processed, the accrual of interest shall be stayed. Interest charges shall be assessed at the rate prescribed in section 3717 of title 31 U.S.C. and shall accrue from the date of the billing. The Secretary shall follow the provisions of the Debt Collection Act of 1982, Pub. L. 97-265 (Oct. 25, 1982), and its implementing procedures, including the use of consumer reporting agencies, collection agencies, and offset.

(i) Other statutes specifically providing for fees.

(1) The fee schedule of this section does not apply with respect to the charging of fees under a statute specifically providing for setting the level of fees for particular types of records-- *i.e.*, any statute that specifically requires a government entity such as the Government Printing Office or the National Technical Information Service, to set and collect fees for particular types of records—in order to:

(i) Serve both the general public and private sector organizations by conveniently making available government information;

(ii) Ensure that groups and individuals pay the cost of publications and other services that are for their special use so that these costs are not borne by the general taxpaying public;

(iii) Operate an information-dissemination activity on a self-sustaining basis to the maximum extent possible; or

(iv) Return revenue to the Treasury for defraying, wholly or in part, appropriate funds used to pay the costs of disseminating government information.

(2) Where records responsive to requests are maintained for distribution by agencies operating statutorily based fee schedule programs, the Secretary shall inform requesters of the steps necessary to obtain records from those sources.

(j) Definitions.

For the purpose of this section:

(1) The term direct costs means those expenditures which the agency actually incurs in searching for and duplicating (and, in the case of commercial use requesters, reviewing) records to respond to a FOIA request. Direct costs include, for example the salary of the employee performing the work (the basic rate of pay for the employee plus 16 percent of that rate to cover benefits) and the cost of operating duplicating machinery. Not included in direct costs are overhead expenses such as costs of space and heating or lighting of the facility in which the records are stored.

(2) The term search includes all time spent looking for material that is responsive to a request, including page-by-page or line-by-line identification of material within documents. The Secretary shall ensure, however, that searches are undertaken in the most efficient and least expensive manner reasonably possible; thus, for example, the Secretary shall not engage in line-by-line search where merely duplicating an entire document would be quicker and less expensive.

(3) The term duplication refers to the process of making a copy of a record necessary to respond to a FOIA request. Such copies can take the form of paper copy, microform, audio-visual materials, or machine-readable documentation (e.g., magnetic tape or disk), among others. The copy provided shall be in a form that is reasonably usable by requesters.

(4) The term review refers to the process of examining a record located in response to a request in order to determine whether any portion of it is permitted to be withheld. It also includes processing any record for disclosure, e.g., doing all that is necessary to excise it and otherwise prepare it for release, although review costs shall be recoverable even where there ultimately is no disclosure of a record. Review time does not include time spent resolving general legal or policy issues regarding the application of exemptions.

(5) The term commercial use in the context of a request refers to a request from or on behalf of one who seeks information for a use or purpose that furthers the commercial, trade, or profit interests of the requester or the person on whose behalf the request is made, which can include furthering those interests through litigation. The Secretary shall determine, as well as reasonably possible, the use to which a requester will put the records requested. Where the circumstances of a request suggest that the requester will put the records sought to a commercial use, either because of the nature of the request itself or because the Secretary otherwise has reasonable

cause to doubt a requester's stated use, the Secretary shall provide the requester a reasonable opportunity to submit further clarification.

(6) The term educational institution refers to a preschool, a public or private elementary or secondary school, an institution of undergraduate higher education, an institution of graduate higher education, an institution of professional education, and an institution of vocational education, which operates a program or programs of scholarly research. To be eligible for inclusion in this category, a requester must show that the request is being made as authorized by and under the auspices of a qualifying institution and that the records are not sought for a commercial use but are sought in furtherance of scholarly research.

(7) The term noncommercial scientific institution refers to an institution that is not operated on a "commercial" basis as that term is referenced in paragraph (j)(5) of this section, and which is operated solely for the purpose of conducting scientific research the results of which are not intended to promote any particular product or industry. To be eligible for inclusion in this category, a requester must show that the request is being made as authorized by and under the auspices of a qualifying institution and that the records are not sought for a commercial use but are sought in furtherance of scientific research.

(8) The term representative of the news media refers to any person actively gathering news for an entity that is organized and operated to publish or broadcast news to the public. The term news means information that is about current events or that would be of current interest to the public. Examples of news media entities include television or radio stations broadcasting to the public at large and publishers of periodicals (but only in those instances where they can qualify as disseminators of "news") who make their products available for purchase or subscription by the general public. For "freelance" journalists to be regarded as working for a news organization, they must demonstrate a clear basis for expecting publication through that organization; a publication contract would be the clearest proof, but the Secretary shall also look to the past publication record of a requester in making this determination. To be eligible for inclusion in this category, a requester also must not be seeking the requested records for a commercial use. In this regard, a request for records supporting the news dissemination function of the requester shall not be considered to be for a commercial use.

(k) Charges for other services and materials.

Apart from the other provisions of this section, where the Secretary elects, as a matter of administrative discretion, to comply with a request for a special service or materials, such as certifying that records are true copies or sending them other than by ordinary mail, the actual direct costs of providing the service or materials shall be charged.

Sec. 201.21 Availability of specific records

(a) Records available.

The following information, on request to the Secretary of the Commission, is available for public inspection and copying: (1) final opinions, including concurring and dissenting opinions, as well as orders, made in the adjudication of cases; (2) those statements of policy and interpretations which have been adopted by the agency; and (3) administrative staff manuals and instructions to staff that affect a member of the public.

Available information includes, but is not limited to: (i) Applications, petitions, and other formal documents filed with the Commission, (ii) notices to the public concerning Commission matters, (iii) transcripts of testimony taken and exhibits submitted at hearings, (iv) reports to the President, to either or both Houses of Congress, or to Committees of Congress, release of which has been authorized by the President or the legislative body concerned, (v) reports and other documents issued for general distribution.

(b) Records not available.

Information specifically exempted from disclosure by 5 U.S.C. 552(b), including reports to the President, to either or both Houses of Congress, or to Committees of Congress, the release of which has not been authorized by the President or the legislative body concerned, and confidential business data as defined in 18 U.S.C. 1905 and 19 CFR 201.06 are not available to the public.

(c) Information requested in cases or matters to which the Commission is not a party.

(1) The procedure specified in this section will apply to all demands directed to Commission employees for the production of documents or for testimony that relates in any way to the employees' official duties. These procedures will also apply to demands directed to former employees if the demands seek nonpublic materials or information acquired during Commission employment. The provisions of paragraph (c)(2) of this section will also apply to demands directed to the agency. For purposes of this section, the term demand means any request, order or subpoena for testimony or production of documents; the term subpoena means any compulsory process in a case or matter to which the Commission is not a party; the term nonpublic includes any material or information which, under Sec. 201.21(b), is exempt from availability for public inspection and copying; the term employee means any current or former officer or employee of the Commission; the term documents means all records, papers or official files, including without limitation, official letters, telegrams, memoranda, reports, studies, calendar and diary entries, graphs, notes, charts, tabulations, data analysis, statistical or information accumulations, records of meetings and conversations, film impressions, magnetic tapes, and sound or mechanical reproductions; the term case or matter means any civil proceeding before a court of law, administrative board, hearing officer, or other body conducting a legal or administrative proceeding in which the Commission is not a named party.

(2) Prior to or simultaneously with a demand to a Commission employee for the production of documents or for testimony concerning matters relating to official duties, the party seeking such production or testimony must serve upon the General Counsel of the Commission an affidavit, or if that is not feasible, then a statement which sets forth the title of the case, the forum, the party's interest in the case, the reasons for the request, and a showing that the desired testimony or documents are not reasonably available from any other source. Where testimony is sought, the party must also provide a summary of the testimony desired, the intended use of the testimony, and show that Commission records could not be provided and used instead of the requested testimony. A subpoena for testimony from a Commission employee concerning official matters or for the production of documents shall be served in accordance with Rule 45 of the Federal Rules of Civil Procedure and a copy of the subpoena shall be sent to the General Counsel.

(3) Any employee or former employee who is served with a subpoena or other demand shall promptly advise the General Counsel of the service of the subpoena or other

demand, the nature of the documents or information sought, and all relevant facts and circumstances.

(4) Absent written authorization from the Chairman of the Commission ("Chairman"), the employee shall respectfully decline to produce the requested documents, to testify, or to otherwise disclose requested information. If a court rules that the demand must be complied with despite the absence of such written authorization, the employee upon whom the demand is made shall respectfully refuse to comply based upon these regulations and *Touhy v. Ragan*, 340 U.S. 462 (1951).

(5) The Chairman will consider and act upon subpoenas under this section with due regard for statutory restrictions, the Commission's rules and the public interest, taking into account such factors as the need to conserve employees' time for conducting official business, the need to prevent the expenditure of the United States government's time and money for private purposes, the need to maintain impartiality between private litigants in cases where no substantial governmental interest is involved, and the relevant legal standards for determining whether justification exists for the disclosure of nonpublic information and documents. If the Chairman determines that the subpoenaed documents or information are protected by a privilege or that the Commission has a duty in law or equity to protect such documents or information from disclosure, the General Counsel shall move the court to quash the subpoena or for other appropriate action.

(6) The General Counsel may consult or negotiate with counsel or the party seeking testimony or documents to refine and limit the demand so that compliance is less burdensome, or obtain information necessary to make the determination described in paragraph (c)(5) of this section. Failure of the counsel or party seeking the testimony or documents to cooperate in good faith to enable the General Counsel to make an informed recommendation to the Chairman under paragraph (c)(5) of this section may serve as the basis for a determination not to comply with the demand.

(7) Permission to testify will, in all cases, be limited to the information set forth in the affidavit as described in paragraph (c)(2) of this section, or to such portions thereof as the Chairman deems proper.

(8) If the Chairman authorizes the testimony of an employee, then the General Counsel shall arrange for the taking of the testimony by methods that are least disruptive of the official duties of the employee. Testimony may, for example, be provided by affidavits, answers to interrogatories, written depositions, or depositions transcribed, recorded, or preserved by any other means allowable by law. Costs of providing testimony, including transcripts, will be borne by the party requesting the testimony. Such costs shall also include reimbursing the Commission for the usual and ordinary expenses attendant upon the employee's absence from his or her official duties in connection with the case or matter, including the employee's salary and applicable overhead charges and any necessary travel expenses.

(9) The Secretary in consultation with the General Counsel is further authorized to charge reasonable fees to parties demanding documents or information. Such fees, calculated to reimburse the government for the expense of responding to such demand, may include the costs of time expended by Commission employees to process and respond to the demand, attorney time for reviewing the demand and for related legal work in connection with the demand, and expenses generated by equipment used to search for, produce and copy the responsive information. In general, such fees will be assessed at the rates and in the manner specified in Sec. 201.20 of this part.

(10) This section does not affect the rights and procedures governing the public access to official documents pursuant to the Freedom of Information Act or the Privacy Act.

(11) This section is intended to provide instructions to Commission employees and does not create any right or benefit, substantive or procedural, enforceable by any party against the Commission.

Subpart D—Safeguarding Individual Privacy Pursuant to 5 U.S.C. 552a

Sec. 201.22 Purpose and scope

This subpart contains the rules that the Commission follows under the Privacy Act of 1974, 5 U.S.C. 552a. The rules in this subpart apply to all records in systems of records maintained by the Commission that are retrieved by an individual's name or other personal identifier. They describe the procedures by which individuals may request access to records about themselves, request amendment or correction of those records, and request an accounting of disclosures of those records by the Commission.

Sec. 201.23 Definitions

For the purpose of these regulations:

(a) The term individual means a citizen of the United States or an alien lawfully admitted for permanent residence;

(b) The term maintain includes maintain, collect, use, or disseminate;

(c) The term record means any item, collection, or grouping of information about an individual that is maintained by the Commission, including, but not limited to, his or her education, financial transactions, medical history, and criminal or employment history and that contains his or her name, or the identifying number, symbol, or other identifying particular assigned to the individual;

(d) The term system of records means a group of any records under the control of the Commission from which information is retrieved by the name of the individual or by some identifying particular assigned to the individual;

(e) The term Privacy Act Officer refers to the Director, Office of Administration, United States International Trade Commission, 500 E Street SW., Washington, DC 20436, or his or her designee.

Sec. 201.24 Procedures for requests pertaining to individual records in a records system

(a) A request by an individual to gain access to his or her record(s) or to any information pertaining to him or her which is contained in a system of records maintained by the Commission shall be addressed to the Privacy Act Officer, United States International Trade Commission, 500 E Street SW., Washington, DC 20436, and shall indicate clearly both on the envelope and in the letter that it is a Privacy Act request.

(b) In order to facilitate location of requested records, whenever possible, the request of the individual shall name the system(s) of records maintained by the Commission which he or she believes contain records pertaining to him or her, shall reasonably describe the requested records, and identify the time period in which the records were compiled.

(c) The Privacy Act Officer shall acknowledge receipt of a request within ten days (excluding Saturdays, Sundays, and legal public holidays), and wherever practicable, indicate whether or not access can be granted. If access is not to be granted, the requestor shall be notified of the reason in writing.

(d) The Privacy Act Officer, or, the Inspector General, if such records are maintained by the Inspector General, shall ascertain whether the systems of records maintained by the Commission contain records pertaining to the individual, and whether access will be granted. Thereupon the Privacy Act Officer shall:

(1) Notify the individual whether or not the requested record is contained in any system of records maintained by the Commission; and

(2) Notify the individual of the procedures as prescribed in Secs. 201.25 and 201.26 of this part by which the individual may gain access to those records maintained by the Commission which pertain to him or her. Access to the records will be provided within 30 days (excluding Saturdays, Sundays, and legal public holidays).

Sec. 201.25 Times, places, and requirements for identification of individuals making requests

(a) If an individual wishes to examine his or her records in person, it shall be the responsibility of the individual requester to arrange an appointment with the Privacy Act Officer for the purpose of inspecting individual records. The time of inspection shall be during the regular office hours of the Commission, 8:45 a.m. to 5:15 p.m., Monday through Friday. The time arranged should be mutually convenient to the requester and to the Commission.

(b) The place where an individual may gain access to records maintained by the Commission which pertain to him or her shall be at the United States International Trade Commission Building, 500 E Street SW., Washington, DC 20436. The Privacy Act Officer shall inform the individual requester of the specific room wherein inspection will take place.

(c) An individual may also request the Privacy Act Officer to provide the individual with a copy of his or her records by certified mail.

(d) An individual who requests to gain access to those records maintained by the Commission which pertain to him or her shall not be granted access to those records without first presenting adequate identification to the Privacy Act Officer. Adequate identification may include, but is not limited to, a government identification card, a driver's license, Medicare card, a birth certificate, or a passport. If requesting records by mail, an individual must provide full name, current address, and date and place of birth. The request must be signed and either notarized or submitted under 28 U.S.C. 1746, which permits statements to be made under penalty of perjury as a substitute for notarization. In order to help the identification and location of requested records, a requestor may also, at his or her option, include the individual's social security number.

Sec. 201.26 Disclosure of requested information to individuals

(a) Once the Privacy Act Officer has made a determination to grant a request for access to individual records, in whole or in part, the Privacy Act Officer shall inform the requesting individual in writing and permit the individual to review the pertinent records and to have a copy made of all or any portion of them. Where redactions due to exemptions pursuant to Sec. 201.32 would render such records or portions thereof incomprehensible, the Privacy Act Officer shall furnish an abstract in addition to an actual copy.

(b) An individual has the right to have a person of his or her own choosing accompany him or her to review his or her records. The Privacy Act Officer shall permit a person of the individual requester's choosing to accompany the individual during inspection.

(c) When the individual requests the Privacy Act Officer to permit a person of the individual's choosing to accompany him or her during the inspection of his or her records, the Privacy Act Officer shall require the individual requester to furnish a written statement authorizing discussion of the records in the accompanying person's presence.

(d) The Privacy Act Officer shall take all necessary steps to insure that individual privacy is protected while the individual requester is inspecting his or her records or while those records are being discussed. Only the Privacy Act Officer shall accompany the individual as representative of the Commission during the inspection of the individual's records. The Privacy Act Officer shall be authorized to discuss the pertinent records with the individual.

Sec. 201.27 Special procedures: Medical records

(a) While an individual has an unqualified right of access to the records in systems of records maintained by the Commission which pertain to him or her, medical and psychological records merit special treatment because of the possibility that disclosure will have an adverse physical or psychological effect upon the requesting individual. Accordingly, in those instances where an individual is requesting the medical and/or psychological records which pertain to him or her, he or she shall, in his or her Privacy Act request to the Privacy Act Officer as called for in Sec. 201.24(a) of this part, specify a physician to whom the medical and/or psychological records may be released.

(b) It shall be the responsibility of the individual requesting medical or psychological records to specify a physician to whom the requested records may be released. If an individual refuses to name a physician and insists on inspecting his or her medical or psychological records in the absence of a doctor's discussion and advice, the individual shall so state in his or her Privacy Act request to the Privacy Act Officer as called for in Sec. 201.24(a) of this part and the Privacy Act Officer shall provide access to or transmit such records directly to the individual.

Sec. 201.28 Requests for correction or amendment of records

(a) If, upon viewing his or her records, an individual disagrees with a portion thereof or feels sections thereof to be erroneous, the individual may request amendment[s] of the records pertaining to him or her. The individual should request such an amendment in writing and should identify each particular record in question, the system[s] of records wherein the records are located, specify the amendment requested, and specify the reasons why the records are not correct, relevant timely or complete. The individual may submit any documentation that would be helpful. The request for amendment of records shall be addressed to the Privacy Act Officer, United States International Trade Commission, 500 E Street SW., Washington, DC 20436, and shall clearly indicate both on the envelope and in the letter that it is a Privacy Act request for amendment of records.

(b) Not later than 10 days (excluding Saturdays, Sundays and legal public holidays) after the date of receipt of a Privacy Act request for amendment of records, the Privacy Act Officer shall acknowledge such receipt in writing. Such a request for amendment will be granted or denied by the Privacy Act Officer or, for records maintained by the Inspector General. If the request is granted, the Privacy Act Officer, or the Inspector General for records maintained by the Inspector General, shall promptly make any correction of any portion of the record which the individual believes is not accurate, relevant, timely, or complete. If, however, the request is denied, the Privacy Act Officer shall inform the individual of the refusal to amend the record in accordance with the individual's request and give the reason(s) for the refusal. In cases where the Privacy Act Officer or the Inspector General has refused to amend in accordance with an individual's request, he or she also shall advise the individual of the procedures under Sec. 201.30 of this part for the individual to request a review of that refusal by the full Commission or by an officer designated by the Commission.

Sec. 201.29 Commission disclosure of individual records, accounting of record disclosures, and requests for accounting of record disclosures

(a) It is the policy of the Commission not to disclose, except as permitted under 5 U.S.C. 552a(b), any record which is contained in any system of records maintained by the Commission to any person, or to another agency, except pursuant to a written request by, or with the prior written consent of, the individual to whom the record pertains.

(b) Except for disclosures either to officers and employees of the Commission, or to contractor employees who, in the Inspector General's or the Privacy Act Officer's judgment, as appropriate, are acting as federal employees, who have a need for the record in the performance of their duties, and any disclosure required by 5 U.S.C. 552, the Privacy Act Officer shall keep an accurate accounting of:

(1) The date, nature, and purpose of each disclosure of a record to any person or to another agency under paragraph (a) of this section; and

(2) The name or address of the person or agency to whom the disclosure is made.

(c) The Privacy Act Officer shall retain the accounting required by paragraph (b) of this section for at least five years or the life of the record, whichever is longer, after such disclosure.

(d) Except for disclosures made to other agencies for civil or criminal law enforcement purposes pursuant to 5 U.S.C. 552a(b)(7), the Privacy Act Officer shall make any accounting made under paragraph (b) of this section available to the individual named in the record at the individual's request.

(e) An individual requesting an accounting of disclosure of his or her records should make the request in writing to the Privacy Act Officer, United States International Trade Commission, 500 E Street SW., Washington, DC 20436. The request should identify each particular record in question and, whenever possible, the system[s] of records wherein the requested records are located, and clearly indicate both on the envelope and in the letter that it is a Privacy Act request for an accounting of disclosure of records.

(f) Where the Commission has provided any person or other agency with an individual record and such accounting as required by paragraph (b) of this section has been made, the Privacy Act Officer shall inform all such persons or other agencies of any correction, amendment, or notation of dispute concerning said record.

Sec. 201.30 Commission review of requests for access to records, for correction or amendment to records, and for accounting of record disclosures

(a) The individual who disagrees with the refusal of the Privacy Act Officer or the Inspector General for access to a record, to amend a record, or to obtain an accounting of any record disclosure, may request a review of such refusal by the Commission within 60 days of receipt of the denial of his or her request. A request for review of such a refusal should be addressed to the Chairman, United States International Trade Commission, 500 E Street, SW., Washington, DC 20436, and shall clearly indicate both on the envelope and in the letter that it is a Privacy Act review request.

(b) Not later than 30 days (excluding Saturdays, Sundays, and legal public holidays) from the date on which the Commission receives a request for review of the Privacy Act Officer's or the Inspector General's refusal to grant access to a record, to amend a record, or to provide an accounting of a record disclosure, the Commission shall complete such a review and make a final determination thereof unless, for good cause shown, the Commission extends the 30-day period.

(c) After the individual's request has been reviewed by the Commission, if the Commission agrees with the Privacy Act Officer's or the Inspector General's refusal to grant access to a record, to amend a record, or to provide an accounting of a record disclosure, in accordance with the individual's request, the Commission shall:

(1) Notify the individual in writing of the Commission's decision;

(2) For requests to amend or correct records, advise the individual that he or she has the right to file a concise statement of disagreement with the Commission which sets forth his or her reasons for disagreement with the refusal of the Commission to grant the individual's request; and

(3) Notify the individual of his or her legal right, if any, to judicial review of the Commission's final determination.

(d) In any disclosure, containing information about which the individual has filed a statement of disagreement regarding an amendment of an individual's record, the Privacy Act Officer, or, for records maintained by the Inspector General, the Inspector General, shall clearly note any portion of the record which is disputed and shall provide copies of the statement and, if the Commission deems it appropriate, copies of a concise statement of the reasons of the Commission for not making the amendments requested, to persons or other agencies to whom the disputed record has been disclosed.

Sec. 201.31 Fees

(a) The Commission shall not charge any fee for the cost of searching for and reviewing an individual's records.

(b) Reproduction, duplication or copying of records by the Commission shall be at the rate of $0.10 per page. There shall be no charge, however, when the total amount does not exceed $25.00.

Sec. 201.32 Specific exemptions

(a) Pursuant to 5 U.S.C. 552a(k)(2), and in order to protect the effectiveness of Inspector General investigations by preventing individuals who may be the subject of an investigation from obtaining access to the records and thus obtaining the opportunity to conceal or destroy evidence or to intimidate witnesses, records contained in the system titled Office of Inspector General Investigative Files (General), insofar as they include investigatory material compiled for law enforcement purposes, shall be exempt from this subpart and from subsections (c)(3), (d), (e)(1), (e)(4)(G), (H), and (I) and (f) of the Privacy Act. However, if any individual is denied any right, privilege, or benefit to which he is otherwise entitled to under Federal law due to the maintenance of this material, such material shall be provided to such individual except to the extent that the disclosure of such material would reveal the identity of a source who furnished information to government investigators under an express promise that the identity of the source would be held in confidence.

(b) Pursuant to 5 U.S.C. 552a(j)(2), and in order to protect the confidentiality and integrity of Inspector General investigations by preventing individuals who may be the subject of an investigation from obtaining access to the records and thus obtaining the opportunity to conceal or destroy evidence or to intimidate witnesses, records maintained in the Office of Inspector General Investigative Files (Criminal), insofar as they contain information pertaining to the enforcement of criminal laws, shall be exempt from this subpart and from the Privacy Act, except that subsections (b), (c)(1) and (2), (e)(4)(A) through (F), (e)(6), (7), (9), (10), and (11) and (i) shall still apply to these records.

(c) Pursuant to 5 U.S.C. 552a(k)(1), (5) and (6), records contained in the system entitled "Personnel Security Investigative Files" have been exempted from subsections (c)(3), (d), (e)(1), (e)(1)(G) through (I) and (f) of the Privacy Act. Pursuant to section 552a(k)(1) of the Privacy Act, the Commission exempts records that contain properly classified information that pertains to national defense or foreign policy and is obtained from other systems of records or another Federal agency. Application of exemption (k)(1) may be necessary to preclude the data subject's access to and amendment of such classified information under 5 U.S.C. 552a(d). All information about individuals in these records that meets the criteria stated in 5 U.S.C. 552a(k)(5) is also exempted because this system contains investigatory material compiled solely for determining suitability, eligibility, and qualifications for Federal civilian employment, Federal contracts or access to classified information. To the extent that the disclosure of such material would reveal the identity of a source who furnished information to the Government under an express promise that the identity of the source would be held in confidence, or, prior to September 27, 1975, under an implied promise that the identity of the source would be held in confidence, the application of exemption (k)(5) will be required to honor such a promise should an individual request access to the accounting of disclosure, or access to or amendment of the record, that would reveal the identity of a confidential source. All information in these records that meets the criteria stated in 5 U.S.C. 552a(k)(6) is also exempt because portions of a case file record may relate to testing and examining material used solely to determine individual qualifications for appointment or promotion in the Federal service. Access to or amendment of this information by the data subject would compromise the objectivity and fairness of the testing or examining process.

Sec. 201.33 Employee conduct

The Privacy Act Officer shall establish rules of conduct for persons involved in the design, development, operation, or maintenance of any system of records, or in maintaining any record, and periodically instruct each such person with respect to such rules and the requirements of the Privacy Act including the penalties for noncompliance.

Subpart E—Opening Commission Meetings to Public Observation Pursuant to 5 U.S.C. 552b

Sec. 201.33 Purpose and scope

(a) Consistent with the principle that the public is entitled to the fullest practicable information regarding the decisionmaking processes of the Federal Government, it is the purpose of this subpart to open the meetings of the United States International Trade Commission to public observation while protecting the rights of individuals and the ability of the Commission to carry out its statutory functions and responsibilities. These regulations are promulgated pursuant to the directive of section (g) of the Government in the Sunshine Act (5 U.S.C. 552b(g)), and specifically implement sections (b) through (f) of said act (5 U.S.C. 552(b) through (f)).

(b) Public access to documents being considered at Commission meetings may be obtained by access to the public files of the Commission or, where documents are not in said public files, shall be obtained in the manner set forth in subpart C of this part (Secs. 201.17 through 201.21).

(c) Unless otherwise provided by the public notices as described in Sec. 201.35 of this subpart, public observation of Commission meetings does not encompass public participation in the deliberations at such meetings.

Sec. 201.34 Definitions

For the purpose of this subpart:

(a)(1) Except as hereinafter provided, the term meeting means the deliberations of at least the number of individual Commissioners required to take action on behalf of the Commission where such deliberations determine or result in the joint conduct or disposition of official Commission business.

(2) The consideration by individual Commissioners of business which is circulated sequentially in writing (circulation by "action jacket") is not considered a meeting under paragraph (a)(1) of this section because circulation by action jacket does not determine or result in the joint conduct or disposition of Commission business until ratification thereof by formal vote of the Commissioners in a meeting as defined by paragraph (a)(1) of this section, although action proposed by action jacket may be taken before or after formal ratification thereof by vote at a Commission meeting.

(3) Conference telephone calls among the Commissioners are considered meetings as defined by paragraph (a)(1) of this section if they involve the number of Commissioners requisite for Commission action.

(4) Deliberations of a majority of the entire membership of the Commission with the sole purpose of determining whether or not to call a meeting at a date earlier than the requisite public notice period as specified in Sec. 201.35 of this subpart are not considered to constitute a meeting or portion of a meeting as defined by paragraph (a)(1) of this section.

(5) Deliberations of a majority of the entire membership of the Commission with the sole purpose of determining whether or not to close a portion or portions of a meeting or series of meetings pursuant to Sec. 201.36 of this subpart are not considered to constitute a meeting or portion of a meeting within the meaning of paragraph (a)(1) of this section.

(6) Deliberations of a majority of the entire membership of the Commission with the sole purpose of determining whether or not to change the subject matter of a publicly announced meeting, or to change the determination of the Commission to open or close a meeting, or portion thereof, to the public, following a public notice, as permitted under Sec. 201.37(b) of this subpart, are not considered to constitute a meeting or portion of a meeting under paragraph (a)(1) of this section.

(b) The terms Secretary and General Counsel mean the Secretary and General Counsel of the Commission and their respective designees within their respective offices.

Sec. 201.35 Notices to the public

(a) At least seven (7) days before each Commission meeting the Commission shall issue a public notice which:

(1) States the time and place of the meeting;

(2) Lists the subjects or agenda items to be discussed at the meeting;

(3) States whether the meeting or portion thereof is to be open or closed to public observation; and

(4) Gives the name and business phone number of the Secretary to the Commission.

(b) When the Commission has voted to close any portion of any meeting in accordance with Sec. 201.36 of this subpart, the notice referred to in paragraph (a) of this section shall also include, or be amended to include, if already issued, (1) A list of the persons reasonably expected to be present at such closed portion or portions of the meeting, (2) A corresponding list of the affiliations of those persons reasonably expected to be present, (3) A written copy of the vote of each Commissioner on whether or not the portion or portions of the meeting or series of meetings should be closed to public observation, (4) A full, written explanation of the Commission's action in closing the portion or portions of the meeting or series of meetings, and (5) A copy of the certification of the General Counsel, called for by Sec. 201.39 of this subpart, that such portion or portions of the meeting or series of meetings were properly closed to the public by the Commission. When a vote to close a portion or portions of a meeting in accordance with Sec. 201.36 of this subpart or a vote to change the subject matter of a meeting or to change a determination to open or close a meeting, or portion thereof, to the public in accordance with Sec. 201.37(b) of this subpart fails for lack of a majority of the entire membership of the Commission, the vote shall also be published as part of the notice required by paragraph (a) of this section.

(c)(1) The 7-day period for public notice provided for in paragraph (a) of this section shall not apply when a majority of the entire membership of the Commission determines by recorded vote that Commission business requires that a particular meeting be called with less than 7 days' notice and that no earlier announcement of such meeting was possible.

(2) When the Commission has voted in conformity with paragraph (c)(1) of this section to shorten the 7-day period for public notice provided for by paragraph (a) of this section with respect to a particular meeting, the Commission shall issue the public notice required by paragraph (a) of this section at the earliest practicable time.

(3) When the Commission not only has voted in conformity with paragraph (c)(1) of this section to shorten the 7-day period for public notice provided for in paragraph (a) of this

section with respect to a particular meeting, but also has voted to close a portion or portions of such meeting in accordance with Sec. 201.36 of this subpart, the public notice required by paragraph (c)(2) of this section shall also include, or be amended to include, if already issued, those items specified in paragraph (b) of this section.

(d)(1) When the Commission has changed the time or place of a publicly announced meeting by acting under Sec. 201.37(a) of this subpart, the public notice required by paragraph (a) or (c)(2) of this section shall be amended to reflect such changed time or place.

(2) When the Commission has changed the subject matter of a meeting or its determination to open or close a meeting, or portion thereof, to the public following a public notice by acting under Sec. 201.37(b) of this subpart, the public notice required by paragraph (a) or (c)(2) of this section shall be amended to (i) Include a statement affirming that Commission business required the change in subject matter and that no earlier announcement of such change was possible and (ii) Indicate the change in subject matter and the vote of each Commissioner upon such change.

(e)(1) The Secretary shall issue the public notices required by this section and such amendments thereto as are appropriate to the specific meeting to which they pertain.

(2) The Secretary (i) Shall promptly post the public notices referred to in paragraph (e)(1) of this section on bulletin boards outside the Office of the Secretary to the Commission, (ii) Shall make copies thereof available to interested members of the public, including mailing copies thereof through a mailing list of those persons desiring to receive such notices and distributing copies to the press, whether of specialized or general readership, and (iii) Shall immediately submit said public notices to the Federal Register for publication.

(3) The Office of the Secretary shall respond to all questions from the public concerning the agendas of Commission meetings. Persons desiring to receive copies of notices of Commission meetings should contact the Office of the Secretary and request to be placed on the mailing list.

Sec. 201.36 Closing a portion or portions of a meeting or a series of meetings

(a) Every meeting of the Commission shall be open to public observation except when the Commission properly determines in the manner specified in paragraph (d) of this section that a portion or portions of a Commission meeting shall be closed to the public for the specific reasons enumerated in paragraph (b) of this section.

(b) The Commission may close a portion or portions of a Commission meeting only when it determines that public disclosure of information to be discussed at such meeting is likely to:

(1) Disclose matters that are (i) Specifically authorized under criteria established by Executive order to be kept secret in the interests of national defense or foreign policy and (ii) in fact properly classified pursuant to such Executive order;

(2) Relate solely to the internal personnel rules and practices of the Commission;

(3) Disclose matters specifically exempted from disclosure by statute (other than the Freedom of Information Act), provided that such statute (i) Requires that the matters be withheld from the public in such a manner as to leave no discretion on the issue, or

(ii) Establishes particular criteria for withholding or refers to particular types of matters to be withheld.

(4) Disclose trade secrets and commercial or financial information obtained from a person and privileged or confidential;

(5) Involve accusing any person of a crime, or formally censuring any person;

(6) Disclose information of a personal nature when disclosure would constitute a clearly unwarranted invasion of personal privacy;

(7) Disclose investigatory records compiled for law-enforcement purposes, or information which, if written, would be contained in such records, but only to the extent that the production of such records or information would: (i) Interfere with enforcement proceedings, (ii) deprive a person of a right to a fair trial or to an impartial adjudication, (iii) constitute an unwarranted invasion of personal privacy, or (iv) disclose the identity of a confidential source, and, in the case of a record compiled by a criminal law-enforcement authority in the course of a criminal investigation or by an agency conducting a lawful national-security intelligence investigation, confidential information furnished only by the confidential source;

(8)(i) Disclose information the premature disclosure of which would, in those instances where the Commission regulates commodities, be likely to lead to significant financial speculation in such commodities;

(ii) Disclose information the premature disclosure of which would be likely to significantly frustrate implementation of a proposed Commission action except (A) When the Commission has already disclosed to the public the content or nature of its proposed action or (B) when the Commission is required by law to make such disclosure on its own initiative prior to taking final Commission action on such proposal; or

(9) Specifically concern: (i) The Commission's issuance of a subpoena, (ii) the Commission's participation in a civil action or proceeding, or (iii) the initiation, conduct, or disposition by the Commission of a particular case of formal Commission adjudication under 19 U.S.C. 1337 pursuant to the procedures of 5 U.S.C. 554 or otherwise involving a determination on the record after opportunity for a hearing.

(c)(1) When the Commission has determined that one or more of the specific reasons enumerated in paragraph (b) of this section for closing a portion or portions of a Commission meeting is applicable to the subject matter or matters to be discussed, the Commission shall consider whether or not the public interest requires that such portion or portions of the meeting be open to public observation.

(2) In making the public-interest determination under paragraph (c)(1) of this section, the Commission shall consider whether public disclosure would (i) Interfere with the Commission's carrying out its statutory responsibilities, (ii) Conflict with the individual right of privacy under the Privacy Act of 1974 (5 U.S.C. 552a), or (iii) Place the Commission in violation of any other applicable provision of law, in addition to any other factors which it deems to be relevant to the particular meeting in question.

(d)(1) Action by the Commission to close a portion or portions of a meeting for one or more of the specific reasons enumerated in paragraphs (b) (1) through (9) of this section shall be taken only when a majority of the entire membership of the Commission has voted to take such action.

(2) A single recorded vote of the Commission shall be taken with respect to: (i) Each Commission meeting of which the Commission proposes to close a portion or portions to the public for one or more of the specific reasons enumerated in paragraphs (b) (1) through (9) of this section, or (ii) any information which the Commission proposes to withhold from the public for one or more of the specific reasons enumerated in paragraphs (b) (1) through (9) of this section. No proxy votes are permissible.

(e)(1) Action by the Commission to close a series of meetings of which the Commission proposes to close a portion or portions to the public for one or more of the specific reasons enumerated in paragraphs (b) (1) through (9) of this section may be taken by a single recorded vote of the Commission to close such portion or portions of the series. No proxy votes are permissible.

(2) A series of meetings may be closed pursuant to paragraph (e)(1) of this section so long as each meeting in such series: (i) Involves the same particular matters and (ii) is scheduled to be held no more than 30 days after the initial meeting in such series.

(f) When the Commission (i) Has voted to close a portion or portions of a meeting in accordance with paragraph (d) of this section or (ii) has voted to close a portion or portions of a series of meetings in accordance with paragraph (e) of this section, the public notices referred to in paragraph (a) or (c)(2) of Sec. 201.35 shall be issued or amended in accordance with paragraph (b) or (c)(3) of Sec. 201.35 at the earliest practicable time, but no later than one (1) working day following such vote.

Sec. 201.37 Changing the time, place, subject matter, or determination to open or close a meeting following a public notice

(a) The time or place of a Commission meeting may be changed following a public announcement required by Sec. 201.35 only if the Commission publicly announces such change or changes at the earliest practicable time by issuing an appropriate amendment to the public notice as required by Sec. 201.35.

(b) The subject matter or matters of a Commission meeting or the determination of the Commission to open or close a meeting, or portion of a meeting, to the public may be changed following a public announcement required by Sec. 201.35 only if: (i) A majority of the entire membership of the Commission determines by recorded vote that Commission business so requires and that no earlier announcement of the change was possible and (ii) the Commission publicly announces such change in subject matter or such change in the determination of the Commission to open or close a meeting, or a portion of a meeting, to the public and the vote of each Commissioner upon such change or changes in a subsequent amendment of the public notice required by Sec. 201.35.

Sec. 201.38 Requests by interested persons that the Commission close a portion of a Commission meeting

(a) Whenever any person whose interests may be directly affected by a portion of a Commission meeting requests that the Commission close such portion to the public for any of the specific reasons enumerated in paragraphs (b) (5), (6), or (7) of Sec. 201.36, the Commission, upon the request of any one of the Commissioners, shall take a vote in the manner specified in Sec. 201.36 of this subpart on whether or not to close such portion of the meeting.

(b) When the Commission votes on a request to close a portion of a meeting under paragraph (a) of this section in the manner specified in Sec. 201.36(d), a public notice as required by paragraphs (a) and (b) of Sec. 201.35 shall be issued.

Sec. 201.39 General Counsel's certification of Commission action in closing a meeting or a series of meetings

Before a Commission meeting may be closed for the specific reasons enumerated in paragraphs (b) (1) through (9) of Sec. 201.36, the General Counsel (i) Shall, in the related public notice, certify that in his or her opinion the meeting may be closed to the public and (ii) Shall state each applicable exemptive provision of paragraphs (b) (1) through (9) of Sec. 201.36.

Sec. 201.40 Records-retention requirements

(a) The Secretary shall maintain a copy of the certification by the General Counsel required by Sec. 201.39 for each Commission meeting of which a portion or portions are closed to the public pursuant to a vote under Sec. 201.36(d).

(b) The Secretary shall also maintain a copy of a statement from the presiding officer of each Commission meeting or portion thereof which was closed to the public for the specific reasons enumerated in paragraphs (b) (1) through (9) of Sec. 201.36(b) setting forth (i) The time and place of the closed meeting, or portion thereof, and (ii) A list of the persons present thereat.

(c) The Secretary shall also maintain a complete transcript or electronic recording of the proceedings of each Commission meeting or portion of a meeting, whether open to public observation or closed to the public. The Secretary shall also maintain a complete transcript or electronic recording of all deliberations conducted under paragraphs (a) (4), (5), and (6) of Sec. 201.34 of this subpart.

(d) Where portions of a Commission meeting are closed for the reasons contained in paragraphs (b) (8)(A) or (9) of Sec. 201.36, the Commission preserves the option to maintain detailed minutes of such portions. Such detailed minutes shall fully and clearly describe all matters discussed and shall provide a full and accurate summary of any actions taken, and the reasons therefor, including a description of each of the views expressed on any item and the record of any rollcall vote (reflecting the vote of each member on the question). All documents considered in connection with any action shall be identified in such minutes.

(e) The retention period for the records required by paragraphs (a), (b), (c), and (d) of this section shall be for a period of at least two (2) years after the particular Commission meeting, or until one (1) year after the conclusion of any Commission proceeding with respect to which the meeting or portion thereof was held, whichever occurs later.

(f) The requirements of paragraphs (c) and (d) of this section shall not affect or supplant the existing duty of the Secretary to maintain permanent minutes of each Commission meeting. The Secretary shall also maintain permanent minutes of all deliberations conducted under paragraphs (a) (4), (5), and (6) of Sec. 201.34 of this subpart.

Sec. 201.41 Public inspection and copying of records; applicable fees

(a) The Secretary shall promptly make available to interested members of the public the transcript or electronic recording of the discussion of any item on the agenda of a Commission meeting or of any item of the testimony of any witness received at the meeting, except for such item or items of such discussion or testimony as the Secretary determines to contain information which may be withheld for reasons specified in paragraphs (b) (1) through (9) of Sec. 201.36. The determination of the Secretary shall be in conformity with a prior vote of the Commission under Sec. 201.36(d) to close a portion or portions of a meeting.

(b) Public inspection of electronic recordings, transcripts, or minutes of Commission meetings shall take place at the United States International Trade Commission, 500 E Street SW., Washington, DC 20436. A room is designated by the Office of the Secretary and tape recorders with earphones are provided by the Commission for public-inspection purposes when proceedings are recorded on tape.

(c)(1) The Secretary shall provide any person with copies of transcripts, minutes of Commission meetings, or transcriptions of electronic recordings of Commission meetings, which disclose the identity of each speaker, at the actual cost of transcription or duplication.

(2) The Secretary shall not include items of discussion or testimony determined by the Secretary to contain information which may be withheld from the public for the reasons specified in paragraphs (b) (1) through (9) of Sec. 201.36 in the copies furnished to the public in accordance with paragraph (c)(1) of this section. The determination of the Secretary shall be in conformity with a prior vote of the Commission under Sec. 201.36(d) to close a portion or portions of a meeting.

Subpart F—National Security Information

Sec. 201.42 Purpose and scope

The following regulation supplements Executive Order 12356, National Security Information, April 2, 1982, as it applies to the Commission.

Sec. 201.43 Program

The Director of Administration is designated as the official of the Commission who is responsible for implementation and oversight of information security programs and procedures, including ensuring conformity with the provisions of Executive Order No. 12356. He shall chair a committee, composed of himself and representatives of the offices of the Secretary, General Counsel, Executive Liaison and Special Adviser for Trade Agreements, and Operations, that will act on all suggestions and complaints with respect to the Commission's administration of the program. All questions, suggestions, and complaints regarding all elements of the information security program shall be directed to the Director of Administration.

Sec. 201.44 Procedures

(a) Mandatory declassification review.

(1) Requests for declassification and release of national security information in the custody of the Commission shall be directed to the Secretary. Requests must reasonably

describe the information that is desired to be declassified. All requests for declassification submitted pursuant to the Freedom of Information Act shall be processed in accordance with the provisions of that act and the applicable regulations of the Commission (19 CFR 201.17 through 201.21).

(2) Because the Commission does not have original classification authority and national security information in its custody has been classified by another Federal agency, the Secretary shall refer all requests for mandatory declassification review of classified information to the originating Federal agency along with his recommendations. Following consultation with the originating agency, the Secretary will notify the requestor of the referral.

(b) Safeguarding.

All classified materials shall be delivered to the addressee or his designee immediately upon receipt at the Commission. In the event that the addressee or his designee is not available to receive the materials, they shall be delivered to the Secretary and secured, unopened, in a combination safe located in his office until the addressee or his designee is available. Under no circumstances shall classified materials that cannot be delivered to the addressee or his designee be stored other than in a GSA approved safe. Access to classified materials at the Commission shall be limited to officers and employees of the Commission on the basis of a favorable determination of trustworthiness on the basis of appropriate personnel security investigations and a need for access in the performance of official duties.

(c) Reproduction.

"Top Secret" documents may not be reproduced without the consent of the originating agency unless otherwise marked by that agency. Documents that have been classified "Secret" or "Confidential" with special dissemination orders may not be reproduced without the permission of the Executive Liaison and Special Adviser for Trade Agreements, and are subject to any limitations imposed by the originator. Reproduced copies shall be subject to the same controls as the original document. The Executive Liaison and Special Adviser for Trade Agreements shall establish a system of recording the number and distribution of copies reproduced from the original documents. Reproduction for the purposes of mandatory review shall not be restricted.

(d) Storage.

All classified material shall be stored in GSA-approved combination safes located at the Commission. The combinations shall be changed as required by section 2001.43(b) of Information Security Oversight Office Directive No. 1. The combinations shall be known only by those employees possessing an appropriate security clearance who have need for access in the performance of official duties.

(e) Employee education.

The Director of Administration shall establish for all employees who have been granted a security clearance an information security education program that will advise them of the handling, reproduction, and storage procedures for these materials. The education program will also enable employees to familiarize themselves with the Order and applicable directives of the Information Security Oversight Office. New employees will be instructed in these procedures as they enter employment with the Commission.

(f) Agency terminology.

The use of the terms "Top Secret", "Secret", and "Confidential" shall be limited to material classified for national security purposes.

Subpart G—Enforcement of Nondiscrimination on the Basis of Handicap in Programs or Activities Conducted by the U.S. International Trade Commission

Sec. 201.101 Purpose

This part effectuates section 119 of the Rehabilitation, Comprehensive Services, and Developmental Disabilities Amendments of 1978, which amended section 504 of the Rehabilitation Act of 1973 to prohibit discrimination on the basis of handicap in programs or activities conducted by Executive agencies or the United States Postal Service.

Sec. 201.102 Application

This part applies to all programs or activities conducted by the agency.

Sec. 201.103 Definitions

For purposes of this part, the term—

Assistant Attorney General means the Assistant Attorney General, Civil Rights Division, United States Department of Justice.

Auxiliary aids means services or devices that enable persons with impaired sensory, manual, or speaking skills to have an equal opportunity to participate in, and enjoy the benefits of, programs or activities conducted by the agency. For example, auxiliary aids useful for persons with impaired vision include readers, Brailled materials, audio recordings, telecommunications devices and other similar services and devices. Auxiliary aids useful for persons with impaired hearing include telephone handset amplifiers, telephones compatible with hearing aids, telecommunication devices for deaf persons (TDD's), interpreters, notetakers, written materials, and other similar services and devices.

Complete complaint means a written statement that contains the complainant's name and address and describes the agency's alleged discriminatory action in sufficient detail to inform the agency of the nature and date of the alleged violation of section 504. It shall be signed by the complainant or by someone authorized to do so on his or her behalf. Complaints filed on behalf of classes or third parties shall describe or identify (by name, if possible) the alleged victims of discrimination.

Facility means all or any portion of buildings, structures, equipment, roads, walks, parking lots, rolling stock or other conveyances, or other real or personal property.

Handicapped person means any person who has a physical or mental impairment that substantially limits one or more major life activities, has a record of such an impairment, or is regarded as having such an impairment.

As used in this definition, the phrase:

(1) Physical or mental impairment includes—

(i) Any physiological disorder or condition, cosmetic disfigurement, or anatomical loss affecting one or more of the following body systems:

Neurological; musculoskeletal; special sense organs; respiratory, including speech organs; cardiovascular; reproductive; digestive; genitourinary; hemic and lymphatic; skin; and endocrine; or

(ii) Any mental or psychological disorder, such as mental retardation, organic brain syndrome, emotional or mental illness, and specific learning disabilities. The term physical or mental impairment includes, but is not limited to, such diseases and conditions as orthopedic, visual, speech, and hearing impairments, cerebral palsy, epilepsy, muscular dystrophy, multiple sclerosis, cancer, heart disease, diabetes, mental retardation, emotional illness, and drug addition and alcoholism.

(2) Major life activities includes functions such as caring for one's self, performing manual tasks, walking, seeing, hearing, speaking, breathing, learning, and working.

(3) Has a record of such an impairment means has a history of, or has been misclassified as having, a mental or physical impairment that substantially limits one or more major life activities.

(4) Is regarded as having an impairment means—

(i) Has a physical or mental impairment that does not substantially limit major life activities but is treated by the agency as constituting such a limitation;

(ii) Has a physical or mental impairment that substantially limits major life activities only as a result of the attitudes of others toward such impairment; or

(iii) Has none of the impairments defined in subparagraph (1) of this definition but is treated by the agency as having such an impairment.

Qualified handicapped person means—

(1) With respect to any agency program or activity under which a person is required to perform services or to achieve a level of accomplishment, a handicapped person who meets the essential eligibility requirements and who can achieve the purpose of the program or activity without modifications in the program or activity that the agency can demonstrate would result in a fundamental alteration in its nature; or

(2) With respect to any other program or activity, a handicapped person who meets the essential eligibility requirements for participation in, or receipt of benefits from, that program or activity.

(3) Qualified handicapped person is defined for purposes of employment in 29 CFR 1613.702(f), which is made applicable to this part by Sec. 201.140.

Section 504 means section 504 of the Rehabilitation Act of 1973 (Pub. L. 93-112, 87 Stat. 394 (29 U.S.C. 794)), as amended by the Rehabilitation Act Amendments of 1974 (Pub. L. 93-516, 88 Stat. 1617), and the Rehabilitation, Comprehensive Services, and Developmental Disabilities Amendments of 1978 (Pub. L. 95-602, 92 Stat. 2955). As used in this part, section 504 applies only to programs or activities conducted by Executive agencies and not to federally assisted programs.

Secs. 201.104-201.109 [Reserved]

Sec. 201.110 Self-evaluation

(a) The agency shall, by April 9, 1987, evaluate its current policies and practices, and the effects thereof, that do not or may not meet the requirements of this part, and, to the extent modification of any such policies and practices is required, the agency shall proceed to make the necessary modifications.

(b) The agency shall provide an opportunity to interested persons, including handicapped persons or organizations representing handicapped persons, to participate in the self-evaluation process by submitting comments (both oral and written).

(c) The agency shall, until three years following the completion of the self-evaluation, maintain on file and make available for public inspections:

(1) A description of areas examined and any problems identified, and

(2) A description of any modifications made.

Sec. 201.111 Notice

The agency shall make available to employees, applicants, participants, beneficiaries, and other interested persons such information regarding the provisions of this part and its applicability to the programs or activities conducted by the agency, and make such information available to them in such manner as the head of the agency finds necessary to apprise such persons of the protections against discrimination assured them by section 504 and this regulation.

Secs. 201.112-201.129 [Reserved]

Sec. 201.130 General prohibitions against discrimination

(a) No qualified handicapped person shall, on the basis of handicap, be excluded from participation in, be denied the benefits of, or otherwise be subjected to discrimination under any program or activity conducted by the agency.

(b)(1) The agency, in providing any aid, benefit, or service, may not, directly or through contractual, licensing, or other arrangements, on the basis of handicap—

(i) Deny a qualified handicapped person the opportunity to participate in or benefit from the aid, benefit, or service;

(ii) Afford a qualified handicapped person an opportunity to participate in or benefit from the aid, benefit, or service that is not equal to that afforded others;

(iii) Provide a qualified handicapped person with an aid, benefit, or service that is not as effective in affording equal opportunity to obtain the same result, to gain the same benefit, or to reach the same level of achievement as that provided to others;

(iv) Provide different or separate aid, benefits, or services to handicapped persons or to any class of handicapped persons than is provided to others unless such action is necessary to provide qualified handicapped persons with aid, benefits, or services that are as effective as those provided to others;

(v) Deny a qualified handicapped person the opportunity to participate as a member of planning or advisory boards; or

(vi) Otherwise limit a qualified handicapped person in the enjoyment of any right, privilege, advantage, or opportunity enjoyed by others receiving the aid, benefit, or service.

(2) The agency may not deny a qualified handicapped person the opportunity to participate in programs or activities that are not separate or different, despite the existence of permissibly separate or different programs or activities.

(3) The agency may not, directly or through contractual or other arrangements, utilize criteria or methods of administration the purpose or effect of which would—

(i) Subject qualified handicapped persons to discrimination on the basis of handicap; or

(ii) Defeat or substantially impair accomplishment of the objectives of a program or activity with respect to handicapped persons.

(4) The agency may not, in determining the site or location of a facility, make selections the purpose or effect of which would—

(i) Exclude handicapped persons from, deny them the benefits of, or otherwise subject them to discrimination under any program or activity conducted by the agency; or

(ii) Defeat or substantially impair the accomplishment of the objectives of a program or activity with respect to handicapped persons.

(5) The agency, in the selection of procurement contractors, may not use criteria that subject qualified handicapped persons to discrimination on the basis of handicap.

(c) The exclusion of nonhandicapped persons from the benefits of a program limited by Federal statute or Executive order to handicapped persons or the exclusion of a specific class of handicapped persons from a program limited by Federal statute or Executive order to a different class of handicapped persons is not prohibited by this part.

(d) The agency shall administer programs and activities in the most integrated setting appropriate to the needs of qualified handicapped persons.

Secs. 201.131-201.139 [Reserved]

Sec. 201.140 Employment

No qualified handicapped person shall, on the basis of handicap, be subjected to discrimination in employment under any program or activity conducted by the agency. The definitions, requirements, and procedures of section 501 of the Rehabilitation Act of 1973 (29 U.S.C. 791), as established by the Equal Employment Opportunity Commission in 29 CFR part 1613, shall apply to employment in federally conducted programs or activities.

Secs. 201.141-201.148 [Reserved]

Sec. 201.149 Program accessibility: Discrimination prohibited

Except as otherwise provided in Sec. 201.150, no qualified handicapped person shall, because the agency's facilities are inaccessible to or unusable by handicapped persons, be denied the benefits of, be excluded from participation in, or otherwise be subjected to discrimination under any program or activity conducted by the agency.

Sec. 201.150 Program accessibility: Existing facilities

(a) General.

The agency shall operate each program or activity so that the program or activity, when viewed in its entirety, is readily accessible to and usable by handicapped persons. This paragraph does not—

(1) Necessarily require the agency to make each of its existing facilities accessible to and usable by handicapped persons; or

(2) Require the agency to take any action that it can demonstrate would result in a fundamental alteration in the nature of a program or activity or in undue financial and administrative burdens. In those circumstances where agency personnel believe that the proposed action would fundamentally alter the program or activity or would result in undue financial and administrative burdens, the agency has the burden of proving that compliance with Sec. 201.150(a) would result in such alteration or burdens. The decision that compliance would result in such alteration or burdens must be made by the agency head or his or her designee after considering all agency resources available for use in the funding and operation of the conducted program or activity, and must be accompanied by a written statement of the reasons for reaching that conclusion. If an action would result in such an alteration or such burdens, the agency shall take any other action that would not result in such an alteration or such burdens but would nevertheless ensure that handicapped persons receive the benefits and services of the program or activity.

(b) Methods.

The agency may comply with the requirements of this section through such means as redesign of equipment, reassignment of services to accessible buildings, assignment of aides to beneficiaries, home visits, delivery of services at alternate accessible sites, alteration of existing facilities and construction of new facilities, use of accessible rolling stock, or any other methods that result in making its programs or activities readily accessible to and usable by handicapped persons. The agency is not required to make structural changes in existing facilities where other methods are effective in achieving compliance with this section. The agency, in making alterations to existing buildings, shall meet accessibility requirements to the extent compelled by the Architectural Barriers Act of 1968, as amended (42 U.S.C. 4151-4157), and any regulations implementing it. In choosing among available methods for meeting the requirements of this section, the agency shall give priority to those methods that offer programs and activities to qualified handicapped persons in the most integrated setting appropriate.

(c) Time period for compliance.

The agency shall comply with the obligations established under this section by June 6, 1986, except that where structural changes in facilities are undertaken, such changes shall be made by April 7, 1989, but in any event as expeditiously as possible.

(d) Transition plan.

In the event that structural changes to facilities will be undertaken to achieve program accessibility, the agency shall develop, by October 7, 1986, a transition plan setting forth the steps necessary to complete such changes. The agency shall provide an opportunity to interested persons, including handicapped persons or organizations representing handicapped persons, to participate in the development of the transition plan by submitting comments (both oral and written). A copy of the transition plan shall be made available for public inspection. The plan shall, at a minimum—

(1) Identify physical obstacles in the agency's facilities that limit the accessibility of its programs or activities to handicapped persons;

(2) Describe in detail the methods that will be used to make the facilities accessible;

(3) Specify the schedule for taking the steps necessary to achieve compliance with this section and, if the time period of the transition plan is longer than one year, identify steps that will be taken during each year of the transition period; and

(4) Indicate the official responsible for implementation of the plan.

Sec. 201.151 Program accessibility: New construction and alterations

Each building or part of a building that is constructed or altered by, on behalf of, or for the use of the agency shall be designed, constructed, or altered so as to be readily accessible to and usable by handicapped persons. The definitions, requirements, and standards of the Architectural Barriers Act (42 U.S.C. 4151-4157), as established in 41 CFR 101-19.600 to 101-19.607, apply to buildings covered by this section.

Secs. 201.152-201.159 [Reserved]

Sec. 201.160 Communications

(a) The agency shall take appropriate steps to ensure effective communication with applicants, participants, personnel of other Federal entities, and members of the public.

(1) The agency shall furnish appropriate auxiliary aids where necessary to afford a handicapped person an equal opportunity to participate in, and enjoy the benefits of, a program or activity conducted by the agency.

(i) In determining what type of auxiliary aid is necessary, the agency shall give primary consideration to the requests of the handicapped person.

(ii) The agency need not provide individually prescribed devices, readers for personal use or study, or other devices of a personal nature.

(2) Where the agency communicates with applicants and beneficiaries by telephone, telecommunication devices for deaf persons (TDD's) or equally effective telecommunication systems shall be used.

(b) The agency shall ensure that interested persons, including persons with impaired vision or hearing, can obtain information as to the existence and location of accessible services, activities, and facilities.

(c) The agency shall provide signage at a primary entrance to each of its inaccessible facilities, directing users to a location at which they can obtain information about accessible facilities. The international symbol for accessibility shall be used at each primary entrance of an accessible facility.

(d) This section does not require the agency to take any action that it can demonstrate would result in a fundamental alteration in the nature of a program or activity or in undue financial and administrative burdens. In those circumstances where agency personnel believe that the proposed action would fundamentally alter the program or activity or would result in undue financial and administrative burdens, the agency has the burden of proving that compliance with Sec. 201.160 would result in such alteration or burdens. The decision that compliance would result in such alteration or burdens must be made by the agency head or his or her designee after considering all agency resources available for use in the funding and operation of the conducted program or activity, and must be accompanied by a written statement of the reasons for reaching that conclusion. If an action required to comply with this section would result in such an alteration or such burdens, the agency shall take any other action that would not result in such an alteration or such burdens but would nevertheless ensure that, to the maximum extent possible, handicapped persons receive the benefits and services of the program or activity.

Secs. 201.161-201.169 [Reserved]

Sec. 201.170 Compliance procedures

(a) Except as provided in paragraph (b) of this section, this section applies to all allegations of discrimination on the basis of handicap in programs or activities conducted by the agency.

(b) The agency shall process complaints alleging violations of section 504 with respect to employment according to the procedures established by the Equal Employment Opportunity Commission in 29 CFR part 1613 pursuant to section 501 of the Rehabilitation Act of 1973 (29 U.S.C. 791).

(c) EEO Director, Office of Operations, Office of Data Systems, Library Division shall be responsible for coordinating implementation of this section. Complaints may be sent to Handicap Coordinator, Office of Operations, Office of Investigations, 500 E Street SW., Washington, DC 20436.

(d) The agency shall accept and investigate all complete complaints for which it has jurisdiction. All complete complaints must be filed within 180 days of the alleged act of discrimination. The agency may extend this time period for good cause.

(e) If the agency receives a complaint over which it does not have jurisdiction, it shall promptly notify the complainant and shall make reasonable efforts to refer the complaint to the appropriate government entity.

(f) The agency shall notify the Architectural and Transportation Barriers Compliance Board upon receipt of any complaint alleging that a building or facility that is subject to the Architectural Barriers Act of 1968, as amended (42 U.S.C. 4151-4157), or section 502 of the Rehabilitation Act of 1973, as amended (29 U.S.C. 792), is not readily accessible to and usable by handicapped persons.

(g) Within 180 days of the receipt of a complete complaint for which it has jurisdiction, the agency shall notify the complainant of the results of the investigation in a letter containing—

(1) Findings of fact and conclusions of law;

(2) A description of a remedy for each violation found;

(3) A notice of the right to appeal.

(h) Appeals of the findings of fact and conclusions of law or remedies must be filed by the complainant within 90 days of receipt from the agency of the letter required by Sec. 201.170(g). The agency may extend this time for good cause.

(i) Timely appeals shall be accepted and processed by the head of the agency.

(j) The head of the agency shall notify the complainant of the results of the appeal within 60 days of the receipt of the request. If the head of the agency determines that additional information is needed from the complainant, he or she shall have 60 days from the date of receipt of the additional information to make his or her determination on the appeal.

(k) The time limits cited in paragraphs (g) and (j) of this section may be extended with the permission of the Assistant Attorney General.

(l) The agency may delegate its authority for conducting complaint investigations to other Federal agencies, except that the authority for making the final determination may not be delegated to another agency.

Secs. 201.171-201.999 [Reserved]

Subpart H—Debt Collection

Sec. 201.201 Definitions

Except where the context clearly indicates otherwise or where the term is defined elsewhere in this section, the following definitions shall apply to this subpart.

(a) Agency means a department, agency, court, court administrative office, or instrumentality in the executive, judicial, or legislative branch of Government, including government corporations.

(b) Certification means a written statement received by a paying agency from a creditor agency that requests the paying agency to offset the salary of an employee and specifies that required procedural protections have been afforded the employee.

(c) Chairman means the Chairman of the Commission.

(d) Compromise means the settlement or forgiveness of a debt.

(e) Creditor agency means an agency of the Federal government to which the debt is owed.

(f) Director means the Director, Office of Finance and Budget of the Commission or an official designated to act on the Director's behalf.

(g) Disposable pay means that part of current basic pay, special pay, incentive pay, retired pay, retainer pay, and, in the case of an employee not entitled to basic pay, other authorized pay, remaining for each pay period after the deduction of any amount required by law to be withheld. The Commission shall allow the following deductions in determining the amount of disposable pay that is subject to salary offset:

(1) Federal employment taxes;

(2) Amounts mandatorily withheld for the United States Soldiers' and Airmen's Home;

(3) Fines and forfeiture ordered by a court-martial or by a commanding officer;

(4) Amounts deducted for Medicare;

(5) Federal, state, or local income taxes to the extent authorized or required by law, but no greater than would be the case if the employee claimed all dependents to which he or she is entitled and such additional amounts for which the employee presents evidence of a tax obligation supporting the additional withholding;

(6) Health insurance premiums;

(7) Normal retirement contributions, including employee contributions to the Thrift Savings Plan;

(8) Normal life insurance premiums (e.g., Serviceman's Group Life Insurance and "Basic Life" Federal Employee's Group Life Insurance premiums), not including amounts deducted for supplementary coverage.

(h) Employee means a current employee of the Commission or other agency, including a current member of the Armed Forces or a Reserve of the Armed Forces of the United States.

(i) Federal Claims Collection Standards (FCCS) means standards published at 4 CFR chapter II.

(j) Hearing official means an individual responsible for conducting any hearing with respect to the existence or amount of a debt claimed and for rendering a decision on the basis of such hearing. A hearing official may not be under the supervision or control of the Chairman when the Commission is the creditor agency but may be an administrative law judge.

(k) Notice of Intent to Offset or Notice of Intent means a written notice from a creditor agency to an employee, organization, or entity stating that the debtor is indebted to the creditor agency and apprising the debtor of certain procedural rights.

(l) Notice of Salary Offset means a written notice from the paying agency to an employee after a certification has been issued by a creditor agency, informing the employee that salary offset will begin at the next officially established pay interval.

(m) Office of Finance and Budget means the Office of Finance and Budget of the Commission.

(n) Paying agency means the agency of the Federal government that employs the individual who owes a debt to an agency of the Federal government. In some cases, the Commission may be both the creditor agency and the paying agency.

Sec. 201.202 Purpose and scope of salary and administrative offset rules

(a) Purpose.

The purpose of Secs. 201.201 through 201.207 is to implement 5 U.S.C. 5514, 31 U.S.C. 3716, and 31 U.S.C. 3720A which authorize the collection by salary offset, administrative offset, or tax refund offset of debts owed by persons, organizations, or entities to the Federal government. Generally, however, a debt may not be collected by such means if it has been outstanding for more than ten years after the agency's right to collect the debt first accrued. These proposed regulations are consistent with the Office of Personnel Management regulations on salary offset, codified at 5 CFR part 550, subpart K, and with regulations on administrative offset codified at 4 CFR part 102.

(b) Scope.

(1) Sections 201.201 through 201.207 establish agency procedures for the collection of certain debts owed the Government.

(2) Sections 201.201 through 201.207 apply to collections by the Commission from:

(i) Federal employees who are indebted to the Commission;

(ii) Employees of the Commission who are indebted to other agencies; and

(iii) Other persons, organizations, or entities that are indebted to the Commission.

(3) Sections 201.201 through 201.207 do not apply:

(i) To debts or claims arising under the Internal Revenue Code of 1986 (26 U.S.C. et seq.), the Social Security Act (42 U.S.C. 301 et seq.), or the tariff laws of the United States;

(ii) To a situation to which the Contract Disputes Act (41 U.S.C. 601 et seq.) applies; or

(iii) In any case where collection of a debt is explicitly provided for or prohibited by another statute (e.g., travel advances in 5 U.S.C. 4108).

(4) Nothing in Secs. 201.201 through 201.207 precludes the compromise, suspension, or termination of collection actions where appropriate under the standards implementing the Federal Claims Collection Act (31 U.S.C. 3711 et seq.), namely, 4 CFR chapter II.

Sec. 201.203 Delegation of authority

Authority to conduct the following activities is hereby delegated to the Director:

(a) Initiate and effectuate the administrative collection process;

(b) Accept or reject compromise offers and suspend or terminate collection actions where the claim does not exceed $100,000 or such higher amount as the Chairman may from time to time prescribe, exclusive of interest, administrative costs, and penalties as provided herein, as set forth in 31 U.S.C. 3711(a)(2);

(c) Report to consumer reporting agencies certain data pertaining to delinquent debts;

(d) Use offset procedures to effectuate collection; and

(e) Take any other action necessary to facilitate and augment collection in accordance with the policies contained herein and as otherwise provided by law.

Sec. 201.204 Salary offset

(a) Notice requirements before offset where the Commission is the creditor agency.

Deductions under the authority of 5 U.S.C. 5514 will not be made unless the Commission provides the employee with a written Notice of Intent to Offset a minimum of 30 calendar days before salary offset is initiated. The Notice of Intent shall state:

(1) That the Director has reviewed the records relating to the claim and has determined that a debt is owed;

(2) The Director's intention to collect the debt by means of deduction from the employee's current disposable pay account until the debt and all accumulated interest is paid in full;

(3) The amount of the debt and the facts giving rise to the debt;

(4) A repayment schedule that includes the amount, frequency, proposed beginning date, and duration of the intended deductions;

(5) The opportunity for the employee to propose an alternative written schedule for the voluntary repayment of the debt, in lieu of offset, on terms acceptable to the Commission. The employee shall include a justification in the request for the

alternative schedule. The schedule shall be agreed to and signed by both the employee and the Director;

(6) An explanation of the Commission's policy concerning interest, penalties, and administrative costs, including a statement that such assessments must be made unless excused in accordance with the Federal Claims Collection Standards;

(7) The employee's right to inspect and copy all records of the Commission not exempt from disclosure pertaining to the debt claimed or to receive copies of such records if the debtor is unable personally to inspect the records, due to geographical or other constraints;

(8) The name, address, and telephone number of the Director to whom requests for access to records relating to the debt must be sent;

(9) The employee's right to a hearing conducted by an impartial hearing official (an administrative law judge or other hearing official not under the supervision or control of the Chairman) with respect to the existence and amount of the debt claimed or the repayment schedule (*i.e.*, the percentage of disposable pay to be deducted each pay period), so long as a request is filed by the employee as prescribed in paragraph (c)(1) of this section;

(10) The name, address, and telephone number of the Director to whom a proposal for voluntary repayment must be sent and who may be contacted concerning procedures for requesting a hearing;

(11) The method and deadline for requesting a hearing;

(12) That the timely filing of a request for a hearing on or before the 15th calendar day following receipt of the Notice of Intent will stay the commencement of collection proceedings;

(13) The name and address of the office to which the request should be sent;

(14) That the Commission will initiate certification procedures to implement a salary offset not less than 30 days from the date of receipt of the Notice of Intent to Offset, unless the employee files a timely request for a hearing;

(15) That a final decision on whether a hearing will be held (if one is requested) will be issued at the earliest practical date;

(16) That any knowingly false or frivolous statements, representations, or evidence may subject the employee to:

(i) Disciplinary procedures appropriate under 5 U.S.C. Chapter 75, 5 CFR part 752, or any other applicable statutes or regulations;

(ii) Penalties under the False Claims Act, 31 U.S.C. 3729-3731, or under any other applicable statutory authority; or

(iii) Criminal penalties under 18 U.S.C. 286, 287, 1001, and 1002 or under any other applicable statutory authority;

(17) Any other rights and remedies available to the employee under statutes or regulations governing the program for which the collection is being made;

(18) That unless there are applicable contractual or statutory provisions to the contrary, amounts paid on or deducted from debts that are later waived or found not to be owed to the United States will be promptly refunded to the employee; and

(19) That proceedings with respect to such debt are governed by 5 U.S.C. 5514.

(b) Review of Commission records related to the debt.

(1) An employee who desires to inspect or copy Commission records related to a debt owed to the Commission must send a letter to the Director as designated in the Notice of Intent requesting access to the relevant records. The letter must be received in the office of the Director within 15 calendar days after the employee's receipt of the Notice of Intent.

(2) In response to a timely request submitted by the debtor, the Director will notify the employee of the location and time when the employee may inspect and copy records related to the debt.

(3) If the employee is unable personally to inspect the records, due to geographical or other constraints, the Director shall arrange to send copies of such records to the employee.

(c) Opportunity for a hearing where the Commission is the creditor agency.

(1) Request for a hearing.

(i) An employee who requests a hearing on the existence or amount of the debt held by the Commission or on the offset schedule proposed by the Commission must send such request to the Director. The request for a hearing must be received by the Director on or before the 15th calendar day following receipt by the employee of the notice.

(ii) The employee must specify whether an oral hearing is requested. If an oral hearing is desired, the request should explain why the matter cannot be resolved by review of the documentary evidence alone. The request must be signed by the employee and must fully identify and explain with reasonable specificity all the facts, evidence,and witnesses, if any, that the employee believes support his or her position.

(2) Failure to timely submit. If the employee files a request for hearing after the expiration of the 15-calendar-day period provided for in paragraph (c)(1) of this section, the Director may accept the request if the employee can show that the delay was the result of circumstances beyond his or her control or that he or she failed to receive actual notice of the filing deadline.

(3) Obtaining the services of a hearing official.

(i) When the debtor is not a Commission employee and the Commission cannot provide a prompt and appropriate hearing before an administrative law judge or other hearing official, the Commission may request a hearing official from an agent of the paying agency, as designated in 5 CFR part 581, appendix A, or as otherwise designated by the paying agency.

(ii) When the debtor is a Commission employee, the Commission may contact any agent of another agency, as designated in 5 CFR part 581, appendix A, or as otherwise designated by the agency, to request a hearing official.

(4) Procedure.

(i) Notice. After the employee requests a hearing, the hearing official shall notify the employee of the form of the hearing to be provided. If the hearing will be oral, the notice shall set forth the date, time, and location of the hearing, which must occur no more than 30 calendar days after the request is received, unless the employee requests that the hearing be delayed. If the hearing will be conducted by examination of documents, the employee shall be notified within 30 calendar days that he or she should submit evidence and arguments in writing to the hearing official.

(ii) Oral hearing. An employee who requests an oral hearing shall be provided an oral hearing if the hearing official determines that the matter cannot be resolved by review of documentary evidence alone (e.g., when an issue of credibility or veracity is involved). The hearing need not be an adversarial adjudication, and rules of evidence need not apply. Witnesses who testify in oral hearings shall do so under oath or affirmation. Oral hearings may take the form of, but are not limited to:

(A) Informal conferences with the hearing official in which the employee and agency representative are given full opportunity to present evidence, witnesses, and argument;

(B) Informal meetings in which the hearing examiner interviews the employee; or

(C) Formal written submissions followed by an opportunity for oral presentation.

(iii) Documentary hearing. If the hearing official determines that an oral hearing is not necessary, he or she shall make the determination based upon a review of the written record.

(iv) Record. The hearing official shall maintain a summary record of any hearing conducted under this section.

(5) Date of decision. The hearing official shall issue a written opinion stating his or her decision, based upon all evidence and information developed at the hearing, as soon as practicable after the hearing, but not later than 60 calendar days after the date on which the request was received by the Commission, unless the hearing was delayed at the request of the employee, in which case the 60 day decision period shall be extended by the number of days by which the hearing was postponed. The decision of the hearing official shall be final.

(6) Content of decision. The written decision shall include:

(i) A summary of the facts concerning the origin, nature, and amount of the debt;

(ii) The hearing official's findings, analysis, and conclusions; and

(iii) The terms of any repayment schedules, if applicable.

(7) Failure to appear. If, in the absence of good cause shown (e.g., illness), the employee or the representative of the Commission fails to appear, the hearing official shall proceed with the hearing as scheduled, and make his or her determination based upon the oral testimony presented and the documentation submitted by both parties. At the request of both parties, the hearing official may schedule a new hearing date. Both parties shall be given reasonable notice of the time and place of this new hearing.

(d) Certification where the Commission is the creditor agency.

(1) The Director shall issue a certification in all cases where:

(i) The hearing official determines that a debt exists; or

(ii) The employee admits the existence and amount of the debt, for example, by failing to request a hearing.

(2) The certification must be in writing and must state:

(i) That the employee owes the debt;

(ii) The amount and basis of the debt;

(iii) The date the Government's right to collect the debt first accrued;

(iv) That the Commission's regulations have been approved by OPM pursuant to 5 CFR part 550, subpart K;

(v) If the collection is to be made by lump-sum payment, the amount and date such payment will be collected;

(vi) If the collection is to be made in installments, the number of installments to be collected, the amount of each installment, and the date of the first installment, if a date other than the next officially established pay period; and

(vii) The date the employee was notified of the debt, the action(s) taken pursuant to the Commission's regulations, and the dates such actions were taken.

(e) Voluntary repayment agreements as alternative to salary offset where the Commission is the creditor agency.

(1) In response to a Notice of Intent, an employee may propose to repay the debt in accordance with scheduled installment payments. Any employee who wishes to repay a debt without salary offset shall submit in writing a proposed agreement to repay the debt. The proposal shall set forth a proposed repayment schedule. Any proposal under paragraph (e) of this section must be received by the Director within 15 calendar days after receipt of the Notice of Intent.

(2) In response to a timely proposal by the debtor, the Director shall notify the employee whether the employee's proposed written agreement for repayment is acceptable. It is within the discretion of the Director to accept, reject, or propose to the debtor a modification of the proposed repayment agreement.

(3) If the Director decides that the proposed repayment agreement is unacceptable, the employee shall have 15 calendar days from the date he or she received notice of the decision in which to file a request for a hearing.

(4) If the Director decides that the proposed repayment agreement is acceptable or the debtor agrees to a modification proposed by the Director, the agreement shall be put in writing and signed by both the employee and the Director.

(f) Special review where the Commission is the creditor agency.

(1) An employee subject to salary offset or a voluntary repayment agreement may, at any time, request a special review by the Director of the amount of the salary offset or voluntary payment, based on materially changed circumstances, including, but not limited to, catastrophic illness, divorce, death, or disability.

(2) In determining whether, as a result of materially changed circumstances, an offset would prevent the employee from meeting essential subsistence expenses (costs incurred for food, housing, clothing, transportation, and medical care), the employee shall submit to the Director a detailed statement and supporting documents for the employee, his or her spouse, and dependents indicating:

(i) Income from all sources;

(ii) Assets;

(iii) Liabilities;

(iv) Number of dependents;

(v) Expenses for food, housing, clothing, and transportation;

(vi) Medical expenses; and

(vii) Exceptional expenses, if any.

(3) If the employee requests a special review under paragraph (f) of this section, the employee shall file an alternative proposed offset or payment schedule and a statement, with supporting documents, showing why the current salary offset or payments result in extreme financial hardship to the employee.

(4) The Director shall evaluate the statement and supporting documents and determine whether the original offset or repayment schedule imposes extreme financial hardship on the employee. The Director shall notify the employee in writing within 30 calendar days of such determination, including, if appropriate, his or her acceptance of a revised offset or payment schedule.

(5) If the special review results in a revised offset or repayment schedule, the Director shall provide a new certification to the paying agency.

(g) Notice of salary offset where the Commission is the paying agency.

(1) Upon issuance of a proper certification by the Director (for debts owed to the Commission) or upon receipt of a proper certification from another creditor agency, the Office of Finance and Budget shall send the employee a written notice of salary offset. Such notice shall advise the employee:

(i) Of the certification that has been issued by the Director or received from another creditor agency;

(ii) Of the amount of the debt and of the deductions to be made; and

(iii) Of the initiation of salary offset at the next officially established pay interval or as otherwise provided for in the certification.

(2) The Office of Finance and Budget shall provide a copy of the notice to the creditor agency and advise such agency of the dollar amount to be offset and the pay period when the offset will begin.

(h) Procedures for salary offset where the Commission is the paying agency.

(1) Generally.

(i) The Director shall coordinate salary deductions under this section.

(ii) The Director shall determine the amount of an employee's disposable pay and the amount of the salary offset subject to the requirements in this paragraph.

(iii) Deductions shall begin the pay period following the issuance of the certification by the Director or the receipt by the Office of Finance and Budget of the certification from another agency or as soon thereafter as possible.

(2) Types of collection.

(i) Lump-sum payment. If the amount of the debt is equal to or less than 15 percent of the employee's disposable pay, such debt ordinarily will be collected in one lump-sum payment.

(ii) Installment deductions. Installment deductions will be made over a period not greater than the anticipated period of employment. The size and frequency of installment deductions will bear a reasonable relation to the size of the debt and the employee's ability to pay. However, the amount deducted for any pay period will not exceed 15 percent of the disposable pay from which the deduction is made unless the employee has agreed in writing to the deduction of a greater amount. The installment payment should normally be sufficient in size and frequency to liquidate the debt in no more than three years. Installment payments of less than $50 should be accepted only in the most unusual circumstances.

(iii) Lump-sum deductions from final check. In order to liquidate a debt, a lump-sum deduction exceeding 15 percent of disposable pay may be made pursuant to 31 U.S.C. 3716 from any final salary payment due a former employee, whether the former employee was separated voluntarily or involuntarily.

(iv) Lump-sum deductions from other sources. Whenever an employee subject to salary offset is separated from the Commission, and the balance of the debt cannot be liquidated by offset of the final salary check, the Commission, pursuant to 31 U.S.C. 3716, may offset any later payments of any kind to the former employee to collect the balance of the debt.

(3) Multiple debts. Where two or more creditor agencies are seeking salary offset, or where two or more debts are owed to a single creditor agency, the Office of Finance and Budget may, at its discretion, determine whether one or more debts should be offset simultaneously within the 15 percent limitation.

(4) Order of precedence for recovery of debts owed the Government.

(i) For Commission employees, subject to paragraph (h)(3) of this section and (paragraph (h)(4)(ii) of this section, offsets to recover debts owed the United States Government shall be made from disposable pay in the following order of precedence:

(A) Indebtedness due the Commission;

(B) Indebtedness due other agencies.

(ii) In the event that a debt to the Commission is certified while an employee is subject to salary offset to repay another agency, the Office of Finance and Budget may, at its discretion, determine whether the debt to the Commission should be repaid before the debt to the other agency, repaid simultaneously, or repaid after the debt to the other agency.

(iii) A levy pursuant to the Internal Revenue Code of 1986 shall take precedence over other deductions under this section, as provided in 5 U.S.C. 5514(d).

(i) Coordinating salary offset with other agencies.

(1) Responsibility of the Commission as the creditor agency.

(i) The Director shall be responsible for:

(A) Arranging for a hearing upon proper request by a Federal employee;

(B) Preparing the Notice of Intent to Offset consistent with the requirements of paragraph (a) of this section;

(C) Obtaining hearing officials from other agencies pursuant to paragraph (c)(3) of this section; and

(D) Ensuring that each certification of debt is sent to a paying agency pursuant to paragraph (d)(2) of this section.

(ii) Upon completion of the procedures established in paragraphs (a) through (f) of this section, the Director shall submit a certified debt claim and an installment agreement or other instruction on the payment schedule, if applicable, to the employee's paying agency.

(iii) If the employee is in the process of separating from Government employment, the Commission shall submit its debt claim to the employee's paying agency for collection by lump-sum deduction from the employee's final check. The paying agency shall certify the total amount of its collection and furnish a copy of the certification to the Commission and to the employee.

(iv) If the employee is already separated and all payments due from his or her former paying agency have been paid, the Commission may, unless otherwise prohibited, request that money due and payable to the employee from the Federal Government be administratively offset to collect the debt.

(v) When an employee transfers to another paying agency, the Commission shall not repeat the procedures described in paragraphs (a) through (f) of this section in order to resume collecting the debt. Instead, the Commission shall review the debt upon receiving the former paying agency's notice of the employee's transfer and shall ensure that collection is resumed by the new paying agency.

(2) Responsibility of the Commission as the paying agency.

(i) Complete claim. When the Commission receives a certified claim from a creditor agency, the employee shall be given written notice of the certification, the date salary offset will begin, and the amount of the periodic deductions. Deductions shall be scheduled to begin at the next officially established pay interval or as otherwise provided for in the certification.

(ii) Incomplete claim. When the Commission receives an incomplete certification of debt from a creditor agency, the Commission shall return the debt claim with notice that procedures under 5 U.S.C. 5514 and 5 CFR 550.1104 must be followed and that a properly certified debt claim must be received before action will be taken to collect from the employee's current pay account.

(iii) Review. The Commission is not authorized to review the merits of the creditor agency's determination with respect to the amount or validity of the debt certified by the creditor agency.

(iv) Employees who transfer from one paying agency to another agency. If, after the creditor agency has submitted the debt claim to the Commission, the employee transfers to an agency outside the Commission before the debt is collected in full, the Commission must certify the total amount collected on the debt. One copy of the certification shall be furnished to the employee and one copy shall be sent to the creditor agency along with notice of the employee's transfer. If the Commission is aware that the employee is entitled to payments from the Civil Service Retirement and Disability Fund, or other similar payments, it must provide written notification to the agency responsible for making such payments that the debtor owes a debt (including the amount) and that the requirements set forth herein and in the Office of Personnel Management's regulation (5 CFR part 550) have been fully met.

(j) Interest, Penalties, and Administrative Costs.

Where the Commission is the creditor agency, it shall assess interest, penalties, and administrative costs pursuant to 31 U.S.C. 3717 and 4 CFR 102.13.

(k) Refunds.

(1) Where the Commission is the creditor agency, it shall promptly refund any amount deducted under the authority of 5 U.S.C. 5514 when:

(i) The debt is compromised or otherwise found not to be owing to the United States; or

(ii) An administrative or judicial order directs the Commission to make a refund.

(2) Unless required by law or contract, refunds under this paragraph (k) shall not bear interest.

(l) Request from a creditor agency for the services of a hearing official.

(1) The Commission may provide a hearing official upon request of the creditor agency when the debtor is employed by the Commission and the creditor agency cannot provide a prompt and appropriate hearing before a hearing official furnished pursuant to another lawful arrangement.

(2) The Commission may provide a hearing official upon request of a creditor agency when the debtor works for the creditor agency and that agency cannot arrange for a hearing official.

(3) The Director shall arrange for qualified personnel to serve as hearing officials.

(4) Services rendered under this paragraph (l) shall be provided on a fully reimbursable basis pursuant to 31 U.S.C. 1535.

(m) Non-waiver of rights by payments.

A debtor's payment, whether voluntary or involuntary, of all or any portion of a debt being collected pursuant to this section shall not be construed as a waiver of any rights that the debtor may have under any statute, regulation, or contract except as otherwise provided by law or contract.

(n) Exception to due process procedures.

The procedures set forth in this section shall not apply to adjustments described in 5 U.S.C. 5514(a)(3).

Sec. 201.205 Salary adjustments

Any negative adjustment to pay arising out of an employee's election of coverage, or a change in coverage, under a Federal benefits program requiring periodic deductions from pay shall not be considered collection of a "debt" for the purposes of this section if the amount to be recovered was accumulated over four pay periods or less. In such cases, the Commission need not comply with Sec. 201.204, but it will provide a clear and concise statement in the employee's earnings statement advising the employee of the previous overpayment at the time the adjustment is made.

Sec. 201.206 Administrative offset

(a) Collection.

The Director may collect a claim pursuant to 31 U.S.C. 3716 from a person, organization, or entity other than an agency of the United States Government by administrative offset of monies payable by the Government. Collection by administrative offset shall be undertaken where the claim is certain in amount, where offset is feasible and desirable and not otherwise prohibited, where the applicable statute of limitations has not expired, and where the offset is in the best interest of the United States.

(b) Offset prior to completion of procedures.

Prior to the completion of the procedures described in paragraph (c) of this section, the Commission may effect offset if:

(1) Failure to offset would substantially prejudice the Commission's ability to collect the debt; and

(2) The time before the payment is to be made does not reasonably permit completion of the procedures described in paragraph (c) of this section. Such prior offsetting shall be followed promptly by the completion of the procedures described in paragraph (c) of this section.

(c) Debtor's rights.

(1) Unless the procedures described in paragraph (b) of this section are used, prior to collecting any claim by administrative offset or referring such claim to another agency for collection through administrative offset, the Director shall provide the debtor with the following:

(i) Written notification of the nature and amount of the claim, the intention of the Director to collect the claim through administrative offset, and a statement of the rights of the debtor under this paragraph;

(ii) An opportunity to inspect and copy the records of the Commission not exempt from disclosure with respect to the claim;

(iii) An opportunity to have the Commission's determination of indebtedness reviewed by the Director. Any request for review by the debtor shall be in writing and be submitted to the Commission within 30 calendar days of the date of the notice of the offset. The Director may waive the time limit for requesting review for good cause shown by the debtor. The Commission shall provide the debtor with a reasonable opportunity for an oral hearing when:

(A) An applicable statute authorizes or requires the Commission to consider waiver of the indebtedness involved, the debtor requests waiver of the indebtedness, and the waiver determination turns on an issue of credibility or veracity; or

(B) The debtor requests reconsideration of the debt and the Commission determines that the question of the indebtedness cannot be resolved by review of the documentary evidence, for example, when the validity of the debt turns on an issue of credibility or veracity. Unless otherwise required by law, an oral hearing under this section is not required to be a formal evidentiary hearing, although the Commission shall document all significant matters discussed at the hearing. In those cases where an oral hearing is not required by this section, the Commission shall nevertheless accord the debtor a "paper hearing," (*i.e.*, the Commission will make its determination on the request for waiver or reconsideration based upon a review of the written record); and

(iv) An opportunity to enter into a written agreement for the repayment of the amount of the claim at the discretion of the Commission.

(2) If the procedures described in paragraph (b) of this section are employed, the procedures described in this paragraph shall be effected after offset.

(d) Interest.

Pursuant to 31 U.S.C. 3717 and 4 CFR 102.3, the Commission shall assess interest, penalties and administrative costs on debts owed to the United States. The Commission is authorized to assess interest and related charges on debts that are not subject to 31 U.S.C. 3717 to the extent authorized under the common law or other applicable statutory authority.

(e) Refunds.

Amounts recovered by offset but later found not to be owed to the Government shall be promptly refunded.

(f) Requests for offset to other Federal agencies.

The Director may request that a debt owed to the Commission be administratively offset against funds due and payable to a debtor by another Federal agency. In requesting administrative offset, the Commission, as creditor, will certify in writing to the Federal agency holding funds of the debtor:

(1) That the debtor owes the debt;

(2) The amount and basis of the debt; and

(3) That the Commission has complied with the requirements of its own administrative offset regulations and the applicable provisions of 4 CFR part 102 with respect to providing the debtor with due process.

(g) Requests for offset from other Federal agencies.

Any Federal agency may request that funds due and payable to its debtor by the Commission be administratively offset in order to collect a debt owed to such Federal agency by the debtor. The Commission shall initiate the requested offset only upon:

(1) Receipt of written certification from the creditor agency:

(i) That the debtor owes the debt;

(ii) The amount and basis of the debt;

(iii) That the agency has prescribed regulations for the exercise of administrative offset; and

(iv) That the agency has complied with its own administrative offset regulations and with the applicable provisions of 4 CFR part 102, including providing any required hearing or review.

(2) A determination by the Commission that collection by offset against funds payable by the Commission would be in the best interest of the United States as determined by the facts and circumstances of the particular case and that such offset would not otherwise be contrary to law.

Sec. 201.207 Administrative offset against amounts payable from Civil Service Retirement and Disability Fund

(a) Unless otherwise prohibited by law, the Commission may request that moneys which are due and payable to a debtor from the Civil Service Retirement and Disability Fund be administratively offset in reasonable amounts in order to collect in one full payment or a minimal number of payments debt owed to the Commission by the debtor. Such requests shall be made to the appropriate officials of the Office of Personnel Management in accordance with such regulations as may be prescribed by the Director of that Office.

(b) When making a request for administrative offset under paragraph (a) of this section, the Commission shall include a written certification that:

(1) The debtor owes the Commission a debt, including the amount of the debt;

(2) The Commission has complied with the applicable statutes, regulations, and procedures of the Office of Personnel Management; and

(3) The Commission has complied with the requirements of 4 CFR 102.3, including any required hearing or review.

(c) Once the Commission decides to request administrative offset under paragraph (a) of this section, it shall make the request as soon as practical after completion of the applicable procedures. This will satisfy any requirement that offset be initiated prior to expiration of the applicable statute of limitations. At such time as the debtor makes a claim for payments from the Fund, if at least a year has elapsed since the offset request was originally made, the debtor shall be permitted to offer a satisfactory repayment plan in lieu of offset upon establishing that changed financial circumstances would render the offset unjust.

(d) If the Commission collects part or all of the debt by other means before deductions are made or completed pursuant to paragraph (a) of this section, the Commission shall act promptly to modify or terminate its request for offset under paragraph (a) of this section.

Sec. 201.208 Tax refund offset

(a) Scope. The provisions of 26 U.S.C. 6402(d) and 31 U.S.C. 3720A authorize the Secretary of the Treasury to offset a delinquent debt owed to the United States Government from the tax refund due a taxpayer when other collection efforts have failed to recover the amount due.

(b) Definitions.

(1) Debt. Debt means money owed by an individual, organization or entity from sources which include loans insured or guaranteed by the United States and all other amounts due the United States from fees, leases, services, overpayments, civil and criminal penalties,

damages, interest, fines, administrative costs, and all other similar sources. A debt becomes eligible for tax refund offset procedures if:

(i) It cannot currently be collected pursuant to the salary offset procedures of 5 U.S.C. 5514(a)(1);

(ii) The debt is ineligible for administrative offset under 31 U.S.C. 3716(a) by reason of 31 U.S.C. 3716(c)(2) or cannot currently be collected by administrative offset under 31 U.S.C. 3716(a); and

(iii) The requirements of this section are otherwise satisfied.

(2) Dispute. A dispute is a written statement supported by documentation or other evidence that all or part of an alleged debt is not past due or legally enforceable, that the amount is not the amount currently owed, that the outstanding debt has been satisfied, or, in the case of a debt reduced to judgment, that the judgment has been satisfied or stayed.

(3) Notice. Notice means the information sent to the debtor pursuant to Sec. 201.208(d). The date of the notice is the date shown on the notice letter as its date of issuance.

(4) Past due. All judgment debts are past due for purposes of this section. Such debts remain past due until paid in full.

(c) The Commission may refer any past due, legally enforceable non-judgment debt of an individual, organization or entity to Treasury for offset if the Commission's or the referring agency's rights of action accrued more than three months but less than ten years before the offset is made. Debts reduced to judgment may be referred at any time. Debts in amounts lower than $25.00 are not subject to referral.

(d) The Commission will provide the debtor with written notice of its intent to offset before initiating the offset. Notice will be mailed to the debtor at the current address of the debtor, as determined from information obtained from the IRS pursuant to 26 U.S.C. 6103(m)(2), (4), (5) or from information regarding the debt maintained by the Commission. The notice sent to the debtor will state the amount of the debt and inform the debtor that:

(1) The debt is past due;

(2) The Commission intends to refer the debt to Treasury for offset from tax refunds that may be due to the taxpayer;

(3) The Commission intends to provide information concerning the delinquent debt exceeding $100 to a consumer reporting bureau unless such debt has already been disclosed; and

(4) The debtor has 65 calendar days from the date of notice in which to present evidence that all or part of the debt is not past due, that the amount is not the amount currently owed, that the outstanding debt has been satisfied, or, if a judgment debt, that the debt has been satisfied, or stayed, before the debt is reported to a consumer reporting agency, if applicable, and referred to Treasury for offset from tax refunds.

(e) If the debtor neither pays the amount due nor presents evidence that the amount is not past due or is satisfied or stayed, the Commission will report the debt to a consumer reporting agency at the end of the notice period, if applicable, and refer the debt to Treasury for offset from the taxpayer's federal tax refund. The Commission shall certify to Treasury that reasonable efforts have been made by the Commission to obtain payment of such debt.

(f) A debtor may request a review by the Commission if the debtor believes that all or part of the debt is not past due or is not legally enforceable, or, in the case of a judgment debt, that the debt has been stayed or the amount satisfied, as follows:

(1) The debtor must send a written request for review to the Director at the address provided in the notice.

(2) The request must state the amount disputed and the reasons why the debtor believes that the debt is not past due, is not legally enforceable, has been satisfied, or, if a judgment debt, has been satisfied or stayed.

(3) The request must include any documents that the debtor wishes to be considered or state that additional information will be submitted within the time permitted.

(4) If the debtor wishes to inspect records establishing the nature and amount of the debt, the debtor must make a written request to the Director for an opportunity for such an inspection. The office holding the relevant records not exempt from disclosure shall make them available for inspection during normal business hours within one week from the date of receipt of the request.

(5) The request for review and any additional information submitted pursuant to the request must be received by the Director at the address stated in the notice within 65 calendar days of the date of issuance of the notice.

(6) The Commission will review disputes and shall consider its records and any documentation and arguments submitted by the debtor. The Commission's decision to refer to Treasury any disputed portion of the debt shall be made by the Chairman. The Commission shall send a written notice of its decision to the debtor. There is no administrative appeal of this decision.

(7) If the evidence presented by the debtor is considered by a non-Commission agent or other entities or persons acting on the Commission's behalf, the debtor will be accorded at least 30 calendar days from the date the agent or other entity or person determines that all or part of the debt is past-due and legally enforceable to request review by an officer or employee of the Commission of any unresolved dispute.

(8) Any debt that previously has been reviewed pursuant to this section or any other section of this subpart, or that has been reduced to a judgment, may not be disputed except on the grounds of payments made or events occurring subsequent to the previous review or judgment.

(g) The Commission will notify Treasury of any change in the amount due promptly after receipt of payments or notice of other reductions.

(h) In the event that more than one debt is owed, the tax refund offset procedure will be applied in the order in which the debts became past due.

CODE OF FEDERAL REGULATIONS
TITLE 19—CUSTOMS DUTIES
CHAPTER II—UNITED STATES INTERNATIONAL TRADE COMMISSION
SUBCHAPTER C—INVESTIGATIONS OF UNFAIR PRACTICES IN IMPORT TRADE
PART 210—ADJUDICATION AND ENFORCEMENT

Subpart A—Rules of General Applicability

Sec. 210.1 Applicability of part

The rules in this part apply to investigations under section 337 of the Tariff Act of 1930 and related proceedings. These rules are authorized by sections 333, 335, or 337 of the Tariff Act of 1930 (19 U.S.C. Secs. 1333, 1335, and 1337) and sections 2 and 1342(d)(1)(B) of the Omnibus Trade and Competitiveness Act of 1988, Pub. L. No. 100-418, 102 Stat. 1107 (1988).

Sec. 210.2 General policy

It is the policy of the Commission that, to the extent practicable and consistent with requirements of law, all investigations and related proceedings under this part shall be conducted expeditiously. The parties, their attorneys or other representatives, and the presiding administrative law judge shall make every effort at each stage of the investigation or related proceeding to avoid delay.

Sec. 210.3 Definitions

As used in this part—

Administrative law judge means the person appointed under section 3105 of title 5 of the United States Code who presides over the taking of evidence in an investigation under this part. If the Commission so orders or a section of this part so provides, an administrative law judge also may preside over stages of a related proceeding under this part.

Commission investigative attorney means a Commission attorney designated to engage in investigatory activities in an investigation or a related proceeding under this part.

Complainant means a person who has filed a complaint with the Commission under this part, alleging a violation of section 337 of the Tariff Act of 1930.

Intervenor means a person who has been granted leave by the Commission to intervene as a party to an investigation or a related proceeding under this part.

Investigation means a formal Commission inquiry instituted to determine whether there is a violation of section 337 of the Tariff Act of 1930. An investigation is instituted upon publication of a notice in the Federal Register. The investigation entails postinstitution adjudication of the complaint. An investigation can also involve the processing of one or more of the following: A motion to amend the complaint and notice of investigation; a motion for temporary relief; a motion to designate "more complicated" the temporary relief stage of the investigation; an interlocutory appeal of an administrative law judge's decision on a particular matter; a motion for sanctions for abuse of process, abuse of discovery, or failure to make or cooperate in discovery, which if granted, would have an impact on the adjudication of the merits of the complaint; a petition for reconsideration of a final Commission determination; a motion for termination of the investigation in whole or part; and procedures undertaken in response to a judgment or judicial order issued in an appeal of a Commission determination or remedial order issued under section 337 of the Tariff Act of 1930.

Party means each complainant, respondent, intervenor, or Commission investigative attorney.

Proposed intervenor means any person who has filed a motion to intervene in an investigation or a related proceeding under this part.

Proposed respondent means any person named in a complaint filed under this part as allegedly violating section 337 of the Tariff Act of 1930.

Related proceeding means preinstitution proceedings, sanction proceedings (for the possible issuance of sanctions that would not have a bearing on the adjudication of the merits of a complaint or a motion under this part), bond forfeiture proceedings, proceedings to enforce, modify, or revoke a remedial or consent order, or advisory opinion proceedings.

Respondent means any person named in a notice of investigation issued under this part as allegedly violating section 337 of the Tariff Act of 1930.

Sec. 210.4 Written submissions; representations; sanctions

(a) Caption; names of parties.

The front page of every written submission filed by a party or a proposed party to an investigation or a related proceeding under this part shall contain a caption setting forth the name of the Commission, the title of the investigation or related proceeding, the docket number or investigation number, if any, assigned to the investigation or related proceeding, and in the case of a complaint, the names of the complainant and all proposed respondents.

(b) Signature.

Every pleading, written motion, and other paper of a party or proposed party who is represented by an attorney in an investigation or a related proceeding under this part shall be signed by at least one attorney of record in the attorney's individual name. A party or proposed party who is not represented by an attorney shall sign, or his duly authorized officer or agent shall sign, the pleading, written motion, or other paper. Each paper shall state the signer's address and telephone number, if any. Pleadings, written motions, and other papers need not be under oath or accompanied by an affidavit, except as provided in Secs. 210.12(a)(1), 210.13(b), 210.18, 210.52(d), 210.59(b), or another section of this part or by order of the administrative law judge or the Commission. If a pleading, motion, or other paper is not signed, it shall be stricken unless it is signed promptly after omission of the signature is called to the attention of the submitter.

(c) Representations.

By presenting to the presiding administrative law judge or the Commission (whether by signing, filing, submitting, or later advocating) a pleading, written motion, or other paper, an attorney or unrepresented party or proposed party is certifying that to the best of the person's knowledge, information, and belief, formed after an inquiry reasonable under the circumstances—

(1) it is not being presented for any improper purpose, such as to harass or to cause unnecessary delay or needless increase in the cost of the investigation or related proceeding;

(2) the claims, defenses, and other legal contentions therein are warranted by existing law or by a nonfrivolous argument for the extension, modification, or reversal of existing law or the establishment of new law;

(3) the allegations and other factual contentions have evidentiary support or, if specifically so identified, are likely to have evidentiary support after a reasonable opportunity for further investigation or discovery; and

(4) the denials of factual contentions are warranted on the evidence or, if specifically so identified, are reasonably based on a lack of information or belief.

(d) Sanctions.

If, after notice and a reasonable opportunity to respond (see paragraphs (d)(1) (i) and (ii) of this section and Sec. 210.25), the presiding administrative law judge or the Commission determines that paragraph (c) of this section has been violated, the administrative law judge or the Commission may, subject to the conditions stated below and in Sec. 210.25, impose an appropriate sanction upon the attorneys, law firms, or parties that have violated paragraph (c) or are responsible for the violation. A representation need not be frivolous in its entirety in order for the administrative law judge or the Commission to determine that paragraph (c) has been violated. If any portion of a representation is found to be false, frivolous, misleading, or otherwise in violation of paragraph (c), a sanction may be imposed. In determining whether paragraph (c) has been violated, the administrative law judge or the Commission will consider whether the representation or disputed portion thereof was objectively reasonable under the circumstances.

(1) How initiated.

(i) By motion. A motion for sanctions under this section shall be made separately from other motions or requests and shall describe the specific conduct alleged to violate paragraph (c). It shall be served as provided in paragraph (g) of this section, but shall not be filed with or presented to the presiding administrative law judge or the Commission unless, within seven days after service of the motion (or such other period as the administrative law judge or the Commission may prescribe), the challenged paper, claim, defense, contention, allegation, or denial is not withdrawn or appropriately corrected. See also Sec. 210.25 (a) through (c). If warranted, the administrative law judge or the Commission may award to the party or proposed party prevailing on the motion the reasonable expenses and attorney's fees incurred in presenting or opposing the motion. Absent exceptional circumstances, a law firm shall be held jointly responsible for violations committed by its partners, associates, and employees.

(ii) On the administrative law judge's or the Commission's initiative. The administrative law judge or the Commission may enter an order *sua sponte* describing the specific conduct that appears to violate paragraph (c) of this section and directing an attorney, law firm, party, or proposed party to show cause why it has not violated paragraph (c) with respect thereto.

(2) Nature of sanctions; limitations. A sanction imposed for violation of paragraph (c) of this section shall be limited to what is sufficient to deter repetition of such conduct or comparable conduct by others similarly situated. Subject to the limitations in paragraphs (d)(2) (i) through (iv) of this section, the sanction may consist of, or include, directives of a nonmonetary nature, an order to pay a penalty, or, if imposed on motion and warranted for effective deterrence, an order directing payment to the movant of some or all of the reasonable attorney's fees and other expenses incurred as a direct result of the violation.

(i) Monetary sanctions shall not be imposed under this section against the United States, the Commission, or a Commission investigative attorney.

(ii) Monetary sanctions may not be awarded against a represented party or proposed party for a violation of paragraph (c)(2) of this section.

(iii) Monetary sanctions may not be imposed on the administrative law judge's or the Commission's initiative unless—

(a) The Commission or the administrative law judge issues an order to show cause before the investigation or related proceeding is terminated, in whole or in relevant part, as to the party or proposed party which is, or whose attorneys are, to be sanctioned; and

(b) such termination is the result of—

(1) A motion to withdraw the complaint, motion, or petition that was the basis for the investigation or related proceeding;

(2) A settlement agreement;

(3) A consent order agreement; or

(4) An arbitration agreement.

(iv) Monetary sanctions imposed to compensate the Commission for expenses incurred by a Commission investigative attorney or the Commission's Office of Unfair Import Investigations will include reimbursement for some or all costs reasonably incurred as a direct result of the violation, but will not include attorney's fees.

(3) Order. When imposing sanctions, the administrative law judge or the Commission shall describe the conduct determined to constitute a violation of this rule and explain the basis for the sanction imposed. See also Sec. 210.25(d)-(f).

(e) Inapplicability to discovery.

Paragraphs (c) and (d) of this section do not apply to discovery requests, responses, objections, and motions that are subject to provisions of Secs. 210.27 through 210.34.

(f) Specifications; filing of documents.

(1) (i) Written submissions that are addressed to the Commission during an investigation or a related proceeding shall comply with Sec. 201.8 of this chapter, except for the provisions regarding the number of copies to be submitted. The required number of copies shall be governed by paragraph (f)(2) of this section. Written submissions may be produced by standard typographic printing or by a duplicating or copying process which produces a clear black image on white paper. If the submission is produced by other than the standard typographical process used by commercial printers, typed matter shall not exceed 6 1/2 by 9 1/2 inches using 10-pitch (pica) or larger pitch type or 5 1/2 by 8 1/2

inches using 11-point or larger proportional spacing type, and shall be double-spaced between each line of text using the standard of 6 lines of type per inch. Text and footnotes shall be in the same size type. Quotations more than two lines long in the text or footnotes may be indented and single-spaced. Headings and footnotes may be single-spaced.

(ii) The administrative law judge may impose any specifications he deems appropriate for submissions that are addressed to the administrative law judge.

(2) Unless the Commission or another section of this part specifically states otherwise, the original and 6 true copies of each submission shall be filed if the investigation or related proceeding is before an administrative law judge, and the original and 14 true copies of each submission shall be filed if the investigation or related proceeding is before the Commission.

(3)(i) If a complaint, a supplement to a complaint, a motion for temporary relief, or the documentation supporting a motion for temporary relief contains confidential business information as defined in Sec. 201.6(a) of this chapter, the complainant shall file nonconfidential copies of the complaint, the supplement to the complaint, the motion for temporary relief, or the documentation supporting the motion for temporary relief concurrently with the requisite confidential copies, as provided in Sec. 210.8(a) of this part.

(ii) Persons who file the following submissions that contain confidential business information covered by an administrative protective order, or that are the subject of a request for confidential treatment, must file nonconfidential copies and serve them on the other parties to the investigation or related proceeding within 10 calendar days after filing the confidential version with the Commission:

(a) A response to a complaint and all supplements and exhibits thereto;

(b) All submissions relating to a motion to amend the complaint or notice of investigation; and

(c) All submissions addressed to the Commission. Other sections of this part may require, or the Commission or the administrative law judge may order, the filing and service of nonconfidential copies of other kinds of confidential submissions. If the submitter's ability to prepare a nonconfidential copy is dependent upon receipt of the nonconfidential version of an initial determination, or a Commission order or opinion, or a ruling by the administrative law judge or the Commission as to whether some or all of the information at issue is entitled to confidential treatment, the nonconfidential copies of the submission must be filed within 10 calendar days after service of the Commission or administrative law judge document in question. The time periods for filing specified in this paragraph apply unless the Commission, the administrative law judge, or another section of this part specifically provides otherwise.

(g) Service.

Unless the Commission, the administrative law judge, or another section of this part specifically provides otherwise, every written submission filed by a party or proposed party shall be served on all other parties in the manner specified in Sec. 201.16(b) of this chapter.

Sec. 210.5 Confidential business information

(a) Definition and submission.

Confidential business information shall be defined and identified in accordance with Sec. 201.6 (a) and (c) of this chapter. Unless the Commission, the administrative law judge, or another section of this part states otherwise, confidential business information shall be submitted in accordance with Sec. 201.6(b) of this chapter. In the case of a complaint, any supplement to the complaint, and a motion for temporary relief filed under this part, the number of nonconfidential copies shall be prescribed by Sec. 210.8(a) of this part.

(b) Restrictions on disclosure.

Information submitted to the Commission or exchanged among the parties in connection with an investigation or a related proceeding under this part, which is properly designated confidential under paragraph (a) of this section and Sec. 201.6(a) of this chapter, may not be disclosed to anyone other than the following persons without the consent of the submitter:

(1) Persons who are granted access to confidential information under Sec. 210.39(a) or a protective order issued pursuant to Sec. 210.34(a);

(2) An officer or employee of the Commission who is directly concerned with—

(i) Carrying out or maintaining the records of the investigation or related proceeding for which the information was submitted;

(ii) The administration of a bond posted pursuant to subsection (e), (f), or (j) of section 337 of the Tariff Act of 1930;

(iii) The administration or enforcement of an exclusion order issued pursuant to subsection (d), (e), or (g), a cease and desist order issued pursuant to subsection (f), or a consent order issued pursuant to subsection (c) of section 337 of the Tariff Act of 1930; or

(iv) Proceedings for the modification or rescission of a temporary or permanent order issued under subsection (d), (e), (f), (g), or (i) of section 337 of the Tariff Act of 1930, or a consent order issued under section 337 of the Tariff Act of 1930;

(3) An officer or employee of the United States Government who is directly involved in a review conducted pursuant to section 337(j) of the Tariff Act of 1930; or

(4) An officer or employee of the United States Customs Service who is directly involved in administering an exclusion from entry under section 337 (d), (e), or (g) of the Tariff Act of 1930 resulting from the investigation or related proceeding in connection with which the information was submitted.

(c) Transmission of certain records to district court.

Notwithstanding paragraph (b) of this section, confidential business information may be transmitted to a district court and be admissible in a civil action, subject to such protective order as the district court determines necessary, pursuant to 28 U.S.C. 1659.

(d) Confidentiality determinations in preinstitution proceedings.

After a complaint is filed under section 337 of the Tariff Act of 1930 and before an investigation is instituted by the Commission, confidential business information designated confidential by the supplier shall be submitted in accordance with Sec. 201.6(b) of this chapter. The Secretary shall decide, in accordance with Sec. 201.6(d) of this chapter, whether the information is entitled to confidential treatment. Appeals from the ruling of the Secretary shall be made to the Commission as set forth in Sec. 201.6(e) and (f) of this chapter.

(e) Confidentiality determinations in investigations and other related proceedings.

(1) If an investigation is instituted or if a related proceeding is assigned to an administrative law judge, the administrative law judge shall set the ground rules for the designation, submission, and handling of information designated confidential by the submitter. When requested to do so, the administrative law judge shall decide whether information in a document addressed to the administrative law judge, or to be exchanged among the parties while the administrative law judge is presiding, is entitled to confidential treatment. The administrative law judge shall also decide, with respect to all orders, initial determinations, or other documents issued by the administrative law judge, whether information designated confidential by the supplier is entitled to confidential treatment. The supplier of the information or the person seeking the information may, with leave of the administrative law judge, request an appeal to the Commission of the administrative law judge's unfavorable ruling on this issue, under Sec. 210.24(b)(2).

(2) The Commission may continue protective orders issued by the administrative law judge, amend or revoke those orders, or issue new ones. All submissions addressed to the Commission that contain information covered by an existing protective order will be given confidential treatment. (See also Sec. 210.72.) New information that is submitted to the Commission, designated confidential by the supplier, and not covered by an existing protective order must be submitted to the Secretary with a request for confidential treatment in accordance with Sec. 201.6(b) and (c) of this chapter. The Secretary shall decide, in accordance with Sec. 201.6(d) of this chapter, whether the information is entitled to confidential treatment. Appeals from the ruling of the Secretary shall be made to the Commission as provided in Sec. 201.6(e) and (f) of this chapter. The Commission shall decide, with respect to all orders, notices, opinions, and other documents issued by or on behalf of the Commission, whether information designated confidential by the supplier is entitled to confidential treatment.

Sec. 210.6 Computation of time, additional hearings, postponements, continuances, and extensions of time

Unless the Commission, the administrative law judge, or another section of this part specifically provides otherwise, the computation of time and the granting of additional hearings, postponements, continuances, and extensions of time shall be in accordance with Secs. 201.14 and 201.16(d) of this chapter. Whenever a party has the right or is required to perform some act or to take some action within a prescribed period after service of a document upon it, and the document was served by mail, the deadline shall be computed by adding to the end of the prescribed period the additional time allotted under Sec. 201.16(d), unless the Commission, the administrative law judge, or another section of this part specifically provides otherwise.

Sec. 210.7 Service of process and other documents; publication of notices

(a) Manner of service.

The service of process and all documents issued by or on behalf of the Commission or the administrative law judge—and the service of all documents issued by parties under Secs. 210.27 through 210.34 of this part—shall be in accordance with Sec. 201.16 of this chapter, unless the Commission, the administrative law judge, or another section of this part specifically provides otherwise.

(b) Publication of notices.

(1) Notice of action by the Commission or an administrative law judge will be published in the Federal Register only as specifically provided in paragraph (b)(2) of this section, by another section in this chapter, or by order of an administrative law judge or the Commission.

(2) When an administrative law judge or the Commission determines to amend or supplement a notice published in accordance with paragraph (b)(1) of this section, notice of the amendment will be published in the Federal Register.

Subpart B—Commencement of Preinstitution Proceedings and Investigations

Sec. 210.8 Commencement of preinstitution proceedings

(a) Upon receipt of complaint.

A preinstitution proceeding is commenced by filing with the Secretary a signed original complaint and the requisite number of true copies. The complainant shall file 14 confidential copies of the complaint, 14 nonconfidential copies, plus one confidential copy and one nonconfidential copy for each person named in the complaint as violating section 337 of the Tariff Act of 1930, and one nonconfidential copy for the government of each foreign country of any person or persons so named. The same requirements apply for the filing of a supplement to the complaint. If the complainant is seeking temporary relief, the complainant must file 14 confidential copies of the motion, 14 nonconfidential copies, plus one additional confidential copy and one additional nonconfidential copy of the motion for such relief for each proposed respondent, and one nonconfidential copy for the government of the foreign country of the proposed respondent. The additional copies of the complaint and motion for temporary relief for each proposed respondent and the appropriate foreign government are to be provided notwithstanding the procedures applicable to a motion for temporary relief, which require service of the complaint and motion for temporary relief by the complainant.

(b) Upon the initiative of the Commission.

The Commission may upon its initiative commence a preinstitution proceeding based upon any alleged violation of section 337 of the Tariff Act of 1930.

Sec. 210.9 Action of Commission upon receipt of complaint

Upon receipt of a complaint alleging violation of section 337 of the Tariff Act of 1930, the Commission shall take the following actions:

(a) Examination of complaint. The Commission shall examine the complaint for sufficiency and compliance with the applicable sections of this chapter.

(b) Informal investigatory activity. The Commission shall identify sources of relevant information, assure itself of the availability thereof, and, if deemed necessary, prepare subpoenas therefore, and give attention to other preliminary matters.

Sec. 210.10 Institution of investigation

(a)(1) The Commission shall determine whether the complaint is properly filed and whether an investigation should be instituted on the basis of the complaint. That determination shall be made within 30 days after the complaint is filed, unless—

(i) Exceptional circumstances preclude adherence to a 30-day deadline;

(ii) Additional time is allotted under other sections of this part in connection with the preinstitution processing of a motion by the complainant for temporary relief;

(iii) The complainant requests that the Commission postpone the determination on whether to institute an investigation; or

(iv) The complainant withdraws the complaint.

(2) If exceptional circumstances preclude Commission adherence to the 30-day deadline for determining whether to institute an investigation on the basis of the complaint, the determination will be made as soon after that deadline as possible.

(3) If additional time is allotted in connection with the preinstitution processing of a motion by the complainant for temporary relief, the Commission will determine whether to institute an investigation and provisionally accept the motion within 35 days after the filing of the complaint or by a subsequent deadline computed in accordance with Sec. 210.53(a), Sec. 210.54, Sec. 210.55(b), Sec. 210.57, or Sec. 210.58 as applicable.

(4) If the complainant desires to have the Commission postpone making a determination on whether to institute an investigation in response to the complaint, the complainant must file a written request with the Secretary. If the request is granted, the determination will be rescheduled for whatever date is appropriate in light of the facts.

(5)(i) The complainant may withdraw the complaint as a matter of right at any time before the Commission votes on whether to institute an investigation. To effect such withdrawal, the complainant must file a written notice with the Commission. If the complaint is being withdrawn pursuant to a settlement agreement, a copy of the agreement must be filed with the Commission along with the notice of withdrawal. If the agreement contains confidential business information within the meaning of Sec. 201.6(a) of this chapter, at least one copy of the agreement with such information deleted shall accompany the motion, in addition to a copy of the confidential version.

(ii) If a motion for temporary relief was filed in addition to the complaint, the motion must be withdrawn along with the complaint, and the complainant must serve copies of the notice of withdrawal on all proposed respondents and on the embassies that were served with copies of the complaint and motion pursuant to Sec. 210.54.

(b) An investigation shall be instituted by the publication of a notice in the Federal Register. The notice will define the scope of the investigation and may be amended as provided in Sec. 210.14 (b) and (c).

(c) If the Commission determines not to institute an investigation on the basis of the complaint, the complaint shall be dismissed, and the complainant and all proposed respondents will receive written notice of the Commission's action and the reason(s) therefor.

Sec. 210.11 Service of complaint and notice of investigation

(a)(1) Notwithstanding the provisions of Sec. 210.54 requiring service of the complaint by the complainant, the Commission, upon institution of an investigation, shall serve copies of the complaint and the notice of investigation (and any accompanying motion for temporary relief) upon each respondent and the embassy in Washington, DC of the government of each foreign country represented by each respondent. All respondents named after an investigation has been instituted and the governments of the foreign countries they represent shall be served as soon as possible after the respondents are named.

(2) The Commission shall serve copies of the notice of investigation upon the U.S. Department of Health and Human Services, the U.S. Department of Justice, the Federal Trade Commission, the U.S. Customs Service, and such other agencies and departments as the Commission considers appropriate.

(b) With leave from the presiding administrative law judge, a party may attempt to effect personal service of the complaint and notice of investigation upon a respondent, if the Secretary's efforts to serve the respondent by certified mail have been unsuccessful. If the party succeeds in serving the respondent by personal service, the party must notify the administrative law judge and file proof of such service with the Secretary.

Subpart C—Pleadings

Sec. 210.12 The complaint

(a) Contents of the complaint.

In addition to conforming with the requirements of Sec. 201.8 of this chapter and Secs. 210.4 and 210.5 of this part, the complaint shall—

(1) Be under oath and signed by the complainant or his duly authorized officer, attorney, or agent, with the name, address, and telephone number of the complainant and any such officer, attorney, or agent given on the first page of the complaint;

(2) Include a statement of the facts constituting the alleged unfair methods of competition and unfair acts;

(3) Describe specific instances of alleged unlawful importations or sales, and shall provide the Tariff Schedules of the United States item number(s) for importations occurring prior to January 1, 1989, and the Harmonized Tariff Schedule of the United States item number(s) for importations occurring on or after January 1, 1989;

(4) State the name, address, and nature of the business (when such nature is known) of each person alleged to be violating section 337 of the Tariff Act of 1930;

(5) Include a statement as to whether the alleged unfair methods of competition and unfair acts, or the subject matter thereof, are or have been the subject of any court or agency litigation, and, if so, include a brief summary of such litigation;

(6)(i) If the complaint alleges a violation of section 337 based on infringement of a U.S. patent, or a federally registered copyright, trademark, or mask work, under section 337(a)(1) (B), (C), or (D) of the Tariff Act of 1930, include a description of the relevant domestic industry as defined in section 337(a)(3) that allegedly exists or is in the process of being established, including the relevant operations of any licensees. Relevant information includes but is not limited to:

(a) Significant investment in plant and equipment;

(b) Significant employment of labor or capital; or

(c) Substantial investment in the exploitation of the subject patent, copyright, trademark, or mask work, including engineering, research and development, or licensing; or

(ii) If the complaint alleges a violation of section 337 of the Tariff Act of 1930 based on unfair methods of competition and unfair acts that have the threat or effect of destroying or substantially injuring an industry in the United States or preventing the establishment of such an industry under section 337(a)(1)(A) (i) or (ii), include a description of the domestic industry affected, including the relevant operations of any licensees; or

(iii) If the complaint alleges a violation of section 337 of the Tariff Act of 1930 based on unfair methods of competition or unfair acts that have the threat or effect of restraining or monopolizing trade and commerce in the United States under section 337(a)(1)(A)(iii), include a description of the trade and commerce affected.

(7) Include a description of the complainant's business and its interests in the relevant domestic industry or the relevant trade and commerce. For every intellectual property based complaint (regardless of the type of intellectual property right involved), include a showing that at least one complainant is the owner or exclusive licensee of the subject intellectual property; and

(8) If the alleged violation involves an unfair method of competition or an unfair act other than those listed in paragraph (a)(6)(i) of this section, state a specific theory and provide corroborating data to support the allegation(s) in the complaint concerning the existence of a threat or effect to destroy or substantially injure a domestic industry, to prevent the establishment of a domestic industry, or to restrain or monopolize trade and commerce in the United States. The information that should ordinarily be provided includes the volume and trend of production, sales, and inventories of the involved domestic article; a description of the facilities and number and type of workers employed in the production of the involved domestic article; profit-and-loss information covering overall operations and operations concerning the involved domestic article; pricing information with respect to the involved domestic article; when available, volume and sales of imports; and other pertinent data.

(9) Include, when a complaint is based upon the infringement of a valid and enforceable U.S. patent—

(i) The identification of each U.S. letters patent and a certified copy thereof (a legible copy of each such patent will suffice for each required copy of the complaint);

(ii) The identification of the ownership of each involved U.S. letters patent and a certified copy of each assignment of each such patent (a legible copy thereof will suffice for each required copy of the complaint);

(iii) The identification of each licensee under each involved U.S. letters patent;

(iv) When known, a list of each foreign patent, each foreign patent application (not already issued as a patent), and each foreign patent application that has been denied corresponding to each involved U.S. letters patent, with an indication of the prosecution status of each such foreign patent application;

(v) A nontechnical description of the invention of each involved U.S. letters patent;

(vi) A reference to the specific claims in each involved U.S. letters patent that allegedly cover the article imported or sold by each person named as violating section 337 of the Tariff Act of 1930, or the process under which such article was produced;

(vii) A showing that each person named as violating section 337 of the Tariff Act of 1930 is importing or selling the article covered by, or produced under the involved process covered by, the above specific claims of each involved U.S. letters patent. The complainant shall make such showing by appropriate allegations, and when practicable, by a chart that applies an exemplary claim of each involved U.S. letters patent to a representative involved domestic article or process and to a representative involved article of each person named as violating section 337 of the Tariff Act or to the process under which such article was produced; and

(viii) Drawings, photographs, or other visual representations of both the involved domestic article or process and the involved article of each person named as violating section 337 of the Tariff Act of 1930, or of the process utilized in pro ducing the imported article, and, when a chart is furnished under paragraph (a)(9)(vii) of this section, the parts of such drawings, photographs, or other visual representations should be labeled so that they can be read in conjunction with such chart; and

(10) Contain a request for relief, and if temporary relief is requested under section 337 (e) and/or (f) of the Tariff Act of 1930, a motion for such relief shall accompany the complaint as provided in Sec. 210.52(a) or may follow the complaint as provided in Sec. 210.53(a).

(b) Submissions of articles as exhibits.

At the time the complaint is filed, if practicable, the complainant shall submit both the domestic article and all imported articles that are the subject of the complaint.

(c) Additional material to accompany each patent-based complaint.

There shall accompany the submission of the original of each complaint based upon the alleged unauthorized importation or sale of an article covered by, or produced under a process covered by, the claims of a valid U.S. letters patent the following:

(1) Three copies of each license agreement arising out of each involved U.S. letters patent, except that, to the extent that a standard license agreement is used, three copies of the standard license agreement and a list of the licensees operating under such agreement will suffice;

(2) One certified copy of the U.S. Patent and Trademark Office prosecution history for each involved U.S. letters patent, plus three additional copies thereof; and

(3) Four copies of each patent and applicable pages of each technical reference mentioned in the prosecution history of each involved U.S. letters patent.

(d) Additional material to accompany each registered trademark-based complaint.

There shall accompany the submission of the original of each complaint based upon the alleged unauthorized importation or sale of an article covered by a Federally registered trademark, one certified copy of the Federal registration and three additional copies, three copies of each license agreement (if any) concerning use of the trademark, except that if a standard license agreement is used, three copies of that agreement and a list of the licensees operating under it will suffice;

(e) Additional material to accompany each complaint based on a non- Federally registered trademark.

There shall accompany the submission of the original of each complaint based upon the alleged unauthorized importation or sale of an article covered by a non-Federally registered trademark the following:

(1) A detailed and specific description of the alleged trademark;

(2) Information concerning prior attempts to register the alleged trademark; and

(3) Information on the status of current attempts to register the alleged trademark.

(f) Additional material to accompany each copyright-based complaint.

There shall accompany the submission of the original of each complaint based upon the alleged unauthorized importation or sale of an article covered by a copyright one certified copy of the Federal registration and three additional copies, three copies of each license agreement (if any) concerning use of the copyright, except that if a standard license agreement is used, three copies of that agreement and a list of the licensees operating under it will suffice;

(g) Additional material to accompany each registered mask work-based complaint.

There shall accompany the submission of the original of each complaint based upon the alleged unauthorized importation or sale of a semiconductor chip in a manner that constitutes infringement of a Federally registered mask work, one certified copy of the Federal registration and three additional copies, three copies of each license agreement (if any) concerning use of the mask work, except that if a standard license agreement is used, three copies of that agreement and a list of the licensees operating under it will suffice;

(h) Duty to supplement complaint.

Complainant shall supplement the complaint prior to institution of an investigation if complainant obtains information upon the basis of which he knows or reasonably should know that a material legal or factual assertion in the complaint is false or misleading.

Sec. 210.13 The response

(a) Time for response.

Except as provided in Sec. 210.59(a) and unless otherwise ordered in the notice of investigation or by the administrative law judge, respondents shall have 20 days from the date of service of the complaint and notice of investigation, by the Commission under Sec. 210.11(a) or by a party under Sec. 210.11(b), within which to file a written response to the complaint and the notice of investigation. When the investigation involves a motion for temporary relief and has not been declared "more complicated," the response to the complaint and notice of investigation must be filed along with the response to the motion for temporary relief—*i.e.*, within 10 days after service of the complaint, notice of investigation, and the motion for temporary relief by the Commission under Sec. 210.11(a) or by a party under Sec. 210.11(b). (See Sec. 210.59.)

(b) Content of the response.

In addition to conforming to the requirements of Sec. 201.8 of this chapter and Secs. 210.4 and 210.5 of this part, each response shall be under oath and signed by respondent or his duly authorized officer, attorney, or agent with the name, address, and telephone number of the respondent and any such officer, attorney, or agent given on the first page of the response. Each respondent shall respond to each allegation in the complaint and in the notice of investigation, and shall set forth a concise statement of the facts constituting each ground of defense. There shall be a specific admission, denial, or explanation of each fact alleged in the complaint and notice, or if the respondent is without knowledge of any such fact, a statement to that effect. Allegations of a complaint and notice not thus answered may be deemed to have been admitted. Each response shall include, when available, statistical data on the quantity and value of imports of the involved article. Respondents who are importers must also provide the Harmonized Tariff Schedule item number(s) for importations of the accused imports occurring on or after January 1, 1989, and the Tariff Schedules of the United States item number(s) for importations occurring before January 1, 1989. Each response shall also include a statement concerning the respondent's capacity to produce the subject article and the relative significance of the United States market to its operations. Respondents who are not manufacturing their accused imports shall state the name and address of the supplier(s) of those imports. Affirmative defenses shall be pleaded with as much specificity as possible in the response. When the alleged unfair methods of competition and unfair acts are based upon the claims of a valid U.S. letters patent, the respondent is encouraged to make the following showing when appropriate:

(1) If it is asserted in defense that the article imported or sold by respondents is not covered by, or produced under a process covered by, the claims of each involved U.S. letters patent, a showing of such noncoverage for each involved claim in each U.S. letters patent in question shall be made, which showing may be made by appropriate allegations and, when practicable, by a chart that applies the involved claims of each U.S. letters patent in question to a representative involved imported article of the respondent or to the process under which such article was produced;

(2) Drawings, photographs, or other visual representations of the involved imported article of respondent or the process utilized in producing such article, and, when a chart is furnished under paragraph (b)(1) of this section, the parts of such drawings, photographs, or other visual representations, should be labeled so that they can be read in conjunction with such chart; and

(3) If the claims of any involved U.S. letters patent are asserted to be invalid or unenforceable, the basis for such assertion, including, when prior art is relied on, a showing of how the prior art renders each claim invalid or unenforceable and a copy of such prior art. For good cause, the presiding administrative law judge may waive any of the substantive requirements imposed under this paragraph or may impose additional requirements.

(c) Submission of article as exhibit.

At the time the response is filed, if practicable, the respondent shall submit the accused article imported or sold by that respondent, unless the article has already been submitted by the complainant.

Sec. 210.14 Amendments to pleadings and notice; supplemental submissions; counterclaims

(a) Preinstitution amendments.

The complaint may be amended at any *sua sponte* time prior to the institution of the investigation.

(b) Postinstitution amendments generally.

(1) After an investigation has been instituted, the complaint or notice of investigation may be amended only by leave of the Commission for good cause shown and upon such conditions as are necessary to avoid prejudicing the public interest and the rights of the parties to the investigation. A motion for amendment must be made to the presiding administrative law judge. If the proposed amendment of the complaint would require amending the notice of investigation, the presiding administrative law judge may grant the motion only by filing with the Commission an initial determination. All other dispositions of such motions shall be by order.

(2) If disposition of the issues in an investigation on the merits will be facilitated, or for other good cause shown, the presiding administrative law judge may allow appropriate amendments to pleadings other than complaints upon such conditions as are necessary to avoid prejudicing the public interest and the rights of the parties to the investigation.

(c) Postinstitution amendments to conform to evidence.

When issues not raised by the pleadings or notice of investigation, but reasonably within the scope of the pleadings and notice, are considered during the taking of evidence by express or implied consent of the parties, they shall be treated in all respects as if they had been raised in the pleadings and notice. Such amendments of the pleadings and notice as may be necessary to make them conform to the evidence and to raise such issues shall be allowed at any time, and shall be effective with respect to all parties who have expressly or impliedly consented.

(d) Supplemental submissions.

The administrative law judge may, upon reasonable notice and on such terms as are just, permit service of a supplemental submission setting forth transactions, occurrences, or events that have taken place since the date of the submission sought to be supplemented and that are relevant to any of the issues involved.

(e) Counterclaims.

At any time after institution of the investigation, but not later than ten business days before the commencement of the evidentiary hearing, a respondent may file a counterclaim at the Commission in accordance with section 337(c) of the Tariff Act of 1930. Counterclaims shall be filed in a separate document. A respondent who files such a counterclaim shall immediately file a notice of removal with a United States district court in which venue for any of the counterclaims raised by the respondent would exist under 28 U.S.C. 1391.

Subpart D—Motions

Sec. 210.15 Motions

(a) Presentation and disposition.

(1) During the period between the institution of an investigation and the assignment of the investigation to a presiding administrative law judge, all motions shall be addressed to the chief administrative law judge. During the time that an investigation or related proceeding is before an administrative law judge, all motions therein shall be addressed to the administrative law judge.

(2) When an investigation or related proceeding is before the Commission, all motions shall be addressed to the Chairman of the Commission. A motion to amend the complaint and notice of investigation to name an additional respondent after institution shall be served on the proposed respondent. All motions shall be filed with the Secretary and shall be served upon each party.

(b) Content.

All written motions shall state the particular order, ruling, or action desired and the grounds therefor.

(c) Responses to motions.

Within 10 days after service of any written motions, or within such longer or shorter time as may be designated by the administrative law judge or the Commission, a nonmoving party, or in the instance of a motion to amend the complaint or notice of investigation to name an additional respondent after institution, the proposed respondent, shall respond or he may be deemed to have consented to the granting of the relief asked for in the motion. The moving party shall have no right to reply, except as permitted by the administrative law judge or the Commission.

(d) Motions for extensions.

As a matter of discretion, the administrative law judge or the Commission may waive the requirements of this section as to motions for extension of time, and may rule upon such motions ex parte.

Sec. 210.16 Default

(a) Definition of default.

(1) A party shall be found in default if it fails to respond to the complaint and notice of investigation in the manner prescribed in Sec. 210.13 or Sec. 210.59(c), or otherwise fails to answer the complaint and notice, and fails to show cause why it should not be found in default.

(2) A party may be found in default as a sanction for abuse of process, under Sec. 210.4(c), or failure to make or cooperate in discovery, under Sec. 210.33(b).

(b) Procedure for determining default.

(1) If a respondent has failed to respond or appear in the manner described in paragraph (a)(1) of this section, a party may file a motion for, or the administrative law judge may issue upon his own initiative, an order directing that respondent to show cause why it should not be found in default. If the respondent fails to make the necessary showing, the

administrative law judge shall issue an initial determination finding the respondent in default. An administrative law judge's decision denying a motion for a finding of default under paragraph (a)(1) of this section shall be in the form of an order.

(2) Any party may file a motion for issuance of, or the administrative law judge may issue on his own initiative, an initial determination finding a party in default for abuse of process under Sec. 210.4(c) or failure to make or cooperate in discovery. A motion for a finding of default as a sanction for abuse of process or failure to make or cooperate in discovery shall be granted by initial determination or denied by order.

(3) A party found in default shall be deemed to have waived its right to appear, to be served with documents, and to contest the allegations at issue in the investigation.

(c) Relief against a respondent in default.

(1) After a respondent has been found in default by the Commission, the complainant may file with the Commission a declaration that it is seeking immediate entry of relief against the respondent in default. The facts alleged in the complaint will be presumed to be true with respect to the defaulting respondent. The Commission may issue an exclusion order, a cease and desist order, or both, affecting the defaulting respondent only after considering the effect of such order(s) upon the public health and welfare, competitive conditions in the U.S. economy, the production of like or directly competitive articles in the United States, and U.S. consumers, and concluding that the order(s) should still be issued in light of the aforementioned public interest factors.

(2) In any motion requesting the entry of default or the termination of the investigation with respect to the last remaining respondent in the investigation, the complainant shall declare whether it is seeking a general exclusion order. The Commission may issue a general exclusion order pursuant to section 337(g)(2) of the Tariff Act of 1930, regardless of the source or importer of the articles concerned, provided that a violation of section 337 of the Tariff Act of 1930 is established by substantial, reliable, and probative evidence, and only after considering the aforementioned public interest factors and the requirements of Sec. 210.50(c).

Sec. 210.17 Failures to act other than the statutory forms of default

Failures to act other than the defaults listed in Sec. 210.16 may provide a basis for the presiding administrative law judge or the Commission to draw adverse inferences and to issue findings of fact, conclusions of law, determinations (including a determination on violation of section 337 of the Tariff Act of 1930), and orders that are adverse to the party who fails to act. Such failures include, but are not limited to:

(a) Failure to respond to a motion that materially alters the scope of the investigation or a related proceeding;

(b) Failure to respond to a motion for temporary relief pursuant to Sec. 210.59;

(c) Failure to respond to a motion for summary determination under Sec. 210.18;

(d) Failure to appear at a hearing before the administrative law judge after filing a written response to the complaint or motion for temporary relief, or failure to appear at a hearing before the Commission;

(e) Failure to file a brief or other written submission requested by the administrative law judge or the Commission during an investigation or a related proceeding;

(f) Failure to respond to a petition for review of an initial determination, a petition for reconsideration of an initial determination, or an application for interlocutory review of an administrative law judge's order;

(g) Failure to file a brief or other written submission requested by the administrative law judge or the Commission; and

(h) Failure to participate in temporary relief bond forfeiture proceedings under Sec. 210.70.

The presiding administrative law judge or the Commission may take action under this rule *sua sponte* or in response to the motion of a party.

Sec. 210.18 Summary determinations

(a) Motions for summary determinations.

Any party may move with any necessary supporting affidavits for a summary determination in his favor upon all or any part of the issues to be determined in the investigation. Counsel or other representatives in support of the complaint may so move at any time after 20 days following the date of service of the complaint and notice instituting the investigation. Any other party or a respondent may so move at any time after the date of publication of the notice of investigation in the Federal Register. Any such motion by any party in connection with the issue of permanent relief, however, must be filed at least 30 days before the date fixed for any hearing provided for in Sec. 210.36(a)(1). Any motion for summary determination filed in connection with the temporary relief phase of an investigation must be filed on or before the deadline set by the presiding administrative law judge.

(b) Opposing affidavits; oral argument; time and basis for determination.

Any nonmoving party may file opposing affidavits within 10 days after service of the motion for summary determination. The administrative law judge may, in his discretion or at the request of any party, set the matter for oral argument and call for the submission of briefs or memoranda. The determination sought by the moving party shall be rendered if pleadings and any depositions, answers to interrogatories, and admissions on file, together with the affidavits, if any, show that there is no genuine issue as to any material fact and that the moving party is entitled to a summary determination as a matter of law.

(c) Affidavits.

Supporting and opposing affidavits shall be made on personal knowledge, shall set forth such facts as would be admissible in evidence, and shall show affirmatively that the affiant is competent to testify to the matters stated therein. Sworn or certified copies of all papers or parts thereof referred to in an affidavit shall be attached thereto or served therewith. The administrative law judge may permit affidavits to be supplemented or opposed by depositions, answers to interrogatories, or further affidavits. When a motion for summary determination is made and supported as provided in this section, a party opposing the motion may not rest upon the mere allegations or denials of the opposing party's pleading, but the opposing party's response, by affidavits, answers to interrogatories, or as otherwise provided in this section, must set forth specific facts showing that there is a genuine issue of fact for the evidentiary hearing under Sec. 210.36(a)(1) or (2). If the opposing party does not so respond, a summary determination, if appropriate, shall be rendered against the opposing party.

(d) Refusal of application for summary determination; continuances and other orders.

Should it appear from the affidavits of a party opposing the motion that the party cannot, for reasons stated, present by affidavit facts essential to justify the party's opposition, the administrative law judge may refuse the application for summary determination, or may order a continuance to permit affidavits to be obtained or depositions to be taken or discovery to be had or may make such other order as is appropriate, and a ruling to that effect shall be made a matter of record.

(e) Order establishing facts.

If on motion under this section a summary determination is not rendered upon the whole case or for all the relief asked and a hearing is necessary, the administrative law judge, by examining the pleadings and the evidence and by interrogating counsel if necessary, shall if practicable ascertain what material facts exist without substantial controversy and what material facts are actually and in good faith controverted. The administrative law judge shall thereupon make an order specifying the facts that appear without substantial controversy and directing such further proceedings in the investigation as are warranted. The facts so specified shall be deemed established.

(f) Order of summary determination.

An order of summary determination shall constitute an initial determination of the administrative law judge.

Sec. 210.19 Intervention

Any person desiring to intervene in an investigation or a related proceeding under this part shall make a written motion. The motion shall have attached to it a certificate showing that the motion has been served upon each party to the investigation or related proceeding in the manner described in Sec. 201.16(b) of this chapter. Any party may file a response to the motion in accordance with Sec. 210.15(c) of this part, provided that the response is accompanied by a certificate confirming that the response was served on the proposed intervenor and all other parties. The Commission, or the administrative law judge by initial determination, may grant the motion to the extent and upon such terms as may be proper under the circumstances.

Sec. 210.20 Declassification of confidential information

(a) Any party may move to declassify documents (or portions thereof) that have been designated confidential by the submitter but that do not satisfy the confidentiality criteria set forth in Sec. 201.6(a) of this chapter. All such motions, whether brought at any time during the investigation or after conclusion of the investigation shall be addressed to and ruled upon by the presiding administrative law judge, or if the investigation is not before a presiding administrative law judge, by the chief administrative law judge or such administrative law judge as he may designate.

(b) Following issuance of a public version of the initial determination on whether there is a violation of section 337 of the Tariff Act of 1930 or an initial determination that would otherwise terminate the investigation (if adopted by the Commission), the granting of a motion, in whole or part, to declassify information designated confidential shall constitute an initial determination, except as to that information for which no submissions in opposition to declassification have been filed.

Sec. 210.21 Termination of investigations

(a) Motions for termination.

(1) Any party may move at any time prior to the issuance of an initial determination on violation of section 337 of the Tariff Act of 1930 for an order to terminate an investigation in whole or in part as to any or all respondents, on the basis of withdrawal of the complaint or certain allegations contained therein, or for good cause other than the grounds listed in paragraph (a)(2) of this section. The presiding administrative law judge may grant the motion in an initial determination upon such terms and conditions as he deems proper.

(2) Any party may move at any time for an order to terminate an investigation in whole or in part as to any or all respondents on the basis of a settlement, a licensing or other agreement, including an agreement to present the matter for arbitration, or a consent order, as provided in paragraphs (b), (c) and (d) of this section.

(b) Termination by settlement.

(1) An investigation before the Commission may be terminated as to one or more respondents pursuant to section 337(c) of the Tariff Act of 1930 on the basis of a licensing or other settlement agreement. A motion for termination by settlement shall contain copies of the licensing or other settlement agreement, any supplemental agreements, and a statement that there are no other agreements, written or oral, express or implied between the parties concerning the subject matter of the investigation. If the licensing or other settlement agreement contains confidential business information within the meaning of Sec. 201.6(a) of this chapter, a copy of the agreement with such information deleted shall accompany the motion.

(2) The motion and agreement(s) shall be certified by the administrative law judge to the Commission with an initial determination if the motion for termination is granted. If the licensing or other agreement or the initial determination contains confidential business information, copies of the agreement and initial determination with confidential business information deleted shall be certified to the Commission simultaneously with the confidential versions of such documents. Notice of the initial determination and the agreement shall be provided to the U.S. Department of Health and Human Services, the U.S. Department of Justice, the Federal Trade Commission, the U.S. Customs Service, and such other departments and agencies as the Commission deems appropriate. If the Commission's final disposition of the initial determination results in termination of the investigation in its entirety, a notice will be published in the Federal Register. An order of termination by settlement need not constitute a determination as to violation of section 337 of the Tariff Act of 1930.

(c) Termination by entry of consent order.

An investigation before the Commission may be terminated pursuant to section 337(c) of the Tariff Act of 1930 on the basis of a consent order. An order of termination by consent order need not constitute a determination as to violation of section 337.

(1) Opportunity to submit proposed consent order—

(i) Prior to institution of an investigation. Where time, the nature of the proceeding, and the public interest permit, any person being investigated pursuant to section 603 of the Trade Act of 1974 (19 U.S.C. Sec. 2482) shall be afforded the opportunity to submit to the Commission a proposal for disposition of the matter under investigation in the form of a consent order stipulation that incorporates a proposed consent order executed by or on behalf of such person and that complies with the requirements of paragraph (c)(3) of this section.

(ii) Subsequent to institution of an investigation. In investigations under section 337 of the Tariff Act of 1930, a proposal to terminate by consent order shall be submitted as a motion to the administrative law judge with a stipulation that incorporates a proposed consent order. If the stipulation contains confidential business information within the meaning of Sec. 201.6(a) of this chapter, a copy of the stipulation with such information deleted shall accompany the motion. The stipulation shall comply with the requirements of paragraph (c)(3)(i) of this section. At any time prior to commencement of the hearing, the motion may be filed by one or more respondents, and may be filed jointly with other parties to the investigation. Upon request and for good cause shown, the administrative law judge may consider such a motion during or after a hearing. The filing of the motion shall not stay proceedings before the administrative law judge unless the administrative law judge so orders. The administrative law judge shall promptly file with the Commission an initial determination regarding the motion for termination if the motion is granted. If the initial determination contains confidential business information, a copy of the initial determination with such information deleted shall be filed with the Commission simultaneously with the filing of the confidential version of the initial determination. Pending disposition by the Commission of a consent order stipulation, a party may not, absent good cause shown, withdraw from the stipulation once it has been submitted pursuant to this section.

(2) Commission disposition of consent order.

(i) If an initial determination granting the motion for termination based on a consent order stipulation is filed with the Commission, notice of the initial determination and the consent order stipulation shall be provided to the U.S. Department of Health and Human Services, the U.S. Department of Justice, the Federal Trade Commission, the U.S. Customs Service, and such other departments and agencies as the Commission deems appropriate.

(ii) The Commission, after considering the effect of the settlement by consent order upon the public health and welfare, competitive conditions in the U.S. economy, the production of like or directly competitive articles in the United States, and U.S. consumers, shall dispose of the initial determination according to the procedures of Secs. 210.42 through 210.45. If the Commission's final disposition of the initial determination results in termination of the investigation in its entirety, a notice will be published in the Federal Register. An order of termination by consent order need not constitute a determination as to violation of section 337. Should the Commission reverse the initial determination, the parties are in no way bound by their proposal in later actions before the Commission.

(3) Contents of consent order stipulation—

(i) Contents.

(A) Every consent order stipulation shall contain, in addition to the proposed consent order, the following:

(1) An admission of all jurisdictional facts;

(2) An express waiver of all rights to seek judicial review or otherwise challenge or contest the validity of the consent order;

(3) A statement that the signatories to the consent order stipulation will cooperate with and will not seek to impede by litigation or other means the Commission's efforts to gather information under subpart I of this part; and

(4) A statement that the enforcement, modification, and revocation of the consent order will be carried out pursuant to subpart I of this part, incorporating by reference the Commission's Rules of Practice and Procedure.

(B) In the case of an intellectual property-based investigation, the consent order stipulation shall also contain—

(1) a statement that the consent order shall not apply with respect to any claim of any intellectual property right that has expired or been found or adjudicated invalid or unenforceable by the Commission or a court or agency of competent jurisdiction, provided that such finding or judgment has become final and nonreviewable; and

(2) a statement that each signatory to the stipulation who was a respondent in the investigation will not seek to challenge the validity of the intellectual property right(s), in any administrative or judicial proceeding to enforce the consent order.

(C) The consent order stipulation may contain a statement that the signing thereof is for settlement purposes only and does not constitute admission by any respondent that an unfair act has been committed.

(ii) Effect, interpretation, and reporting. The consent order shall have the same force and effect and may be enforced, modified, or revoked in the same manner as is provided in section 337 of the Tariff Act of 1930 and this part for other Commission actions. The Commission may require periodic compliance reports pursuant to subpart I of this part to be submitted by the person entering into the consent order stipulation.

(d) Termination based upon arbitration agreement.

Upon filing of a motion for termination with the administrative law judge or the Commission, a section 337 investigation may be terminated as to one or more respondents pursuant to section 337(c) of the Tariff Act of 1930 on the basis of an agreement between complainant and one or more of the respondents to present the matter for arbitration. The motion and a copy of the arbitration agreement shall be certified by the administrative law judge to the Commission with an initial determination if the motion for termination is granted. If the agreement or the initial determination contains confidential business information, copies of the agreement and initial determination with confidential business information deleted shall be certified to the Commission with the confidential versions of such documents. A notice will be published in the Federal Register if the Commission's final disposition of the initial determination results in termination of the investigation in its entirety. An order of termination based on an arbitration agreement does not constitute a determination as to violation of section 337 of the Tariff Act of 1930.

(e) Effect of termination.

An order of termination issued by the administrative law judge shall constitute an initial determination.

Sec. 210.22 Designating an investigation "more complicated"

(a) Definition.

A more complicated investigation is an investigation that is of an involved nature owing to the subject matter, difficulty in obtaining information, the large number of parties involved, or other significant factors.

(b) Temporary relief.

The Commission or the presiding administrative law judge, pursuant to Sec. 210.60, may declare an investigation "more complicated" in order to have up to 60 days of additional time to adjudicate a motion for temporary relief. See also Sec. 210.51(b). The Commission's or the administrative law judge's reasons for designating the investigation "more complicated" for that purpose shall be published in the Federal Register. The extended deadline for concluding an investigation that has been designated "more complicated" under this paragraph shall be computed in the manner specified in Sec. 210.51(c).

Sec. 210.23 Suspension of investigation

Any party may move to suspend an investigation under this part, because of the pendency of proceedings before the Secretary of Commerce or the administering authority pursuant to section 337(b)(3) of the Tariff Act of 1930. The administrative law judge or the Commission also may raise the issue *sua sponte*. An administrative law judge's decision granting a motion for suspension shall be in the form of an initial determination.

Sec. 210.24 Interlocutory appeals

Rulings by the administrative law judge on motions may not be appealed to the Commission prior to the administrative law judge's issuance of an initial determination, except in the following circumstances:

(a) Appeals without leave of the administrative law judge. The Commission may in its discretion entertain interlocutory appeals, except as provided in Sec. 210.64, when a ruling of the administrative law judge:

(1) Requires the disclosure of Commission records or requires the appearance of Government officials pursuant to Sec. 210.32(c)(2); or

(2) Denies an application for intervention under Sec. 210.19. Appeals from such rulings may be sought by filing an application for review, not to exceed 15 pages, with the Commission within five days after service of the administrative law judge's ruling. An answer to the application for review may be filed within five days after service of the application. The application for review should specify the person or party taking the appeal, designate the ruling or part thereof from which appeal is being taken, and specify the reasons and present arguments as to why review is being sought. The Commission may, upon its own motion, enter an order

staying the return date of an order issued by the administrative law judge pursuant to Sec. 210.32(c)(2) or may enter an order placing the matter on the Commission's docket for review. Any order placing the matter on the Commission's docket for review will set forth the scope of the review and the issues that will be considered and will make provision for the filing of briefs if deemed appropriate by the Commission.

(b) Appeals with leave of the administrative law judge.

(1) Except as otherwise provided in paragraph (a) of this section, Sec. 210.64, and paragraph (b)(2) of this section, applications for review of a ruling by an administrative law judge may be allowed only upon request made to the administrative law judge and upon determination by the administrative law judge in writing, with justification in support thereof, that the ruling involves a controlling question of law or policy as to which there is substantial ground for difference of opinion, and that either an immediate appeal from the ruling may materially advance the ultimate completion of the investigation or subsequent review will be an inadequate remedy.

(2) Applications for review of a ruling by an administrative law judge under Sec. 210.5(e)(1) as to whether information designated confidential by the supplier is entitled to confidential treatment under Sec. 210.5(b) may be allowed only upon request made to the administrative law judge and upon determination by the administrative law judge in writing, with justification in support thereof.

(3) A written application for review under paragraph (b)(1) or (b)(2) of this section shall not exceed 15 pages and may be filed within five days after service of the administrative law judge's determination. An answer to the application for review may be filed within five days after service of the application for review. Thereupon, the Commission may, in its discretion, permit an appeal. Unless otherwise ordered by the Commission, Commission review, if permitted, shall be confined to the application for review and answer thereto, without oral argument or further briefs.

(c) Investigation not stayed. Application for review under this section shall not stay the investigation before the administrative law judge unless the administrative law judge or the Commission shall so order.

Sec. 210.25 Sanctions

(a)(1) Any party may file a motion for sanctions for abuse of process under Sec. 210.4(d)(1), abuse of discovery under Sec. 210.27(d)(3), failure to make or cooperate in discovery under Sec. 210.33 (b) or (c), or violation of a protective order under Sec. 210.34(c). A motion alleging abuse of process should be filed promptly after the requirements of Sec. 210.4(d)(1)(i) have been satisfied. A motion alleging abuse of discovery, failure to make or cooperate in discovery, or violation of a protective order should be filed promptly after the allegedly sanctionable conduct is discovered.

(2) The administrative law judge (when the investigation or related proceeding is before him) or the Commission (when the investigation or related proceeding is before it) also may raise the sanction issue *sua sponte*. (See also Secs. 210.4(d)(1)(ii), 210.27(d)(3), 210.33(c), and 210.34(c).)

(b) A motion for sanctions shall be addressed to the presiding administrative law judge, if the allegedly sanctionable conduct occurred and is discovered while the administrative law judge is presiding in an investigation or in a related proceeding. During an investigation, the administrative law judge's ruling on the motion shall be in the form of an order, if it is issued before or concurrently with the initial determination concerning violation of section 337 of the Tariff Act of 1930 or termination of the investigation. In a related proceeding, the administrative law judge's ruling shall be in the form of an order, regardless of the point in time at which the order is issued.

(c) A motion for sanctions shall be addressed to the Commission, if the allegedly sanctionable conduct occurred while the Commission is presiding or is filed after the subject investigation or related proceeding is terminated. The Commission may assign the motion to an administrative law judge for issuance of a recommended determination. The deadlines and procedures that will be followed in processing the recommended determination will be set forth in the Commission order assigning the motion to an administrative law judge.

(d) If an administrative law judge's order concerning sanctions is issued before the initial determination concerning violation of section 337 of the Tariff Act of 1930 or termination of the investigation, it may be appealed under Sec. 210.24(b)(1) with leave from the administrative law judge, if the requirements of that section are satisfied. If the order is issued concurrently with the initial determination, the order may be appealed by filing a petition meeting the requirements of Sec. 210.43(b). The periods for filing such petitions and responding to the petitions will be specified in the Commission notice issued pursuant to Sec. 210.42(i), if the initial determination has granted a motion for termination of the investigation, or in the Commission notice issued pursuant to Sec. 210.46(a), if the initial determination concerns violation of section 337. The Commission will determine whether to adopt the order after disposition of the initial determination concerning violation of section 337 or termination of the investigation.

(e) If the administrative law judge's ruling on the motion for sanctions is in the form of a recommended determination pursuant to paragraph (c) of this section, the deadlines and procedures for parties to contest the recommended determination will be set forth in the Commission order assigning the motion to an administrative law judge.

(f) If a motion for sanctions is filed with the administrative law judge during an investigation, he may defer his adjudication of the motion until after he has issued a final initial determination concerning violation of section 337 of the Tariff Act of 1930 or termination of investigation. If the administrative law judge defers his adjudication in such a manner, his ruling on the motion for sanctions must be in the form of a recommended determination and shall be issued no later than 90 days after issuance of the aforesaid initial determination on violation of section 337 or termination of the investigation. To aid the Commission in determining whether to adopt a recommended determination, any party may file written comments with the Commission 14 days after service of the recommended determination. Replies to such comments may be filed within seven days after service of the comments. The Commission will determine whether to adopt the recommended determination after reviewing the parties' arguments and taking any other steps the Commission deems appropriate.

Sec. 210.26 Other motions

Motions pertaining to discovery shall be filed in accordance with Sec. 210.15 and the pertinent provisions of subpart E of this part (Secs. 210.27 through 210.34). Motions pertaining to evidentiary hearings and prehearing conferences shall be filed in accordance with Sec. 210.15 and the pertinent provisions of subpart F of this part (Secs. 210.35 through 210.40). Motions for temporary relief shall be filed as provided in subpart H of this part (see Secs. 210.52 through 210.57).

Subpart E—Discovery and Compulsory Process

Sec. 210.27 General provisions governing discovery

(a) Discovery methods.

The parties to an investigation may obtain discovery by one or more of the following methods: depositions upon oral examination or written questions; written interrogatories; production of documents or things or permission to enter upon land or other property for inspection or other purposes; and requests for admissions.

(b) Scope of discovery.

Regarding the scope of discovery for the temporary relief phase of an investigation, see Sec. 210.61. For the permanent relief phase of an investigation, unless otherwise ordered by the administrative law judge, a party may obtain discovery regarding any matter, not privileged, that is relevant to the following:

(1) The claim or defense of the party seeking discovery or to the claim or defense of any other party, including the existence, description, nature, custody, condition, and location of any books, documents, or other tangible things;

(2) The identity and location of persons having knowledge of any discoverable matter;

(3) The appropriate remedy for a violation of section 337 of the Tariff Act of 1930 (see Sec. 210.42(a)(1)(ii)(A)); or

(4) The appropriate bond for the respondents, under section 337(j)(3) of the Tariff Act of 1930, during Presidential review of the remedial order (if any) issued by the Commission (see Sec. 210.42(a)(1)(ii)(B)).

It is not grounds for objection that the information sought will be inadmissible at the hearing if the information sought appears reasonably calculated to lead to the discovery of admissible evidence.

(c) Supplementation of Responses.

(1) A party who has responded to a request for discovery with a response is under a duty to supplement or correct the response to include information thereafter acquired if ordered by the administrative law judge or the Commission or in the following circumstances: A party is under a duty seasonably to amend a prior response to an interrogatory, request for production, or request for admission if the party learns that the response is in some material respect incomplete or incorrect and if the additional or corrective information has not otherwise been made known to the other parties during the discovery process or in writing.

(2) A duty to supplement responses also may be imposed by agreement of the parties, or at any time prior to a hearing through new requests for supplementation of prior responses.

(d) Signing of Discovery Requests, Responses, and Objections.

(1) The front page of every request for discovery or response or objection thereto shall contain a caption setting forth the name of the Commission, the title of the investigation or related proceeding, and the docket number or investigation number, if any, assigned to the investigation or related proceeding.

(2) Every request for discovery or response or objection thereto made by a party represented by an attorney shall be signed by at least one attorney of record in the attorney's individual name, whose address shall be stated. A party who is not represented by an attorney shall sign the request, response, or objection and shall state the party's address. The signature of the attorney or party constitutes a certification that to the best of the signer's knowledge, information, and belief formed after a reasonable inquiry, the request, objection, or response is:

(i) Consistent with Sec. 210.5(a) (if applicable) and other relevant provisions of this chapter, and warranted by existing law or a good faith argument for the extension, modification, or reversal of existing law;

(ii) Not interposed for any improper purpose, such as to harass or to cause unnecessary delay or needless increase in the cost of litigation; and

(iii) Not unreasonable or unduly burdensome or expensive, given the needs of the case, the discovery already had in the case, and the importance of the issues at stake in the litigation.

If a request, response, or objection is not signed, it shall be stricken unless it is signed promptly after the omission is called to the attention of the party making the request, response, or objection, and a party shall not be obligated to take any action with respect to it until it is signed.

(3) If without substantial justification a request, response, or objection is certified in violation of paragraph (d)(2) of this section, the administrative law judge or the Commission, upon motion or *sua sponte* under Sec. 210.25 of this part, may impose an appropriate sanction upon the person who made the certification, the party on whose behalf the request, response, or objection was made, or both.

(4) An appropriate sanction may include an order to pay to the other parties the amount of reasonable expenses incurred because of the violation, including a reasonable attorney's fee, to the extent authorized by Rule 26(g) of the Federal Rules of Civil Procedure. Monetary sanctions shall not be imposed under this section against the United States, the Commission, or a Commission investigative attorney.

(5) Monetary sanctions may be imposed under this section to reimburse the Commission for expenses incurred by a Commission investigative attorney or the Commission's Office of Unfair Import Investigations. Monetary sanctions will not be imposed under this section to reimburse the Commission for attorney's fees.

Sec. 210.28 Depositions

(a) When depositions may be taken.

Following publication in the Federal Register of a Commission notice instituting the investigation, any party may take the testimony of any person, including a party, by deposition upon oral examination or written questions. The presiding administrative law judge will determine the permissible dates or deadlines for taking such depositions.

(b) Persons before whom depositions may be taken.

Depositions may be taken before a person having power to administer oaths by the laws of the United States or of the place where the examination is held.

(c) Notice of examination.

A party desiring to take the deposition of a person shall give notice in writing to every other party to the investigation. The administrative law judge shall determine the appropriate period for providing such notice. The notice shall state the time and place for taking the deposition and the name and address of each person to be examined, if known, and, if the name is not known, a general description sufficient to identify him or the particular class or group to which he belongs. A notice may provide for the taking of testimony by telephone, but the administrative law judge may, on motion of any party, require that the deposition be taken in the presence of the deponent. The parties may stipulate in writing, or the administrative law judge may upon motion order, that the testimony at a deposition be recorded by other than stenographic means. If a subpoena duces tecum is to be served on the person to be examined, the designation of the materials to be produced as set forth in the subpoena shall be attached to or included in the notice.

(d) Taking of deposition.

Each deponent shall be duly sworn, and any adverse party shall have the right to cross-examine. Objections to questions or documents shall be in short form, stating the grounds of objections relied upon. Evidence objected to shall be taken subject to the objections, except that privileged communications and subject matter need not be disclosed. The questions propounded and the answers thereto, together with all objections made, shall be reduced to writing, after which the deposition shall be subscribed by the deponent (unless the parties by stipulation waive signing or the deponent is ill or cannot be found or refuses to sign) and certified by the person before whom the deposition was taken. If the deposition is not subscribed by the deponent, the person administering the oath shall state on the record such fact and the reason therefor. When a deposition is recorded by stenographic means, the stenographer shall certify on the transcript that the witness was sworn in the stenographer's presence and that the transcript is a true record of the testimony of the witness. When a deposition is recorded by other than stenographic means and is thereafter transcribed, the person transcribing it shall certify that the person heard the witness sworn on the recording and that the transcript is a correct writing of the recording. Thereafter, that person shall forward one copy to each party who was present or represented at the taking of the deposition. See paragraph (i) of this section concerning the effect of errors and irregularities in depositions.

(e) Depositions of nonparty officers or employees of the Commission or of other Government agencies.

A party desiring to take the deposition of an officer or employee of the Commission other than the Commission investigative attorney, or of an officer or employee of another Government agency, or to obtain documents or other physical exhibits in the custody, control, and possession of such officer or employee, shall proceed by written motion to the administrative law judge for leave to apply for a subpoena under Sec. 210.32(c). Such a motion shall be granted only upon a showing that the information expected to be obtained thereby is within the scope of discovery permitted by Sec. 210.27(b) or Sec. 210.61 and cannot be obtained without undue hardship by alternative means.

(f) Service of deposition transcripts on the Commission staff.

The party taking the deposition shall promptly serve one copy of the deposition transcript on the Commission investigative attorney.

(g) Admissibility of depositions.

The fact that a deposition is taken and filed with the Commission investigative attorney as provided in this section does not constitute a determination that it is admissible in evidence or that it may be used in the investigation. Only such part of a deposition as is received in evidence at a hearing shall constitute a part of the record in such investigation upon which a determination may be based. Objections may be made at the hearing to receiving in evidence any deposition or part thereof for any reason that would require exclusion of the evidence if the witness were then present and testifying.

(h) Use of depositions.

A deposition may be used as evidence against any party who was present or represented at the taking of the deposition or who had reasonable notice thereof, in accordance with any of the following provisions:

(1) Any deposition may be used by any party for the purpose of contradicting or impeaching the testimony of a deponent as a witness;

(2) The deposition of a party may be used by an adverse party for any purpose;

(3) The deposition of a witness, whether or not a party, may be used by any party for any purposes if the administrative law judge finds—

(i) That the witness is dead; or

(ii) That the witness is out of the United States, unless it appears that the absence of the witness was procured by the party offering the deposition; or

(iii) That the witness is unable to attend or testify because of age, illness, infirmity, or imprisonment; or

(iv) That the party offering the deposition has been unable to procure the attendance of the witness by subpoena; or

(v) Upon application and notice, that such exceptional circumstances exist as to make it desirable in the interest of justice and with due regard to the importance of presenting the oral testimony of witnesses at a hearing, to allow the deposition to be used.

(4) If only part of a deposition is offered in evidence by a party, an adverse party may require him to introduce any other part that ought in fairness to be considered with the part introduced, and any party may introduce any other parts.

(i) Effect of errors and irregularities in depositions—

(1) As to notice. All errors and irregularities in the notice for taking a deposition are waived unless written objection is promptly served upon the party giving notice.

(2) As to disqualification of person before whom the deposition is to be taken. Objection to taking a deposition because of disqualification of the person before whom it is to be taken is waived unless made before the taking of the deposition begins or as soon thereafter as the disqualification becomes known or could be discovered with reasonable diligence.

(3) As to taking of depositions.

(i) Objections to the competency of a witness or the competency, relevancy, or materiality of testimony are not waived by failure to make them before or during the deposition, unless the ground of the objection is one which might have been obviated or removed if presented at that time.

(ii) Errors and irregularities occurring at the oral examination in the manner of taking the deposition, in the form of the questions or answers, in the oath or affirmation, or in the conduct of parties, and errors of any kind which might be obviated, removed, or cured if promptly presented, are waived unless seasonable objection thereto is made at the taking of the deposition.

(iii) Objections to the form of written questions submitted under this section are waived unless served in writing upon the party propounding them. The presiding administrative law judge shall set the deadline for service of such objections.

(4) As to completion and return of deposition. Errors and irregularities in the manner in which the testimony is transcribed or the deposition is prepared, signed, certified, sealed, indorsed, transmitted, filed, or otherwise dealt with by the person before whom it is taken are waived unless a motion to suppress the deposition or some part thereof is made with reasonable promptness after such defect is, or with due diligence might have been, ascertained.

Sec. 210.29 Interrogatories

(a) Scope; use at hearing.

Any party may serve upon any other party written interrogatories to be answered by the party served. Interrogatories may relate to any matters that can be inquired into under Sec. 210.27(b) or Sec. 210.61, and the answers may be used to the extent permitted by the rules of evidence.

(b) Procedure.

(1) Interrogatories may be served upon any party after the date of publication in the Federal Register of the notice of investigation.

(2) Parties answering interrogatories shall repeat the interrogatories being answered immediately preceding the answers. Each interrogatory shall be answered separately and fully in writing under oath, unless it is objected to, in which event the reasons for objection shall be stated in lieu of an answer. The answers are to be signed by the person making them, and the objections are to be signed by the attorney making them. The party upon whom the interrogatories have been served shall serve a copy of the answers, and objections if any, within the time specified by the administrative law judge. The party submitting the interrogatories may move for an order under Sec. 210.33(a) with respect to any objection to or other failure to answer an interrogatory.

(3) An interrogatory otherwise proper is not necessarily objectionable merely because an answer to the interrogatory involves an opinion or contention that relates to fact or the application of law to fact, but the administrative law judge may order that such an interrogatory need not be answered until after designated discovery has been completed or until a prehearing conference or a later time.

(c) Option to produce records.

When the answer to an interrogatory may be derived or ascertained from the records of the party upon whom the interrogatory has been served or from an examination, audit, or inspection of such records, or from a compilation, abstract, or summary based thereon, and the burden of deriving or ascertaining the answer is substantially the same for the party serving the interrogatory as for the party served, it is a sufficient answer to such interrogatory to specify the records from which the answer may be derived or ascertained and to afford to the party serving the interrogatory reasonable opportunity to examine, audit, or inspect such records and to make copies, compilations, abstracts, or summaries. The specifications provided shall include sufficient detail to permit the interrogating party to locate and to identify, as readily as can the party served, the documents from which the answer may be ascertained.

Sec. 210.30 Requests for production of documents and things and entry upon land

(a) Scope.

Any party may serve on any other party a request:

(1) To produce and permit the party making the request, or someone acting on his behalf, to inspect and copy any designated documents (including writings, drawings, graphs, charts, photographs, and other data compilations from which information can be obtained), or to inspect and copy, test, or sample any tangible things that are in the possession, custody, or control of the party upon whom the request is served; or

(2) To permit entry upon designated land or other property in the possession or control of the party upon whom the request is served for the purpose of inspecting and measuring, surveying, photographing, testing, or sampling the property or any designated object or operation thereon, within the scope of Sec. 210.27(b).

(b) Procedure.

(1) The request may be served upon any party after the date of publication in the Federal Register of the notice of investigation. The request shall set forth the items to be inspected, either by individual item or by category, and describe each item and category

with reasonable particularity. The request shall specify a reasonable time, place, and manner of making the inspection and performing the related acts.

(2) The party upon whom the request is served shall serve a written response within the time specified by the administrative law judge. The response shall state, with respect to each item or category, that inspection and related activities will be permitted as requested, unless the request is objected to, in which event the reasons for objection shall be stated. If objection is made to part of any item or category, the part shall be specified. The party submitting the request may move for an order under Sec. 210.33(a) with respect to any objection to or other failure to respond to the request or any part thereof, or any failure to permit inspection as requested. A party who produces documents for inspection shall produce them as they are kept in the usual course of business or shall organize and label them to correspond to the categories in the request.

(c) Persons not parties.

This section does not preclude issuance of an order against a person not a party to permit entry upon land.

Sec. 210.31 Requests for admission

(a) Form, content, and service of request for admission.

Any party may serve on any other party a written request for admission of the truth of any matters relevant to the investigation and set forth in the request that relate to statements or opinions of fact or of the application of law to fact, including the genuineness of any documents described in the request. Copies of documents shall be served with the request unless they have been otherwise furnished or are known to be, and in the request are stated as being, in the possession of the other party. Each matter as to which an admission is requested shall be separately set forth. The request may be served upon a party whose complaint is the basis for the investigation after the date of publication in the Federal Register of the notice of investigation. The administrative law judge will determine the period within which a party may serve a request upon other parties.

(b) Answers and objections to requests for admissions.

A party answering a request for admission shall repeat the request for admission immediately preceding his answer. The matter may be deemed admitted unless, within the period specified by the administrative law judge, the party to whom the request is directed serves upon the party requesting the admission a sworn written answer or objection addressed to the matter. If objection is made, the reason therefor shall be stated. The answer shall specifically deny the matter or set forth in detail the reasons why the answering party cannot truthfully admit or deny the matter. A denial shall fairly meet the substance of the requested admission, and when good faith requires that a party qualify his answer or deny only a part of the matter as to which an admission is requested, he shall specify so much of it as is true and qualify or deny the remainder. An answering party may not give lack of information or knowledge as a reason for failure to admit or deny unless he states that he has made reasonable inquiry and that the information known to or readily obtainable by him is insufficient to enable him to admit or deny. A party who considers that a matter as to which an admission has been requested presents a genuine issue for a hearing may not object to the request on that ground alone; he may deny the matter or set forth reasons why he cannot admit or deny it.

(c) Sufficiency of answers.

The party who has requested the admissions may move to determine the sufficiency of the answers or objections. Unless the objecting party sustains his burden of showing that the objection is justified, the administrative law judge shall order that an answer be served. If the administrative law judge determines that an answer does not comply with the requirements of this section, he may order either that the matter is admitted or that an amended answer be served. The administrative law judge may, in lieu of these orders, determine that final disposition of the request be made at a prehearing conference or at a designated time prior to a hearing under this part.

(d) Effect of admissions; withdrawal or amendment of admission.

Any matter admitted under this section may be conclusively established unless the administrative law judge on motion permits withdrawal or amendment of the admission. The administrative law judge may permit withdrawal or amendment when the presentation of the issues of the investigation will be subserved thereby and the party who obtained the admission fails to satisfy the administrative law judge that withdrawal or amendment will prejudice him in maintaining his position on the issue of the investigation. Any admission made by a party under this section is for the purpose of the pending investigation only and is not an admission by him for any other purpose, nor may it be used against him in any other proceeding.

Sec. 210.32 Subpoenas

(a) Application for issuance of a subpoena.

(1) Subpoena ad testificandum. An application for issuance of a subpoena requiring a person to appear and depose or testify at the taking of a deposition or at a hearing shall be made to the administrative law judge.

(2) Subpoena duces tecum. An application for issuance of a subpoena requiring a person to appear and depose or testify and to produce specified documents, papers, books, or other physical exhibits at the taking of a deposition, at a prehearing conference, at a hearing, or under any other circumstances, shall be made in writing to the administrative law judge and shall specify the material to be produced as precisely as possible, showing the general relevancy of the material and the reasonableness of the scope of the subpoena.

(3) The administrative law judge shall rule on all applications filed under paragraph (a)(1) or (a)(2) of this section and may issue subpoenas when warranted.

(b) Use of subpoena for discovery.

Subpoenas may be used by any party for purposes of discovery or for obtaining documents, papers, books or other physical exhibits for use in evidence, or for both purposes. When used for discovery purposes, a subpoena may require a person to produce and permit the inspection and copying of nonprivileged documents, papers, books, or other physical exhibits that constitute or contain evidence relevant to the subject matter involved and that are in the possession, custody, or control of such person.

(c) Application for subpoenas for nonparty Commission records or personnel or for records and personnel of other Government agencies.

(1) Procedure. An application for issuance of a subpoena requiring the production of nonparty documents, papers, books, physical exhibits, or other material in the records of

the Commission, or requiring the production of records or personnel of other Government agencies shall specify as precisely as possible the material to be produced, the nature of the information to be disclosed, or the expected testimony of the official or employee, and shall contain a statement showing the general relevancy of the material, information, or testimony and the reasonableness of the scope of the application, together with a showing that such material, information, or testimony or their substantial equivalent could not be obtained without undue hardship or by alternative means.

(2) Ruling. Such applications shall be ruled upon by the administrative law judge, and he may issue such subpoenas when warranted. To the extent that the motion is granted, the administrative law judge shall provide such terms and conditions for the production of the material, the disclosure of the information, or the appearance of the official or employee as may appear necessary and appropriate for the protection of the public interest.

(3) Application for subpoena grounded upon the Freedom of Information Act. No application for a subpoena for production of documents grounded upon the Freedom of Information Act (5 U.S.C. Sec. 552) shall be entertained by the administrative law judge.

(d) Motion to limit or quash.

Any motion to limit or quash a subpoena shall be filed within such time as the administrative law judge may allow.

(e) Ex parte rulings on applications for subpoenas.

Applications for the issuance of the subpoenas pursuant to the provisions of this section may be made ex parte, and, if so made, such applications and rulings thereon shall remain ex parte unless otherwise ordered by the administrative law judge.

(f) Witness Fees

(1) Deponents and witnesses. Any person compelled to appear in person to depose or testify in response to a subpoena shall be paid the same mileage as are paid witnesses with respect to proceedings in the courts of the United States; provided, that salaried employees of the United States summoned to depose or testify as to matters related to their public employment, irrespective of the party at whose instance they are summoned, shall be paid in accordance with the applicable Federal regulations.

(2) Responsibility. The fees and mileage referred to in paragraph (f)(1) of this section shall be paid by the party at whose instance deponents or witnesses appear. Fees due under this paragraph shall be tendered no later than the date for compliance with the subpoena issued under this section. Failure to timely tender fees under this paragraph shall not invalidate any subpoena issued under this section.

(g) Obtaining judicial enforcement.

In order to obtain judicial enforcement of a subpoena issued under paragraphs (a)(3) or (c)(2) of this section, the administrative law judge shall certify to the Commission, on motion or *sua sponte*, a request for such enforcement. The request shall be accompanied by copies of relevant papers and a written report from the administrative law judge concerning the purpose, relevance, and reasonableness of the subpoena. The Commission will subsequently issue a notice stating whether it has granted the request and authorized its Office of the General Counsel to seek such enforcement.

Sec. 210.33 Failure to make or cooperate in discovery; sanctions

(a) Motion for order compelling discovery.

A party may apply to the administrative law judge for an order compelling discovery upon reasonable notice to other parties and all persons affected thereby.

(b) Non-monetary sanctions for failure to comply with an order compelling discovery.

If a party or an officer or agent of a party fails to comply with an order including, but not limited to, an order for the taking of a deposition or the production of documents, an order to answer interrogatories, an order issued pursuant to a request for admissions, or an order to comply with a subpoena, the administrative law judge, for the purpose of permitting resolution of relevant issues and disposition of the investigation without unnecessary delay despite the failure to comply, may take such action in regard thereto as is just, including, but not limited to the following:

(1) Infer that the admission, testimony, documents, or other evidence would have been adverse to the party;

(2) Rule that for the purposes of the investigation the matter or matters concerning the order or subpoena issued be taken as established adversely to the party;

(3) Rule that the party may not introduce into evidence or otherwise rely upon testimony by the party, officer, or agent, or documents, or other material in support of his position in the investigation;

(4) Rule that the party may not be heard to object to introduction and use of secondary evidence to show what the withheld admission, testimony, documents, or other evidence would have shown;

(5) Rule that a motion or other submission by the party concerning the order or subpoena issued be stricken or rule by initial determination that a determination in the investigation be rendered against the party, or both; or

(6) Order any other non-monetary sanction available under Rule 37(b) of the Federal Rules of Civil Procedure. Any such action may be taken by written or oral order issued in the course of the investigation or by inclusion in the initial determination of the administrative law judge. It shall be the duty of the parties to seek, and that of the administrative law judge to grant, such of the foregoing means of relief or other appropriate relief as may be sufficient to compensate for the lack of withheld testimony, documents, or other evidence. If, in the administrative law judge's opinion such relief would not be sufficient, the administrative law judge shall certify to the Commission a request that court enforcement of the subpoena or other discovery order be sought.

(c) Monetary sanctions for failure to make or cooperate in discovery.

(1) If a party or an officer, director, or managing agent of the party or person designated to testify on behalf of a party fails to obey an order to provide or permit discovery, the administrative law judge or the Commission may make such orders in regard to the failure as are just. In lieu of or in addition to taking action listed in paragraph (b) of this section and to the extent provided in Rule 37(b)(2) of the Federal Rules of Civil Procedure, the administrative law judge or the Commission, upon motion or *sua sponte* under Sec. 210.25, may require the party failing to obey the order or the attorney advising that party or both to pay reasonable expenses, including attorney's fees, caused by the failure,

unless the administrative law judge or the Commission finds that the failure was substantially justified or that other circumstances make an award of expenses unjust. Monetary sanctions shall not be imposed under this section against the United States, the Commission, or a Commission investigative attorney.

(2) Monetary sanctions may be imposed under this section to reimburse the Commission for expenses incurred by a Commission investigative attorney or the Commission's Office of Unfair Import Investigations. Monetary sanctions will not be imposed under this section to reimburse the Commission for attorney's fees.

Sec. 210.34 Protective orders

(a) Issuance of protective order.

Upon motion by a party or by the person from whom discovery is sought or by the administrative law judge on his own initiative, and for good cause shown, the administrative law judge may make any order that may appear necessary and appropriate for the protection of the public interest or that justice requires to protect a party or person from annoyance, embarrassment, oppression, or undue burden or expense, including one or more of the following:

(1) That discovery not be had;

(2) That the discovery may be had only on specified terms and conditions, including a designation of the time or place;

(3) That discovery may be had only by a method of discovery other than that selected by the party seeking discovery;

(4) That certain matters not be inquired into, or that the scope of discovery be limited to certain matters;

(5) That discovery be conducted with no one present except persons designated by the administrative law judge;

(6) That a deposition, after being sealed, be opened only by order of the Commission or the administrative law judge;

(7) That a trade secret or other confidential research, development, or commercial information not be disclosed or be disclosed only in a designated way; and

(8) That the parties simultaneously file specified documents or information enclosed in sealed envelopes to be opened as directed by the Commission or the administrative law judge. If the motion for a protective order is denied, in whole or in part, the Commission or the administrative law judge may, on such terms and conditions as are just, order that any party or person provide or permit discovery. The Commission also may, upon motion or *sua sponte*, issue protective orders or may continue or amend a protective order issued by the administrative law judge.

(b) Unauthorized disclosure of information.

If confidential business information submitted in accordance with the terms of a protective order is disclosed to any person other than in a manner authorized by the protective order, the party responsible for the disclosure must immediately bring all pertinent facts relating to such disclosure to the attention of the submitter of the information and the administrative law judge or the Commission, and, without prejudice to other rights and remedies of the submitter of the information, make every effort to prevent further disclosure of such information by the party or the recipient of such information.

(c) Violation of protective order.

Any individual who has agreed to be bound by the terms of a protective order issued pursuant to paragraph (a) of this section, and who is determined to have violated the terms of the protective order, may be subject to one or more of the following:

(1) An official reprimand by the Commission;

(2) Disqualification from or limitation of further participation in a pending investigation;

(3) Temporary or permanent disqualification from practicing in any capacity before the Commission pursuant to Sec. 201.15(a) of this chapter;

(4) Referral of the facts underlying the violation to the appropriate licensing authority in the jurisdiction in which the individual is licensed to practice;

(5) Sanctions of the sort enumerated in Sec. 210.33(b), or such other action as may be appropriate.

The issue of whether sanctions should be imposed may be raised on a motion by a party, the administrative law judge's own motion, or the Commission's own initiative in accordance with Sec. 210.25(a)(2). The Commission or the administrative law judge shall allow the parties to make written submissions and, if warranted, to present oral argument bearing on the issues of violation of a protective order and sanctions therefor. When the motion is addressed to the administrative law judge, he shall grant or deny a motion for sanctions by issuing an order.

(d) Reporting requests for confidential business information.

(1) Reporting Requirement. Each person subject to protective order issued pursuant to paragraph (a) of this section shall report in writing to the Commission immediately upon learning that confidential business information disclosed to him or her pursuant to the protective order is the subject of a subpoena, court or administrative order (other than an order of a court reviewing a Commission decision), discovery request, agreement, or other written request seeking disclosure, by him or any other person, of that confidential business information to persons who are not, or may not be, permitted access to that information pursuant to either a Commission protective order or Sec. 210.5(b).

(2) Sanctions and other actions. After providing notice and an opportunity to comment, the Commission may impose a sanction upon any person who willfully fails to comply with paragraph (d)(1) of this section, or it may take other action.

Subpart F—Prehearing Conferences and Hearings

Sec. 210.35 Prehearing conferences

(a) When appropriate.

The administrative law judge in any investigation may direct counsel or other representatives for all parties to meet with him for one or more conferences to consider any or all of the following:

(1) Simplification and clarification of the issues;

(2) Scope of the hearing;

(3) Necessity or desirability of amendments to pleadings subject, however, to the provisions of Sec. 210.14 (b) and (c);

(4) Stipulations and admissions of either fact or the content and authenticity of documents;

(5) Expedition in the discovery and presentation of evidence including, but not limited to, restriction of the number of expert, economic, or technical witnesses; and

(6) Such other matters as may aid in the orderly and expeditious disposition of the investigation including disclosure of the names of witnesses and the exchange of documents or other physical exhibits that will be introduced in evidence in the course of the hearing.

(b) Subpoenas.

Prehearing conferences may be convened for the purpose of accepting returns on subpoenas duces tecum issued pursuant to Sec. 210.32(a)(3).

(c) Reporting.

In the discretion of the administrative law judge, prehearing conferences may or may not be stenographically reported and may or may not be public.

(d) Order.

The administrative law judge may enter in the record an order that recites the results of the conference. Such order shall include the administrative law judge's rulings upon matters considered at the conference, together with appropriate direction to the parties. The administrative law judge's order shall control the subsequent course of the hearing, unless the administrative law judge modifies the order.

Sec. 210.36 General provisions for hearings

(a) Purpose of hearings.

(1) An opportunity for a hearing shall be provided in each investigation under this part, in accordance with the Administrative Procedure Act. At the hearing, the presiding administrative law judge will take evidence and hear argument for the purpose of determining whether there is a violation of section 337 of the Tariff Act of 1930, and for the purpose of making findings and recommendations, as described in Sec. 210.42(a)(1)(ii), concerning the appropriate remedy and the amount of the bond to be posted by respondents during Presidential review of the Commission's action, under section 337(j) of the Tariff Act.

(2) An opportunity for a hearing in accordance with the Administrative Procedure Act shall also be provided in connection with every motion for temporary relief filed under this part.

(b) Public hearings.

All hearings in investigations under this part shall be public unless otherwise ordered by the administrative law judge.

(c) Expedition.

Hearings shall proceed with all reasonable expedition, and, insofar as practicable, shall be held at one place, continuing until completed unless otherwise ordered by the administrative law judge.

(d) Rights of the parties.

Every hearing under this section shall be conducted in accordance with the Administrative Procedure Act (*i.e.*, 5 U.S.C. Secs. 554 through 556). Hence, every party shall have the right of adequate notice, cross-examination, presentation of evidence, objection, motion, argument, and all other rights essential to a fair hearing.

(e) Presiding official.

An administrative law judge shall preside over each hearing unless the Commission shall otherwise order.

Sec. 210.37 Evidence

(a) Burden of proof.

The proponent of any factual proposition shall be required to sustain the burden of proof with respect thereto.

(b) Admissibility.

Relevant, material, and reliable evidence shall be admitted. Irrelevant, immaterial, unreliable, or unduly repetitious evidence shall be excluded. Immaterial or irrelevant parts of an admissible document shall be segregated and excluded as far as practicable.

(c) Information obtained in investigations.

Any documents, papers, books, physical exhibits, or other materials or information obtained by the Commission under any of its powers may be disclosed by the Commission investigative attorney when necessary in connection with investigations and may be offered in evidence by the Commission investigative attorney.

(d) Official notice.

When any decision of the administrative law judge rests, in whole or in part, upon the taking of official notice of a material fact not appearing in evidence of record, opportunity to disprove such noticed fact shall be granted any party making timely motion therefor.

(e) Objections.

Objections to evidence shall be made in timely fashion and shall briefly state the grounds relied upon. Rulings on all objections shall appear on the record.

(f) Exceptions.

Formal exception to an adverse ruling is not required.

(g) Excluded evidence.

When an objection to a question propounded to a witness is sustained, the examining party may make a specific offer of what he expects to prove by the answer of the witness, or the administrative law judge may in his discretion receive and report the evidence in full. Rejected exhibits, adequately marked for identification, shall be retained with the record so as to be available for consideration by any reviewing authority.

Sec. 210.38 Record

(a) Definition of the record.

The record shall consist of all pleadings, the notice of investigation, motions and responses, all briefs and written statements, and other documents and things properly filed with the Secretary, in addition to all orders, notices, and initial determinations of the administrative law judge, orders and notices of the Commission, hearing and conference transcripts, evidence admitted into the record, and any other items certified into the record by the administrative law judge or the Commission.

(b) Reporting and transcription.

Hearings shall be reported and transcribed by the official reporter of the Commission under the supervision of the administrative law judge, and the transcript shall be a part of the record.

(c) Corrections.

Changes in the official transcript may be made only when they involve errors affecting substance. A motion to correct a transcript shall be addressed to the administrative law judge, who may order that the transcript be changed to reflect such corrections as are warranted, after consideration of any objections that may be made. Such corrections shall be made by the official reporter by furnishing substitute typed pages, under the usual certificate of the reporter, for insertion in the transcript. The original uncorrected pages shall be retained in the files of the Commission.

(d) Certification of record.

The record shall be certified to the Commission by the administrative law judge upon his filing of an initial determination or at such earlier time as the Commission may order.

Sec. 210.39 In camera treatment of confidential information

(a) Definition.

Except as hereinafter provided and consistent with Secs. 210.5 and 210.34, confidential documents and testimony made subject to protective orders or orders granting in camera treatment are not made part of the public record and are kept confidential in an in camera record. Only the persons identified in a protective order, persons identified in Sec. 210.5(b), and court personnel concerned with judicial review shall have access to confidential information in the in camera record. The right of the administrative law judge and the Commission to disclose confidential data under a protective order (pursuant to Sec. 210.34) to the extent necessary for the proper disposition of each proceeding is specifically reserved.

(b) Transmission of certain Commission records to district court.

In a civil action involving parties that are also parties to a proceeding before the Commission under section 337 of the Tariff Act of 1930, at the request of a party to the civil action that is also a respondent in the proceeding before the Commission, the district court may stay, until the determination of the Commission becomes final, proceedings in the civil action with respect to any claim that involves the same issues involved in the proceeding before the Commission under certain conditions. If such a stay is in effect, after the determination of the Commission becomes final, the Commission shall certify to the district court such portions of the record of its proceeding as the district court may request. Notwithstanding paragraph (a) of this section, the in camera record may be transmitted to a district court and be admissible in a civil action, subject to such protective order as the district court determines necessary, pursuant to 28 U.S.C. 1659.

(c) In camera treatment of documents and testimony.

The administrative law judge shall have authority to order documents or oral testimony offered in evidence, whether admitted or rejected, to be placed in camera.

(d) Part of confidential record.

In camera documents and testimony shall constitute a part of the confidential record of the Commission.

(e) References to in camera information.

In submitting proposed findings, briefs, or other papers, counsel for all parties shall make an attempt in good faith to refrain from disclosing the specific details of in camera documents and testimony. This shall not preclude references in such proposed findings, briefs, or other papers to such documents or testimony including generalized statements based on their contents. To the extent that counsel consider it necessary to include specific details of in camera data in their presentations, such data shall be incorporated in separate proposed findings, briefs, or other papers marked "Business Confidential," which shall be placed in camera and become a part of the confidential record.

Sec. 210.40 Proposed findings and conclusions and briefs

At the time a motion for summary determination under Sec. 210.18(a) or a motion for termination under Sec. 210.21(a) is made, or when it is found that a party is in default under Sec. 210.16, or at the close of the reception of evidence in any hearing held pursuant to this part (except as provided in Sec. 210.63), or within a reasonable time thereafter fixed by the administrative law judge, any party may file proposed findings of fact and conclusions of law, together with reasons therefor. When appropriate, briefs in support of the proposed findings of fact and conclusions of law may be filed with the administrative law judge for his consideration. Such proposals and briefs shall be in writing, shall be served upon all parties in accordance with Sec. 210.4(g), and shall contain adequate references to the record and the authorities on which the submitter is relying.

Subpart G—Determinations and Actions Taken

Sec. 210.41 Termination of investigation

Except as provided in Sec. 210.21 (b)(2), (c), and (d), an order of termination issued by the Commission shall constitute a determination of the Commission under Sec. 210.45(c). The Commission shall publish in the Federal Register notice of each Commission order that terminates an investigation in its entirety.

Sec. 210.42 Initial determinations

(a)(1)(i) On issues concerning violation of section 337. Unless otherwise ordered by the Commission, the administrative law judge shall certify the record to the Commission and shall file an initial determination on whether there is a violation of section 337 of the Tariff Act of 1930 no later than 3 months before the target date set pursuant to Sec. 210.51(a) if the target date is 15 months or less from the date of institution, and no later than 4 months before the target date if the target date is more than 15 months from the date of institution.

(ii) Recommended determination on issues concerning permanent relief and bonding. Unless the Commission orders otherwise, within 14 days after issuance of the initial determination on violation of section 337 of the Tariff Act of 1930, the administrative law judge shall issue a recommended determination containing findings of fact and recommendations concerning—

(a) The appropriate remedy in the event that the Commission finds a violation of section 337, and

(b) The amount of the bond to be posted by the respondents during Presidential review of Commission action under section 337(j) of the Tariff Act.

(2) On certain motions to declassify information. Following issuance of the public version of an initial determination under paragraph (a)(1)(i) of this section, the decision of an administrative law judge granting a motion to declassify information, in whole or in part, shall be in the form of an initial determination as provided in Sec. 210.20(b).

(b) On issues concerning temporary relief or forfeiture of temporary relief bonds.

Certification of the record and the disposition of an initial determination concerning a motion for temporary relief are governed by Secs. 210.65 and 210.66. The disposition of an initial determination concerning possible forfeiture or return of a complainant's temporary relief bond, in whole or in part, is governed by Sec. 210.70.

(c) On other matters.

The administrative law judge shall grant the following types of motions by issuing an initial determination or shall deny them by issuing an order: a motion to amend the complaint or notice of investigation pursuant to Sec. 210.14(b); a motion for a finding of default pursuant to Sec. 210.16; a motion for summary determination pursuant to Sec. 210.18; a motion for intervention pursuant to Sec. 210.19; a motion for termination pursuant to Sec. 210.21; a motion to suspend an investigation pursuant to Sec. 210.23; a motion for forfeiture or return of respondents' bonds pursuant to Sec. 210.50(d); a motion to set a target date exceeding 15 months pursuant to Sec. 210.51(a); or a motion for forfeiture or return of a complainant's temporary relief bond pursuant to Sec. 210.70.

(d) Contents.

The initial determination shall include: an opinion stating findings (with specific page references to principal supporting items of evidence in the record) and conclusions and the reasons or bases therefor necessary for the disposition of all material issues of fact, law, or discretion presented in the record; and a statement that, pursuant to Sec. 210.42(h), the initial determination shall become the determination of the Commission unless a party files a petition for review of the initial determination pursuant to Sec. 210.43(a) or the Commission, pursuant to Sec. 210.44, orders on its own motion a review of the initial determination or certain issues therein.

(e) Notice to and advice from other departments and agencies.

Notice of each initial determination granting a motion for termination of an investigation in whole or part on the basis of a consent order or a settlement, licensing, or other agreement pursuant to Sec. 210.21 of this part, and notice of such other initial determinations as the Commission may order, shall be provided to the U.S. Department of Health and Human Services, the U.S. Department of Justice, the Federal Trade Commission, the U.S. Customs Service, and such other departments and agencies as the Commission deems appropriate. The Commission shall consider comments, limited to issues raised by the record, the initial determination, and the petitions for review, received from such agencies when deciding whether to initiate review or the scope of review. The Commission shall allow such agencies 10 days after the service of an initial determination to submit their comments.

(f) Initial determination made by the administrative law judge.

An initial determination under this section shall be made and filed by the administrative law judge who presided over the investigation, except when that person is unavailable to the Commission and except as provided in Sec. 210.20(a).

(g) Reopening of proceedings by the administrative law judge.

At any time prior to the filing of the initial determination, the administrative law judge may reopen the proceedings for the reception of additional evidence.

(h) Effect.

(1) An initial determination filed pursuant to Sec. 210.42(a)(2) shall become the determination of the Commission 45 days after the date of service of the initial determination, unless the Commission has ordered review of the initial determination or certain issues therein, or by order has changed the effective date of the initial determination.

(2) An initial determination under Sec. 210.42(a)(1)(i) shall become the determination of the Commission 45 days after the date of service of the initial determination, unless the Commission, within 45 days after the date of such service shall have ordered review of the initial determination or certain issues therein or by order has changed the effective date of the initial determination. The findings and recommendations made by the administrative law judge in the recommended determination issued pursuant to Sec. 210.42(a)(1)(ii) will be considered by the Commission in reaching determinations on remedy and bonding by the respondents pursuant to Sec. 210.50(a).

(3) An initial determination filed pursuant to Sec. 210.42(c) shall become the determination of the Commission 30 days after the date of service of the initial determination, except as provided in paragraph (h)(5) of this section, Sec. 210.50(d)(3) and Sec. 210.70(c), unless the Commission, within 30 days after the date of such service shall have ordered review of the initial determination or certain issues therein or by order has changed the effective date of the initial determination.

(4) The disposition of an initial determination granting or denying a motion for temporary relief is governed by Sec. 210.66.

(5) The disposition of an initial determination concerning possible forfeiture of a complainant's temporary relief bond is governed by Sec. 210.70(c).

(i) Notice of determination.

A notice stating the Commission's decision on whether to review an initial determination will be issued by the Secretary and served on the parties. Notice of the Commission's decision will be published in the Federal Register if the decision results in termination of the investigation in its entirety.

Sec. 210.43 Petitions for review of initial determinations on matters other than temporary relief

(a) Filing of the petition.

(1) Except as provided in paragraph (a)(2) of this section, any party to an investigation may request Commission review of an initial determination issued under Sec. 210.42(a)(1) or (c), Sec. 210.50(d)(3) or Sec. 210.70(c) by filing a petition with the Secretary. A petition for review of an initial determination issued under Sec. 210.42(a)(1) must be filed within 10 days after service of the initial determination. A petition for review of an initial determination issued under Sec. 210.42(c) must be filed within five business days after issuance of the initial determination. A petition for review of an initial determination issued under Sec. 210.50(d)(3) or Sec. 210.70(c) must be filed within 10 days after issuance of the initial determination.

(2) A party may not petition for review of any issue as to which the party has been found to be in default. Similarly, a party or proposed respondent who did not file a response to the motion addressed in the initial determination may be deemed to have consented to the relief requested and may not petition for review of the issues raised in the motion.

(b) Content of the petition.

(1) A petition for review filed under this section shall identify the party seeking review and shall specify the issues upon which review of the initial determination is sought, and shall, with respect to each such issue, specify one or more of the following grounds upon which review is sought:

(i) That a finding or conclusion of material fact is clearly erroneous;

(ii) That a legal conclusion is erroneous, without governing precedent, rule or law, or constitutes an abuse of discretion; or

(iii) That the determination is one affecting Commission policy.

The petition for review must set forth a concise statement of the facts material to the consideration of the stated issues, and must present a concise argument providing the reasons that review by the Commission is necessary or appropriate to resolve an important issue of fact, law, or policy.

(2) Any issue not raised in a petition for review will be deemed to have been abandoned by the petitioning party and may be disregarded by the Commission in reviewing the initial determination (unless the Commission chooses to review the issue on its own initiative under Sec. 210.44).

(3) Any petition designated by the petitioner as a "contingent" petition for review shall be deemed to be a petition under paragraph (a)(1) of this section and shall be processed accordingly.

(4) A party's failure to file a petition for review of an initial determination shall constitute abandonment of all issues decided adversely to that party in the initial determination.

(c) Responses to the petition.

Any party may file a response to a petition for review within five business days after service of the petition, except that a party who has been found to be in default may not file a response to any issue as to which the party has defaulted.

(d) Grant or denial of review.

(1) The Commission shall decide whether to grant, in whole or in part, a petition for review of an initial determination filed pursuant to Sec. 210.42(a)(1), Sec. 210.50(d)(3) or Sec. 210.70(c) within 45 days of the service of the initial determination on the parties, or by such other time as the Commission may order. The Commission shall decide whether to grant, in whole or in part, a petition for review of an initial determination filed pursuant to Sec. 210.42(c) within 30 days of the service of the initial determination on the parties, or by such other time as the Commission may order.

(2) The Commission shall decide whether to grant a petition for review, based upon the petition and response thereto, without oral argument or further written submissions unless the Commission shall order otherwise. A petition will be granted and review will be ordered if it appears that an error or abuse of the type described in paragraph (b)(1) of this section is present or if the petition raises a policy matter connected with the initial determination, which the Commission thinks it necessary or appropriate to address.

(3) The Commission shall grant a petition for review and order review of an initial determination or certain issues therein when at least one of the participating Commissioners votes for ordering review. In its notice, the Commission shall establish the scope of the review and the issues that will be considered and make provisions for filing of briefs and oral argument if deemed appropriate by the Commission. If the notice solicits written submissions from interested persons on the issues of remedy, the public interest, and bonding in addition to announcing the Commission's decision to grant a petition for review of the initial determination, the notice shall be served by the Secretary on all parties, the U.S. Department of Health and Human Services, the U.S. Department of Justice, the Federal Trade Commission, the U.S. Customs Service, and such other departments and agencies as the Commission deems appropriate.

Sec. 210.44 Commission review on its own motion of initial determinations on matters other than temporary relief

Within the time provided in Sec. 210.43(d)(1), the Commission on its own initiative may order review of an initial determination, or certain issues in the initial determination, when at least one of the participating Commissioners votes for ordering review. A self-initiated Commission review of an initial determination will be ordered if it appears that an error or abuse of the kind described in Sec. 210.43(b)(1) is present or the initial determination raises a policy matter which the Commission thinks is necessary or appropriate to address.

Sec. 210.45 Review of initial determinations on matters other than temporary relief

(a) Briefs and oral argument.

In the event the Commission orders review of an initial determination pertaining to issues other than temporary relief, the parties may be requested to file briefs on the issues under review at a time and of a size and nature specified in the notice of review. The parties, within the time provided for filing the review briefs, may submit a written request for a hearing to present oral argument before the Commission, which the Commission in its discretion may grant or deny. The Commission shall grant the request when at least one of the participating Commissioners votes in favor of granting the request.

(b) Scope of review.

Only the issues set forth in the notice of review, and all subsidiary issues therein, will be considered by the Commission.

(c) Determination on review.

On review, the Commission may affirm, reverse, modify, set aside or remand for further proceedings, in whole or in part, the initial determination of the administrative law judge. The Commission also may make any findings or conclusions that in its judgment are proper based on the record in the proceeding. If the Commission's determination on review terminates the investigation in its entirety, a notice will be published in the Federal Register.

Sec. 210.46 Petitions for and *sua sponte* review of initial determinations on violation of section 337 or temporary relief

(a) Violation of section 337.

An initial determination issued under Sec. 210.42(a)(1)(i) on whether respondents have violated section 337 of the Tariff Act of 1930 will be processed as provided in Sec. 210.42(e), (h)(2), and (i) and Secs. 210.43 through 210.45. The Commission will issue a notice setting deadlines for written submissions from the parties, other Federal agencies, and interested members of the public on the issues of remedy, the public interest, and bonding by the respondents. In those submissions, the parties may assert their arguments concerning the recommended determination issued by the administrative law judge pursuant to Sec. 210.42(a)(ii) on the issues of remedy and bonding by respondents.

(b) Temporary relief.

Commission action on an initial determination concerning temporary relief is governed by Sec. 210.66.

Sec. 210.47 Petitions for reconsideration

Within 14 days after service of a Commission determination, any party may file with the Commission a petition for reconsideration of such determination or any action ordered to be taken thereunder, setting forth the relief desired and the grounds in support thereof. Any petition filed under this section must be confined to new questions raised by the determination or action ordered to be taken thereunder and upon which the petitioner had no opportunity to submit arguments. Any party desiring to oppose such a petition shall file an answer thereto within five days after service of the petition upon such party. The filing of a petition for reconsideration shall not stay the effective date of the determination or action ordered to be taken thereunder or toll the running of any statutory time period affecting such determination or action ordered to be taken thereunder unless specifically so ordered by the Commission.

Sec. 210.48 Disposition of petitions for reconsideration

The Commission may affirm, set aside, or modify its determination, including any action ordered by it to be taken thereunder. When appropriate, the Commission may order the administrative law judge to take additional evidence.

Sec. 210.49 Implementation of Commission action.

(a) Service of Commission determination upon the parties

A Commission determination pursuant to Sec. 210.45(c) or a termination on the basis of a licensing or other agreement, a consent order or an arbitration agreement pursuant to Sec. 210.21(b), (c) or (d), respectively, shall be served upon each party to the investigation.

(b) Publication and transmittal to the President.

A Commission determination that there is a violation of section 337 of the Tariff Act of 1930 or that there is reason to believe that there is such a violation, together with the action taken relative to such determination, or Commission action taken pursuant to subpart I of this part, shall promptly be published in the Federal Register and transmitted to the President, together with the record upon which the determination and the action are based.

(c) Enforceability of Commission action.

Unless otherwise specified, any Commission action other than an exclusion order or an order directing seizure and forfeiture of articles imported in violation of an outstanding exclusion order shall be enforceable upon receipt by the affected party of notice of such action. Exclusion orders and seizure and forfeiture orders shall be enforceable upon receipt of notice thereof by the Secretary of the Treasury.

(d) Finality of affirmative Commission action.

If the President does not disapprove the Commission's action within a 60-day period beginning the day after a copy of the Commission's action is delivered to the President, or if the President notifies the Commission before the close of the 60-day period that he approves the Commission's action, such action shall become final the day after the close of the 60-day period or the day the President notifies the Commission of his approval, as the case may be.

(e) Duration.

Final Commission action shall remain in effect as provided in subpart I of this part.

Sec. 210.50 Commission action, the public interest, and bonding by respondents

(a) During the course of each investigation under this part, the Commission shall.

(1) Consider what action (general or limited exclusion of articles from entry or a cease and desist order, or exclusion of articles from entry under bond or a temporary cease and desist order), if any, it should take, and, when appropriate, take such action;

(2) Consult with and seek advice and information from the U.S. Department of Health and Human Services, the U.S. Department of Justice, the Federal Trade Commission, the U.S. Customs Service, and such other departments and agencies as it considers appropriate, concerning the subject matter of the complaint and the effect its actions (general or limited exclusion of articles from entry or a cease and desist order, or exclusion of articles from entry under bond or a temporary cease and desist order) under section 337 of the Tariff Act of 1930 shall have upon the public health and welfare, competitive conditions in the U.S. economy, the production of like or directly competitive articles in the United States, and U.S. consumers;

(3) Determine the amount of the bond to be posted by a respondent pursuant to section 337(j)(3) of the Tariff Act of 1930 following the issuance of temporary or permanent relief under section 337(d), (e), (f), or (g) of the Tariff Act of 1930, taking into account the requirement of section 337(e) and (j)(3) that the amount of the bond be sufficient to protect the complainant from any injury.

(4) Receive submissions from the parties, interested persons, and other Government agencies and departments with respect to the subject matter of paragraphs (a)(1), (a)(2), and (a)(3), of this section.

When the matter under consideration pursuant to paragraph (a)(1) of this section is whether to grant some form of permanent relief, the submissions described in paragraph (a)(4) of this section shall be filed by the deadlines specified in the Commission notice issued pursuant to Sec. 210.46(a). When the matter under consideration is whether to grant some form of temporary relief, such submissions shall be filed by the deadlines specified in Sec. 210.67(b), unless the Commission orders otherwise. Any submission from a party shall be served upon the other parties in accordance with Sec. 210.4(g). The parties' submissions, as well as any filed by interested persons or other agencies shall be available for public inspection in the Office of the Secretary. The Commission will consider motions for oral argument or, when necessary, a hearing with respect to the subject matter of this section, except that no hearing or oral argument will be permitted in connection with a motion for temporary relief.

(b)(1) With respect to an administrative law judge's ability to take evidence or other information and to hear arguments from the parties and other interested persons on the issues of appropriate Commission action, the public interest, and bonding by the respondents for purposes of an initial determination on temporary relief, see Secs. 210.61, 210.62, and 210.66(a). For purposes of the recommended determination required by Sec. 210.42(a)(1)(ii), an administrative law judge shall take evidence or other information and hear arguments from the parties and other interested persons on the issues of appropriate Commission action and bonding by the respondents. Unless the Commission orders otherwise, and except as provided in paragraph (b)(2) of this section, an administrative law judge shall not address the issue of the public interest for purposes of an initial determination on violation of section 337 of the Tariff Act under Sec. 210.42(a)(1)(i).

(2) Regarding terminations by settlement agreement, consent order, or arbitration agreement under Sec. 210.21 (b), (c) or (d), the parties may file statements regarding the impact of the proposed termination on the public interest, and the administrative law judge may hear argument, although no discovery may be compelled with respect to issues relating solely to the public interest. Thereafter, the administrative law judge shall consider and make appropriate findings in the initial determination regarding the effect of the proposed settlement on the public health and welfare, competitive conditions in the U.S. economy, the production of like or directly competitive articles in the United States, and U.S. consumers.

(c) No general exclusion from entry of articles shall be ordered under paragraph (a)(1) of this section unless the Commission determines that—

(1) Such exclusion is necessary to prevent circumvention of an exclusion order limited to products of named persons; or

(2) There is a pattern of violation of section 337 of the Tariff Act of 1930 and it is difficult to identify the source of infringing products.

(d) Forfeiture or return of respondents' bonds.

(1)(i) If one or more respondents posts a bond pursuant to 19 U.S.C. 1337(e)(1) or 1337(j)(3), proceedings to determine whether a respondent's bond should be forfeited to a complainant in whole or part may be initiated upon the filing of a motion by a complainant within 30 days after expiration of the Presidential review period under 19 U.S.C. 1337(j).

(ii) A respondent may file a motion for the return of its bond.

(2) Any nonmoving party may file a response to a motion filed under paragraph (d)(1) of this section within 15 days after filing of the motion, unless otherwise ordered by the administrative law judge.

(3) A motion for forfeiture or return of a respondent's bond in whole or part will be adjudicated by the administrative law judge in an initial determination with a 45-day effective date, which shall be subject to review under the provisions of Secs. 210.42 through 210.45. In determining whether to grant the motion, the administrative law judge and the Commission will be guided by practice under Rule 65 of the Federal Rules of Civil Procedure (taking into account that the roles of the parties are reversed in this instance).

(4) If the Commission determines that a respondent's bond should be forfeited to a complainant, and if the bond is being held by the Secretary of the Treasury, the Commission Secretary shall promptly notify the Secretary of the Treasury of the Commission's determination.

Sec. 210.51 Period for concluding investigation

(a) Permanent relief.

Within 45 days after institution of the investigation, the administrative law judge shall issue an order setting a target date for completion of the investigation. If the target date does not exceed 15 months from the date of institution of the investigation, the order of the administrative law judge shall be final and not subject to interlocutory review. If the target date exceeds 15 months, the order of the administrative law judge shall constitute an initial determination. After the target date has been set, it can be modified by the administrative law judge for good cause shown before the investigation is certified to the Commission or by the Commission after the investigation is certified to the Commission. Any extension of the target date beyond 15 months, before the investigation is certified to the Commission, shall be by initial determination.

(b) Temporary relief.

The temporary relief phase of an investigation shall be concluded and a final order issued no later than 90 days after publication of the notice of investigation in the Federal Register, unless the temporary relief phase of the investigation has been designated "more complicated" by the Commission or the presiding administrative law judge pursuant to Sec. 210.22(c) and Sec. 210.60. If that designation has been made, the temporary relief phase of the investigation shall be concluded and a final order issued no later than 150 days after publication of the notice of investigation in the Federal Register.

(c) Computation of time.

In computing the deadlines imposed in paragraph (b) of this section, there shall be excluded any period during which the investigation is suspended pursuant to Sec. 210.23.

Subpart H—Temporary Relief

Sec. 210.52 Motions for temporary relief

Requests for temporary relief under section 337 (e) or (f) of the Tariff Act of 1930 shall be made through a motion filed in accordance with the following provisions:

(a) A complaint requesting temporary relief shall be accompanied by a motion setting forth the complainant's request for such relief. In determining whether to grant temporary relief, the Commission will apply the standards the U.S. Court of Appeals for the Federal Circuit uses in determining whether to affirm lower court decisions granting preliminary injunctions. The motion for temporary relief accordingly must contain a detailed statement of specific facts bearing on the factors the Federal Circuit has stated that a U.S. District Court must consider in granting a preliminary injunction.

(b) The motion must also contain a detailed statement of facts bearing on:

(1) Whether the complainant should be required to post a bond as a prerequisite to the issuance of temporary relief; and

(2) The appropriate amount of the bond, if the Commission determines that a bond will be required.

(c) In determining whether to require a bond as a prerequisite to the issuance of temporary relief, the Commission will be guided by practice under Rule 65 of the Federal Rules of Civil Procedure.

(d) The following documents and information also shall be filed along with the motion for temporary relief:

(1) A memorandum of points and authorities in support of the motion;

(2) Affidavits executed by persons with knowledge of the facts asserted in the motion; and

(3) All documents, information, and other evidence in complainant's possession that complainant intends to submit in support of the motion.

(e) If the complaint, the motion for temporary relief, or the documentation supporting the motion for temporary relief contains confidential business information as defined in Sec. 201.6(a) of this chapter, the complainant must follow the procedure outlined in Secs. 210.4(a), 210.5(a), 201.6 (a) and (c), 210.8(a), and 210.55 of this part.

Sec. 210.53 Motion filed after complaint

(a) A motion for temporary relief may be filed after the complaint, but must be filed prior to the Commission determination under Sec. 210.10 on whether to institute an investigation. A motion filed after the complaint shall contain the information, documents, and evidence described in Sec. 210.52 and must also make a showing that extraordinary circumstances exist that warrant temporary relief and that the moving party was not aware, and with due diligence could not have been aware, of those circumstances at the time the complaint was filed. When a motion for temporary relief is filed after the complaint but before the Commission has determined whether to institute an investigation based on the complaint, the 35-day period allotted under Sec. 210.58 for review of the complaint and informal investigatory activity will begin to run anew from the date on which the motion was filed.

(b) A motion for temporary relief may not be filed after an investigation has been instituted.

Sec. 210.54 Service of motion by the complainant

Notwithstanding the provisions of Sec. 210.11 regarding service of the complaint and motion for temporary relief by the Commission upon institution of an investigation, on the day the complainant files a complaint and motion for temporary relief with the Commission (see Sec. 201.8(a) of this chapter), the complainant must serve nonconfidential copies of both documents (as well as nonconfidential copies of all materials or documents attached thereto) on all proposed respondents and on the embassy in Washington, DC of each country from which the allegedly unfair imports come. The complaint and motion shall be served by messenger, courier, express mail, or equivalent means. A signed certificate of service must accompany the complaint and motion for temporary relief. If the certificate does not accompany the complaint and the motion, the Secretary shall not accept the complaint or the motion and shall promptly notify the submitter. Actual proof of service on each respondent and embassy (e.g., certified mail return receipts, courier or overnight delivery receipts, or other proof of delivery)—or proof of a serious but unsuccessful effort to make such service—must be filed within 10 days after the filing of the complaint and motion. If the requirements of this section are not satisfied, the Commission may extend its 35-day deadline under Sec. 210.58 for determining whether to provisionally accept the motion for temporary relief and institute an investigation on the basis of the complaint.

Sec. 210.55 Content of service copies

(a) Any purported confidential business information that is deleted from the nonconfidential service copies of the complaint and motion for temporary relief must satisfy the requirements of Sec. 201.6(a) of this chapter (which defines confidential information for purposes of Commission proceedings). For attachments to the complaint or motion that are confidential in their entirety, the complainant must provide a nonconfidential summary of what each attachment contains. Despite the redaction of confidential material from the complaint and motion for temporary relief, the nonconfidential service copies must contain enough factual information about each element of the violation alleged in the complaint and the motion to enable each proposed respondent to comprehend the allegations against it.

(b) If the Commission determines that the complaint, motion for temporary relief, or any exhibits or attachments thereto contain excessive designations of confidentiality that are not warranted under Sec. 201.6(a) of this chapter, the Commission may require the complainant to file and serve new nonconfidential versions of the aforesaid submissions and may determine that the 35-day period under Sec. 210.58 for deciding whether to institute an investigation and to provisionally accept the motion for temporary relief for further processing shall begin to run anew from the date the new nonconfidential versions are filed with the Commission and served on the proposed respondents.

Sec. 210.56 Notice accompanying service copies

(a) Each service copy of the complaint and motion for temporary relief shall be accompanied by a notice containing the following text:

> Notice is hereby given that the attached complaint and motion for temporary relief will be filed with the U.S. International Trade Commission in Washington, DC on ________, 19__. The filing of the complaint and motion will not institute an investigation on that date, however, nor will it begin the period for filing responses to the complaint and motion pursuant to 19 CFR 210.13 and 210.59.
>
> Upon receipt of the complaint, the Commission will examine the complaint for sufficiency and compliance with 19 CFR 201.8, 210.4, 210.5, 210.8, and 210.12. The Commission's Office of Unfair Import Investigations will conduct informal investigatory activity pursuant to 19 CFR 210.9 to identify sources of relevant information and to assure itself of the availability thereof. The motion for temporary relief will be examined for sufficiency and compliance with 19 CFR 201.8, 210.4, 210.5, 210.52, 210.53(a) (if applicable), 210.54, 210.55, and 210.56, and will be subject to the same type of preliminary investigative activity as the complaint.
>
> The Commission generally will determine whether to institute an investigation on the basis of the complaint and whether to provisionally accept the motion for temporary relief within 35 days after the complaint and motion are filed or, if the motion is filed after the complaint, within 35 days after the motion is filed—unless the 35-day deadline is extended pursuant to 19 CFR 210.53, 210.54, 210.55(b), 210.57, or 210.58. If the Commission determines to institute an investigation and provisionally accept the motion, the motion will be assigned to a Commission administrative law judge for issuance of an initial determination in accordance with 19 CFR 210.66. See 19 CFR 210.10 and 210.58.
>
> If the Commission determines to conduct an investigation of the complaint and the motion for temporary relief, the investigation will be formally instituted on the date the Commission publishes a notice of investigation in the Federal Register pursuant to 19 CFR 210.10(b). If an investigation is instituted, copies of the complaint, the notice of investigation, the motion for temporary relief, and the Commission's Rules of Practice and Procedure (19 CFR Part 210) will be served on each respondent by the Commission pursuant to 19 CFR 210.11(a). Responses to the complaint, the notice of investigation, and the motion for temporary relief must be filed within 10 days after Commission service thereof, and must comply with 19 CFR 201.8, 210.4, 210.5,

210.13, and 210.59. See also 19 CFR 201.14 and 210.6 regarding computation of the 10-day response period.

If, after reviewing the complaint and motion for temporary relief, the Commission determines not to institute an investigation, the complaint and motion will be dismissed and the Commission will provide written notice of that decision and the reasons therefor to the complainant and all proposed respondents pursuant to 19 CFR 210.10.

For information concerning the filing and processing of the complaint and its treatment, and to ask general questions concerning section 337 practice and procedure, contact the Office of Unfair Import Investigations, U.S. International Trade Commission, 500 E Street SW., Room 401, Washington, DC 20436, telephone 202-205-2560. Such inquiries will be referred to the Commission investigative attorney assigned to the complaint. (See also the Commissions's Rules of Practice and Procedure set forth in 19 CFR Part 210.)

To learn the date that the Commission will vote on whether to institute an investigation and the publication date of the notice of investigation (if the Commission decides to institute an investigation), contact the Office of the Secretary, U.S. International Trade Commission, 500 E Street SW., room 112, Washington, DC 20436, telephone 202-205-2000.

This notice is being provided pursuant to 19 CFR 210.56.

(b) In the event that the complaint and motion for temporary relief are filed after the date specified in the above notice, the complainant must serve a supplementary notice to all proposed respondents and embassies stating the correct filing date. The supplementary notice shall be served by messenger, courier, express mail, or equivalent means. The complainant shall file a certificate of service and a copy of the supplementary notice with the Commission.

Sec. 210.57 Amendment of the motion

A motion for temporary relief may be amended at any time prior to the institution of an investigation. All material filed to amend the motion (or the complaint) must be served on all proposed respondents and on the embassies in Washington, DC, of the foreign governments that they represent, in accordance with Sec. 210.54. If the amendment expands the scope of the motion or changes the complainant's assertions on the issue of whether a bond is to be required as a prerequisite to the issuance of temporary relief or the appropriate amount of the bond, the 35-day period under Sec. 210.58 for determining whether to institute an investigation and provisionally accept the motion for temporary relief shall begin to run anew from the date the amendment is filed with the Commission. A motion for temporary relief may not be amended to expand the scope of the temporary relief inquiry after an investigation is instituted.

Sec. 210.58 Provisional acceptance of the motion

The Commission shall determine whether to accept a motion for temporary relief at the same time it determines whether to institute an investigation on the basis of the complaint. That determination shall be made within 35 days after the complaint and motion for temporary relief are filed, unless the 35-day period is restarted pursuant to Sec. 210.53(a), 210.54, 210.55, or 210.57, or exceptional circumstances exist which preclude adherence to the prescribed deadline. (See Sec. 210.10(a)(1).) Before the Commission determines whether to provisionally accept a motion for temporary relief, the motion will be examined for sufficiency and compliance with Secs. 210.52, 210.53(a) (if applicable), 210.54 through 210.56, as well as Secs. 201.8, 210.4, and 210.5. The motion will be subject to the same type of preliminary investigatory activity as the complaint. (See Sec. 210.9(b).) Acceptance of a motion pursuant to this paragraph constitutes provisional acceptance for referral of the motion to the chief administrative law judge, who will assign the motion to a presiding administrative law judge for issuance of an initial determination under Sec. 210.66(a). Commission rejection of an insufficient or improperly filed complaint will preclude acceptance of a motion for temporary relief. Commission rejection of a motion for temporary relief will not preclude institution of an investigation of the complaint.

Sec. 210.59 Responses to the motion and the complaint

(a) Any party may file a response to a motion for temporary relief. Unless otherwise ordered by the administrative law judge, a response to a motion for temporary relief in an ordinary investigation must be filed not later than 10 days after service of the motion by the Commission. In a "more complicated" investigation, the response shall be due within 20 days after such service, unless otherwise ordered by the presiding administrative law judge.

(b) The response must comply with the requirements of Sec. 201.8 of this chapter, as well as Secs. 210.4 and 210.5 of this part, and shall contain the following information:

(1) A statement that sets forth with particularity any objection to the motion for temporary relief;

(2) A statement of specific facts concerning the factors the U.S. Court of Appeals for the Federal Circuit would consider in determining whether to affirm lower court decisions granting or denying preliminary injunctions;

(3) A memorandum of points and authorities in support of the respondent's response to the motion;

(4) Affidavits, where possible, executed by persons with knowledge of the facts specified in the response. Each response to the motion must address, to the extent possible, the complainant's assertions regarding whether a bond should be required and the appropriate amount of the bond. Responses to the motion for temporary relief also may contain counter-proposals concerning the amount of the bond or the manner in which the bond amount should be calculated.

(c) Each response to the motion for temporary relief must also be accompanied by a response to the complaint and notice of investigation. Responses to the complaint and notice of investigation must comply with Sec. 201.8 of this chapter, Secs. 210.4 and 210.5 of this part, and any protective order issued by the administrative law judge under Sec. 210.34 of this part.

Sec. 210.60 Designating an investigation "more complicated" for the purpose of adjudicating a motion for temporary relief

At the time the Commission determines to institute an investigation and provisionally accepts a motion for temporary relief pursuant to Sec. 210.58, the Commission may designate the investigation "more complicated" pursuant to Sec. 210.22(c) for the purpose of obtaining up to 60 additional days to adjudicate the motion for temporary relief. In the alternative, after the motion for temporary relief is referred to the administrative law judge for an initial determination under Sec. 210.66(a), the administrative law judge may issue an order, *sua sponte* or on motion, designating the investigation "more complicated" for the purpose of obtaining additional time to adjudicate the motion for temporary relief. Such order shall constitute a final determination of the Commission, and notice of the order shall be published in the Federal Register. As required by section 337(e)(2) of the Tariff Act of 1930, the notice shall state the reasons that the temporary relief phase of the investigation was designated "more complicated." The "more complicated" designation may be conferred by the Commission or the presiding administrative law judge pursuant to this paragraph on the basis of the complexity of the issues raised in the motion for temporary relief or the responses thereto, or for other good cause shown.

Sec. 210.61 Discovery and compulsory process

The presiding administrative law judge shall set all discovery deadlines. The administrative law judge's authority to compel discovery includes discovery relating to the following issues:

(a) Any matter relevant to the motion for temporary relief and the responses thereto, including the issues of bonding by the complainant; and

(b) The issues the Commission considers pursuant to sections 337 (e)(1), (f)(1), and (j)(3) of the Tariff Act of 1930, viz.,

(1) The appropriate form of relief (notwithstanding the form requested in the motion for temporary relief),

(2) Whether the public interest precludes that form of relief, and

(3) The amount of the bond to be posted by the respondents to secure importations or sales of the subject imported merchandise while the temporary relief order is in effect. The administrative law judge may, but is not required to, make findings on the issues specified in sections 337 (e)(1), (f)(1), or (j)(3) of the Tariff Act of 1930. Evidence and information obtained through discovery on those issues will be used by the parties and considered by the Commission in the context of the parties' written submissions on remedy, the public interest, and bonding by respondents, which are filed with the Commission pursuant to Sec. 210.67(b).

Sec. 210.62 Evidentiary hearing

An opportunity for a hearing in accordance with the Administrative Procedure Act and Sec. 210.36 of this part will be provided in connection with every motion for temporary relief. If a hearing is conducted, the presiding administrative law judge may, but is not required to, take evidence concerning the issues of remedy, the public interest, and bonding by respondents under section 337 (e)(1), (f)(1), and (j)(3) of the Tariff Act of 1930.

Sec. 210.63 Proposed findings and conclusions and briefs

The administrative law judge shall determine whether and, if so, to what extent the parties shall be permitted to file proposed findings of fact, proposed conclusions of law, or briefs under Sec. 210.40 concerning the issues involved in adjudication of the motion for temporary relief.

Sec. 210.64 Interlocutory appeals

There will be no interlocutory appeals to the Commission under Sec. 210.24 on any matter connected with a motion for temporary relief that is decided by an administrative law judge prior to the issuance of the initial determination on the motion for temporary relief.

Sec. 210.65 Certification of the record

When the administrative law judge issues an initial determination concerning temporary relief pursuant to Sec. 210.66(a), he shall also certify to the Commission the record upon which the initial determination is based.

Sec. 210.66 Initial determination concerning temporary relief; Commission action thereon

(a) On or before the 70th day after publication of the notice of investigation in an ordinary investigation, or on or before the 120th day after such publication in a "more complicated" investigation, the administrative law judge will issue an initial determination concerning the issues listed in Secs. 210.52 and 210.59. If the 70th day or the 120th day is a Saturday, Sunday, or Federal holiday, the initial determination must be received in the Office of the Secretary no later than 12:00 noon on the first business day after the 70-day or 120-day deadline. The initial determination may, but is not required to, address the issues of remedy, the public interest, and bonding by the respondents pursuant under sections 337 (e)(1), (f)(1), and (j)(3) of the Tariff Act of 1930.

(b) If the initial determination on temporary relief is issued on the 70-day or 120-day deadline imposed in paragraph (a) of this section, the initial determination will become the Commission's determination 20 calendar days after issuance thereof in an ordinary case, and 30 calendar days after issuance in a "more complicated" investigation, unless the Commission modifies, reverses, or sets aside the initial determination in whole or part within that period. If the initial determination on temporary relief is issued before the 70-day or 120-day deadline imposed in paragraph (a) of this section, the Commission will add the extra time to the 20-day or 30-day deadline to which it would otherwise have been held. In computing the deadlines imposed by this paragraph, intermediary Saturdays, Sundays, and Federal holidays shall be included. If the last day of the period is a Saturday, Sunday, or Federal holiday as defined in Sec. 201.14(a) of this chapter, the effective date of the initial determination shall be extended to the next business day.

(c) The Commission will not modify, reverse, or set aside an initial determination concerning temporary relief unless the Commission finds that a finding of material fact is clearly erroneous, that the initial determination contains an error of law, or that there is a policy matter warranting discussion by the Commission. All parties may file written comments concerning any clear error of material fact, error of law, or policy matter warranting such action by the Commission. Such comments must be limited to 35 pages in an ordinary investigation and 45 pages in a "more complicated" investigation. The comments must be filed no later than seven calendar days after issuance of the initial determination in an ordinary case and 10 calendar days after issuance of the initial determination in a "more complicated" investigation. In computing the aforesaid 7-day and 10-day deadlines, intermediary Saturdays, Sundays, and Federal holidays shall be included. If the initial determination is issued on a Friday, however, the filing deadline for comments shall be measured from the first business day after issuance. If the last day of the filing period is a Saturday, Sunday, or Federal holiday as defined in Sec. 201.14(a) of this chapter, the filing deadline shall be extended to the next business day. The parties shall serve their comments on other parties by messenger, courier, express mail, or equivalent means.

(d) Notice of the initial determination shall be served on the other agencies listed in Sec. 210.50(a)(2). Those agencies will be given 10 calendar days from the date of service of the notice to file comments on the initial determination.

(e)(1) Each party may file a response to each set of comments filed by another party. All such reply comments must be filed within 10 calendar days after issuance of the initial determination in an ordinary case and within 14 calendar days after issuance of an initial determination in a "more complicated" investigation. The deadlines for filing reply comments shall be computed in the manner described in paragraph (c) of this section, except that in no case shall a party have fewer than two calendar days to file reply comments.

(2) Each set of reply comments will be limited to 20 pages in an ordinary investigation and 30 pages in a "more complicated" case.

(f) If the Commission determines to modify, reverse, or set aside the initial determination, the Commission will issue a notice and, if appropriate, a Commission opinion. If the Commission does not modify, reverse, or set aside the administrative law judge's initial determination within the time provided under paragraph (b) of this section, the initial determination will automatically become the determination of the Commission. Notice of the Commission's determination concerning the initial determination will be issued on the statutory deadline for determining whether to grant temporary relief, or as soon as possible thereafter, and will be served on the parties. Notice of the determination will be published in the Federal Register if the Commission's disposition of the initial determination has resulted in a determination that there is reason to believe that section 337 has been violated and a temporary remedial order is to be issued. If the Commission determines (either by reversing or modifying the administrative law judge's initial determination, or by adopting the initial determination) that the complainant must post a bond as a prerequisite to the issuance of temporary relief, the Commission may issue a supplemental notice setting forth conditions for the bond if any (in addition to those outlined in the initial determination) and the deadline for filing the bond with the Commission.

Sec. 210.67 Remedy, the public interest, and bonding by respondents

The procedure for arriving at the Commission's determination of the issues of the appropriate form of temporary relief, whether the public interest factors enumerated in the statute preclude such relief, and the amount of the bond under which respondents' merchandise will be permitted to enter the United States during the pendency of any temporary relief order issued by the Commission, is as follows:

(a) While the motion for temporary relief is before the administrative law judge, he may compel discovery on matters relating to remedy, the public interest, and bonding by respondents (as provided in Sec. 210.61). The administrative law judge also is authorized to make findings pertaining to the public interest, as provided in Sec. 210.66(a). Such findings may be superseded, however, by Commission findings on that issue as provided in paragraph (c) of this section.

(b) On the 65th day after institution in an ordinary case or on the 110th day after institution in a "more complicated" investigation, all parties shall file written submissions with the Commission addressing those issues. The submissions shall refer to information and evidence already on the record, but additional information and evidence germane to the issues of appropriate relief, the statutory public interest factors, and bonding by respondents may be provided along with the parties' submissions. Pursuant to Sec. 210.50(a)(4), interested persons may also file written comments, on the aforesaid dates, concerning the issues of remedy, the public interest, and bonding by the respondents.

(c) On or before the 90-day or 150-day statutory deadline for determining whether to order temporary relief under section 337 (e)(1) and/or (f)(1) of the Tariff Act of 1930, the Commission will determine what relief is appropriate in light of any violation that appears to exist, whether the public interest factors enumerated in the statute preclude the issuance of such relief, and the amount of the bond under which the respondents' merchandise will be permitted to enter the United States during the pendency of any temporary relief order issued by the Commission. In the event that Commission's findings on the public interest pursuant to this paragraph are inconsistent with findings made by the administrative law judge in the initial determination pursuant to Sec. 210.66(a), the Commission's findings are controlling.

Sec. 210.68 Complainant's temporary relief bond

(a) In every investigation under this part involving a motion for temporary relief, the question of whether the complainant shall be required to post a bond as a prerequisite to the issuance of such relief shall be addressed by the parties, the presiding administrative law judge, and the Commission in the manner described in Secs. 210.52, 210.59, 210.61, 210.62, and 210.66. If the Commission determines that a bond should be required, the bond may consist of one or more of the following:

(1) The surety bond of a surety or guarantee corporation that is licensed to do business with the United States in accordance with 31 U.S.C. 9304-9306 and 31 CFR Parts 223 and 224;

(2) The surety bond of an individual, a trust, an estate, or a partnership, or a corporation, whose solvency and financial responsibility will be investigated and verified by the Commission; or

(3) A certified check, a bank draft, a post office money order, cash, a United States bond, a Treasury note, or other Government obligation within the meaning of 31 U.S.C. 9301 and 31 CFR Part 225, which is owned by the complainant and tendered in lieu of a surety bond, pursuant to 31 U.S.C. 9303(c) and 31 CFR Part 225.

The same restrictions and requirements applicable to individual and corporate sureties on Customs bonds, which are set forth in 19 CFR Part 113, shall apply with respect to sureties on bonds filed with the Commission by complainants as a prerequisite to a temporary relief under section 337 of the Tariff Act of 1930. If the surety is an individual, the individual must file an affidavit of the type shown in Appendix A to Sec. 210.68. Unless otherwise ordered by the Commission, while the bond of the individual surety is in effect, an updated affidavit must be filed every four months (computed from the date on which the bond was approved by the Secretary or the Commission).

(b) The bond and accompanying documentation must be submitted to the Commission within the time specified in the Commission notice, order, determination, or opinion requiring the posting of a bond, or within such other time as the Commission may order. If the bond is not submitted within the specified period (and an extension of time has not been granted), temporary relief will not be issued.

(c) The corporate or individual surety on a bond or the person posting a certified check, a bank draft, a post office money order, cash, a United States bond, a Treasury note, or other Government obligation in lieu of a surety bond must provide the following information on the face of the bond or in the instrument authorizing the Government to collect or sell the bond, certified check, bank draft, post office money order, cash, United States bond, Treasury note, or other Government obligation in response to a Commission order requiring forfeiture of the bond pursuant to Sec. 210.70:

(1) The investigation caption and docket number;

(2) The names, addresses, and seals (if appropriate) of the principal, the surety, the obligee, as well as the "attorney in fact" and the registered process agent (if applicable) (see Customs Service regulations in 19 CFR Part 113 and Treasury Department regulations in 31 CFR Parts 223, 224, and 225);

(3) The terms and conditions of the bond obligation, including the reason the bond is being posted, the amount of the bond, the effective date and duration of the bond (as prescribed by the Commission order, notice, determination, or opinion requiring the complainant to post a bond); and

(4) A section at the bottom of the bond or other instrument for the date and authorized signature of the Secretary to reflect Commission approval of the bond.

(d) Complainants who wish to post a certified check, a bank draft, a post office money order, cash, a United States bond, a Treasury note, or other Government obligation in lieu of a surety bond must notify the Commission in writing immediately upon receipt of the Commission document requiring the posting of a bond, and must contact the Secretary to make arrangements for Commission receipt, handling, management, and deposit of the certified check, bank draft, post office money order, cash, United States bond, Treasury note, or other Government obligation tendered in lieu of a surety bond, in accordance with 31 U.S.C. Sec. 9303, 31 CFR Parts 202, 206, and 225 and other governing Treasury regulations and circular(s). If required by the governing Treasury regulations and circular, a certified check, a bank draft, a post office money order, cash, a United States bond, a Treasury note, or other government obligation tendered in lieu of a surety bond may have to be collateralized. See, e.g., 31 CFR 202.6 and the appropriate Treasury Circular.

Appendix A to Sec. 210.68 Affidavit by Individual Surety

United States International Trade Commission Affidavit by Individual Surety 19 CFR 210.68

State of County SS: ______________________________

I, the undersigned, being duly sworn, depose and say that I am a citizen of the United States, and of full age and legally competent; that I am not a partner in any business of the principal on the bond or bonds on which I appear as surety; and that the information herein below furnished is true and complete to the best of my knowledge. This affidavit is made to induce the United States International Trade Commission to accept me as surety on the bond(s) filed or to be filed with the United States International Trade Commission pursuant to 19 CFR 210.68. I agree to notify the Commission of any transfer or change in any of the assets herein enumerated.

____

1. Name (First, Middle, Last)

____

2. Home Address

____

3. Type & Duration of Occupation

____

4. Name of Employer (If Self-Employed)

____

5. Business Address

____

6. Telephone No.

Home____________________________________

Business __________________________________

7. The following is a true representation of my assets, liabilities, and net worth and does not include any financial interest I have in the assets of the principal on the bond(s) on which I appear as surety.

a. Fair value of solely owned real estate *..

b. All mortgages or other encumbrances on the real estate included in Line a ....

c. Real estate equity (subtract Line b from Line a)...

d. Fair value of all solely owned property other than real estate...

e. Total of the amounts on Lines c and d ....

f. All other liabilities owing or incurred not included in Line b...

g. Net worth (subtract Line f from Line e) ....

*Do not include property exempt from execution and sale for any reason. Surety's interest in community property may be included if not so exempt.

8. LOCATION AND DESCRIPTION OF REAL ESTATE OF WHICH I AM SOLE OWNER, THE VALUE OF WHICH IS IN LINE a, ITEM 7 ABOVE \1\

Amount of assessed value of above real estate for taxation purposes:

____

9. DESCRIPTION OF PROPERTY INCLUDED IN LINE d, ITEM 7 ABOVE (List the value of each category of property separately) \2\

____

10. ALL OTHER BONDS ON WHICH I AM SURETY (State character and amount of each bond; if none, so state) \3\

____

11.SIGNATURE

---

12. BOND AND COMMISSION INVESTIGATION TO WHICH THIS AFFIDAVIT RELATES

SUBSCRIBED AND SWORN TO BEFORE ME AS FOLLOWS:

DATE OATH ADMINISTERED

MONTH DAY YEAR

CITY ____________________

STATE (Or Other Jurisdiction) ____________________

NAME & TITLE OF OFFICIAL
ADMINISTERING OATH ____________________

SIGNATURE ____________________

MY COMMISSION EXPIRES ____________________

INSTRUCTIONS

1. Here describe the property by giving the number of the lot and square or block, and addition or subdivision, if in a city, and, if in the country, after showing state, county, and township, locate the property by metes and bounds, or by part of section, township, and range, so that it may be identified.

2. Here describe the property by name so that it can be identified—for example "Fifteen shares of the stock of the "National Metropolitan Bank, New York City," or "Am. T. & T. s. f.5's 60."

3. Here state what other bonds the affiant has already signed as surety, giving the name and address of the principal, the date, and the amount and character of the bond.

Sec. 210.69 Approval of complainant's temporary relief bond

(a) In accordance with 31 U.S.C. Sec. 9304(b), all bonds posted by complainants must be approved by the Commission before the temporary relief sought by the complainant will be issued. See also 31 U.S.C. Sec. 9303(a) and 31 CFR 225.1 and 225.20. The Commission's bond approval officer for purposes of those provisions shall be the Secretary.

(b) The bond approval process may entail investigation by the Secretary or the Commission's Office of Investigations to determine the veracity of all factual information set forth in the bond and the accompanying documentation (e.g., powers of attorney), as well as any additional verification required by 31 CFR Parts 223, 224, or 225. The Secretary may reject a bond on one or more of the following grounds:

(1) Failure to comply with the instructions in the Commission determination, order, or notice directing the complainant to post a bond;

(2) Failure of the surety or the bond to provide information or supporting documentation required by the Commission, the Secretary, Sec. 210.68 of this part, 31 CFR Parts 223 or 224, or other governing statutes, regulations, or Treasury circulars, or because of a limitation prescribed in a governing statute, regulation, or circular;

(3) Failure of an individual surety to execute and file with the bond, an affidavit of the type shown in Appendix A to Sec. 210.68, which sets forth information about the surety's assets, liabilities, net worth, real estate and other property of which the initial surety is the sole owner, other bonds on which the individual surety is a surety (and which must be updated at 4-month intervals while the bond is in effect, measured from the date on which the bond is approved by the Secretary on behalf of the Commission or by the Commission);

(4) Any question about the solvency or financial responsibility of the surety, or any question of fraud, misrepresentation, or perjury which comes to light as a result of the verification inquiry during the bond approval process; and

(5) Any other reason deemed appropriate by the Secretary.

(c) If the complainant believes that the Secretary's rejection of the bond was erroneous as a matter of law, the complainant may appeal the Secretary's rejection of the bond by filing a petition with the Commission in the form of a letter to the Chairman, within 10 days after service of the rejection letter.

(d) After the bond is approved and temporary relief is issued, if any question concerning the continued solvency of the individual or the legality or enforceability of the bond or undertaking develops, the Commission may take the following action(s), *sua sponte* or on motion;

(1) Revoke the Commission approval of the bond and require complainant to post a new bond; or

(2) Revoke or vacate the temporary remedial order for public interest reasons or changed conditions of law or fact (criteria that are the basis for modification or rescission of final Commission action pursuant to Sec. 210.76(a)(1) and (b)); or

(3) Notify the Treasury Department if the problem involves a corporate surety licensed to do business with the United States under 31 U.S.C. Secs. 9303-9306 and 31 CFR Parts 223 and 224; or

(4) Refer the matter to the U.S. Department of Justice if there is a suggestion of fraud, perjury, or related conduct.

Subpart I—Enforcement Procedures and Advisory Opinions

Sec. 210.70 Forfeiture or return of complainant's temporary relief bond

(a)(1) If the Commission determines that one or more of the respondents whose merchandise was covered by the temporary relief order has not violated (153section 337 of the Tariff Act of 1930 to the extent alleged in the motion for temporary relief and provided for in the temporary relief order, proceedings to determine whether the complainant's bond should be forfeited to one or more respondents in whole or part may be initiated upon the filing of a motion by a respondent within 30 days after filing of the aforesaid Commission determination on violation.

(2) A complainant may file a motion for the return of its bond.

(b) Any nonmoving party may file a response to a motion filed under paragraph (a) of this section within 15 days after filing of the motion, unless otherwise ordered by the administrative law judge.

(c) A motion for forfeiture or return of a complainant's temporary relief bond in whole or part will be adjudicated by the administrative law judge in an initial determination with a 45-day effective date, which shall be subject to review under the provisions of Secs. 210.42 through 210.45. In determining whether to grant the motion, the administrative law judge and the Commission will be guided by practice under Rule 65 of the Federal Rules of Civil Procedure.

Sec. 210.71 Information gathering

(a) Power to require information.

(1) Whenever the Commission issues an exclusion order, the Commission may require any person to report facts available to that person that will help the Commission assist the U.S. Customs Service in determining whether and to what extent there is compliance with the order or whether and to what extent the conditions that led to the order are changed. Similarly, whenever the Commission issues a cease and desist order or a consent order, it may require any person to report facts available to that person that will aid the Commission in determining whether and to what extent there is compliance with the order or whether and to what extent the conditions that led to the order are changed.

(2) The Commission may also include provisions that exercise any other information-gathering power available to the Commission by law, regardless of whether the order at issue is an exclusion order, a cease and desist order, or a consent order. The Commission may at any time request the cooperation of any person or agency in supplying it with information that will aid the Commission or the U.S. Customs Service in making the determinations described in paragraph (a)(1) of this section.

(b) Form and detail of reports.

Reports under paragraph (a) of this section are to be in writing, under oath, and in such detail and in such form as the Commission prescribes.

(c) Power to enforce informational requirements.

Terms and conditions of exclusion orders, cease and desist orders, and consent orders for reporting and information gathering shall be enforceable by the Commission by a civil action under 19 U.S.C. Sec. 1333, or, at the Commission's discretion, in the same manner as any other provision of the exclusion order, cease and desist order, or consent order is enforced.

(d) Term of reporting requirement.

An exclusion order, cease and desist order, or consent order may provide for the frequency of reporting or information gathering and the date on which these activities are to terminate. If no date for termination is provided, reporting and information gathering shall terminate when the exclusion order, cease and desist order, or consent order or any amendment to it expires by its own terms or is terminated.

Sec. 210.72 Confidentiality of information

Confidential information (as defined in Sec. 201.6(a) of this chapter) that is provided to the Commission pursuant to exclusion order, cease and desist order, or consent order will be received by the Commission in confidence. Requests for confidential treatment shall comply with Sec. 201.6 of this chapter. The restrictions on disclosure and the procedures for handling such information (which are set out in Secs. 210.5 and 210.39) shall apply and, in a proceeding under Secs. 210.75 or 210.76, the Commission or the presiding administrative law judge may, upon motion or *sua sponte*, issue or continue appropriate protective orders.

Sec. 210.73 Review of reports

(a) Review to insure compliance.

The Commission, through the Office of Unfair Import Investigations, will review reports submitted pursuant to any exclusion order, cease and desist order, or consent order and conduct such further investigation as it deems necessary to insure compliance with its orders.

(b) Extension of time.

The Director of the Office of Unfair Import Investigations may, for good cause shown, extend the time in which reports required by exclusion orders, cease and desist orders, and consent orders may be filed. An extension of time within which a report may be filed, or the filing of a report that does not evidence full compliance with the order, does not in any circumstances suspend or relieve a respondent from its obligation under the law with respect to compliance with such order.

Sec. 210.74 Modification of reporting requirements

(a) Exclusion and cease and desist orders.

The Commission may modify reporting requirements of exclusion and cease and desist orders as necessary:

(1) To help the Commission assist the U.S. Customs Service in ascertaining that there has been compliance with an outstanding exclusion order;

(2) To help the Commission ascertain that there has been compliance with a cease and desist order;

(3) To take account of changed circumstances; or

(4) To minimize the burden of reporting or informational access.

An order to modify reporting requirements shall identify the reports involved and state the reason or reasons for modification. No reporting requirement will be suspended during the pendency of such a modification unless the Commission so orders. The Commission may, if the public interest warrants, announce that a modification of reporting is under consideration and ask for comment, but it may also modify any reporting requirement at any time without notice, consistent with the standards of this section.

(b) Consent orders.

Consistent with the standards set forth in paragraph (a) of this section, the Commission may modify reporting requirements of consent orders. The Commission shall serve notice of any proposed change, together with the reporting requirements to be modified and the reasons therefor, on each party subject to the consent order. Such parties shall be given the opportunity to submit briefs to the Commission, and the Commission may hold a hearing on the matter. Notice of any proposed change in the reporting requirements will be published in the Federal Register if the Commission determines to solicit public comment on the proposed change.

Sec. 210.75 Proceedings to enforce exclusion orders, cease and desist orders, consent orders, and other Commission orders

(a) Informal enforcement proceedings.

Informal enforcement proceedings may be conducted by the Commission, through the Office of Unfair Import Investigations, with respect to any act or omission by any person in possible violation of any provision of an exclusion order, cease and desist order, or consent order. Such matters may be handled by the Commission through correspondence or conference or in any other way that the Commission deems appropriate. The Commission may issue such orders as it deems appropriate to implement and insure compliance with the terms of an exclusion order, cease and desist order, or consent order, or any part thereof. Any matter not disposed of informally may be made the subject of a formal proceeding pursuant to this subpart.

(b) Formal enforcement proceedings.

(1) The Commission may institute an enforcement proceeding at the Commission level upon the filing by the complainant in the original investigation or his successor in interest, by the Office of Unfair Import Investigations, or by the Commission of a complaint setting forth alleged violations of any exclusion order, cease and desist order, or consent order. If a proceeding is instituted, the complaint shall be served upon the alleged violator and a notice of institution published in the Federal Register. Within 15 days after the date of service of such a complaint, the named respondent shall file a response to it. Responses shall fully advise the Commission as to the nature of any defense and shall admit or deny each allegation of the complaint specifically and in detail unless the respondent is without knowledge, in which case its answer shall so state and the statement shall operate as a denial. Allegations of fact not denied or controverted may be deemed admitted. Matters alleged as affirmative defenses shall be separately stated and numbered.

(2) Upon the failure of a respondent to file and serve a response within the time and in the manner prescribed herein the Commission, in its discretion, may find the facts alleged in the complaint to be true and take such action as may be appropriate without notice or hearing, or, in its discretion, proceed without notice to take evidence on the allegations set forth in the complaint, provided that the Commission (or administrative law judge, if one is appointed) may permit late filings of an answer for good cause shown.

(3) The Commission, in the course of a formal enforcement proceeding under this section may hold a public hearing and afford the parties to the enforcement proceeding the opportunity to appear and be heard. The hearing will not be subject to sections 554, 555, 556, 557, and 702 of title 5 of the United States Code. The Commission may delegate the hearing to the chief administrative law judge for designation of a presiding administrative law judge, who shall certify an initial determination to the Commission. That initial determination shall become the determination of the Commission 90 days after the date of service of the initial determination, unless the Commission, within 90 days after the date of such service shall have ordered review of the initial determination on certain issues therein, or by order shall have changed the effective date of the initial determination.

(4) Upon conclusion of a formal enforcement proceeding under this section, the Commission may:

(i) Modify a cease and desist order, consent order, and/or exclusion order in any manner necessary to prevent the unfair practices that were originally the basis for issuing such order;

(ii) Bring civil actions in a United States district court pursuant to paragraph (c) of this section (and section 337(f)(2) of the Tariff Act of 1930) requesting the imposition of a civil penalty or the issuance of injunctions incorporating the relief sought by the Commission; or

(iii) Revoke the cease and desist order or consent order and direct that the articles concerned be excluded from entry into the United States.

(5) Prior to effecting any modification, revocation, or exclusion under this section, the Commission shall consider the effect of such action upon the public health and welfare, competitive conditions in the U.S. economy, the production of like or directly competitive articles in the United States, and U.S. consumers.

(6) In lieu of or in addition to taking the action provided for in paragraph (b)(1) of this section, the Commission may issue, pursuant to section 337(i) of the Tariff Act of 1930, an order providing that any article imported in violation of the provisions of section 337 of the Tariff Act of 1930 and an outstanding final exclusion order issued pursuant to section 337(d) of the Tariff Act of 1930 be seized and forfeited to the United States, if the following conditions are satisfied:

(i) The owner, importer, or consignee of the article (or the agent of such person) previously attempted to import the article into the United States;

(ii) The article previously was denied entry into the United States by reason of a final exclusion order; and

(iii) Upon such previous denial of entry, the Secretary of the Treasury provided the owner, importer, or consignee of the article (or the agent of such person) with written notice of the aforesaid exclusion order and the fact that seizure and forfeiture would result from any further attempt to import the article into the United States.

(c) Court enforcement.

To enforce an exclusion order, a cease and desist order, a consent order, or a sanctions order, the Commission may initiate a civil action in the U.S. district court pursuant to section 337(f)(2) of the Tariff Act of 1930, requesting the imposition of such civil penalty or the issuance of such injunctions as the Commission deems necessary to enforce its orders and protect the public interest. The Commission may initiate a proceeding to obtain judicial enforcement without any other type of proceeding otherwise available under section 337 or this subpart or without prior notice to any person, except as required by the court in which the civil action is initiated.

Sec. 210.76 Modification or rescission of exclusion orders, cease and desist orders, and consent orders

(a) Petitions for modification or rescission of exclusion orders, cease and desist orders, and consent orders.

(1) Whenever any person believes that changed conditions of fact or law, or the public interest, require that an exclusion order, cease and desist order, or consent order be

modified or set aside, in whole or in part, such person may file with the Commission a petition requesting such relief. The Commission may also on its own initiative consider such action. The petition shall state the changes desired and the changed circumstances warranting such action, shall include materials and argument in support thereof, and shall be served on all parties to the investigation in which the exclusion order, cease and desist order, or consent order was issued. Any person may file an opposition to the petition within 10 days of service of the petition.

(2) If the petitioner previously has been found by the Commission to be in violation of section 337 of the Tariff Act of 1930 and if its petition requests a Commission determination that the petitioner is no longer in violation of that section or requests modification or rescission of an order issued pursuant to section 337 (d), (e), (f), (g), or (i) of the Tariff Act of 1930, the burden of proof in any proceeding initiated in response to the petition pursuant to paragraph (b) of this section shall be on the petitioner. In accordance with section 337(k)(2) of the Tariff Act, relief may be granted by the Commission with respect to such petition on the basis of new evidence or evidence that could not have been presented at the prior proceeding or on grounds that would permit relief from a judgment or order under the Federal Rules of Civil Procedure.

(b) Commission action upon receipt of petition.

The Commission may thereafter institute a proceeding to modify or rescind the exclusion order, cease and desist order, or consent order by issuing a notice. The Commission may hold a public hearing and afford interested persons the opportunity to appear and be heard. After consideration of the petition, any responses thereto, and any information placed on the record at a public hearing or otherwise, the Commission shall take such action as it deems appropriate. The Commission may delegate any hearing under this section to the chief administrative law judge for designation of a presiding administrative law judge, who shall certify a recommended determination to the Commission.

Sec. 210.77 Temporary emergency action

(a) Whenever the Commission determines, pending a formal enforcement proceeding under Sec. 210.75(b), that without immediate action a violation of an exclusion order, cease and desist order, or consent order will occur and that subsequent action by the Commission would not adequately repair substantial harm caused by such violation, the Commission may immediately and without hearing or notice modify or revoke such order and, if it is revoked, replace the order with an appropriate exclusion order.

(b) Prior to taking any action under this section, the Commission shall consider the effect of such action upon the public health and welfare, competitive conditions in the U.S. economy, the production of like or directly competitive articles in the United States, and U.S. consumers. The Commission shall, if it has not already done so, institute a formal enforcement proceeding under Sec. 210.75(b) at the time of taking action under this section or as soon as possible thereafter, in order to give the alleged violator and other interested parties a full opportunity to present information and views regarding the continuation, modification, or revocation of Commission action taken under this section.

Sec. 210.78 Notice of enforcement action to Government agencies

(a) Consultation.

The Commission may consult with or seek information from any Government agency when taking any action under this subpart.

(b) Notification of Treasury.

The Commission shall notify the Secretary of the Treasury of any action under this subpart that results in a permanent or temporary exclusion of articles from entry, or the revocation of an order to such effect, or the issuance of an order compelling seizure and forfeiture of imported articles.

Sec. 210.79 Advisory opinions

(a) Advisory opinions.

Upon request of any person, the Commission may, upon such investigation as it deems necessary, issue an advisory opinion as to whether the person's proposed course of action or conduct would violate a Commission exclusion order, cease and desist order, or consent order. The Commission will consider whether the issuance of such an advisory opinion would facilitate the enforcement of section 337 of the Tariff Act of 1930, would be in the public interest, and would benefit consumers and competitive conditions in the United States, and whether the person has a compelling business need for the advice and has framed his request as fully and accurately as possible. Advisory opinion proceedings are not subject to sections 554, 555, 556, 557, and 702 of title 5 of the United States Code.

(b) Revocation.

The Commission may at any time reconsider any advice given under this section and, where the public interest requires, revoke its prior advice. In such event the person will be given notice of the Commission's intent to revoke as well as an opportunity to submit its views to the Commission. The Commission will not proceed against a person for violation of an exclusion order, cease and desist order, or consent order with respect to any action that was taken in good faith reliance upon the Commission's advice under this section, if all relevant facts were accurately presented to the Commission and such action was promptly discontinued upon notification of revocation of the Commission's advice.

ABOUT THE COMMISSIONERS

The USITC is headed by six Commissioners who are nominated by the President and confirmed by the U.S. Senate. No more than three Commissioners may be of any one political party. Currently three Democrats and two Republicans serve as Commissioners, and there is one vacancy.

The Commissioners serve overlapping terms of nine years each, with a new term beginning every 18 months. The Chairman and Vice Chairman are designated by the President from among the current Commissioners for two-year terms. The Chairman and Vice Chairman must be from different political parties, and the Chairman cannot be from the same political party as the preceding Chairman.

The current Commissioners of the USITC are:

Stephen Koplan

Stephen Koplan, a Democrat of Virginia, is the Chairman of the United States International Trade Commission.

Chairman Koplan was nominated to the ITC by President Clinton on March 3, 1998, and confirmed by the U.S. Senate on July 30, 1998. He was sworn in as a member of the Commission on August 4, 1998, for a term expiring on June 16, 2005.

Chairman Koplan has been admitted to practice law in both Massachusetts and the District of Columbia. He began his career as a prosecutor in the Tax Division of the U.S. Department of Justice. He served in the Department for a total of 12 years (Tax Division, five years; Civil Rights Division, seven years). While there, he gained both criminal and civil trial experience and ultimately headed up a section responsible for the enforcement of those laws intended to assure nondiscrimination in federal financial assistance programs. Subsequently, he served for six and one-half years as the Legislative Representative for tax and international trade issues for the AFL-CIO.

Chairman Koplan also served as staff attorney for three years to former U.S. Senator Lee Metcalf (D-Montana), for whom he had the responsibility for all federal tax and foreign trade legislation referred to the Senate Committee on Finance. Koplan returned to the Senate to serve as the General Counsel of what was formerly the Post Office and Civil Service Committee. His business experience includes five years as the Vice President of Governmental Affairs of Joseph E. Seagram & Sons, Inc., where he directed the federal legislative and regulatory operations of the corporation with an emphasis on tax and foreign trade. He has also served as a principal in two Washington, D.C., law firms, Bayh & Connaughton and the McNair Law Firm, for a total of five and one-half years. Most recently, he was the Director for Governmental and Conservation Affairs of Safari Club International.

Chairman Koplan is originally from Belmont, Massachusetts. He holds a Bachelor of Arts degree from Brandeis University, a Juris Doctor degree from Boston University School of Law, and a Master of Laws (in Taxation) degree from the Graduate Law Division of New York University. He resides in Fairfax, Virginia, with his wife, Harriet. They have four sons, Michael, Bruce, David, and Adam, and two grandchildren, Jacob and Zoe.

June 2000

Jennifer A. Hillman

Jennifer A. Hillman, a Democrat of Indiana, was nominated to the United States International Trade Commission by President Clinton in March 1998 and confirmed by the U.S. Senate on July 30, 1998. Commissioner Hillman was sworn in as a member of the Commission on August 4, 1998, for a term expiring on December 16, 2006.

Commissioner Hillman served as General Counsel for the United States Trade Representative (USTR) from 1995-1997, where she was responsible for a wide variety of trade matters, including all U.S. government submissions in dispute settlement cases pending before either the World Trade Organization or North American Free Trade Agreement panels as well as all legal work done in connection with trade negotiations.

Prior to that position, she served as Chief Textile Negotiator with the Rank of Ambassador for the USTR. As Chief Textile Negotiator, Commissioner Hillman was responsible for negotiating bilateral textile agreements with 38 countries in 1993-1994. Prior to joining the USTR, Commissioner Hillman served as the Deputy Cluster Coordinator for Financial Institutions for the Presidential and Vice Presidential transition.

Before joining the transition, Commissioner Hillman was the Legislative Director and Counsel to U.S. Senator Terry Sanford of North Carolina. On the Hill, she was responsible for all international trade issues, as well as matters coming before the Committee on Banking, Housing and Urban Affairs, including thrift banking securities, export control, international finance, and housing matters. She began her professional career as an attorney in the Washington firm of Patton, Boggs & Blow.

Commissioner Hillman is originally from South Bend, Indiana. She holds a Bachelor of Arts degree in political science and a Master of Education degree in higher education administration from Duke University; she received her J.D. from Harvard Law School. She resides in Washington, DC, with her husband, Mitchell Berger, and two sons.

August 1998

Marcia E. Miller

Marcia E. Miller, a Democrat of Indiana, was nominated to the United States International Trade Commission by President Clinton on May 16, 1996, for the term ending December 16, 2003. Her nomination was confirmed by the U.S. Senate on June 26, 1996, and she was sworn in as a member of the Commission on August 5, 1996.

Commissioner Miller served as Chairman of the Commission from August 5, 1996, through June 16, 1998. She also served as Vice Chairman of the Commission from June 17, 1998, through June 16, 2000.

Prior to her appointment, Commissioner Miller was the Minority Chief International Trade Counselor with the U.S. Senate Committee on Finance. The Committee has jurisdiction over U.S. foreign trade policy, customs and import matters, and the budgets of several related agencies, as well as tax and other fiscal matters. Ms. Miller was named Chief International Trade Counselor to the Finance Committee by then-Chairman Daniel Patrick Moynihan in February 1993 following six years of service as a professional staff member with the Committee.

Earlier in her career, Commissioner Miller was an international economist with the law firm of Wilmer, Cutler, and Pickering. Prior to that, she handled international trade issues for the American Textile Manufacturers Institute.

Commissioner Miller holds a master of arts degree from the School of Advanced International Studies, Johns Hopkins University, and a bachelor of arts degree from Miami University in Oxford, Ohio. She is married, has one son, and resides in McLean, VA.

June 2000

Lynn M. Bragg

Lynn Munroe Bragg, a Republican of Maryland, was appointed to the United States International Trade Commission by President Clinton for the term that will expire on June 16, 2002. She served as Chairman of the ITC from June 17, 1998, through June 16, 2000. She also served as Vice Chairman of the ITC from August 5, 1996, through June 16, 1998. She has served as a Commissioner since March 31, 1994.

Prior to her appointment, Commissioner Bragg served in a senior management position with the Edison Electric Institute (EEI), a trade association representing the investor-owned electric utility industry. As a director of government affairs, she advised member companies on legislative matters relating to fossil fuels and industry structure issues.

From 1981 to 1991, Commissioner Bragg served on the staff of former Senator Malcolm Wallop (R-WY). In that position, she worked extensively on energy, tax, and trade issues as the legislative director and a legislative assistant. Before joining Senator Wallop's staff, Bragg held several positions in the corporate affairs department of the Potomac Electric Power Company (PEPCO) in Washington, D.C.

Commissioner Bragg holds a master's degree from Boston University and a bachelor's degree with final honors from Mary Washington College in Fredericksburg, Virginia.

Commissioner Bragg was born on June 15, 1954, at Fort Leonard Wood, Missouri. She is married to Ray Bragg; has three children, Rachael, Braxton, and Hudson; and currently lives in Chevy Chase, Maryland.

June 2000

Deanna Tanner Okun

Deanna Tanner Okun, a Republican of Idaho, is the Vice Chairman of the United States International Trade Commission.

Vice Chairman Okun was nominated to the ITC by President Clinton on November 10, 1999, and confirmed by the U.S. Senate on November 19, 1999. She was sworn in as a member of the Commission on January 3, 2000, for a term expiring on June 16, 2008.

Prior to her appointment, Vice Chairman Okun served as counsel for international affairs to Senator Frank Murkowski (R-AK) from 1993-1999, where she was responsible for the international trade issues with which the Senator was involved as a member of the Senate Finance Committee. She also handled international energy and foreign relations issues for the Senator in his position as Chairman of the Senate Energy and Natural Resources Committee.

Earlier, Vice Chairman Okun served as a legislative assistant to Senator Murkowski, where she was responsible for his Foreign Relations Committee work, with an emphasis on East Asian affairs. Prior to her work with the Senator, Ms. Okun was an associate attorney and member of the International Trade Group at the Washington, DC, law firm of

Hogan & Hartson. Earlier in her career, Ms. Okun was a research associate specializing in trade at the Competitive Enterprise Institute in Washington, DC.

Vice Chairman Okun holds a Bachelor of Arts degree in political science with honors from Utah State University and received her J.D. with honors from the Duke University School of Law. She is originally from Paul, Idaho. Currently, Vice Chairman Okun resides in McLean, Virginia, with her husband, Bob Okun, and two daughters, Rachel and Kelsi.

July 2001

APPENDIX B
CUSTOMS SERVICE STATUTES AND REGULATIONS

UNITED STATES CODE
TITLE 15—COMMERCE AND TRADE
CHAPTER 22—TRADEMARKS
SUBCHAPTER III—GENERAL PROVISIONS

Sec. 1124 Importation of goods bearing infringing marks or names forbidden

Except as provided in subsection (d) of section 1526 of Title 19, no article of imported merchandise which shall copy or simulate the name of the domestic manufacture, or manufacturer, or trader, or of any manufacturer or trader located in any foreign country which, by treaty, convention, or law affords similar privileges to citizens of the United States, or which shall copy or simulate a trade-mark registered in accordance with the provisions of this Act or shall bear a name or mark calculated to induce the public to believe that the article is manufactured in the United States, or that it is manufactured in any foreign country or locality other than the country or locality in which it is in fact manufactured, shall be admitted to entry at any customhouse of the United States; and, in order to aid the officers of the customs in enforcing this prohibition, any domestic manufacturer or trader, and any foreign manufacturer or trader, who is entitled under the provisions of a treaty, conviction, declaration, or agreement between the United States and any foreign country to the advantages afforded by law to citizens of the United States in respect to trademarks and commercial names, may require his name and residence, and the name of the locality in which his goods are manufactured, and a copy of the certificate of registration of his trademark, issued in accordance with the provisions of this Act, to be recorded in books which shall be kept for this purpose in the Department of the Treasury, under such regulations as the Secretary of the Treasury shall prescribe, and may furnish to the Department facsimiles of his name, the name of the locality in which his goods are manufactured, or of his registered trade-mark, and thereupon the Secretary of the Treasury shall cause one or more copies of the same to be transmitted to each collector or other proper officer of customs.

Sec. 1125 False designations of origin, false descriptions, and dilution forbidden

(a) Civil action

(1) Any person who, on or in connection with any goods or services, or any container for goods, uses in commerce any word, term, name, symbol, or device, or any combination thereof, or any false designation of origin, false or misleading description of fact, or false or misleading representation of fact, which—

(A) is likely to cause confusion, or to cause mistake, or to deceive as to the affiliation, connection, or association of such person with another person, or as to the origin, sponsorship, or approval of his or her goods, services, or commercial activities by another person, or

(B) in commercial advertising or promotion, misrepresents the nature, characteristics, qualities, or geographic origin of his or her or another person's goods, services, or commercial activities,

shall be liable in a civil action by any person who believes that he or she is or is likely to be damaged by such act.

(2) As used in this subsection, the term "any person" includes any State, instrumentality of a State or employee of a State or instrumentality of a State acting in his or her official capacity. Any State, and any such instrumentality, officer, or employee, shall be subject to the provisions of this chapter in the same manner and to the same extent as any nongovernmental entity.

(3) In a civil action for trade dress infringement under this chapter for trade dress not registered on the principal register, the person who asserts trade dress protection has the burden of proving that the matter sought to be protected is not functional.

(b) Importation

Any goods marked or labeled in contravention of the provisions of this section shall not be imported into the United States or admitted to entry at any customhouse of the United States. The owner, importer, or consignee of goods refused entry at any customhouse under this section may have any recourse by protest or appeal that is given under the customs revenue laws or may have the remedy given by this chapter in cases involving goods refused entry or seized.

(c) Remedies for dilution of famous marks

(1) The owner of a famous mark shall be entitled, subject to the principles of equity and upon such terms as the court deems reasonable, to an injunction against another person's commercial use in commerce of a mark or trade name, if such use begins after the mark has become famous and causes dilution of the distinctive quality of the mark, and to obtain such other relief as is provided in this subsection. In determining whether a mark is distinctive and famous, a court may consider factors such as, but not limited to—

(A) the degree of inherent or acquired distinctiveness of the mark;

(B) the duration and extent of use of the mark in connection with the goods or services with which the mark is used;

(C) the duration and extent of advertising and publicity of the mark;

(D) the geographical extent of the trading area in which the mark is used;

(E) the channels of trade for the goods or services with which the mark is used;

(F) the degree of recognition of the mark in the trading areas and channels of trade used by the marks' owner and the person against whom the injunction is sought;

(G) the nature and extent of use of the same or similar marks by third parties; and

(H) whether the mark was registered under the Act of March 3, 1881, or the Act of February 20, 1905, or on the principal register.

(2) In an action brought under this subsection, the owner of the famous mark shall be entitled only to injunctive relief as set forth in section 1116 of this title unless the person against whom the injunction is sought willfully intended to trade on the owner's reputation or to cause dilution of the famous mark. If such willful intent is proven, the owner of the famous mark shall also be entitled to the remedies set forth in sections 1117(a) and 1118 of this title, subject to the discretion of the court and the principles of equity.

(3) The ownership by a person of a valid registration under the Act of March 3, 1881, or the Act of February 20, 1905, or on the principal register shall be a complete bar to an action against that person, with respect to that mark, that is brought by another person under the common law or a statute of a State and that seeks to prevent dilution of the distinctiveness of a mark, label, or form of advertisement.

(4) The following shall not be actionable under this section:

(A) Fair use of a famous mark by another person in comparative commercial advertising or promotion to identify the competing goods or services of the owner of the famous mark.

(B) Noncommercial use of a mark.

(C) All forms of news reporting and news commentary.

(d) Cyberpiracy prevention

(1)(A) A person shall be liable in a civil action by the owner of a mark, including a personal name which is protected as a mark under this section, if, without regard to the goods or services of the parties, that person—

(i) has a bad faith intent to profit from that mark, including a personal name which is protected as a mark under this section; and

(ii) registers, traffics in, or uses a domain name that—

(I) in the case of a mark that is distinctive at the time of registration of the domain name, is identical or confusingly similar to that mark;

(II) in the case of a famous mark that is famous at the time of registration of the domain name, is identical or confusingly similar to or dilutive of that mark; or

(III) is a trademark, word, or name protected by reason of section 706 of title 18 or section 220506 of title 36.

(B)(i) In determining whether a person has a bad faith intent described under subparagraph (A), a court may consider factors such as, but not limited to—

(I) the trademark or other intellectual property rights of the person, if any, in the domain name;

(II) the extent to which the domain name consists of the legal name of the person or a name that is otherwise commonly used to identify that person;

(III) the person's prior use, if any, of the domain name in connection with the bona fide offering of any goods or services;

(IV) the person's bona fide noncommercial or fair use of the mark in a site accessible under the domain name;

(V) the person's intent to divert consumers from the mark owner's online location to a site accessible under the domain name that could harm the goodwill represented by the mark, either for commercial gain or with the intent to tarnish or disparage the mark, by creating a likelihood of confusion as to the source, sponsorship, affiliation, or endorsement of the site;

(VI) the person's offer to transfer, sell, or otherwise assign the domain name to the mark owner or any third party for financial gain without having used, or having an intent to use, the domain name in the bona fide offering of any goods or services, or the person's prior conduct indicating a pattern of such conduct;

(VII) the person's provision of material and misleading false contact information when applying for the registration of the domain name, the person's intentional failure to maintain accurate contact information, or the person's prior conduct indicating a pattern of such conduct;

(VIII) the person's registration or acquisition of multiple domain names which the person knows are identical or confusingly similar to marks of others that are distinctive at the time of registration of such domain names, or dilutive of famous marks of others that are famous at the time of registration of such domain names, without regard to the goods or services of the parties; and

(IX) the extent to which the mark incorporated in the person's domain name registration is or is not distinctive and famous within the meaning of subsection (c)(1) of this section.

(ii) Bad faith intent described under subparagraph (A) shall not be found in any case in which the court determines that the person believed and had reasonable grounds to believe that the use of the domain name was a fair use or otherwise lawful.

(C) In any civil action involving the registration, trafficking, or use of a domain name under this paragraph, a court may order the forfeiture or cancellation of the domain name or the transfer of the domain name to the owner of the mark.

(D) A person shall be liable for using a domain name under subparagraph (A) only if that person is the domain name registrant or that registrant's authorized licensee.

(E) As used in this paragraph, the term "traffics in" refers to transactions that include, but are not limited to, sales, purchases, loans, pledges, licenses, exchanges of currency, and any other transfer for consideration or receipt in exchange for consideration.

(2)(A) The owner of a mark may file an in rem civil action against a domain name in the judicial district in which the domain name registrar, domain name registry, or other domain name authority that registered or assigned the domain name is located if—

(i) the domain name violates any right of the owner of a mark registered in the Patent and Trademark Office, or protected under subsection (a) or (c) of this section; and

(ii) the court finds that the owner—

(I) is not able to obtain in personam jurisdiction over a person who would have been a defendant in a civil action under paragraph (1); or

(II) through due diligence was not able to find a person who would have been a defendant in a civil action under paragraph (1) by—

(aa) sending a notice of the alleged violation and intent to proceed under this paragraph to the registrant of the domain name at the postal and e-mail address provided by the registrant to the registrar; and

(bb) publishing notice of the action as the court may direct promptly after filing the action.

(B) The actions under subparagraph (A)(ii) shall constitute service of process.

(C) In an in rem action under this paragraph, a domain name shall be deemed to have its situs in the judicial district in which—

(i) the domain name registrar, registry, or other domain name authority that registered or assigned the domain name is located; or

(ii) documents sufficient to establish control and authority regarding the disposition of the registration and use of the domain name are deposited with the court.

(D)(i) The remedies in an in rem action under this paragraph shall be limited to a court order for the forfeiture or cancellation of the domain name or the transfer of the domain name to the owner of the mark. Upon receipt of written notification of a filed, stamped copy of a complaint filed by the owner of a mark in a United States district court under this paragraph, the domain name registrar, domain name registry, or other domain name authority shall—

(I) expeditiously deposit with the court documents sufficient to establish the court's control and authority regarding the disposition of the registration and use of the domain name to the court; and

(II) not transfer, suspend, or otherwise modify the domain name during the pendency of the action, except upon order of the court.

(ii) The domain name registrar or registry or other domain name authority shall not be liable for injunctive or monetary relief under this paragraph except in the case of bad faith or reckless disregard, which includes a willful failure to comply with any such court order.

(3) The civil action established under paragraph (1) and the in rem action established under paragraph (2), and any remedy available under either such action, shall be in addition to any other civil action or remedy otherwise applicable.

(4) The in rem jurisdiction established under paragraph (2) shall be in addition to any other jurisdiction that otherwise exists, whether in rem or in personam.

UNITED STATES CODE
TITLE 17—COPYRIGHTS
CHAPTER 5—COPYRIGHT INFRINGEMENT AND REMEDIES

Sec. 506 Criminal offenses

(a) Criminal infringement. Any person who infringes a copyright willfully either—

(1) for purposes of commercial advantage or private financial gain, or

(2) by the reproduction or distribution, including by electronic means, during any 180-day period, of 1 or more copies or phonorecords of 1 or more copyrighted works, which have a total retail value of more than $1,000, shall be punished as provided under section 2319 of title 18, United States Code. For purposes of this subsection, evidence of reproduction or distribution of a copyrighted work, by itself, shall not be sufficient to establish willful infringement.

(b) Forfeiture and destruction. When any person is convicted of any violation of subsection (a), the court in its judgment of conviction shall, in addition to the penalty therein prescribed, order the forfeiture and destruction or other disposition of all infringing copies or phonorecords and all implements, devices, or equipment used in the manufacture of such infringing copies or phonorecords.

(c) Fraudulent copyright notice. Any person who, with fraudulent intent, places on any article a notice of copyright or words of the same purport that such person knows to be false, or who, with fraudulent intent, publicly distributes or imports for public distribution any article bearing such notice or words that such person knows to be false, shall be fined not more than $2,500.

(d) Fraudulent removal of copyright notice. Any person who, with fraudulent intent, removes or alters any notice of copyright appearing on a copy of a copyrighted work shall be fined not more than $ 2,500.

(e) False representation. Any person who knowingly makes a false representation of a material fact in the application for copyright registration provided for by section 409, or in any written statement filed in connection with the application, shall be fined not more than $ 2,500.

(f) Rights of attribution and integrity. Nothing in this section applies to infringement of the rights conferred by section 106A(a).

Sec. 509 Seizure and forfeiture

(a) All copies or phonorecords manufactured, reproduced, distributed, sold, or otherwise used, intended for use, or possessed with intent to use in violation of section 506 (a), and all plates, molds, matrices, masters, tapes, film negatives, or other articles by means of which such copies or phonorecords may be reproduced, and all electronic, mechanical, or other devices for manufacturing, reproducing, or assembling such copies or phonorecords may be seized and forfeited to the United States.

(b) The applicable procedures relating to (i) the seizure, summary and judicial forfeiture, and condemnation of vessels, vehicles, merchandise, and baggage for violations of the customs laws contained in title 19, (ii) the disposition of such vessels, vehicles, merchandise, and baggage or the proceeds from the sale thereof, (iii) the remission or mitigation of such forfeiture, (iv) the compromise of claims, and (v) the award of compensation to informers in respect of such forfeitures, shall apply to seizures and forfeitures incurred, or alleged to have been incurred, under the provisions of this section, insofar as applicable and not inconsistent with the provisions of this section; except that such duties as are imposed upon any officer or employee of the Treasury Department or any other person with respect to the seizure and forfeiture of vessels, vehicles, merchandise; and baggage under the provisions of the customs laws contained in title 19 shall be performed with respect to seizure and forfeiture of all articles described in subsection (a) by such officers, agents, or other persons as may be authorized or designated for that purpose by the Attorney General.

CHAPTER 6—MANUFACTURING REQUIREMENTS AND IMPORTATION

Sec. 602 Infringing importation of copies or phonorecords

(a) Importation into the United States, without the authority of the owner of copyright under this title, of copies or phonorecords of a work that have been acquired outside the United States is an infringement of the exclusive right to distribute copies or phonorecords under section 106, actionable under section 501. This subsection does not apply to—

(1) importation of copies or phonorecords under the authority or for the use of the Government of the United States or of any State or political subdivision of a State, but not including copies or phonorecords for use in schools, or copies of any audiovisual work imported for purposes other than archival use;

(2) importation, for the private use of the importer and not for distribution, by any person with respect to no more than one copy or phonorecord of any one work at any one time, or by any person arriving from outside the United States with respect to copies or phonorecords forming part of such person's personal baggage; or

(3) importation by or for an organization operated for scholarly, educational, or religious purposes and not for private gain, with respect to no more than one copy of an audiovisual work solely for its archival purposes, and no more than five copies or phonorecords of any other work for its library lending or archival purposes, unless the importation of such copies or phonorecords is part of an activity consisting of systematic reproduction or distribution, engaged in by such organization in violation of the provisions of section 108(g)(2).

(b) In a case where the making of the copies or phonorecords would have constituted an infringement of copyright if this title had been applicable, their importation is prohibited. In a case where the copies or phonorecords were lawfully made, the United States Customs Service has no authority to prevent their importation unless the provisions of section 601 are applicable. In either case, the Secretary of the Treasury is authorized to prescribe, by regulation, a procedure under which any person claiming an interest in the copyright in a particular work may, upon payment of a specified fee, be entitled to notification by the Customs Service of the importation of articles that appear to be copies or phonorecords of the work.

Sec. 603 Importation prohibitions: Enforcement and disposition of excluded articles

(a) The Secretary of the Treasury and the United States Postal Service shall separately or jointly make regulations for the enforcement of the provisions of this title prohibiting importation.

(b) These regulations may require, as a condition for the exclusion of articles under section 602—

(1) that the person seeking exclusion obtain a court order enjoining importation of the articles; or

(2) that the person seeking exclusion furnish proof, of a specified nature and in accordance with prescribed procedures, that the copyright in which such person claims an interest is valid and that the importation would violate the prohibition in section 602; the person seeking exclusion may also be required to post a surety bond for any injury that may result if the detention or exclusion of the articles proves to be unjustified.

(c) Articles imported in violation of the importation prohibitions of this title are subject to seizure and forfeiture in the same manner as property imported in violation of the customs revenue laws. Forfeited articles shall be destroyed as directed by the Secretary of the Treasury or the court, as the case may be; however, the articles may be returned to the country of export whenever it is shown to the satisfaction of the Secretary of the Treasury that the importer had no reasonable grounds for believing that his or her acts constituted a violation of law.

UNITED STATES CODE
TITLE 19—CUSTOMS DUTIES
CHAPTER 4—TARIFF ACT OF 1930

Sec. 1526 Merchandise bearing American trademark

(a) Importation prohibited. Except as provided in subsection (d) of this section, it shall be unlawful to import into the United States any merchandise of foreign manufacture if such merchandise, or the label, sign, print, package, wrapper, or receptacle, bears a trade-mark owned by a citizen of, or by a corporation or association created or organized within, the United States, and registered in the Patent and Trademark Office by a person domiciled in the United States, under the provisions of sections 81 to 109 of Title 15, and if a copy of the certificate of registration of such trade-mark is filed with the Secretary of the Treasury, in the manner provided in section 106 of said Title 15, unless written consent of the owner of such trade-mark is produced at the time of making entry.

(b) Seizure and forfeiture. Any such merchandise imported into the United States in violation of the provisions of this section shall be subject to seizure and forfeiture for violation of the customs laws.

(c) Injunction and damages. Any person dealing in any such merchandise may be enjoined from dealing therein within the United States or may be required to export or destroy such merchandise or to remove or obliterate such trademark and shall be liable for the same damages and profits provided for wrongful use of a trademark, under the provisions of sections 81 to 109 of Title 15.

(d) Exemptions; publication in Federal Register; forfeitures; rules and regulations.

(1) The trademark provisions of this section and section 1124 of Title 15, do not apply to the importation of articles accompanying any person arriving in the United States when such articles are for his personal use and not for sale if (A) such articles are within the limits of types and quantities determined by the Secretary pursuant to paragraph (2) of this subsection, and (B) such person has not been granted an exemption under this subsection within thirty days immediately preceding his arrival.

(2) The Secretary shall determine and publish in the Federal Register lists of the types of articles and the quantities of each which shall be entitled to the exemption provided by this subsection. In determining such quantities of particular types of trade-marked articles, the Secretary shall give such consideration as he deems necessary to the numbers of such articles usually purchased at retail for personal use.

(3) If any article which has been exempted from the restrictions on importation of the trade-mark laws under this subsection is sold within one year after the date of importation, such article, or its value (to be recovered from the importer), is subject to forfeiture. A sale pursuant to a judicial order or in liquidation of the estate of a decedent is not subject to the provisions of this paragraph.

(4) The Secretary may prescribe such rules and regulations as may be necessary to carry out the provisions of this subsection.

(e) Merchandise bearing counterfeit mark; seizure and forfeiture; disposition of seized goods. Any such merchandise bearing a counterfeit mark (within the meaning of section 1127 of Title 15 imported into the United States in violation of the provisions of section 1124 of Title 15, shall be seized and, in the absence of the written consent of the trademark owner, forfeited for violations of the customs laws. Upon seizure of such merchandise, the Secretary shall notify the owner of the trademark, and shall, after forfeiture, destroy the merchandise. Alternatively, if the merchandise is not unsafe or a hazard to health, and the Secretary has the consent of the trademark owner, the Secretary may dispose of the goods seized—

(1) by delivery to such Federal, State, and local government agencies as in the opinion of the Secretary have a need for such merchandise,

(2) by gift to such eleemosynary institutions as in the opinion of the Secretary have a need for such merchandise, or

(3) more than 90 days after the date of forfeiture, by sale by the Customs Service at public auction under such regulations as the Secretary prescribes, except that before making any such sale the Secretary shall determine that no Federal, State, or local government agency or eleemosynary institution has established a need for such merchandise under paragraph (1) or (2).

(4) Repealed.

(f) Civil Penalties.

(1) Any person who directs, assists financially or otherwise, or aids and abets the importation of merchandise for sale or public distribution that is seized under subsection (e) shall be subject to a civil fine.

(2) For the first such seizure, the fine shall be not more than the value that the merchandise would have had if it were genuine, according to the manufacturer's suggested retail price, determined under regulations promulgated by the Secretary.

(3) For the second seizure and thereafter, the fins shall be not more than twice the value that the merchandise would have had if it were genuine, as determined under the regulations promulgated by the Secretary.

(4) The imposition of a fine under this subsection shall be within the discretion of the Customs Service, and shall be in addition to any other civil or criminal penalty or other remedy authorized by law.

CODE OF FEDERAL REGULATIONS
TITLE 19—CUSTOMS DUTIES
CHAPTER I—UNITED STATES CUSTOMS SERVICE, DEPARTMENT OF THE TREASURY
PART 133—TRADEMARKS, TRADE NAMES, AND COPYRIGHTS

Sec. 133.1 Recordation of trademarks

(a) Eligible trademarks. Trademarks registered by the U.S. Patent and Trademark Office under the Trademark Act of March 3, 1881, the Trademark Act of February 20, 1905, or the Trademark Act of 1946 (15 U.S.C. 1051 *et seq.*) except those registered on the supplemental register under the 1946 Act (15 U.S.C. 1096), may be recorded with the U.S. Customs Service if the registration is current.

(b) Notice of recordation and other action. Applicants and recordants will be notified of the approval or denial of an application filed in accordance with §§ 133.2, 133.5, 133.6, and 133.7 of this subpart.

Sec. 133.2 Application to record trademark

An application to record one or more trademarks shall be in writing, addressed to the Intellectual Property Rights Branch, U.S. Customs Service, 1300 Pennsylvania Avenue, NW., Washington, DC 20229, and shall include the following information:

(a) The name, complete business address, and citizenship of the trademark owner or owners (if a partnership, the citizenship of each partner; if an association or corporation the State, country, or other political jurisdiction within which it was organized, incorporated, or created);

(b) The places of manufacture of goods bearing the recorded trademark;

(c) The name and principal business address of each foreign person or business entity authorized or licensed to use the trademark and a statement as to the use authorized; and

(d) The identity of any parent or subsidiary company or other foreign company under common ownership or control which uses the trademark abroad. For this purpose:

(1) "Common ownership"' means individual or aggregate ownership of more than 50 percent of the business entity; and

(2) "Common control" means effective control in policy and operations and is not necessarily synonymous with common ownership.

(e) "Lever-rule" protection. For owners of U.S. trademarks who desire protection against gray market articles on the basis of physical and material differences (*see Lever Bros. Co. v. United States,* 981 F.2d 1330 (D.C. Cir. 1993)), a description of any physical and material difference between the specific articles authorized for importation or sale in the United States and those not so authorized. In each instance, owners who assert that physical and material differences exist must state the basis for such a claim with particularity, and must support such assertions by competent evidence and provide summaries of physical and material differences for publication. Customs determination of physical and material differences may include, but is not limited to, considerations of:

(1) The specific composition of both the authorized and gray market product(s) (including chemical composition);

(2) Formulation, product construction, structure, or composite product components, of both the authorized and gray market product;

(3) Performance and/or operational characteristics of both the authorized and gray market product;

(4) Differences resulting from legal or regulatory requirements, certification, etc.;

(5) Other distinguishing and explicitly defined factors that would likely result in consumer deception or confusion as proscribed under applicable law.

(f) Customs will publish in the Customs Bulletin a notice listing any trademark(s) and the specific products for which gray market protection for physically and materially different products has been requested. Customs will examine the request(s) before issuing a determination whether gray market protection is granted. For parties requesting protection, the application for trademark protection will not take effect until Customs has made and issued this determination. If protection is granted, Customs will publish in the Customs Bulletin a notice that a trademark will receive *Lever*-rule protection with regard to a specific product.

Sec. 133.3 Documents and fee to accompany application

(a) Documents. The application shall be accompanied by:

(1) A status copy of the certificate of registration certified by the U.S. Patent and Trademark Office showing title to be presently in the name of the applicant; and

(2) Five copies of this certificate, or of a U.S. Patent and Trademark Office facsimile. The copies may be reproduced privately and shall be on paper approximately 8" x 101/2" in size. If the certificate consists of two or more pages, the copies may be reproduced on both sides of the paper.

(b) Fee. The application shall be accompanied by a fee of $190 for each trademark to be recorded. However, if the trademark is registered for more than one class of goods (based on the class, or classes, first stated on the certificate of registration, without consideration of any class, or classes, also stated in parentheses) the fee for recordation shall be $190 for each class for which the applicant desires to record the trademark with the United States Customs Service. For example, to secure recordation of a trademark registered for three classes of goods, a fee of $570 is payable. A check or money order shall be made payable to the United States Customs Service.

Sec. 133.4 Effective date, term, and cancellation of trademark recordation and renewals

(a) Effective date. Recordation of trademark and protection thereunder shall be effective on the date an application for recordation is approved, as shown on the recordation notice issued by the United States Customs Service instructing Customs officers as to the terms and conditions of import protection appropriate.

(b) Term. The recordation or renewal of an existing recordation of a trademark shall remain in force concurrently with the 20-year current registration period[1] or last renewal thereof in the U.S. Patent and Trademark Office.

(c) Cancellation of recordation. Recordation of a trademark with the United States Customs Service shall be canceled if the trademark registration is finally canceled or revoked.

Sec. 133.5 Change of ownership of recorded trademark

If there is a change in ownership of a recorded trademark and the new owner wishes to continue the recordation with the United States Customs Service, he shall apply therefor by:

(a) Complying with § 133.2;

(b) Describing any time limit on the rights of ownership transferred;

(c) Submitting a status copy of the certificate of registration certified by the U.S. Patent and Trademark Office showing title to be presently in the name of the new owner; and

(d) Paying a fee of $80, which covers all trademarks included in the application which have been previously recorded with the United States Customs Service. A check or money order shall be made payable to the United States Customs Service.

Sec. 133.6 Change in name of owner of recorded trademark

If there is a change in the name of the owner of a recorded trademark, but no change in ownership, written notice thereof shall be given to the Intellectual Property Rights Branch, accompanied by:

(a) A status copy of the certificate of registration certified by the U.S. Patent and Trademark Office showing title to be presently in the name as changed; and

(b) A fee of $80, which covers all trademarks included in the application which have been previously recorded with the United States Customs Service. A check or money order shall be made payable to the United States Customs Service.

Sec. 133.7 Renewal of trademark recordation

(a) Application to renew. To continue uninterrupted Customs protection for trademarks, the trademark owner shall submit a written application to renew Customs recordation to the Intellectual Property Rights Branch not later than 3 months after the date of expiration of the current 20-year trademark registration issued by the U.S. Patent and Trademark Office.[2] A timely application to renew a Customs recordation must include the following:

(1) A status copy of the certificate of registration certified by the U.S. Patent and Trademark Office showing renewal of the trademark and title to be in the name of the applicant;

(2) A statement describing any change of ownership or in the name of owner, in compliance with §§ 133.5 and 133.6 of this part, and any change of addresses of owners or places of manufacture; and

(3) A fee of $80 for each renewal of a trademark recordation. Where the trademark covers several classes, a fee of $80 is required for each class. A check or money order shall be made payable to the United States Customs Service.

(b) Delayed application. Upon request made during the grace period of 3 months afforded by paragraph (a) of this section, a trademark owner whose application for renewal of

---

2 *Id.*

recordation is unavoidably delayed may be afforded a reasonable extended period within which to comply with the requirements of paragraph (a) of this section. The request shall be in writing, addressed to the Intellectual Property Rights Branch, and shall set forth the circumstances due to which application is delayed.

(c) Untimely application. Failure of the trademark owner to submit a renewal application within the 3-month grace period afforded in accordance with paragraph (a) of this section or within an extension of time granted in accordance with paragraph (b) of this section, shall deprive the trademark owner of the renewal process. A delinquent applicant will be required to apply anew to record the renewed trademark in accordance with the procedures and requirements of §§ 133.2 and 133.3.

Sec. 133.11 Trade names eligible for recordation

The name or trade style used for at least 6 months to identify a manufacturer or trader may be recorded with the United States Customs Service. Words or designs used as trademarks, whether or not registered in the U.S. Patent and Trademark Office shall not be accepted for recordation as a trade name. Generally, the complete business name will be recorded unless convincing proof establishes that only a part of the complete name is customarily used.

Sec. 133.12 Application to record a trade name

An application to record a trade name shall be in writing addressed to the Intellectual Property Rights Branch, U.S. Customs Service, 1300 Pennsylvania Avenue, NW., Washington, DC 20229, and shall include the following information:

(a) The name, complete business address, and citizenship of the trade name owner or owners (if a partnership, the citizenship of each partner; if an association or corporation, the State, country, or other political jurisdiction within which it was organized, incorporated or created);

(b) The name or trade style to be recorded;

(c) The name and principal business address of each foreign person or business entity authorized or licensed to use the trade name and a statement as to the use authorized;

(d) The identity of any parent or subsidiary company, or other foreign company under common ownership or control which uses the trade name abroad (*see* § 133.2(d)); and

(e) A description of the merchandise with which the trade name is associated.

Sec. 133.13 Documents and fee to accompany application

(a) Documents. The application shall be accompanied by a statement of the owner, partners, or principal corporate officer, and by statements by at least two other persons not associated with or related to the applicant but having actual knowledge of the facts, stating that to his best knowledge and belief:

(1) The applicant has used the trade name in connection with the class or kind of merchandise described in the application for at least 6 months;

(2) The trade name is not identical or confusingly similar to any other trade name or registered trademark used in connection with such class or kind of merchandise; and

(3) The applicant has the sole and exclusive right to the use of such trade name in connection with the merchandise of that class or kind.

(b) Fee. The application shall be accompanied by a fee of $190 for each trade name to be recorded. A check or money order shall be made payable to the United States Customs Service.

Sec. 133.14 Publication of trade name recordation

(a) Notice of tentative recordation. Notice of tentative recordation of a trade name shall be published in the Federal Register and the Customs Bulletin. The notice shall specify a procedure and a time period within which interested parties may oppose the recordation.

(b) Notice of final action. After consideration of any claims, rebuttals, and other relevant evidence, notice of final approval or disapproval of the application shall be published in the Federal Register and the Customs Bulletin.

Sec. 133.15 Term of Customs trade name recordation

Protection for a recorded trade name shall remain in force as long as the trade name is used. The recordation shall be canceled upon request of the recordant or upon evidence of disuse. From time to time, the Intellectual Property Rights Branch may request the trade name owner to advise whether the name is still in use. The failure of a trade name owner to respond to such a request shall be regarded as evidence of disuse.

Sec. 133.21 Articles bearing counterfeit trademarks

(a) Counterfeit trademark defined. A "counterfeit trademark" is a spurious trademark that is identical to, or substantially indistinguishable from, a registered trademark.

(b) Seizure. Any article of domestic or foreign manufacture imported into the United States bearing a counterfeit trademark shall be seized and, in the absence of the written consent of the trademark owner, forfeited for violation of the customs laws.

(c) Notice to trademark owner. When merchandise is seized under this section, Customs shall disclose to the owner of the trademark the following information, if available, within 30 days, excluding weekends and holidays, of the date of the notice of seizure:

(1) The date of importation;

(2) The port of entry;

(3) A description of the merchandise;

(4) The quantity involved;

(5) The name and address of the manufacturer;

(6) The country of origin of the merchandise;

(7) The name and address of the exporter; and

(8) The name and address of the importer.

(d) Samples available to the trademark owner. At any time following seizure of the merchandise, Customs may provide a sample of the suspect merchandise to the owner of the trademark for examination, testing, or other use in pursuit of a related private civil remedy for trademark infringement. To obtain a sample under this section, the trademark/trade name owner must furnish Customs a bond in the form and amount specified by the port director, conditioned to hold the United States, its officers and employees, and the importer or owner of the imported article harmless from any loss or damage resulting from the furnishing of a sample by Customs to the trademark owner. Customs may demand the return of the sample at any time. The owner must return the sample to Customs upon demand or at the conclusion of the examination, testing, or other use in pursuit of a related private civil remedy for trademark infringement. In the event that the sample is damaged, destroyed, or lost while in the possession of the trademark owner, the owner shall, in lieu of return of the sample, certify to Customs that: "The sample described as [insert description] and provided pursuant to 19 CFR 133.21(d) was (damaged/destroyed/lost) during examination, testing or other use."

(e) Failure to make appropriate disposition. Unless the trademark owner, within 30 days of notification, provides written consent to importation of the articles, exportation, entry after obliteration of the trademark, or other appropriate disposition, the articles shall be disposed of in accordance with § 133.52, subject to the importer's right to petition for relief from the forfeiture under the provisions of part 171 of this chapter.

Sec. 133.22 Restrictions on importation of articles bearing copying or simulating trademarks

(a) Copying or simulating trademark or trade name defined. A "copying or simulating" trademark or trade name is one which may so resemble a recorded mark or name as to be likely to cause the public to associate the copying or simulating mark with the recorded mark or name.

(b) Denial of entry. Any articles of foreign or domestic manufacture imported into the United States bearing a mark or name copying or simulating a recorded mark or name shall be denied entry and subject to detention as provided in § 133.25.

(c) Relief from detention of articles bearing copying or simulating trademarks. Articles subject to the restrictions of this section shall be detained for 30 days from the date on which the goods are presented for Customs examination, to permit the importer to establish that any of the following circumstances are applicable:

(1) The objectionable mark is removed or obliterated as a condition to entry in such a manner as to be illegible and incapable of being reconstituted, for example by:

(i) Grinding off imprinted trademarks wherever they appear;

(ii) Removing and disposing of plates bearing a trademark or trade name;

(2) The merchandise is imported by the recordant of the trademark or trade name or his designate;

(3) The recordant gives written consent to an importation of articles otherwise subject to the restrictions set forth in paragraph (b) of this section or § 133.23(c) of this subpart, and such consent is furnished to appropriate officials;

(4) The articles of foreign manufacture bear a recorded trademark and the one-item personal exemption is claimed and allowed under § 148.55 of this chapter.

(d) Exceptions for articles bearing counterfeit trademarks. The provisions of paragraph (c)(1) of this section are not applicable to articles bearing counterfeit trademarks at the time of importation (*see* § 133.26).

(e) Release of detained articles. Articles detained in accordance with § 133.25 may be released to the importer during the 30-day period of detention if any of the circumstances allowing exemption from trademark or trade name restriction set forth in paragraph (c) of this section are established.

(f) Seizure. If the importer has not obtained release of detained articles within the 30-day period of detention, the merchandise shall be seized and forfeiture proceedings instituted. The importer shall be promptly notified of the seizure and liability to forfeiture and his right to petition for relief in accordance with the provisions of part 171 of this chapter.

Sec. 133.23 Restrictions on importation of gray market articles

(a) Restricted gray market articles defined. "Restricted gray market articles" are foreign-made articles bearing a genuine trademark or trade name identical with or substantially indistinguishable from one owned and recorded by a citizen of the United States or a corporation or association created or organized within the United States and imported without the authorization of the U.S. owner. "Restricted gray market goods" include goods bearing a genuine trademark or trade name which is:

(1) Independent licensee. Applied by a licensee (including a manufacturer) independent of the U.S. owner, or

(2) Foreign owner. Applied under the authority of a foreign trademark or trade name owner other than the U.S. owner, a parent or subsidiary of the U.S. owner, or a party otherwise subject to common ownership or control with the U.S. owner (*see* §§ 133.2(d) and 133.12(d) of this part), from whom the U.S. owner acquired the domestic title, or to whom the U.S. owner sold the foreign title(s); or

(3) "Lever-rule". Applied by the U.S. owner, a parent or subsidiary of the U.S. owner, or a party otherwise subject to common ownership or control with the U.S. owner (*see* §§ 133.2(d) and 133.12(d) of this part), to goods that the Customs Service has determined to be physically and materially different from the articles authorized by the U.S. trademark owner for importation or sale in the U.S. (as defined in § 133.2 of this part).

(b) Labeling of physically and materially different goods. Goods determined by the Customs Service to be physically and materially different under the procedures of this part, bearing a genuine mark applied under the authority of the U.S. owner, a parent or subsidiary of the U.S. owner, or a party otherwise subject to common ownership or control with the U.S. owner (*see* §§ 133.2(d) and 133.12(d) of this part), shall not be detained under the provisions of paragraph (c) of this section where the merchandise or its packaging bears a conspicuous and legible label designed to remain on the product until the first point of sale to a retail consumer in the United States stating that: "This product is not a product authorized by the United States trademark owner for importation and is physically and materially different from the authorized product." The label must be in close proximity to the trademark as it appears in its most prominent location on the article itself or the retail package or container. Other information designed to dispel consumer confusion may also be added.

(c) Denial of entry. All restricted gray market goods imported into the United States shall be denied entry and subject to detention as provided in § 133.25, except as provided in paragraph (b) of this section.

(d) Relief from detention of gray market articles. Gray market goods subject to the restrictions of this section shall be detained for 30 days from the date on which the goods are presented for Customs examination, to permit the importer to establish that any of the following exceptions, as well as the circumstances described above in § 133.22(c), are applicable:

(1) The trademark or trade name was applied under the authority of a foreign trademark or trade name owner who is the same as the U.S. owner, a parent or subsidiary of the U.S. owner, or a party otherwise subject to common ownership or control with the U.S. owner (in an instance covered by §§ 133.2(d) and 133.12(d) of this part); and/or

(2) For goods bearing a genuine mark applied under the authority of the U.S. owner, a parent or subsidiary of the U.S. owner, or a party otherwise subject to common ownership or control with the U.S. owner, that the merchandise as imported is not physically and materially different, as described in § 133.2(e), from articles authorized by the U.S. owner for importation or sale in the United States; or

(3) Where goods are detained for violation of § 133.23(a)(3), as physically and materially different from the articles authorized by the U.S. trademark owner for importation or sale in the U.S., a label in compliance with § 133.23(b) is applied to the goods.

(e) Release of detained goods. Articles detained in accordance with § 133.25 may be released to the importer during the 30-day period of detention if any of the circumstances allowing exemption from trademark restriction set forth in § 133.22(c) of this subpart or in paragraph (d) of this section are established.

(f) Seizure. If the importer has not obtained release of detained articles within the 30-day period of detention, the merchandise shall be seized and forfeiture proceedings instituted. The importer shall be notified of the seizure and liability of forfeiture and his right to petition for relief in accordance with the provisions of part 171 of this chapter.

Sec. 133.24 Restrictions on articles accompanying importer and mail importations

(a) Detention. Articles accompanying an importer and mail importations subject to the restrictions of §§ 133.22 and 133.23 shall be detained for 30 days from the date of notice that such restrictions apply, to permit the establishment of whether any of the circumstances described in § 133.22(c) or 133.23(d) are applicable.

(b) Notice of detention. Notice of detention shall be given in the following manner:

(1) Articles accompanying importer. When the articles are carried as accompanying baggage or on the person or persons arriving in the United States, the Customs inspector shall orally advise the importer that the articles are subject to detention.

(2) Mail importations. When the articles arrive by mail in noncommercial shipments, or in commercial shipments valued at $250 or less, notice of the detention shall be given on Customs Form 8.

(c) Release of detained goods.

(1) General. Articles detained in accordance paragraph (a) of this section may be released to the importer during the 30-day period of detention if any of the

circumstances allowing exemption from trademark or trade name restriction(s) set forth in § 133.22(c) or 133.23(d) of this subpart are established.

(2) Articles accompanying importer. Articles arriving as accompanying baggage or on the person of the importer may be exported or destroyed under Customs supervision at the request of the importer, or may be released if:

(i) The importer removes or obliterates the marks in a manner acceptable to the Customs officer at the time of examination of the articles; or

(ii) The request of the importer to obtain skillful removal of the marks is granted by the port director under such conditions as he may deem necessary, and upon return of the article to Customs for verification, the marks are found to be satisfactorily removed.

(3) Mail importations. Articles arriving by mail in noncommercial shipments, or in commercial shipments valued at $250 or less, may be exported or destroyed at the request of the addressee or may be released if:

(i) The addressee appears in person at the appropriate Customs office and at that time removes or obliterates the marks in a manner acceptable to the Customs officer; or

(ii) The request of the addressee appearing in person to obtain skillful removal of the marks is granted by the port director on such conditions as he may deem necessary, and upon return of the article to Customs for verification, the marks are found to be satisfactorily removed.

(d) Seizure. If the importer has not obtained release of detained articles within the 30-day period of detention, the merchandise shall be seized and forfeiture proceedings instituted. The importer shall be promptly notified of the seizure and liability to forfeiture and his right to petition for relief in accordance with the provisions of part 171 of this chapter.

Sec. 133.25 Procedure on detention of articles subject to restriction

(a) In general. Articles subject to the restrictions of §§ 133.22 and 133.23 shall be detained for 30 days from the date on which the merchandise is presented for Customs examination. The importer shall be notified of the decision to detain within 5 days of the decision that such restrictions apply. The importer may, during the 30-day period, establish that any of the circumstances described in § 133.22(c) or § 133.23(d) are applicable. Extensions of the 30-day time period may be freely granted for good cause shown.

(b) Notice of detention and disclosure of information. From the time merchandise is presented for Customs examination until the time a notice of detention is issued, Customs may disclose to the owner of the trademark or trade name any of the following information in order to obtain assistance in determining whether an imported article bears an infringing trademark or trade name. Once a notice of detention is issued, Customs shall disclose to the owner of the trademark or trade name the following information, if available, within 30 days, excluding weekends and holidays, of the date of detention:

(1) The date of importation;

(2) The port of entry;

(3) A description of the merchandise;

(4) The quantity involved; and

(5) The country of origin of the merchandise.

(c) Samples available to the trademark or trade name owner. At any time following presentation of the merchandise for Customs examination, but prior to seizure, Customs may provide a sample of the suspect merchandise to the owner of the trademark or trade name for examination or testing to assist in determining whether the article imported bears an infringing trademark or trade name. To obtain a sample under this section, the trademark/trade name owner must furnish Customs a bond in the form and amount specified by the port director, conditioned to hold the United States, its officers and employees, and the importer or owner of the imported article harmless from any loss or damage resulting from the furnishing of a sample by Customs to the trademark owner. Customs may demand the return of the sample at any time. The owner must return the sample to Customs upon demand or at the conclusion of the examination or testing. In the event that the sample is damaged, destroyed, or lost while in the possession of the trademark or trade name owner, the owner shall, in lieu of return of the sample, certify to Customs that: "The sample described as [insert description] and provided pursuant to 19 CFR 133.25(c) was (damaged/destroyed/lost) during examination or testing for trademark infringement."

(d) Form of notice. Notice of detention of articles found subject to the restrictions of § 133.22 or § 133.23 shall be given the importer in writing.

Sec. 133.26 Demand for redelivery of released merchandise

If it is determined that merchandise which has been released from Customs custody is subject to the restrictions of § 133.22 or § 133.23 of this subpart, the port director shall promptly make demand for the redelivery of the merchandise under the terms of the bond on Customs Form 301, containing the bond conditions set forth in § 113.62 of this chapter, in accordance with § 141.113 of this chapter. If the merchandise is not redelivered to Customs custody, a claim for liquidated damages shall be made in accordance with § 141.113(g) of this chapter.

Sec. 133.27 Civil fines for those involved in the importation of counterfeit trademark goods

In addition to any other penalty or remedy authorized by law, Customs may impose a civil fine on any person who directs, assists financially or otherwise, or aids and abets the importation of merchandise bearing a counterfeit mark (within the meaning of § 133.21 of this part) as follows:

(a) First violation. For the first seizure of such merchandise, the fine imposed will not be more than the domestic value of the merchandise, (*see* § 162.43(a) of this chapter), as if it had been genuine, based on the manufacturer's suggested retail price of the merchandise at the time of seizure.

(b) Second and subsequent violations. For the second and each subsequent seizure of such merchandise, the fine imposed will not be more than twice the domestic value of the merchandise as if it had been genuine, based on the manufacturer's suggested retail price of the merchandise at the time of seizure.

APPENDIX C
SECTION 301 STATUTES AND REGULATIONS

UNITED STATES CODE
TITLE 19. CUSTOMS DUTIES
CHAPTER 12—TRADE ACT OF 1974
SUBCHAPTER I—NEGOTIATING AND OTHER AUTHORITY
PART 8—IDENTIFICATION OF MARKET BARRIERS AND CERTAIN UNFAIR TRADE ACTIONS

Sec. 2242 Identification of countries that deny adequate protection, or market access, for intellectual property rights

(a) In general

By no later than the date that is 30 days after the date on which the annual report is submitted to Congressional committees under section 2241(b) of this title, the United States Trade Representative (hereafter in this section referred to as the "Trade Representative") shall identify—

(1) those foreign countries that—

(A) deny adequate and effective protection of intellectual property rights, or

(B) deny fair and equitable market access to United States persons that rely upon intellectual property protection, and

(2) those foreign countries identified under paragraph (1) that are determined by the Trade Representative to be priority foreign countries.

(b) Special rules for identifications

(1) In identifying priority foreign countries under subsection (a)(2) of this section, the Trade Representative shall only identify those foreign countries—

(A) that have the most onerous or egregious acts, policies, or practices that—

(i) deny adequate and effective intellectual property rights, or

(ii) deny fair and equitable market access to United States persons that rely upon intellectual property protection,

(B) whose acts, policies, or practices described in subparagraph (A) have the greatest adverse impact (actual or potential) on the relevant United States products, and

(C) that are not—

(i) entering into good faith negotiations, or

(ii) making significant progress in bilateral or multilateral negotiations, to provide adequate and effective protection of intellectual property rights.

(2) In identifying priority foreign countries under subsection (a)(2), of this section, the Trade Representative shall—

(A) consult with the Register of Copyrights, the Commissioner of Patents and Trademarks, other appropriate officers of the Federal Government, and

(B) take into account information from such sources as may be available to the Trade Representative and such information as may be submitted to the Trade Representative by interested persons, including information contained in reports submitted under section 2241(b) of this title and petitions submitted under section 2412 of this title.

(3) The Trade Representative may identify a foreign country under subsection (a)(1)(B) of this section only if the Trade Representative finds that there is a factual basis for the denial of fair and equitable market access as a result of the violation of international law or agreement, or the existence of barriers, referred to in subsection (d)(3) of this section.

(4) In identifying foreign countries under paragraphs (1) and (2) of subsection (a) of this section, the Trade Representative shall take into account—

(A) the history of intellectual property laws and practices of the foreign country, including any previous identification under subsection (a)(2) of this section, and

(B) the history of efforts of the United States, and the response of the foreign country, to achieve adequate and effective protection and enforcement of intellectual property rights.

(c) Revocations and additional identifications

(1) The Trade Representative may at any time—

(A) revoke the identification of any foreign country as a priority foreign country under this section, or

(B) identify any foreign country as a priority foreign country under this section,

if information available to the Trade Representative indicates that such action is appropriate.

(2) The Trade Representative shall include in the semi-annual report submitted to the Congress under section 2419(3) of this title a detailed explanation of the reasons for the revocation under paragraph (1) of the identification of any foreign country as a priority foreign country under this section.

(d) Definitions

For purposes of this section—

(1) The term "persons that rely upon intellectual property protection" means persons involved in—

(A) the creation, production or licensing of works of authorship (within the meaning of sections 102 and 103 of Title 17) that are copyrighted, or

(B) the manufacture of products that are patented or for which there are process patents.

(2) A foreign country denied adequate and effective protection of intellectual property rights if the foreign country denied adequate and effective means under the laws of the foreign country for persons who are not citizens or nationals of such foreign country to secure, exercise, and enforce rights relating to patents, process patents, registered trademarks, copyrights and mask works.

(3) A foreign country denies fair and equitable market access if the foreign country effectively denies access to a market for a product protected by a copyright or related right, patent, trademark, mask work, trade secret, or plant breeder's right, through the use of laws, procedures, practices, or regulations which—

(A) violate provisions of international law or international agreements to which both the United States and the foreign country are parties, or

(B) constitute discriminatory nontariff trade barriers.

(4) A foreign country may be determined to deny adequate and effective protection of intellectual property rights, notwithstanding the fact that the foreign country may be in compliance with the specific obligations of the Agreement on Trade-Related Aspects of Intellectual Property Rights referred to in section 3511(d)(5) of this title.

(e) Publication

The Trade Representative shall publish in the Federal Register a list of foreign countries identified under subsection (a) of this section and shall make such revisions to the list as may be required by reason of action under subsection (c) of this section.

(f) Special rule for actions affecting United States cultural industries

(1) In general

By no later than the date that is 30 days after the date on which the annual report is submitted to Congressional committees under section 2241(b) of this title, the Trade Representative shall identify any act, policy, or practice of Canada which—

(A) affects cultural industries,

(B) is adopted or expanded after December 17, 1992, and

(C) is actionable under article 2106 of the North American Free Trade Agreement.

(2) Special rules for identifications

For purposes of section 2412(b)(2)(A) of this title, an act, policy, or practice identified under this subsection shall be treated as an act, policy, or practice that is the basis for identification of a country under subsection (a)(2) of this section, unless the United States has already taken action pursuant to article 2106 of the North American Free Trade Agreement in response to such act, policy, or practice. In deciding whether to identify an act, policy, or practice under paragraph (1), the Trade Representative shall—

(A) consult with and take into account the views of representatives of the relevant domestic industries, appropriate committees established pursuant to section 2155 of this title, and appropriate officers of the Federal Government, and

(B) take into account the information from such sources as may be available to the Trade Representative and such information as may be submitted to the Trade

Representative by interested persons, including information contained in reports submitted under section 2241(b) of this title.

(3) Cultural industries

For purposes of this subsection, the term "cultural industries" means persons engaged in any of the following activities:

(A) The publication, distribution, or sale of books, magazines, periodicals, or newspapers in print or machine readable form but not including the sole activity of printing or typesetting any of the foregoing.

(B) The production, distribution, sale, or exhibition of film or video recordings.

(C) The production, distribution, sale, or exhibition of audio or video music recordings.

(D) The publication, distribution, or sale of music in print or machine readable form.

(E) Radio communications in which the transmissions are intended for direct reception by the general public, and all radio, television, and cable broadcasting undertakings and all satellite programming and broadcast network services.

(g) Annual report

The Trade Representative shall, by not later than the date by which countries are identified under subsection (a) of this section, transmit to the Committee on Ways and Means of the House of Representatives and the Committee on Finance of the Senate, a report on actions taken under this section during the 12 months preceding such report, and the reasons for such actions, including a description of progress made in achieving improved intellectual property protection and market access for persons relying on intellectual property rights.

UNITED STATES CODE
TITLE 19—CUSTOMS DUTIES
CHAPTER 12—TRADE ACT OF 1974
SUBCHAPTER III—ENFORCEMENT OF UNITED STATES RIGHTS UNDER TRADE AGREEMENTS AND RESPONSE TO CERTAIN FOREIGN TRADE PRACTICES

Sec. 2411 Actions by United States Trade Representative

(a) Mandatory action

(1) If the United States Trade Representative determines under section 2414(a)(1) of this title that—

(A) the rights of the United States under any trade agreement are being denied; or

(B) an act, policy, or practice of a foreign country—

(i) violates, or is inconsistent with, the provisions of, or otherwise denies benefits to the United States under, any trade agreement, or

(ii) is unjustifiable and burdens or restricts United States commerce;

the Trade Representative shall take action authorized in subsection (c) of this section subject to the specific direction, if any, of the President regarding any such action, and shall take all other appropriate and feasible action within the power of the President that the President may direct the Trade Representative to take under this subsection, to enforce such rights or to obtain the elimination of such act, policy, or practice. Actions may be taken that are within the power of the President with respect to trade in any goods or services, or with respect to any other area of pertinent relations with the foreign country.

(2) The Trade Representative is not required to take action under paragraph (1) in any case in which—

(A) The Dispute Settlement Body (as defined in section 3531(5) of this title) has adopted a report, or a ruling issued under the formal dispute settlement proceeding provided under any other trade agreement finds, that—

(i) the rights of the United States under a trade agreement are not being denied, or

(ii) the act, policy, or practice—

(I) is not a violation of, or inconsistent with, the rights of the United States, or

(II) does not deny, nullify, or impair benefits to the United States under any trade agreement; or

(B) the Trade Representative finds that—

(i) the foreign country is taking satisfactory measures to grant the rights of the United States under a trade agreement,

(ii) the foreign country has—

(I) agreed to eliminate or phase out the act, policy, or practice, or

(II) agreed to an imminent solution to the burden or restriction on United States commerce that is satisfactory to the Trade Representative,

(iii) it is impossible for the foreign country to achieve the results described in clause (i) or (ii), as appropriate, but the foreign country agrees to provide to the United States compensatory trade benefits that are satisfactory to the Trade Representative,

(iv) in extraordinary cases, where the taking of action under this subsection would have an adverse impact on the United States economy substantially out of proportion to the benefits of such action, taking into account the impact of not taking such action on the credibility of the provisions of this subchapter, or

(v) the taking of action under this subsection would cause serious harm to the national security of the United States.

(3) Any action taken under paragraph (1) to eliminate an act, policy, or practice shall be devised so as to affect goods or services of the foreign country in an amount that is equivalent in value to the burden or restriction being imposed by that country on United States commerce.

(b) Discretionary action

If the Trade Representative determines under section 2414(a)(1) of this title that—

(1) an act, policy, or practice of a foreign country is unreasonable or discriminatory and burdens or restricts United States commerce, and

(2) action by the United States is appropriate, the Trade Representative shall take all appropriate and feasible action authorized under subsection (c) of this section, subject to the specific direction, if any, of the President regarding any such action, and all other appropriate and feasible action within the power of the President that the President may direct the Trade Representative to take under this subsection, to obtain the elimination of that act, policy, or practice. Actions may be taken that are within the power of the President with respect to trade in any goods or services, or with respect to any other area of pertinent relations with the foreign country.

(c) Scope of authority

(1) For purposes of carrying out the provisions of subsection (a) or (b) of this section, the Trade Representative is authorized to—

(A) suspend, withdraw, or prevent the application of, benefits of trade agreement concessions to carry out a trade agreement with the foreign country referred to in such subsection;

(B) impose duties or other import restrictions on the goods of, and, notwithstanding any other provision of law, fees or restrictions on the services of, such foreign country for such time as the Trade Representative determines appropriate;

(C) in a case in which the act, policy, or practice also fails to meet the eligibility criteria for receiving duty-free treatment under subsections (b) and (c) of section 2462 of this title, subsections (b) and (c) of section 2702 of this title, or subsections (c) and (d) of section 3202 of this title, withdraw, limit, or suspend such treatment under such provisions, notwithstanding the provisions of subsection (a)(3) of this section; or

(D) enter into binding agreements with such foreign country that commit such foreign country to—

(i) eliminate, or phase out, the act, policy, or practice that is the subject of the action to be taken under subsection (a) or (b) of this section,

(ii) eliminate any burden or restriction on United States commerce resulting from such act, policy, or practice, or

(iii) provide the United States with compensatory trade benefits that—

(I) are satisfactory to the Trade Representative, and

(II) meet the requirements of paragraph (4).

(2)(A) Notwithstanding any other provision of law governing any service sector access authorization, and in addition to the authority conferred in paragraph (1), the Trade Representative may, for purposes of carrying out the provisions of subsection (a) or (b) of this section—

(i) restrict, in the manner and to the extent the Trade Representative determines appropriate, the terms and conditions of any such authorization, or

(ii) deny the issuance of any such authorization.

(B) Actions described in subparagraph (A) may only be taken under this section with respect to service sector access authorizations granted, or applications therefor pending, on or after the date on which—

(i) a petition is filed under section 2412(a) of this title, or

(ii) a determination to initiate an investigation is made by the Trade Representative under section 2412(b) of this title.

(C) Before the Trade Representative takes any action under this section involving the imposition of fees or other restrictions on the services of a foreign country, the Trade Representative shall, if the services involved are subject to regulation by any agency of the Federal Government or of any State, consult, as appropriate, with the head of the agency concerned.

(3) The actions the Trade Representative is authorized to take under subsection (a) or (b) of this section may be taken against any goods or economic sector—

(A) on a nondiscriminatory basis or solely against the foreign country described in such subsection, and

(B) without regard to whether or not such goods or economic sector were involved in the act, policy, or practice that is the subject of such action.

(4) Any trade agreement described in paragraph (1)(D)(iii) shall provide compensatory trade benefits that benefit the economic sector which includes the domestic industry that would benefit from the elimination of the act, policy, or practice that is the subject of the action to be taken under subsection (a) or (b) of this section, or benefit the economic sector as closely related as possible to such economic sector, unless—

(A) the provision of such trade benefits is not feasible, or

(B) trade benefits that benefit any other economic sector would be more satisfactory than such trade benefits.

(5) If the Trade Representative determines that actions to be taken under subsection (a) or (b) of this section are to be in the form of import restrictions, the Trade Representative shall—

(A) give preference to the imposition of duties over the imposition of other import restrictions, and

(B) if an import restriction other than a duty is imposed, consider substituting, on an incremental basis, an equivalent duty for such other import restriction.

(6) Any action taken by the Trade Representative under this section with respect to export targeting shall, to the extent possible, reflect the full benefit level of the export targeting to the beneficiary over the period during which the action taken has an effect.

(d) Definitions and special rules

For purposes of this chapter—

(1) The term "commerce" includes, but is not limited to—

(A) services (including transfers of information) associated with international trade, whether or not such services are related to specific goods, and

(B) foreign direct investment by United States persons with implications for trade in goods or services.

(2) An act, policy, or practice of a foreign country that burdens or restricts United States commerce may include the provision, directly or indirectly, by that foreign country of subsidies for the construction of vessels used in the commercial transportation by water of goods between foreign countries and the United States.

(3)(A) An act, policy, or practice is unreasonable if the act, policy, or practice, while not necessarily in violation of, or inconsistent with, the international legal rights of the United States, is otherwise unfair and inequitable.

(B) Acts, policies, and practices that are unreasonable include, but are not limited to, any act, policy, or practice, or any combination of acts, policies, or practices, which—

(i) denies fair and equitable—

(I) opportunities for the establishment of an enterprise,

(II) provision of adequate and effective protection of intellectual property rights notwithstanding the fact that the foreign country may be in compliance with the specific obligations of the Agreement on Trade-Related Aspects of Intellectual Property Rights referred to in section 3511(d) of this title,

(III) nondiscriminatory market access opportunities for United States persons that rely upon intellectual property protection, or

(IV) market opportunities, including the toleration by a foreign government of systematic anticompetitive activities by enterprises or among enterprises in the foreign country that have the effect of restricting, on a basis that is inconsistent with commercial considerations, access of United States goods or services to a foreign market,

(ii) constitutes export targeting, or

(iii) constitutes a persistent pattern of conduct that—

(I) denies workers the right of association,

(II) denies workers the right to organize and bargain collectively,

(III) permits any form of forced or compulsory labor,

(IV) fails to provide a minimum age for the employment of children, or

(V) fails to provide standards for minimum wages, hours of work, and occupational safety and health of workers.

(C)(i) Acts, policies, and practices of a foreign country described in subparagraph (B)(iii) shall not be treated as being unreasonable if the Trade Representative determines that—

(I) the foreign country has taken, or is taking, actions that demonstrate a significant and tangible overall advancement in providing throughout the foreign country (including any designated zone within the foreign country) the rights and other standards described in the subclauses of subparagraph (B)(iii), or

(II) such acts, policies, and practices are not inconsistent with the level of economic development of the foreign country.

(ii) The Trade Representative shall publish in the Federal Register any determination made under clause (i), together with a description of the facts on which such determination is based.

(D) For purposes of determining whether any act, policy, or practice is unreasonable, reciprocal opportunities in the United States for foreign nationals and firms shall be taken into account, to the extent appropriate.

(E) The term "export targeting" means any government plan or scheme consisting of a combination of coordinated actions (whether carried out severally or jointly) that are bestowed on a specific enterprise, industry, or group thereof, the effect of which is to assist the enterprise, industry, or group to become more competitive in the export of a class or kind of merchandise.

(F)(i) For the purposes of subparagraph (B)(i)(II), adequate and effective protection of intellectual property rights includes adequate and effective means under the laws of the foreign country for persons who are not citizens or nationals of such country to secure, exercise, and enforce rights and enjoy commercial benefits relating to patents, trademarks, copyrights and related rights, mask works, trade secrets, and plant breeder's rights.

(ii) For purposes of subparagraph (B)(i)(IV), the denial of fair and equitable nondiscriminatory market access opportunities includes restrictions on market access related to the use, exploitation, or enjoyment of commercial benefits derived from exercising intellectual property rights in protected works or fixations or products embodying protected works.

(4)(A) An act, policy, or practice is unjustifiable if the act, policy, or practice is in violation of, or inconsistent with, the international legal rights of the United States.

(B) Acts, policies, and practices that are unjustifiable include, but are not limited to, any act, policy, or practice described in subparagraph (A) which denies national or most-favored-nation treatment or the right of establishment or protection of intellectual property rights.

(5) Acts, policies, and practices that are discriminatory include, when appropriate, any act, policy, and practice which denies national or most-favored-nation treatment to United States goods, services, or investment.

(6) The term "service sector access authorization" means any license, permit, order, or other authorization, issued under the authority of Federal law, that permits a foreign supplier of services access to the United States market in a service sector concerned.

(7) The term "foreign country" includes any foreign instrumentality. Any possession or territory of a foreign country that is administered separately for customs purposes shall be treated as a separate foreign country.

(8) The term "Trade Representative" means the United States Trade Representative.

(9) The term "interested persons", only for purposes of sections 2412(a)(4)(B), 2414(b)(1)(A), 2416(c)(2), and 2417(a)(2) of this title, includes, but is not limited to, domestic firms and workers, representatives of consumer interests, United States product exporters, and any industrial user of any goods or services that may be affected by actions taken under subsection (a) or (b) of this section.

Sec. 2412 Initiation of investigations

(a) Petitions

(1) Any interested person may file a petition with the Trade Representative requesting that action be taken under section 2411 of this title and setting forth the allegations in support of the request.

(2) The Trade Representative shall review the allegations in any petition filed under paragraph (1) and, not later than 45 days after the date on which the Trade Representative received the petition, shall determine whether to initiate an investigation.

(3) If the Trade Representative determines not to initiate an investigation with respect to a petition, the Trade Representative shall inform the petitioner of the reasons therefor and shall publish notice of the determination, together with a summary of such reasons, in the Federal Register.

(4) If the Trade Representative makes an affirmative determination under paragraph (2) with respect to a petition, the Trade Representative shall initiate an investigation regarding the issues raised in the petition. The Trade Representative shall publish a summary of the petition in the Federal Register and shall, as soon as possible, provide opportunity for the presentation of views concerning the issues, including a public hearing—

(A) within the 30-day period beginning on the date of the affirmative determination (or on a date after such period if agreed to by the petitioner) if a public hearing within such period is requested in the petition, or

(B) at such other time if a timely request therefor is made by the petitioner or by any interested person.

(b) Initiation of investigation by means other than petition

(1)(A) If the Trade Representative determines that an investigation should be initiated under this subchapter with respect to any matter in order to determine whether the matter is actionable under section 2411 of this title, the Trade Representative shall publish such determination in the Federal Register and shall initiate such investigation.

(B) The Trade Representative shall, before making any determination under subparagraph (A), consult with appropriate committees established pursuant to section 2155 of this title.

(2)(A) By no later than the date that is 30 days after the date on which a country is identified under section 2242(a)(2) of this title, the Trade Representative shall initiate an investigation under this subchapter with respect to any act, policy, or practice of that country that—

(i) was the basis for such identification, and

(ii) is not at that time the subject of any other investigation or action under this subchapter.

(B) The Trade Representative is not required under subparagraph (A) to initiate an investigation under this subchapter with respect to any act, policy, or practice of a foreign country if the Trade Representative determines that the initiation of the investigation would be detrimental to United States economic interests.

(C) If the Trade Representative makes a determination under subparagraph (B) not to initiate an investigation, the Trade Representative shall submit to the Congress a written report setting forth, in detail—

(i) the reasons for the determination, and

(ii) the United States economic interests that would be adversely affected by the investigation.

(D) The Trade Representative shall, from time to time, consult with the Register of Copyrights, the Commissioner of Patents and Trademarks, and other appropriate officers of the Federal Government, during any investigation initiated under this chapter by reason of subparagraph (A).

(c) Discretion

In determining whether to initiate an investigation under subsection (a) or (b) of this section of any act, policy, or practice that is enumerated in any provision of section 2411(d) of this title, the Trade Representative shall have discretion to determine whether action under section 2411 of this title would be effective in addressing such act, policy, or practice.

Sec. 2413 Consultation upon initiation of investigation

(a) In general

(1) On the date on which an investigation is initiated under section 2412 of this title, the Trade Representative, on behalf of the United States, shall request consultations with the foreign country concerned regarding the issues involved in such investigation.

(2) If the investigation initiated under section 2412 of this title involves a trade agreement and a mutually acceptable resolution is not reached before the earlier of—

(A) the close of the consultation period, if any, specified in the trade agreement, or

(B) the 150th day after the day on which consultation was commenced,

the Trade Representative shall promptly request proceedings on the matter under the formal dispute settlement procedures provided under such agreement.

(3) The Trade Representative shall seek information and advice from the petitioner (if any) and the appropriate committees established pursuant to section 2155 of this title in preparing United States presentations for consultations and dispute settlement proceedings.

(b) Delay of request for consultations

(1) Notwithstanding the provisions of subsection (a) of this section—

(A) the United States Trade Representative may, after consulting with the petitioner (if any), delay for up to 90 days any request for consultations under subsection (a) of this section for the purpose of verifying or improving the petition to ensure an adequate basis for consultation, and

(B) if such consultations are delayed by reason of subparagraph (A), each time limitation under section 2414 of this title shall be extended for the period of such delay.

(2) The Trade Representative shall—

(A) publish notice of any delay under paragraph (1) in the Federal Register, and

(B) report to Congress on the reasons for such delay in the report required under section 2419(a)(3) of this title.

Sec. 2414 Determinations by the Trade Representative

(a) In general

(1) On the basis of the investigation initiated under section 2412 of this title and the consultations (and the proceedings, if applicable) under section 2413 of this title, the Trade Representative shall—

(A) determine whether—

(i) the rights to which the United States is entitled under any trade agreement are being denied, or

(ii) any act, policy, or practice described in subsection (a)(1)(B) or (b)(1) of section 2411 of this title exists, and

(B) if the determination made under subparagraph (A) is affirmative, determine what action, if any, the Trade Representative should take under subsection (a) or (b) of section 2411 of this title.

(2) The Trade Representative shall make the determinations required under paragraph (1) on or before—

(A) in the case of an investigation involving a trade agreement, the earlier of—

(i) the date that is 30 days after the date on which the dispute settlement procedure is concluded, or

(ii) the date that is 18 months after the date on which the investigation is initiated, or

(B) in all cases not described in subparagraph (A) or paragraph (3), the date that is 12 months after the date on which the investigation is initiated.

(3)(A) If an investigation is initiated under this subchapter by reason of section 2412(b)(2) of this title and the Trade Representative does not consider that a trade agreement, including the Agreement on Trade-Related Aspects of Intellectual Property Rights (referred to in section 3511(d)(15) of this title), is involved or does not make a determination described in subparagraph (B) with respect to such investigation, the Trade Representative shall make the determinations required under paragraph (1) with respect to such investigation by no later than the date that is 6 months after the date on which such investigation is initiated.

(B) If the Trade Representative determines with respect to an investigation initiated by reason of section 2412(b)(2) of this title (other than an investigation involving a trade agreement) that—

(i) complex or complicated issues are involved in the investigation that require additional time,

(ii) the foreign country involved in the investigation is making substantial progress in drafting or implementing legislative or administrative measures that will provide adequate and effective protection of intellectual property rights, or

(iii) such foreign country is undertaking enforcement measures to provide adequate and effective protection of intellectual property rights,

the Trade Representative shall publish in the Federal Register notice of such determination and shall make the determinations required under paragraph (1) with respect to such investigation by no later than the date that is 9 months after the date on which such investigation is initiated.

(4) In any case in which a dispute is not resolved before the close of the minimum dispute settlement period provided for in a trade agreement, the Trade Representative, within 15 days after the close of such dispute settlement period, shall submit a report to Congress setting forth the reasons why the dispute was not resolved within the minimum dispute settlement period, the status of the case at the close of the period, and the prospects for resolution. For purposes of this paragraph, the minimum dispute settlement period provided for under any such trade agreement is the total period of time that results if all stages of the formal dispute settlement procedures are carried out within the time limitations specified in the agreement, but computed without regard to any extension authorized under the agreement at any stage.

(b) Consultation before determinations

(1) Before making the determinations required under subsection (a)(1) of this section, the Trade Representative, unless expeditious action is required—

(A) shall provide an opportunity (after giving not less than 30 days notice thereof) for the presentation of views by interested persons, including a public hearing if requested by any interested person,

(B) shall obtain advice from the appropriate committees established pursuant to section 2155 of this title, and

(C) may request the views of the United States International Trade Commission regarding the probable impact on the economy of the United States of the taking of action with respect to any goods or service.

(2) If the Trade Representative does not comply with the requirements of subparagraphs (A) and (B) of paragraph (1) because expeditious action is required, the Trade Representative shall, after making the determinations under subsection (a)(1) of this section, comply with such subparagraphs.

(c) Publication

The Trade Representative shall publish in the Federal Register any determination made under subsection (a)(1) of this section, together with a description of the facts on which such determination is based.

CODE OF FEDERAL REGULATIONS
TITLE 15—COMMERCE AND FOREIGN TRADE
CHAPTER XX—OFFICE OF THE UNITED STATES TRADE REPRESENTATIVE
PART 2006—PROCEDURES FOR FILING PETITIONS FOR ACTION UNDER SECTION 301 OF THE TRADE ACT OF 1974, AS AMENDED

Sec. 2006.0 Submission of petitions requesting action under section 301

(a) Section 301 of the Trade Act of 1974, as amended (the "Trade Act") requires the United States Trade Representative, subject to the specific direction, if any, of the President regarding such action, to take appropriate and feasible action in response to a foreign government's violation of a trade agreement, or any other international agreement the breach of which burdens or restricts United States commerce; and authorizes the Trade Representative, subject to the specific direction of the President, if any, to take action to obtain the elimination of acts, policies, and practices of foreign countries that are unjustifiable, unreasonable, or discriminatory and burden or restrict United States commerce. Section 302 of the Trade Act provides for petitions to be filed with the Trade Representative requesting that action be taken under section 301. Petitions filed under section 302 will be treated as specified in these regulations.

(b) Petitions may be submitted by an interested person. An interested person is deemed to be any party who has a significant interest affected by the act, policy, or practice complained of, for example: A producer, a commercial importer, or an exporter of an affected product or service; a United States person seeking to invest directly abroad, with implications for trade in goods or services; a person who relies on protection of intellectual property rights; a trade association, a certified union or recognized union or group of workers which is representative of an industry engaged in the manufacture, production or wholesale distribution in the United States of a product or service so affected; or any other private party representing a significant economic interest affected directly by the act, policy or practice complained of in the petition.

(c) The petitioner shall submit 20 copies of the petition in English, clearly typed, photocopied, or printed to: Chairman, Section 301 Committee, Office of the United States Trade Representative, 600 17th Street, NW., Washington, DC 20506.

To ensure proper docketing, petitions may be filed only during the following hours on days when the Federal Government is open for business: between 9 a.m. and 12 noon and 1 p.m. to 5 p.m.

(d) Recorded information on section 302 petitions and investigations may be obtained by calling (202) 395-3871.

Sec. 2006.1 Information to be included in petition

(a) General information.

Petitions submitted pursuant to section 302 of the Trade Act shall clearly state on the first page that the petition requests that action be taken under section 301 of the Trade Act and shall contain allegations and information reasonably available to petitioner in support of the request, in the form specified below. Petitioners for whom such information is difficult or impossible to obtain shall provide as much information as possible, and assistance in filing their petition may be obtained through the Chairman of the Section 301 Committee. All petitions shall:

(1) Identify the petitioner and the person, firm or association, if any, which petitioner represents and describe briefly the economic interest of the petitioner which is directly affected by the failure of a foreign government or instrumentality to grant rights of the United States under a trade agreement, or which is otherwise directly affected economically by an act, policy, or practice which is actionable under section 301.

(2) Describe the rights of the United States being violated or denied under the trade agreement which petitioner seeks to enforce or the other act, policy or practice which is the subject of the petition, and provide a reference to the particular part of section 301 related to the assertion in the petition.

(3) Include, wherever possible, copies of laws or regulations which are the subject of the petition. If this is not possible, the laws and regulations shall be identified with the greatest possible particularity, such as by citation.

(4) Identify the foreign country or instrumentality with whom the United States has an agreement under which petitioner is asserting rights claimed to be denied or whose acts, policies or practices are the subject of the petition.

(5) Identify the product, service, intellectual property right, or foreign direct investment matter for which the rights of the United States under the agreement claimed to be violated or denied are sought, or which is subject to the act, policy or practice of the foreign government or instrumentality named in paragraph (a)(4) of this section.

(6) Demonstrate that rights of the United States under a trade agreement are not being provided; or show the manner in which the act, policy or practice violates or is inconsistent with the provisions of a trade agreement or otherwise denies benefits accruing to the United States under a trade agreement, or is unjustifiable, unreasonable, or discriminatory and burdens or restricts United States commerce.

(7) Provide information concerning:

(i) The degree to which U.S. commerce is burdened or restricted by the denial of rights under a trade agreement or by any other act, policy, or practice which is actionable under section 301,

(ii) The volume of trade in the goods or services involved, and

(iii) A description of the methodology used to calculate the burden or restriction on U.S. commerce.

(8) State whether petitioner has filed or is filing for other forms of relief under the Trade Act or any other provision of law. If the foreign government practice at issue is the subject of investigation under any other provision of law, the USTR may determine not to initiate an investigation; or if the same matter is subsequently subject to investigation under some other provision of law, USTR may terminate the section 302 investigation.

(b) Additional specific information.

(1) Subsidies. If the petition includes an assertion that subsidy payments are having an adverse effect upon products or services of the United States in United States' markets or in other foreign markets, it shall include an analysis supporting any claim

that the subsidy complained of is inconsistent with any trade agreement and describe the manner in which it burdens or restricts United States commerce.

(2) Certain unreasonable practices. If the petition asserts that an unreasonable practice defined in section 301(d) (3) denies fair and equitable opportunities for the establishment of an enterprise, or denies adequate and effective protection of intellectual property rights, or denies fair and equitable market opportunities, and burdens or restricts U.S. commerce, the petition should include, to the extent possible, identification of reciprocal opportunities in the United States that may exist for foreign nationals and firms; and

(i) If the petition asserts that fair and equitable opportunities for the establishment of an enterprise in a foreign country are denied, the petition shall:

(A) Describe in detail the nature of any foreign direct investment proposed by the United States person, including estimates of trade in goods and services that could reasonably be expected to result from that investment,

(B) Indicate the manner in which the foreign government is denying the United States person a fair and equitable opportunity for the establishment of an enterprise,

(C) State whether action by the foreign government is in violation of or inconsistent with the international legal rights of the United States, citing the relevant provisions of any international agreements to which the United States and the foreign government are party, and

(D) To the extent possible, provide copies of all relevant foreign government statutes, regulations, directives, public policy statements and correspondence with the United States person with respect to the proposed investment.

(ii) If the petition asserts that fair and equitable provision of adequate and effective protection of intellectual property rights in a foreign country is denied, the petition shall:

(A) Identify the intellectual property right for which protection has been sought,

(B) Indicate how persons who are not citizens or nationals of such foreign country are denied the opportunity to secure, exercise, and enforce rights relating to patents, process patents, registered trademarks, copyrights, or mask works, and

(C) Provide information on the relevant laws of the foreign country and an analysis of how the foreign country's law or policies conform to provisions of international law or international agreements to which both the United States and the foreign country are parties;

(iii) If the petition asserts that fair and equitable market opportunities are denied through the toleration by a foreign government of systematic private anticompetitive activities, the petition shall specifically:

(A) Identify the private firms in the foreign country whose systematic anticompetitive activities have the effect of restricting access of United States goods to purchasing by those firms, inconsistent with commercial considerations,

(B) Describe in detail the private activities in question,

(C) State whether evidence of such activities has been provided (by petitioner or others) to the appropriate foreign government authorities, and describe the evidence indicating that the foreign government is aware of and supports, encourages, or tolerates such activities,

(D) Describe the duration and pervasiveness of such activities,

(E) Indicate whether such activities are inconsistent with the laws of the foreign country involved, making specific reference to any laws in question, and

(F) Indicate whether the foreign government's enforcement of (or failure to enforce) its relevant laws with respect to the private activities at issue is inconsistent with its enforcement practices in other situations;

(iv) If the petition asserts that an act, policy or practice, or combination thereof constitutes export targeting, the petition shall:

(A) Identify the specific enterprise, industry, or group thereof which has been assisted in becoming more competitive in the export of the affected product or products,

(B) Describe the elements of the foreign government's plan or scheme consisting of coordinated actions to assist that enterprise, industry, or group, and

(C) Provide information on how and to what degree exports of the affected products by that enterprise, industry, or group have become more competitive as a result of the foreign government's plan or scheme; and

(v) If the petition asserts that an act, policy or practice, or combination thereof constitutes a persistent pattern of conduct that denies workers the right of association or the right to organize and bargain collectively, or permits forced or compulsory labor, or fails to provide a minimum age for employment of children or standards for minimum wages, hours, and occupational safety and health of workers, the petition shall:

(A) Describe the rights or standards denied and provide information on the laws, policies and practices of the foreign country involved, if any, that relate to such rights or standards, and

(B) Indicate, to the extent such information is available to petitioner, whether the foreign country has taken, or is taking, actions that demonstrate a significant and tangible overall advancement in providing these rights or standards.

Sec. 2006.2 Adequacy of the petition

If the petition filed pursuant to section 302 does not conform substantially to the requirements of Secs. 2006.0 and 2006.1, the Chairman of the Section 301 Committee may decline to docket the petition as filed and, if requested by petitioner, return it to petitioner with guidance on making the petition conform to the requirements, or may nevertheless determine that there is sufficient information on which to proceed to a determination whether to initiate an investigation.

Sec. 2006.3 Determinations regarding petitions

Within 45 days after the day on which the petition is received, the Trade Representative shall determine, after receiving the advice of the Section 301 Committee, whether to initiate an investigation.

(a) If the Trade Representative determines not to initiate an investigation, the Section 301 Chairman shall notify the petitioner of the reasons and shall publish notice of the negative determination and a summary of the reasons therefor in the Federal Register.

(b) If the Trade Representative determines to initiate an investigation regarding the petition, the Section 301 Chairman shall publish a summary of the petition in the Federal Register, and provide an opportunity for the presentation of views concerning the issues, including a public hearing if requested. A hearing may be requested by the petitioner or any interested person, including but not limited to a domestic firm or worker, a representative of consumer interests, a United States product exporter, or any industrial user of any goods or services that may be affected by actions taken under section 301 with respect to the act, policy or practice that is the subject of the petition.

Sec. 2006.4 Requests for information made to Foreign Governments or Instrumentalities

If the U.S. Trade Representative receives a petition alleging violations of any international agreement, he will notify the foreign government or instrumentality of the allegations and may request information, in English, necessary to a determination under section 304(a)(1)(A) of the Trade Act. The Trade Representative may proceed on the basis of best information available if, within a reasonable time, no information is received in response to the request.

Sec. 2006.5 Consultations with the Foreign Government

(a) If the Trade Representative determines to initiate an investigation on the basis of a petition he shall, on behalf of the United States, request consultations with the foreign country concerned regarding the issues involved in such an investigation. In preparing United States presentations for consultations and dispute settlement proceedings, the Trade Representative shall seek information and advice from the petitioner and any appropriate private sector representatives, including committees established pursuant to section 135 of the Trade Act.

(b) To ensure an adequate basis for consultation, the Trade Representative may, after consulting with the petitioner, delay requests for consultations for up to 90 days in order to verify or improve the petition. If consultations are delayed, the time limits referred to in Sec. 2006.12 below shall be extended for the period of such delay.

Sec. 2006.6 Formal dispute settlement

If the issues in a petition are covered by a trade agreement between the United States and the foreign government involved and a mutually acceptable resolution cannot be reached within the consultation period provided for in the agreement, or by 150 days after consultations begin, whichever is earlier, the Trade Representative shall institute the formal dispute settlement proceedings, if any, provided for in the trade agreement.

Sec. 2006.7 Public hearings

(a) A public hearing for the purpose of receiving views on the issues raised in a petition shall be held by the Section 301 Committee:

(1) Within 30 days after the date that an investigation is initiated under section 302(a)(2) if a hearing is requested in the petition (or later, if agreed to by the petitioner); or

(2) Within a reasonable period if, after the investigation is initiated, a timely request is made by the petitioner, or any other interested person as defined in Sec. 2006.3(b).

(b) Prior to making a recommendation on what action, if any, should be taken in response to issues raised in the petition, the Section 301 Committee shall hold a public hearing upon the written request of any interested person. An interested person should submit an application to the Section 301 Chairman stating briefly the interest of the person requesting the hearing, the firm, person, or association he represents, and the position to be taken. A hearing so requested shall be held:

(1) Prior to determining what action should be taken under section 301, and after at least 30 days' notice; or

(2) Within 30 days after the determination of action is made, if the Trade Representative determines that expeditious action is required.

(c) After receipt of a request for a public hearing under sections 302(a)(4)(B) or 304(b)(1)(A) of the Trade Act, the Chairman of the Section 301 Committee will notify the applicant whether the request meets the requirements of this part, and if not, the reasons therefor. If the applicant has met the requirements of this part, he will receive at least 30 days' notice of the time and place of the hearing.

(d) Notice of public hearings to be held under sections 302(a)(4)(B) and 304(b)(1)(A) shall be published in the Federal Register by the Chairman of the Section 301 Committee.

Sec. 2006.8 Submission of written briefs

(a) In order to participate in the presentation of views either at a public hearing or otherwise, an interested person must submit a written brief before the close of the period of submission announced in the public notice. The brief may be, but need not be, supplemented by the presentation of oral testimony in any public hearing scheduled in accordance with Sec. 2006.7.

(b) The brief shall state clearly the position taken and shall describe with particularity the supporting rationale. It shall be submitted in 20 copies, which must be legibly typed, printed, or duplicated.

(c) In order to assure each interested person an opportunity to contest the information provided by other parties, the Section 301 Committee will entertain rebuttal briefs filed by any interested person within a time limit specified in the public notice. Rebuttal briefs should be strictly limited to demonstrating errors of fact or analysis not pointed out in the briefs or hearing and should be as concise as possible.

Sec. 2006.9 Presentation of oral testimony at public hearings

(a) A request by an interested person to present oral testimony at a public hearing shall be submitted in writing before the close of the period of submission announced in the public notice and shall state briefly the interest of the applicant. Such request will be granted if a brief has been submitted in accordance with Sec. 2006.8.

(b) After consideration of a request to present oral testimony at a public hearing, the Chairman of the Section 301 Committee will notify the applicant whether the request conforms to the requirements of Sec. 2006.8(a) and, if it does not, will give the reasons. If the applicant has submitted a conforming request he shall be notified of the time and place for the hearing and for his oral testimony.

INDEX

The manufacturer's authorised representative in the EU for product safety is Oxford University Press España S.A. of El Parque Empresarial San Fernando de Henares, Avenida de Castilla, 2 - 28830 Madrid (www.oup.es/en or product.safety@oup.com). OUP España S.A. also acts as importer into Spain of products made by the manufacturer.
Printed and bound by CPI Group (UK) Ltd, Croydon, CR0 4YY
14/09/2026
02216286-0020